CURRENT ISSUES IN MONETARY THEORY AND POLICY

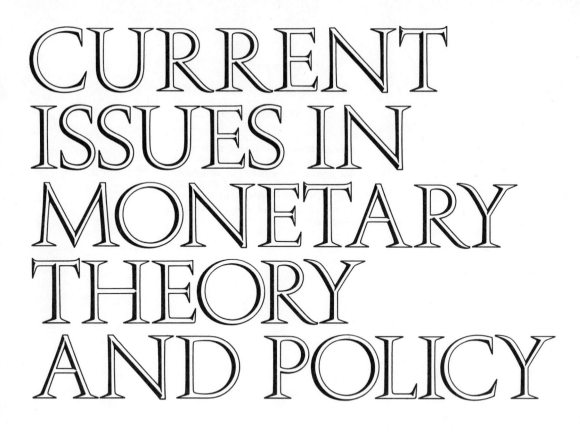

CURRENT ISSUES IN MONETARY THEORY AND POLICY

EDITED BY

THOMAS M. HAVRILESKY
DUKE UNIVERSITY

JOHN T. BOORMAN
INTERNATIONAL MONETARY FUND

AHM Publishing Corporation
Arlington Heights, Illinois 60004

ISBN: 0-88295-402-4

Library of Congress Card Number: 76-1296

PRINTED IN THE UNITED STATES OF AMERICA
736

Contents

B. The Transmission Process and Policy Implications

II. EMPIRICAL EVIDENCE

B. Monetary Policy in an Open Economy

C. Monetary Policy in Public Debate

Preface

DATE: 1976

Monetary theory and policy have been among the more controversial areas in economics in recent years. The continuing debate between Keynesians and Monetarists rages not only in scholarly journals but also in the financial press and increasingly in the political sphere.

As the struggle goes on, it becomes more difficult to identify the ever-shifting lines of battle: the latest Monetarist thrust or Keynesian parry. Perhaps confusion in the din of combat is characteristic of all wars—even intellectual ones. Nevertheless, many economists earn at least part of their living off the intellectual battlefield—by explaining the issues to others. Thus, such difficulty makes life especially trying for the teacher of money and banking, macroeconomic theory, or monetary economics. As the Monetarist versus Keynesian debate takes on new dimensions (as theoretical refinement and empirical work uncover new perspectives), it is no easy task for teachers to illuminate the issues. In the classroom, where one once could simply focus on disagreement over the stability of the demand for money and the implications of flexible money wages and prices, the instructor must now address crucial new questions.

This book of readings focuses on those questions. The articles have been selected to guide the student through recent developments in monetary theory and policy. We have chosen works on the basis of their lucidity, representativeness, relevance, ability to stimulate discussion and debate, and complementarity with other readings. We have tried to sustain balance between theoretical and empirical work and to avoid exceedingly complex formulations that would be beyond the ken of most students. We have attempted in each subject area to choose articles that present the issues most cogently, regardless of the Monetarist or Keynesian leanings of the author or his or her place of employment.

In our selection process we were not bound by traditional formulas for books of readings in monetary economics and money and banking. There are, for instance, no readings on debt management, the incidence of monetary policy, rules versus discretion, or incomes policy. Nor are there lengthy critiques of the "tools" of monetary policy. These subjects were more important at one time and may very well come into prominence again, but they are topics that most current textbooks cover in timely detail. In an effort to keep the book reasonably sized (and reasonably priced), we have not emphasized topics that are adequately developed in textbooks, nor have we concentrated on topical areas that, command an entire volume of readings by themselves, such as recent developments in commercial banking.

The collection is divided into four parts. Part I is devoted to monetary theory. It is addressed to the contrasting views of the macroeconomy, their analytical description, and how these views are reflected in basic areas of theoretical analysis. Part II is concerned with empirical estimation of many of the theoretical constructs discussed in Parts I and III. Part III examines the evidence on money supply, money demand, and interest rates that underlie many of the issues discussed in Parts I, II, and IV. Part IV is concerned with the implementation of monetary policy.

We are grateful to Ralph Byrnes, Joseph Crews, Richard Froyen, Edward Kane, Raymond Lombra, Robert Schweitzer, and William Yohe for their guidance during the selection of readings. We acknowledge Paul Funk, James Johnson, Maxine McGee, Katie Frye, and Jean Peek in Durham, Annie Sarino and Ziska Lalamentik in Jakarta and Maureen Trobec in Arlington Heights for their assistance in the production process. A note of thanks is due our editors, Harry Metzger and Harlan Davidson, for their encouragement and help during all stages of this preparation. Finally, we congratulate all contributors to this volume for their contribution to scholarship.

THOMAS M. HAVRILESKY
Durham, North Carolina

JOHN T. BOORMAN
Jakarta, Indonesia

October, 1975

I

MONETARY THEORY

A. Analytical Models and Descriptive Overview

In the opening article Warren L. Smith presents the seminal exposition of the Keynesian version of the aggregate demand (LM–IS analysis) and aggregate supply sectors of a global model of the macroeconomy. The underemployment equilibrium of Keynes is shown fundamentally to be a result of rigidity of money wages, and the neoclassical (often called Monetarist) propositions are shown to be a result of money wage and price flexibility. Robert H. Rasche's sketch of the Monetarist analytical framework is in accord with the main implications of Smith's article. Rasche's analysis, however, appends to the basic aggregate demand–aggregate supply model two key Monetarist features: (1) explicit treatment of the price (and money wage) perceptions that lie behind the underemployment-creating "rigidities" (discussed by Smith) and (2) inclusion of a government sector and an outstanding stock of government debt to allow for fuller examination of the effects of fiscal and monetary policy. Together, the material in these two readings is an important supplement to treatments found in the standard textbooks in the fields of macroeconomics, money and banking, and monetary theory. In addition, many of the issues introduced in these opening readings are explored in greater detail later in the book.

The standard paradigms of economic theory have received a new challenge from the work of Axel Leijonhufvud, Robert Clower, and others who have reexamined Keynesian models (represented here by Warren L. Smith's reading) and Monetarist models (represented here by Robert H. Rasche's contribution) and contrasted them with the original work of John Maynard Keynes. Is Keynes' work a special (e.g. rigid nominal wage) case of a more general neoclassical theory, or did it represent a rather unique world view? In a brilliant exposition featured as the third essay in this section, A. J. Hines represents the growing number of economists who opt for the latter position. Hines succinctly reveals the new and exciting perspective on macroeconomic theory expounded by the new students of Keynes' system.

"There is but one macroeconomics (or monetary theory), and it has been around for over two hundred years." This statement characterizes the brisk and provocative final essay in this section. John H. Wood argues that there is fundamentally no paradigmatic conflict between the world views of Keynes and Monetarist Milton Friedman. Wood contends that Keynes *and* Friedman would both agree that it is an unstable monetary environment that produces the general uncertainty of future prices that allows changes in aggregate demand to have short-run effects on output and employment.

1

A Graphical Exposition of the Complete Keynesian System

*Warren L. Smith**

The purpose of this paper is chiefly expository. A simple graphical technique is employed to exhibit the working of several variants of the Keynesian model. Many of the issues discussed have been dealt with elsewhere,[1] but it is hoped that the analysis presented here will clarify some of the issues and be useful for pedagogical purposes.

Reprinted from the *Southern Economic Journal*, Vol. 23, No. 3 (October, 1956), pp. 115-125, by permission of the Southern Economic Association and the estate of Warren L. Smith.

* The development of the technique employed in this paper is a result of discussions with many persons, particularly Professor Daniel B. Suits of the University of Michigan, to whom the writer wishes to express his thanks.

[1]See particularly L. R. Klein, "Theories of Effective Demand and Employment," *Journal of Political Economy*, Vol. LV (April 1947), pp. 108-31, reprinted in R. V. Clemence (ed.), *Readings in Economic Analysis*, Vol. I (Cambridge, Mass.: Addison-Wesley Press, 1950), pp. 260-83, and *The Keynesian Revolution* (New York: Macmillan Co., 1950), esp. Technical Appendix; F. Modigliani, "Liquidity Preference and the Theory of Interest and Money," *Econometrica*, Vol. XII (Jan. 1944), pp. 45-88, reprinted in F. A. Lutz and L. W. Mints (eds.), *Readings in Monetary Theory* (Homewood, Ill.: Richard D. Irwin, Inc., 1951), pp. 186-239; also V. Lutz, "Real and Monetary Factors in the Determination of Employment Levels," *Quarterly Journal of Economics*, Vol. LXVI (May 1952), pp. 251-72; L. Hough, "The Price Level in Macroeconomic Models," *American Economic Review*, Vol. LXIV (June 1954), pp. 269-86.

I. The Keynesian System with Flexible Wages

This system can be represented symbolically by the following five equations:

$$y = c(y,r) + i(y,r) \tag{1}$$

$$\frac{M}{p} = L(y,r) \tag{2}$$

$$y = f(N) \tag{3}$$

$$\frac{w}{p} = f'(N) \tag{4}$$

$$N = \phi\left(\frac{w}{p}\right) \tag{5}$$

Here y = real GNP (at constant prices), r = an index of interest rates, M = money supply (in current dollars), p = index of the price level applicable to GNP, N = the volume of employment (in equivalent full-time workers), w = the money wage. The model represents a theory of short-run income determination with capital stock fixed and labor the only variable factor of production.

The working of this model is illustrated in Figure I. Figure I should be studied in clockwise fashion, beginning with Chart I(a) in the lower lefthand corner. In I(a), *DD* represents the demand for labor [equation (4)] and *SS* represents the supply of labor [equation (5)]. The level of employment and the real wage are determined at the full employment levels, N_f and $(w/p)_f$. Proceeding to I(b), the curve *OP* represents the aggregate production function [equation (3)], its shape reflecting diminishing returns.[2] With employment of N_f, y would be at the level y_f, indicated in I(b).

Chart I(c) is the type of diagram developed by Hicks and utilized by others to depict the condition of monetary equilibrium in the Keynesian system.[3] The *IS* curve in I(c) depicts equation (1) and indicates for each possible level of the interest rate (r) the equilibrium level of income (y) which would prevail after the multiplier had

[2]According to the mathematical formulation of our model in equations (1)-(5), the curve *DD* in I(a) is the derivative of curve *OP* in I(b), the relation reflecting the operation of the marginal productivity law under competitive conditions. This precise condition is not important, however, and we shall make no attempt to draw the curves in such a way as to fulfill it. For one thing, the presence of monopoly in the economy or failure of entrepreneurs to seek maximum profits would destroy the precision of the equations, but relations of the type depicted in Figure I would in all probability continue to hold.

[3]For a detailed discussion of this diagram, see J. R. Hicks, "Mr. Keynes and the 'Classics': A Suggested Interpretation," *Econometrica*, Vol. V (April 1937), pp. 147-59; also A. H. Hansen, *Monetary Theory and Fiscal Policy* (New York: McGraw-Hill, 1949), chap. 5. The reader's attention is directed to the fact that we have reversed the axes of the Hicks diagram; we measure the interest rate on the horizontal axis and income on the vertical axis.

worked itself out fully.[4] We treat the stock of money as an exogenous variable determined by the monetary authority. Given M, the LM curves in I(c), of which there would be one for each possible price level (p) which might prevail, represent equation (2) in our model. For example, if the price level were held constant at p_o, the curve $LM(p_o)$ depicts the different interest rates that would be required to preserve equilibrium in the money market at different income levels. The fact that rising income levels are associated with higher interest rates reflects the presumption that as income rises, transactions cash requirements are larger, leaving less of the fixed (in real terms) quantity of money to satisfy demands for idle balances, thus pushing up the interest rate.

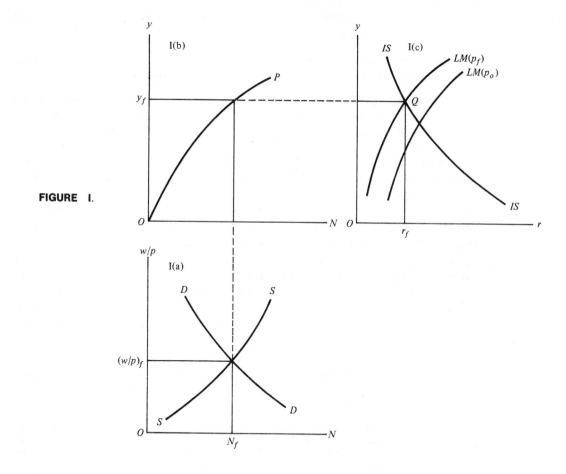

FIGURE I.

[4]It should be noted that the formal analysis in this paper falls entirely in the category of comparative statics, that is, it refers to conditions of equilibrium and changes in the equilibrium values of the variables brought about by changes in data or exogenous variables and does not pretend to describe the *paths* followed by the variables as they move from one equilibrium position to another.

If prices and wages are flexible and the situation is as depicted in Figure I, full employment will automatically be maintained, since the price level will adjust to the level p_f, establishing the *LM* curve in the position $LM(p_f)$ where it will intersect the *IS* curve at point Q which corresponds to the full employment level of income (y_f). If, for example, the real wage is initially above $(w/p)_f$, money wages will fall due to the excess of supply of labor. This will reduce costs, resulting in increased output and employment and lower prices. Falling prices shift the *LM* curve upward by increasing the real value of cash balances (M/p), thus lowering the interest rates and expanding aggregate demand to the point where the market will absorb the output corresponding to full employment.[5]

Two important and related propositions can be set down concerning interest and money in the above model:

1. The rate of interest is determined solely by saving and investment and is independent of the quantity of money and liquidity preference.

2. The quantity theory of money holds for this model—that is, a change in the quantity of money will bring about an equal proportional change in the price level and will have no effect on real income or employment.

In other words, the quantity of money and liquidity preference serve not to determine the interest rate, as alleged by Keynes, but the price level. As can readily be seen from Figure I, income is established at the full employment level [I(a) and I(b)], the interest rate adjusts to equate savings and investment [on the *IS* curve in I(c)] at this income level, and the price level adjusts so as to satisfy liquidity requirements at this interest rate [establishing the *LM* curve at the appropriate position in I(c)].

It is a comparatively simple matter to modify the analysis of Figure I to take account of the possible effect of changes in the real value of liquid assets on consumption (the Pigou effect).[6] The real value of the stock of liquid assets would be included in equation (1), and falling prices would then shift the *IS* curve to the right, thus strengthening the tendency toward full employment equilibrium. This suggests the question: Does the introduction of the Pigou effect give the quantity of money the power to change the rate of interest when prices and wages are flexible? The answer to this question cannot be deduced from the curves of Figure I, but it is not difficult to find the answer with the aid of the following simple model:

[5]We abstract from the possibility of dynamic instability which may arise due to falling prices if the public has elastic expectations. See D. Patinkin, "Price Flexibility and Full Employment," *American Economic Review*, Vol. XXXVII (September 1948), pp. 543-64, reprinted with slight modification in Lutz and Mints, *op. cit.*, pp. 252-83.

[6]On the Pigou effect, see A. C. Pigou, "Economic Progress in a Stable Environment," *Economica*, New Series, Vol. XIV (August 1947), pp. 180-88, reprinted in Lutz and Mints, *op. cit.*, pp. 241-51; Patinkin, *op. cit.*, G. Ackley, "The Wealth-Saving Relationship," *Journal of Political Economy*, Vol. LIX (April 1951), pp. 154-61; M. Cohen, "Liquid Assets and the Consumption Function," *Review of Economics and Statistics*, Vol. XXXVI (May 1954), pp. 202-11; and bibliography in the latter two articles.

$$\bar{y} = c(\bar{y},r,a) + i(\bar{y},r)$$

$$\frac{M}{p} = L(\bar{y},r)$$

$$a = \frac{A}{p}$$

Here a = the real value of liquid assets which is included in the consumption function and A = their money value. The last three equations of our original model are assumed to determine the real wage, employment, and real income. These equations are dropped and y is treated as a constant (having value $\bar{y}$) determined by those equations. We can now treat M and A as parameters and r, a, and p as variables, differentiate these three equations with respect to M, and solve for dr/dM. This gives the following expression:

$$\frac{dr}{dM} = \frac{\dfrac{c_a}{i_r} \dfrac{A}{M} (1 - \eta_{AM})}{p\left(1 + \dfrac{c_r}{i_r} + \dfrac{A}{M} \dfrac{L_r c_a}{i_r}\right)} \tag{6}$$

In this expression, the subscripts refer to partial derivates, e.g., $c_a = \delta c/\delta a$. Normally, the following conditions would be satisfied: $c_a > 0$, $i_r < 0$, $L_r < 0$. We cannot be sure about the sign of c_r, but it is likely to be small in any case. The coefficient η_{AM} has the following meaning:

$$\eta_{AM} = \frac{M}{A} \frac{dA}{dM} = \frac{\dfrac{dA}{A}}{\dfrac{dM}{M}}$$

For example, if a change in M is brought about in such a way as to produce an exactly proportionate change in A, η_{AM} will be unity. Or if the change in M is not accompanied by any change in A, η_{AM} will be zero. It is apparent from the above expression that a change in the quantity of money will not affect the rate of interest if $\eta_{AM} = 1$, while an increase (decrease) in the quantity of money will lower (raise) the rate of interest if $\eta_{AM} < 1$.[7] Thus, the way in which changes in the quantity of

[7]We assume that $c_r < 0$, or if $c_r > 0$,

$$1 + \frac{A}{M} \frac{L_r c_a}{i_r} > \frac{c_r}{i_r}$$

so that the denominator of (6) is positive.

money affect the rate of interest depends upon what asset concept is included in the consumption function (i.e., what is included in A) and how the volume of these assets is affected by monetary change. If M itself is the appropriate asset concept to include in the consumption function (i.e., if $A = M$), changes in M will not affect the interest rate, since in this case η_{AM} is equal to unity. However, the consensus of opinion seems to be that some other aggregate, such as currency, deposits, and government securities held by the nonbank public minus the public's indebtedness to the banks, is more appropriate.[8] If this concept is employed, most of the usual methods of increasing the money supply will ordinarily either leave A unchanged ($\eta_{AM} = 0$) or cause it to increase less than in proportion to the increase in M ($0 < \eta_{AM} < 1$).[9] We may conclude that the Pigou effect gives monetary changes power to influence the rate of interest, even if wages and prices are fully flexible. An increase (decrease) in the quantity of money will ordinarily lower (raise) the rate of interest and also increase (decrease) investment and decrease (increase) consumption, but will not change income and employment which are determined by real forces (the last three equations of our complete model).[10,11]

II. Possibilities of Underemployment Disequilibrium

There are several possible circumstances arising from the shapes of the various schedules which might produce a situation in which, even though the relations in the above model held true, it might be impossible, at least temporarily, for equilibrium (full employment or otherwise) to be reached. The most widely discussed of these possibilities is depicted in Figure II.

[8]The question of what asset concept is appropriate is discussed in Patinkin, *op. cit.,* Cohen, *op. cit.,* and J. Tobin, "Asset Holdings and Spending Decisions," *American Economic Review Papers and Proceedings,* Vol. XLII (May 1952), pp. 109-23.

[9]Open market purchases of government securities by the central bank from the nonbank public will leave A unchanged, since the initial purchase transaction will result in a decline in the public's security holdings and an equal increase in M, while any induced expansion of loans and investments by the banks will result in an increase in M offset by an equal increase in the public's indebtedness to the banks. On the other hand, if the Treasury prints currency and gives it to the public, A will be increased by the same absolute amount as M but the increase in A will be proportionately smaller than the increase in M (provided the public's holdings of government securities exceed its indebtedness to the banks so that $A > M$).

[10]The fact that the existence of a wealth effect on savings may confer upon the quantity of money the power to affect the rate of interest even with flexible wages is demonstrated in L. A. Metzler, "Wealth, Saving, and the Rate of Interest," *Journal of Political Economy,* Vol. LIX (April 1951), pp. 93-116. Metzler's conclusions, which differ from those given here, can be attributed to assumptions that he makes, particularly the assumption that the only assets are money and common stock.

[11]If the supply of labor is affected by the real value of wealth held by workers, changes in the quantity of money may affect output and employment by shifting the SS curve in Figure I(a). Also, even though monetary change does not affect the *current* level of income and employment, if, due to the operation of the Pigou effect, it changes the interest rate and thereby investment, it may affect the *future* level of employment, since the change in capital stock will ordinarily shift the demand for labor [DD curve in Figure I(a)] at a future date. Both these points are mentioned in V. Lutz, *op. cit.*

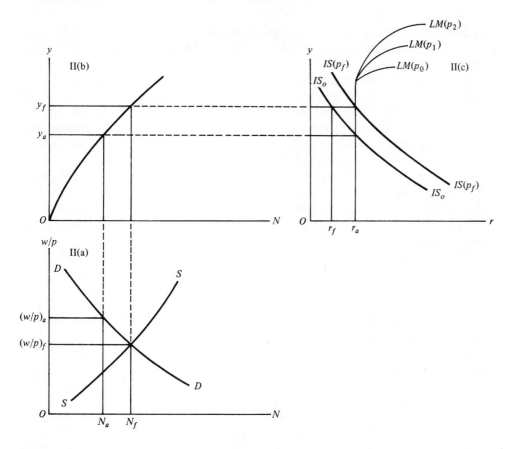

FIGURE II.

II(a) and II(b) are similar to I(a) and I(b). However, the *LM* curves in II(c) are drawn to reflect the much-discussed possibility mentioned by Keynes[12] that the liquidity preference schedule might become infinitely elastic at some low level of interest rates [r_a in II(c)], due either to the unanimous expectations of investors that interest rates would rise when they reached this extremely low level relative to future expectations or to the cost of investments. In the case depicted, full employment (N_f) would involve a level of income of y_f. If the *IS* curve were at the level IS_0, the interest rate required to make investment equal to saving at income y_f would be r_f. But the infinite elasticity of the *LM* schedule prevents the interest rate from falling below r_a. The result would be that employment and income would be prevented from rising above the level N_a and y_a by inadequate effective demand. The real wage would hold at the level $(w/p)_a$ which is above the full employment level $(w/p)_f$. Competition for employment would reduce money wages, costs, and prices. But the falling price level, although it would increase the quantity of money in real terms, would not affect the

[12]J. M. Keynes, *General Theory of Employment, Interest, and Money* (New York: Harcourt, Brace and Co., 1936), pp. 201–4.

interest rate, hence would not increase investment. As prices fell, the *LM* curve would take successive positions, such as $LM(p_0)$, $LM(p_1)$, $LM(p_2)$, etc., leaving the interest rate unaffected.[13]

A special case of the situation depicted in Figure II may arise if a negative interest rate is required to equate investment to full employment savings. In this case, the *IS* curve would cut the *y*-axis and lie to the left of it at an income corresponding to full employment. Then, even if there were nothing to prevent the rate of interest from approaching zero, it could not go below zero,[14] and the *LM* curve would have a floor at a zero rate, thus preventing full employment from being attained.

It is interesting to note that if the Pigou effect is operative, a full employment equilibrium may be attainable even in the case illustrated in Figure II. As prices fall, the real value of liquid assets increases. If this increases consumption expenditures, the *IS* curve will shift to the right until it attains the position $IS(p_f)$, where a full employment equilibrium is reached.

Certain other conceivable situations which might lead to an underemployment disequilibrium are worthy of brief mention. One possibility is that the supply of labor might exceed the demand at all levels of real wages. Such a situation seems very improbable, however, since there is reason to believe that the short-run aggregate labor supply is quite inelastic over a considerable range of wage rates and declines when wage rates become very low.[15]

Disequilibrium situations could also arise if (*a*) the demand curve for labor had a steeper slope than the supply curve at their point of intersection, or (*b*) the *IS* curve cut the *LM* curve in such a way that *IS* lay to the right of *LM* above their intersection and to the left of *LM* below their intersection in Figure I(c) or II(c). Actually, these are situations of unstable equilibrium rather than of disequilibrium. However, in these cases, a slight departure from equilibrium would produce a cumulative movement away from it, and the effect would be similar to a situation of disequilibrium.

III. Underemployment Equilibrium Due to Wage Rigidity

Next we may consider the case in which the supply of and demand for labor are essentially the same as in Figures I and II, but for institutional or other reasons the

---

[13]Equations (1)-(5) above apply to the situations covered in both Figure I and Figure II. In the latter case, however, the equations are mathematically inconsistent and do not possess a solution. Mathematics does not tell us what will happen in this case (although the additional conditions necessary to describe the results could be expressed mathematically). The statements made above concerning the results (i.e., that income will be y_a, prices and wages will fall together, etc.) are propositions in economics.

[14]Since the money rate of interest cannot be negative, as long as it costs nothing to hold money. In fact, a zero rate of interest would be impossible, since in this case property value would be infinite; however, the rate might *approach* zero. The *real* rate of interest, *ex post*, may be negative due to inflation, but this is not relevant to our problem. On this, see I. Fisher, *The Theory of Interest* (New York: Macmillan Co., 1930), chaps. ii, xix, and pp. 282–86.

[15]On the probable shape of the short-run aggregative supply of labor, see G. F. Bloom and H. R. Northrup, *Economics of Labor Relations* (Homewood, Ill.: Richard D. Irwin, Inc., 1954), pp. 250–53.

money wage does not fall when there is an excess supply of labor.[16] This rigidity of money wages may be due to various factors, including (*a*) powerful trade unions which are able to prevent money wages from falling, at least temporarily, (*b*) statutory provisions, such as minimum wage laws, (*c*) failure of employers to reduce wages due to a desire to retain loyal and experienced employees and to maintain morale,[17] or (*d*) unwillingness of unemployed workers to accept reduced money wages even though they would be willing to work at lower real wages brought about by a rise in prices.[18]

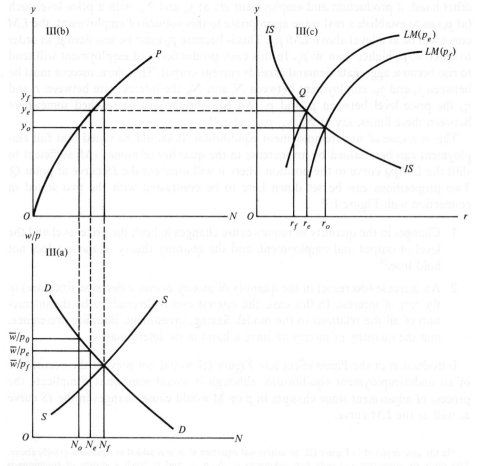

FIGURE III.

---

[16]We will assume that this rigidity does not prevail in an upward direction—i.e., money wages will rise when there is an excess demand for labor.

[17]See A. Rees, "Wage Determination and Involuntary Unemployment, *Journal of Political Economy*, Vol. LIX (April 1951), pp. 143-53.

[18]Keynes, *op. cit.,* chap. 2; J. Tobin, "Money Wage Rates and Employment," in S. E. Harris (ed.), *The New Economics* (New York: Knopf, 1947), pp. 572-87.

A situation of this kind is depicted in Figure III. The fixed money wage is designated by $\bar{w}$. In order for full employment (N_f) to be attained, the price level must be at p_f (such as to make $\bar{w}/p_f$ equal to the real wage corresponding to full employment), income will be y_f, and the interest rate must reach r_f. However, in the case shown in Figure III, the quantity of money, M, is such that when p is at the level p_f, the LM curve [$LM(p_f)$] intersects the IS curve at an income (y_0) below the full employment level and an interest rate (r_0) above the full employment level. Hence, full employment cannot be sustained due to inadequate effective demand. On the other hand, if production and employment are at y_0 and N_0, with a price level such (at p_0) as to establish a real wage appropriate to this volume of employment, the LM curve will be at a level above $LM(p_f)$. This is because p_0 must be less than p_f in order to make $\bar{w}/p_0$ higher than $\bar{w}/p_f$. In this case, production and employment will tend to rise because aggregate demand exceeds current output. Therefore, income must be between y_f and y_0, employment between N_f and N_0, the interest rate between r_f and r_0, the price level between p_f and p_0. An equilibrium will be reached somewhere between these limits, say at N_e, y_e, p_e, and r_e.[19]

This is a case of underemployment equilibrium. It should be noted that full employment can be attained by an increase in the quantity of money (M) sufficient to shift the $LM(p_f)$ curve to the position where it will intersect the IS curve at point Q. Two propositions can be set down here to be contrasted with the two stated in connection with Figure I:[20]

1. Changes in the quantity of money cause changes in both the price level and the level of output and employment, and the quantity theory of money does not hold true.[21]

2. An increase (decrease) in the quantity of money causes a decrease (increase) in the rate of interest. In this case, the interest rate is determined by the interaction of all the relations in the model. Saving, investment, liquidity preference, and the quantity of money all have a hand in its determination.

Introduction of the Pigou effect into Figure III would not prevent the occurrence of an underemployment equilibrium, although it would somewhat complicate the process of adjustment since changes in p or M would cause changes in the IS curve as well as the LM curve.

---

[19]In the case depicted in Figure III, an additional equation $\bar{w} = w$ is added to equations (1)–(5) above. This gives six equations and only five unknowns (y, N, p, w, and r). Such a system of equations is *overdetermined* and does not, in general, possess a solution. If the quantity of money is treated as a variable which is adjusted so as to maintain full employment, we have six equations and six unknowns and there will be a solution (unless the equations are inconsistent).

[20]See p. 5, *supra.*

[21]In the limiting case in which the DD curve has a horizontal stage which includes the current level of employment, the entire effect of an increase in M is on y, with no change in p. A considerable part of Keynes' *General Theory* (prior to the discussion of wages and prices in Book V) has reference primarily to this situation.

To summarize, our analysis of Figures I and III indicates that rigidity of money wages is, in general, a necessary condition for (*a*) the occurrence of an underemployment equilibrium, (*b*) the quantity of money to have an effect on the level of real income and employment. The rate of interest will not be affected by the quantity of money and liquidity preference unless (*a*) there is rigidity of money wages or (*b*) the Pigou effect is operative with $\eta_{AM} \neq 1$. Monetary theories of the rate of interest, whether of the loanable funds or liquidity preference variety, ordinarily assume rigidity (or at least stickiness) in the structure of money wages.[22]

IV. Concluding Comments

In conclusion, we would like to call the reader's attention to further uses to which our graphical technique can be put. With appropriate modifications to suit the occasion, it can be used to analyze other variations of the Keynesian model.[23] Additional factors affecting the income, employment, and price levels, such as those suggested by Hough[24] and by Lutz[25] can be quite easily introduced into the analysis through appropriate shifts in the schedules shown in our system of graphs. Fiscal policy and its relation to monetary policy can be dealt with, since fiscal policy influences the level and shape of the *IS* curve. Finally, it provides a useful starting point for the study of economic growth. Factors affecting the rate of growth, such as capital accumulation, population growth, technological change, etc., can be brought in by allowing for their effects on the various schedules.

[22]The relative merits of loanable funds and liquidity preference types of monetary interest theories we do not consider, except to say that when appropriately formulated, the two are equivalent.

[23]For example, the models with which Modigliani begins his analysis (*op. cit.,* pp. 46-48 in original, pp. 187-90 in *Readings in Monetary Theory*). Analysis of these models requires some alteration in the graphical technique, since he assumes that consumption, investment, and the demand for money, all in current dollars, depend upon money income and the rate of interest, thus introducing "money illusions" into his scheme at several points.

[24]L. Hough, "The Price Level in Macroeconomic Models," *American Economic Review,* Vol. LXIV (June 1954), pp. 269-86.

[25]V. Lutz, "Real and Monetary Factors in the Determination of Employment Levels," *Quarterly Journal of Economics,* Vol. LXVI (May 1952), pp. 251-72.

2

A Comparative Static Analysis of Some Monetarist Propositions

Robert H. Rasche

The typical textbook approach to macroeconomic analysis is almost completely barren with respect to what has become characterized as the "monetarist position" on the effects of monetary and fiscal policy actions. These propositions might be summarized as follows:

(1) the long-run impact of monetary actions is on nominal variables, such as nominal GNP, the general price level, and nominal interest rates;

(2) long-run movements in real economic variables, such as output and employment, are little influenced, if at all, by monetary actions;

(3) in the short run, actions of the central bank exert an impact on both real and nominal variables;

(4) fiscal actions have little lasting influence on nominal GNP but can affect short-run movements in output and employment; and

(5) government expenditures financed by taxes or borrowing from the public tend to crowd out, over a fairly short period of time, an equal amount of private expenditures.[1]

Reprinted from the Federal Reserve Bank of St. Louis, *Review* (December, 1973), pp. 15-23, by permission of the publisher and the author.

[1]These propositions have been gleaned from Leonall C. Andersen, "A Monetarist View of Demand Management: The United States Experience," this *Review* (September 1971), pp. 3-11.

It would seem that a static analytic framework could be developed which could shed some light on the theoretical underpinnings of monetarism, although the mode of analysis is obviously insufficient to cope with the dynamic propositions which are associated with this school. Unfortunately, the literature is extremely scarce. Milton Friedman has set forth a static framework, and alleges that the differences between monetarists and post-Keynesians have to do with assumptions about price (and wage) behavior. Monetarism, he alleges, assumes that the aggregate price level is determined in such a way as to clear all markets in the long run. For the short run, he alleges that neither the monetarist nor the fiscalist has a satisfactory theory of the response of real output and the general price level to monetary shocks. Unfortunately, Friedman's excursion into dynamics and differential equations is difficult, if not impossible, to relate to individual market forces.[2]

Thus, the issue remains unsettled. On the one hand, we are left without a clearly specified analytical framework for the monetarist approach which can be contrasted with the well-developed static income determination model. On the other hand, and even more importantly, there is no general model which can produce the post-Keynesian model as a particular case and the monetarist and classical models as alternative cases. Such a framework is useful in order to discriminate between alternative hypotheses and to construct empirical tests which have the potential to refute one or both positions.

This study attempts to develop a general model by examining equilibria which differ by the length of the "run." This Marshallian tool should be clearly defined as applying to the behavior which is assumed to be embodied in the *ceteris paribus* assumptions: the more behavior which is embodied in *ceteris paribus*, the shorter the "run." Traditional macrostatics has been of the Marshallian "short-run" variety; that is, the real capital stock has been held constant. This leads to some unfortunately confusing terminology. Most of the traditional analysis from which the "long-run" monetarist propositions can be gleaned is not long-run analysis in the Marshallian sense. At the risk of adding further confusion to the discussion we shall stay with the traditional short-run definition as the "short run," and compare the results of this model with those of an even shorter run, or "monetary-run" model.

It is well established that a Patinkin-type four market model (labor services, commodities, bonds, and money), under assumptions of complete price flexibility, absence of money illusion, unitary elasticity of price expectations, and perfect information on market prices, will exhibit propositions (1), (2), and (5) above, in comparison of "short-run" equilibria which differ because of a shock to some policy variable.[3]

[2]Milton Friedman, "A Theoretical Framework for Monetary Analysis," *Journal of Political Economy* (March/April 1970), pp. 193-238.

[3]For a derivation of these propositions and a discussion of the effects of the presence or absence of government bonds in the model, see Don Patinkin, *Money, Interest, and Prices: An Integration of Monetary and Value Theory,* 2nd ed. (New York: Harper & Row, 1965), chap. 10; Robert L. Crouch, *Macroeconomics* (New York: Harcourt Brace Jovanovich, 1972), chaps. 6-9; and Franco Modigliani, "The Monetary Mechanism and Its Interaction with Real Phenomena," *Review of Economics and Statistics, Supplement* (February 1963), pp. 79-107.

However, these analyses have nothing to contribute to the discussion of propositions (3) and (4).

Basic Elements of Model

More than a decade ago, it appears that the assumption of perfect information on prices was implicitly relaxed in some of the research work of leading monetarists. Friedman, in his work on the demand for money, distinguished between the current commodity price index and a longer-run concept which he called the "permanent price level." He argued that:

> . . . holders of money presumably judge the "real" amount of cash balances in terms of the quantity of goods and services to which the balances are equivalent, not at any given moment of time, but over a sizable and indefinite period; that is, they evaluate them in terms of "expected" or "permanent" prices, not in terms of the current price level. This consideration does not, of course, rule out some adjustment to temporary movements in prices.[4]

Recently, following the pioneering work of George Stigler and Armen A. Alchian, considerable theoretical and empirical work on labor market behavior and the Phillips curve has been produced.[5] These studies assume that workers do not possess perfect information on the wages available to them in return for their labor services, and it is costly for workers to search out information on the opportunities available to them. Within this framework it is necessary to distinguish between the nominal wage rate which is actually offered for labor services at a point in time, W, and the wage rate which is perceived by suppliers of labor services, W_e. In this paper we employ a wage rate information parameter, λ_1, to relate the perceived wage rate to the currently offered rate and an exogenous, or predetermined, component, W_o.

The relationship we postulate is:

$$W_e = W^{\lambda_1} (W_o)^{1 - \lambda_1}$$

so the perceived nominal wage rate is a geometric average of the current wage rate and a predetermined wage rate, presumably based on the history of previous wage experience. If the wage information parameter, λ_1, is set equal to 1.0, there is costless information and the perceived wage rate is the current nominal wage. At the other

---

[4]Milton Friedman, "The Demand for Money: Some Theoretical and Empirical Results," *Journal of Political Economy* (August 1959), pp. 327–351.

[5]George J. Stigler, "Information in the Labor Market," *Journal of Political Economy, Supplement* (October 1962), pp. 94–105, and Armen A. Alchian, "Information Costs, Pricing, and Resource Unemployment," Edmund Phelps et al., *Microeconomic Foundations of Employment and Inflation Theory* (New York: Norton, 1970), pp. 27–52.

extreme, if λ_1 is set equal to zero, information about the current wage rate has an infinite price and there is total ignorance of current market conditions.

This cost of information approach can be extended to the commodity market. We assume that households make their consumption and portfolio decisions on the basis of their perceived commodity price index, P_e, which can differ from the actual commodity price index if information on commodity prices is imperfect and costly to gather.[6] Analogous to the case of the wage rate, we postulate a price information parameter, λ_2, which relates the perceived price index to the current price index as follows:

$$P_e = P^{\lambda_2}(P_o)^{1 - \lambda_2}$$

Again the perceived commodity price index is a geometric average of the current price index and an exogenously determined price level. When λ_2 equals one, information on the commodity price is free, and all information on current prices can be incorporated into decision making. When λ_2 is equal to zero, the cost of information is infinite, and no current market behavior is incorporated into decision making.

Once we allow the perceived price level and perceived wage rate to differ from the respective current market value, we must explicitly introduce P_e and W_e into the model. This is indicated in Table 1, where the labor supply function of households is expressed as a function of the perceived real wage rate (W_e/P_e), real consumption demand is a function of perceived real net worth (V/P_e) and perceived real disposable income, as are real bond demand and the demand for real cash balances. If we interpret P_e as equivalent to Friedman's "permanent" price index concept, the money demand equation (equation XII in Table 1) is the money demand function used by Friedman with the exception of his use of a per capita specification and an explicit functional form.[7] All other functions are specified exactly as in the Patinkin model. In particular it should be noted that the interest elasticity of the demand for real cash balances has not been constrained to zero.

First, the behavior of the labor market has to be considered. As indicated in Figure 1, there is a single labor demand curve plotted as a function of the prevailing real wage (W/P). We have to analyze how the labor supply curve interacts with this labor demand curve. Consider a situation in which the movement from one equilibrium to another involves a rise in the commodity price index, P. If, under these circumstances, the labor supply function shifts to the right, from N^s_1 to N^s_2, then the new equilibrium of the system is characterized by higher employment and a lower real wage rate than the initial equilibrium. Since employment is higher, real output is also higher in the new equilibrium relative to the initial equilibrium.

---

[6]For simplicity, we assume firms have zero information costs with respect to wages and prices.
[7]Friedman, "The Demand for Money," pp. 327-351.

It can be shown that a sufficient condition for the labor supply curve to shift to the right in the real wage-employment plane in response to increases in the commodity price index is that λ_1, the information parameter for the perceived nominal wage rate, be greater than λ_2, the information parameter for the perceived commodity price

Table 1. Equations for the Complete Macroeconomic Model
(excluding a Government Sector)

	Equation	Name	Market
(I)	$N^d = N^d\left(\dfrac{W}{P}, \bar{K}\right)$	Labor demand function	
(II)	$N^s = N^s\left(\dfrac{W_e}{P_e}\right)$	Labor supply function	Labor market
(III)	$N^d = N^s = N$	Labor market equilibrium condition	
(IV)	$X^s = X^s\,(N, \bar{K})$	Production (or commodity supply) function	
(V)	$C = C\left(X_d, \dfrac{V}{P_e}\right)$	Commodity demand function for consumption (the consumption function)	
(VI)	$I = I\,(X, r)$	Commodity demand function for investment (the investment function)	Commodity market
(VII)	$X = C + I$	Total (or aggregate) commodity demand function	
(VIII)	$X = X^s$	Commodity market equilibrium condition	
(IX)	$\dfrac{B^d}{rP_e} = B^d\left(X_d, \dfrac{1}{r}, \dfrac{V}{P_e}\right)$	Bond demand function	
(X)	$\dfrac{B^s}{rP} = B^s\left(X^s, \dfrac{1}{r}, \dfrac{V}{P}\right)$	Bond supply function	Bond market
(XI)	$B^d = B^s$	Bond market equilibrium condition	
(XII)	$\dfrac{M^d}{P_e} = L\left(X_d, r, \dfrac{V}{P_e}\right)$	Money demand function	
(XIII)	$M^d = \overline{M^s}$	Money market equilibrium condition and (exogenous) money supply function	Money market

Table 1. (continued)

	Equation	Name	Market
(XIV)	$S = X^s - C$	Definition of saving	
(XV)	$Y = PX^s$	Definition of money income	
(XVI)	$V = P \bar{K} + \bar{M}^s$	Definition of money wealth (net assets or net worth)	Definitions of supplementary variables
(XVII)	$X_d = \dfrac{Y}{P_e}$	Definition of real perceived disposable income	
(XVIII)	$W_e = W^{\lambda_1} W_0^{(1 - \lambda_1)}$	Definition of perceived wage rate	
(XIX)	$P_e = P^{\lambda_2} P_0^{(1 - \lambda_2)}$	Definition of perceived price level	

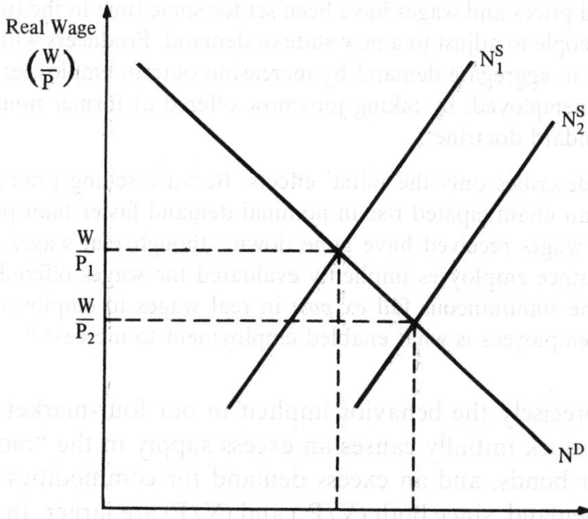

FIGURE 1.

index.[8] In the analysis which follows, we shall characterize the "momentary" equilibrium as one in which information on both wages and prices is not free—that is, $0 < \lambda_2 < \lambda_1 < 1$. The short-run equilibrium will be characterized by perfect information on both wages and prices—that is, $\lambda_1 = \lambda_2 = 1$. In the short run, there are no shifts

[8]For a proof of this proposition see Appendix A, which is available only in the reprint [no. 82, Spring 1974] to this article.[At the time of this printing, copies of this Reprint were available from the Research Department of the Federal Reserve Bank of St. Louis, St. Louis, Missouri.—Ed.]

of the labor supply curve in response to changes in commodity prices and the equilibrium level of employment remains at N*, the initial equilibrium level. This phenomenon appears to be identical to that conceived by Friedman in his discussion of the natural unemployment rate.[9] N* could be termed the "natural level of employment" in this static model.

Changes in the Money Stock

It remains to be seen how the model reacts in a momentary equilibrium after the money stock has changed. A monetarist scenario has been provided by Friedman:

> . . . suppose . . . that the "natural" [unemployment] rate is higher than 3 percent. Suppose also that we start out at a time when prices have been stable and when unemployment is higher than 3 percent. Accordingly, the [monetary] authority increases the rate of monetary growth. This will be expansionary. By making nominal cash balances higher than people desire, it will tend initially to lower interest rates and in this and other ways to stimulate spending. Income and spending will start to rise.
>
> To begin with, much or most of the rise in income will take the form of an increase in output and employment rather than in prices. People have been expecting prices to be stable, and prices and wages have been set for some time in the future on that basis. It takes time for people to adjust to a new state of demand. Producers will tend to react to the initial expansion in aggregate demand by increasing output, employees by working longer hours, and the unemployed, by taking jobs now offered at former nominal wages. This much is pretty standard doctrine.
>
> But it describes only the initial effects. Because selling prices of products typically respond to an unanticipated rise in nominal demand faster than prices of factors of production, real wages received have gone down—though real wages anticipated by employees went up, since employees implicitly evaluated the wages offered at the earlier price level. Indeed, the simultaneous fall *ex post* in real wages to employers and rise *ex ante* in real wages to employees is what enabled employment to increase.[10]

This is precisely the behavior implicit in our four-market model. The increase in the money stock initially causes an excess supply in the "money market," an excess demand for bonds, and an excess demand for commodities through increased consumption demand, since both (V/P_e) and (V/P) are larger. In the momentary equilibrium, real output, commodity prices, and money wages are all higher than their initial equilibrium values.[11] However, the change in W, the money wage rate, is less than proportional to the change in P, and the actual real wage rate declines. The real wage perceived by suppliers of labor services (W_e/P_e) increases as long as the cost of

---

[9]Milton Friedman, "The Role of Monetary Policy," *American Economic Review* (March 1968), p. 8.
[10]Friedman, "The Role of Monetary Policy," pp. 9-10.
[11]The mathematical proof of these propositions, with a statement of sufficiency conditions, can be found in Appendix B, which appears only in the [original 1974] reprint to this article. [See footnote 8.]

obtaining information about prices is greater than the cost of obtaining information about wages ($\lambda_2 < \lambda_1$). Thus, the labor supply curve shifts to the right. The momentary equilibrium results correspond quite closely to the monetarist scenario outlined by Friedman and to the third proposition taken from Andersen.

An interesting question remains on the extent to which prices respond to a change in the money stock in this momentary equilibrium. In particular, we wish to consider the percentage change in the commodity price index generated by a one percent change in the money stock. In Appendix B (included only in reprint)* it is shown that when (1) a set of sufficient conditions for a positive change in real output in response to a positive change in the money stock is satisfied and (2) the money

Table 2. Notation

I. Endogenous Variables
  A. Flow variables
    1. N^d, demand for labor (labor services per time period)
    2. N^s, supply of labor (labor services per time period)
    3. X^s, real income (total output of commodities per time period)
    4. C, real consumption (commodities consumed per time period)
    5. I, real investment (commodities invested, added to the capital stock, per time period)
    6. X, real aggregate demand (total demand for commodities per time period)
    7. S, real saving (output of commodities not consumed per time period)
    8. Y, money income (money value of total output of commodities per time period)
    9. X_d, perceived real disposable income
  B. Stock variables
    1. B^d, demand for bonds (number of bonds demanded to hold)
    2. B^s, supply of bonds (number of bonds planned to be outstanding)
    3. M^d, demand for nominal money (number of dollars demanded to hold)
    4. V, nominal wealth, or net worth (dollar value of real assets and money)
  C. Price variables
    1. P, the absolute, or nominal, price level (the price of commodities)
    2. W, the absolute, or nominal, wage level (the price of labor or wage rate)
    3. $1/r$, the absolute, or nominal, price of bonds

II. Exogenous Variables
  A. Flow variables
    1. G, government demand for commodities (commodities per time period)
    2. $\$B^g$, interest cost of the outstanding government debt (equals B^g times one dollar per time period)
    3. T, real tax receipts (per time period)
  B. Stock variables
    1. $\bar{K}$, the real capital stock (the number of commodities that have been accumulated up to the beginning of the present time period)
    2. $\bar{M}^s$, the supply of nominal money (the number of dollars available to be held)
    3. B^g, supply of government bonds (number of government bonds outstanding)
  C. Price variables
    1. P_0, predetermined component of the perceived price level
    2. W_0, predetermined component of the perceived wage rate

* See footnote 8.

demand function is elastic with respect to perceived real disposable income, then the elasticity of the price level with respect to the money stock is less than one. Hence, the change in the price level between the two equilibrium states is less than proportional to the change in the money stock.

This result allows some interesting comparative static results to be obtained between the momentary equilibrium and the short-run equilibrium in which perceptions have been allowed to adjust fully to the change in the actual price level. In this state money can be shown to be neutral. Therefore, in comparison to the initial equilibrium, the percentage change in the commodity price index must be equal to the percentage change in the money stock. Thus, P must be higher in the short-run equilibrium than it is in the momentary equilibrium for a given change in the money stock. On the other hand, in the short-run equilibrium real output and employment must be unchanged from the initial equilibrium and, therefore, employment must be *lower* than in the momentary equilibrium.

This simultaneous increase in the price level and reduction in employment is a close analog to the dynamic phenomena of increasing inflation and increasing unemployment which perplexed economists and policymakers during 1970–1971. In the model, the cause of this type of behavior is not price rigidity or monopolistic market power, but rather the correction of false perceptions.

Open Market Operations in Existing Government Debt

The analysis of the previous section applies to an economy in which there is no government debt, and money has to be created by some artificial construct such as throwing it out of airplanes. This is frequently the convention with textbook models. More realistically, the model should be expanded to include a government sector and an outstanding stock of government debt. In such an economy, open market operations can be conducted with the monetary authorities purchasing or selling government debt in exchange for cash balances. The modifications to the equations of Table 1, necessary to incorporate the government sector, are given in Table 3.

There are three basic additions to the model of Table 1. First, the commodity demand equation has to be expanded to incorporate the government demand for goods and services, G. Second, we assume that the public does not discount future tax liabilities which will be required to pay the interest on the outstanding debt, so that the value of the stock of government debt is a component of private wealth. Third, the definition of perceived real disposable income must be modified to allow for the taxing of income by the government, T, and the payment of interest on the outstanding debt.

The remaining problem is to define what is meant by a pure open market operation. Open market operations are defined as exchanges of government debt and cash balances of equal value between the monetary authorities and the private sector of

Table 3. Modified Equations to Incorporate a Government Sector in the Macroeconomic Model

VIIa	$X = C + I + G$	Aggregate commodity demand function
XIa	$B^d = B^s + B^g$	Bond market equilibrium condition
XVIa	$V = P\bar{K} + \bar{M}^s + \dfrac{B^g}{r}$	Definition of money wealth
XVIIa	$X_d = \dfrac{P}{P_e}(X - T) + \dfrac{\$B^g}{P_e}$	Definition of real perceived disposable income

Government financing constraint:

$$P(G - T) + \$B^g = \frac{dB^g}{r} + dM$$

the economy. Unfortunately, we cannot leave the definition at this point. It is now well established that macroeconomic models frequently have been careless in the treatment of the relationships between government fiscal and monetary operations which are implicit in a financing constraint on the government sector.[12] In the model developed here, the government must finance the difference between its tax receipts and the value of its purchases of goods and services plus the interest payments on the outstanding debt either by issuing new debt or by printing new money. This relationship is indicated as the government financing constraint in Table 3.

Consider an initial equilibrium of the economy where the right-hand side of the equation for the financing constraint is zero; that is, tax receipts just cover government expenditures and interest cost. Now consider an open market operation which changes the amount of government debt held by the public. Since debt and cash balances of equal value are exchanged in the transactions, if the right-hand side of the financing constraint was zero initially, it remains zero. Since the stock of debt held by the private sector has changed, the left-hand side of the equation can no longer sum to zero without some changes in either G or T, to offset the direct effect on the financing constraint of the change in the interest cost, and the indirect effect of the change in value of government purchases and taxes through induced changes in commodity prices. We shall define a *pure open market operation* as an exchange of government debt and cash balances between the monetary authorities and the private sector, which is *simultaneously* accompanied by whatever change in T is necessary to maintain the government financing constraint, with G remaining unchanged.

The effects of a pure open market operation in the momentary equilibrium are analyzed in Appendix C (included only in reprint).* The sufficiency conditions for positive responses of real output, employment, and commodity prices to an open market operation which increases the stock of money held by the public are the same

[12]Carl Christ, "A Simple Macroeconomic Model with a Government Budget Restraint," *Journal of Political Economy* (January/February 1968), pp. 53-67.

* See footnote 8.

as those for the situation where the stock of money was increased in the absence of government debt.

It is well known that in the Patinkin-type model with which we are working money will not be neutral in the short run in the presence of interest-bearing government debt. Therefore, the response of prices to open market operations in the short run must be analyzed before we can determine that all of the results of the first model carry over to this case.[13] There are no real output or employment responses relative to the initial equilibrium in this case, since the classical labor market behavior without any money illusion is present.

It can be shown that the conditions which are sufficient for a positive output response to an open market operation which increases the stock of money in the momentary equilibrium are also sufficient to insure that the elasticity of the price index to the increase in the money stock is greater in the short run than in the momentary run. Thus, the result of the first model that prices are higher in the short run relative to the momentary equilibrium, even though employment is lower between the two equilibria, carries over to the model including government debt in the presence of a pure open market operation.

Fiscal Policy: Tax-Financed Changes in Real Government Expenditures

The conclusions for the comparative static impacts of fiscal policy in the momentary equilibrium are quite similar to those of monetary policy. A tax-financed increase in real government purchases of goods and services generates an initial excess demand in the commodity market which causes commodity prices to rise. The increased commodity price causes a shift of the labor supply function as in Figure 1, since the same type of money illusion prevails here as in the monetary policy case. In the momentary equilibrium real output, employment, prices, and money wages are higher than in the initial equilibrium, but real wages are lower. In this case, since the stock of money has not changed, we can conclude unambiguously that the interest rate, r, must be higher for the "money" and bond markets to be restored to equilibrium.

It is well known that in the short-run equilibrium the increases in real government purchases and taxes do not have any impact on real output and employment. Hence, output and employment must be lower relative to the momentary equilibrium. Real government purchases, in the short run, "crowd out" an equal amount of real private expenditures. This "crowding out" comes about through increases in P and r which reduce both private consumption demand and private investment demand. Since in

[13]This analysis is carried out in Appendix D, which is available only as part of the [original 1974] reprint to this article. See footnote 8.

the short-run equilibrium, as compared to the initial equilibrium, P is higher and X remains unchanged, "crowding out" does not in general occur in nominal terms.[14]

In this model, crowding out occurs in nominal terms only if P remains unchanged, and all the adjustment of private demand comes about through interest rate changes. This occurs only if additional assumptions are made about the nature of the demand for real cash balances. In particular, complete nominal "crowding out" of tax-financed changes in government purchases of goods and services occurs in this model only if both the interest elasticity of the demand for real cash balances and the real wealth elasticity of the demand for real cash balances are equal to zero. In addition, the demand for real cash balances must be specified as a function of real output, and not real disposable income, to the extent that there exists a current real income elasticity of this function. Under these circumstances, if P were to rise (fall), the supply of real cash balances would decline (rise), but the demand for real cash balances would remain unchanged. Hence, any P other than the initial P would be inconsistent with equilibrium in the "money" market.

Fiscal Policy: Changes in Real Government Expenditures Financed by Selling Debt or Printing Money

The impacts of changes in government expenditures financed by debt issue or money creation are similar to those of the tax financing case, but the magnitudes are different. In the debt financing case, there exists a problem of definition similar to that encountered in the open market operation discussed above. Changes in outstanding debt imply changes in interest costs. Also, to the extent that there are induced effects on the commodity price level, the value of government purchases of goods and services and the value of tax receipts are changed, upsetting the financing constraint. We have assumed that a debt-financed change in government expenditures is accompanied by changes in real taxes which leaves real disposable income in the short-run equilibrium unchanged from the initial equilibrium value. Using this convention, a situation of financing by printing money, which can be thought of as a debt financing situation simultaneously accompanied by a pure open market purchase of government debt, requires no change in taxes.

---

[14]Nominal "crowding out" is implied by Andersen's fourth proposition. It is not clear how generally this proposition is accepted among "monetarists." The implication of the St. Louis model (Leonall C. Andersen and Keith M. Carlson, "A Monetarist Model for Economic Stabilization," this *Review* (April 1970), pp. 7-25), is that changes in nominal *high employment* government expenditures, if unaccompanied by changes in the money stock, will ultimately leave nominal GNP unchanged. Since high employment government expenditures differ from actual government expenditures only by some adjustments to unemployment compensation, this equation might be interpreted as implying complete "nominal crowding out." For a further defense of the nominal crowding out position, see Roger W. Spencer and William P. Yohe, "The 'Crowding Out' of Private Expenditures by Fiscal Policy Actions," this *Review* (October 1970), pp. 12-24.

As noted above, the effects of changes in government expenditures on the commodity price level in the short-run equilibrium differ depending on the financing mode. In particular, debt financing has a smaller impact on the price level than printing money. Further, the impact of a debt-financed change in government expenditures on the price level is not zero, unless both the interest elasticity and the wealth elasticity of the demand for real cash balances are zero. Again, complete nominal crowding out of real government expenditures requires extreme assumptions in this model.

The Relation of This Model to the Textbook Post-Keynesian Model

The model presented in Tables 1 and 3 has been discussed in terms of the monetarist propositions stated in the introduction. It has been shown that comparison of a momentary run, in which information costs are positive, with a short run, in which information is perfect, can produce conclusions similar to those alleged by the proponents of monetarism.

Consider a situation in which, no matter what the length of the run, households remain perfectly ignorant with respect to commodity prices ($\lambda_2 = 0$). In contrast, assume households possess perfect information on money wages ($\lambda_1 = 1$). The perceived real wage rate in all runs is then $(W_e/P_e) = (W/P_o)$, and the labor supply function states that the quantity of labor services supplied is a function solely of the nominal wage rate, regardless of the length of the run. This, however, is just the usual post-Keynesian assumption about the labor supply function.

Theoretical consistency suggests that these assumptions about the information parameters be carried over to the other household behavior functions. This implies that the consumption function and asset demand functions should not be homogenous of degree zero in money income, nominal wealth, and commodity prices. The post-Keynesian literature on these functions is not completely consistent on this interpretation. Modigliani states that the homogeneity restrictions should be applied to both the consumption functions and asset demand equations, even though the labor supply function depends only on the nominal wage rate.[15]

In empirical studies, the approach has been mixed. At least one study of the consumption function has taken the approach that the specification should allow for the existence of money illusion in the consumption function and the data should be allowed to indicate the result.[16] More frequently, the homogeneity restrictions have been applied *a priori*. In the empirical literature on the money demand function, the approach has been less one sided, with both homogeneous and nonhomogeneous functions prevalent in the literature.[17]

[15]Modigliani, "The Monetary Mechanism," pp. 79-107.

[16]William H. Branson and Alvin K. Klevorick, "Money Illusion and the Aggregate Consumption Function," *American Economic Review* (December 1969), pp. 832-849.

[17]See David Laidler, "The Rate of Interest and the Demand for Money: Some Empirical Evidence," *Journal of Political Economy* (December 1966), pp. 543-555.

The assumption that $\lambda_2 = 0$ and $\lambda_1 = 1$ is of course just a particular case of the general case of $\lambda_2 < \lambda_1 \leq 1$, which we use to characterize the momentary equilibrium case above. Thus, all of the results which were discussed for the momentary equilibrium are characteristic of the post-Keynesian case. Within this framework, the main difference between the post-Keynesians and the monetarists appears to be how rapidly households develop correct perceptions of price and wage developments.

The Relation of This Model to Other Monetarist Issues

It was noted at the beginning of this analysis that the results which were generated from this framework would satisfy many of the monetarist propositions about the working of the macroeconomy. However, it was emphasized that this should not be considered as "the" monetarist model. In particular, there are many aspects of it which monetarists would allege are incomplete. Since the analysis is confined to comparative statics, nothing has been said, nor can anything be said, about real versus nominal interest rates.

In addition, the analysis is restricted to the four-market model which is usually presented, implicitly or explicitly, in the commonly used macroeconomics texts. This has been done purposefully in the attempt to maintain comparability. On the other hand, the model definitely will appear deficient to many monetarists because of this restriction. In particular, no banking sector has been explicitly developed, so all cash balances in the economy are high-powered money. Thus, all problems associated with the relationship between money and a monetary base concept are swept aside.

Recently, Karl Brunner and Allan Meltzer have alleged that the four-market model is an inadequate framework within which to discuss the working of the macroeconomy because it omits an essential market, the market for existing real capital.[18] The analysis presented above could be extended to include an additional market and an additional price, that of existing assets. Obviously, such a model can have different implications on the results of various policy actions, and it is possible that a thorough analysis of such a model along the lines presented here would produce considerably more optimistic results for those who are persuaded that "nominal crowding out" of real government expenditures, in the absence of monetary financing, is an important feature of the economic picture.

Conclusions

All of the "monetarist" propositions about the results of monetary policy actions, and all but one of the propositions about the results of fiscal policy actions (the

[18]Karl Brunner and Allan Meltzer, "Money, Debt, and Economic Activity," *Journal of Political Economy* (September/October 1972), pp. 951-977.

exception being nominal "crowding out"), have been derived without any explicit restrictions on the interest elasticity of the demand function for real cash balances. In particular, the results *do not* require that this elasticity be zero, either at momentary equilibrium or at short-run equilibrium. Rather, the propositions are derived from explicit and differing assumptions about price perceptions. Furthermore, the original model, with the labor supply curve replaced by the assumption of a permanently rigid money wage rate, is easily recognizable as the textbook "complete" Keynesian model.

The rather pessimistic conclusion suggested by this analysis is that a decade of academic debate on the relative stability of monetary velocity and the autonomous expenditure multiplier has been totally extraneous to the basic problem. On balance, the debate has probably been harmful to our understanding of the impact of alternative stabilization policies. The issues involved in these debates just do not discriminate between alternative hypotheses of macroeconomic behavior.

3

The (Neo)-Classical Resurgence and the Reappraisal of Keynes' Theory of Employment

A. G. Hines

The (Neo)-Classical Resurgence

Within the past five years the work of Clower, Leijonhufvud and others has re-awakened interest in the question of what constitutes the theoretical basis of the "Keynesian" revolution.

Before this there had been a consensus among the majority and perhaps dominant school in the profession as to the nature of Keynes' contribution to economics. That consensus was not very flattering to Keynes' claim to have produced a general theory which provided a synthesis between the theory of value and the theory of money. For the consensus asserted that Keynes had really taken the then current model, and had arbitrarily imposed certain restrictions upon it—converting certain functions into constraints, setting certain price elasticities equal to infinity or to zero—and then had claimed not only to have refuted the Classical model but also to have provided a more general theory. As was pointed out during the great debate, to make that kind of claim and to make it stick, one has to take on a theory on its own grounds. According to the consensus, this is precisely what Keynes had failed to do. It would not be overstating the position to say that the prevailing view was that so far as pure theory was concerned Keynes would have been well advised not to have written the

Reprinted with deletion of footnotes from *On the Reappraisal of Keynesian Economics* (London: Martin Robertson, 1971), pp. 7-22, by permission of the publisher and the author.

General Theory at all. He should have written a note in the Economic Journal (or perhaps more appropriately written a letter to *The Times*) making the rather obvious observation that in modern capitalist economies money wages are rigid in a downward direction. It would also have helped if he had not clouded the issue by making incantatory noises about the "dark forces, of time and ignorance, which envelop our times," and by introducing funny mechanical toys such as the multiplier.

If proof were required that this was in fact the dominant view of the Keynesian revolution, one has only to look at the Neo-Classical resurgence, the revival of the Quantity Theory or the work of Patinkin and the character of the debate which surrounded it. True, there still existed in various corners of England some followers of Keynes. But then the English are well known for their love and reverence for ancient monuments and relics.

The standard models in terms of which the debate was conducted are well known and it is not necessary to write them down. The usual argument is familiar. Given wage and price flexibility, the equations of the labour market determine a market clearing real wage rate at full employment of labour. Since the historically given capital stock is thrown on to the market in perfectly inelastic supply, the production function determines the maximum obtainable level of output. Given output, the equilibrium condition in the market for commodities simultaneously determines the rate of interest and the proportion of its income which the community wishes to consume currently, and the proportion which it wishes to use to add to the man-made means of production. With real income and the rate of interest determined, the equilibrium condition in the money market determines the price level for a given stock of money. This result is not vitiated by adding to the model an asset demand for money and by setting its partial derivative with respect to the rate of interest equal to infinity. Nor is it affected by setting the elasticities of the expenditure sector with respect to the rate of interest close to, or equal to, zero. So long as there is a stock of outside government debt, which is assumed to be the net worth of the private sector, under a regime of wage and price flexibility, the solution state of the model exhibits full employment, i.e., it lies on the physical transformation frontier of society.

Naturally, if one assumes that one price, the money price of labour, is rigid because workers are organised in trade unions and/or suffer from money illusion, then it follows trivially that for a given stock of money the model no longer necessarily yields a unique full-employment solution. In this context the introduction of a speculative demand for money together with the money illusion which is allegedly built into it does not matter. It simply weakens the strong version of the quantity theory of money.

It had to be admitted that the logical validity of the Classical model depended ultimately on the existence of a stock of outside money and the indifference of the public sector to the size of its liabilities. It was agreed that this was a slender reed on which to lean in a situation in which the real wage rate was too high. Consideration of time lags, the relevant magnitudes of the response of aggregate expenditure to changes in net worth, possible perverse expectations and so on indicated that both social justice and efficiency in the choice of instruments required the use of fiscal and monetary policies to correct any chance departure from the equilibrium state. As Leijonhufvud points out, it was this admission which was responsible for the recent truce and the burial of the Keynes vs. Classics debate. For the theorists were prepared to concede to those with a more practical turn of mind that the so called "Keynes special case" is the one which is empirically relevant for short-run policy. The Classics won the intellectual battle; Keynes won the policy war. Again the victorious theorists were too polite to point out that "Keynesian" policies were being advocated by a varied assortment of men long before the General Theory appeared.

This state of affairs has been rudely shattered by the work of Clower and Leijonhufvud. For, if they are correct—as indeed they are correct—Keynes' claim is substantiated or, at the very least, is still on the agenda. A major revision and abandonment of certain well-entrenched views is in order, and the theoretical questions which Keynes posed still stand at the frontier of on-going research in our subject. For their thesis is that Keynes' under-employment state (it is a matter of semantics whether we call it an equilibrium state, since equilibrium is nothing more than a short-hand term for the set of values of the variables that satisfies the equations of a given model) can be shown to exist independently of liquidity traps, the equality of savings and investment requiring a non-feasible negative price vector, money illusion, rigid wages, etc.

Let me summarise, or rather give my own interpretation of, the core of their contention.

The Reappraisal of Keynes' Theory of Employment

Keynes was well aware that if he was to show that he had a theory which was more general than that of his predecessors, he had to take on their theory on its own grounds. Consequently, he accepted the following (Neo)-Classical assumptions.

(a) Households are rational in the sense that they maximise well-ordered utility functions irrespective of whether the arguments of these functions are contemporaneously available commodities or present and future commodities.

(b) Firms maximise profits.

(c) Well-behaved physical transformation functions exist.

(d) There is a "large" number of traders on each side of each market.

(e) Price incentives are effective.

(f) Transactors do not suffer from money illusion.

His challenge went to the very heart of Neo-Classical theory, for as Leijonhufvud points out: "in a large system where decision making is decentralised, the efficient working of the price mechanism requires that it fulfils two functions simultaneously: (a) prices should *disseminate the information* necessary to co-ordinate the economic activities and plans of the independent transactors and (b) prices should *provide the incentives* for transactors to adjust their activities in such manner that they become consistent in the aggregate." In other words, if the market clearing vector of relative prices (which is assumed to exist) is known by all transactors, and if each transactor adjusts to these parameters, the system simultaneously generates an optimal allocation of resources and ensures that they are fully employed. To demonstrate his thesis Keynes was willing to accept the proposition that price incentives are effective. What he denied was that the price system disseminates the appropriate information with sufficient efficiency to guarantee the full employment of the economy's resources, at any rate in the short run.

The question of the dissemination of information concerning the market clearing price vector has worried the truly great minds of our profession. Adam Smith thought that it was all done by "the invisible hand"; Edgeworth allowed his traders to "re-contract"; Walras had an auctioneer who, without cost to the system, called out the prices. Walras made the proviso, which is very apposite in this context, that contracts were not binding and no trade was to take place until the market clearing vector of prices was finally announced. Moreover, if the system was subjected to some exogenous disturbance, say a change in tastes or in technology, the auctioneer would immediately announce the new market clearing price vector and, given the implied infinite velocity of price adjustments, the system would immediately adjust to its new optimal position. If we extend the argument to an economy in which accumulation is taking place and in which expenditure plans extend over n time periods, the optimal operation of such an economy requires that the Walrasian auctioneer should disseminate the information concerning the vector of inter-temporal relative prices which would simultaneously clear all present and future markets.

But what is the situation if, as Keynes insisted, there is no such auctioneer? We immediately face a dilemma. For, as Arrow points out, if each transactor is a price taker, who is left over to make the price? Let us imagine that the going price vector is somehow correct; then everything is satisfactory. But now let the system be subject to some exogenous disturbance such that it requires a new market clearing vector if plans are to mesh in the aggregate. What then? It is clear that we are no longer in a state of perfect competition. Perfect competition requires that each transactor be able to buy and sell as much as he wishes at going prices and this clearly cannot happen at a wrong set of relative prices. As long as disequilibrium exists, each optimising transactor must behave like a monopolist, since he faces downward sloping demand and upward sloping supply curves along which he must search for the correct combination of prices and/or quantities. And we are immediately faced with the probability that trade may take place at false prices.

In an attempt to be more realistic than Walras and Edgeworth, Hicks wished to generalise his analysis of the determination of relative prices to markets in which there is no auctioneer and/or in which re-contracting is not permitted. He therefore had to admit the possibility of false trading at disequilibrium prices. However, he wished to show that the same equilibrium price set is attainable as in the case in which all trade takes place at equilibrium prices. Consequently, he assumed that the only effect of false trading would be a re-distribution of income between buyers and sellers and that the income effects of such re-distribution would be small, because the volume of false trading would be small and would occur at prices which did not deviate much from the set of equilibrium prices and would in any case tend to cancel out on both sides of the market "if any intelligence is shown in price fixing." Hicks observed "that a certain degree of indeterminateness is nearly always imparted by income effects to the laws of economic theory" and that false trading intensifies this indeterminateness. However, he did not really offer a solution to the question of how the system behaves when there is false trading. For this theoretical issue cannot be settled by the introduction of an empirical assumption which amounts to saying no more than "that income effects can be ignored if they are sufficiently unimportant to be neglected."

What then are we to assume about the behaviour of the typical transactor who holds stocks of assets such as labour, money, bonds, capital goods, etc., and who must in a disequilibrium situation make some assumption about expected market prices and/or quantities? The assumption made by Keynes' predecessors and by the majority of post-Keynesians is that the elasticity of price expectations is unity. Each transactor regards the first set of prices that emerge in the wake of a disturbance as correct. If each transactor acts immediately upon this belief, then unemployed resources cannot emerge even though the resulting situation may not be Pareto optimal. But is this the most reasonable assumption to make? Why, as this argument implies, should transactors regard the present value of their assets as being perfectly variable? Why is it rational for transactors who have some memory and who make plans for the future to regard passively such changes in their net worth as normal?

Imagine a worker who, because of some change which results in a reduction in the demand for his labour, is made unemployed or can only keep his present job by accepting a substantial cut in his money wages. He must decide whether to accept this cut or choose to become unemployed. To make a decision, he has to form a view as to whether the new situation is local or is generalised, is permanent or is temporary. If he regards the situation as localised and temporary, so that the previous wage rate will presently be restored, then this implies that he regards that previous wage as normal. He will, therefore, choose to become unemployed (or more likely to be laid off by his employers without being offered the alternative of accepting a lower wage). He must then begin a search for employment at the expected wage, balancing the cost of search against the probability of obtaining a better offer. At each stage he must compare the present value of the income streams which will emerge if he accepts the next offer against that which he would obtain at his expected best offer, the expected wage itself being a decreasing function of the length of search. Several writers have shown that the inescapable consequence of such phenomena is the emergence of unemployed resources which can be regarded at the *micro* level as a reservation demand on the part of the owner for the services of his own assets.

Or again, consider the position of a bond holder. The typical ultimate asset holder in Keynes' theory is an individual in the middle of his life cycle who owns a share in the system's physical capital. Given the assumption that more roundabout processes are physically more productive than less roundabout ones—a Cassellian proposition which begs the index number question—the economy is tempted by the profitability of "long" processes to carry a stock of illiquid assets. But this stock will turn over more slowly than households want. Our typical asset holder from some future date onwards plans to consume in excess of current gross incomes, the amounts and dates of the necessary encashments being presently uncertain. But the maturity structure of his representative share in the system's capital stock is assumed to be too long to match this encashment schedule. He is subject to capital uncertainty since assets may have to be sold at a loss to meet planned encashments. The representative transactor who is presumed to be a risk averter must be offered some compensation for the risk which this speculative position entails, just as a bank must be offered a yield differential between deposits and earning assets in order to borrow short and lend long. Now suppose that there is a fall in bond prices. The bond holder (who like the worker is assumed to have inelastic price expectations) will, as a risk-averting optimiser, buy bonds on the expectation of a capital gain if he regards the previous price as normal, i.e., he will re-arrange his portfolio so that on balance it moves towards the less liquid end of the maturity spectrum. (The argument is symmetrical for a fall in the interest rate.) This is, of course, the basis of the doctrine of liquidity preference.

Exactly the same analysis holds for the owner of any other asset, including entrepreneurs who invest directly in capital goods. Thus in Keynes' short-run model *every* transactor is assumed to have inelastic price expectations; it is not an assumption which applies exclusively to the holders of bonds.

We are, therefore, in a world whose differences from its classical predecessors flow from the failure of the price mechanism to disseminate the information which is required to co-ordinate the plans of transactors both now and in the future. It is a world of inelastic expectations, reservation demands and adjustment costs. Instead of a known vector of relative prices of currently produced commodities, prices are the outcome of a non-*tâtonnement* search procedure. Moreover, whereas one can conceive of changes in institutional arrangements which would improve the dissemination of information concerning the market clearing vector of current relative prices, *in principle* the provision of adequate information concerning the appropriate inter-temporal price vector of an uncertain future appears to be impossible. Instead of a known vector of inter-temporal prices we, therefore, have two phenomena: (a) the long-term state of expectations, alias the marginal efficiency of capital which summarises entrepreneurial conjectures about the prospective income streams to be obtained from outlays on physical capital; (b) liquidity preference which determines the composition of portfolios with respect to the continuum of assets with varying dates to maturity. Hence, if plans are to be consistent in the aggregate in the absence of the appropriate forward markets, both the marginal efficiency of capital and the structure of asset prices—"the rate of interest"—must correctly anticipate and reflect future prices and quantities in commodity and financial markets.

Now there is a forward market of sorts in the economy. It is the stock exchange. But this market does not transmit the information that would be provided by the Walrasian auctioneer. For, as Keynes pointed out, although there is the activity of "enterprise" in this market—the genuine attempt, on imperfect information, to forecast the future yields from sources of income and to act upon such forecasts—there is also the activity of "speculation." And in times of disequilibrium the latter easily dominate the former. But it is just at such times that the activity of enterprise should dominate if the effects of the workings of this market are to be stabilising rather than de-stabilising.

Keynes' problem then was to analyse "the economic behaviour of the present under the influence of changing ideas about the future," noting that "it is by reason of the existence of durable equipment that the future is linked to the present." What triggers off a cumulative contraction in the General Theory is a failure in the co-ordination of production, trading and consumption plans in the future. The exogenous disturbances with which Keynes was concerned were either a change in the long-run state of expectations or a change in tastes which altered the propensity to save or the form in which wealth holders chose to hold their assets.

We must now investigate the system-wide implications with respect to the level of aggregate output and employment of any such disturbance.

In a barter system, where all commodities are directly tradeable against each other, the system-wide consequences of such disturbances are not clear. But the Keynesian system is a monetary economy, i.e., it is a system in which money is the only commodity which is directly tradeable in all markets. Here the system-wide implications are abundantly clear.

In a money economy it is necessary to distinguish between *desire* (which may be based on feasible transformation possibilities) and effective demand—desires backed by the ability to pay in *cash*. In such an economy it is money offers to buy and to sell which take over the role of the system of relative prices and act as the mechanism which transmits the relevant market signals to transactors. But this means, as Clower has pointed out, that we must now distinguish between *notional* excess *demands*—excess demands which reflect the underlying real transformation possibilities of the system—and actual or *effective* excess demands—those which are backed by the ability to pay in money and which, therefore, constitute relevant market signals. These two sets of excess demands are only equal when the system is in a full equilibrium. What this means is that except in a full equilibrium in which each excess demand is zero, Walras' Law does not hold as between notional and effective excess demands.

Walras' Law is the proposition that the sum of the value of all excess demands is zero, i.e.,

$$\sum_{i=1}^{n} P_i q_i = 0, \quad q_i \equiv D_i - S_i.$$

In a barter economy with a *tâtonnement* mechanism such that trade never takes place at 'false' prices, all excess demand functions hold simultaneously and "the offer of any commodity is an exercise of effective purchasing power over any other commodity." Hence, Walras' Law follows by logical necessity. This is not the case in a money economy since every act of exchange between two non-monetary commodities is necessarily indirect. All this does not matter in full equilibrium when all excess demands are zero. Then Walras' Law does hold. However, in a state of transactor disequilibrium, Walras' Law as usually defined does not hold. Thus, consider an equilibrium which is disturbed by the decision of some transactor to increase his consumption (or holdings) or some commodity i by supplying some other commodity j to the market. In a barter economy with all other excess demand functions equal to zero, we would simply write $X_i = - X_j$ where X_i and X_j are the value of the excess demand for the ith and jth good, respectively. But in a monetary economy, this procedure is not appropriate unless the jth commodity is money. If it is not money, then in order to make his plans effective the individual must first exchange the jth commodity for money and, *if he is successful,* he then exchanges money for the ith commodity. And, since in a non-*tâtonnement* system the actual vector of prices might be such that plans to demand money (plans to supply goods, bonds or factor services) may not be achieved, i.e., actual sales may fall short of or exceed planned sales, the contingent plans to demand goods, bonds and money to hold as an asset stand subject to revision. Clower has analysed what this involves for the optimising transactor as a "*dual decision hypothesis.*" Transactors maximise their utility subject to the constraint of their notional income. If their realised and notional incomes are equal, the system is in a full equilibrium and the excess demand functions generated by the solution to the familiar constrained maximisation problem yield relevant market signals. But if actual incomes are not equal to notional incomes, a second round of decision making is in order: the transactor must maximise utility subject to the constraint of realised income, which is the money value of the receipts from the sale of factor services. It is the resulting income-constrained excess demand functions which provide relevant market signals.

Now suppose that, starting from a position of equilibrium, there is an exogenous change in the state of long-term expectations such that entrepreneurs re-evaluate in a downward direction the prospective yields from the services of capital goods and that this results in a reduction in planned investment expenditures at each level of the rate of interest. In the classical full information system, there is a fall in the interest rate which increases the consumption income ratio at an unchanged level of output and employment. In Keynes' theory there is an implication for the level of output and employment. The rate of interest does fall: but its fall is insufficient to equate savings and investment at an unchanged level of income. The limitation in the fall of the interest rate is due to the existence of liquidity preference. Speculators who consider that the rise in bond prices will be reversed offer savers existing bonds from their portfolios (equal in value to the reduced supply of the investors in capital goods) in exchange for money and hoard the proceeds of sale. In these circumstances, there is a fall in expenditure on new capital goods and, given the assumptions which we have already made, unemployed resources emerge in this sector before any countervailing effects of the possible unwinding of the speculative position taken up by the "bears" can make itself felt.

Unemployed resources emerge because of the sequence of trades which is assumed to take place in a production economy in which contracts are made in terms of money. In the absence of a market clearing vector of prices which is known, entrepreneurs plan their output on the basis of the level of demand which they expect to rule in the future and which depends in part upon a weighted average of past levels of sales. Given planned output, firms enter into price contracts, fixed for a stated period, for the services of productive resources. Faced with an unexpected fall in demand, entrepreneurs who are assumed to have inelastic price expectations do not reduce the price of their output within the unit period by an amount which is sufficient to dispose of their current output. They are, therefore, faced with an unintended accumulation of inventories at the end of the period. Even if they plan to make some reduction in the price of output in the next period, they will now reduce the amount of factor services for which they will contract at the end of the current period, especially since the assumption of inelastic price expectations also applies to the owners of these productive services so that they would not accept a reduction in rates of remuneration sufficient to keep their factors employed in the same establishment.

Now consider an unemployed worker in this sector who now begins a search for a wage rate which is consistent with his current estimate of the present value of his labour services. His notional excess supply of labour does not provide him with the means to transmit relevant information concerning his corresponding excess demand for goods. How is he to maintain his desired levels of expenditure? He could run down any accumulated non-labour assets. But then he must do this in a situation in which uncertainty about their realisable value has increased. He could try to borrow, offering as collateral his human and/or non-human wealth. But, in addition to his uncertain but inelastic expectations about their present values, lending institutions themselves have no hard knowledge but must conjecture about the value of the collateral which is being offered. Moreover, in the postulated situation, lending institutions are also attempting to increase the liquidity of their portfolios. The costs of being unemployed are high and we may expect downward revisions in the worker's reservation price as the unemployment state persists. But so long as the elasticity of expectations is less than unity in Keynes' short period, the worker in the sector in which the disturbance first occurs will have an actual income which is less than his notional income and, since actual income now constitutes a binding constraint on actual behaviour, effective demands are now reduced in markets in which the initial shock may have had no impact. Unemployed resources now emerge in these markets and "the search instituted by unemployed workers and producers with excess capacity will yield information on 'effective' demands not on 'notional' demands. The 'multiplier' repercussions thus set in motion make the information acquired 'dated' even while it is being gathered." To each set of trades which takes place there corresponds a set of wrong relative prices which are themselves unknown to all transactors. There is no reason to assume (at any rate without further specification) that in the short run the system is converging to the correct vector of relative prices.

Rather, as Keynes' theory implies, the observed price and quantity changes are *deviation amplifying* and the system probably contracts to a floor which is set by the given stock of money.

The same analysis holds if there is an increase in the propensity to save which is the result of a change in tastes such that households wish to alter the time profile of their consumption stream in favour of future consumption. In the Classical system the rate of interest now falls so that the increased demand for bonds which is assumed to be the analogue of the increase in savings is met by new issues by investors. Savings and investment are equated at a higher investment to income ratio and full employment is maintained. In Keynes' theory the level of output and employment falls. An act of saving is a plan to increase the transactor's future command over *purchasing power in general.* Unlike money expenditure on currently produced goods and services, it does not transmit relevant information to producers concerning the specific goods and the combination thereof which will be demanded in the future. In the absence of this information, the relevant inter-temporal price vector is unknown. Consequently, entrepreneurs do not have the same incentive as in the Classical system to shift the composition of their portfolios towards the less liquid end of the maturity spectrum. The rate of interest does fall, but because of liquidity preference its fall is partially stabilised. Just as in the case of the fall in the marginal efficiency of capital, "bear" speculators offer those who wish to increase their current savings existing bonds from their portfolios and hoard the proceeds of sale. Thus, only a fraction of the increased demand for bonds is met by new issues. In these circumstances there is a fall in expenditure on consumer goods which is not offset by the increased expenditure on investment goods. Unemployed resources emerge; the process which we have already described is under way, and when the equality of savings and investment does come about, it is the result of a cumulative contraction in incomes and employment.

Thus, contrary to what has become standard doctrine, liquidity preference—or rather the hypothesis of inelastic price expectations which underlies the notion of liquidity preference—can explain under-employment equilibrium. The multiplier does amplify initial disturbances. For we have been analysing the consequences of false trading in a situation in which the actual vector of relative prices is not only wrong but is unknown. To generate Keynes' under-employment state, we simply relinquish the strong, but in the context inappropriate, Classical assumption of infinite velocity of prices and zero velocity of quantities within the unit period. A reversal of the ranking of price and quantity velocities is sufficient. Specifically, the assumption of an absolute rigidity in the money wage rate is not necessary to explain under-employment. Indeed the Keynesian analysis leads to the distinctly non-Classical conclusion that in a general equilibrium model unemployed resources may emerge in the ith market at a correct money price in that market because the money price is wrong in the jth market. In this case, the ith market is the labour market: the jth market is the market for "bonds." Moreover, contrary to Walras' Law, the system can attain a (temporary) equilibrium with an excess supply of labour which is not matched by an equivalent value of *effective* excess demand for goods. The unemployed workers may be said to have an excess demand for money. However, it is notional rather than effective inasmuch as it cannot work "directly on the price system to offset prevailing elements of excess supply." The contingent excess demand for goods is also notional since it cannot be communicated to producers unless and until labour is successfully exchanged for money.

In such a situation a policy of cutting money wages is a faulty prescription based on a wrong diagnosis. For in Keynes' analysis of advanced capitalist economies, a disequilibrium is usually assumed to originate in a change in long-run expectations or in liquidity preference, which generates a rate of interest too high for a general equilibrium. A sufficient cut in money wages would, *ceteris paribus,* restore a correct relative price between "bonds" and labour services. But since we are in a general equilibrium model, this would clearly not achieve the appropriate price ratios between "bonds" and the other commodities of the model. Moreover, the Pigou effect—the direct effect on aggregate expenditure of a change in the value of the nominal money stock—is irrelevant in this setting. For, as we have seen, Keynes' diagnosis of the malady is that relative prices are "wrong"; and, if this is the case, an all-round deflation will not help. A priori it could only work if it affected relative prices, i.e., if it lowers the rate of interest relative to the money wage rate. This is possible since the rate of interest has the highest ranking in terms of velocity among the set of prices in Keynes' short-period model. But now we are really talking about the Keynes' wealth effect, i.e., the effect on aggregate consumption of changes in the rate of interest. Leijonhufvud's dismissal of the Pigou effect is very neat.

4

Money and Output: Keynes and Friedman in Historical Perspective

J. H. Wood*

It's not quite the Montagues and the Capulets, even the Hatfields and the McCoys, again, but a long-time feud has been raging between two prominent "families" of economists.

Money—its quantity, importance, and efficacy—is the root of the squabble. Each camp, armed with logic, statistics, and other essential academic trappings, has dug in for a long and running battle—or debate—over the effectiveness of governmental monetary and fiscal policies as means of influencing economic activity.

One clan—the Keynesians, self-styled followers (or disciples) of John Maynard Keynes—argues that money and monetary policy have little or no impact on income and employment, particularly during severe economic downturns; and that government taxation and spending are the most effective remedies for inflation and unemployment, especially the latter.

The other group—the Monetarists, largely rallying around Milton Friedman of the University of Chicago—emphasizes money's role in the economic process. Spurning the notion that fiscal policy is paramount, they argue that a rule which requires the

Reprinted with deletions, from the Federal Reserve Bank of Philadelphia, *Business Review* (September, 1972), pp. 3-12, by permission of the publisher and the author.

* This article is adapted from an inaugural lecture delivered at the University of Birmingham, March 21, 1972. The author wishes to express his deep appreciation to the Esmée Fairbairn Charitable Trust, whose generosity made possible the research leading to this lecture, and to Douglas Vickers for encouragement and helpful discussions in the early stages of that research.

monetary authorities to cause the stock of money to increase at some constant rate, say 3 percent annually, would effectively reduce fluctuations in prices, output, and employment.

It is curious that when the dust settles on this debate, the problems that have interested Keynes and Friedman, the policy tools each has used, and the principal results each has obtained resemble not only each other but those of eighteenth-century British economists as well. In short—and this may jolt some economists and noneconomists—*there are no fundamental theoretical differences between Keynes and Friedman.* As with such controversies, the differences between Keynes and Friedman on the employment of fiscal and monetary policies to achieve economic stability hinge on differences in economic conditions existing at the times that each economist wrote and from dissimilar political philosophies rather than from any theoretical differences over money's influence on output. Moreover, the genesis of most of these "differences" can be found in the positions taken by many British economists of previous centuries.

Enter Keynes

In his *Tract on Monetary Reform* (1923), Keynes was highly critical of the pre-1914 theory of Ricardo, Mill, and others.

> Now "in the long run" this theory is probably true. If, after the American Civil War, the dollar had been stabilized and defined by law at 10 percent below its present value, it would be safe to assume that M [money] and P [prices] would now be just 10 percent greater than they actually are and that the present values of V [velocity] and T [volume of transactions] would be entirely unaffected. But this *long run* is a misleading guide to current affairs. *In the long run* we are all dead. Economists set themselves too easy, too useless a task if in tempestuous seasons they can only tell us that when the storm is long past the ocean is flat again.[1]

But things were different after 1914. Keynes began his *Tract* in the same way that he had begun the *Economic Consequences of the Peace* (1919), discussing what he believed had been the extremely delicate, short-lived, and essentially unstable economic system existing before 1914:

> For a hundred years the system worked throughout Europe with an extraordinary success and facilitated the growth of wealth on an unprecedented scale. To save and to invest became at once the duty and the delight of a large class.[2]

Keynes wrote during a time of extraordinary upheaval. Between 1914 and 1920 prices tripled, then dropped by nearly one-half by 1922. He pointed out that the

[1]John Maynard Keynes, *The Collected Writings of Keynes* (London: Macmillan Ltd., 1971), p. 6.
[2]Ibid., p. xiv.

arrangements of the nineteenth century could not work properly if money, the assumed standard, is not dependable.

> Unemployment, the precarious life of the worker, the disappointment of expectation, the sudden loss of savings, the excessive windfalls to individuals, the speculator, the profiteer—all proceed, in large measure, from the instability of the standard of value.[3]

If businessmen are to develop their productive capacity and if the savings of households are to be converted into investment projects, then businessmen must be able to foresee with a reasonable degree of assurance the prices of the products coming out of their new plants and the costs of the inputs from which those products will be made.

To Keynes, the overriding determinant of investment is price expectations. Expectations of price increases encourage investment; expected deflation discourages investment. Uncertainty is the worst offender. If rapid monetary changes have occurred in the past and are expected to be repeated in the future—in which direction no one knows—businessmen will refuse to bear the risk of investment.

The problems that Keynes considered as well as the remedies proposed in his *Treatise on Money* (1930) were the same as those analyzed and advanced in the *Tract.* Only his methodology had changed; it had become more sophisticated. He traced in detail the effects of changes in the quantity of money on the level and composition of output. Some passages in the *Treatise* echo Cantillon. Like the latter, Keynes always carefully specified the source of an assumed monetary disturbance before discussing its effects. For him, most increases in money resulted from increases in bank loans to businessmen. He stressed that the failure of different prices to move together is the essence of short-period fluctuations and that an easier monetary policy that leads to low interest rates and rising prices results in higher profits and increases investment.

The processes through which monetary disturbances lead to variations in output in the first instance are the same in the *General Theory of Employment, Interest and Money* as in the *Tract* and the *Treatise:* namely, through price changes and their influence on expectations of future prices. He argued that the relation between current and future prices influences investment decisions most.

Keynes came to the conclusion that in a world of rapidly fluctuating prices uncertainty on the part of businessmen would be so great that the state would have to undertake the investment necessary for growth and economic stability. Since 1924 he had advocated public works in a supporting role to monetary policy as an antideflationary device. But, from the behavior of the Bank of England—from its determination to accept and enforce whatever price fluctuations were consistent, first with the return to gold at the prewar par and then with the maintenance of the gold standard at a fixed rate—Keynes became convinced that the nation would have to rely on means other than monetary policy to stabilize prices and output.

[3]Ibid.

. . . Then Friedman

Reading Milton Friedman and Anna Jacobson Schwartz's *A Monetary History of the United States* (1963) is a frustrating experience. On the one hand, the authors present a wealth of highly suggestive and expertly handled historical data. But, on the other hand, just as they seem to be on the verge of explaining causal relationships (that is, of giving an explicit statement of the processes through which, in their view, money affects economic activity), they descend into a quagmire of algebraic manipulations. But, if we carefully examine the way in which Friedman handles the data in this and other historical discussions, we can get an inkling of how, in his view, money matters.

In comparing the two periods 1865–1879 and 1879–1897 as well as other lengthy intervals, Friedman and Schwartz conclude that over long periods "generally declining or generally rising prices had little impact on the rate of growth [of output], but the period of great monetary uncertainty in the early nineties produced sharp deviations from the long-term trend."

They make this point again and again, concluding:

Apparently, the forces determining the long-run rate of growth of real income are largely independent of the long-run rate of growth of the stock of money, so long as both proceed fairly smoothly. But marked instability of money is accompanied by instability of economic growth.[4]

Surprise is the key word in all this. To the extent that changes in money and prices proceed smoothly and are foreseen, money does not influence economic activity. But sudden and unforeseen monetary disturbances produce fluctuations in output.

There is a close connection here and elsewhere between Friedman's descriptions of historical periods and Mill's argument that changes in the money supply that people expect and upon which they can plan allow employment, output, and other economic variables to be determined by nonmonetary forces.

Parallel in Theory but Parting in Prescription

Both Keynes and Friedman, therefore, fear monetary instability. They both desire a stable growth rate in the money supply as a way of minimizing fluctuations in prices, output, and employment. But they part ways in approach and emphasis on how to achieve the benefits of monetary stability.

Keynes, on the one hand, was pragmatic. He was a man of a thousand plans. If one was impractical, he would try another. To him monetary policy was important

[4]Milton Friedman and Anna Jacobson Schwartz, *A Monetary History of the United States, 1867–1960* (Princeton: Princeton University Press, 1963), p. 678.

but not the "be-all and end-all." And so he moved from a reliance on monetary to fiscal policy when he thought it unrealistic on political or other grounds to expect a stable growth in the money supply.

Friedman, on the other hand, has less confidence than Keynes in the willingness or ability of the authorities—monetary or fiscal—to make the economy work smoothly. That is why Friedman wants to tie both the monetary and fiscal authorities to certain specific rules—not because the people who would make the rules are more intelligent than those who formulate and implement discretionary policies, but because, whatever the rule, it will be known. People can formulate plans on the basis of what they can expect the future money supply and price level to be. In such a way, Friedman hopes, as Keynes did with fiscal policy, that money *CAN BE MADE* not to matter.

B. The Transmission Process and Policy Implications

The contrasting models presented in the previous section provide clues to the challenging and fascinating world of monetary theory. The readings in this section, without requiring the extensive use of mathematical and graphical analysis, will survey slightly more sophisticated views of the monetary economy.

An important subject in monetary analysis concerns the various ways (through short-term interest rates, long-term interest rates, wealth, etc.) in which monetary impulses may be transmitted to spending, production, employment, and prices. The first three essays will examine the major contributions regarding the channels through which monetary stimuli affect the economy.

The opening reading by Yung Chul Park is a most interesting survey of this "transmission" mechanism. Park's analysis is invaluable because of its fairly intensive examination of the views of Boris Pesek and Thomas Saving (and their critics) on the contribution of bank deposits to private wealth. Park's article is further unique because it offers a specific model representing Milton Friedman's theoretical conceptualization of the transmission mechanism. The essay ends with an examination of the "reduced-form" versus the "structural" approach to the effect of monetary and fiscal impulses on the economy.

The second essay by David I. Fand is a critique of macroeconomic models that fail to distinguish between real and nominal values. Fand contrasts the postulates of the modern quantity theory with those of Keynesian income-expenditure theory and scores macroeconomists who omit capital market and money market effects from their analysis of fiscal policy.

Roger W. Spencer's article on the transmission process, the third in this section, complements those of Park and Fand. Spencer provides an interesting historical background by surveying the work of Knut Wicksell, Irving Fisher, and John Maynard Keynes on this problem. Like Park, Spencer compares and contrasts the views of Milton Friedman, James Tobin, Karl Brunner and Allan Meltzer, and others on the effect of monetary impulses on relative prices and portfolio adjustments in the transmission process. Spencer then presents a rather extensive survey of the effect of monetary impulses on wealth. Here he examines the contributions of A. C. Pigou, Don Patinkin, John Hicks, Boris Pesek and Thomas Saving, James Tobin, Lloyd Metzler, Milton Friedman and Karl Brunner, and Allan Meltzer. His article ends with an appendix containing helpful numerical examples of how the relative price and wealth effects work.

What is the effect of fiscal policy on economic activity? In recent years the work of Carl Christ and others has demonstrated that neither fiscal nor monetary policy can be viewed independently of one another. The stimulatory effect of increases in government expenditures on aggregate demand should not be analyzed without regard to their concomitants of either raising taxes, increasing the stock of money, or expanding the supply of interest-bearing government debt. The fourth article in this section by Alan S. Blinder and Robert M. Solow is a direct challenge to the Monetarist assertion that in models where these factors are included fiscal policy does not significantly affect aggregate spending. The authors develop a model that implies that fiscal policy *does* have an effect unless that model is unstable; they then outline the conditions under which it is stable. In the fifth essay, Roger W. Spencer and Keith M. Carlson survey recent theoretical and empirical literature pertaining to the influence of fiscal actions on economic activity. They argue that stability conditions, as featured by Blinder and Solow, are of limited importance with respect to the "crowding out effect" and point out the need for further work in this area.

Thomas M. Humphrey's penetrating discussion of the inflation-employment tradeoff, or Phillips curve, is the final reading in this section. Humphrey carefully analyzes the accelerationist views (often identified with the Monetarists) and nonaccelerationist views (often identified with the Keynesians) of the notion that the lower unemployment can be attained if added price inflation is acceptable.

5

Some Current Issues on the Transmission Process of Monetary Policy

Yung Chul Park

There is widespread agreement that money is of some importance in determining the course of economic events. There is, however, substantial disagreement concerning the extent to which money matters (that is, the size of the money multiplier). Monetarists argue that changes in the stock of money are a primary determinant of changes in total spending. On the other hand, nonmonetarists, although they may readily admit that money matters, also regard changes in the various components of aggregate demand as having an important influence on the level of economic activity; they, therefore, place as much emphasis on fiscal policy as on monetary controls. In fact, a spectrum of views on the importance of money ranges from "money matters little" at one extreme to "money alone matters" at the other extreme. An important question is the extent to which these differences in opinion may be traced to differences in models of the monetary process (that is, the transmission mechanism explaining how monetary influences affect real output, employment, and the price level). The objective of this paper is to examine this question by reviewing critically

Reprinted, with deletions, from the *Staff Papers,* International Monetary Fund (March 1972), pp. 1–43 by permission of the publisher and the author.

the analytical bases for the different views among monetarists and nonmonetarists;[1] only casual reference will be made to the vast and growing empirical literature. Since the transmission process is an integral part of the entire operational structure of the economy, the survey cannot be carried out without discussing divergent views on how the economy in general operates. While this may lengthen the paper, it will help us to analyze the mechanism in a proper context. The review begins in Section I with a discussion of post-Keynesian developments, followed in Section II by an analysis of the nonmonetarist views of the neo-Keynesians and the neo-Fisherians. The monetarist view is elaborated in Section III, and a summary and concluding remarks comprise Section IV.

I. Post-Keynesian Analysis: The Wealth Effect, Credit Rationing, and Portfolio Balance

The Cost-of-Capital Channel

The main process by which monetary forces influence the real economy in Keynesian income/expenditure models is through the cost-of-capital channel. In a simple Keynesian framework, monetary policy operates through changes in the rate of interest. The change in the volume of money alters "the" rate of interest—a rate of interest usually approximated by the long-term government bond rate—so as to equate the demand for money with the supply. The change in the rate of interest affects investment and possibly consumption; the change in aggregate demand, in turn, has a multiple effect on equilibrium income. Thus, the rate of interest is viewed as a measure of the cost of capital, as the indicator of the stance of monetary policy, and as the key linkage variable between the real and financial sectors.

In addition to the cost-of-capital channel, post-Keynesians also recognized two other channels, namely, the wealth effect on consumption expenditure and the credit rationing linkage between the financial and real sectors.

The Wealth Effect

THE POST-KEYNESIAN VIEW

One of the most significant post-Keynesian developments has been the emphasis on net private wealth as well as income as a factor influencing real flows of expendi-

---

[1]Readers are also referred to other excellent reviews on this topic and on recent developments in monetary economics: Maurice Mann, "How Does Monetary Policy Affect the Economy?" *Federal Reserve Bulletin,* Vol. 54 (1968), pp. 803-14; Allan H. Meltzer, "Money, Intermediation, and Growth," *The Journal of Economic Literature,* Vol. VII (1969), pp. 27-56; Harry G. Johnson, "Recent Developments in Monetary Theory—A Commentary," in *Money in Britain, 1959-1969,* ed. by David R. Croome and Harry G. Johnson (Oxford University Press, 1970), pp. 83-114; Warren L. Smith, "On Some Current Issues in Monetary Economics: An Interpretation," *The Journal of Economic Literature,* Vol. VIII (1970), pp. 767-82; Harry G. Johnson, "The Keynesian Revolution and the Monetarist Counter-Revolution," American Economic Association, *Papers and Proceedings of the Eighty-third Annual Meeting* (*The American Economic Review,* Vol. LXI, May 1971), pp. 1-14.

tures. The connection between net wealth of the private sector and consumption was first pointed out by Pigou[2] and Haberler,[3] and in a more rigorous manner by Patinkin,[4] in the form of real cash balance effect: changes in the real quantity of money could affect real aggregate demand even if they did not alter the rate of interest. The central feature of the real cash balance effect is the assumption that the stock of money is a component of the net wealth of the economy. However, the stock of money that these economists considered as part of net wealth was not the usually defined concept of narrow money (currency outside banks *plus* demand deposits) but rather the monetary base, or, in Gurley and Shaw's terminology, outside money alone.[5] The justification for excluding demand deposits (inside money) as part of wealth is that these deposits are claims of the public on the banking system that are counterbalanced by the debts of the public to the banking sector. Therefore, when the balance sheets of all economic units are consolidated, inside money disappears and, hence, should not be considered as part of wealth.

This justification, however, brings out immediately the question of why the same logic should not be applied to outside money, which is, after all, the noninterest-bearing debt of the government. If, indeed, outside money is government debt, as it has been treated in the post-Keynesian literature,[6] a consolidation of the balance sheet of the private and government sectors must result in the cancellation of outside money as an item of net wealth. It then follows that a change in outside money cannot exert a wealth effect, since the change cannot cause a simultaneous change in net wealth. To establish that the change in outside money does indeed have economic consequences, one has to provide an explanation other than that outside money is part of wealth. The explanation that has had widest support has been that the government, unlike other debtors, is unconcerned about the size of its debt and makes its economic decisions accordingly.[7] Thus, the only effect of the change in

[2]A. C. Pigou, "Economic Progress in a Stable Environment," *Economica,* New Series, Vol. XIV (1947), pp. 180-88.

[3]Gottfried Haberler, *Prosperity and Depression* (New York, Third Edition, 1946), pp. 242, 403, and 491-503.

[4]Don Patinkin, "Price Flexibility and Full Employment," in *Readings in Monetary Theory,* ed. by Friedrich A. Lutz and Lloyd W. Mints (New York, 1951), pp. 252-83.

[5]Outside money is defined as the money that is backed by foreign or government securities or gold, or fiat money issued by the government, whereas inside money—commercial bank demand deposits—is based on private domestic securities. See John G. Gurley and Edward S. Shaw, *Money in a Theory of Finance,* The Brookings Institution (Washington, 1960), pp. 363-64.

[6]See James Tobin, "Money, Capital, and Other Stores of Value," American Economic Association, *Papers and Proceedings of the Seventy-third Annual Meeting (The American Economic Review,* Vol. LI, May 1961), pp. 26-37; James Tobin, "Commercial Banks as Creators of 'Money'," Chapter 1 in *Financial Markets and Economic Activity,* ed. by Donald D. Hester and James Tobin, Cowles Foundation, Monograph 21 (New York, 1967), pp. 1-11, also included in *Banking and Monetary Studies,* ed. by Deane Carson (Homewood, Illinois, 1963); James Tobin, "Money and Economic Growth," *Econometrica,* Vol. 33 (1965), pp. 671-84; Gurley and Shaw, *Money in a Theory of Finance* (cited in footnote 5); Don Patinkin, *Money, Interest, and Prices: An Integration of Monetary and Value Theory* (New York, Second Edition, 1965).

[7]The government, the argument claims, ignores the real value of its debt because it can pay its debts by issuing new debts; the government is able to do so since (1) it controls the supply of money and (2) it possesses the taxing power. See Harry G. Johnson, "Monetary Theory and Policy," in his *Essays in Monetary Economics* (Harvard University Press, 1967), p. 24.

outside money is the effect of the increase in assets of the private sector. This explanation reduces the wealth effect of changes in outside money to a distribution effect of a wealth transfer between the private and government sectors. This explanation also suggests that the traditional distinction between inside and outside money is based not on a measure of wealth applicable to all types of assets but rather on asymmetric responses of various economic decision-making units to changes in assets and debts.[8]

Later developments have extended this wealth effect beyond money to other forms of wealth, such as the real market values of equities and interest-bearing government debt. It is fairly easy to appreciate the wealth effect or distribution effect associated with outside money. However, it is not evident whether the same argument could be applied to interest-bearing government debt. There is an important difference between the two assets. Unlike outside money, the interest burden on interest-bearing government debt must be financed by future taxes. Hence, if the private sector discounts its future tax liabilities in the same way in which it discounts future interest receipts, the existence of government bonds represents an asset as well as a liability to the public and will, therefore, not generate any net wealth effect.[9] However, if the public considers only a constant fraction of total interest-bearing government debt as a liability, then an open market purchase of government bonds will increase net private wealth and thereby directly affect aggregate demand.

At the theoretical level, the link between the net wealth of consumers and real consumption has been refined as in the life cycle hypothesis of Ando, Brumberg, and Modigliani, which holds that consumers allocate consumption over their lifetime, given initial net worth, a rate of time preference, and expectations regarding labor income.[10]

The Keynesian approach uses the rate of interest on long-term bonds as the representative rate on all types of earning asset. "This implicitly assumes that equities, government bonds, and private debt are all perfect substitutes for one another."[11] As a result, the Keynesian analysis considers only substitution between money and bonds important but ignores entirely the substitutability between money and real assets or real expenditures. The intellectual importance of the real cash balance effect lies in the fact that it allowed the possibility of substitution between money, on the one hand, and real expenditures, on the other hand, in macroeconomic analysis.[12]

---

[8]For a further elaboration on this point, see the following section.

[9]Patinkin, *Money, Interest, and Prices* (cited in footnote 6), p. 289.

[10]Albert Ando and Franco Modigliani, "The 'Life Cycle' Hypothesis of Saving: Aggregate Implications and Tests," *The American Economic Review,* Vol. LIII (March 1963), pp. 55-84; Franco Modigliani and Richard Brumberg, "Utility Analysis and the Consumption Function: An Interpretation of Cross-Section Data," in *Post Keynesian Economics,* ed. by Kenneth K. Kurihara (Rutgers University Press, 1954), pp. 388-436; Franco Modigliani and Albert Ando, "The 'Permanent Income' and the 'Life Cycle' Hypothesis of Saving Behavior: Comparison and Tests," in *Consumption and Saving,* Vol. II, ed. by Irwin Friend and Robert Jones (Wharton School, University of Pennsylvania, 1960), pp. 49-174.

[11]Tobin, "Money, Capital, and Other Stores of Value" (cited in footnote 6), p. 30.

[12]Milton Friedman, "Postwar Trends in Monetary Theory and Policy," in *Money and Finance: Readings in Theory, Policy, and Institutions,* ed. by Deane Carson (New York, 1966), p. 187.

This fact has, to a great extent, contributed to the explicit treatment of real capital goods in portfolio analysis and to a reemphasis on the role of money.

THE PESEK AND SAVING THESIS

In a recent book by Pesek and Saving,[13] the authors argue that commercial bank demand deposits (inside money) should also be treated as part of the net wealth of the economy, because demand deposits are an asset produced by banks and sold by them to the public in exchange for the latter's statements of indebtedness.[14] Demand deposits, unlike outside money, carry an "instant repurchase clause"—an obligation by the banks to repurchase them with outside money. But this characteristic, Pesek and Saving argue, does not affect the basic fact that demand deposits are part of net wealth.

If Pesek and Saving's thesis is valid, then their analysis will have important implications for the effects of monetary policy. Their analysis literally means that monetary authorities can directly create or destroy nominal private wealth at will through monetary policy. This, in turn, implies that monetary policy can affect aggregate demand *directly* and in theory can have strong effects on the level of economic activity. For instance, a central bank's open market purchase of government bills, given the money supply multiplier, will generate a multiple expansion of the initial increase in outside money. The increase in money supply should be considered an increase in nominal private wealth, which will, in turn, increase consumption expenditure. This means that the open market operation has a direct wealth effect in addition to the conventional liquidity effect[15] and the interest-rate-induced wealth effects (capital gains or losses on government bonds and equities) on total spending. For this reason, Pesek and Saving's argument deserves careful examination.

Pesek and Saving's view is based on the principle that the economically relevant measure of wealth is the capitalized value of a stream of net income. When this measure of wealth is applied to outside money, it is shown that outside money is a component of net wealth because it yields a net flow of services to the user—not because the government is unconcerned with its outstanding debt. The flow of services of outside money is the saving of time in barter transactions, which stems from the role of money as a medium of exchange. The saving of time may be used either for leisure or for the production of capital goods. Hence, outside money generates a positive stream of income; the capitalized value of this income is then an addition to the net wealth of the economy. The same reasoning applies to demand deposits, the basic difference between government fiat money and demand deposits being one of institutional arrangements. The arrangement is that government fiat money is produced by the government, whereas demand deposits are produced by the government agents, namely, commercial banks that have received the monopoly right of producing money. From this point of view, there is no difference between outside money

---

[13]Boris P. Pesek and Thomas R. Saving, *Money, Wealth, and Economic Theory* (New York, 1967).

[14]*Ibid.*, Chapter 4, "Bank Money as Wealth," pp. 79-102.

[15]The liquidity effect, or the substitution effect, refers to changes in interest rates that are brought about by changes in money supply via a liquidity preference relation.

and demand deposits. To put it differently, inside money also represents a stream of net income, since demand deposits, as a medium of exchange, yield a flow of services that banks have agreed to provide. For inside money, however, the net income takes the form of the earnings of the banks through the process of money creation or intermediation. The capitalized value of the earnings is then an increase in the net wealth of the economy.[16]

To elaborate further on this point, let us assume that a commercial bank receives $5,000 of demand deposits and that the bank is subject to a reserve requirement of 20 percent. The bank then retains $1,000 in cash reserves and creates demand deposits amounting to $4,000 by lending this amount to the private nonfinancial sector of the economy. Suppose that there is a single rate of interest, say, 5 percent, in this economy. This means that, *ceteris paribus,* the bank is earning an additional $200. The present value of this interest earning, given the 5 percent interest rate, is $4,000, which is exactly equal to the increase in demand deposits held by the public. This present value represents an increase in the net worth of the bank. Since the bank is a private one, the increase should be reflected also in the balance sheets of its stockholders; *ceteris paribus,* the increase in the net worth of the bank will be reflected in an increase in the market value of the bank's stocks, which is equivalent to an increase in the public's wealth.

The argument so far is based on the assumption that the costs of producing (or servicing) demand deposits are negligible. However, in reality the commercial banking industry has operating costs just like any other industry and is fairly competitive. To the extent that there are operating costs connected with demand deposits (or outside money, for that matter), the whole value of demand deposits is not necessarily part of the net wealth of the economy. In the extreme case where the banking industry is fully competitive and is not subject to government controls and regulations, Patinkin shows that the capitalized value of the banks' operating costs (the sum of the present values of the current operating costs and of the imputed annual interest charge on the fixed assets) is equal to the value of demand deposits and that, consequently, demand deposits should be excluded from net national wealth.[17] The implication of the perfect competition case is, of course, that the true origin of the net worth of the banking sector is in its monopoly right of creating demand deposits.

However, if the assumption of zero costs of managing demand deposits is unrealistic, so is the assumption of perfect competition in the banking sector. A reasonable assumption would then be that, since entry into the banking industry is restricted by the necessity of obtaining a license, the present value of the income from creating demand deposits should be regarded, in part, as a component of net private wealth.

---

[16]Reviewing the book by Pesek and Saving, Patinkin points out that the true origin of the net worth of the banking sector lies not in the production of demand deposits per se but in the monopoly right of producing demand deposits, which this sector has received from the government. See Don Patinkin, "Money and Wealth: A Review Article," *The Journal of Economic Literature,* Vol. VII (1969), pp. 1140–60. See also the reviews by Meltzer, "Money, Intermediation, and Growth" (cited in footnote 1), pp. 32–36, and Smith, "On Some Current Issues in Monetary Economics: An Interpretation" (cited in footnote 1), pp. 769–70.

[17]Patinkin, "Money and Wealth" (cited in footnote 16), pp. 1147–54.

This conclusion, in turn, raises an important question as to whether the conventional specification of the economically relevant wealth equation for theoretical as well as empirical studies is a proper one, and if it is not, how it should be modified.[18]

Net private (nonhuman) wealth (W) is generally defined as the sum of outside money and the market values of interest-bearing government debt and of the existing stock of physical capital:

$$W = PK + M_0 + B,$$

where P = price level; K = real stock of capital; M_0 = outside money; B = supply of government bonds.[19]

The market value of real assets or equities (V) has been defined, for instance, as

$$V = 100 \left(\frac{Y_{cd}}{R_d} \right),$$

where Y_{cd} = corporate dividend payments; R_d = dividend/price ratio on common stock (percentage).[20]

On the other hand, Pesek and Saving define real nonhuman wealth for the purpose of general analysis as

$$W = \frac{M}{P} + \frac{y_n}{r_n} + \frac{g}{r_g},$$

where M = nominal quantity of money (narrow definition of currency *plus* demand deposits); P = price level; y_n = real nonhuman income; g = real nonhuman income yielded by government securities; r_n = capitalization rate applicable to real nonhuman income; r_g = capitalization rate applicable to real government interest payments.[21]

Brunner and Meltzer, following Pesek and Saving's reasoning, also explicitly introduce the net worth of the commercial banking sector into their definition of nonhuman wealth:

$$W = PK + B + (1 + \sigma)M_0,$$

where σ = the banking system's net worth multiplier; σM_0 = the net worth contri-

---

[18]Once the monopoly is broken and perfect competition is restored in the banking sector, the monopoly profits (earnings) of banks will be transferred to the owners of demand deposits in the form of nonpecuniary services. See Meltzer, "Money, Intermediation, and Growth" (cited in footnote 1), p. 34.

[19]See, for example, Franco Modigliani, "The Monetary Mechanisn and Its Interaction with Real Phenomena," *The Review of Economics and Statistics,* Vol. XLV (Supplement, February 1963), p. 80.

[20]Frank de Leeuw and Edward M. Gramlich, "The Channels of Monetary Policy," *Federal Reserve Bulletin,* Vol. 55 (1969), p. 481.

[21]Pesek and Saving, *Money, Wealth, and Economic Theory* (cited in footnote 13), pp. 289-90.

bution of the banking sector, or the capitalized value of net earnings of the banking system.[22]

The basic difference between the definition of Pesek and Saving (or of Brunner and Meltzer) and the conventional one is, of course, that the former includes demand deposits (in whole or in part) as a component of net private wealth whereas the latter does not. At first sight, it may appear that the appropriate definition of wealth is the specification of either Pesek and Saving or Brunner and Meltzer. But that is not so. It was pointed out that any increase in the net worth of the banking sector would, *ceteris paribus,* lead to a corresponding increase in the net worth of the nonbanking private sector in the form of an increase in the market value of bank stocks. This means that the value of demand deposits in Pesek and Saving's definition, or the net worth contribution of the banking sector (σM_0) in Brunner and Meltzer's, is already included in the market value of equities (*PK, V,* or Y_n/r_n) to the extent that demand deposits (in whole or in part) are part of net wealth; adding the net worth of the banking sector to the market value of equities amounts to a double counting of the market value of commercial bank stocks. For this reason, the wealth definitions of Pesek and Saving and of Brunner and Meltzer should probably be rejected. One might then conclude that the conventional definition of net wealth is economically appropriate regardless of the validity of Pesek and Saving's thesis and that the direct wealth effect of monetary policy implied by their analysis has been accounted for in traditional analysis without being explicitly recognized.

Credit Rationing

Keynesian income/expenditure models assume a well-functioning competitive capital market in which desired investments are equilibrated to desired savings through the mechanism of the interest rate. In these models there exists a single short-run equilibrium rate of interest that simultaneously measures the rate of return to lenders, the cost of borrowings, the internal marginal rate of return from investments, and the opportunity cost of holding money. No one would question that the assumption of perfectly competitive capital markets is unrealistic; in reality, capital markets are not well functioning, and the price allocation mechanism may not work. It is, however, the proposition of the credit rationing channel that the Keynesian view of the transmission process of monetary policy and its consequences may have to be modified when market imperfections in capital markets are properly taken into consideration.

The most widely accepted view of the credit rationing channel appears to be the following proposition: under imperfect capital markets interest rates charged to borrowers by financial intermediaries, including commercial banks, are controlled by institutional forces, not by market forces, and tend not to change even when there is a change in the demand for funds, so that lenders ration the available supply of

[22]Karl Brunner and Allan H. Meltzer, "Fiscal and Monetary Policy in a Non-Keynesian World" (unpublished paper, 1970).

credit (by various nonprice terms). Accordingly, the demand for credit is limited "not by the borrowers' willingness to borrow at the given rate but by the lenders' willingness to lend—or, more precisely, by the funds available to them to be rationed out among the would-be borrowers."[23] Under these circumstances the single short-run equilibrium rate of interest in the perfect capital market framework is replaced by a plurality of rates—one for the lending units (depositors) and another for the rationed borrowers. This proposition implies that monetary policy could affect total expenditures directly by changing the degree of credit rationing and consequently the volume of lending, even if monetary controls did not change interest rates appreciably or if aggregate demand was interest inelastic. It also implies that insofar as "sticky" lending rates prevail, monetary policy would be less effective if it were geared to control the power of banks to create money rather than the actual money supply.[24]

While the credit rationing phenomenon has been well known, it has proved to be rather difficult to deal with effectively in macroeconomic analyses. One difficulty is that what is observed as credit availability is actually only a temporary disequilibrium situation in the capital market, one that may cause changes in interest rates in other parts of the capital market to levels that will eventually clear the market. Another difficulty is the empirical problem of measuring and identifying the degree of credit rationing. In most cases the specific details of credit rationing are not observable or recorded, so that indirect—often unsatisfactory—means must be used to represent credit rationing.

Portfolio Balance Approach

A more fundamental and basic development in monetary theory subsequent to Keynes' liquidity preference theory has been the capital theoretic formulation of the demand for money. This analysis emphasizes money as an asset that can be compared with other real as well as financial assets; its emphasis is on what is called portfolio balance. The analysis of portfolio and balance sheet adjustments has been extended beyond the Keynesian two-asset (money and bonds) models to include various financial and real assets other than bonds and has been integrated with varying degrees of complexity into the Keynesian income/expenditure framework.

The portfolio approach to monetary theory involves a new view of how the influence of monetary policy is transmitted to the real economy. The general view that has been emerging from the writings of both neo-Keynesians and monetarists stresses the impact of monetary policy changes on the composition of assets held by the public and the influence of these changes on interest rates on these assets and ultimately on the rate of return from investing in the production of new physical assets. In the portfolio view the impact on the real sector of an initial monetary disturbance is the result of changing relative prices among a wide array of financial and real

[23]Modigliani, "The Monetary Mechanism and Its Interaction with Real Phenomena" (cited in footnote 19), p. 98.
[24]*Ibid.*, p. 100.

assets. An increase in the supply of money, following an open market purchase of government securities, results in excessive holdings of money relative to other forms of wealth. Holders of wealth will be induced to exchange these excessive balances for other assets, which will in turn raise asset prices and lower rates of return across the board. As a result, an increase in the supply of money may eventually stimulate new investment in many directions.

This broad description of the transmission mechanism appears to be acceptable to both monetarists and nonmonetarists. There is, however, considerable disagreement as to the major variables and interest rates that must be defined in order to take account of all the ways in which monetary policy works out its effects. In what follows, focusing on this aspect, we will review and compare the views of nonmonetarists and monetarists on the transmission process of monetary policy.

II. The Nonmonetarist View

Neo-Keynesian Analysis: The Yale School View

It is always misleading to classify economists, who do not necessarily have common views about the subject matter concerned, under a single label as we do in this paper. It should be understood that the nomenclature is introduced solely for the convenience and clarity of exposition. Some economists whom we consider neo-Keynesians could take substantially different positions on particular issues. With this risk in mind, we summarize what appear to be the major arguments and findings of neo-Keynesians, or the Yale school.

(1) Neo-Keynesians consider that the stock of money, conventionally defined, is not an exogenous variable completely controlled by the monetary authorities but is partly an endogenous quantity that reflects the economic behavior of financial intermediaries and nonfinancial private economic units.[25]

(2) The sharp traditional distinctions between money and other assets and between commercial banks and other financial intermediaries are not warranted. Instead, monetary analysis should

> focus on demands for supplies of the whole spectrum of assets rather than on the quantity and velocity of "money"; and to regard the structure of interest rates, asset yields, and credit availability rather than the quantity of money [or the rate of interest] as the linkage between monetary and financial institutions and policies on the one hand and the real economy on the other.[26]

[25] *Financial Markets and Economic Activity* (cited in footnote 6), "Foreword," p. viii. See also Lyle E. Gramley and Samuel B. Chase, Jr., "Time Deposits in Monetary Analysis," *Federal Reserve Bulletin,* Vol. 51 (1965), pp. 1380-1406; John H. Kareken, "Commercial Banks and the Supply of Money: A Market-Determined Demand Deposit Rate," *Federal Reserve Bulletin,* Vol. 53 (1967), pp. 1699-1712; J. A. Cacy, "Alternative Approaches to the Analysis of the Financial Structure," Federal Reserve Bank of Kansas City, *Monthly Review* (March 1968), pp. 3-9; Richard G. Davis, "The Role of the Money Supply in Business Cycles," Federal Reserve Bank of New York, *Monthly Review* (April 1968), pp. 63-73.

[26] Tobin, "Commercial Banks as Creators of 'Money' " (cited in footnote 6), p. 3.

This argument has been known as the New View, a view that clearly is related to, if not similar to, the Radcliffe Committee's position some years ago. In fact, Johnson claims that the Yale school has provided the intellectual foundations of the Radcliffe position on monetary theory and policy.[27]

(3) Proposition (2) implies that the crucial distinction in a neo-Keynesian framework is between the financial sector and the real sector rather than between the banking system and the rest of the economy or between liquid and illiquid assets. The construction of the financial sector reflects the theory of portfolio management by economic units. The theory takes as its subject matter stocks of assets and debts, and their framework is the balance sheet; the decision variables in this sector are stocks.[28] The real sector deals with flows of income, saving, expenditures, and the production of goods and services. Its accounting framework is the income statement, and the decision variables are flows. The two sectors are linked by "accounting identities—e.g., increase in net worth equals saving plus capital appreciation—and by technological and financial stock-flow relations."[29] This, together with proposition (2), implies a rather complicated relationship between the two sectors in the linkage sequence. Some attempts have been made to synthesize the two sectors with varying degrees of simplification, but none of them seems satisfactory. Considering the emphasis on and the amount of attention paid to the building and analyzing of the interactions within the financial sector, it is indeed surprising to find that there has been no satisfactory attempt to bridge the gap. In our discussion we will consider perhaps the most widely accepted of these attempts, the synthesis developed by Brainard and Tobin.[30]

(4) While there is still considerable debate on the link between the real and financial sectors, there appears to be a consensus among neo-Keynesians that monetary policy operates through changes in the market price of equities that represent claims on existing real assets, such as plant and equipment.[31] The prime indicator of stance and the proper target of monetary policy is thus "the required rate of return on capital," or the equity yield. "Nothing else, whether it is the quantity of 'money' or some financial interest rate, can be more than an imperfect and derivative indicator of the effective thrust of monetary events and policies."[32] In a neo-Keynesian framework an expansionary monetary policy, for example, raises the price of equities (that is, reduces the yield on equities), thereby generating a positive discrepancy between the valuation of real assets on these markets (the price of equities) and their costs of production. The discrepancy provides an incentive to expand production of these

[27]Johnson, "Recent Developments in Monetary Theory—A Commentary" (cited in footnote 1), p. 101.

[28]*Financial Markets and Economic Activity* (cited in footnote 6), "Foreword," pp. v-vi.

[29]Tobin, "Money, Capital, and Other Stores of Value" (cited in footnote 6), p. 28.

[30]William C. Brainard and James Tobin, "Pitfalls in Financial Model Building," American Economic Association, *Papers and Proceedings of the Eightieth Annual Meeting* (*The American Economic Review,* Vol. LVIII, May 1968), pp. 99-122.

[31]Neo-Keynesians assume that capital goods have two separate market prices: the prices of existing (secondhand) capital goods represented by the price of equities and the output prices of these goods (or the prices of newly produced capital goods).

[32]Brainard and Tobin, "Pitfalls in Financial Model Building" (cited in footnote 30), p. 104.

capital goods. Suppose that the existing plant and equipment of a corporation that could be reproduced for $1 million is valued at $2 million in the stock market. This margin between the market valuation and the cost of reproducing the existing capital goods will then stimulate new investment in these goods.[33] On this reasoning, the stock market plays a significant role in influencing economic activity, and indeed changes in the Dow-Jones averages give some measure of the stance of monetary policy.[34]

The most serious criticism that may be made of the neo-Keynesian analysis is that despite the very complex financial sector, incorporating detailed specifications of asset preferences, its transmission mechanism remains naïve and simple. The synthesis by Brainard and Tobin assumes that the equity rate is the major link between money and the level of economic activity. Compared with the Keynesian transmission process, this simply involves replacing the rates of interest on financial assets by the equity yield—a yield that is now taken to represent the influence of monetary forces. Also, neo-Keynesians appear to ignore the relative importance of borrowing costs and, hence, the importance of debt financing in business firms.

The Neo-Fisherian View

All of the major empirical studies have found that the demand for money and velocity are responsive to interest rates, although the choice of rates between short-term and long-term is not clear cut. However, neither Keynes' speculative motive of holding money nor Tobin's portfolio selection theory provides a rational explanation of the nonzero interest elasticity of the demand for money in an economy where there exist short-term securities—such as time deposits, savings and loan shares, treasury bills, high-grade commercial paper, and negotiable certificates of deposit for large investors—that dominate money. When these assets are readily available, the public—faced, for example, with a low current rate of interest and an expectation of capital losses owing to an expected rise in the current rate of interest—will be induced to shift from long-term to short-term securities, but not to money. This is so because these short-term assets possess the same properties as money—near perfect liquidity and no risk of default—while yielding a positive rate of return.[35]

Given these short-term securities, changes in the current rate of interest and expec-

[33]For further discussion on this investment behavior, see Brainard and Tobin, "Pitfalls in Financial Model Building" (cited in footnote 30), p. 112; Hyman P. Minsky, "Private Sector Asset Management and the Effectiveness of Monetary Policy: Theory and Practice," *The Journal of Finance*, Vol. XXIV (1969), p. 229; W. L. Smith, "A Neo-Keynesian View of Monetary Policy," in *Controlling Monetary Aggregates* (Proceedings of a monetary conference in Massachusetts), Federal Reserve Bank of Boston (June 1969), p. 106; Ralph Turvey, *Interest Rates and Asset Prices* (London, 1960); James Tobin, "An Essay on Principles of Debt Management," in *Fiscal and Debt Management Policies,* Commission on Money and Credit (Englewood Cliffs, New Jersey, 1963), p. 150; James Tobin, "Monetary Semantics," in *Targets and Indicators of Monetary Policy,* ed. by Karl Brunner (San Francisco, 1969), pp. 173-74.

[34]Tobin, "Monetary Semantics" (cited in footnote 33), p. 174. See the Appendix for a systematic discussion on the neo-Keynesian transmission process of monetary policy.

[35]See Smith, "On Some Current Issues in Monetary Economics: An Interpretation" (cited in footnote 1), pp. 774-75.

tation of capital gains or losses no longer explain the substitution between long-term securities and money but the substitution between long-term and short-term securities.[36] Therefore, the only plausible theory of the demand for money that is consistent with the existing empirical evidence seems to be the transactions cost approach of the demand for money, developed by Baumol and Tobin.[37] The basic hypothesis of this approach, which has been labeled as neo-Fisherian, is that "the demand for money is basically related to the flow of transactions and arises from a lack of synchronization between receipts and payments, coupled with the transactions costs involved in exchanging money for short-term assets."[38] This hypothesis implies that (i) the wealth variable does not appear in the demand for money function, since money is held primarily to facilitate transactions and that (ii) the demand for money is sensitive to short-term interest rates.

The financial sector of the Federal Reserve–MIT econometric model embodies the neo-Fisherian hypothesis.[39] In the financial sector of the model the reciprocal of velocity (the Cambridge k) is related to the rates of interest on short-term assets relative to transactions costs. Assuming no significant variation in transactions costs, the demand for money is then expressed as $M^d = k(i)Y$, where i = a set of available rates of return on short-term assets, Y = nominal gross national product (GNP), and M is narrow money.[40]

Within the neo-Fisherian framework, changes in the quantity of money have their direct impact on short-term interest rates.[41] Through the process of portfolio substitutions, changes in short-term interest rates affect, in turn, the long-term interest rates, equity yields, and possibly other rates of return on real assets.[42] Changes in these variables then influence aggregate demand for goods and services. This transmission process indicates that the full effect of monetary policy is subject to a considerable

[36]The Keynesian speculative demand for money ceases to be an explanation of holding money but becomes the basis for an expectational theory of the term structure of interest rates.

[37]William J. Baumol, "The Transactions Demand for Cash: An Inventory Theoretic Approach," *The Quarterly Journal of Economics,* Vol. LXVI (1952), pp. 545-56; James Tobin, "The Interest-Elasticity of Transactions Demand for Cash," *The Review of Economics and Statistics,* Vol. XXXVIII (1956), pp. 241-47.

[38]Franco Modigliani, Robert Rasche, and J. Philip Cooper, "Central Bank Policy, the Money Supply, and the Short-Term Rate of Interest," *Journal of Money, Credit and Banking,* Vol. II (1970), p. 167. The neo-Fisherian model of the demand for money developed by these authors is basically the one in the Federal Reserve–MIT econometric model.

[39]Robert H. Rasche and Harold T. Shapiro, "The F.R.B.–M.I.T. Econometric Model: Its Special Features," American Economic Association, *Papers and Proceedings of the Eightieth Annual Meeting (The American Economic Review,* Vol. LVIII, May 1968), pp. 123-49.

[40]*Ibid.,* p. 137.

[41]However, if the monetary authorities dealt in the long-term bond market, changes in the quantity of money resulting from open market operations would affect the long-term interest rate directly.

[42]The process through which changes in short-term interest rates affect long-term interest rates may be explained directly by an equation from the term structure of interest rates based on the expectations hypothesis. This approach allows us to omit the equations of supply and demand for many financial assets. The Federal Reserve–MIT model follows this approach, relying on the term structure hypothesis developed by Franco Modigliani and Richard Sutch, "Innovations in Interest Rate Policy," American Economic Association, *Papers and Proceedings of the Seventy-eighth Annual Meeting (The American Economic Review,* Vol. LVI, May 1966), pp. 178-97.

lag, because it takes time for changes in monetary policy to be reflected in long-term interest rates and equity yields and also requires additional delay for this rate change to be reflected in various components of aggregate demand.[43]

III. The Monetarist View

The theoretical framework used by nonmonetarists to explain how monetary and fiscal policies affect economic activity is a variant of the Keynesian income/expend-iture model. While nonmonetarists are rather explicit in their theoretical argument, monetarists have not been very precise in providing a convincing explanation of how money affects the economy and how changes in the supply of money could have markedly more potent and direct effects than changes in fiscal variables. Instead, their argument seems to be based on several kinds of empirical evidence, the most widely publicized being the findings of the reduced form equation studies. These studies relate changes in GNP to the simultaneous and lagged changes in the supply of money and a budget variable or autonomous expenditures.

In this section we will discuss the views of Friedman, Brunner and Meltzer, and other monetarists. The general view that emerges from the writings of these monetar-ists is that "changes in the money stock are a primary determinant of changes in total spending, and should thereby be given major emphasis in economic stabilization programs."[44] In addition to this, monetarists emphasize the following three points: (1) The monetary authorities can dominate movements in the stock of money over time and over business cycles. (2) Movements in the quantity of money are the most reliable measure of the thrust of monetary impulses. (3) Monetary impulses are transmitted to the real economy through a relative price process (portfolio adjust-ment process), which operates on a vast array of financial and real assets.[45]

---

[43]In the Federal Reserve-MIT model the costs of capital are defined to be linear combinations of various long-term interest rates and the dividend/price ratio. The effect of monetary policy is felt immedi-ately in the short-term interest rates. Through the term structure equation, changes in short-term rates affect the long-term rates with a time lag. The long-term rate in turn affects the cost of capital directly as one of its components and indirectly through the dividend/price ratio. The cost of capital influences the demand functions for final output with an additional time lag. See Rasche and Shapiro, "The F. R. B.-M. I. T. Econometric Model" (cited in footnote 39), p. 146. See also de Leeuw and Gramlich, "The Channels of Monetary Policy" (cited in footnote 20), pp. 485-90.

[44]Leonall C. Andersen and Keith M. Carlson, "A Monetarist Model for Economic Stabilization," Federal Reserve Bank of St. Louis, *Review,* Vol. 52 (April 1970), p. 7. An important qualification of this is Friedman's view that, notwithstanding the importance of money, monetary policy—because it operates with a long and variable lag—should not be used for short-run stabilization. Instead, money should be allowed to grow at a constant rate over time.

On the general view of monetarists, see Milton Friedman, *The Counter-Revolution in Monetary Theory,* first Wincott Memorial Lecture, delivered at the Senate House, University of London, September 16, 1970, Occasional Paper 33, Institute of Economic Affairs (London, 1970); Karl Brunner, "The 'Monetarist Revolution' in Monetary Theory," *Weltwirtschaftliches Archiv,* Band 105, Heft 1 (1970), pp. 1-30.

[45]Karl Brunner, "The Role of Money and Monetary Policy," Federal Reserve Bank of St. Louis, *Review,* Vol. 50 (July 1968), pp. 9, 18, and 24.

Friedman: The Monetary Theory of
Nominal Income

Professor Milton Friedman, as the chief architect of the monetarist view, is responsible for the intellectual revival of the quantity theory in the postwar period—a
revival that has for some years provoked a good deal of commentary and critical
interpretation. Much of this controversy has been attributed to his failure to make
explicit the theoretical framework that encompasses his views on the role of money.
In two recent articles,[46] he has responded to this criticism, but it is not clear to what
extent he has succeeded in answering his critics.[47]

Friedman's theoretical framework in the most recent expression of his views is a
Keynesian income/expenditure model, which, he claims, is acceptable to both monetarists and nonmonetarists.[48]

The model is given as follows:

$$\frac{C}{P} = f\left(\frac{Y}{P}, r\right) \tag{1}$$

$$\frac{I}{P} = g(r) \tag{2}$$

$$\frac{Y}{P} = \frac{C}{P} + \frac{I}{P} \tag{3}$$

$$M^d = P\,L\left(\frac{Y}{P}, r\right) \tag{4}$$

$$M^s = h(r) \tag{5}$$

$$M^d = M^s, \tag{6}$$

where Y = money income; C = consumption; I = investment; r = the rate of
interest; P = the price level; M^s = supply of money; M^d = demand for money.

Equations (1)–(3) describe the real sector of the economy, while equations (4)–(6)
outline the monetary sector. In this model, real consumption expenditure is ex-

[46]Milton Friedman, "A Theoretical Framework for Monetary Analysis," *Journal of Political Economy*,
Vol. 78 (March/April 1970), pp. 193–238; "A Monetary Theory of Nominal Income," *Journal of Political
Economy*, Vol. 79 (March/April 1971), pp. 323–37.

[47]Prior to this, Patinkin had shown conclusively that Friedman's reformulation of the quantity theory
was an elegant exposition of the modern portfolio approach to the demand for money, which can be seen
as a continuation of the Keynesian liquidity preference theory. (See Don Patinkin, "The Chicago Tradition, the Quantity Theory, and Friedman," *Journal of Money, Credit and Banking*, Vol. I 1969, pp. 46–70.)
In recent writings, Friedman himself has acknowledged that his reformulation was much influenced by the
Keynesian liquidity analysis. (See Friedman, "Postwar Trends in Monetary Theory and Policy" (cited in
footnote 12) p. 188. See also Milton Friedman, "Money: Quantity Theory," *International Encyclopedia of
the Social Sciences*, Vol. 10 (New York, 1968), pp. 432–47.

[48]See Friedman, "A Theoretical Framework for Monetary Analysis" (cited in footnote 46), pp.
217–18.

plained by real income and the interest rate (equation 1) and real investment is explained by the interest rate (equation 2). Equation (3) is the equilibrium condition in the commodity market, or the income identity. Real money balances are a function of real income and the rate of interest (equation 4), while the nominal supply of money is assumed to be an increasing function of the interest rate (equation 5). The equilibrium condition in the money market is given by equation (6).

The model consists of six independent equations with seven endogenous variables (C, I, Y, P, M^d, M^s, r), so that the system of equations cannot determine simultaneously the solution values of these variables. One of these variables must be determined exogenously by relationships outside the system. Friedman discusses three different ways of solving the system that correspond to three different macroeconomic theories. The first two methods are well known in the literature; they are the income/expenditure theory and the quantity theory approach. The difference between the two theories is the condition that is added to make the model determine the solution values of the seven endogenous variables. The Keynesian income/expenditure theory assumes that the general level of prices is determined outside the system—the Keynesian assumption of price or wage rigidity ($P = P_0$). Given this assumption, the system of equations determines simultaneously the solution for the level of income and the rate of interest, as usually described in the familiar Hicksian *IS/LM* apparatus.[49] The quantity theory approach, on the other hand, assumes that real income is determined outside the system—the classical assumption of full employment. This assumption allows a dichotomy of the system into the real and monetary sectors, with the result that the demand for and supply of money functions determine the price level.[50] Friedman takes the view that the quantity theory model is valid for long-run equilibrium, so that, in the long run, variations in the rate of change in the quantity of money will change only the rate of inflation and not growth of real output.[51]

According to Friedman, neither the quantity theory nor the income/expenditure theory model is satisfactory as a framework for short-run analysis. This is so, Fried-

---

[49]The price rigidity assumption, $P = P_0$, allows equations (1)-(3) to define one relation between r and real income (*IS* curve) and equations (4)-(6) to define a second such relation (*LM* curve). Their simultaneous solution gives the rate of interest and real income.

[50]Given the level of real income, $Y/P = y$, equations (1)-(3) determine the rate of interest. Equations (4)-(6) then yield an equation relating the price level to the quantity of money.

[51]In conditions where the rate of growth of real output is determined independently by real forces in the economy, conditions that are assumed to prevail in the long run, changes in the money supply will dominate only changes in the price level, notwithstanding the fact that the demand for money is interest sensitive. Specifically, Friedman argues that in the long run monetary policy cannot control real variables—the real rate of interest, the level of unemployment, and real income—but can control only nominal quantities—the price level, money rate of interest, and nominal income. See Milton Friedman, "The Role of Monetary Policy," in his *The Optimum Quantity of Money and Other Essays* (Chicago, 1969), p. 105.

Critics of Friedman have frequently pointed out that his extreme view of the role of money is valid only if the demand for money is insensitive to interest rates, implying a close linkage between the stock of money and income. In the light of the above discussion and his recent reformulation on the demand for money, this kind of criticism seems no longer valid. See also Milton Friedman, "Interest Rates and the Demand for Money" in his *The Optimum Quantity of Money and Other Essays*, pp. 141-55.

man claims, mainly because neither theory can explain "(*a*) the short-run division of a change in nominal income between prices and output, (*b*) the short-run adjustment of nominal income to a change in autonomous variables, and (*c*) the transition between this short-run situation and a long-run equilibrium described essentially by the quantity-theory model."[52]

The third alternative way to determine the system of equations is given by the monetary theory of nominal income—a theory that, Friedman claims, is superior to either the income/expenditure or the quantity theory as an approach to closing the system for the purpose of analyzing short-period changes. This third approach synthesizes Irving Fisher's ideas on the nominal and real interest rates and Keynes' view that the current market rate of interest (long-term) is determined largely by the rate that is expected to prevail over a long period. The Keynes and Fisher synthesis is then integrated into a quantity theory model together with the empirical assumption (i) that the real income elasticity of the demand for money is unity and (ii) that a difference between the anticipated real interest rate and the anticipated growth rate of real income is determined outside the system.[53] The result is a monetary model in which current income is related to current and prior nominal quantities of money.

The monetary model may be described as follows:[54]

THE MONETARY SECTOR

Given the assumption of unitary real income elasticity of the demand for money, equation (4) can be rewritten as

$$M^d = F(r)Y \tag{4$'$}$$

In order to simplify the exposition of the model, let us assume that the supply of money is determined exogenously:

$$M^s = M \tag{5$'$}$$

Then equations (4)$'$, (5)$'$, and equilibrium conditions (6) yield

$$M = F(r)Y \tag{7}$$

Equation (7) can be written as

$$Y = \frac{1}{F(r)} M = H(r)M \tag{8}$$

[52]Friedman, "A Theoretical Framework for Monetary Analysis" (cited in footnote 46), p. 223. Both theories analyze short-run adjustments in terms of shifts from one static equilibrium position to another without explaining a dynamic adjustment process involved in such a change in equilibrium positions.

[53]This assumption is the counterpart of the third approach of the full employment and rigid-price assumptions of the quantity theory and income/expenditure theory.

[54]See Friedman, "A Monetary Theory of Nominal Income" (cited in footnote 46), pp. 325-32.

The Fisherian distinction between the nominal and real rate of interest is given by the following identity:

$$r = q + \left(\frac{1}{P}\frac{dP}{dt}\right), \tag{9}^{55}$$

where q = the real rate of interest; $(1/P\ dP/dt)$ = the rate of change of the price level.

From equation (9), it also follows that

$$r^* = q^* + \left(\frac{1}{P}\frac{dP}{dt}\right)^*, \tag{10}$$

where the variables with an asterisk refer to anticipated (or expected) values.

Following Keynes' argument that market rates of interest are determined largely by speculators with firmly held expectations, Friedman assumes that

$$r = r^* \tag{11}^{56}$$

From the identity, $Y = yP$, it follows that

$$\left(\frac{1}{P}\frac{dP}{dt}\right)^* = \left(\frac{1}{Y}\frac{dY}{dt}\right)^* - \left(\frac{1}{y}\frac{dy}{dt}\right)^* \tag{12}$$

Combining equations (10), (11), and (12) we obtain

$$r = q^* - g^* + \left(\frac{1}{Y}\frac{dY}{dt}\right)^*, \tag{13}$$

where $g^* = (1/y\ dy/dt)^*$ = the anticipated rate of growth of real income.

Substitution of equation (13) into (8) yields

$$Y = H\left[q^* - g^* + \left(\frac{1}{Y}\frac{dY}{dt}\right)^*\right]M \tag{14}$$

Equation (14) states that the level of income Y is determined by q^*, g^*, $(1/Y\ dY/dt)^*$, and M. Friedman assumes that the difference between q^* and g^* is a constant. In a static framework, the expected rate of growth of nominal income

---

[55]Notice that both the simple quantity and income/expenditure theories assume a stable price level; hence, real and nominal rates of interest are the same.

[56]Suppose that a substantial number of asset owners have the same expectation on the future rate of interest and hold the expectation firmly, then the demand for money will become perfectly elastic at the current rate of interest that is equal to the expected rate of interest, namely, when $r = r^*$. Money and other earning assets (bonds in the Keynesian analysis) would become perfect substitutes; the demand for money has a liquidity trap at $r = r^*$. In this situation, the monetary authorities would not be able to change the rate of interest by changing the quantity of money; no matter what the monetary authorities do with the supply of money, asset owners will force the current rate of interest into conformity with their expectations on the future rate of interest. Friedman argues that this is the basic idea behind the Keynes' short-run liquidity trap. See Friedman, "A Theoretical Framework for Monetary Analysis" (cited in footnote 46), p. 214.

$(1/Y\ dY/dt)^*$ may be treated as a predetermined variable. Then equation (14) determines the level of nominal income for a given supply of money without any reference to the real sector of the model.[57] In a dynamic framework, however, it would be natural to regard $(1/Y\ dY/dt)^*$ as determined by the past history of nominal income. Since the past history of nominal income is in turn a function of the past history of money as implied by equation (8) for earlier dates, equation (14) becomes a relation between the level of nominal income at each point in time and the past history of the quantity of money.

This dynamic character of the model may be better understood by analyzing an example given by Friedman. Take the logarithm of equation (14) and differentiate with respect to time.

This gives

$$\frac{1}{Y}\frac{dY}{dt} = s \cdot \frac{d}{dt}\left(\frac{1}{Y}\frac{dY}{dt}\right)^* + \frac{1}{M}\frac{dM}{dt}, \tag{15}$$

where $s = 1/H\ dH/dr =$ the slope of the regression of log H on the rate of interest.

Suppose that the expected rate of growth of nominal income is determined by an adaptive expectation process:

$$\frac{d}{dt}\left(\frac{1}{Y}\frac{dY}{dt}\right)^* = \beta\left[\frac{1}{Y}\frac{dY}{dt} - \left(\frac{1}{Y}\frac{dY}{dt}\right)^*\right] \tag{16}[58]$$

---

[57]Once we make the distinction between the nominal and real rate of interest, the rate of interest relevant to the consumption and investment functions is the real rate of interest, q. Hence, the equations describing the real sector of the model are modified as

$$\frac{C}{P} = f\left(\frac{Y}{P},\ q\right) \tag{1$'$}$$

$$\frac{I}{P} = g(q) \tag{2$'$}$$

$$\frac{Y}{P} = \frac{c}{P} + \frac{I}{P} \tag{3}$$

Assume that the realized real rate of interest q is constant,

$$q = q^* = q_o \tag{15}$$

Then equations (1)$'$-(3) become a self-contained system of three equations with three unknowns: C/P, I/P, and Y/P. The price level would then be determined by substituting Y/P obtained from the real sector and Y from the monetary sector into the following identity, $Y = y \cdot P$.

Friedman considers this way of combining the monetary and real sectors as highly unsatisfactory for two reasons: the assumption of a constant real rate of interest is likely to introduce serious errors, particularly through the real sector, and the consumption function (1) ignores several important arguments, such as wealth and expected rate of inflation. See Friedman, "A Monetary Theory of Nominal Income" (cited in footnote 46), p. 330.

[58]Equation (16) is analogous to

$$\left(\frac{1}{Y}\frac{dY}{dt}\right)^*_T = \int_{-\infty}^{T} e^{\beta(t-T)}\left(\frac{1}{Y}\frac{dY}{dt}\right)_t dt,$$

Substituting equation (16) into equation (15) and solving for $(1/Y \, dY/dt)$, we have

$$\frac{1}{Y}\frac{dY}{dt} = \left(\frac{1}{Y}\frac{dY}{dt}\right)^* + \frac{1}{(1-\beta s)}\left[\frac{1}{M}\frac{dM}{dt} - \left(\frac{1}{Y}\frac{dY}{dt}\right)^*\right] \tag{17}$$

When
$(1/Y \, dY/dt)^* = 1/M \, dM/dt$, equation (17) gives the quantity theory result that nominal income changes at the same rate as money supply.

Friedman states that his monetary model of nominal income corresponds to the broader framework implicit in much of the theoretical and empirical work that he and others have done in analyzing monetary experience in the short run and is consistent with many of their empirical findings.[59]

However, Friedman's model sheds little light on his view concerning the precise mechanism through which changes in the quantity of money affect income. This is so because the model is designed primarily for empirical analysis of the relation between money and income. What this model reflects is rather his view on the appropriate empirical approach to evaluating the role of money—a view that is in sharp contrast to the more common one held by nonmonetarists. Contrary to the impression that one might gather from his model—possibly a rigid and mechanical connection between money and income—his view on the transmission mechanism in a conceptual framework is a complicated portfolio adjustment process that involves many uncertain channels and impinges on a wide array of assets and expenditures. The process[60] following an exogenous change in the supply of money begins with changes in the prices and yields of financial assets and spreads to nonfinancial assets. These changes in the prices of financial and nonfinancial assets influence spending to produce new assets and spending on current services. At the same time, these changes alter real wealth of the public relative to income and thereby affect consumption. This is, in a simple fashion, the way in which the initial impulse is diffused from the financial markets to the markets for goods and services. The exposition stresses portfolio adjustment and is strikingly similar to that described by many economists.

The transmission process is also essentially consistent with the Keynesian liquidity

---

which means that the expected rate of growth of nominal income at T is a weighted average of past growth rates of nominal income, the weights $(e^{\beta(t-T)})$ declining exponentially where t is the time of the observation weighted. See Edgar L. Feige, "Expectations and Adjustments in the Monetary Sector," American Economic Association, *Papers and Proceedings of the Seventy-ninth Annual Meeting* (*The American Economic Review*, Vol. LVII, May 1967), pp. 463–67.

[59]Friedman, "A Monetary Theory of Nominal Income" (cited in footnote 46), pp. 324 and 334.

[60]Milton Friedman and Anna J. Schwartz, "Money and Business Cycles," *The Review of Economics and Statistics,* Vol. XLV (Supplement, February 1963), pp. 59–63; Milton Friedman and David Meiselman, "The Relative Stability of Monetary Velocity and the Investment Multiplier in the United States, 1877–1958," *Stabilization Policies,* Commission on Money and Credit (Englewood Cliffs, New Jersey, 1963), pp. 217–22; Milton Friedman, "The Role of Monetary Policy," in his *The Optimum Quantity of Money and Other Essays* (cited in footnote 51), p. 100, and *The Counter-Revolution in Monetary Theory* (cited in footnote 44), pp. 24–25.

preference doctrine as to how money affects income. As in the income/expenditure theory, interest rates play a key role. This being so, it has been pointed out that Friedman cannot be saying anything different from Keynes[61] and that there is no clear reason why one should look at money supply as a target as Friedman insists rather than at interest rates directly.[62] However, these criticisms miss the fundamental points of Friedman's view. The difference between Friedman and the non-monetarists concerning the transmission process is not whether changes in the supply of money operate through interest rates but rather (i) the range of interest rates considered and (ii) the empirical approach to estimating the actual influence of monetary policy. Friedman argues that the impact of monetary policy is likely to be understated in magnitude and narrowed in scope in the Keynesian income/expenditure theory. One reason is that, since monetary policy impinges on a broad range of capital assets and a correspondingly broad range of associated expenditures, the Keynesian practice of looking only at recorded market interest rates, which are only part of a much broader spectrum of rates, makes one underestimate the actual impact of monetary policy. The rates of interest that influence investment decisions are for the most part implicit yields and hence not observable, so that one cannot hope to obtain useful results by looking at relations between market interest rates and the categories of spending associated with these rates. Also, recorded market interest rates may not provide an appropriate measure of the cost of capital, since these interest rates are not real rates of interest that reflect the basic forces of productivity but nominal rates that are influenced by the expected rate of inflation. Moreover, monetary influences may work through channels that we have not been able to identify. In fact, it may not be possible to trace through any particular channel, as monetary policy operates through an extremely complicated process of portfolio adjustments.

For all these reasons, Friedman considers that even the most complex structure of a general equilibrium model cannot be expected to capture actual monetary influences adequately. A more reliable empirical approach would be to pursue the methodology of positive economies, the essence of which is to select the crucial and simple theoretical relationships that allow one to predict something large (such as GNP) from something small (for instance, the supply of money), regardless of the intervening chain of causation. One such relationship is claimed to be the velocity function relating income to money, which is the essence of the quantity theory; another is the multiplier relationship relating income to autonomous expenditure, which is the essence of the income/expenditure theory.[63]

[61]Nicholas Kaldor, "The New Monetarism," *Lloyd's Bank Review* (July 1970), p. 9.
[62]H. C. Wallich, "Quality Theory and Quantity Policy," Chapter 10 in *Ten Economic Studies in the Tradition of Irving Fisher* (New York, 1967), p. 260.
[63]This is Johnson's interpretation of Friedman's view. See Johnson, "Recent Developments in Monetary Theory—A Commentary" (cited in footnote 1), pp. 86-87; see also Johnson, "The Keynesian Revolution and the Monetarist Counter-Revolution" (cited in footnote 1), p. 9.

Friedman argues that the velocity function (that is, the relationship between money and nominal income) has been shown, on average, to be more stable and less affected by institutional and historical change than the multiplier relationship and that, consequently, the velocity function may be the key relationship in understanding macroeconomic developments.[64] It then follows that a much more promising approach to the question of evaluating the affects of monetary policy on the economy is to try to relate changes in income directly to changes in the quantity of money. Friedman's monetary model of nominal income seems to reflect this point of view.

Friedman's view, however, raises two important issues. One issue is concerned with the conditions under which one could derive a simple relationship between income and money. It has been argued frequently that Friedman's view is valid only if the demand for money is not significantly influenced by the rate of interest. As indicated earlier, Friedman now states clearly and repeatedly that the rate of interest is an important determinant of the demand for money. If indeed the demand for money depends on the rate of interest, then one cannot—critics of Friedman argue— hope to find such a simple relationship between money and income, unless one specifies an independent theory of the determination of the rate of interest.

The Keynes and Fisher synthesis that Friedman incorporates into his monetary model appears to be one such independent theory. It is an independent theory in the sense that the determination of the nominal rate of interest depends on relationships outside the system of six equations. According to Friedman's monetary model, the rate of interest is determined solely by the anticipated rate of growth of money income $(1/Y\ dY/dt)^*$, given the assumptions that $r = r^*$ and that $q^* - g^* = k_0$. While these assumptions are crucial to a model that allows one to relate current money income directly to current and prior quantities of money, it should be realized that they are also responsible for several defects of the model. One serious defect is that the model rules out liquidity or substitution effects of a change in the quantity of money on the interest rate.

In Friedman's monetary model, a change in the rate of change of money supply $(1/M\ dM/dt)$ directly affects the rate of growth of nominal income $(1/Y\ dY/dt)$ (see equation 17) with little direct effect on change in the interest rates, that is, the change does not initially produce the liquidity effect but immediately produces an income effect. The change in $(1/Y\ dY/dt)$ then causes a change in the expected rate of growth of nominal income $(1/Y\ dY/dt)^*$ (equation 16), which, in turn, influences the nominal rate of interest (equation 13). In other words, the change in the rate of change in money supply affects market rates of interest only as it influences the courses of current and expected nominal income and, in consequence, the expected rate of inflation. This process does not appear to be supported by the existing empirical evidence on the effects of changes in money supply on the interest rates and

---

[64]See Friedman and Meiselman, "The Relative Stability of Monetary Velocity and the Investment Multiplier in the United States, 1877-1958" (cited in footnote 60).

income.[65] Nor does it seem to be consistent with Friedman's own earlier exposition on the transmission mechanism of monetary policy, in which he argues that a change in the supply of money has its first impact on the financial markets and much later on the market for goods and services.[66]

However, the failure of the model to explain the liquidity effect is clearly not a point of disagreement with Friedman, for he admits that the model neglects the effects of changes in the nominal quantity of money on interest rates.[67] Yet, it is not clear to what extent he appreciates the analytical significance of relaxing either of his two critical assumptions to permit a strong liquidity effect in the model. Relaxation of these assumptions would mean that Friedman's model would be modified in such a way that the rate of interest is determined within the model through the interaction of demand for and supply of money together with other behavioral relationships in the real sector of the economy. Such a modification would then suggest that one may not utilize velocity to derive a simple relation between money income and the quantity of money.

The other issue that Friedman's monetary model raises is whether the methodology of positive economics embodied in the model is a scientifically acceptable method. The general consensus seems to be that the methodology is seriously inadequate. We shall return to this topic in some detail in the final section of this paper.

Brunner and Meltzer

The transmission process described by Brunner and Meltzer is basically a process of portfolio (balance sheet) adjustment, which is, on a general level of discussion, shared by both neo-Keynesians and other monetarists.[68] The difference between

[65]In examining the relationship betweeh changes in the rate of change in money supply and changes in the commercial paper rates, Cagan found that an increase in the monetary growth rate initially exerts a negative liquidity effect on the interest rate. The negative effect is then offset by positive income and price effects within about one year, following the increase in the monetary growth rate. See Phillip Cagan, "The Channels of Monetary Effects on Interest Rates" (mimeographed, National Bureau of Economic Research, 1966).

Friedman himself acknowledges that change in the rate of change in the quantity of money will have no appreciable effect on the rate of change in money income for six months to nine months, on average, in the United States. See Friedman, "A Monetary Theory of Nominal Income" (cited in footnote 46), p. 335.

In a recent study by Gibson, however, the initial liquidity effects are shown to be fully offset by positive effects only after a period of three or five months, depending on which definition of money one uses. See William E. Gibson, "Interest Rates and Monetary Policy," *Journal of Political Economy,* Vol. 78 (May/June, 1970), pp. 431-55.

[66]See footnote 60.

[67]See Friedman, "A Monetary Theory of Nominal Income" (cited in footnote 46), p. 333. He also states that the model cannot explain satisfactorily the movements of interests and velocity in the first nine months or so after a distinct change in the rate of monetary growth. (*Ibid.,* p. 335.)

[68]For a more detailed discussion, see Karl Brunner, "The Report of the Commission on Money and Credit," *The Journal of Political Economy,* Vol. LXIX (December 1961), pp. 605-20; Karl Brunner, "Some Major Problems in Monetary Theory," American Economic Association, *Papers and Proceedings of the Seventy-third Annual Meeting (The American Economic Review,* Vol. LI, May 1961), pp. 47-56; Karl Brunner and Allan H. Meltzer, "The Place of Financial Intermediaries in the Transmission of Monetary

Brunner and Meltzer and other economists, if any, may be found in the different degrees of emphasis on the importance of real capital in the mechanism. Brunner and Meltzer point out that the analysis of portfolio balance reveals that changes in the level of output emerge fundamentally from this balance sheet adjustment, particularly in response to the public's decision to adjust its real capital holdings. In order, then, to capture the total effects of monetary policy changes, it is necessary to specify the appropriate stock-flow relationship centered on real capital goods, since changes in the asset price of real capital relative to its output price form a crucial linkage in the transmission process. Accordingly, they distinguish four classes of output—output for real consumption and for Types I, II, and III of capital goods—and also consider various financial assets together with the stocks of real capital disaggregated into the three types.

Type I capital goods are those that have separate market prices for equity claims on existing stock and for new output. (Examples under this category would be machinery, plant, and equipment.)[69] Type II capital goods have a single price for existing assets and new output of comparable quality (housing and automobiles); Type III has a price for new output only, and there is no market for existing assets or claims to them (consumer durables, such as washing machines). Corresponding to these different types of capital goods are different paths through which monetary policy can affect the real economy. An increase in the supply of money, for example, will, through portfolio substitutions, lead to an overall increase in the asset prices of all these types of real capital goods. The increase in the equity price for Type I real capital relative to its output price accelerates the actual rate of accumulation of this type of capital goods.[70] The increase in the asset price of Type II capital, *ceteris paribus*, stimulates the production of Type II capital goods. Furthermore, the rise in the asset prices of real capital and the fall in the rates of return on financial assets result in an increase in the market value of public wealth, which, in turn, raises the desired stock of Type III capital and consumption expenditure. The total effects of the expansionary monetary policy will then be the sum of these influences.[71]

The income/expenditure theory as represented by the conventional *IS/LM* framework, in Brunner and Meltzer's view, fails to accommodate the public's stock-flow behavior bearing on its real capital position, which they consider crucial in the transmission process. Because of this failure, Brunner and Meltzer argue that the Keynesian approach of relating investment expenditure to interest rates in some financial assets as a measure of the costs of borrowing—supplemented by the wealth

---

Policy," American Economic Association, *Papers and Proceedings of the Seventy-fifth Annual Meeting* (*The American Economic Review,* Vol. LIII, May 1963), pp. 372-82; Karl Brunner, "The Relative Price Theory of Money, Output, and Employment" (unpublished, based on a paper presented at the Midwestern Economic Association Meetings, April 1967); Brunner and Meltzer, "Fiscal and Monetary Policy in a Non-Keynesian World" (cited in footnote 22).

[69]The transmission mechanism identified in the analysis of the neo-Keynesian portion centers around Type I capital goods.

[70]This process is analogous to the one described and emphasized by neo-Keynesians.

[71]Brunner and Meltzer, "The Place of Financial Intermediaries in the Transmission of Monetary Policy" (cited in footnote 68), pp. 374-77. Brunner and Meltzer do not emphasize the interest rate effect on the desired stock of Type II capital but only the wealth effect.

effect—can hardly capture the actual impact of monetary policy and that, thus, the Keynesian approach should be rejected.

A more satisfactory approach that would be consistent with Brunner and Meltzer's view would require a structural model of general equilibrium—a model that specifies the whole spectrum of real and financial assets and the explicit relations between the production of new real capital goods and the existing ones. In a recent unpublished paper,[72] Brunner and Meltzer attempt to construct such a model. However, in formulating the model they choose to ignore entirely the markets for Types II and III of real capital goods and focus on the market for Type I real capital, the equity market. The result of this modification, or simplification, of their view is a model that is, in all important aspects, analogous to the neo-Keynesian model discussed in the Appendix.*

Therefore, the model suggests that Brunner and Meltzer—contrary to their claim—accept the Keynesian view on the nature of the transmission process; what they seem to reject is the heuristic simplification of reality with regard to the range of assets considered in the Keynesian income/expenditure theory . . .

IV. Concluding Remarks

The main purpose of this paper has been to review divergent views on the transmission process of monetary policy. The review indicates that at the level of general description there appear to be no significant differences in the transmission process of monetary influences among a variety of monetary economists. Both monetarists and nonmonetarists appear to support some version of the portfolio adjustment process as a framework to describe the effects of monetary policy on the real economy. The disagreement between them on this process centers on the range of assets and interest rates that should be considered and the technical relationships involving the stocks of real assets and the flows of real expenditure corresponding to these assets. The range of assets and interest rates considered by nonmonetarists is rather limited, whereas monetarists stress a broad range of assets and the expenditures associated with these assets. Also, both monetarists and nonmonetarists emphasize the wealth effect channel and, in various forms, the credit rationing channel.

From these observations one might conclude that the question of the relative effectiveness of monetary and fiscal policy is essentially an empirical issue, not a theoretical one. Although the issue has evoked a great deal of empirical study in recent years, the controversy still is far from being settled. The evidence from several of the large-scale econometric models—the estimation method favored by nonmonetarists—is that monetary variables are, in general, less important than fiscal variables in influencing aggregate expenditures.[73]

[72]Brunner and Meltzer, "Fiscal and Monetary Policy in a Non-Keynesian World" (cited in footnote 22).

[73]A notable exception is the Federal Reserve-MIT quarterly econometric model for the United States. It shows that monetary policy has a powerful effect, although less powerful than suggested by monetarists. See de Leeuw and Gramlich, "The Channels of Monetary Policy" (cited in footnote 20).

* The Appendix to this article is not reprinted here.—Ed.

On the other hand, monetarists have produced an imposing volume of empirical evidence of several kinds in support of their central proposition. One kind of evidence draws on historical case studies, such as the one by Friedman and Schwartz,[74] and the experience of a number of countries with easy-money policies that led to inflation after World War II. A second type of evidence is the "statistical stability" of the demand function for money in several industrial countries, notably in the United States. Some monetarists view the demand function for money as the crucial relationship in the understanding of macroeconomic developments. The stability of this function is then presented as evidence in favor of the traditional quantity theory as opposed to the income/expenditure theory, and the function is then used to explain and to predict the level of money income.[75] The demand function for money may well be of central importance to economic activity. However, insofar as the money demand is sensitive to interest rates, evidence for which has been demonstrated beyond any reasonable doubt in all of the major empirical studies on the demand function for money, one has to provide a theory of the determination of interest rates along with its interrelationship with a theory of income determination to prove that money indeed matters. A third type of empirical evidence bearing on this question is the reduced form equation studies, which invariably show that the quantity of money is far more significant than various exogenous components of aggregate demand in explaining the movements in money income.

The debate on the reduced form approach, or the direct estimation method, also reflects a sharp disagreement between nonmonetarists and monetarists on the methodological questions of how best to estimate the effects of monetary and fiscal actions on the level of economic activity. As noted above, nonmonetarists favor estimation through large-scale econometric models. Monetarists, however, argue that the channels through which monetary policy operates are so diverse and complicated that it is inherently impossible to identify and to measure them with structural equation models, no matter how detailed they may be. Basically, for this reason, they contend that a more reliable method would be the direct estimation technique whereby final demand variables, such as money GNP, are regressed upon monetary and fiscal variables.

No one would deny the complexity involved in the channels of monetary policy; however, the important questions are whether this complexity justifies the use of the reduced form approach and, if it does, whether the approach is a scientifically acceptable method. Judging by the prevailing standards of academic economics, indeed, the direct estimation approach is seriously inadequate as an empirical methodology.[76]

One of the most serious weaknesses of the approach is that the structural model

[74]Milton Friedman and Anna Jacobson Schwartz, *Monetary History of the United States, 1867-1960,* National Bureau of Economic Research, Studies in Business Cycles, No. 12 (Princeton University Press, 1963).
[75]See Karl Brunner and Allan H. Meltzer, "Predicting Velocity: Implications for Theory and Policy," *The Journal of Finance,* Vol. XVIII (1963), pp. 319-54.
[76]Johnson, "The Keynesian Revolution and the Monetarist Counter-Revolution" (cited in footnote 1), p. 12.

from which a reduced form equation is derived may not be consistent internally. The direct estimation approach completely ignores a priori restrictions on the coefficients of the independent variables of the equation, for example, the restrictions that are built into general equilibrium models through identities, lags, omitting variables, etc. Because of the absence of these restrictions, there is no way of knowing whether the structural model is consistent internally.[77] If it is not, the reduced form equation is no more than a linear equation relating an "alleged" endogenous variable, such as money GNP, to a set of "alleged" exogenous variables with no meaningful economic causations between the endogenous and exogenous variables.

Another equally damaging weakness is the problem of selecting exogenous monetary and fiscal variables. Depending upon which variable one assumes to be exogenous—monetary base, free reserves, narrow money, or broad money on the monetary side and the various definitions of autonomous expenditures on the fiscal side—one can take a "money mostly" stance, a "fiscal policy mostly" stance, or a "both matter" stance.[78]

In response to the first defect, some monetarists have begun to extend their efforts in specifying the details of the structural models that underlie the various reduced form equations that they estimate. These models are invariably some version of Keynesian income/expenditure models.[79] Therefore, the response may be an open admission that monetarists are increasingly compromising with the Keynesian income/expenditure theory, which they had set out to question. The response also suggests that monetarists are, in compromising with nonmonetarists, burdening themselves with another difficult task, namely, giving a convincing explanation as to why such a great divergence exists in empirical evidence between the reduced form and structural model approaches. A satisfactory answer has yet to come.

In view of these assessments of the monetarist view, it appears that one cannot read too much into the results of various reduced form equation studies. These assessments also suggest that a more promising road toward the settlement of the controversy concerning the relative strengths of fiscal and monetary actions lies in further development and refinement of existing econometric models. In this regard, the monetarist view suggests a number of factors that have been inadequately treated

---

[77]A good example of the internal inconsistency of a reduced form equation may be found in the recent study by Leonall C. Andersen and J. Jordan, "Monetary and Fiscal Actions: A Test of Their Relative Importance in Economic Stabilization," Federal Reserve Bank of St. Louis *Review,* Vol. L (November 1968), pp. 11-24. They show that the impact coefficient of government expenditure on the level of money income is less than unity. Given that money income should rise by at least the same amount as the increase in government expenditure, Andersen and Jordan's finding means that some private endogenous spending is falling by a larger amount as a consequence of the government expenditure. Since they do not specify the structural model of their reduced form equation, one cannot determine what expenditure is falling and why. One possible reason for such a low impact coefficient may be that the structural model is not consistent internally. See Edward M. Gramlich, "The Usefulness of Monetary and Fiscal Policy as Discretionary Stabilization Tools," *Journal of Money, Credit and Banking,* Vol. III (1971), p. 514.

[78]*Ibid.,* pp. 523-24.

[79]This type of response can be found in a series of unpublished articles by Andersen in which he develops a Keynesian income/expenditure model and then derives from the model a reduced form equation. See Leonall C. Andersen, "Influence of Monetary and Fiscal Actions in a Financially Constrained Economy" (unpublished paper, May 1971).

in existing models and that may account partly for the sluggish response of monetary influences in these models.

We may point out two such factors relevant to our subject matter. One possible factor is the failure of existing econometric models to include implicit rates of return on real capital and consumer durables. The other is the failure to distinguish between nominal and real interest rates in some of these models. The rates of interest used in these models are nominal rates that are affected by the expectation on future prices. However, interest rates that are relevant to the consumption and investment functions are clearly the real rates of interest that are relatively unaffected by changes in the level of prices. It has been shown empirically that high nominal interest rates are accompanied by a high rate of increase in money supply—an easy stance of monetary policy—and vice versa.[80] This is so because a high growth rate of money supply causes a rise in current prices and then the expectation of future inflation, which ultimately leads to a higher nominal rate of interest. It is, therefore, questionable whether nominal interest rates are meaningful indicators of the monetary posture, except perhaps in the very short run.

When these and other factors[81] are properly taken into consideration, it is quite possible that econometric models may turn up a much sharper and more rapid response of monetary influence than has been shown in the past.

[80]See, for example, William P. Yohe and Denis S. Karnosky, "Interest Rates and Price Level Changes, 1952-69," Federal Reserve Bank of St. Louis, *Review,* Vol. 51 (December 1969), pp. 18-38; William E. Gibson, "Price Expectations Effects on Interest Rates," *The Journal of Finance,* Vol. XXV (1970), pp. 19-34; Gibson, "Interest Rates and Monetary Policy" (cited in footnote 65).

[81]For other factors, see David I. Fand, "The Monetary Theory of Nine Recent Quarterly Econometric Models of the United States: A Comment," *Journal of Money, Credit and Banking,* Vol. III (1971), pp. 450-60.

6

Some Issues in Monetary Economics: The Income-Expenditure Theory and the Quantity Theory: Nominal and Real Quantities

David I. Fand

There is considerable agreement on the proposition in monetary theory that the *real* value of the money stock is an *endogenous* variable, determined by the interaction of the financial and real sectors, and therefore outside the control of the monetary authorities. This is in sharp contrast to the theoretical (and practical) disagreements concerning the extent to which the central bank can control the behavior of the (nominal) money stock. In equilibrium, the stock of real cash balances has a value—analogous to, say, the real wage—which the stabilization authorities cannot readily influence, except in those special cases where nominal and real variables move together. Figure 1 demonstrates that such is not always the case. For instance, the nominal money stock was unchanged during the latter half of 1966, while real money balances activity declined.

Income-expenditure theorists in their macroeconomic models often use nominal balances when the analysis requires real balances. This substitution of a nominal quantity (which can be easily changed) for a real quantity (with a determinate equilibrium value) has two consequences: it suggests that an increase in nominal balances will always tend to lower market interest rates; it also implies that changes in market rates correspond to, and reflect, changes in real rates. This procedure is sometimes justified by a special interpretation of the demand for money, an interpretation that is often attributed to Keynes' *General Theory*.

Reprinted from the Federal Reserve Bank of St. Louis *Review* (January, 1970), pp. 16–23, by permission of the publisher and the author.

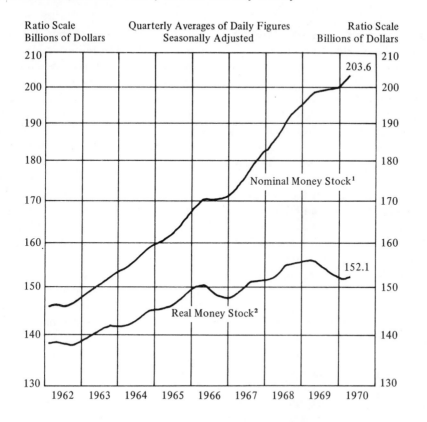

FIGURE 1. Nominal and Real Money Stock

[1]Private demand deposits and currency held by the nonbank public.
[2]Nominal money stock divided by the implicit price deflator.
Latest data plotted: 2nd quarter preliminary.
Prepared by Federal Reserve Bank of St. Louis.

It is therefore useful to recall the transformation of the demand for money in Keynes' *General Theory.* Instead of defining a demand for a *quantity* of real balances, the demand for money (or real balances) was transformed into the liquidity preference function and a basic determinant of the interest rate: the liquidity preference function together with the (real) quantity of money determines the interest rate; and since Keynes assumed explicitly that the price level was given, he could move from nominal to real balances to determine the *market* (or nominal) interest rate, the *real* interest rate (or return on capital), and the equilibrium quantity of real balances.[1] The post-Keynesian income models follow the *General Theory* in treating the

[1]For an elaboration of this theme see D. Fand, "Keynesian Monetary Theories, Stabilization Policy and the Recent Inflation," *Journal of Money, Credit and Banking,* Vol. 1 (August 1969), Section II on "The Demand for Money and Liquidity Preference: Real Balances and Interest Rates," which discusses the changing role of real cash balances in the Keynesian and quantity theories, the shifting emphasis from the price level to the level of employment, and the transformation of the money demand function into a liquidity preference function.

demand for money as a liquidity preference function, but they do not determine explicitly the equilibrium quantity of real cash balances. The failure to define an equilibrium value for the real money stock opens up the possibility of treating both the real and nominal money stock as policy variables[2] and as close substitutes.

The substitution of nominal balances for real balances in many post-Keynesian income-expenditure models has extremely important consequences. To assume that nominal and real balances may be interchanged is to assume that the authorities have the power to print real capital and wealth: it exaggerates the control of the authorities over *real* interest rates (and rates of return); and it necessarily abstracts from any *direct* effects of money on prices (note that the link between the money stock and prices requires that we distinguish between nominal and real values). This tendency to abstract from the price level, to substitute freely nominal and real variables, and to equate market interest rates with real rates (of return) reflects the analytical *failure to define equilibrium conditions for real balances*, and is a striking feature of the post-Keynesian income models.

In sharp contrast to the income-expenditure theory, we have the following postulates concerning real balances in the modern quantity theory: (1) the money demand function defines the demand for real cash balances; (2) the quantity of real cash balances is an endogenous variable and not under the control of the monetary authorities (except for the very short run); and (3) changes in nominal balances will generally have effects on market interest rates, on income, and on prices.[3] For the analysis of transition periods it assumes that an increase in nominal balances will have a compound effect on interest rates—including a short-run liquidity (Keynes) effect, an income effect, and a longer-run (Fisher) price expectation effect.[4] The modern quantity theory also assumes that the demand for money is quite stable, and that a velocity function (derived from the money demand function) may provide a useful link between (changes in) money and (changes in) money income; and, in

[2]For a penetrating analysis emphasizing the originality and generality of the Keynes theory, in contrast to the rigidities, traps, and elasticity pessimism in many of the post-Keynesian income models, see A. Leijonhufvud, *On Keynesian Economics and the Economics of Keynes* (Oxford, 1968). See also D. Fand, "Keynesian Monetary Theories, Stabilization Policy and the Recent Inflation," *op. cit.,* Section III on "Three Keynesian Liquidity Preference Theories," and J. Tobin's seminal article on "Money, Capital, and Other Stores of Value," American Economic Association, *Papers and Proceedings* of the *Seventy-third Annual Meeting (American Economic Review,* May 1961), for his illuminating analysis of an aggregative model with three assets.

[3]See L. Mints, *Monetary Policy for a Competitive Society* (McGraw-Hill, 1950); M. Friedman (ed.), *Studies in the Quantity Theory of Money* (Chicago, 1958) and *The Optimum Quantity of Money* (Aldine, 1969), especially chapters 6-9; H. Johnson, *Essays in Monetary Economics* (Harvard, 1967), chapters 1-3; D. Patinkin, *Money, Interest and Prices,* 2nd ed. (Harper, 1965), chapter 15; and C. Warburton, *Depression, Inflation, and Monetary Policy,* (Johns Hopkins Press, 1966).

[4]For a more explicit statement of the relation between changes in the nominal money stock and interest rates, see M. Friedman and A. Schwartz, *Trends in Money, Income and Prices* (forthcoming); M. Friedman, *Dollars and Deficits* (Prentice Hall, 1968); P. Cagan and A. Gandolfi, "The Channels of Monetary Effects on Interest Rates," *American Economic Review,* May 1969; W. Gibson and G. Kaufman, "The Sensitivity of Interest Rates to Changes in Money and Income," *Journal of Political Economy,* May 1968; D. Meiselman, "Bond Yields and the Price Level: The Gibson Paradox" in *Banking and Monetary Studies, op. cit.*; and D. I. Fand, "A Monetarist Model of the Monetary Process," *The Journal of Finance,* Vol. 25 (May 1970), pp. 275-289.

contrast to the earlier quantity theory, postulates a stable velocity function, but allows marginal velocity to differ from average velocity.

Taken together, these quantity theory propositions have two important implications. They suggest: (1) that the monetary authorities do not control *real* interest rates or the stock of real balances, even if they can always control the stock of nominal money and thereby influence nominal or market interest rates; (2) that money is an important variable for explaining changes in prices, since the equilibrium quantity of real balances links changes in nominal money with changes in the price level. Accordingly, the modern quantity theory uses the money demand function to predict the level of money income and prices if output is given, or *changes* in money income if output varies with changes in the money stock.

The modern quantity theory and income-expenditure theory thus differ sharply in their analysis of the money demand function. In the modern quantity theory it serves as a velocity function relating either money and money income, or marginal *changes* in money and money income (if both output and marginal velocity vary with the money stock); in the income-expenditure theory it serves as a liquidity preference theory of interest rates, or of *changes* in interest rates (if the price level is given and determined independently of the monetary sector). Accordingly, the modern quantity theory focuses on discrepancies between actual and desired real balances, distinguishes between (exogenous) nominal balances and (endogenous) real balances, emphasizes monetary aggregates rather than interest rates, and highlights nominal money as the operational policy variable; the income-expenditure theory focuses on discrepancies between actual and full-employment output, abstracts from price-level changes, emphasizes an interest rate transmission mechanism, views the monetary aggregates as endogenous variables, and highlights the full-employment surplus as the operational policy variable.[5]

Viewed as general theories of income determination, both theories have deficiencies. The modern quantity theory seeks to explain prices, or money income, but often abstracts from the level of employment; the income-expenditure theory seeks to

[5]The mnemonic statements that money is or is not important do not bring out the essential monetary differences between the income and quantity theories. In some ways the income-expenditure theory attaches greater significance to money than does the quantity theory. Thus, the income-expenditure theory assumes that it is often possible to permanently lower interest rates, or rates of return, by an increase in nominal money, while the quantity theory is more inclined to view nominal money changes as having a permanent effect mainly on money income and prices. Yet because quantity theorists are often analyzing situations where inappropriate monetary policies may have caused severe difficulties (e.g., in the 1930's), they may foster the impression that errors in monetary policy are always associated with such drastic consequences.

One other paradox may be noted. Many income-expenditure theorists treat the nominal money stock as an endogenous variable because they believe that this approach assumes less and is therefore more accurate. But while this treatment of the money stock is most appropriate in this formal sense, it may apparently also lead to substantive errors. For example, the large-scale econometric models treat the nominal money stock as an endogenous variable, but do not restrict the movements in real balances by well-defined equilibrium conditions. The assumption that an increase in nominal balances will increase real balances may have been responsible for some of the forecasting errors and policy mistakes in 1968. This assumption may involve a more serious error, substantively and analytically, than treating the nominal money stock, formally, as an exogenous variable.

explain the levels of employment, but often abstracts from the price level; this difference in focus mirrors the change in the analytical roles of real balances and interest
rates in the two theories. The quantity theory emphasis on real balances as an endogenous variable implies that the attempt by the monetary authorities to raise the
money stock may cause prices to rise and also cause *nominal* and *real* interest rates
to diverge. In contrast, the income-expenditure theory, by de-emphasizing the endog-
geneity of real balances, implies that real balances and interest rates can be controlled (within limits) by the authorities—an impression that is reinforced by their
failure to distinguish between nominal and real rates.

The analysis of money, interest rates, and prices in the post-Keynesian income
theories may explain several of the troublesome features of recent stabilization policy: the use of market interest rates as an indicator of monetary policy; the tendency
to minimize the price-level consequences of excessive monetary growth; the failure to
recognize the impact of inflationary expectations on market interest rates; the reluctance to distinguish between nominal and real quantities; and the conviction that the
rise in market interest rates since 1966 was due to an increased demand for money,
and not the result of excessive growth in the money supply.[6]

The failure of income-expenditure theorists to consider the impact of accelerated
(excessive) monetary growth on rising (or high) market interest rates, and to distinguish between market and real interest rates, is especially relevant for analyzing the
post-1965 inflation and the stabilization difficulties since June 1968. The surprising
failure of the Revenue and Expenditure Control Act of June 1968 to cool the economy thus far could be explained by noting that the fiscal "refrigeration" effect was
offset by the monetary "boiler" effect.[7] The authorities, while fighting inflation with
the surcharge, also wished to lower interest rates and move toward a tighter fiscal
and easier monetary policy during this period, and this led to a very substantial
increase in the monetary aggregates.

Many who favored monetary expansion after the June tax package based their
case on the desirability (and social necessity) of lowering market interest rates. In
retrospect, it seems difficult to suppose that an increase in nominal money will raise
real balances, lower interest rates, curtail disintermediation, facilitate residential construction, and somehow not raise aggregate demand or prices. But an increase in the
money stock which takes place in the midst of an inflation will not only raise prices
but also raise market interest rates. Nevertheless, if true, it suggests that an incredibly

---

[6]For a recent, and very useful, statement of the income theory approach to stabilization, incorporating
a commitment to economic growth and viewing it as a key aspect of government policy, see W. Heller
(ed.), *Perspectives on Economic Growth* (Random House, 1968). Because the contributors to this volume are
outstanding, it may not be inappropriate to mention that the chapters dealing with stabilization policy and
monetary theory provide examples illustrating the several questionable tendencies just summarized. Obviously these tendencies are not just limited to those whose understanding of the income theory may be
questioned. It is for this reason that I do not regard these characteristics as analytical errors, but think of
them as "methodological commitments" that may have become burdensome, and perhaps analytically
oppressive.

[7]See the cogent analysis by A. Wojnilower. "Blowing Hot and Cold," First Boston Corporation (September 1968).

optimistic theory—based on a refusal to acknowledge the endogeneity of real cash balances and its implications for diverging nominal and real rates—may have contributed directly to the inflationary pressures which are still continuing, and it may also have contributed to our 1966 stabilization difficulties, if the authorities believed that monetary expansion would bring about lower interest rates.[8]

The stabilization difficulties that we have experienced since 1965 may be related to two questionable propositions about money, which are implicit in many income-expenditure models: (1) that the authorities can affect real balances if they can control the nominal stock of money; and (2) that the authorities can influence *real* rates through central bank operations which change *nominal* market rates. Although both of these propositions are generally accepted, they have only a limited validity, and may lead to serious policy errors when applied to a high-pressure economy such as the United States in the post-1965 period.

In an underemployed economy, *nominal* quantities and *nominal* rates may move with *real* quantities and *real* rates, and real balances may be sufficiently flexible to be treated as a policy variable. But in a high-pressure economy with rising prices, nominal and real quantities no longer coincide; the real (value of the) money stock cannot be treated as a policy variable, and an increase in the money stock will not only raise prices but will raise market interest rates as well. A similar question arises regarding the behavior of interest rates. In a slack economy market interest rates and real rates move together; but in a high-employment economy with rising prices, *market* rates and *real* rates may diverge (see Figure 2). Indeed, in a period of price inflation, constant *real* rates are necessarily associated with rising *market* rates, so that movements in the market rates cannot always correspond to real rates.

The endogeneity of the real (value of the) money stock, as indicated by the divergence between nominal and real balances and by the divergence between real and market interest rates, is thus a manifestation of an economy approaching full utilization. And we need to investigate empirically when movements in interest rates and in money balances begin to diverge, and whether the divergence between real and nominal interest rates is related to the divergence between real and nominal balances.[9]

Many investigators have commented on the monetary lag, and have suggested that because of this lag we would expect very sharp movements in interest rates—as the initial response to changes in the money stock. It is not clear how the monetary lag may be affected by the divergence between *market* and *real* interest rates and between nominal and real balances. Knowledge of the conditions when real and nomi-

---

[8]The fear of *overkill* articulated by influential sources in the summer of 1968 may have served to reconcile the views of those who favored the tax increase primarily as a stabilization measure to cool the inflation with the views of those who favored the tax increase to shift the policy mix to achieve lower interest rates and stimulate socially desirable capital expenditures.

[9]Somewhere between the slack economy and the inflationary high-pressure economy there is a change in the relation between nominal and real balances and between nominal and real rates. Responsible policy officials must, therefore, identify and take account of the divergence between nominal and real rates, especially if they follow an interest rate criterion and use money market rates in the implementation of monetary policy decisions.

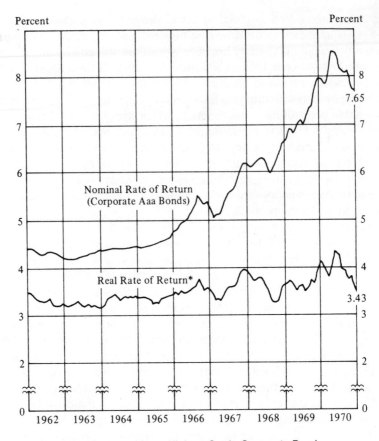

FIGURE 2. Yields on Highest-Grade Corporate Bonds

*Estimates of "real" interest rates were obtained from statistical regressions of nominal interest rates on current and lagged price changes and on variables thought to influence "real" interest rates (i.e., the level of and changes in output and changes in the deflated money stocks). See William P. Yohe and Denis S. Karnosky, "Interest Rates and Price Level Changes, 1952-69," *Review*, Federal Reserve Bank of St. Louis, December 1969.
  Latest data plotted: December.
  Prepared by Federal Reserve Bank of St. Louis.

nal balances diverge, of the process that causes interest rates to diverge, and of the mechanism through which the monetary lag operates, should be useful in improving stabilization policy. It would also help reconcile the income-expenditure and modern quantity theories and thus help complete the work initiated by Keynes by providing us with a truly general theory of employment, interest and money.

7

Channels of Monetary Influence: A Survey

*Roger W. Spencer**

Among the numerous controversies surrounding "money," few are further from resolution than the issue of how money affects the economy. Compounding the controversy is the fact that the arguments advanced are not divided neatly along so-called
monetarist and nonmonetarist lines, but are separated by other criteria.

To be sure, monetarists have long taken exception to the intellectual strait jacket
of the Keynesian framework which limited the influence of monetary actions to the
response of investment to interest rate changes. However, the monetarist alternatives
offered have been far from uniform. Certainly, monetary actions result in the change
of more than one relative price—the interest rate—and one type of spending—investment. However, substantial disagreement among monetarists (as well as other economists) persists beyond this point.

There is basic agreement that at less than full employment changes in the rate of
growth of the money supply affect output and employment before prices, a proposition which may be traced back at least two hundred years (Hume [48]), but this tells
nothing about how total spending and its components react to monetary actions. It is

Reprinted from the Federal Reserve Bank of St. Louis, *Review* (November, 1974), pp. 8-26, by permission of the publisher.

* The author acknowledges the helpful comments on earlier drafts of George Kaufman, Thomas Mayer, John Pippinger, Robert Rasche, William Rawson, Clark Warburton, and William Yohe. They are
blameless for remaining errors.

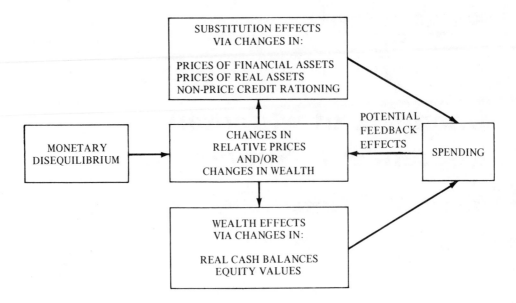

FIGURE 1. The Monetary Transmission Process

necessary to examine the changes in relative prices and wealth associated with monetary impulses to gain insight into the money-spending relation.

When the existing money stock (however defined) either exceeds or falls short of the quantity demanded, wealth and/or relative prices change and this sets off both substitution and wealth effects, as indicated in Figure 1.[1] The changes in relative prices typically involve changes in the rates of return on real capital and financial assets as well as changes in the prices of goods and services. Ways in which changes in wealth may influence spending include movements in real cash balances and changes in the market value of equities.

There remains considerable disagreement about the relative importance of these factors in the transmission of monetary impulses. This is not surprising, given the history of the relative price and wealth relations. Keynes, as well as prominent economists who preceded him, was ambiguous on the subject. This article first traces the early development of these two factors and then analyzes more recent work in each area.

---

[1]The "correct" definition of money and the determinants of money demand and supply functions are matters closely related to, but beyond the scope of the present article. Another limitation is that because of the large number of authors surveyed, only the briefest of summaries can be given here. In some cases, this results in considerable oversimplification of complex analyses.

Substitution and wealth effects are treated here as essentially equivalent to substitution and income effects of generally-accepted price theory. Although monetary-induced changes in relative prices or changes in wealth may generate both substitution and wealth effects, the relative price change has often been associated more with substitution effects and the wealth change more with wealth effects; we will follow that practice.

Historical Background

Among the better early efforts to explain the money-spending linkages were those of Irving Fisher and Knut Wicksell. Writing around the turn of the century, they both maintained a short-run view of the transmission process which was dominated by interest rate movements and a long-run view in which the key role was played by changes in real cash balances (Money/Price Level).

Fisher and Wicksell

Fisher, like other neoclassical writers, determined that output was at its full-employment level in the long run. In the short (or transitional) run, however, business cycles occurred in Fisher's time, as well as in other periods before and since. Consequently, macroeconomic analysts have continued to attempt explanations of this phenomenon. Fisher's view of the business cycle depended strongly on "sticky" interest rates.[2]

This relative price effect (via interest rates) was set off by an increase in the money stock relative to the quantity of money demanded. The nominal money supply may be assumed to have increased due to a rise in the gold stock and, consequently, bank reserves. With the additional assumption that output and velocity were fixed initially, a rise in the commodity price level was expected to be associated with the money supply increase. Because Fisher assumed that the commodity price rise preceded the increase in interest rates, with interest costs being viewed as a significant component of firms' operating costs, the rise in the price level produced an increase in firms' profits.

A continued increase in demand deposits (through business investment loan demand) relative to currency resulted in yet further increases in prices and profits. Eventually, however, excess reserves would run out; the interest rate would become "unstuck" and would rise even faster than commodity prices. With the rise in firms' costs of operation, there would occur a decline in profits and investment and a sharp increase in bankruptcies. The downward phase of the cycle was reversed when excess reserves again rose and the interest rate had fallen accordingly.

Wicksell's well-known "cumulative process" also captured cyclical movements of the economy largely through interest rate changes. Some initial disturbance, such as an innovation or technological breakthrough would foster an increase in the desire to invest at the prevailing interest rate. The demand for loanable funds would then rise as would the "normal" or "natural" rate of interest, the rate "at which *the demand for loan capital and the supply of savings* exactly agree" (Wicksell [89], p. 193). If, however, the banking community failed to realize that investment demand had risen, they would maintain the same *market* rate of interest through increases in the money

---

[2]See especially Fisher's Chapter 4, "Disturbance of Equation and of Purchasing Power During Transition Periods," in Fisher [25]. In later years, Fisher [24] associated severe swings of the business cycle with changes in debt activity.

supply which, given the usual classical assumptions, would result in commodity price rises.

Note that at this point the money supply has risen, observed interest rates have been kept low in relation to the normal rate, and business spending has been the component of aggregate demand which has increased. After some period of time, the banks' reserve position deteriorates and monetary growth is curbed. The market rate of interest rises to the level of the natural rate, an action which leads to the elimination of excess aggregate demand and price level increases.

In the above short-run dynamic analyses, both Fisher and Wicksell relied on the relative price mechanism inherent in a money-interest rates-investment framework. However, in their approach to the determination of long-run equilibrium, interest rates and investment were replaced by a treatment of the role of real cash balances.

Fisher's real balance explanation began with an assumed doubling of the money supply:

> Suppose, for a moment, that a doubling in the currency in circulation should not at once raise prices, but should halve the velocities instead; such a result would evidently upset for each individual the adjustment which he had made of cash on hand. Prices being unchanged, he now has double the amount of money and deposits which his convenience had taught him to keep on hand.[3]

With the apparent increase in wealth, everyone tries to reduce their cash balances by purchasing goods and services, according to Fisher. Because velocity (V) and output (Q) in the equation of exchange $MV = PQ$ are determined to be fixed in the long run, a doubling of the money supply (M) cannot generate any increased holdings of goods and services, but must result in a doubling of the price level (P).

Wicksell also saw real balances as the adjusting variable on the return path to restoring long-run equilibrium after the economy had been disturbed by an exogenous shock.

> Now let us suppose that for some reason or other commodity prices rise while the stock of money remains unchanged, or that the stock of money is diminished while prices remain temporarily unchanged. The cash balances will gradually appear to be *too small in relation to the new level of prices.* . . . I therefore seek to enlarge my balance. This can only be done— neglecting for the present the possibility of borrowing, etc.—through a *reduction* in my *demand* for goods and services, or through an *increase* in the *supply* of my own commodity . . . or through both together.[4]

The reduction in demand and/or increase in supply will cause commodity prices to fall until they have reached their equilibrium level. Neither Wicksell nor Fisher mentioned the money-interest rates-investment spending channel of monetary influ-

[3]Fisher [25], p. 153.

[4]Wicksell, [90], pp. 39–40. Wicksell's treatment of the real balance effect is considered superior to Fisher's because the former avoided the trap of dichotomizing the determination of relative prices and the absolute price level. See Patinkin [63].

ence in their analyses of movements to long-run equilibrium. Both focused on changes in real cash balances without explaining in detail the substitution and wealth processes involved. Although their long-run vs. short-run analyses were similar in many respects, Fisher was probably more noted for his long-run quantity theory views and Wicksell more for his short-run cumulative process.

Keynes

Like Wicksell and Fisher, Keynes' position on the monetary transmission mechanism was somewhat ambiguous. Some critics have contended that he found little or no role for either wealth or relative price effects while others have credited Keynes with having advanced a significant role for both.

Keynes' substitution effect, which was a part of a relatively early portfolio choice model, stressed the money-interest rates-investment spending channel. Did Keynes think changes in the rate of growth of the money supply affected interest rates? There seems to be little doubt that he did. The principal evidence to the contrary may be found in the following passage from *The General Theory of Employment, Interest and Money:*

> There is the possibility, for the reasons discussed above, that, after the rate of interest has fallen to a certain level, liquidity-preference may become virtually absolute in the sense that almost everyone prefers cash to holding a debt which yields so low a rate of interest. In this event the monetary authority would have lost effective control over the rate of interest. But whilst this limiting case might become practically important in future, I know of no example of it hitherto. Indeed, owing to the unwillingness of most monetary authorities to deal boldly in debts of long term, there has not been much opportunity for a test. Moreover, if such a situation were to arise, it would mean that the public authority itself could borrow through the banking system on an unlimited scale at a nominal [very low] rate of interest.[5]

Note that after raising the possibility that a "liquidity trap" situation could conceivably arise in the future, Keynes immediately disavowed its existence under conditions (the low-employment, low-interest rate period of the 1930s) in which Keynesian analysis suggested it would likely occur.

Regarding the second part of the money-interest rates-investment channel, there is considerable evidence that Keynes thought investment to be quite responsive to interest rate changes (Leijonhufvud [53], pp. 157-185). However, the interest sensitivity of investment was restricted in the main to long-term rates, which changed only slowly.

There are a number of wealth effects to be found in *The General Theory* which relate to either price-induced changes in wealth (changes in wealth associated with changes in the absolute price level) or interest-induced movements in wealth (changes in wealth associated with changes in yields). Of the basic price-induced and interest-induced wealth effects, it has been alleged that "Keynes stated both parts of

---

[5]Keynes [51], p. 207. Bracketed expression supplied.

the wealth effect, emphasized their importance, and then let wealth slip through his fingers by his failure to build it into his analysis." (Pesek and Saving [64], p. 21). This criticism is unjustified to the extent that those parts of Keynes' analyses which subsequently enjoyed sustained popularity are not necessarily those parts favored by Keynes. For example, the "liquidity trap" was not an intrinsic part of Keynes' analysis (he denied its occurrence); yet it became closely associated with his name as one of his major contributions.

It is easy to see how Keynes' wealth effects were overlooked by those analysts quick to interpret and popularize his basic theory. Keynes brought up the price-induced wealth effect and minimized its significance in the same passage: "It is, therefore, on the effect of a falling wage- and price-level on the demand for money that those who believe in the self-adjusting quality of the economic system must rest the weight of their argument; though I am not aware that they have done so. If the quantity of money is itself a function of the wage- and price-level [a variant of the real bills doctrine], there is indeed, nothing to hope in this direction."[6]

Keynes endorsed interest-induced wealth effects more vigorously, but made it clear that even these were of secondary importance. As a man well acquainted with the stock market and windfall gains and losses, he thought interest-induced "windfall effects" had only a minor influence on spending habits.

> For if a man is enjoying a windfall increment in the value of his capital, it is natural that his motives towards current spending should be strengthened, even though in terms of income his capital is worth no more than before; ... Apart from this, the main conclusion suggested by experience is, I think, that the short-period influence of the rate of interest ... is secondary and relatively unimportant, except, perhaps, where unusually large changes are in question.[7]

There is, however, sufficient question about Keynes' view of wealth effects, which appear frequently in *The General Theory*, to spark a continuing debate.[8] What Keynes actually meant is less significant than his failure to give either monetary-induced substitution or wealth effects a leading part in his attack against orthodox, classical theory. By vacillating on the importance of the two major channels of monetary influence, Keynes in effect was inviting his interpreters to close off the channels completely.

The Relative Price Relation

The most frequently cited of the relative price relations, money-interest rates-investment, obviously consists of a money-interest rates channel and an interest rates-

---

[6]Keynes [51], p. 206. Bracketed expression supplied.
[7]Keynes [51], p. 94.
[8]See Keynes [51], pp. 92–93, 319. Among the participants in the Keynes wealth effect debate have been Ackley [1], Patinkin [63], Pesek and Saving [64] and Leijonhufvud [53].

investment channel. Closure of either of these channels would eliminate a basic route through which money is presumed to affect spending. This route was virtually sealed off by early interpreters of Keynes (among others) and not reopened for about a quarter of a century.

Closed and Reopened

The initial part of the money-interest rates-investment channel was attacked indirectly through innuendo rather than directly either by overpowering theory or evidence. Although Keynes repeatedly stressed the importance of the money-interest rates linkage, J. R. Hicks, the chief architect of the IS-LM "Keynesian" framework, failed to pass along Keynes' emphasis. In Hicks' [44] relatively brief article which became the most popular condensed version of Keynes, Hicks focused on the liquidity trap as one of Keynes' major contributions upsetting neoclassical theory. Nowhere did he indicate that Keynes was unaware of any such situation actually having occurred. The adoption of such slogans as "you can't push on a string" or "you can lead a horse to water, but you can't make him drink" provided popular support for Hicks' interpretation of Keynes' view of the money-interest rates channel in periods of economic slack.

Empirical studies of the late 1930s were the main instrument employed to seal off the interest rates-investment channel. Researchers in England and the United States published results of surveys in which businessmen were questioned about the importance of the interest rate in their investment decisions.[9] A vast majority indicated that interest rates had little or no effect on their decisions to invest. These studies were cited prominently by Alvin Hansen [39] in his 1938 American Economic Association presidential address as evidence of the impotence of monetary policy. Moreover, as Samuelson recently noted, ". . . people like Sir John Hicks said that as far as short-term investment is concerned, interest is of no consequence as a cost; and as far as long-term investment is concerned, uncertainty is so great that it completely swamps interest, which leaves you with only a miniscule of intermediate investment that is interest elastic."[10]

The eventual rebirth of the relative price channel did not occur until well into the 1950s, although the seeds were planted long before. The emergence of portfolio choice models in the 1950s and 1960s ushered in, among other channels, the old money-interest rates-investment route.

Much of the literature dealing with portfolio choice models has been associated with money demand studies. Portfolio choice theory, however, provides the rationale for the holding of any asset in one's portfolio, including money. Instead of focusing on the individual's or firm's income statement which deals with flows, portfolio

---

[9]See Henderson [42], Meade and Andrews [57], and Ebersole [21]. For a humorous criticism of the survey approach, see Eisner [22], pp. 29-40. A more recent example of the survey approach is found in Crockett, Friend, and Shavell [18].

[10]Samuelson [70], p. 41.

choice analysis stresses the stock relationships which are found on the asset and liability sides of the balance sheet. The basic assumptions are that: (1) other things equal, everyone equates the marginal rate of return on each asset in the portfolio—allowing for risk (in terms of variance of return and *exclusive* of price level movements), costs of acquiring information and of conducting transactions; and (2) an increase in the supply of any asset (on a macro level) will lower the price of that asset relative to all others. The increased supply of the asset leads to diminishing marginal returns per unit of the asset, thereby motivating the wealth holder to attempt to substitute or exchange some of the asset whose price has fallen for some of those whose price has not.

Changes in relative prices are a consequence of wealth holders' efforts to restore equilibrium to their portfolio—that is, equate all marginal rates of return. The initial disturbance, a change in the stock of any asset, may produce a chain of substitution effects as wealth holders react to changing asset yields.

Although certain types of money have a zero nominal rate of return by law, money continues to be held in the portfolio for at least two reasons. First, as opposed to equities, for example (which may carry substantial risk along with a relatively high mean rate of return), money holding is less risky. Second, money economizes on the use of real resources in the gathering of information and in the conduct of transactions. An implication of this latter characteristic is that money is held to bridge the gap between income receipts and expenditures.[11]

Which assets, besides money, are included in the portfolio? Much of the controversy surrounding the portfolio choice framework has centered on the answer to this question. The early portfolio choice models greatly limited the range of assets and rates of return. Pigou [65] sketched a rough money-capital model, while Keynes [51] added government and private debt to the menu. By assuming perfect substitutability between capital and bonds, Keynes had only the yield differential between money and one other asset (he chose bonds) to explain. Patinkin's model [63] was similar to Keynes' in terms of assets included and yields explained.

A major change in the approach to the number of assets and yields to be examined occurred in the early 1960s. Tobin [77], Brunner and Meltzer [9], and Friedman [28] all expanded the portfolio menu, but in varying degrees.[12] The differing approaches of these contemporary monetary economists will be examined in some detail.

[11]To pursue further these distinctions would require a detailed analysis of money demand, a project much beyond the scope of this article. The interested reader may wish to consult Pigou [65], Hicks [43], Tobin [77] and Brunner-Meltzer [10].

[12]Cagan [13] also introduced a sketchy portfolio choice scenario. More recently, he focused on money-interest rate influences [14].

The relative price mechanism was also employed by Warburton as early as 1946 to explain the transmission process. "In practice the effects of a change in demand or in supply, either of a specific commodity or of money (circulating medium), are felt, first in some particular part of the economy and spread from that part to the rest of the economy through the medium of price differentials created at each stage of adjustment." Warburton [88], p. 85.

Three Views on the Relative Price Relation

Tobin ([77], p. 36) suggested that "a minimal program for a theory of the capital account" should include six assets—all of which, except the capital stock, are financial assets—and six yields. The number of assets is only slightly greater than the earlier models, but a substantial step toward reality is taken with the elimination of Keynes' perfect substitutability assumption. The choice of assets is closely restricted to facilitate "purchasing definiteness in results at the risk of errors of aggregation" (Tobin [77], p. 28). If increases in the money supply happen to reduce the supply price of capital—the rate which wealth holders require in order to hold in their portfolios the current capital stock—below its marginal productivity, the capital stock will rise. This is the sole linkage between the financial and real sectors. The "if" is necessary because the increase in the supply of money—which lowers the price of money relative to other assets—may simply result in an increased demand for financial assets, rather than for the capital stock (real assets).

One infers from Tobin that an increase in the stock of *any* of the financial assets in the macro portfolio is about as likely to stimulate investment expenditures as is money.[13] In this view it is unclear as to whether an increase in the money stock can lower the supply price of capital *directly* without setting off a chain of substitution effects ranging all through the spectrum of assets with different shades of risk-return characteristics. It is apparent from Tobin's comparative static framework, however, that no feedback from the real to the financial sector occurs.

The types of real capital which are affected by portfolio shuffling are delineated closely by Brunner-Meltzer [9], although the number of assets and relevant yields in the macro portfolio are not. They classify three types of capital according to the relation between asset prices and output prices—language somewhat comparable with Tobin's supply price of capital and marginal productivity.[14]

Increases in real capital occur as (not "if") a rise in the stock of base money lowers the relative price of base money and that of its close substitutes, resulting in an increased demand for other assets, those assets being dominated by real capital. "The increase in the price of financial assets simultaneously raises real capital's market value relative to the capital stock's replacement costs and increases the desired stock relative to the actual stock." (Brunner [5], p. 612.) Real capital is defined to exclude consumer nondurable goods and services.[15] Unlike Tobin (with regard to his comparative static models), Brunner–Meltzer ([19], p. 379) view the monetary transmission mechanism as having important feedback effects.

---

[13]The view that financial or liquid assets other than money (M_1) can about as likely affect the real sector, is advocated more strongly by the Radcliffe Committee [17], Gurley and Shaw [37], and Gramley and Chase [35], in what became known as the "New View" (from Tobin [78]).

[14]Friedman's [28] terminology is prices of services and prices of sources as explained in the excerpt from Friedman on page 90. A parallel semantic issue is Tobin's preference for the term "demand debt," Friedman for "high-powered money," and Brunner-Meltzer for "base money."

[15]Brunner added the general thought that "The wealth, income, and relative price effects involved in the whole transmission process also tend to raise demand for nondurable goods." Brunner [5], p. 612.

Friedman [28], in his portfolio choice–relative price analysis, is less formal than either Tobin or Brunner-Meltzer in that he attempts no classification of types of real capital, portfolio assets, or relevant yields. Friedman acknowledges that an increase in the money supply affects the portfolio of the financial sector first, but the subsequent increase in demand may be as likely reflected next in consumer nondurables as in any areas of real capital. Possible scenarios are outlined by Friedman in several places.[16] Initially, the prices of sources are raised relative to the prices of services, thereby inducing investment and consumer expenditures.

> The key feature of this process is that it tends to raise the prices of sources of both producer and consumer services relative to the prices of the services themselves; for example, to raise the prices of houses relative to the rents of dwelling units, or the cost of purchasing a car relative to the cost of renting one. It therefore encourages the production of such sources (this is the stimulus to "investment" conceived broadly as including a much wider range of items than are ordinarily included in that term) and, at the same time, the direct acquisition of services rather than of the source (this is the stimulus to "consumption" relative to "savings"). But these reactions in their turn tend to raise the prices of services relative to the prices of sources, that is, to undo the initial effects on interest rates [broadly defined]. The final result may be a rise in expenditures in all directions without any change in interest at all.[17]

A Comparison of Three Views

The Friedman, Tobin, and Brunner-Meltzer views of the monetary substitution effect are distinguished by a number of points of agreement and disagreement. The three views are coincident in the following: (1) the total response of the financial sector to a change in the money supply occurs *before* the total response of the real sector; (2) money as a medium of exchange is of less significance than money as an asset with regard to the portfolio choice transmission mechanism; (3) changes in rates of return or yields on real or financial assets are the key elements in the transmission process.

To a large extent, the differences in the three views are due not so much to contradictory theories, but rather to shades of emphasis among similar approaches. Because Tobin insists on a formal separation of the capital account (stocks) from the production and income account (flows), he is led to highlight different aspects of the portfolio choice process than Friedman and Brunner-Meltzer.[18]

Tobin gives the impression that portfolio choice analysis adds little to the Keynesian (not Keynes') view of money-interest rates-investment. Given a consumption

---

[16]Friedman [28], Friedman-Meiselman [33], Friedman-Schwartz [34]. Other attempts at pinning down the open market purchase-bank reserves-interest rates, etc., channels can be found in Cagan [13], Davis [19], and Ettin [23].

[17]Friedman [28], p. 462. Bracketed expression supplied. The latter part of this quote represents one of Friedman's interpretations of the feedback effect.

[18]"Treatment of the capital account separately from the production and income account of the economy is only a first step, a simplification to be justified by convenience rather than realism" (Tobin [81], p. 15). It appears, however, that Tobin's efforts at moving toward greater realism (Tobin [84]) are inhibited by the "General Equilibrium Approach" (Tobin [81]).

function dependent on income, but not wealth or relative prices, consumption can be affected by monetary actions only *after* investment via the standard Keynesian multiplier. In his portfolio choice analysis, the potential end result of the shuffling of portfolios is a change in real capital;[19] feedback effects from the real to the financial sector do not fit into Tobin's capital account approach. Tobin specifically draws attention to the insignificance of money's medium of exchange property *vis a vis* its zero nominal rate of return in his portfolio analysis and generally denigrates money's "uniqueness." Changes in money may set off a chain of portfolio reverberations which results in a change in desired real capital, or it may not.

Friedman's avoidance of formal, structural models which specify any unique monetary transmission process has probably contributed significantly to the charge that monetarists' views of how money works are locked in a "black box."[20] Friedman's informal tracing of possible monetary channels stresses the point that consumer spending is as likely to be the real sector component first to respond to monetary actions as is investment spending. Although changes in yields are the key to portfolio adjustments, "These effects can be described as operating on 'interest rates,' if a more cosmopolitan interpretation of 'interest rates' is adopted than the usual one which refers to a small range of marketable securities" (Friedman [28], p. 462).

Brunner-Meltzer tread a path between Tobin and Friedman in their methodological approach to portfolio analysis. Like Tobin, they attempt to organize the pattern of response of the real sector to monetary impulses and eventually construct a formal model (Brunner-Meltzer [12]). They also emphasize the significance of real capital in the process with only minor references to such spending components as consumer nondurable goods and services.

Like Friedman, Brunner-Meltzer do not attach "if" considerations to the money-real sector linkage, nor do they stress long substitution chains relating money and other financial assets. Their view is also similar to Friedman's in that they: (1) emphasize financial sector-real sector feedbacks; (2) do not denigrate money as an indicator of monetary actions; and (3) stress relative prices, of which yields on securities are only a part. Brunner points out that "every change in relative prices of assets (that is, durables) with different temporal yield streams involves also a change in suitably defined interest rates."[21]

In their money demand theory, Brunner-Meltzer [10] dwell on the medium of exchange property of money, but this property does not appear specifically in their formal model [12] of the *transmission* mechanism. Relative prices in the 1972 model take the form of asset (including securities) prices and output prices, but no distinction is made between investment and consumer goods prices. Finally, in spite of their

---

[19]In an informal analysis, Tobin added consumer durables to the list of "storable and durable" goods—or real capital—influenced in the monetary transmission process. See Tobin [80].

[20]Friedman's formal model [30], [31] sheds little light on specific monetary transmission linkages.

[21]Brunner [8], p. 27. He adds, "The general role of interest rates does not distinguish therefore between the Keynesian and non-Keynesian positions. The crucial difference occurs in the range of the interest rates recognized to operate in the process. The Keynesian position restricts this range to a narrow class of financial assets, whereas the relative price theory includes interest rates over the whole spectrum of assets and liabilities occurring in balance-sheets of households and firms" (Brunner [8], p. 27).

criticism of IS–LM models which reflect a "Keynesian" approach to the transmission mechanism, they grant that if changes in the stock of government debt were presumed to have no effect on wealth, "our model could be pressed into the standard, IS–LM framework" (Brunner-Meltzer [11], p. 953).

In summation, these three approaches to tracing monetary impulses are probably not as different as they at first appear. Once the semantic issues are put aside and the preferences for formal vs. informal models are understood, the Tobin, Brunner-Meltzer, Friedman approaches to the relative price channels of monetary influence are quite similar. It remains to be resolved, however, if more is to be gained by Tobin's admittedly heroic abstractions from reality, Friedman's apparent presumption that the channels are too complex to be captured in any economic model, or Brunner-Meltzer's approach somewhere between these two in terms of answering the questions of the academic fraternity and the general public of how money works.

Other Developments in the Relative Price Relation

Two extensions of the relative price relation which, although out of the mainstream of monetary transmission research, merit elaboration are (1) credit rationing and (2) the overshoot, or feedback, phenomenon. The former involves the allocation of resources by price *and* nonprice criteria, and the latter is a consequence of the dynamic adjustment of the economy to a monetary shock.

CREDIT RATIONING

So long as the price mechanism functions in an open market with complete factor and product homogeneity, resources (including credit) are rationed by price. In so-called "imperfect" markets, however, nonprice discriminatory practices abound. Among borrowers who are the same in every respect but one, net worth for example, lenders may advance one borrower credit at an X percent rate and another borrower zero credit at any interest rate. At least, that is one implication of the term "credit rationing." As used here, "global" credit rationing is defined to indicate a reduction in (the rate of) total spending due to a rise in the non-observed interest price of loans.

Traditionally, "local" credit rationing has been associated with the behavior of commercial banks in extending loans in a period of "tight credit." Arguments for commercial bank credit rationing were advanced in 1951 by Robert Roosa [68]. He asserted that in periods of falling security prices (rising interest rates), bankers prefer to pass over relatively more lucrative commercial loans and continue to hold on to their securities in order to avoid a recorded capital loss. Moreover, Roosa contended that banks preferred to hold securities as a means of countering the uncertainty fostered by the monetary authorities during critical, high-interest rate periods.

Paul Samuelson [69] objected to this analysis on the grounds that it did not conform to the usual tenets of profit-maximizing behavior of the firm. He argued that the usual way of rationing anything in "short supply" was to allow a higher price to do the rationing. Samuelson would not agree that over any other than a very brief period, bankers would hold their assets in relatively low-yielding securities, while rationing a set volume of loans at a fixed interest rate.

Subsequently, additional arguments were employed to buttress the credit rationing view.[22] One of these was that default risk increased relatively more for loans than for securities in tight credit periods. Another was that the banking industry is oligopolistic and is better off to restrict the volume of loans rather than lend out to the point required by the competitive market solution.

Legal interest ceilings have been invoked more recently in explanations of the working of credit rationing. The basic idea is that a financial institution might be perfectly willing to lend to a borrower at X percent in accord with such criteria as size of loan, default risk, and compensating balance requirements, but if usury or other laws set a ceiling at Y percent which happens to be below X percent, the prospective borrower will not obtain the loan. He may be able to obtain funds from some other source, such as from a lending facility in a state whose ceiling is higher, or from an effectively unregulated private individual. There are, however, considerable costs of information involved in addition to the higher interest costs which may cause the potential borrower to drop out (that is, be rationed out) of the funds market.

Interest ceilings also affect the flows of funds into financial and nonfinancial institutions. When market interest rates rise above rates payable (considering liquidity, risk, maturity, and tax factors) by savings institutions and state and local governments, many savers put their funds into less regulated securities markets. The bypassed institutions accordingly cut back their lending activities. Whether the rechanneling of credit results in a reduction of total spending, however, is another matter—one which is rarely treated in the credit rationing literature.

One study, for example, found that Regulation Q ceilings encouraged savers to bypass commercial banks in certain tight credit situations, allegedly forcing commercial banks to curtail credit extensions.[23] Since bank credit is only one component of total credit, it cannot be assumed that a reduction in total credit or total spending could be attributed to the workings of Regulation Q. According to the authors of the study, the reduction of credit available to commercial bank customers "would presumably occur to the benefit of customers of other intermediaries and/or of those firms able to raise funds directly in the market."[24]

If it is presumed that credit rationing at one institution is *not* offset by increased loan activity elsewhere, then "global" credit rationing, which is accompanied by a slowing in the rate of total spending, occurs. Because all observed interest rates do

---

[22]Lindbeck [55], Hodgman [47], and Kane [50] are among those who have substantially advanced the credit rationing literature.

[23]Federal Reserve Regulation Q places a ceiling on interest rates payable by member banks on time and savings accounts.

[24]Jaffee and Modigliani [49], pp. 871–72. Although Jaffee and Modigliani suggest that credit rationing of commercial banks is offset by increased loan activity in other areas, the reverse does not necessarily hold. The FRB-MIT model, with which Modigliani has been closely associated, finds a credit rationing effect through noncommercial bank savings institutions *not* offset by increased commercial bank activity. See deLeeuw and Gramlich [20].

not necessarily capture a rise in the relative price of credit as represented by greater information and transactions costs (which are assumed to include such costs as increased compensating balances), interest rate changes alone would not give a complete picture of the effectiveness of monetary actions. In certain tight credit situations, interest rates rise to slow down spending. But after some point at which interest yields are confronted by legal rate ceilings, interest rates would not give a correct picture of the true cost of credit. An important implication of this analysis is that interest rates likely emit inconsistent signals with respect to monetary influences on spending via relative price changes.

OVERSHOOT EFFECT

The "overshoot effect" is analogous to the previously-mentioned feedback effect, in which the real sector reacts back upon the financial sector, with the original disturbance having come from the financial sector. Although the overshoot may occur by way of relative price or wealth influences, the vast majority of the literature on this topic is couched in a relative price framework. The term "overshoot' is indicative of the tendency of the initial adjustment of such economic variables as interest rates and income to exceed the steady-state levels. Friedman is often identified as the current leading advocate of this thesis, but the argument has its roots in studies by Fisher, Wicksell, Keynes, and Tooke.[25]

Friedman [28], [29], [33] pointed out in several places that changes in the money supply and interest rates are inversely related for only a short period. A rise in the money supply, for example, is associated with a fall in interest rates initially. After some period of time, the fall in interest rates will have stimulated spending and the demand for credit. The rise in the demand for credit will tend to reverse the initial fall in interest rates. If spending is continually stimulated, demand pressures will force up the price level and price anticipations which, in turn, add upward pressures to interest yields.

The extent to which interest rates overshoot their equilibrium value is dependent on many factors, including initial conditions and the duration and degree of monetary stimulus. It should be noted that the rise in the price level lowers the real value of monetary assets. At the higher price level, the quantity of money demanded is less in real terms. Also, the rate of increase of the money supply tends to slow automatically due to "feedback effects through the monetary mechanism" (Friedman and Schwartz [34], p. 562). Thus, prices, interest rates, money, and general economic activity are all subject to the overshoot phenomenon.

Similar dynamic analysis has been offered by Brunner-Meltzer. Through changes in wealth and relative prices, they postulate that monetary impulses alter the magnitude of and rate of return on the capital stock. "Variations in the stock of real capital, of income expected from human wealth, or the yield expected from real capital affect the allocation pattern of financial assets, trigger the interest mechanism,

---

[25]See Fisher [25], Wicksell [89] (natural interest rate vs. market interest rate), Keynes [51] (the Gibson paradox), and Tooke [86] (the Ricardo-Tooke Conundrum).

and generate a feedback to the asset prices of real capital." Thus, "monetary impulses not only affect the real processes but real impulses feed back to financial processes."[26] Brunner also noted the role of price anticipations in the feedback process and postulated that without continuing money growth acceleration, initial output and employment gains would be offset over time.[27]

Tobin's basic comparative static framework revealed no role for the overshoot effect. On at least two occasions (Tobin [82], [84]), however, he engaged in dynamic analysis. On both occasions he pointed out that initial disturbances in the real sector which affect the money supply (endogenity of money) are a plausible explanation of observed money-income relationships. In one instance (Tobin and Brainard [84], p. 119), he noted that an exogenous change in bank reserves would produce an adjustment path of the yield on real capital which overshoots and oscillates.

Even the standard IS–LM framework can be altered so as to give interest rate and income overshoots.[28] It can be shown that differences in the adjustment pattern of investment to interest rates and money demand to interest rates are capable of producing interest rate and income overshoots. If investment is dependent at all on the current interest rate, a sharp drop in interest rates can cause investment to expand and income to rise; if money demand is a function of income, there ensues a rise in money demand which reacts back on interest rates.

It is possible to conjecture fairly complicated reaction patterns to relative price changes, even without such complications as an accelerator effect, or changes in the absolute price level. Even working within a simple analytical framework, it would be difficult for policymakers to attempt to stabilize incomes or interest rates if they did not know whether the adjustment paths were monotonic or cyclical. Considerable empirical verification of the overshoot or cyclical process in the "real" economy has been provided.[29]

The Wealth Relation

The monetary channel of influence which operates through changes in wealth is best approached by examination of the linkages between wealth and consumption. Although the substitution effect, in some versions, is seen to work through consumer spending as well as investment, the wealth effect has been typically limited to the consumer sector. One definition of nonhuman money wealth is

$$W_{NH} = PK + D + \frac{G}{r}$$

[26]Brunner-Meltzer [9], p. 379.

[27]Brunner [7], p. 13. Friedman ([29], p. 10) made the same point regarding monetary acceleration via a comparison of the market unemployment rate-natural unemployment rate with the market interest rate-natural interest rate.

The feedback effects noted in the formal Brunner-Meltzer model [12] are started by an initial disturbance in the *output* market, and thus are not quite comparable to earlier analysis.

[28]See Laidler [52], Smith [73], Tanner [74], and Tucker [87].

[29]See Silber [72] and Christ's ([16], pp. 444–45) review of large econometric models.

where

      P = price of real capital

      K = stock of capital (PK = market value of equity)

      D = monetary base plus fraction of bank debt not counted in PK

      G = government debt (one dollar multiplied by the number of securities outstanding, each of which is assumed to be a consol)

      r = market interest rate (G/r = market value of outstanding debt).

Monetary factors affect each of these components of nonhuman money wealth in varying degrees.

Real human wealth, w_H, is determined by the present value of one's expected lifetime income, a concept related to permanent income or even disposable income (with the appropriate lags), but not directly related to monetary actions. Real consumption (c) is assumed to be a function of both types of wealth as described by

$$c = c(w_H, \frac{W_{NH}}{p}).$$

The human wealth concept forms the typical Keynesian element in the consumption function. The relation between nonhuman wealth (divided by the price level) and consumption is probably less well accepted.

Because the arguments for the D and G/r elements of the wealth effect are closely intertwined, they will be discussed together as "Real Balance Effects." The PK section follows under the heading "Equity Effects."

Real Balance Effects

As mentioned earlier, Keynes discussed several different real balance effects, but made little use of them in his general framework. Ironically, it was the work of a prominent Keynesian interpreter which sparked renewed interest in real cash balances. Pigou, who generally receives the lion's share of the credit for reviving real cash balances,[30] was disturbed by Alvin Hansen's stagnation thesis.

Hansen [40] charged that even *with* flexible prices and wages a perpetual state of less than full employment could well be the natural resting place for the economy. Such neoclassical economists as Pigou were willing to concede that an assumption of inflexible prices and wages could be consistent with the thesis of a less than full-employment state, but only given this important assumption. Pigou demonstrated that the rise in real cash balances associated with a falling price level and unchanged money stock would increase consumer spending, reduce saving, and thereby permit the rate of interest to rise above some assumed "liquidity trap" level.

[30]Pigou [66]. See also Haberler [38] and Scitovszky [71].

By associating consumption with real cash balances, Pigou drove a wedge into the small opening left for monetary policy by the Keynesians of the late 1930s. Because consumption comprises a much larger percentage of total spending than business fixed investment, the potential for monetary policy to affect total spending was greatly expanded. Pigou and others who formulated real cash balance theories in the early 1940s did not claim much empirical significance for this effect. Their concern was only to show that it was theoretically plausible for the economy to return to full employment under the assumption of price and wage flexibility. They did not take up Keynes' windfall effect or any other aspect of the monetary wealth effect. Thus, their concern was limited to the "D" portion of the nonhuman wealth definition, with the relevant debt typically taken to be the government's demand debt (or monetary base).

Don Patinkin took up the discussion of real cash balances in the postwar period.[31] He also ignored the interest-induced wealth effects and focused on theoretical rather than empirical considerations. Patinkin's chief contribution to the channels of influence controversy was to spell out the interplay between the positive real cash balance effect and the negative real cash balance effect which combine to produce proportionality between money and prices (the "quantity theory") between periods of short-run equilibrium.[32]

Prominent among those disputing the usefulness of the real cash balance approach have been Hicks and Hansen, who also downgraded the monetary relative price channel. Hansen's [41] criticism of the real balance effect was limited to a short note in which he agreed that the effect could theoretically bring a halt to a downturn, but could not generate the spending required to attain full employment.

Hicks devoted more effort to wealth considerations, as demonstrated by the important role of wealth in his landmark book, *Value and Capital* [45]. However, neither in *Value and Capital* nor subsequently did he attach much significance to a monetary wealth effect. Hicks omitted real balance effects in *Value and Capital* and only thirty years later did he find any use for the concept at all.[33] The dominant channel of

---

[31]Patinkin [63]. Patinkin's first articles on real cash balances appeared in the late 1940s.

[32]The positive real balance effect associates the demand for real balances (positively) with money and the negative real balance effect associates the demand for real balances (inversely) with prices. The demand for goods is related to one's holding of real cash balances.

[33]Leijonhufvud noted Hicks' lack of consideration for either price-induced or interest-induced wealth effects in *Value and Capital*. "It is interesting to note that the first edition of *Value and Capital* did not take the real balance effect into account. In the second edition, Hicks responded to the criticisms of Lange and Mosak on that issue by admitting: 'I was too much in love with the simplification which comes from assuming that income-effects [Pigou effects] cancel out when they appear on both sides of the market' (p. 334). While this did not lead him to reconsider also the assumption that the wealth effects of interest changes cancel, it may well be that the same remark applies also to this problem." (Leijonhufvud [53], p. 275.)

Hicks eventually took note of the real cash balance version of the wealth effect in a review of the first edition of Patinkin's book. Hicks missed the point initially that a rise in real cash balances stimulates spending, as he later admitted in his *Critical Essays* ([46], p. 52). In 1967 he recognized the existence of a 'liquidity pressure effect'—but thought it had merit only in restraining an expanding economy. This concept, of course, is a variation on the monetary policy "can't push on a string" thesis.

monetary influence, so long as no liquidity trap exists, was through his portfolio choice-relative price route.

Exactly what should be included in the "D" portion of the real balance wealth definition has been the subject of debate in more recent years. In most cases, private debt typically is assumed to cancel out. However, Pesek and Saving [64] maintained that because no interest is paid for demand deposits, wealth (which accrues to bank stockholders) increases in proportion to demand deposits. Thus, they would count both inside money (demand deposits) and outside money (monetary base) in net private wealth, contrary to the traditional view which counts only outside money. To include all inside money as wealth, however, would likely result in some double counting.

If the inside money benefits to banks are capitalized in the value of the banks' stock, as are the typical gains to nonbank firms, the same inside money would be found in the "D" portion and the "PK" portion of the wealth equation. To the extent that demand deposit gains are *not* capitalized instantaneously, there should be some allowance made for the addition of inside money to net wealth. The effect on spending would be through additional outlays by bank stockholders.

What about government securities (G) held by the public? Do these represent private wealth? They only represent private wealth to the extent that the public does not anticipate offsetting future tax increases to eliminate such debt. The G/r term in the wealth equation may have some effect on spending through: (1) changes in the magnitude of G; (2) changes in the composition of G; and (3) changes in r.

One source of controversy concerning changes in wealth has been the relation between G and D. The two have frequently been summed (interest-bearing debt plus noninterest-bearing debt) in empirical and theoretical investigations of the effects of "liquidity" on the economy. If it can be assumed that G and D are good substitutes, their composition is of less concern than their sum.[34] Early empirical investigations of wealth effects published shortly after the accumulation of much government debt in World War II often tested the real balance effect as the sum of G and D.[35] Many found a strong relation between liquid wealth and consumption. If this can be called a direct channel, a more indirect route, via interest rates, has been envisioned by others.

---

[34]Proponents of the "New View" also add nongovernment, nonbank liabilities, such as savings and loan shares, to the total. See Brunner [6].

The Radcliffe Committee [17] found a role for money to affect spending *if* it added to total liquidity, to include funds made available by nonbank financial institutions. John Gurley noted that the Committee "believes that changes in these [interest] rates have had little direct effect on spending; and it does not think that there is any direct, close connection between the money supply and spending. But while money is shoved out of the house through the front door, for all to see, it does make its reappearance surreptitiously through the back door as a part of general liquidity: and the most important source of liquidity is the large group of financial institutions." (Gurley [36], p. 685. Bracketed expression supplied.)

[35]See Patinkin's empirical chapter [63]. Lerner [54] theorized that continued growth of government debt, as in World War II, would eventually induce sufficient consumer expenditures as to eliminate any excess of savings over investment at full-employment income. He did not attempt an empirical test, however.

Tobin [79] emphasized aggregate monetary wealth and its composition with respect to the effect on interest rates. Not only does an increase in monetary wealth relative to real assets lower the supply price of capital and thereby induce investment, but an increase in short-term government debt relative to long-term debt (no change in aggregate debt) may achieve the same result. These actions are closer to fiscal policy or debt management policy than to what is normally labeled monetary policy.

To the extent that monetary actions affect the yields on government debt, there is an interest-induced monetary wealth effect on consumption. If expansive monetary actions lower the "r" component of G/r proportionately more than "G" in the wealth definition, nonhuman money wealth rises, as does (under typical assumptions) consumption. Of course, a monetary overshoot effect would reverse the fall in interest rates and subsequently work in the opposite direction on consumer expenditures. Also, if the rise in the price of securities (fall in interest rates), induces those wealth holders who have not yet purchased securities to pay a higher price for their securities, this particular group may *curtail* their outlays for consumer goods.[36]

As far as the real balance effect, especially that part which pertains to "D" is concerned, there is little indication that Tobin, Brunner-Meltzer, or Friedman envision monetary influences as having much impact through this channel.[37] In at least two cases, however, these leading monetary economists have found a strong role for the money-equity channel. Their views on the money-equity route will be discussed after mention of some of the earlier proponents of this channel.

Equity Effect

How can monetary actions affect the market value of equity, "PK"? One answer was provided by Lloyd Metzler, who reopened the equity channel in 1951 which had been described earlier by Keynes. Metzler [58] was probably the first economist whose formal model included the investment-borrowing costs channel and both aspects of the wealth channel—real cash balances and private equities.[38] Metzler, however, made the unusual assumption that the Federal Reserve increases the money stock through purchases of privately held common stock.

An increase in the money stock (in the Metzler model), given full employment,

---

[36]See Leijonhufvud ([53], pp. 241–42) for a discussion of this effect. Lawrence Klein, who recognized the potential of interest-induced changes in wealth to affect consumption inversely, related to the author recently that an inverse relation is more likely in the depression state, such as the 1930s, than today.

[37]"Like Friedman (1970, pp. 206–7) we believe that the real-balance effect is one of several explanations of long-run changes in the IS curve. We agree, also, that the short-run importance of the real-balance effect is small enough to neglect in most developed economies where real balances are a small part of wealth. In our analysis the size of the traditional real-balance effect depends on the proportion of money to total nonhuman wealth, a factor that is less than .05 for the United States." (Brunner and Meltzer [11], p. 847.)

[38]Tinbergen provided the first empirical test of an equities-consumption relation. Dividing consumption into that by income earners and nonworkers, he found that "a fall in capital gains had already caused a decline in consumption between 1928 and 1929" (Tinbergen [75], p. 78).

results in a proportional increase in prices and thus no change in consumption with real balances remaining constant. The Federal Reserve's purchase of common stock *lowers* net private wealth (the volume of securities in private hands falls) and consequently, consumer spending. The fall in consumer expenditures is accompanied by a rise in saving, a fall in the rate of interest, and the consequent increase in capital intensity. Criticism of Metzler's model centered on his unusual assumptions, which, among other results, gave a negative association between monetary growth and consumer spending.

The more orthodox conjecture, that monetary growth, the market valuation of equities, and consumer spending are all positively related, has been given theoretical and empirical support by Franco Modigliani. Modigliani [59], [60] advanced formal theoretical models in 1944 and 1963. He recognized a role for wealth-consumption influences in his revised model of the economy (called the "mid-50s" model) which he acknowledged had been omitted from the 1944 model. His new consumption equation was

$$C = C(X, \frac{NW}{p}, r, \left[\frac{Vo}{p}\right])$$

where

$$X = \text{real income}$$
$$\frac{NW}{p} = \text{Modigliani's life-cycle aggregate labor income variable[39]}$$
$$r = \text{the rate of return on (or cost of) capital}$$
$$\frac{Vo}{p} = \text{the net worth of the private sector.}$$

The two latter monetary-related terms, the borrowing cost variable and the wealth variable, appeared in much the same form in the FRB–MIT model of the later 1960s, a model with which Modigliani has been closely identified.

The money-equities-consumption channel in the FRB–MIT model hinges on the substitutability of bonds and stocks. If an increase in demand for, say, Treasury securities, by the Federal Reserve results in lower yields and higher prices for these securities, other investors could well be discouraged from purchasing the now higher-priced Treasury securities, but securities whose price was not initially affected by the Federal Reserve action. To the extent that demand is shifted to equities from Treasury securities because of their higher price, there is a rise in common stock prices, which is reflected in a rise in PK.

The higher equity prices represent capital gains to equity owners. The wealth effect

---

[39]Modigliani-Brumberg [62] in 1954 related consumption to one's expected income over his life span. The discounted value of "permanent" income is human wealth, or $Y/r = W$.

Neither Modigliani-Brumberg nor Friedman [27] related monetary-induced nonhuman wealth to consumption at this early stage.

portion of this process is the inducement to spend on the part of equity owners because of their increased net worth. Over a sixteen-quarter period, the equity channel represents 45 percent of the entire monetary influence on total spending in the FRB–MIT model.[40]

It is not likely that Friedman would credit any sort of *monetary-induced* nonhuman wealth effect as having that much influence on spending. The relative price channel dominates his discussion of the channels of monetary influence in numerous articles (Friedman [28], [33], [34]). In more recent studies in which Friedman developed a formal economic model, he omitted wealth from the consumption function, using only $C/p = f(Y/p, r)$.[41] One indication that nonhuman wealth is of some significance in his view of the transmission process emerged in a recent article in which he attempted to delineate initial and subsequent shifts in the IS-LM apparatus.[42]

Until recently, Tobin apparently shared Friedman's lack of enthusiasm for monetary-induced wealth effects on consumption. His omission of wealth influences on consumption may be found in his informal models of the early 1960s as well as his more detailed models of the late 1960s.[43] It is not so much that Tobin denied a wealth effect, rather that he preferred to keep stock and flow variables separate. Thus, consumption (and saving) were functions of flow variables—specifically income—and not wealth, a stock concept. "The propensity to consume may depend upon interest rates, but it does not depend *directly* on the existing mix of asset supplies or on the rates at which these supplies are growing."[44]

In a significant departure from most of his previous studies, Tobin [85] stressed the importance of wealth effects in an article co-authored with Dolde in 1971. They considered the "two major recognized channels of monetary influence on consumption: (A) changes in wealth and in interest rates, (B) changes in liquidity constraints."[45] They recognized the historical significance of the Pigou effect, but wealth

[40]deLeeuw and Gramlich [20], p. 487. Other simulations by Modigliani of the FRB–MIT model indicate an even stronger equities effect when alternate forms of the money-equities-consumption equations are run. Modigliani [61], however, did not accept these as realistic.

[41]Friedman recognized the inadequacy of the above consumption function ([30], p. 223) and ([31], p. 331) "in a full statement" ([30], p. 223), because it excluded wealth, but he stated he was attempting to stick to Keynesian short-period analysis. In a much earlier study, Friedman [26] endorsed the real balance effect more vigorously.

[42]Friedman ([32], p. 916) discussed shifts in IS-LM curves (first-round effects vs. subsequent effects) in a manner consistent with the view that wealth influences subsequent shifts. Friedman did not mention "wealth," but Blinder-Solow [2] interpreted his discussion in that context.

[43]See Tobin's early models [77], [78] and later models [81], [84]. He did mention monetary influences on saving/consumption in "Money, Capital, and Other Stores of Value" [77], and gave the relation somewhat more prominence in the earlier "Relative Income, Absolute Income, and Saving" [76].

[44]Tobin [81], p. 16.

[45]Tobin-Dolde [85], p. 100. Tobin's comments concerning the volatility of the marginal propensity to consume, especially with respect to the 1968 tax surcharge, provide a clue as to why he chose to include wealth in the consumption function. "Now if it had been true that the income-flow theory of consumption was a resounding success, and that its indications were being borne out all the time, then we wouldn't need to go into the wealth theory or the life-cycle theory and all that. We wouldn't need to seek a fundamental theory about why savings ratios are what they are and how they relate to various parameters. But we all know that the cash income theory is not a resounding success." (Tobin [83], p. 159.)

changes in their study were associated with capital gains (equity effect). Their liquidity effect referred to the cost of converting nonliquid assets to liquid form in a world of imperfect capital markets. The level of the penalty rate of interest (a relative price) inhibits or encourages conversion of nonliquid to liquid assets.

Using a Modigliani-Brumberg life-cycle model, they concluded that wealth (equity values), interest rates, and the liquidity constraint all have important influences on consumer spending. Their model was basically a reduced form, in that they did not provide the linkages between monetary policy actions and monetary effects.

Brunner-Meltzer have long included a prominent role for wealth effects in their view of the monetary transmission process. "PK" is the component of nonhuman wealth mentioned most favorably in their analysis. For example, in discussing the chain of events following an injection of base money, Brunner-Meltzer noted that "the resulting rise in the market value of the public's (nonhuman) wealth raises the desired stock of capital III and the desired rate of real consumption."[46] They further stated that relative price effects also operate to increase real consumption following the expansive monetary action.

At a later date Brunner again stressed the importance of "PK" relative to the real balance effect in the transmission process. "The dominant portion of the wealth adjustment induced by a monetary impulse occurs beyond a real balance effect and depends on the relative price change of existing real capital. The monetarist analysis of the transmission mechanism determines that this portion of the total wealth effect thoroughly swamps the real balance or even the financial asset effects."[47]

Real balances are included, however, in Brunner-Meltzer's [12] formal model. Total spending (which includes consumer spending) in that model is influenced by, among other factors, nonhuman wealth. Their nonhuman wealth variables include real capital, the monetary base, the stock of government debt, and the value of commercial banks' monopoly position excluded from real capital (Pesek and Saving effect).

Formal economic models now routinely include wealth and/or substitution effects on consumption.[48] Few, if any, of the empirically-oriented, structural models permit all the wealth effects on consumption described above. For example, the FRB–MIT model (Board of Governors [3]) has an equities effect but no real balance effect; the Wharton Mark III model (McCarthy [56]) has a real balance effect but no equities effect. Only when model builders make allowance for all possible monetary effects are so-called structurally rich models as likely to reflect as significant a money-spending impact as reduced form models. There is, of course, a good possibility that yet undiscovered wealth, relative price, and even monetary income effects will be found in the monetary channels of the future.

---

[46]Brunner and Meltzer [9], p. 377. Capital III refers primarily to certain types of consumer durable goods. Examples of the other two types of capital delineated by Brunner and Meltzer are machinery and equipment (Type I) and houses (Type II).

[47]Brunner [7], p. 5.

[48]See, for example, Christ [15] and Rasche [67].

Summary

This article surveyed the relative price and wealth changes set in motion when the quantity of money supplied changes relative to money demanded. Relative price and wealth changes were viewed as major elements of the monetary transmission mechanism around the turn of the century (in rudimentary fashion) and in recent years, but in much of the intervening period their role was subjected to considerable question.

Fisher and Wicksell favored one approach in which wealth was the dominant monetary force and another in which relative prices were of more significance. Keynes amplified both views, but his major interpreters were not so inclined. It is, in fact, ironic that J. R. Hicks, who formulated the IS-LM interpretation of Keynes, downgraded both monetary wealth and relative price influences, despite his pioneering research into basic wealth [45] and portfolio choice fields [43].

Real balance wealth effects were revived by Pigou, Patinkin, and others while Metzler reformulated the equity wealth effect. Tobin, Brunner-Meltzer, and Friedman advanced the portfolio choice-relative price effect in the early 1960s, and with the exception of Friedman, have also highlighted the equity wealth effect.

These hardly exhaust all the ways in which monetary impulses affect spending. For example, an income effect occurs when the Treasury draws down its bank balances to purchase goods and services. A decline in Treasury deposits relative to demand deposits increases the money supply (other things equal) and income.

Alternatively, a rise in the money supply may be associated with a change in relative prices and no change in wealth. For example, a fall in currency relative to demand deposits increases the money supply and lowers bank loan rates, but there is no rise in real balances—if defined only as outside money—and no change in government debt.

Thus, depending on how the money supply is caused to change relative to money demand, some effects on spending are set in motion, but not necessarily all. Moreover, the fact that initial conditions, to include all relative prices, are never the same suggests that under one set of circumstances initial monetary effects may be on, say, consumer durable goods expenditures and under another set, state and local government purchases. To follow explicitly the channels of monetary influence whenever there occurs a change in the quantity of money supplied relative to the quantity demanded, one would have to know as a minimum the cause of the change in the money supply, all relevant relative prices, and the impact of other exogenous events on spending units. Add to this the effect of feedback forces, both relative price and wealth, and it becomes less surprising that the contents of the monetary black box have been difficult to unravel.

The complexity of the forces at work, however, does not mean that one should despair of *forecasting* the effect of monetary influences on total spending and rely on (presumably) more elementary tools to guide economic activity. The effects of other policy actions are also difficult to trace with certainty.[49]

---

[49]It has become clear in recent years that simply *forecasting* the result of fiscal policy effects on total

The likelihood is that all possible channels of monetary or other policy actions have not been spelled out completely in any one model. There remains much room for research which would narrow the gap between economic reality and economic models.

Examples of How Money Works

The following is an oversimplified description of monetary impulses working through the relative price and wealth channels. The numbers are chosen entirely for illustrative purposes and bear no relation to current actual magnitudes. This hypothesized scenario represents some of the possible ways in which spending might respond to a monetary injection. To begin, assume a sale of government bonds by the Treasury to bond dealers, the bonds being subsequently purchased by the Federal Reserve.

Relative Price Channel

The purchase of government debt by the Federal Reserve (Fed) increases bank reserves and lowers the yield (raises the price) on Treasury securities. The banks lend out (increase demand deposits) some multiple of the higher level of reserves by lowering bank loan rates; the higher price of Treasury securities encourages investors to purchase securities whose prices have not yet risen.

At this point the money supply has risen and interest rates have declined. Borrowers obtained money balances in order to purchase real assets (cars, houses, machinery) and/or financial assets (stocks, bonds), depending on the current and expected relative prices of the assets. If real assets are purchased through either consumer or investment expenditures, the price of existing real capital rises. If financial assets are purchased, the price of existing real capital rises via capitalization of the assets. The rise in the price of existing real capital encourages the production of additional capital. Observed declines in interest rates also represent lower borrowing costs, an additional stimulus to the production of goods and services. The lower costs may be interpreted as a fall in the rental price for the services rendered by an asset. More-

---

spending requires more than reliance on some variation of the deceptively simple relations $Y = C + I + G$ and $C = C(Y - T)$. These relations imply a direct link between government spending (G) and total spending (Y), and between disposable income $(Y - T)$, which includes tax changes, and consumption (C). What does not appear in these simple relations are the vector of relative prices, the type of government spending involved, how the government spending is to be financed, and whether the tax changes are presumed to be temporary or permanent.

Fiscal policy actions may also influence wealth and interest rates in addition to income, the income effect presumably being what is referred to as the *direct* effect of fiscal actions on spending. Although monetary and fiscal channels of influence are both complex, only monetary actions have typically been viewed as operating within a black box.

over, a fall in interest rates could eliminate the effects of credit rationing, which are presumed to occur at high levels of interest rates.

In other terms, if both consumption (c) and investment (i) depend on interest rates (r) and the price of existing real capital (P) relative to the price level (p), then $c = f(r, P/p)$ and $i = g(r, P/p)$. Both c and i are stimulated if r falls from say, 0.04 to 0.02 and P/p rises from 1/1 to 2/1.

As the money supply rises, however, and new recipients of money balances hire more workers, buy more equipment, pay out larger dividends, or pay higher wages, the price level begins to rise. The closer the economy is to capacity operations, the more rapid the increase in the price level. Moreover, demand for credit expands, and this, together with the price-level rise, puts upward pressure on market interest rates. The result may be a return of the interest rate and price variables to their earlier relations; that is

$$\bar{c} = f(.04, \frac{2}{2}) \text{ and } \bar{i} = g(.04, \frac{2}{2}).$$

Wealth Channel

The issuance of government debt by the Treasury results in a transfer of assets from transactor A (who purchased the debt) to transactor B (paid by the government with the proceeds from A). A holds an asset, interest and principal on which can be paid off by the government through, among other means, an increase in taxes. To the extent that the public does *not* anticipate the government raising taxes to pay off its outstanding debt, government debt represents wealth to the private sector. Whether taxes are anticipated or not, the value of a unit of government debt falls with the rise in interest rates caused by the issuance of new debt.

Federal Reserve purchase of government debt, however, unambiguously increases wealth because the Fed cannot raise taxes, and its purchase of government debt initially lowers interest rates. In other words, if monetary nonhuman wealth consists of outside money (D), government bonds (G) divided by the market rate of interest (r), and the price of capital (P) times the capital stock (K), then $W = D + \beta G/r + PK$. $\beta < 1$ indicates that wealth holders believe some portion of the government debt will be paid off by increased future taxes. Real nonhuman wealth, w, is obtained by deflating the above by the price level, p, or $w = D/p + \beta G/pr + PK/p$. Given initial values of $D = 100$, $G = 200$, $K = 10,000$, $r = .04$, $\beta = .5$, $p = 1$ and $P = 1$, then $w = 100/1 + (.5)(200)/1(.04) + 1(10,000)/1$, and therefore, $w = 100 + 2500 + 10,000$. It is assumed that $c = c(w)$ where $c' > 0$; that is, wealth positively influences consumption expenditures.

Issuance of new government debt by the Treasury of 5 bonds is assumed to raise interest rates to 0.041, such that this component of wealth remains unchanged: $\beta G/pr = 0.5(205)/1(.041) = 2500$. If the Fed purchases the government debt, however, the change in the first two wealth components is: $D/p + \beta G/pr = 105/1 + 0.5(200)/1(0.04) = 105 + 2500$.

A number of other wealth effects may be distinguished, some of which are not related to a Fed purchase of Treasury debt:

1) The Pigou effect normally associates a fall in the price level with a constant level of D. Example:
Value of D/p rises from $100/1 = 100$ to $100/0.5 = 200$.

2) The real financial effect associates a fall in the price level with a constant level of G. Example:
Value of $\beta G/pr$ rises from $0.5(200)/1(0.04) = 2500$ to $0.5(200)/0.5(0.04) = 5000$. There is also a Keynes effect which goes beyond the Pigou effect by assuming the rise in real cash balances lowers interest rates and stimulates investment.

3) Keynes' windfall effect may apply to either the government bonds or the capital stock portion of nonhuman wealth:

   A. a fall in interest rates. Example: Value of $\beta G/pr$ rises from $0.5(200)/1(0.04) = 2500$ to $0.5(200)/1(0.02) = 5000$.

   B. a rise in the price of real capital. Example: Value of PK/p rises from $1(10,000)/1 = 10,000$ to $2(10,000)/1 = 20,000$.*

4) The Pesek-Saving effect takes into account the possibility that some commercial bank debt (demand deposits) is not adequately capitalized in the PK/p term and should be included as a part of D. Example: Assume $\alpha = 0.5$ is the fraction of demand deposits (dd) to be included in the wealth term, such that if there is a rise in demand deposits, the value of the $D + \alpha(dd)/p$ term rises from $100 + 0.5(150)/1 = 175$ to $100 + 0.5(160)/1 = 180$.

5) It should be noted that just as a rising price level tends to offset the initially expansive effects of monetary actions through the relative price effect, a rising price level also tends to counter a monetary-induced wealth effect. Example: An increase of the (outside) money stock (D) initially increased the value of nonhuman wealth from $w = D/p + \beta G/pr + PK/p = 100/1 + 0.5(200)/1(0.04) + 1(10,000)/1 = 12,600$ to $200/1 + 0.5(200)/$

---

* Leijonhufvud ([53], pp. 324-25) provides a more detailed description of effects 1-3 in the context of Keynes' views on wealth-consumption influences.

1(0.02) + 2(10,000)/1 = 25,200. But if the price level also in-creases, w = 200/2 + 0.5(200)/2(0.04) + 2(10,000)/2 = 11,350, which is a decline from the initial value of wealth due to the effect of the price rise on government debt.

REFERENCES

1. ACKLEY, GARDNER. "The Wealth-Saving Relationship." *The Journal of Political Economy* 59 (1951).
2. BLINDER, ALAN S., and SOLOW, ROBERT M. "Does Fiscal Policy Matter?" *Journal of Public Economics* 2 (1973).
3. Board of Governors of the Federal Reserve System. *Equations In The MIT-PENN-SSRC Econometric Model Of The United States.* (1973).
4. BROWN, A. J. "The Liquidity-Preference Schedules of the London Clearing Banks." *Oxford Economic Papers* 1 (1938).
5. BRUNNER, KARL. "The Report of The Commission On Money and Credit." *The Journal of Political Economy* 69 (1961).
6. ———. "The Role of Money and Monetary Policy." this *Review* 50 (1968).
7. ———. "The 'Monetarist Revolution' in Monetary Theory." *Weltwirtschaftliches Archiv* 105 (1970).
8. ———. "A Survey of Selected Issues in Monetary Theory." *Schweizerische Zeitschrift für Volkswirtschaft und Statistik* 107 (1971).
9. BRUNNER, KARL, and MELTZER, ALLEN H. "The Place of Financial Intermediaries In The Transmission of Monetary Policy." *The American Economic Review* 53 (1963).
10. ———. "The Uses of Money: Money in the Theory of an Exchange Economy." *The American Economic Review* 61 (1971).
11. ———. "Friedman's Monetary Theory." *The Journal of Political Economy* 80 (1972).
12. ———. "Money, Debt, and Economic Activity." *The Journal of Political Economy* 80 (1972).
13. CAGAN, PHILLIP. "Why Do We Use Money In Open Market Operations?" *The Journal of Political Economy* 66 (1958).
14. ———. *The Channels of Monetary Effects on Interest Rates.* New York: National Bureau of Economic Research, 1972.
15. CHRIST, CARL F. "A Model of Monetary and Fiscal Policy Effects on the Money Stock, Price Level, and Real Output." *Journal of Money, Credit and Banking* 1 (1969).
16. ———. "Econometric Models of the Financial Sector." *Journal of Money, Credit and Banking* 3 (1971).
17. Committee on the Working of the Monetary System. *Report.* London: Her Majesty's Stationary Office, 1959.
18. CROCKETT, JEAN; FRIEND, IRWIN; and SHAVELL, HENRY. "The Impact of Monetary Stringency on Business Investment." *Survey of Current Business* 47 (1967).
19. DAVIS, RICHARD G. "The Role of the Money Supply in Business Cycles." Federal Reserve Bank of New York *Monthly Review* 50 (1968).
20. DELEEUW, FRANK, and GRAMLICH, EDWARD M. "The Channels of Monetary Policy." Federal Reserve *Bulletin* 55 (1969).

21. EBERSOLE, J. FRANKLIN. "The Influence of Interest Rates Upon Enterpreneurial Decisions In Business—A Case Study." *Harvard Business Review* 17 (1939).

22. EISNER, ROBERT. "Factors Affecting The Level of Interest Rates: Part II." United States Savings and Loan League. *Savings and Residential Financing: 1968 Conference Proceedings,* 1968.

23. ETTIN, EDWARD C. "A Qualitative Analysis of the Relationships Between Money and Income." *Weltwirtschaftliches Archiv* 96 (1966).

24. FISHER, IRVING. *Booms and Depressions: Some First Principles.* New York: Adelphi Company, 1932.

25. ———. *The Purchasing Power of Money: Its Determination And Relation To Credit Interest And Crises.* rev. ed. New York: Reprints of Economic Classics, 1963.

26. FRIEDMAN, MILTON. "A Monetary and Fiscal Framework for Economic Stability." *The American Economic Review* 38 (1948).

27. ———. *A Theory of the Consumption Function.* New York: The National Bureau of Economic Research, 1957.

28. ———. "The Lag in Effect of Monetary Policy." *The Journal of Political Economy* 69 (1961).

29. ———. "The Role of Monetary Policy." *The American Economic Review* 58 (1968).

30. ———. "A Theoretical Framework for Monetary Analysis." *The Journal of Political Economy* 78 (1970).

31. ———. "A Monetary Theory of Nominal Income." *The Journal of Political Economy* 79 (1971).

32. ———. "Comments on the Critics." *The Journal of Political Economy* 80 (1972).

33. FRIEDMAN, MILTON, and MEISELMAN, DAVID. "The Relative Stability of Monetary Velocity and the Investment Multiplier In The United States." In *Stabilization Policies,* Commission on Money and Credit. Englewood Cliffs, New Jersey: Prentice-Hall, Inc., 1963.

34. FRIEDMAN, MILTON, and SCHWARTZ, ANNA J. "Money And Business Cycles." *The Review of Economics and Statistics* 45 (1963).

35. GRAMLEY LYLE E., and CHASE, SAMUEL B., JR. "Time Deposits in Monetary Analysis." Federal Reserve *Bulletin* 51 (1965).

36. GURLEY, JOHN G. "The Radcliffe Report and Evidence: A Review Article." *The American Economic Review* 50 (1960).

37. GURLEY, JOHN G. and SHAW, EDWARD S. *Money in a Theory of Finance.* Washington, D.C.: The Brookings Institution, 1960.

38. HABERLER, GOTTFRIED. *Prosperity and Depression: A Theoretical Analysis of Cyclical Movements.* 3d ed. Geneva: League of Nations, 1941.

39. HANSEN, ALVIN H. "Economic Progress and Declining Population Growth." *The American Economic Review* 29 (1939).

40. ———. *Fiscal Policy and Business Cycles.* New York: W. W. Norton & Company, Inc., 1941.

41. ———. "The Pigouvian Effect." *The Journal of Political Economy* 59 (1951).

42. HENDERSON, H. D. "The Significance of the Rate of Interest." *Oxford Economic Papers* 1 (1938).

43. HICKS, J(OHN) R. "A Suggestion for Simplifying The Theory of Money." *Economica* 2 (1935).

44. ———. "Mr. Keynes and the 'Classics'; A Suggested Interpretation." *Econometrica* 5 (1937).

45. ———. *Value and Capital: An Inquiry into. Some Fundamental Principles of Economic Theory.* 2d ed. Oxford: The Clarendon Press, 1946.

46. ———. *Critical Essays in Monetary Theory.* Oxford: The Clarendon Press, 1967.

47. HODGMAN, DONALD R. *Commercial Bank Loan and Investment Policy.* Champaign, Illinois: Bureau of Economic And Business Research, 1963.

48. HUME, DAVID. *Writings on Economics.* Edited by Eugene Rotwein. Madison: The University of Wisconsin Press, 1970.

49. JAFFEE, DWIGHT M., and MODIGLIANI, FRANCO. "A Theory and Test of Credit Rationing." *The American Economic Review* 59 (1969).

50. KANE, EDWARD J. "Is There a Predilected Lock-In Effect?" *National Tax Journal* 21 (1968).

51. KEYNES, JOHN MAYNARD. *The General Theory of Employment, Interest and Money.* New York: Harcourt, Brace and Company, 1936.

52. LAIDLER, DAVID. "Expectations, Adjustment, and the Dynamic Response of Income to Policy Changes." *Journal of Money, Credit and Banking* 5 (1973).

53. LEIJONHUFVUD, AXEL. *On Keynesian Economics and the Economics of Keynes: A Study in Monetary Theory.* New York: Oxford University Press, 1968.

54. LERNER, A. P. "The Burden of the National Debt." *Income, Employment and Public Policy: Essays in Honor of Alvin H. Hansen.* New York: W. W. Norton & Company, Inc., 1948.

55. LINDBECK, ASSAR. "The 'New' Theory Of Credit Control In The United States." 2d ed. Stockholm Economic Studies Pamphlet Series I. Stockholm: Almqvist & Wiksell, 1962.

56. MCCARTHY, MICHAEL D. *The Wharton Quarterly Econometric Forecasting Model: Mark III.* Philadelphia: University of Pennsylvania, 1972.

57. MEADE, J. E., and ANDREWS, P. W. S. "Summary of Replies to Questions on Effects of Interest Rates." *Oxford Economic Papers* 1 (1938).

58. METZLER, LLOYD A. "Wealth, Saving, And The Rate Of Interest." *The Journal of Political Economy* 59 (1951).

59. MODIGLIANI, FRANCO. "Liquidity Preference and the Theory of Interest and Money." *Econometrica* 12 (1944).

60. ———. "The Monetary Mechanism and Its Interaction with Real Phenomena." *The Review of Economics and Statistics* 45 (1963).

61. ———. "Monetary Policy and Consumption: Linkages via Interest Rate and Wealth Effects in the FMP Model." Federal Reserve Bank of Boston. *Consumer Spending and Monetary Policy: The Linkages,* 1971.

62. MODIGLIANI, FRANCO, and BRUMBURG, RICHARD. "Utility Analysis and the Consumption Function: An Interpretation of Cross-Section Data." *Post Keynesian Economics.* Edited by Kenneth K. Kurihara. New Brunswick, New Jersey: Rutgers University Press, 1954.

63. PATINKIN, DON. *Money, Interest, and Prices: An Integration of Monetary and Value Theory.* 2d ed. New York: Harper & Row, 1965.

64. PESEK, BORIS P., and SAVING, THOMAS R. *Money, Wealth, and Economic Theory.* New York: The Macmillan Company, 1967.

65. PIGOU, A. C. "The Value of Money." *The Quarterly Journal of Economics* 32 (1917-1918).

66. ———. "The Classical Stationary State." *Economic Journal* 1943.

67. RASCHE, ROBERT H. "A Comparative Static Analysis of Some Monetarist Propositions." this *Review* 55 (1973).

68. ROOSA, ROBERT V. "Interest Rates and the Central Bank." *Money, Trade, and Economic Growth: In Honor of John Henry Williams.* New York: The Macmillan Company, 1951.

69. SAMUELSON, PAUL A. U.S., Congress, Joint Economic Committee. *Monetary Policy and the Management of The Public Debt: Their Role in Achieving Price Stability And High-Level Employment.* 82nd Congress, 2nd session, 1952.

70. ———. "Money, Interest Rates and Economic Activity: Their Interrelationship in a Market Economy." The American Bankers Association. *A Symposium on Money, Interest Rates and Economic Activity,* 1967.

71. SCITOVSZKY, T. DE. "Capital Accumulation, Employment and Price Rigidity." *The Review of Economic Studies* 8 (1940-1941).

72. SILBER, WILLIAM L. "The St. Louis Equation: 'Democratic' and 'Republican' Version And Other Experiments." *The Review of Economics and Statistics* 53 (1971).

73. SMITH, PAUL E. "Lags in the Effects of Monetary Policy: Comment." *The American Economic Review* 62 (1972).

74. TANNER, ERNEST J. "Lag in the Effects of Monetary Policy: A Statistical Investigation." *The American Economic Review* 59 (1969).

75. TINBERGEN, JAN. *Statistical Testing of Business-Cycle Theories.* Geneva: League of Nations, 1938.

76. TOBIN, JAMES. "Relative Income, Absolute Income and Saving." *Money, Trade and Economic Growth: In Honor of John Henry Williams.* New York: The Macmillan Company, 1951.

77. ———. "Money, Capital, and Other Stores of Value." *The American Economic Review* 51 (1961).

78. ———. "Commercial Banks as Creators of 'Money'." *Banking and Monetary Studies.* Edited by Deane Carson. Homewood, Illinois: R. D. Irwin, Inc., 1963.

79. ———. "An Essay on Principles of Debt Management." In *Fiscal and Debt Management Policies,* Commission on Money and Credit. Englewood Cliffs, New Jersey: Prentice-Hall, Inc., 1963.

80. ———. "Monetary Semantics." *Targets and Indicators of Monetary Policy.* Edited by Karl Brunner. San Francisco: Chandler Publishing Company, 1969.

81. ———. "A General Equilibrium Approach to Monetary Theory." *Journal of Money, Credit and Banking* 1 (1969).

82. ———. "Money and Income: Post Hoc Ergo Propter Hoc?" *The Quarterly Journal of Economics* 84 (1970).

83. ———. "Rebuttal." Federal Reserve Bank of Boston. *Consumer Spending and Monetary Policy: The Linkages,* 1971.

84. TOBIN, JAMES, and BRAINARD, WILLIAM C. "Pitfalls in Financial Model Building." *The American Economic Review* 58 (1968).

85. TOBIN, JAMES, and DOLDE, WALTER. "Wealth, Liquidity and Consumption." Federal Reserve Bank of Boston. *Consumer Spending and Monetary Policy: The Linkages,* 1971.

86. TOOKE, THOMAS. *A History of Prices and of the State of the Circulation from 1792 to 1856.* London: P. S. King and Son, Ltd., 1928.

87. TUCKER, DONALD P. "Dynamic Income Adjustment to Money-Supply Changes." *The American Economic Review* 56 (1966).

88. WARBURTON, CLARK. *Depression, Inflation, and Monetary Policy: Selected Papers, 1945-1953.* Baltimore: The John Hopkins Press, 1966.
89. WICKSELL, KNUT. *Lectures on Political Economy: Money.* Vol. 2. Edited by Lionel Robbins. London: Routledge & Kegan Paul Ltd., 1950.
90. ———. *Interest and Prices: A Study of the Causes Regulating the Value of Money.* Translated by R. F. Kahn. New York: Reprints of Economic Classics, 1962.

8

Does Fiscal Policy Matter?

Alan S. Blinder and Robert M. Solow[*]

Perhaps the most fundamental achievement of the Keynesian revolution was the reorientation of the way economists view the influence of government activity on the private economy. Before Keynes, it was commonplace that government spending and taxation were powerless to affect the aggregate levels of spending and employment in the economy; they could only redirect resources from the private to the public sector. This, of course, is an immediate corollary of Say's Law. In a full-employment context, each dollar of additional government spending can only "crowd out" exactly one dollar of private spending; it cannot alter the overall level of aggregate income.

The Keynesian demonstration that with sticky wages unemployment can persist changed all this. Economists began to stress the macroeconomic effects of government spending and taxation. It became commonplace that not only would a dollar of additional government spending raise national income by the original dollar, but that this expenditure would have multiplier effects of perhaps several dollars more. The old view that government spending simply crowded out private spending was ban-

Reprinted from the *Journal of Public Economics,* Vol. 2 (1973), pp. 319-337, by permission of the North Holland Publishing Company and the authors.

* This paper is an outgrowth of work we are doing for The Brookings Institution. Support from Brookings and from the National Science Foundation under Grant GS 32003X is gratefully acknowledged. We are also indebted to A. B. Atkinson for an important suggestion which led to a substantial revision of this paper.

ished. At the same time a new question arose: Does monetary policy matter, or, at least, does it matter much?

Lately, however, the resurgence of the quantity theory of money—under the new name of "monetarism"—has brought with it both a renewed belief in the power of monetary policy and a resurgence of interest in the crowding-out effect. Both the theoretical and empirical work of the monetarists has called into question the basic Keynesian principle that government spending can alter the aggregate level of employment. The current question appears to be: Does fiscal policy matter?[1]

The purpose of this note is to reexamine the underlying basis of the Keynesian multiplier in view of the monetarist critique. We hope to show that there are still good theoretical reasons to believe in the efficacy of fiscal policy in an economy with underemployed resources.

1. The Problem Defined

There are several levels at which crowding out has been alleged to occur. The most obvious is the possibility that government will engage in productive activities which would otherwise be provided by the private sector, so that public spending would simply supplant private investment. It can be argued, for example, that total investment in electrical utilities in the Tennessee Valley area would be much the same today had the government never created the Tennessee Valley Authority. However, for the bulk of government expenditures—on national defense, courts, and the like— it is hard to imagine that public-sector outlays are simply replacing potential private outlays on a *dollar-for-dollar basis*. In any case, this is not the sort of crowding out we wish to discuss, and it would occur whether the spending were financed by taxes, bonds, or money.

A second level of crowding out is an integral part of the Keynesian tradition and is, in fact, disputed by almost no one. This is the notion that deficit spending *not accompanied by new issues of money* carries with it the need for the government to float debt issues which compete with private debt instruments in financial markets. The resulting upward pressure on interest rates will reduce any private expenditures which are interest-elastic—which may include some spending by state and local governments as well as private spending on consumer durables, business fixed investment and residential construction. This financial side effect will partially offset the expansionary effect of the original increase in public spending. Thus in a monetary economy the government spending multiplier is certainly lower than the naive Keynesian formula, multiplier = $1/(1 -$ marginal propensity to spend), and is lower for bond-financed spending than it is for money-financed spending.

There is no theoretical controversy over this second level of crowding out. The only contested issues are empirical. How much will interest rates rise in response to

[1]See, for example, L. C. Andersen and J. L. Jordan (1968); R. W. Spencer and W. A. Yohe (1970); and many of the writings of Milton Friedman.

the greater demand for money and supply of bonds engendered by the government spending? How much will investment fall in response to the rise in interest rates? It is by now well known that only a zero interest-elasticity of the demand for money will give rise to a multiplier of zero, that is, make fiscal policy impotent. While this assumption was formerly associated with the new quantity theorists,[2] there is by now an overwhelming accumulation of empirical evidence against it, and the monetarists have more or less disavowed it.[3]

Yet monetarists still cling to the view that fiscal policy is powerless, that is, that the multiplier for bond-financed government spending is approximately zero. How can this be so? A possible answer is that when there are significant wealth effects the simple Keynesian story (as summarized, say, in the *IS-LM* model) closes the books too soon. Any government deficit requires the issuance of some sort of debt instrument—outside money or interest-bearing bonds—and this increase in private wealth will have further reverberations in the economy. It is precisely these wealth effects—which provide the rationale for the third level of crowding out—that we wish to investigate in this paper.

Figures 1 and 2 illustrate the problem. In Figure 1 IS_0 and LM_0 represent the initial equilibrium of the economy in the ordinary Hicks-Hansen model. Government spending is indicated by an outward shift of the *IS* curve to IS_1. Income rises by $Y_1 - Y_0$. Income does not rise all the way to Y_2—which represents the naive multiplier effect—because of the second level of crowding out alluded to above.

This is where the usual textbook story ends, and if there are no significant wealth effects, that is correct. However, when wealth effects exist, Y_1 is not an equilibrium position. Greater wealth will, presumably, mean higher levels of consumption out of any given income flow; thus the *IS* curve will shift out further to IS_2 in Figure 2. This

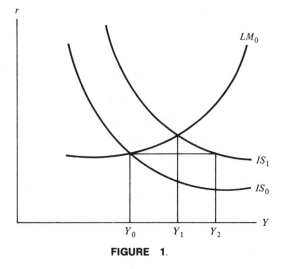

FIGURE 1.

[2]See Friedman (1956, 1959).
[3]Friedman (1966, 1972), Fand (1970).

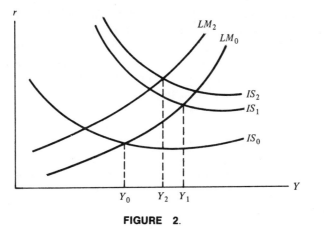

FIGURE 2.

augments the ordinary multiplier. But the greater wealth will also affect the financial markets. Increased household wealth will presumably mean increased demands for money (and bonds) at any level of income and interest rates, represented by a shift in the *LM* curve to LM_2 in Figure 2.

The outcome of these last two shifts may be either expansionary or contractionary on balance as Silber (1970) has stressed. Advocates of complete crowding out, of course, believe the results to be contractionary. If they are correct, as long as a budgetary deficit exists there will be increases in private wealth which have deflationary impacts on the level of national income. In the long run the fiscal policy multiplier is negative.

In response to a recent criticism by Tobin (1972), Friedman has indicated that he now believes that these wealth effects, rather than the oft-cited slope of the *LM* curve, constitute the main issue separating monetarists from Keynesians. He contrasts the initial impact of the fiscal policy in Figure 1 with the wealth-induced shifts in Figure 2—shifts which continue as long as the budget is unbalanced—and he asks: "Is there any doubt that this (latter) effect must swamp the once-for-all shift of the *IS* curve?" (Friedman, 1972, p. 916.) He summarizes his new view of the monetarist-Keynesian debate as follows (Friedman, 1972, p. 922):

> One way to characterize the Keynesian approach is that it gives almost exclusive importance to the first-round effect. This leads it to attach importance primarily to flows of spending rather than to stocks of assets. Similarly, one way to characterize the quantity-theory approach is to say that it gives almost no importance to first-round effects.
>
> The empirical question is how important the first-round effects are compared to the ultimate effects. Theory cannot answer that question.

Friedman believes that the answer for deficit spending financed by printing money is that the subsequent asset effects are (a) much larger than and (b) in the same direction as the initial expansionary thrust of government spending. By contrast, if the deficits are financed by floating government bonds, he apparently believes that wealth effects are (a) about equal in magnitude and (b) opposite in direction to the initial movement of the *IS* curve. On the other hand, it has always been a central tenet of Keynesian macroeconomics that bond-financed government spending has a net expansionary impact on the level of economic activity.[4] After all, if this were not so, symmetry would imply that reducing spending in order to pay off part of the national debt would be expansionary.

But is it only faith that supports this view? In this paper, we hope to show that while Friedman may be correct in describing the issue as an empirical one, certain theoretical arguments can be adduced in support of the conventional view that fiscal policy works. Furthermore, we suggest that it is also an empirical question whether the subsequent wealth effects of bond-financed deficits, while less expansionary than money-financed deficits in the short run (Friedman's "first round") are actually more expansionary in the long run.[5]

In the following section we consider the long-run impact of government spending, under the two alternative modes of financing, in an *IS-LM* model with wealth effects. This analysis, however, utilizes a funny concept of the "long run" since, in conformity with the *IS-LM* rules, the capital stock is held fixed (despite positive net investment) while the stocks of the other two assets (money and bonds) adjust to their final equilibrium. So, in section 3, we rectify this error by considering a true long-run equilibrium where all three asset stocks are free to adjust. We find that, in a sense to be specified later, the case for fiscal policy is somewhat stronger in this more sophisticated model.

2. Crowding Out in the Simple *IS-LM* Model

The conventional *IS-LM* model,[6] with wealth effects added, consists of the following ingredients:

$$\text{(goods–market equilibrium)} \quad Y \equiv NNP = C + I + G \qquad (1)$$

[4]There is no controversy over government spending financed by printing money. Both sides agree that it will be expansionary; but one group likes to call it fiscal policy, while the other prefers to call it monetary policy. Nothing much hinges on this distinction. In terms of Figure 2, the *LM* curve would shift outward instead of inward if financing were by money instead of by bonds.

[5]So far as we know, this conclusion was first suggested in a paper by Sean Murray (forthcoming).

[6]The *IS-LM* model usually treats the price level as exogenously fixed, and we shall adhere to this convention. However, it should be noted that we do this strictly for simplicity. There are no real difficulties in adding a production function and a labor market and allowing the price level to be endogenously determined. The result would be that expansionary fiscal policy causes some inflation of the price level which reduces the value of the multiplier for (at least) three reasons: (1) With prices higher, the real value of the money stock is lower, which shifts the *LM* curve inward. (2) Higher prices reduce the real wealth of the private sector, which has a negative "Pigou effect" on consumption, shifting the *IS* curve inward. (3) If taxes are progressive in terms of money income, inflation will increase the real yield of the tax system at each level of real income, again lowering the *IS* curve. While each of these serves to reduce the absolute value of the fiscal multiplier, none of them has any bearing on its sign, which is what is at issue here.

(consumption function)	$C = C(Y - T, W)$	(2)
(net investment function)	$I = I(r)$	(3)
(tax function)	$T = T(Y)$	(4)
(demand for real balances)	$\dfrac{M^d}{P} = L(r, Y, W)$	(5)
(exogenous money supply)[7]	$M^s = M$	(6)
(money-market equilibrium)	$M^s = M^d$	(7)
(definition of wealth)[8]	$W = K + \dfrac{M}{P} + \dfrac{V(r)}{P}.$	(8)

Here $V(r)$ is the nominal market value of the supply of government bonds. The only additions to the classical textbook treatment which we have made are to include wealth as an argument in both the consumption and demand for money functions.

To this model, we must append a somewhat different version of what Carl Christ (1967, 1968) has called the "government budget restraint." As it usually appears in the work of Christ and others, the restraint is a simple differential (or difference) equation equating the changes in the nominal stocks of bonds and money to the nominal government deficit:

$$P[G - T(Y)] = \dot{B} + \dot{M}, \qquad (9')$$

where B is the number of bonds (each of face value \$1). But $(9')$ commits an oversight: it ignores the fact that interest paid on bonds is an expense item in the government's budgetary accounts along with G. If we assume for simplicity that each bond is a perpetuity paying \$1 per year, interest payments will be B and the market value of the stock of bonds will be B/r. The government budget restraint can therefore be written:

$$P[G + B - T] = \dot{B}/r + \dot{M}. \qquad (9)$$

Note that the bond term on the righthand side is the change in the number of bonds, evaluated at the current market price. This differs from $(\dot{B}/r)$, which is the change in the market value of the stock of bonds, if there are capital gains or losses on pre-existing bonds.

Two other minor alterations in the model are necessary. First, in the definition of wealth we can write B/r for $V(r)$. Second, both consumption and taxes presumably

---

[7]This is again a simplification made solely for the purpose of notational convenience. We here ignore the banking system, and thus the distinction between inside and outside money, and we treat the money stock as exogenous. These complications could all be brought in, and would in no way affect the central conclusions.

[8]This includes government bonds as a net asset to the public. We are well aware of, but not persuaded by, the arguments which hold that such bonds are not seen as net worth by individuals because of the implied future tax liability. If that view were correct, the wealth effects of new bonds, illustrated in Figure 2, would simply not occur.

depend upon personal income, which includes the interest paid on the national debt; thus (2') and (4') become:

$$C = C(Y + B - T, W) \tag{2}$$

$$T = T(Y + B). \tag{4}$$

The first model which we shall study consists of equations (1)-(9). Since we shall treat the price level as fixed throughout, we can set $P = 1$ with no loss of generality and reduce the nine equations to the following three-equation dynamic system:

$$Y = C\left[Y + B - T(Y + B), M + \frac{B}{r} + K\right] + I(r) + G \tag{10}$$

$$M = L\left(r, Y, M + \frac{B}{r} + K\right) \tag{11}$$

$$\dot{M} + \frac{\dot{B}}{r} = G + B - T(Y + B). \tag{12}$$

Equations (10) and (11) are the static *IS* and *LM* equations which hold at each instant; equation (12) drives the model from one instantaneous equilibrium to the next by changing the stocks of money and/or bonds.

The unmodified model which ignores interest payments as a budgetary expense item—equations (1), (2'), (3), (4'), (5)-(8), and (9')—has an implication which has attracted attention in recent years. Suppose that we ignore the dynamics of the model and look only at the long-run steady-state solution. This means that $\dot{M} = \dot{B} = 0$, so that (9') implies $G = T(Y)$, that is, the government budget must be balanced in long-run equilibrium. But this immediately implies that the steady-state multiplier for government spending not financed by higher tax rates (but ultimately financed by higher tax revenues at unchanged rates) must be, as Christ has pointed out:

$$\frac{dY}{dG} = \frac{1}{T'(Y)}.$$

Observe that this long-run multiplier expression holds regardless of how the deficit is financed and is independent of all functional relations in the model except the tax function. In a word, if the model is stable under each mode of financing (so that it actually approaches its steady state), the long-run multipliers for bond and money-financed deficit spending are identical.

What happens when we add interest to the budget constraint? Setting $\dot{B} = \dot{M} = 0$ in (9) gives: $G + B = T(Y + B)$, from which it follows that:

$$\frac{dY}{dG} = \frac{1 + (1 - T')\dfrac{dB}{dG}}{T'}.$$

If deficits are financed by money creation, so that $dB/dG = 0$, we obtain the same long-run multiplier as before. But if bond financing is used, so that $dB/dG > 0$, the long-run multiplier exceeds $1/T'$. In words, contrary to the usual supposition, the long-run multiplier for bond-financed deficit spending exceeds that for money-financed deficit spending.

What is the reason for this paradoxical result? Simply this: starting from any long-run equilibrium income level with a balanced budget, an initial surge in government spending will cause income to rise as in normal *IS-LM* analysis. It is well known that, if the *LM* curve has positive slope, the impact multiplier will be larger if the deficit is financed by creating money. But, this is only Friedman's "first round." Since the budget will be in deficit, new assets will have to be created. If financing is by bonds, the subsequent deficit financing will have to be larger than in the money case for two reasons. First, income will rise less so the induced increase in tax receipts will be smaller. Second, a larger outstanding debt will require greater interest payments. Provided that the net impact of the wealth effects is expansionary, the "second-round" increase in income will be greater under bond financing than under money financing, and this will continue to be true in subsequent rounds. The basic intuition is that under bond financing any given budgetary gap is harder to close because every increase in the number of bonds outstanding requires more expenditure on debt service. It therefore takes a greater rise in income to induce tax receipts sufficient to close the budgetary gap.

Thus one is tempted to conclude that Friedman's "empirical question" can be resolved on purely theoretical grounds after all—not only is deficit spending financed by bonds expansionary in the long run, it is even more expansionary than the same spending financed by the creation of new money.[9] However, this would be jumping too hastily to a conclusion which may not be warranted. Steady-state equilibria are of interest only if the system under consideration is stable. And it turns out that the stability of the system of equations (10)-(12) may depend on the way in which deficits are financed. As we shall see, the model is always stable under money finance, but there are three possibilities under bond finance:

(a) If the parameters of the system are such that the net wealth effect of a new bond issue is contractionary (as depicted in Figure 2), the monetarists will be vindicated; but the more important consequence is that the system will then be unstable.

(b) For some other values of the crucial parameters, bonds will have an expansionary impact on the level of national income (so that the monetarists are wrong), but this impact will not be sufficiently strong to close the budgetary gap. Again the system will be unstable.

(c) Finally, if the parameters are such that the system is stable, additional bonds must have a positive net impact on GNP (Y_2 must lie to the right of Y_1 in Figure 2) so that fiscal policy works as expected. Only in this case can we appeal to the steady-

---

[9]An interesting corollary of this is that an open-market purchase, i.e., a swap of B for M by the government with G unchanged, will be contractionary! This is because, with less debt service, the existing levels of G and Y will imply a budgetary surplus which, in turn, must lead to a reduction in the supplies of money and/or bonds.

state result that bond-financed deficits are more expansionary than money-financed deficits. And it is an empirical question as to which case actually obtains.

To prove these assertions it will be useful to consider the static equilibrium equations (10)-(11) as defining Y and r as functions of M and B, for given K and G:

$$Y(t) = F(M, B, \overline{K}; G) \tag{13}$$

$$r(t) = H(M, B, \overline{K}; G). \tag{14}$$

It is a routine exercise in comparative statics to find that the partial derivatives of these functions are:

$$F_M = \mu\alpha \qquad H_M = \mu\frac{\lambda}{L_r}(S' - h) \tag{I}$$

$$F_B = \mu\beta \qquad H_B = -\mu\frac{\lambda}{L_r}\left[\frac{h}{r} + (1 - S')L_y\right]$$

where

$$h \equiv S'L_w + C_wL_y > 0$$

$$0 < S' \equiv 1 - C_y(1 - T') < 1$$

$$\alpha \equiv C_w + (1 - L_w)\sigma > 0 \text{ since } 0 < L_w < 1$$

$$\beta \equiv C_w - L_w\sigma$$

$$0 < \lambda \equiv L_r\bigg/\left(L_r - \frac{B}{r^2}L_w\right) < 1$$

$$\sigma = \frac{I_r - (B/r^2)C_w}{L_r - (B/r^2)L_w} > 0$$

and μ is the basic multiplier:[10]

$$\mu \equiv 1/(S' + \sigma L_y).$$

So the short-run multiplier for increases in M is $\partial Y/\partial M = \mu\alpha$, which is unambiguously positive; while the corresponding multiplier for bonds B is $\partial Y/\partial B = \mu\beta$, which is ambiguous on a priori grounds. Monetarists, of course, believe $\beta < 0$, but correctly emphasize that the sign of β is an empirical question.

[10]Note that if, as is typically done in *IS-LM* analysis, we ignored the capital gains on bonds when interest rates change, σ would simplify to I_r/L_r, so that μ would be the more familiar $1/(S' + I_rL_y/L_r)$.

We now turn to the issue of stability. Equations (13)-(14) enable us to reduce the dynamic system (10)-(12) to a single nonlinear differential equation:

$$\dot{M} = G + \overline{B} - T[F(M, \overline{B}, \overline{K}) + \overline{B}]$$

under money finance, or (15a)

$$\dot{B} = H(\overline{M}, B, \overline{K})\{G + B - T[F(\overline{M}, B, \overline{K}) + B]\}$$

under bond finance. (15b)

Under a regime of pure money finance, the stability condition for differential equation (15a) is simply:

$$\frac{\partial \dot{M}}{\partial M} = - T'F_M = - T' \mu\alpha < 0,$$ (16a)

which is obviously satisfied. However, if deficits are financed by floating bonds, the corresponding condition is:

$$\frac{\partial \dot{B}}{\partial B} = r\{1 - T'(F_B + 1)\} + H_B \{G + B - T\} < 0$$

$$= r(1 - T' - T'F_B) \text{ in the neighborhood of equilibrium.}$$

So the necessary and sufficient condition for local stability is:

$$F_B = \mu\beta > \frac{1 - T'}{T'}.$$ (16b)

We find that the stability of the *IS-LM* model under bond financing of deficits is indeed an empirical question. However, since $\beta > 0$ is necessary (but not sufficient) for stability, *in a stable system* the discovery of a hitherto unsuspected government bond must lead to a higher level of national income. The three possibilities enumerated above are immediately apparent from condition (16b). If $F_B < 0$ as the monetarists claim, fiscal policy does not work, but the system is unstable. The economy does not return to its initial equilibrium before the deficit spending, as monetarist doctrine holds; instead income falls cumulatively and without limit. If $0 < F_B < (1 - T')/T'$, fiscal policy works as Keynesians have always believed, but the increases in GNP are not sufficient to close the budgetary gap. Each new bond leads to a rise in income of $F_B dB$ and a rise in tax revenues of $T'F_B dB$, but costs the government $(1 - T')dB$. Only if $T'F_B$ exceeds $(1 - T')$, i.e., only if (16b) is satisfied, will the budget deficit be falling, and thus only in this case will the system approach its new steady state equilibrium.[11]

---

[11]In a model where interest payments are omitted from the budget restraint, the stability condition turns out to be simply $F_B < 0$, so that there is a direct correspondence between whether fiscal policy works as expected and whether the system is stable.

3. Crowding Out When the Capital Stock May Vary

We now wish to make only two small alterations in the *IS-LM* model of equations (10)-(12). First, we recognize that the change in the capital stock *(K)* is identical to net investment *(I)*. Second, in line with modern investment theory which envisions an equilibrium demand for capital stock and a disequilibrium demand for investment, we alter the investment function of equation (3) to read:

$$I = I(r, K), \quad I_r < 0, \ I_K < 0; \tag{3'}$$

with the property that $I(r^*, K^*) = 0$ if r^* is the long-run equilibrium interest rate corresponding to any long-run equilibrium capital stock, K^*.

With these modifications, our dynamic system becomes:

$$Y = C[Y + B - T(Y + B), M + \frac{B}{r} + K] + I(r, K) + G \tag{17}$$

$$M = L(r, Y, M, + \frac{B}{r} + K) \tag{18}$$

$$\dot{M} + \frac{\dot{B}}{r} = G + B - T(Y + B) \tag{19}$$

$$\dot{K} = I(r, K). \tag{20}$$

Once again, we can treat the static *IS-LM* equations (17) and (18), as defining Y and r as functions of M, B, and K, for a given G:

$$Y = F(M, B, K; G) \tag{21}$$

$$r = H(M, B, K; G) \tag{22}$$

with the following comparative-static derivatives:

$$F_M = \mu\alpha > 0; \qquad\qquad H_M = \mu \frac{\lambda}{L_r} (S' - h)$$

$$F_B = \mu\beta; \qquad\qquad H_B = - \mu \frac{\lambda}{L_r} [\frac{h}{r} + (1 - S')] \, L_y > 0$$

$$F_K = \mu(\beta + I_K) < F_B; \quad H_K = - \mu \frac{\lambda}{L_r} (h + I_K L_y). \tag{II}$$

Note that the derivatives with respect to M and B are the same as in equations (I). In particular, $\partial Y / \partial B = \mu \beta$ remains ambiguous. Substitution of (21)-(22) into (19)-(20) reduces our system to two nonlinear differential equations:

$$\dot{K} = I[H(M, B, K), K] \tag{23}$$

and either:

$$\dot{M} = G + \bar{B} - T[F(M, \bar{B}, K) + \bar{B}] \tag{24a}$$

in the case of money financing, or:

$$\dot{B} = H(\bar{M}, B, K)\{G + B - T[F\bar{M}, B, K) + B]\} \tag{24b}$$

in the case of bond financing.

Let us take up the case of monetary finance first. Linearizing the nonlinear system (23)-(24a) about its equilibrium:

$$M^*, \bar{B}, K^*, T(Y^* + \bar{B}) = G + \bar{B}, I(r^*, K^*) = 0,$$

gives:

$$\begin{pmatrix} \dot{m} \\ \dot{k} \end{pmatrix} = \begin{pmatrix} -T'F_M & -T'F_K \\ I_r H_M & I_r H_K + I_K \end{pmatrix} \begin{pmatrix} m \\ k \end{pmatrix} \tag{25}$$

where $m \equiv M - M^*$ and $k \equiv K - K^*$. Denoting the matrix in (25) by D, the stability conditions are:

$$\operatorname{tr}(D) < 0 \tag{26a}$$

$$\det(D) > 0 \tag{26b}$$

where $\operatorname{tr}(D)$ and $\det(D)$ denote respectively the trace and determinant of D. Substituting from (II) into (26a) yields:

$$\operatorname{tr}(D) = -T'\mu\alpha - \mu\lambda \frac{I_r}{L_r}(h + I_K L_y) + I_K < 0$$

$$= -T'\mu\alpha - \mu\lambda \frac{I_r}{L_r} h + I_K \left(1 - \mu\lambda \frac{I_r}{L_r} L_y\right) < 0.$$

A sufficient condition is therefore:

$$\lambda \frac{I_r}{L_r} L_y < \frac{1}{\mu} = S' + \sigma L_y,$$

which is true since $\lambda(I_r/L_r) < \sigma$.

The proof that the determinant is positive is as follows. From equations (II):

$$\det (D) = - T' \mu \begin{vmatrix} \alpha & \beta + I_K \\ \mu\lambda \frac{I_r}{L_r} (S' - h) & I_K(1 - \mu\lambda\frac{I_r}{L_r} L_y) - \mu\lambda \frac{I_r}{L_r} h \end{vmatrix}$$

So we need to prove:

$$\alpha I_K - \lambda \frac{I_r}{L_r} \mu [\alpha I_K L_y + \alpha h + (\beta + I_K)(S' - h)] < 0.$$

The term in square brackets can be written:

$$I_K (\alpha L_y - h) + S'(\beta + I_K) + (\alpha - \beta)h$$
$$= I_K (\alpha L_y - h) + S'(\beta + I_K) + \sigma h \qquad \text{since } \alpha - \beta = \sigma.$$

Expanding this by using the definitions of α, β and h yields:

$$I_K [C_w L_y + (1 - L_w) \sigma L_y - S' L_w - C_w L_y]$$
$$+ S' (C_w - \sigma L_w + I_K) + \sigma(S' L_w + C_w L_y)$$
$$= [I_K (1 - L_w + C_w] (S' + \sigma L_y)$$
$$= \frac{I_K (1 - L_w) + C_w}{\mu}.$$

Thus the entire expression simplifies to:

$$\alpha I_K - \lambda \frac{I_r}{L_r} (I_K (1 - L_w) + C_w) < 0$$

$$C_w (I_K - \lambda \frac{I_r}{L_r}) + (1 - L_w) I_K (\sigma - \lambda \frac{I_r}{L_r}) < 0,$$

which is again true since $\lambda(I_r/L_r) < \sigma$. Q.E.D. This establishes (26b) and thus the stability of the system (25).

Now turn to the system under bond financing of deficits, equation (23) and (24b). Linearizing around equilibrium as before results in:

$$
\begin{bmatrix} \dot{b} \\ \dot{k} \end{bmatrix} = \begin{bmatrix} r(1 - T' - T'F_B) & -T'rF_K \\ I_rH_B & I_rH_K + I_K \end{bmatrix} \begin{bmatrix} b \\ k \end{bmatrix}
\tag{27}
$$

where $\dot{b} = B(t) - B^*$. Defining Δ as the matrix in (27), the stability conditions for the system are:

$$
\operatorname{tr}(\Delta) < 0
\tag{28a}
$$

$$
\det(\Delta) > 0.
\tag{28b}
$$

It is not possible, in general, to prove that these inequalities must hold. That is, as in the case where the capital stock was fixed, stability under bond finance is an empirical matter. We can, however, derive a set of intuitively plausible sufficient conditions for stability.

Consider first the trace. The upper left term will be negative if and only if condition (16b) holds. The lower right term is simply the total effect of an increase in the capital stock on investment, including any indirect effects through changing interest rates. It seems intuitively plausible that this should be negative. If this condition is met, then the model with variable capital stock is "more stable" than the model with fixed capital stock in the sense that (16b) is sufficient but no longer necessary.

Only one other condition is required to insure stability. Let us pose the following question: What would be the effect on aggregate demand of the discovery of an additional dK of capital? First, it would increase consumption through the wealth effect by $C_w dK$. Second, it would decrease investment by $I_K dK$. It seems intuitively plausible that the net effect should be contractionary, that is, $I_K + C_w < 0$. As the reader can verify from (II), this assumption suffices to establish that $H_K < 0$, and thus that (28a) holds. In fact, it proves (28b) as well. From (II) we find that $I_K + C_w < 0$ implies $F_K < 0$, which, in view of the fact that $H_B > 0$ establishes that the determinant is positive.

To recapitulate, two jointly sufficient conditions (neither one necessary) for the stability of the economy under bond finance are:

$$
F_B > \frac{1 - T'}{T'}
\tag{16b}
$$

$$
I_K + C_w < 0.
\tag{29}
$$

We would argue that both are likely to be satisfied in practice.

The argument for (29) has already been given: it asserts that the depressing effect of more capital on investment outweighs the expansionary wealth effect on consumption.[12] In considering (16b), the reader is reminded that B is the volume of interest

---

[12]Note that this is not *necessary* for stability since more capital also has a contractionary impact through the *LM* curve.

payments on the national debt, so $F_B = dY/dB$ is analogous to an ordinary multiplier for transfer payments. A number between 1.0 and 2.0 seems plausible for F_B, at least for the United States. These limits would imply that T' must exceed some number between 0.33 and 0.50 in order to satisfy (16b). The appropriate interpretation of T' is as the *marginal propensity to tax and reduce income-conditioned transfer payments* as GNP rises. According to Modigliani (1971, p. 30) when U.S. GNP rises by \$1, the combined increase in federal income taxes, state and local income taxes, social security contributions, and corporate income taxes amounts to about 50¢. Since there are also transfer payments which decline automatically with rising incomes—unemployment insurance, welfare payments of various kinds, and farm subsidies are just a few examples—it would appear that $T' > 0.50$. And this would imply that any F_B greater than unity would mean that the system is stable.[13]

4. Summary and Conclusions

The cutting edge of monetarism is the assertion that fiscal policy can not affect aggregate spending; otherwise monetarism is hardly distinguishable from an eclectic Keynesian view. The latest version of the monetarist challenge appears to accept the interest-elasticity of the demand for money and to rest, instead, on the perverse wealth effects associated with bond-financed government spending.

We have analyzed the question in the framework of an *IS-LM* model extended to allow for wealth effects and for the need of the government to finance its budget deficit or surplus. The economy can be at rest only when the budget is balanced, else the stock of financial assets in the hands of the private economy will necessarily be changing, and there will be wealth effects on private spending. In this context, an analysis of the effectiveness of fiscal and monetary policy has to cover both the comparative-static multiplier for bond-financed or money-financed government spending and the stability of the process touched off by an unbalanced government budget.

As a preparatory exercise, we study a conventional "short-run" model in which the stock of fixed capital is assumed to be constant, although net investment may be going on for as long as it takes the economy to reach a new equilibrium. Our conclusion is that if such an economy is stable at all under bond finance, fiscal policy is normally effective. If the monetarists are right, the system must be unstable. And then fiscal policy is worse than impotent: bond-financed spending drives income down without limit. Both the stability of the economy and the effectiveness of fiscal policy are in principle empirical matters. But equation (16b) provides an empirically plausible condition that guarantees both. The case of monetarist instability—deficit

[13]In the oversimplified model which omits interest payments from the budget restraint, stability under bond finance can be established on purely theoretical grounds in the case where the capital stock varies. The proof is given in the original working draft upon which the present paper is based: "Does Fiscal Policy Matter?" Econometric Research Program Memorandum No. 144, Princeton, New Jersey, August 1972.

spending contracts the economy, thus enlarging the deficit and contracting the economy still more, thus . . . —hardly sounds plausible.

Allowing the capital stock to vary complicates the story, but changes the result only slightly. It remains true that both the stability of the economy and the positivity of the multiplier for bond-financed deficit spending are empirical matters. But (16b) and (29) are a pair of plausible restrictions on the behavior functions that suffice to insure both. In this extended model, $dY/dB > 0$ is no longer a necessary condition for convergence, so that it is logically possible for the economy to be stable and fiscal policy ineffective. However, we regard this as a curiosum rather than as a vindication of monetarism. For the empirical values characteristic of the United States, at least, the evidence seems to require a comfortable "yes" in answer to the question posed in the title of this paper.

BIBLIOGRAPHY

ANDERSEN, L. C., and J. L. JORDAN, 1968, Monetary and fiscal actions: a test of their relative importance in economic stabilization, Federal Reserve Bank of St. Louis Review 51 (November), 11-24.

CHRIST, C. F., 1967, A short-run aggregate—demand model of the interdependence of monetary and fiscal policies with Keynesian and classical interest elasticities, American Economic Review 57 (May), 434-443.

CHRIST, C. F., 1968, A simple macroeconomic model with a government budget restraint, Journal of Political Economy 76, 53-67.

FAND, D. I., 1970, A monetarist model of the monetary process, Journal of Finance 25, 275-289.

FRIEDMAN, M., 1956, The quantity theory of money—a restatement, in: Friedman, M., ed., Studies in the quantity theory of money (University of Chicago Press, Chicago), 3-21.

FRIEDMAN, M., 1959, The demand for money: some theoretical and empirical results, Journal of Political Economy 67, 327-351.

FRIEDMAN, M., 1966, Interest rates and the demand for money, Journal of Law and Economics 9, 71-85.

FRIEDMAN, M., 1972, Comments on the critics, Journal of Political Economy 80, 906-950.

MODIGLIANI, F., 1971, Monetary policy and consumption, in: Federal reserve bank of Boston, Consumer spending and monetary policy: the linkages, Conference Series No. 5 (Boston), 9-84.

MURRAY, S., (forthcoming), Financing the government budget deficit, Journal of Money, Credit, and Banking.

SILBER, W. L., 1970, Fiscal policy in *IS-LM* analysis: a correction, Journal of Money, Credit and Banking 2, 461-472.

SPENCER, R. W., and W. P. YOHE, 1970, The 'crowding out' of private expenditures by fiscal policy actions, Federal Reserve Bank of St. Louis Review 52 (October), 12-24.

TOBIN, J., 1972, Friedman's theoretical framework, Journal of Political Economy 80, 852-863.

9

Crowding Out and Its Critics

*Keith M. Carlson and Roger W. Spencer**

Does Government spending displace a near-equal amount of private spending? This notion, popularly known as the "crowding-out" effect of government expenditures, has recently gained widespread attention at two levels. First, at the policy level, public officials have expressed concern that massive current and projected federal deficits will have a deleterious effect on private capital expenditures for some time to come. Second, at the academic level, "crowding out" is at least one of the issues which helps to distinguish between followers of the two major macroeconomic schools of thought—Keynesians and monetarists.

This article focuses on "crowding out" from more of an academic than a practical policy point of view. Policy implications can be drawn from this discussion, but, for the most part, the abstract economic models used in academic circles are not easily adaptable to observable phenomena. Yet the origins of the recent crowding-out controversy at the academic level are traceable to certain empirical results based on U.S. experience.

New research has been conducted in this area and some old arguments have been

Reprinted from the Federal Reserve Bank of St. Louis *Review,* (December 1975), by permission of the publisher.

* The authors acknowledge the helpful comments of James Barth, William Dewald, Dean Dutton, Thomas Havrilesky, Robert Rasche, Paul Smith, Frank Steindl, and William Yohe, none of whom should be held responsible for remaining errors.

revived.[1] Many of the developments in the crowding-out controversy can be described in the context of the standard IS-LM analytic framework. In this framework, which is the cornerstone of most macroeconomics courses taught throughout the Western world, the IS curve represents the locus of points (pairs of interest rates and real income) in which the real sector of the economy is in equilibrium and the LM curve represents a similar locus of points for which the demand for money equals the supply. The IS-LM apparatus has distinct limitations, but because of its widespread use as a pedagogical device, it serves a useful function in highlighting the issues in the crowding-out controversy.[2]

The subject of crowding out is approached by first investigating a number of separate "cases" which provide various explanations of how crowding out might occur. Next, the role of stability considerations in the controversy is assessed. Finally, several econometric models are examined to determine what empirical implications they have for the crowding-out issue.

Some Preliminaries

To set the stage for the discussion, two matters of a preliminary nature are taken up in this section. First, crowding out is defined for the purposes at hand. Much of the recent discussion of crowding out has been confusing simply because the term has not been carefully defined. Second, since the controversy has moved through several stages in recent years and has oftentimes involved complex and subtle arguments, an overview is provided as a guide to the reader.

What Is Crowding Out?

Crowding out generally refers to the economic effects of expansionary fiscal actions. If an increase in government demand, financed by either taxes or debt issuance to the public, fails to stimulate total economic activity, the private sector is said to have been "crowded out" by the government action. The presumption of a constant money supply insures that the policy action accompanying the increase in government demand is fiscal and not monetary.

The analysis may be conducted in either real or nominal terms. The crowding-out hypothesis maintains that if prices are held constant, as in typical IS-LM fashion, an increase in real government demand financed by real taxes or debt has no lasting

[1]For a survey that includes a discussion of the views of the classical economists on crowding out, see Roger W. Spencer and William P. Yohe, "The 'Crowding Out' of Private Expenditures by Fiscal Policy Actions," Federal Reserve Bank of St. Louis *Review* (October 1970), pp. 12-24.

[2]For discussion of the limitations of the IS-LM framework, see Karl Brunner and Allan Meltzer, "Monetarism: The Principal Issues, Areas of Agreement and the Work Remaining," Jerome L. Stein, ed., *Monetarism* (Amsterdam: North Holland Publishing Co., forthcoming), and "Mr. Hicks and the 'Monetarists'," *Economica* (February 1973), pp. 44-59.

effect on real income. Alternatively, crowding out implies that an increase in government spending, given flexible prices and a constant money supply, has no lasting effect on nominal income. In other words, the steady-state government spending multiplier, under the above conditions, is approximately zero.[3]

By approximately zero, we mean that increased government demand may crowd out exactly the same amount of private demand, or slightly less, or slightly more. There is complete crowding out if $1 of government demand displaces $1 of private demand, partial crowding out if $1 of government demand displaces less than $1 of private demand, and over crowding out if $1 of government demand displaces more than $1 of private demand. The increased government demand may increase aggregate demand temporarily, permanently, or not at all, as will be explained below.

Overview

The origins of the recent controversy are traceable primarily to the empirical results published by Andersen and Jordan in 1968 and supporting studies by Keran in 1969 and 1970.[4] These results indicated that nominal crowding out occurs, that is, a change in federal spending financed by either borrowing or taxes has only a negligible effect on GNP over a period of about a year. These studies did not suggest that fiscal actions have no effect, but showed instead that the initial effect of an expansionary fiscal action is positive, and this positive effect is followed in later quarters by an approximately offsetting negative effect.

The response to these empirical results took place at two levels—statistical and theoretical. At the statistical level the validity of the results was questioned.[5] Were proper statistical procedures followed in their derivation? On the theoretical level the question was whether or not the results were consistent with what seemed to be the accumulated evidence on certain theoretical propositions.[6]

Although all the returns regarding the validity of the Andersen-Jordan empirical procedures are not yet in, this article focuses on the theoretical arguments that have

[3]These definitional issues are explored in more detail in the Appendix.

[4]Leonall C. Andersen and Jerry L. Jordan, "Monetary and Fiscal Actions: A Test of Their Relative Importance in Economic Stabilization," Federal Reserve Bank of St. Louis, *Review* (November 1968), pp. 11-24; Michael W. Keran, "Monetary and Fiscal Influences on Economic Activity—The Historical Evidence," Federal Reserve Bank of St. Louis *Review* (November 1969), pp. 5-24, and "Monetary and Fiscal Influences on Economic Activity: The Foreign Experience," Federal Reserve Bank of St. Louis *Review* (February 1970), pp. 16-28.

[5]See E. Gerald Corrigan, "The Measurement and Importance of Fiscal Policy Changes," Federal Reserve Bank of New York, *Monthly Review* (June 1970), pp. 133-45: Richard G. Davis, "How Much Does Money Matter? A Look at Some Recent Evidence," Federal Reserve Bank of New York, *Monthly Review* (June 1969), pp. 119-31; and Edward M. Gramlich, "The Usefulness of Monetary and Fiscal Policy as Discretionary Stabilization Tools," *Journal of Money, Credit and Banking* (May 1971), pp. 506-32.

[6]James Tobin, "Friedman's Theoretical Framework," *Journal of Political Economy* (September/October 1972), pp. 852-63; Warren L. Smith, "A Neo-Keynesian View of Monetary Policy," in Federal Reserve Bank of Boston, *Controlling Monetary Aggregates* (June 1969), pp. 105-26; and Ronald L. Teigen, "A Critical Look at Monetarist Economics," Federal Reserve Bank of St. Louis *Review* (January 1972), pp. 10-25.

since evolved. The first theoretical argument offered in response to the crowding-out concept was an alleged inconsistency between such results and the prevailing estimates of the interest elasticity of the demand for money.[7] The critics charged, on the basis of the IS-LM framework, that in order for crowding out to occur, the proponents of these results must be assuming that the demand for money is nearly perfectly interest-inelastic. This allegation meant acceptance of the proposition that the LM curve is vertical. According to the critics, most empirical estimates do not support an interest elasticity of money demand of zero.

In answer to this charge of inconsistency, Milton Friedman and others argued that the slope of the LM curve was largely irrelevant to the crowding-out discussion.[8] In particular, Friedman pointed out the necessity of distinguishing between initial and subsequent effects of fiscal actions. According to Friedman, an "expansionary" fiscal action might first be reflected in a rise in output, but the financing of the deficit would set in motion contractionary forces which would eventually offset the initial stimulative effect.[9]

In response to the Friedman explanation, the critics developed still another argument, again pointing out an alleged inconsistency. This time the critics attempted to demonstrate that the Friedman argument, which stemmed from explicit consideration of the government's financing requirements, is not consistent with generally accepted assumptions concerning stability of the economic system (as represented by the IS-LM apparatus).[10] In particular, a debt-financed increase in government spending in a world where crowding out occurs does not set in motion a set of forces that will drive the IS-LM model to a new equilibrium once it is disturbed from an initial equilibrium.

All of these arguments are reviewed in some detail in this article. Several alternative explanations are offered as to how crowding out might occur regardless of the slope of the LM curve. A number of shortcomings of the recently advanced arguments based on stability analysis are introduced. Finally, returning to the empirical level, the results of some well-known econometric models are examined to see what light they shed on the crowding-out controversy.

[7]Tobin, "Friedman's Theoretical Framework."

[8]Milton Friedman, "Comments on the Critics," *Journal of Political Economy* (September/October 1972), pp. 906-50; and Karl Brunner and Allan H. Meltzer, "Money, Debt, and Economic Activity," *Journal of Political Economy* (September/October 1972), pp. 951-77.

[9]For further discussion of the role of the Government financing constraint, see Spencer and Yohe, "The 'Crowding Out' of Private Expenditures"; Carl F. Christ, "A Short-Run Aggregate-Demand Model of the Interdependence and Effects of Monetary and Fiscal Policies with Keynesian and Classical Interest Elasticities," *The American Economic Review* (May 1967), pp. 434-43, and "A Simple Macroeconomic Model with a Government Budget Restraint," *The Journal of Political Economy* (January/February 1968), pp. 53-67; and William L. Silber, "Fiscal Policy in IS-LM Analysis: A Correction," *Journal of Money, Credit and Banking* (November 1970), pp. 461-72.

[10]Alan S. Blinder and Robert M. Solow, "Does Fiscal Policy Matter?" *Journal of Public Economics* (November 1973), pp. 319-37; and James Tobin and Willem Buiter, "Long-Run Effects of Fiscal and Monetary Policy on Aggregate Demand," Cowles Foundation Discussion Paper No. 384 (December 13, 1974).

Crowding Out and the Slope of the LM Curve

Until recently, it was suggested by a number of analysts that contemporary monetarists view the vertical LM curve as a requirement for the existence of crowding out. James Tobin, for example, observed that a vertical LM curve leads to the "characteristic monetarist" proposition that "a shift of the *IS* locus, whether due to fiscal policy or to exogenous change in consumption and investment behavior, cannot alter Y."[11] William Branson, in his popular macroeconomics textbook, noted that

> The monetarist position is that the interest elasticities of the demand for and supply of money are zero, so that the *LM* curve is vertical. In this case fiscal policy changes the composition, but not the level of national output, while monetary policy, shifting a vertical *LM* curve, can change the level of output.[12]

Similar statements can be found in other texts.

This classical case of crowding out is examined in some detail because of its presumed importance in the crowding-out discussion. Following discussion of this classical case, several alternative explanations are offered as to how crowding can occur in the IS-LM framework, even if the interest elasticity of money demand is not zero.

The Classical Case: A Vertical LM Curve

In order for government spending to stimulate economic activity, it must either foster increases in the money stock (however defined) or increases in the rate at which the existing money stock turns over. Because the former possibility does not involve net debt purchases by the private sector or increases in taxes, there is no reason to think that private spending would be crowded out. However, if the money stock does not increase, government spending must be financed by debt issuance or increased tax revenue, either of which could result in a reduction in private spending. If private spending is not curbed by such actions, total spending rises, which implies a rise in velocity—the rate at which the money stock turns over.

It is an axiom of classical economics that velocity is virtually constant and cannot be increased by government actions. In particular, the rise in interest rates, which is associated with the issuance of government debt, does not induce the private sector to attempt to hold less money balances because the demand for money is not sensitive to interest rate changes. This idea can be illustrated graphically with the Hicksian IS-LM apparatus in Figure 1.

[11]Tobin, "Friedman's Theoretical Framework," p. 853.

[12]William H. Branson, *Macroeconomic Theory and Policy* (New York: Harper & Row, Publishers, 1972), p. 281. It is of interest to note that Tobin labels the case in which only monetary policy can affect income as characteristically monetarist and the situation in which *both* monetary and fiscal policies can alter income as characteristically neo-Keynesian. Branson symmetrically views the vertical LM case as "extreme" monetarist, and the vertical IS case as "extreme" neo-Keynesian (or "fiscalist").

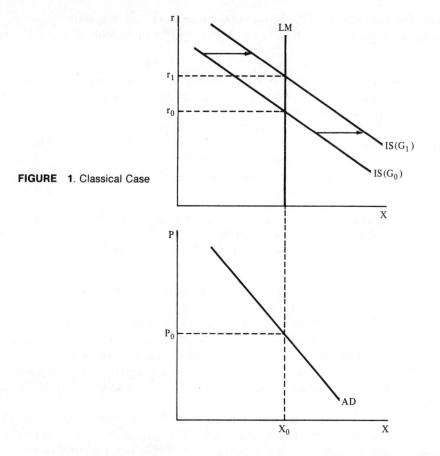

FIGURE 1. Classical Case

The LM curve is vertical (drawn for a given price level, P_0) in the classical case, reflecting a zero interest elasticity of the demand for (and supply of) money. Thus, an increase in government spending which shifts the IS curve to the right can only increase the interest rate, but does not stimulate velocity. Consequently, aggregate demand, as shown in the bottom half of Figure 1, does not shift.* One or more components of private spending are crowded out by an amount equal to the amount of the government spending increase. As a result, with aggregate demand failing to shift in response to the increase in government spending, crowding out occurs in both real and nominal terms.

Alternative Cases: Crowding Out Without a Vertical LM Curve

Five cases are presented which represent economic situations conducive to government displacement of private spending *without* the requirement of a vertical LM

---

* Although shown as a straight line, the true spirit of the classical case would be better preserved if aggregate demand were drawn as a rectangular hyperbola.

curve. The architects of these frameworks range from such disparate figures as the Chicago economists, Frank Knight and Milton Friedman, to John Maynard Keynes.

THE KEYNES CASE: EXPECTATIONS EFFECTS

John Maynard Keynes in 1936 provided the thrust for the proposition that government spending does *not* crowd out private spending in his landmark book, *The General Theory of Employment, Interest and Money*.[13] It is ironic that certain passages in that book provide strong support for the opposite contention.

Keynes, throughout his *General Theory*, was much concerned with expectations and confidence. He did not overlook the possibility, even in those times of relatively small budget deficits, that government spending could adversely affect the confidence of the private sector in its economic future.

> With the confused psychology which often prevails, the Government programme may, through its effect on "confidence," increase liquidity-preference or diminish the marginal efficiency of capital, which, again, may retard other investment unless measures are taken to offset it.[14]

An increase in liquidity preference is depicted in the IS-LM framework (see Figure 2) by a leftward shift of the LM curve, and a diminished marginal efficiency of investment schedule is reflected by the subsequent backward shift of the IS curve to the position denoted as IS (G_1).[15] If these shifts in the IS and LM curves result in no change in aggregate demand at the given price level P_o, both nominal and real crowding out will occur. However, the actual shift in aggregate demand could be positive, negative, or negligible, depending on the relative shifts of the IS and LM curves.

A number of analysts have recently invoked the Keynes case to explain the sluggishness of capital expenditures in recent years. They, however, are not the first since Keynes to attribute lackluster investment plans to stepped-up government spending. Describing a situation with some similarities to the present, Daniel Throop Smith observed (in 1939) that

> A continued experience with deficits which do not produce sustained recovery, as in this country, or a recent inflation and collapse, as in continental European countries, is likely to make a deficit matter for concern and anxiety. And if there is disbelief in the benefits of a deficit, then the new money spent by the government may well be more than offset by additional withdrawals of private money which would otherwise be spent. Likewise, if consumer incomes do increase immediately as a result of the deficit, business may anticipate that the increase is temporary and refrain from long-term commitments.[16]

[13]John Maynard Keynes, *The General Theory of Employment, Interest and Money* (New York: Harcourt, Brace and Company, 1936), pp. 119-20.

[14]Ibid., p. 120.

[15]For an algebraic analysis that takes into account some of the relevant aspects of this Keynes case, see Richard J. Cebula, "Deficit Spending, Expectations, and Fiscal Policy Effectiveness," *Public Finance* (3-4/1973), pp. 362-70.

[16]Daniel Throop Smith, "Is Deficit Spending Practical?" *Harvard Business Review* (Autumn 1939), p. 38.

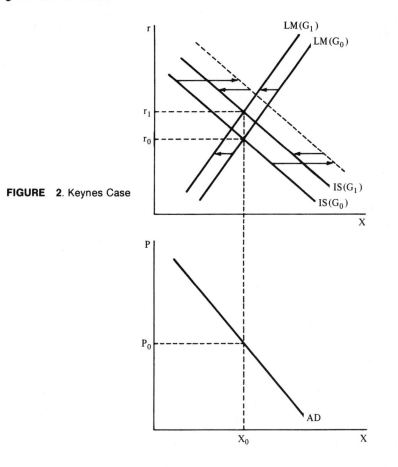

FIGURE 2. Keynes Case

THE KNIGHT CASE: A HORIZONTAL IS CURVE

This case is constructed on the basis of the writings of Frank Knight.[17] The analysis does not do justice to the complex theories of Knight but is offered as being roughly consistent with the spirit of his theory of capital and interest.[18] Though Knight certainly did not conduct his analysis within an IS-LM framework, an attempt is made to translate his ideas into such terms.

[17]No attempt is made to cite all of Knight's articles on interest and capital, but a summary is contained in Frank H. Knight, "Capital and Interest," in *Readings in the Theory of Income Distribution,* American Economic Association (Philadelphia: The Blakiston Company, 1949), pp. 384–417. The Knight case was suggested to the authors by William Dewald of Ohio State University, but he is absolved of any responsibility for the particular analysis here.

[18]The difficulty of interpreting Knight's writing is illustrated by Friedrich A. Lutz, *The Theory of Interest* (Chicago: Aldine Publishing Company, 1968), p. 104, where he introduces his chapter on Knight as follows:

It is not easy to give an exposition of Knight's theory of capital and interest. Over a number of years Knight devoted many papers to the subject; and, as anyone who ever attempted to work his way through Knight's theory knows, these writings have passages which are very difficult to understand and also, either apparently or really, contradictory.

According to Knight, we should expect no diminishing returns from investment. One reason for a nearly perfectly interest-elastic investment function is that the quantity of capital is so large relative to the additions to it that these additions should not be expected to have much of an effect on the yield of capital.[19] Another reason, according to Knight, is that investment carries with it an investment in knowledge, including research and development. As a result, a declining marginal product of capital is approximately offset by technological advances so that an aggregate invest-ment curve is drawn as nearly horizontal with respect to the yield on capital.

When translated into an IS-LM frame of reference, the Knight case introduces an interesting element to the crowding-out controversy. A perfectly flat IS curve (see Figure 3) means that fiscal actions are incapable of shifting the IS curve. An increase in government spending, for example, absorbs saving and reduces the amount avail-able for private investment (any increase in government spending shows up as a one for one displacement of private investment). Combining the flat IS curve with the LM curve provides a case where monetary policy dominates the determination of output. Fiscal actions have no effect on either output or the interest rate.[20] It is of interest to note that monetary policy has no effect on the interest rate either, an implication which runs counter to some statements by Knight.[21] But because fiscal actions do not shift aggregate demand for this so-called Knight case, the implication is that both nominal and real crowding out occur.[22]

THE ULTRARATIONAL CASE: DIRECT SUBSTITUTION EFFECTS

Recently, Professors Paul David and John Scadding developed some arguments for crowding out that are derived from an assumption of ultrarationality on the part of households.[23] The notion of ultrarationality is based on the assumption that house-

---

[19]For a discussion of the relationship between stocks and flows in the market for capital goods, see James G. Witte, Jr., "The Micro Foundations of the Social Investment Function," *The Journal of Political Economy* (October 1963), pp. 441-56.

To add to the confusion relating to the interpretation of Knight's writings, it should be noted that Knight did not accept the three-part division of resources into land, labor, and capital. His interpretation, rather, was that anyone who has control over productive capacity will employ any or all sources in such a way as to maximize the return for their use. For an analysis that preserves this broad definition of capital, see Milton Friedman, *Price Theory: A Provisional Text* (Chicago: Aldine Publishing Company, 1962), pp. 244-63.

[20]It is surprising that this case has not received more attention in the literature because it is every bit as monetarist as the vertical LM case. For an example of one writer who does mention this case, see Martin Bronfenbrenner, *Income Distribution Theory* (Chicago: Aldine-Atherton, 1971), pp. 339-40. However, Bronfenbrenner dismisses it as a long-run case with little short-run significance.

[21]See Knight, "Capital and Interest," p. 406.

[22]Though the Knight case has not been empirically tested, it has implications which are consistent with the results of a number of empirical studies. The Andersen-Jordan results relating changes in GNP to monetary and fiscal actions are consistent with such a case. The inability to find a stable relationship between interest rates and various measures of fiscal action is also consistent. And finally, the stability of real interest rates over time—at least to the extent real rates have been measured—provides indirect evidence in support of the Knight model.

[23]Paul A. David and John L. Scadding, "Private Savings; Ultrarationality, Aggregation, and 'Denison's Law,'" *Journal of Political Economy* (March/April 1974), pp. 225-50.

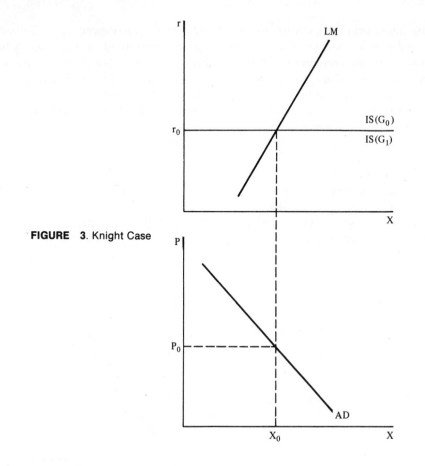

FIGURE 3. Knight Case

holds regard the corporate and government sectors as extensions of themselves—as instruments of their private interests. This fundamental behavioral assumption is offered as an explanation for Denison's Law—the observed stability of the ratio of gross private saving to GNP in the United States.[24]

The David-Scadding article is of relevance to the crowding-out controversy because of its fiscal policy implications. The assumption of ultrarationality implies displacement effects of government spending which the authors call "*ex ante* crowding out." They argue that stability of the gross private saving ratio in the face of substantial variation in the government deficit suggests that private debt and public debt are close substitutes. An extra dollar of government deficit displaces a dollar of

---

[24]Edward F. Denison, "A Note on Private Saving," *The Review of Economics and Statistics* (August 1958), pp. 261-67. David and Scadding suggest that if government and corporate activity simply substitute for, rather than augment, household activity, there should be virtually no change in such broad aggregates as the ratio of gross private saving to GNP.

private investment expenditure because deficit financing is viewed as public investment and substitutes for private investment, in that households tend to classify both
in terms of future consumption benefits. This case is shown in Figure 4, where an
increase in government spending financed by borrowing induces an offsetting change
in private investment so that the IS curve does not shift on balance.

Similarly, government consumption has a displacement effect on private consumption. Tax-financed expenditures are viewed in terms of their present consumption
benefits and substitute perfectly for private consumption. With an increase in government spending for consumption financed by increased taxes, the increase in taxes
reduces private consumption with no effect on private saving. As a result, there is a
shift in the composition of output from the private sector to the government, but
there is no shift in aggregate demand.

Consequently, with tax-financed government expenditures displacing private consumption and government bond issues (deficit financing) displacing private debt
issues, there is no way that fiscal actions can affect total demand for goods and

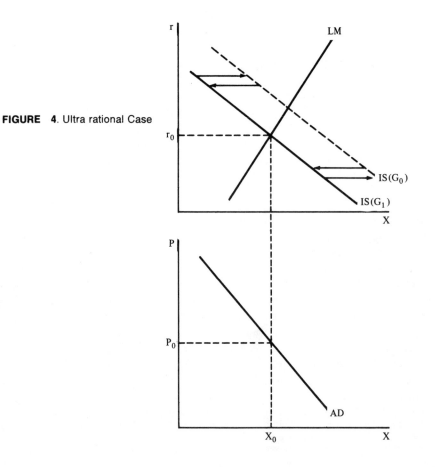

FIGURE   4. Ultra rational Case

services. In the parlance of the IS-LM framework, fiscal actions (defined as either tax- or debt-financed government expenditures) have no net effect on the IS curve or on aggregate demand, which implies both nominal and real crowding out. Also, for this case, fiscal actions have no influence on interest rates.

Whether the David-Scadding ultrarational case is to be taken as a serious explanation of crowding out is an open question. Yet it is important to note the implications of this model because it represents a departure from the severe restrictions implicit in the IS-LM model. In particular, the IS-LM model allows for no substitution between private spending and public spending, and David-Scadding have shown that moving away from these restrictive assumptions acts in the direction of reducing the fiscal policy multipliers. Furthermore, by way of Denison's Law, they conclude that the evidence leans more toward the extreme of ultrarationality than the extreme of the IS-LM model.

THE EXTENDED IS-LM CASE: PRICE FLEXIBILITY

All cases discussed thus far have not presented any conflicts with respect to the nominal versus real crowding-out issue because aggregate demand typically does not shift. There is, however, another way in which crowding out might occur, reflecting a response of the price level to a step-up in government spending. This case argues that crowding out is possible even without the assumption that aggregate demand does not shift. The implication for nominal versus real crowding out is ambiguous for this case, however.

Robert Rasche constructed a sophisticated version of the IS-LM apparatus, which was based primarily on the textbook presentation of Robert Crouch.[25] The model included wealth in the consumption and money demand functions, a government budget constraint, and a labor sector, as well as an endogenous price level. According to Rasche's analysis, an increase in real government purchases, financed either by taxes or debt issuance, increases aggregate demand and, consequently, the commodity price level. Although there may also be a rise in consumption owing to a presumed positive effect of debt issuance on wealth, there is an offsetting increase in the demand for money associated with such wealth gains (see Figure 5). The rise in the price level reduces private consumption as well as the real supply of money. Together with a decline in the amount of private investment owing to an increase in interest rates, these factors tend to crowd out an amount of real private expenditures equivalent to the increase in government purchases. Crowding out occurs in this model in real terms, but with a higher price level; crowding out is not likely to occur in nominal terms.

These results lead Rasche to conclude that nominal crowding out requires "extreme" assumptions about the interest elasticity and the wealth elasticity of the demand for real cash balances. It should be pointed out, however, that Rasche, in his

---

[25]Robert H. Rasche, "A Comparative Static Analysis of Some Monetarist Propositions," *Federal Reserve Bank of St. Louis Review* (December 1973), pp. 15-23; and Robert L. Crouch, *Macroeconomics* (New York: Harcourt Brace Jovanovich, Inc., 1972).

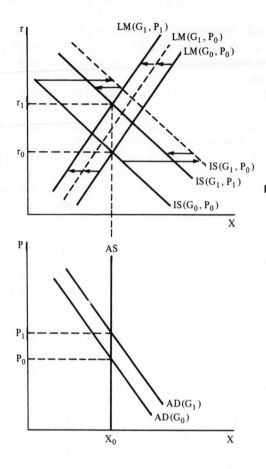

FIGURE 5. Extended IS-LM Case

manipulation of the model, did not allow for a Keynes expectation effect, an ultrarational direct substitution effect, or a Knight effect, all of which leave the aggregate demand curve unmoved in response to an initial increase in government spending.

THE FRIEDMAN CASE: INITIAL VS. SUBSEQUENT EFFECTS

Milton Friedman's role in the crowding-out controversy was established in a series of articles published in the *Journal of Political Economy* over the period 1970 to 1972.[26] Friedman did not rely solely on the IS-LM model as a framework for his analysis, but most of his ideas can be summarized in such a context. Friedman denied emphatically that the monetarist propositions rested on the shape of the LM locus.

[26]Friedman, "Comments on the Critics"; "A Theoretical Framework for Monetary Analysis," *Journal of Political Economy* (March/April 1970), pp. 193–238; and "A Monetary Theory of Nominal Income," *Journal of Political Economy* (March/April 1971), pp. 323–37.

Instead, Friedman stressed the continuing effects of deficit finance and a fundamental distinction between stocks and flows.

Friedman dealt with a large number of complex issues in his reply to the critics,
and it is difficult to determine to what extent he supported the notion of fiscal
crowding out. His chief point seems to have been that the power of monetary actions
far surpasses that of fiscal actions, which is not the same thing as declaring a belief in
crowding out. Nevertheless, he concluded that the expansionary effect of an increase
in government spending by borrowing is likely to be minor.

To show the Friedman case, consider Figure 6. The IS curve is drawn quite flat,
reflecting Friedman's statement that " 'saving' and 'investment' have to be interpreted much more broadly than neo-Keynesians tend to interpret it. . . ."[27] Though
Friedman does not emphasize it, this interpretation puts him close to the Knight case
because the implication of more inclusive investment tends to flatten the IS curve

[27]Friedman, "Comments on the Critics," pp. 915.

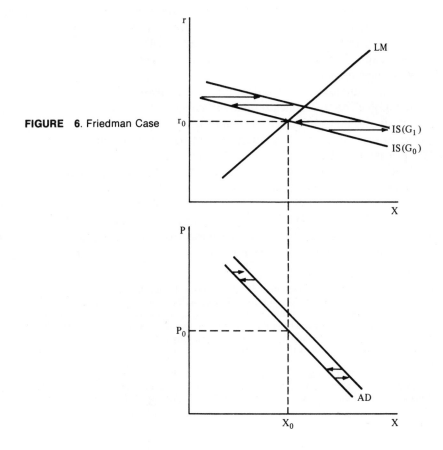

FIGURE　6. Friedman Case

and dampen the power of fiscal actions.[28] In addition, Friedman indicates that the wealth effects of increased bond holdings on spending will be minimal because increases in debt would tend to be offset by an increase in expected tax liabilities.

Perhaps an even more important reason to doubt the long-run expansive capacity of increased government spending is its effect on the future production of goods and services. Friedman notes that debt-supported government spending leads to a "reduction in the physical volume of assets created because of lowered private productive investment."[29] In other words, potential output in the future will be lowered relative to what it would otherwise be with the transfer of resources from private investment, which generates the future capital stock, to government spending, which absorbs it.

Apart from these objections to the idea of stimulative government actions, an initial shift of the IS curve (see Figure 6) may still be consistent with crowding out over the longer term. For a given LM curve, the relatively flat IS curve, which Friedman apparently envisions, yields a shift of aggregate demand which is very small. In addition, Friedman notes that "the evidences of government debt are largely in place of evidences of private debt—people hold Treasury bills instead of bills issued by, for example, U.S. Steel."[30] If this statement is given the ultrarational interpretation discussed earlier, private expenditure is cut back, offsetting the initial increase in government spending. Whether such an effect is a partial or complete offset is not made clear, but if it exists, the IS and aggregate demand curves move back toward their original positions.

These are the initial effects of a debt-financed increase in government spending, but Friedman goes on to emphasize that subsequent effects will continue as long as a deficit exists. In later periods the IS curve will continue shifting back to the left because private expenditures continue to be cut back as government debt is substituted for private debt. Eventually, the stock of private wealth will be reduced relative to what it otherwise would be because of reduced investment, thereby reinforcing the leftward movement of the IS curve.[31]

Because Friedman is not clear with regard to the role of commodity prices in his analysis, it is difficult to assess his view of real versus nominal crowding out. It is perhaps best simply to conclude that the impact of an increase in debt-financed government spending is very small and that there is little difference between the

[28]Norman Van Cott and Gary Santoni, "Friedman versus Tobin: A Comment," *Journal of Political Economy* (July/August 1974), pp. 883-85. In this article the authors show that the effect of broadening the interpretation of saving and investment is to make the IS schedule flatter. They demonstrate this by adding the interest rate as an argument in the consumption function and then showing that the extent to which the IS curve is shifted is unaffected by fiscal actions; only the slope is changed.
[29]Friedman, "Comments on the Critics," p. 917.
[30]Ibid.
[31]For a recent paper that works out a numerical example of the first-round and subsequent effects of a fiscal action in an IS-LM framework, see Laurence H. Meyer, "The Balance Sheet Identity, the Government Financing Constraint, and the Crowding-Out Effect," *Journal of Monetary Economics* (January 1975), pp. 65-78.

effects of debt versus tax-financed expenditure. A relatively flat IS curve yields these results, and any ultrarational effects would reinforce them.

Crowding Out and Stability Considerations

The Friedman emphasis on the longer-run effects of monetary and fiscal actions prompted two major papers (one by Alan Blinder and Robert Solow and the other by James Tobin and Willem Buiter) that attempted to demonstrate that the crowding-out effect of fiscal actions is not consistent with the assumption of stability of the economic system, as represented by the IS-LM model.[32] Both of these papers are discussed in this section along with a third—by Karl Brunner and Allan Meltzer—which actually antedates the other two.[33] All three models essentially employ comparative static tools to examine a dynamic phenomenon.

The Long-Run Balanced Budget Models

BLINDER AND SOLOW
Recently, Blinder and Solow developed a rigorous theoretical attack on the crowding-out thesis.[34] They envisioned three possible levels of crowding out:

1. The government undertakes activities which would otherwise be provided, on a one-for-one basis, by the private sector. They point out that this sort of crowding out (to the extent it exists) would occur regardless of how the government spending was financed;

2. Debt issues floated by the government to finance its spending drive up interest rates and crowd out private borrowing;

3. Increases in wealth, derived from the issuance of government bonds, increase money demand, that is, shift the LM curve leftward sufficiently to negate the rightward shifts of the IS curve.

Blinder-Solow constructed an extended version of the IS-LM framework which incorporated consumption and money demand as functions of wealth, and a government budget constraint providing for government debt interest payments. They ad-

---

[32]Blinder and Solow, "Does Fiscal Policy Matter?" and Tobin and Buiter, "Long-Run Effects."

[33]Brunner and Meltzer, "Money, Debt, and Economic Activity."

[34]Many of the ideas in the Blinder-Solow article did not originate with them. See Frank G. Steindl, "Wealth, Fiscal Policy and the Government Budget Restraint," unpublished (April 1973). For papers criticizing the Blinder-Solow analysis, see Albert Ando, "Some Aspects of Stabilization Policies, The Monetarist Controversy, and the MPS Model," *International Economic Review* (October 1974), pp. 541-71; Paul E. Smith, "The Government Budget Constraint, Crowding Out, and Stability of Equilibrium," unpublished (May 1975); and James R. Barth, James T. Bennett, and Richard H. Sines, "Fiscal Policy and Macroeconomic Activity," paper presented at the meetings of the Southern Economic Association, New Orleans, Louisiana, November 14, 1975.

hered to the usual IS-LM customs of treating the price level as fixed and of ignoring the existence of a banking system.

Blinder-Solow then attempted to discern the likelihood of crowding-out phenomena occurring by investigating the stability properties of the model. They arrived at the following theoretical implications:

1. If government spending financed by bond issuance is contractionary, as (according to Blinder-Solow) monetarists claim, the IS-LM model is unstable;

2. If government spending is expansive, as neo-Keynesians claim, but *less* expansive than government spending financed by money creation, the model is unstable;

3. If government spending financed by bond issuance is *more* expansive than government spending financed by money creation, the model is stable.

The unusual result that theoretical stability conditions imply that bond-financed government spending is more stimulative than money-financed government spending comes about because of the inclusion of interest payments on outstanding debt in the government budget constraint. For the model to be stable, the budget must be in balance in the long run to insure unchanging stocks of money and debt. In order for the budget gap to close after the initial shock of fiscal stimulus, income must rise by a larger amount in the bond-financed case than in the money-financed case. This result follows because higher tax receipts must be induced to offset the increased interest payments on the government debt.

TOBIN AND BUITER

Recently Tobin and Buiter also formulated an IS-LM model for the purpose of examining the crowding-out thesis. Although some of the equations differ from those employed by Blinder-Solow, the basic assumptions, such as a constant price level, and the methodology, which is marked by the stability requirement of a balanced budget process, are virtually the same.[35] Their analysis is also marked by the stability requirement of a balanced budget process. Like Blinder-Solow, Tobin-Buiter utilized more than one variation of the basic IS-LM model, and, like Blinder-Solow, they arrived at the conclusion that the stability considerations inherent in the balanced budget requirement generate a positive government spending multiplier. Tobin-Buiter emphasized that the analysis is conducted for periods in which the economy is less than fully employed.

BRUNNER AND MELTZER

Another model has recently been developed which is adaptable to analysis of the crowding-out question. Brunner and Meltzer constructed a model of the economy along IS-LM lines, but with a number of significant differences. The Brunner-Meltzer model contains markets for real assets, financial assets, and current ouput and

[35]Although the bulk of their analysis assumes a constant price level, as does an earlier model on which their paper was based, Tobin-Buiter present one version of the model which employs a variable price level.

permits wealth owners to choose among money, bonds, real capital, and current expenditures. In contrast with the Blinder-Solow and basic Tobin-Buiter models, the Brunner-Meltzer model permits the price level to be determined endogenously and includes a banking sector. The analysis also features, as do the other models, stability considerations and a government sector which issues interest-bearing debt.

Apparently, these common elements of the models are the elements which lead to the unusual results already noted in the Blinder-Solow model and which also emerge in the Brunner-Meltzer model. In particular, Brunner-Meltzer find that government spending financed by debt issuance is more stimulative than government spending accompanied by expansionary monetary actions. Such a result is again dictated by the requirement of a balanced budget. Once disturbed by, say, an increase in government spending, the budget is required to return to balance, and the presence of interest payments in the budget constraint means that a larger increase in income is required for bond financing than for money financing.

Brunner-Meltzer recognized this obvious discrepancy between their model's results and the historical evidence, particularly as interpreted by monetarists. They note that their model results imply "that inflation or deflation can occur without any change in B [the monetary base, which is the prime determinant of the money supply]."[36] Brunner-Meltzer take a markedly different view of the causes of inflation *outside* their model construct and in the context of observable phenomena: "Our analysis of inflation, presented at the Universities–National Bureau Conference on Secular Inflation, analyzes the issue in more detail and explains why most inflations or deflations have resulted from changes in money."[37]

One must bear in mind that the results of the Brunner-Meltzer model are predicated on: (1) the absence of money illusion (in the usual sense), but the existence of a possible wealth illusion by way of incomplete discounting of future tax liabilities; (2) the requirement of a balanced budget; (3) a fixed capital stock (Blinder-Solow, in contrast, present a variation of their model in which the capital stock is permitted to grow); (4) no labor sector (to facilitate changes in output in lieu of the absence of a changing capital stock); and (5) the presumption that asset prices respond more strongly to an increase in government debt than to an increase in the monetary base.[38]

Shortcomings of the Stability Models

The recent attack on the crowding-out thesis by way of stability analysis introduces a new element into the controversy. There are several reasons to question the impli-

---

[36]Brunner and Meltzer, "Money, Debt, and Economic Activity," p. 973 (bracketed words supplied).
[37]Ibid.
[38]The last-mentioned item is particularly critical for the Brunner-Meltzer results. Whereas asset prices can be expected to respond in a positive manner to increases in the monetary base, there is ambiguity in the response of asset prices to the issuance of government debt. A positive wealth effect (given incomplete discounting of a future tax liabilities) must outweigh a negative substitution effect (caused by government debt competing in asset markets with private debt) for the Brunner-Meltzer results to hold.

cations of these models of the economy which indicate that crowding out is not consistent with model stability.

Treatment of Price Level Changes

The Blinder-Solow model and the basic Tobin-Buiter model, which are somewhat sophisticated versions of the basic IS-LM apparatus, permit no rule for price level changes.[39] Considering world-wide economic developments over the past decade, one must question the relevance of so-called "structural" models which omit the existence of inflationary pressures and inflationary expectations. Moreover, an important channel through which crowding out might occur is closed off when price level changes are forbidden to emerge.

Blinder-Solow recognized this deficiency of their model to some extent, as indicated by their acknowledgment that the fiscal policy multiplier would be lowered in several ways by the inclusion of an endogenously determined price level: (1) higher prices lower the real value of the money stock and shift the LM curve to the left; (2) higher prices reduce real wealth, and thus consumption, shifting the IS curve to the left; (3) progressive taxes combined with inflation increase the real yield of the tax system, which also tends to shift the IS curve leftward; (4) a rising price level depresses exports and induces imports in an open economy, which again pushes the IS curve to the left.[40]

Blinder-Solow maintained that although the fiscal multiplier will be less than before with the inclusion of price level changes, the sign of the multiplier will remain positive. Because it is their view that the crowding-out hypothesis requires the fiscal multiplier to be negative, the authors considered only the sign of the coefficient to be at issue. This, however, is a gross exaggeration. To our knowledge, there have been no claims that the crowding-out hypothesis requires that a dollar of government spending, unsupported by monetary expansion, *must* reduce private spending by *more* than a dollar, which is the implication of a negative fiscal policy multiplier.[41] Crowding out of the private sector occurs not only when $1 of government spending reduces private spending by $1 (a multiplier of zero), but when $1 of government spending reduces private spending by 50 cents (a multiplier of 0.50). Crowding out, then, is a matter of degree rather than of absolute magnitudes. A negative multiplier is not a necessary condition for crowding out. And the omission of changing price levels in various IS-LM models contributes to the likelihood that crowding-out tendencies will not emerge.

---

[39]The Brunner-Meltzer model permits price level flexibility but excludes a labor sector, which presumably plays an important part in realistic attempts to capture the economic structure.

[40]Blinder-Solow added this final price effect in "Analytical Foundations of Fiscal Policy," in *The Economics of Public Finance* (Washington, D.C.: The Brookings Institution, 1974), p. 47.

[41]It should be pointed out that various econometric models indeed have uncovered negative fiscal multipliers.

BALANCED BUDGET EQUILIBRIUM

The three models under consideration show that in order for the budget to be balanced, and for the model to be in long-run equilibrium, the fiscal policy multiplier must be positive. A full equilibrium requires that the levels of stocks and flows be unchanging. But the question remains, How does such a formal analysis contribute to an explanation of the empirical results that imply crowding out occurs?

Tobin-Buiter made two significant points in this connection. First, they questioned the ability of economic analysis—presumably, as incorporated in abstract models—to track changing economic variables to some logical end. "The trouble with such discussions, including this one, is that a long run constructed to track the ultimate consequences of anything is a never-never land. For that abstraction we apologize in advance."[42] If one is really interested in tracking changes in economic variables over time, the better approach would be to construct dynamic models rather than comparative static models.

Second, Tobin-Buiter questioned the stability requirements (including a balanced budget) associated with the IS-LM investigations into the crowding-out controversy. Their concluding remarks were:

> Finally, we observe again that it is disturbing that the qualitative properties of models—the signs of important system-wide multipliers, the stability of equilibria—can turn on relatively small changes of specifications or on small differences in values of coefficients. We do not feel entitled to use the "correspondence principle" assumption of stability to derive restrictions on structural equations and parameters. *There is no divine guarantee that the economic system is stable.*[43]

The economic system may be stable in the sense that the U.S. economy has not exploded, but it is a long jump from that sort of stability to one which requires stock-flow equilibrium including a balanced budget. Indeed, the budget of the U.S. government has been in deficit in eleven of the past fifteen years.

Stock-flow equilibrium models, then, are basically empty of empirical content. Although there may have been periods in which some of the relevant flows were approximately in balance, one would be hard pressed to uncover data points corresponding to periods of unchanging stocks. Without the necessary data, it is impossible to confirm or refute the hypotheses associated with stock-flow equilibrium models.

FISCAL VS. MONETARY STIMULUS

The underlying assumptions and stability requirements of the models in question combine to produce a most curious result: government spending financed by debt issuance is more expansionary than government spending accompanied by money

---

[42]Tobin-Buiter, "Long-Run Effects," p. 1.
[43]Ibid., p. 42 (italics supplied).

creation. The expansionary effect is summarized in terms of real output in the Blinder-Solow model and in terms of prices in the Brunner-Meltzer model.

These theoretical implications run contrary to virtually every investigation conducted into the impacts of fiscal and monetary policy actions on economic activity. None of the architects of these models attempted to reconcile the model implications with the mass of empirical studies contradicting them.

Brunner-Meltzer acknowledged this discrepancy. However, they offered no explanation for the fact that even though their model implies that bond-financed government spending is more inflationary than money-financed spending, their own empirical studies indicate just the opposite.[44] One is led to conclude that manipulation of these theoretical models constitutes an interesting academic exercise but contributes little of practical significance to the crowding out controversy. With empirical considerations coming to the fore, the discussion now turns to the econometric literature to determine what evidence that approach has brought to bear on the issue of crowding out.

Econometric Models and Crowding Out

In a recent study of a number of econometric models, Gary Fromm and Lawrence Klein published simulation results showing the implied government expenditure and tax multipliers for these models.[45] The results showed long-run government spending multipliers ranging from about 1 to 5 when measured in terms of impact on current dollar GNP.[46] However, the majority of the large models surveyed revealed that crowding out did occur in real terms over time. Some indicated $1 of government spending for goods and services crowded out even more than $1 of private spending.

For example, the Wharton Mark III Model yielded a multiplier of minus 3 after forty quarters, and the Bureau of Economic Analysis (U.S. Department of Commerce) Model gave a real government spending multiplier over the same time period of minus 23. These results go well beyond monetarists' contentions that complete crowding out gives a multiplier of approximately zero, though these results are less than clear on the issue of nominal crowding out.

Fromm and Klein's survey of the empirical results suggested that crowding out typically occurred because of a rising price level, capacity constraints, and rising

[44]Karl Brunner, Michele Fratianni, Jerry L. Jordan, Alan H. Meltzer, and Manfred J. Neumann, "Fiscal and Monetary Policies in Moderate Inflation," *Journal of Money, Credit and Banking* (February 1973), pp. 313-53.

[45]Gary Fromm and Lawrence R. Klein, "A Comparison of Eleven Econometric Models of the United States," *The American Economic Review* (May 1973), pp. 385-93. These models, unlike the IS-LM abstractions discussed earlier, were not forced to a full stock-flow equilibrium.

[46]Blinder and Solow cited these results as attesting to the absence of crowding out in large income-expenditure models. Acknowledging the nonexistence of government budget constraints in the models, they added that despite this deficiency, "All we can do now is render a verdict on the basis of the evidence already in." They ignored the real crowding out results implied by the econometric models, which is surprising, in that their own model emphasized the crowding out issue in real terms. Blinder and Solow, "Analytical Foundations of Fiscal Policy," p. 47.

nominal interest rates. These results are consistent with those implied by the extended IS-LM case described above, and they do not necessarily corroborate crowding out of the nonshifting aggregate demand variety, that is, those cases which imply that crowding out occurs because fiscal actions are offset by other components of aggregate demand.

However, Fromm and Klein recognized that the model simulations produced evidence not in accord with the usual standard Keynesian presumption of positive government spending multipliers:

> Conventional textbook expositions generally depict real expenditure multipliers approaching positive asymptotes. In fact, most of the models here show such multipliers reaching a peak in two or three years and then declining thereafter in fluctuating paths. At the end of five to ten years, some of the models show that continued sustained fiscal stimulus has ever-increasing *perverse* impacts.[47]

Klein suggested elsewhere that perhaps these new estimates of the fiscal multiplier are not as damaging to the Keynesian position as they initially appear.[48] After all, it takes a considerable length of time in some of the models for the government spending multiplier to approach zero or turn negative, and policymakers historically have shown little concern for the long run. We would only add that this argument reflects the progression of the debate on crowding out from "Does it exist?" to "What is the time period?"

As far as small models are concerned, the monetarist model of the Federal Reserve Bank of St. Louis set off much of the current controversy. Fiscal crowding out emerges in the reduced-form equations published in the St. Louis *Review* only after a period of time, even though it is a much shorter period of time than that of the large income-expenditure models, and it occurs in nominal terms rather than in just real terms. Government spending, as measured by high-employment expenditures, exercises a relatively strong influence on GNP (assuming a constant change in the money supply) in the current quarter and the next quarter, but it is approximately offset within a year's time.

These results, which are confirmed by regression analysis employing data through mid-1975, should not be interpreted to suggest that "government spending doesn't matter"; it matters very much over a certain period. Moreover, if government spending were to accelerate or decelerate rapidly rather than be held to a steady rate of change, the impact on GNP would be considerable.

The chief reason that these reduced-form results are of interest is that they do not follow from a structural model that constrains the channels of transmission from fiscal actions to economic activity. Government expenditures cover a wide range of activities, some of which substitute for private consumption and investment and

---

[47]Fromm and Klein, "A Comparison," p. 393 (italics supplied).

[48]See Lawrence R. Klein, "Commentary on 'The State of the Monetarist Debate,'" Federal Reserve Bank of St. Louis, *Review* (September 1973), pp. 9–12.

others which serve as substitutes or complements to private factors of production.[49] With such diverse effects, any model which restricts the transmission of fiscal actions to income and/or interest rate channels runs the risk of missing the full effects of government interaction with the private sector.[50] The St. Louis results certainly do not do justice to the measurement of the effects of the complexities of the government-spending process, but they serve the function of questioning the results from models which restrict the operation of fiscal actions via fixed channels.

Summary and Conclusions

This article has surveyed the recent literature on the subject of the crowding-out effect of fiscal actions. Crowding out was defined as a steady-state government spending multiplier of near zero, a definition which was extended to differentiate the terms "nominal" and "real" crowding out.

This survey indicates that the controversy has taken place on two fronts—theoretical and empirical. First, the theoretical literature has developed primarily with reference to the IS-LM model or modifications thereof. Several cases were examined which serve as candidates providing theoretical support for the crowding-out hypothesis. In addition, the role of stability conditions in the crowding-out controversy was examined. In general, the conclusion was that stability considerations are of limited relevance with respect to the acceptance or rejection of the crowding-out hypothesis.

The empirical literature, on the other hand, has taken the form of simulations of government actions and has yielded results that show signs of being consistent with the crowding-out hypothesis. This crowding out tends to be very slow in developing, however, and occurs in real rather than nominal terms. The St. Louis results still stand out relative to the large econometric models in that crowding out occurs more quickly and also in nominal terms.

As a result of this survey, it is clear that the crowding-out controversy continues to exist. Apparently these issues will not approach resolution until additional structural models are developed and tested. The Keynesians have developed many models, but

[49]We, like most other analysts, have had little to say about the effect of fiscal actions on aggregate supply. For an attempt to enrich standard macroeconomic analysis with such considerations, see Kenneth J. Arrow and Mordecai M. Kurz, *Public Investment, the Rate of Return, and Optimal Fiscal Policy* (Baltimore: Johns Hopkins Press, 1970), and Lowell E. Gallaway and Paul E. Smith, "The Government Budget Constraint and Aggregate Supply," paper presented at the meetings of the Southern Economic Association, New Orleans, Louisiana, November 14, 1975.

[50]See R. L. Basmann, "Remarks Concerning the Application of Exact Finite Sample Distribution Functions for GCL Estimates in Econometric Statistical Inference," *Journal of the American Statistical Association* (December 1963), p. 944, where he says:

"... the entire burden of statistical inference in econometric simultaneous equations models falls on the unconstrained estimates and test statistics associated with the reduced-form, at least, if empirical confirmation of the underlying economic postulates is the goal aimed at. Whenever the unconstrained reduced-form statistics are judged to be in good agreement with the propositions (theorems) deduced from the underlying economic postulates, then do the structural estimates emerge as sound and convenient summaries of that part of the sample statistical information which is relevant to the numerical values of structural parameters, but generally not otherwise."

these models have not been tested as interdependent units.[51] Monetarists, on the other hand, have not offered structural models to go along with their reduced-form results.[52] Such a turn toward hypothesis testing could lead toward a resolution of the issues in the crowding-out controversy. Although the controversy has been explored in this article primarily on a theoretical level, the implications of these issues for practical matters of stabilization policy are of great significance.

Appendix

For purposes of definition consider Figure 7, Panel (A) which is a representation of the market for total output of goods and services. The intersection of aggregate supply (AS_o) and demand (AD_o) determine the equilibrium level of output, X_o, and the price, P_o, at which it will be sold. Label this intersection as point A and interpret it as an initial equilibrium. Now, introduce an expansionary fiscal action like increased government demand for goods and services financed by sales of government debt to the public.

Assume that the net effect of increased government demand and the issuance of debt is an increased demand for goods and services, as indicated by the shift of the demand curve to AD_1. Further, suppose that the expanded government sector adversely affects efficiency and productive capacity, resulting in a shift of the supply curve to AS_1. If the new equilibrium occurs anywhere on the vertical line through point A, say at point B, we say that *real* crowding out has occurred, that is, increased real government demand has been completely offset by a decline in real private demand.

Consider now Panel (B) in Figure 7. The curved line drawn through point A is a rectangular hyperbola indicating that P times X, which is defined as the nominal value of total output (that is, GNP), is constant and equal to $P_o X_o$. In other words, there is an infinite number of combinations of P and X, besides P_o and X_o, which would give the same dollar value of total output as at point A. Suppose that in response to an expansionary fiscal action, aggregate demand and aggregate supply shift in various directions (depending on the assumptions made) and the new equilibrium settles on the curved line, say at point B or C. Under these conditions, *nominal* crowding out is said to occur. That is, an increase in government spending has been offset by a decline in the dollar amount of spending by the private sector.

This distinction between nominal and real crowding out is important because clearly one does not imply the other. This is shown in Panel (C), which combines the

---

[51]See Keith M. Carlson, "Monetary and Fiscal Actions in Macroeconomic Models," this *Review* (January 1974), pp. 8–18. A suggested testing of models as interdependent units requires that the model be specified in structural form but that the testing of the model focuses on the reduced form. For further discussion of this approach, see James L. Murphy, *Introductory Econometrics* (Homewood, Ill.: Richard D. Irwin, Inc., 1974).

[52]For recent efforts in this direction, however, see Leonall C. Andersen, "A Monetary Model of Nominal Income Determination," this *Review* (June 1975), pp. 9–19.

definitions of real and nominal crowding out from Panels (A) and (B). The lines are not demand and supply curves; they are the loci of points defining real and nominal crowding out.

Note that the lines are now drawn as the midpoint of a shaded band. This is done to reflect the crowding-out hypothesis, that is, an increase in government demand, not supported by monetary expansion, results in a steady-state income multiplier of *approximately* zero. The middle of these bands represents those points at which $1 of government demand crowds out exactly $1 of private demand. The shading to the right of either line describes that area in which partial crowding out (a multiplier between 0 and $+1$) occurs; the shading to the left of either line describes that area in

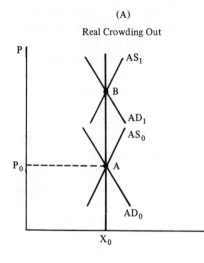

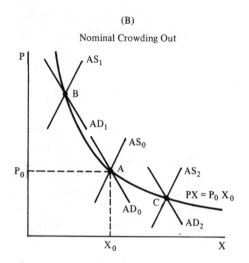

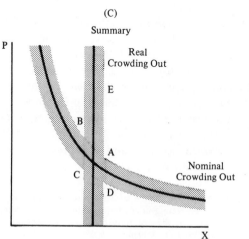

FIGURE 7.

which over crowding out (a multiplier between 0 and −1) occurs. Of course, it is possible that $1 of government spending might crowd out more than $2 of private spending, resulting in a multiplier of less than −1 and an equilibrium point to the left of either of the bands.

Various combinations of real and nominal crowding out are possible, given an expansionary fiscal action. For example, at point A there is partial nominal and partial real crowding out. At point B there is partial nominal, but over real, crowding out and so on around the intersection of the two bands through point D. At some point outside this area such as point E, there is partial real crowding out, but a complete absence of any sort of nominal crowding out. It is clear that a complete analysis of the fiscal process requires an assessment of both the demand and supply factors involved in order to describe accurately the extent to which nominal and real crowding out might occur.

10

Changing Views of the Phillips Curve

Thomas M. Humphrey

One of the more fashionable tools of contemporary macroeconomic analysis is the so-called "Phillips curve," named after its originator, British economist A. W. Phillips. An empirical relation between the rate of wage-price change and the rate of unemployment, the Phillips curve purportedly shows the set of inflation-unemployment "trade-offs," or feasible policy choices, available to the economic stabilization authorities. First introduced in 1958, the Phillips curve gained swift acceptance by economists who used it to analyze the persistent problems plaguing economic policy-makers attempting to achieve simultaneously society's apparently conflicting goals of high employment and stable prices.

Over the past fifteen years the Phillips curve has played a prominent role in policy discussion and formulation. For example, Phillips curve analysis provided a rationale for the incomes (wage-price) and labor-market (manpower) policies implemented during the past decade. The recent Phase I and II programs, as well as the earlier wage-price guidepost, job-training, and retraining programs, were designed within a framework that can be described in terms of the Phillips curve.

. . . The rapid penetration and assimilation of early Phillips curve analysis in the non-technical economic literature has been matched by equally rapid recent shifts in

Reprinted with deletions from the Federal Reserve Bank of Richmond, *Monthly Review* (July, 1973), pp. 2–13, by permission of the publisher and the author.

economists' understanding and interpretation of the Phillips curve. Initially, the Phillips curve was interpreted as a simple, stable, and permanent empirical relationship between wage-price changes and unemployment. Subsequent research and experience, however, have revealed that the relation was neither as simple nor as stable as originally thought. Instead of a unique, invariant relation, economists have found a variety of shifting short-run Phillips curves, each corresponding to different underlying conditions and expectations in the labor and product markets. Economists now acknowledge the importance of a host of other variables ("shift parameters") influencing the position of the Phillips curve. Changes in these shift parameters have rendered the curve quite unstable.

The findings of the short-run instability of the inflation-unemployment trade-off have served to provoke a lively controversy over the usefulness and validity of the Phillips curve concept. Some economists have even gone so far as to deny the existence of a permanent trade-off between inflation and unemployment. Other economists, however, contend that a long-run trade-off exists and that, given a more sophisticated interpretation, the Phillips curve remains a valid and useful concept. Consequently, much ingenuity and a large proportion of recent research in the field of macroeconomics have been devoted to establishing theoretical and empirical support for a reformulated Phillips curve that may have relevancy in long-run economic analysis.

. . . This article traces, with the aid of a sequence of charts, the development of the Phillips curve concept from its origins in 1958 to its current interpretation in policy analysis.

The Original Phillips Curve (Chart 1)

The first Phillips curve appeared in a 1958 study investigating the influence of the rate of unemployment (taken as an index of the degree of excess demand or "labor shortage" in the labor market) on the rate of change of wages. In that study, Professor A. W. Phillips of the London School of Economics fitted an empirical curve to a statistical scatter diagram of time series data for annual percentage rates of money wage changes (w) and unemployment (u) for the British economy over the interval 1861–1913. The resulting curve was downward-sloping, indicating an inverse relation between the two variables. Thus, Phillips' data showed that in years when the labor market was tight and unemployment low, money wages tended to rise at a rapid clip. But when the labor market was slack and unemployment high, wage changes tended to be very slight.

The chief novelty of the Phillips curve, however, was its apparent demonstration that inflation could coexist with unemployment. This finding had important policy implications. In the 1940's and 1950's, the policymakers' mission was viewed as one of achieving full employment without inflation. Price stability and full employment would indeed be attainable, compatible goals if inflation and unemployment were

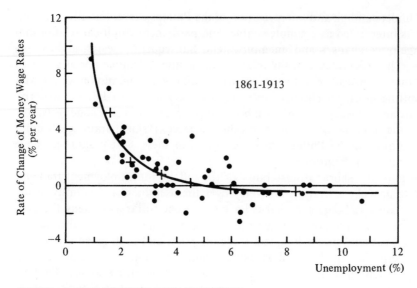

CHART 1   THE ORIGINAL PHILLIPS CURVE.

Source: A. W. Phillips. "The Relation Between Unemployment and the Rate of Change of Money Wage Rates in the United Kingdom, 1861-1957," *Economica*, 25, No. 100 (November 1958) 285.

mutually exclusive phenomena. In this ideal case one could eradicate unemployment without generating inflation. According to the Phillips curve, however, wage-price increases in the United Kingdom actually would start to occur long before absolute full employment was reached. Wages would begin to rise at an unemployment rate of just under 5½ percent, the point at which the Phillips curve crossed the horizontal axis. And to the left of this intersection, progressively lower rates of unemployment would provoke faster wage inflation. The policy implications were unmistakable: it would be impossible for the authorities to hit the twin targets of zero inflation and full capacity. Price stability and full employment were incompatible, conflicting goals. More of one objective could be obtained only at the cost of less of the other, but it would be impossible to attain both. Thus, the hope of simultaneous achievement of stable prices and full employment gave way to the notion of trade-offs between these goals.

Demand-Pull and Cost-Push Cases
(Chart 2)

Phillips himself contended that wages tend to be pulled up by rising demand. As numerous economists have since pointed out, however, the rising segment of the Phillips curve is consistent with the operation of supply-oriented cost-push, as well as demand-pull, forces. In conditions of excess demand for labor, money wages can be advanced by sellers, forced up by frictional or structural impediments ("bottle-necks") to labor mobility, and bid up by buyers. More generally, wage escalation is now viewed as partly stemming from a variety of market imperfections including labor-capital immobilities, job-information deficiencies, and employer-union monopoly power. Because of these imperfections or rigidities on the supply side, rising

Percent Rate of
Change of Wages (w)

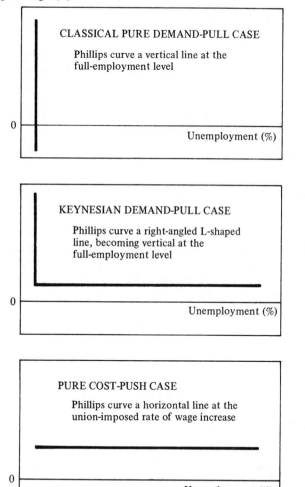

CLASSICAL PURE DEMAND-PULL CASE

Phillips curve a vertical line at the
full-employment level

0

Unemployment (%)

KEYNESIAN DEMAND-PULL CASE

Phillips curve a right-angled L-shaped
line, becoming vertical at the
full-employment level

0

Unemployment (%)

PURE COST-PUSH CASE

Phillips curve a horizontal line at the
union-imposed rate of wage increase

0

Unemployment (%)

CHART 2 PHILLIPS CURVES FOR CRUDE DEMAND-PULL AND COST-PUSH CASES.

demand can exert upward pressure on wages even when sizable numbers of workers are still unemployed.

Although both cost-push and demand-pull elements can be used to explain the rising portion of the Phillips schedule, there is more to the Phillips curve interpretation of inflation than just simple demand-pull and cost-push conceptions. The essence of the Phillips curve approach is that it expresses an interdependent *relationship* between unemployment and wage changes that yields the dilemma of conflicting policy goals: less unemployment is attainable only at the cost of faster wage inflation. By contrast, these variables were treated as completely independent, unrelated, and therefore non-conflicting in crude demand-pull and cost-push theories that predated the Phillips interpretation.

Prior to Phillips' analysis, the chief explanations of wage-level determination were two versions of the demand-pull theory. The *Classical* version of this theory assumed that full employment would be maintained continuously by the operation of complete and instantaneous wage-price flexibility. Production and labor utilization would always be tied to full employment, and prices and money wages would float with the level of aggregate demand. In this extreme Classical case, the only magnitudes that could vary would be money wages and prices. With the economy always at full capacity, any increases or decreases in demand would be matched solely by rises or declines in money wages and prices. Consequently, the Phillips curve corresponding to the Classical demand-pull case would be a vertical line at the full-employment level.

The *Keynesian* version of the demand-pull theory combined the Classical postulate of upward wage-price flexibility at full employment with the assumption of rigid downward inflexibility of wages and prices at less than full employment. In the Keynesian system, falling aggregate demand would result in declines in output and employment rather than reductions in wages and prices. Thus, as shown by the right-angled Phillips curve, one could distinguish sharply between two mutually exclusive situations: (1) unemployment with wage-price stability and (2) full employment with inflation. No policy conflicts could develop in the Keynesian case because wage-price increases could not occur before full employment was reached. Consequently, macro-economic policy could eliminate unemployment without provoking inflation by maintaining aggregate demand just at the point of full capacity.

At the opposite extreme of the Classical demand-pull case was the hypothetical pure cost-push case. Here the rate of wage inflation would be determined solely by union wage demands, which are assumed to be independent of the level of unemployment. According to the simplistic pure cost-push theory, unions would adhere tenaciously to inflationary wage claims regardless of whether the labor market was brisk or slack. As in the Classical and Keynesian cases, the rate of wage change would be completely independent of the level of unemployment. Again, there would be no policy conflicts: unemployment could be reduced without causing additional inflation. The Phillips curve in this case would be a horizontal line at the union-determined rate of wage increase.

Derivation of the Inflation-Unemployment Trade-Off Via Conversion from Wages to Prices (Chart 3)

The original Phillips curve related unemployment to wage changes. Other econo-mists, however, soon transformed the wage-unemployment relation into a price-un-employment relation by assuming that the rate of change of prices (p) was simply the difference between the rate of change of wages (w) and the constant trend rate of increase of man-hour productivity (q), i.e., $p = w - q$. On the Phillips chart this

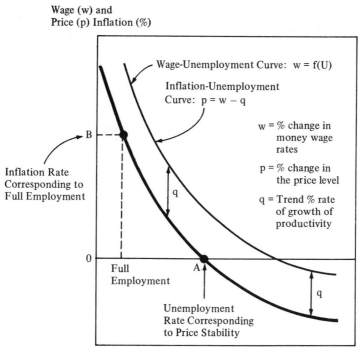

CHART 3 DERIVATION OF THE INFLATION-UNEMPLOYMENT TRADE-OFF VIA CONVERSION FROM WAGES TO PRICES. The inflation-unemployment curve (heavy line) is derived from the wage-unemployment curve by subtracting the trend rate of growth of productivity (q) from the latter. Note that point A shows the unemployment rate at which prices would be stable, while point B shows the rate of price inflation correspond-ing to full employment.

conversion was accomplished via a vertical downward shift of the schedule in such a way that the new price-unemployment curve was located q percentage points below the old wage-unemployment curve.

The transformed Phillips curve, it was thought, would be more useful to the policymakers since policy goals tend to be specified in terms of target rates of change of prices rather than of wages. From the inflation-unemployment curve, the authorities could determine how much unemployment would be associated with any given target rate of inflation and vice versa. For example, the curve would permit the policymakers to calculate both the rate of unemployment required to achieve complete price stability (point A) and the rate of inflation that would have to be tolerated as the price for maintaining a specified full-employment target (point B).

Trade-Offs and Attainable Combinations (Chart 4)

Phillips curve analysis stresses the distinction between the *location* (i.e., distance from origin) and the *slope* of the curve. The location fixes the inner boundary, or frontier, of feasible (attainable) combinations of inflation and unemployment rates. Determined by the structure of labor and product markets, the position of the curve defines the set of all coordinates of inflation rates and unemployment rates the au-

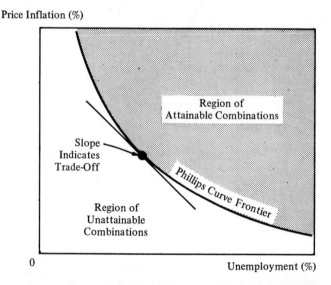

CHART 4 TRADE-OFFS AND ATTAINABLE COMBINATIONS. The location of the curve fixes the inner boundary of attainable combinations. The slope of the curve shows the trade-offs or rates of exchange between policy goals.

thorities could achieve via implementation of monetary and fiscal policies. Using these macroeconomic policies, the authorities could put the economy anywhere on or to the right of the curve. But, according to the Phillips curve analysis of the early 1960's, the authorities would reject all combinations to the right of the curve because superior positions involving less unemployment and/or inflation would be available on the curve. Moreover, whereas the policymakers *would not* operate to the right of the curve, they *could not* operate to the left of it. The Phillips curve could be viewed as a constraint preventing the authorities from achieving still lower levels of both inflation and unemployment. Given the structure of labor and product markets, it would be impossible for monetary-fiscal policy alone to reach combinations in the region to the left of the curve.

The *slope* of the curve was thought to be of critical importance since it shows the relevant policy trade-offs (rates of exchange between policy goals) available to the authorities. As explained by early advocates of the Phillips curve approach to policy problems, these trade-offs arise because of the existence of irreconcilable conflicts among policy objectives. When the goals of full employment and price stability are not simultaneously achievable, then attempts to move the economy closer to one will necessarily move it further away from the other. The rate at which one objective must be given up to obtain a little bit more of the other is measured by the slope of the Phillips curve. For example, when the Phillips curve is steeply sloped, it means that a small reduction in unemployment would be purchased at the cost of a large increase in the rate of inflation. Conversely, when the curve is flat, considerably lower unemployment could be obtained at a relatively cheap sacrifice of inflation objectives. Knowledge of these trade-offs would enable the authorities to determine the price-stability sacrifice necessary to buy any given reduction in the unemployment rate.

The Best Selection on the Phillips Frontier (Chart 5)

In the 1960's it was frequently said that the Phillips curve offered policymakers a menu of feasible policy choices between the two evils, unemployment and inflation. If so, the policymakers had to select from the menu the particular inflation-unemployment mix resulting in the smallest social cost. To do this, they would have to assign relative weights to the twin evils in accordance with society's views of the comparative harm caused by each. Then the authorities could move along the Phillips curve, trading off unemployment for inflation (or vice versa) until they arrived at the optimum, or least undesirable, combination. At this point on the Phillips constraint, they would have reached the lowest attainable social disutility contour (shown as the convex or bowed-out curves radiating outward from the origin of Chart 5). Here the unemployment-inflation combination chosen would be the one that minimized social harm.

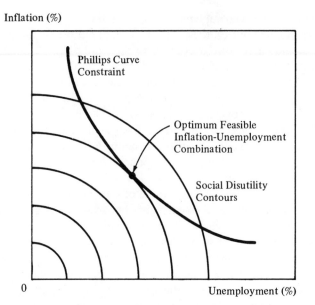

Inflation (%)

0   Unemployment (%)

CHART 5 THE BEST SELECTION ON THE MENU OF CHOICES. The bowed-out curves are social disutility contours. Each contour shows all the combinations of inflation and unemployment resulting in a given level of social disutility. The closer to the origin the lower will be the level of disutility. The slopes of these contours reflect the relative weights that society (or the policymakers) assigns to the evils of inflation and unemployment. The best combination of inflation and unemployment that the policymakers can reach, given the Phillips curve constraint, is the mix appearing on the lowest attainable social disutility contour.

Different Preferences, Different Outcomes (Chart 6)

It was recognized, of course, that policymakers would differ in their assessment of the comparative social disutility of inflation vs. unemployment. Thus, different policymakers might assign different weights to the two evils depending on their evaluation of the relative harmfulness of each. Policymakers who considered joblessness to be more undesirable than rising prices would assign a much higher relative weight to the former than would policymakers who judged inflation to be the worse evil. Hence, those with a marked aversion to unemployment would prefer a point much higher up on the Phillips curve than would those more anxious to avoid inflation, as shown in Chart 6. Whereas one administration might try to run a high-pressure economy because it thought the social benefits of low unemployment exceeded the harm done

Inflation (%)

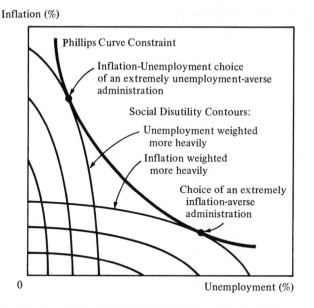

Phillips Curve Constraint

Inflation-Unemployment choice
of an extremely unemployment-averse
administration

Social Disutility Contours:

Unemployment weighted
more heavily

Inflation weighted
more heavily

Choice of an extremely
inflation-averse
administration

0   Unemployment (%)

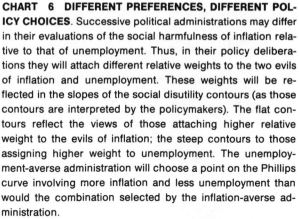

**CHART 6 DIFFERENT PREFERENCES, DIFFERENT POL-
ICY CHOICES**. Successive political administrations may differ
in their evaluations of the social harmfulness of inflation relative to that of unemployment. Thus, in their policy deliberations they will attach different relative weights to the two evils
of inflation and unemployment. These weights will be reflected in the slopes of the social disutility contours (as those
contours are interpreted by the policymakers). The flat contours reflect the views of those attaching higher relative
weight to the evils of inflation; the steep contours to those
assigning higher weight to unemployment. The unemployment-averse administration will choose a point on the Phillips
curve involving more inflation and less unemployment than
would the combination selected by the inflation-averse administration.

by inflation, another administration might deliberately shoot for a low-pressure economy because it believed that some economic slack was a relatively painless means of
eradicating harmful inflation. Both groups of policymakers of course would prefer
combinations to the southwest of the Phillips constraint, down closer to the diagram's origin (the ideal point of zero inflation and zero unemployment). But this
would be impossible, however, given the structure of the economy, which determines
the position or location of the Phillips frontier. Thus, as previously mentioned, the
policymakers would be constrained to combinations lying on (or to the right of) this
boundary, unless they were prepared to alter the economy's structure.

Pessimistic Phillips Curves and the "Cruel Dilemma" (Chart 7)

In the mid-1960's, there was much discussion of the so-called "cruel-dilemma" problem imposed by an unfavorable Phillips curve. The cruel dilemma refers to certain pessimistic situations where *none* of the available combinations on the menu of policy choices is socially acceptable. For example, suppose there is some maximum rate of inflation, A, that society is willing to tolerate. Likewise, suppose there is some maximum tolerable rate of unemployment, B. As shown in the chart, these limits define the zone of acceptable or socially tolerable combinations of inflation and unemployment. An economy that occupies a position anywhere within this zone will have performed adequately in satisfying society's demands for reasonable price stability and high employment. But if either of these limits is exceeded and the economy ends up outside the region of satisfactory outcomes, the system's performance will have fallen short of what was expected of it, and the resulting discontent may severely aggravate political and social tensions.

If, as some analysts alleged, the Phillips curve tended to be located so far to the right in the chart that no portion of it fell within the zone of acceptable combina-

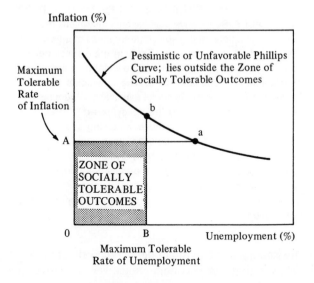

CHART 7 PESSIMISTIC PHILLIPS CURVE AND THE "CRUEL DILEMMA". Given the unfavorable Phillips curve, policymakers are confronted with a cruel choice. They can achieve acceptable rates of inflation (point a) or unemployment (point b) but not both. The rationale for the wage-price guideposts and manpower policies, implemented in the 1960's, was to shift the Phillips curve down into the zone of acceptable outcomes.

tions, then the policymakers would indeed be confronted with a painful dilemma. At best they could hold *either* inflation or unemployment down to acceptable levels. But they could not hold both simultaneously within the limits of toleration. Faced with such a pessimistic Phillips curve, policymakers would find it impossible to achieve combinations of inflation and unemployment acceptable to society.

It was this concern and frustration over the seeming inability of monetary-fiscal policy to resolve the unemployment-inflation dilemma that induced some economists in the 1960's to urge the adoption of incomes (wage-price) and labor-market (man-power) policies. Monetary-fiscal policies alone were thought to be insufficient to resolve the cruel dilemma. The most these policies could do, it was feared, was enable the economy to occupy alternative positions on the pessimistic Phillips curve. That is, monetary-fiscal policies could move the economy *along* the given curve, but they could not move the curve itself into the zone of tolerable outcomes. What was needed, it was argued, were new policies that would shift the Phillips frontier toward the origin of the diagram. Thus, the rationale for such measures as wage-price guide-posts, job-training, and retraining programs was to shift the Phillips frontier down into the zone of toleration so that the economy could choose more socially acceptable inflation-unemployment combinations.

Doubts about the Phillips Curve

Up until the late 1960's, the Phillips curve had received widespread and largely uncritical acceptance. Despite a lack of convincing statistical evidence of a signifi-cant inverse inflation-unemployment relation for the United States, few questioned the usefulness, let alone the existence, of this construct. In policy discussion as well as economic textbooks, the Phillips schedule was treated as a unique, consistent, and stable relation. In fact, so influential was this concept of a unique and stable trade-off, that it was instrumental in shaping several basic tenets of economic stabilization policy in the 1960's including (1) the idea that permanently lower unemployment could be preserved at the price of some constant rate of inflation and (2) the notion that guidepost and/or manpower policies should be used to shift the Phillips curve down and to the left.

In the late 1960's, however, doubts about the Phillips curve began to develop. Contributing to the mounting skepticism were two major factors. The first of these was the inflationary experience in the closing years of the decade, when events con-sistently went counter to the predictions of the conventional trade-off view. Accord-ing to the standard Phillips curve analysis of the 1960's, one would expect rising rates of inflation to be accompanied by falling unemployment; or, conversely, one should expect to observe an unchanged rate of unemployment maintained at a constant rate of inflation. Neither of these things happened, however. Instead, the record for 1967–1969 shows that although inflation accelerated sharply, the unemployment rate remained unchanged. Far from purchasing lower unemployment, escalating inflation evidently was required just to keep the unemployment rate fixed in place. In short,

Phillips curve forecasts parted company with experience. And the forecasting errors were even worse in 1970 when *both* inflation and unemployment increased.

A second source of skepticism was the steady accumulation of statistical findings that indicated that the Phillips relation might not be as stable or as consistent as was commonly believed. In numerous empirical studies conducted during the 1960's, Phillips curves had been statistically fitted to inflation-unemployment data for the United States. These efforts, however, had not been entirely successful. The trouble was that there was usually a large degree of dispersion, or variance, of the actual inflation-unemployment observations about the fitted Phillips curves. In other words, the simple, two-variable Phillips relationship was shown to be very loose and inexact. Additional variables—including, among others, corporate profits, the rate of change of unemployment, lagged changes in the cost of living, indexes of the dispersion of unemployment across separate labor markets, trade union membership, vacancy rates—had to be introduced to explain this variance and improve the statistical fit. Unfortunately, these studies proved that numerous, different Phillips curves could be fitted to the same set of inflation-unemployment observations, depending on which specific additional variables were used in the curve-fitting procedure. This discovery, of course, made it difficult to determine which, if any, was *the* true Phillips curve.

These findings ultimately led an increasing number of economists to question the consistency, uniqueness, and stability of short-run Phillips curves. Apparently, there was not one Phillips curve but rather numerous families of short-run Phillips curves corresponding to the host of other variables (shift parameters) influencing the inflation-unemployment relation. Because of these influences, a given observed short-run Phillips curve did not stand still but, instead, shifted over time as the values of the other variables changed. But which of these underlying variables exercised the dominant influence? In his 1967 Presidential address to the American Economic Association, Milton Friedman suggested the answer: inflation expectations. He argued that expectation-induced shifts in the Phillips curve would, in every case, render trade-off policy ineffective. Thus, in the hands of Friedman and others, the expectations hypothesis emerged as the main challenge to the validity of the Phillips curve. By the late 1960's many other observers also had begun to suspect that price expectations might be the most important factor causing the short-run Phillips curve to shift.

Accelerationists, the Expectations Hypothesis, and the Vertical Phillips Curve (Chart 8)

In its most extreme version, the expectations hypothesis denies the existence of a permanent trade-off between inflation and unemployment and asserts the accelerationist view that policymakers' attempts to preserve low unemployment will provoke explosive, ever-accelerating inflation. Led by Milton Friedman of the University of Chicago and Edmund Phelps of the University of Pennsylvania, accelerationists argue that in the long run the Phillips curve is a vertical line at the natural rate of

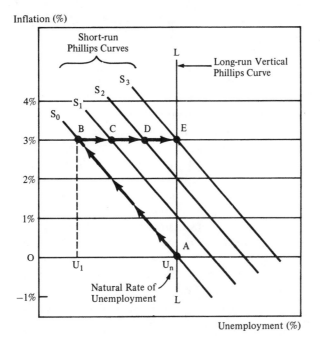

Inflation (%)

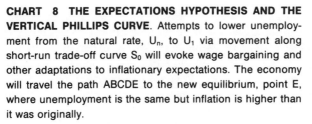

CHART 8 THE EXPECTATIONS HYPOTHESIS AND THE VERTICAL PHILLIPS CURVE. Attempts to lower unemployment from the natural rate, U_n, to U_1 via movement along short-run trade-off curve S_0 will evoke wage bargaining and other adaptations to inflationary expectations. The economy will travel the path ABCDE to the new equilibrium, point E, where unemployment is the same but inflation is higher than it was originally.

unemployment, i.e., the rate of unemployment at which the rate of change of prices is steady (neither accelerating nor decelerating) and *real* wages are in equilibrium (money wages having been fully adjusted to allow for correctly-anticipated inflation).

Accelerationists, of course, do not deny the existence of short-run trade-offs. But they think those trade-offs are transitory phenomena that arise from *unexpected* inflation and vanish as soon as expectations adapt to inflationary experience. Accordingly, accelerationists argue that movements along a short-run Phillips curve would alter expectations, thereby inducing *shifts* in the schedule in the direction of the vertical zero-trade-off line.

The sequence envisioned by accelerationists can be illuminated with the aid of Chart 8. On the chart is shown the vertical long-run Phillips curve (labeled L) passing through the natural rate of unemployment. The natural rate of unemployment is that particular rate of unemployment at which expected inflation equals actual inflation and where the real wage rate is at its equilibrium level. Also shown on the chart are four short-run Phillips curves, labeled S_0, S_1, S_2, S_3, corresponding to expected rates of inflation of zero, 1, 2, and 3 percent, respectively. The position of each short-run curve depends on the expected rate of inflation; the higher the expected rate of inflation, the higher the short-run Phillips curve. Note that at the point where each short-run Phillips curve cuts the vertical long-run curve expected and actual rates of inflation would be identical. For example, S_3, the short-run curve corresponding to an expected rate of inflation of 3 percent, would intersect the vertical curve at an actual rate of inflation of 3 percent. Similarly, S_0, the short-run curve along which inflationary expectations are zero, cuts the vertical curve at a zero rate of inflation.

Now suppose the economy is initially at point A, where there is complete price stability and the rate of unemployment is at its natural level. The authorities, intending to reduce unemployment from the natural rate to some lower level like U_1, then engineer an expansion in aggregate demand. This expansion in aggregate demand initially bids up both product prices (which rise at a rate of 3 percent) and wages. According to accelerationists, and many other observers, however, product prices initially tend to respond to increased demand more rapidly than money wages. With prices rising more rapidly than money or nominal wages, real wage rates fall.[1] The decline in real wages induces employers to expand production and employment, thereby lowering unemployment temporarily to U_1. Inflation has temporarily stimulated the economy, moving it from point A to point B on the short-run Phillips curve, S_0.

In the accelerationist model, however, such an inflationary stimulus would be short-lived. The stimulus will start to weaken almost immediately as price expectations are revised in light of actual inflationary experience. At first workers were fooled by the 3 percent inflation; they did not anticipate that rising prices would erode their real wages. But workers cannot be fooled for long. Over time, as inflation persists at the 3 percent rate, workers learn to adjust their expectations to the actual rate of inflation and to incorporate these price anticipations in their wage bargains. Thus, as the gap between anticipated and actual inflation narrows, so too does the discrepancy between the rates of increase of prices and money wages. Money wage increases begin to catch up with price increases, thereby tending to lift the real wage rate back to its pre-inflation level. This rise in the real wage induces employers to cut back employment, thus reversing the initial downward movement of unemployment. As the unemployment rate rises back to its original natural level, the economy moves along the path BCDE to long-run equilibrium. In the long run, (1) price changes will be fully anticipated, i.e., the 3 percent expected rate of inflation will equal the actual rate of inflation; (2) the expected rate of inflation will be completely incorporated in wage demands, i.e., money wages will be rising at the same rate as prices; (3) the original real wage will be reestablished and the old natural rate of unemployment restored; but (4) the steady-state rates of wage and price inflation will be higher than originally.

[1]For simplicity, productivity growth is assumed to be zero in this example. Thus the percentage change in real wage rates is just the difference between the percentage changes in nominal wages (w) and the price level (p), that is, w − p.

Policy Implications of the Accelerationist View (Chart 9)

Several important policy implications arise from the accelerationist analysis. The first is that attempts to hold unemployment below the natural rate will result in explosive, ever-accelerating inflation. Maintenance of unemployment at some target level U_1 (Chart 9) requires that real wage rates be kept low enough to induce employers to add sufficient numbers of jobseekers to their work forces. But the required permanent reduction in real wage rates can be achieved only if rising prices continually outstrip money wage increases. Since past rates of price increase (a proxy for expected inflation) tend to feed back into current money wage increases, however, the rate of price increase must be ever escalating to stay a step ahead of money wage increases. Alternatively stated, actual inflation must be kept running continually ahead of expected inflation, which workers incorporate in their wage demands. But since expected inflation is always rising in an attempt to catch up with actual inflation, the latter must be continually accelerated, from P_1 to P_2 to P_3, etc., in order to keep the gap open and continually frustrate workers' attempts to close it.

A second policy implication is that a stable rate of inflation purchases little in the way of lower unemployment. Since any steady rate of inflation would eventually be

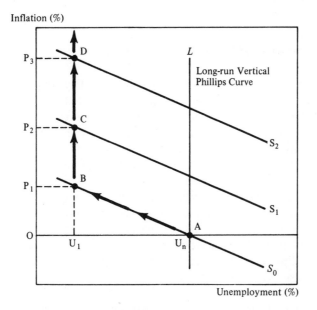

CHART 9 THE ACCELERATIONIST HYPOTHESIS. Attempts to maintain unemployment at some lower than natural rate, u_1, will provoke explosive, ever-accelerating inflation. The economy will travel the path ABCD with the rate of inflation rising from P_1 to P_2 to P_3, etc.

fully anticipated, inflation could have no lasting impact on unemployment. This conclusion is in direct conflict with the Phillips trade-off view that a permanently low rate of unemployment could be achieved at the price of some constant rate of inflation. Accelerationists claim that the trade-off view offers a treacherous guide to policy. For if the policymakers follow it, they will find that in the long run, they will have institutionalized inflation without permanently lowering unemployment.

A third policy implication is that since the natural rate of unemployment is consistent with *any* stable rate of inflation, the best thing the policymakers could do would be to choose the zero rate of inflation. But this means that the authorities should never try to reduce unemployment below the natural rate, since attempts to do so inevitably lead, via shifting expectations, to positive steady-state rates of inflation.

Finally, accelerationists also argue that the best path the economy can take in returning to its long-run, natural rate equilibrium is the path that leads to the zero rate of inflation. Since an economy in disequilibrium can return to equilibrium at *any* rate of steady, permanent inflation along the vertical Phillips curve, it might as well be the zero rate. Thus, accelerationists are willing to tolerate a deflationary policy that keeps unemployment high for as long as it takes to eliminate inflationary expectations and bring the economy to long-run equilibrium at the zero permanent rate of inflation. But they argue that inflationary expectations would vanish quickly, thereby necessitating only a short interval of high unemployment.[2]

The Non-Accelerationist Rebuttal (Chart 10)

Many economists have been unwilling to accept the policy conclusions flowing from the accelerationist model. They acknowledge that accelerationists have successfully demonstrated the crucial importance of price expectations in shifting the short-run Phillips curves. (Virtually no one believes in the existence of naive, stable short-run Phillips curves any more.) But they think accelerationists have adopted too extreme a position regarding price and employment policy. In particular, they dispute the accelerationists' interpretation of the natural rate of unemployment as corresponding to full employment in the labor market. Moreover, they point out that the natural rate of unemployment is a poor policy guide, not only because it results in too much joblessness, but also because it cannot be measured with precision.

The main challenge to the accelerationist position, however, focuses on the issue of the long-run Phillips curve. Anti-accelerationists point out that, contrary to the natural rate hypothesis, recent econometric studies indicate that a long-run trade-off

---

[2]When the economy is in the high-unemployment region to the right of the long-run vertical Phillips curve, actual inflation will always fall *below* anticipated inflation, thus inducing people to revise expectations downward. But how *fast* will these expectations be adjusted? Some accelerationists contend that the speed of adjustment is directly proportional to the discrepancy between expected and experienced inflation. Since this disparity tends to vary systematically with the rate of unemployment, high unemployment may be required for the swift dampening of inflationary expectations.

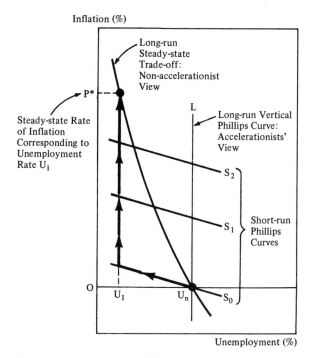

Inflation (%)

Long-run
Steady-state
Trade-off:
Non-accelerationist
View

P*

Steady-state Rate
of Inflation
Corresponding to
Unemployment
Rate U_1

L

Long-run Vertical
Phillips Curve:
Accelerationists'
View

S_2

Short-run
Phillips
Curves

S_1

O

U_1 U_n S_0

Unemployment (%)

**CHART 10 NON-ACCELERATIONIST VIEW OF LONG-
RUN STEADY-STATE TRADE-OFF**. Non-accelerationists argue that a downward sloping steady-state Phillips curve does
exist to prevent ever-accelerating inflation. Hence, unemployment can be maintained permanently at U_1, yet inflation will
never exceed its stable, steady-state rate p*.

curve *does* exist. This curve, while steeper than short-run Phillips curves, is not
completely vertical. Instead, it is negatively sloped, still providing trade-off opportunities for the policymakers.

These findings, if correct, would be extremely damaging to the accelerationist
position. If a steady-state trade-off does exist, then permanent reductions in the level
of unemployment will not require ever-accelerating inflation. Instead, for each level
of unemployment, including *low* levels, there will be some stable, constant, permanently sustainable rate of inflation. Thus, when unemployment is lowered, inflation
will start to climb and will continue to rise until it reaches the long-run, steady-state
Phillips curve, at which point it stops rising. Chart 10 illustrates this case. As indicated in the chart, when unemployment is lowered from U_N to U_1, price expectations
are set in motion, causing inflation to rise until it reaches its steady-state rate of p*.
Thereafter, unemployment can be maintained permanently at U_1 without the rate of
price increase exceeding p*.

Accelerationists have not been slow in responding to this challenge. Downward-sloping, steady-state Phillips curves, they point out, imply that workers never fully adjust to inflation. Incomplete adjustment could occur if workers have irrational *money illusion* and fail to perceive the discrepancy between nominal (money) and real wages. If workers have succumbed to money illusion, this is tantamount to a willingness on their part to let real wages be eroded by inflation in order to induce employers to hire the unemployed. Accelerationists, however, do not believe that workers behave that way. Workers, they contend, are free from money illusion and actively seek to *protect* the purchasing power of their wages from erosion by inflation. Therefore, in the long run, correctly anticipated inflation will be completely incorporated in money wage bargains, thereby maintaining real wages. And if expected price increases feed back completely into money wage increases, a downward-sloping long-run Phillips curve is logically impossible. Something must be wrong with the econometric models or empirical techniques that generate such curves. Perhaps the flaw in the empirical models is their assumption that people form expectations of future inflation by looking at a weighted average of past rates of inflation. If it were true that expectations are based solely on *past* experience and are adjusted with a lag, then in periods of monotonically rising inflation people would always expect inflation to be less than it actually is.

But this may not be an accurate description of how anticipations are formulated. Expectations are as likely to be generated from direct forecasts of the future as from mere projections of the past. Moreover, people probably base their anticipations at least as much on new information about a variety of current developments as on old data pertaining to past price changes only. Accelerationists contend that if the expectations formation process were correctly specified, then empirical models would not show systematic underestimation of inflation by workers.

Non-accelerationists acknowledge this latter shortcoming in their models, but they point out that accelerationists likewise have been unsuccessful in formulating satisfactory models of the formation of expectations. Moreover, Phillips curve advocates even concede that given sufficient time, e.g., several decades, steady inflation might conceivably cause the curve to become vertical. But they maintain that this very long run is of little practical importance. They still insist that over the policymakers' time horizon the trade-off does exist.[3] Finally, trade-off adherents argue that workers *are* willing to accept reductions in real wages if accomplished by inflation. Yet this does not necessarily signify irrational behavior or money illusion. Why? Because, it is claimed, workers care more about *relative* (comparative) real wages than about the absolute level of their wages. And inflation, which supposedly hits all wage earners alike, is a means of reducing absolute real wages without altering relative wage relationships. Debate on these issues continues, and the controversy over the existence of the long-run Phillips curve remains unresolved.

[3]Frequent disturbances, triggered by exogenous events, may prevent the economy from ever reaching long-run equilibrium. If so, then the intermediate-run Phillips curve may be most appropriate for policy purposes—and this curve could be negatively sloped.

Optimal Paths Off the Phillips Curve (Chart 11)

Even if long-run trade-offs do exist, however, there still remains the very real problem of what to do if the curve is unfavorable, i.e., if it falls outside the zone of socially acceptable inflation-unemployment combinations. Several possible strategies have been suggested to deal with this likely situation. The simplest calls for the policymakers to pick a point on the bad Phillips curve and then stay there. This strategy, however, would probably be rejected by most policymakers.

A better alternative, perhaps, would be for the policymakers to chart a course *off* the curve. Instead of choosing the best *point* on a bad long-run Phillips curve, the authorities can select the optimum *path* around the Phillips curve, deliberately abandoning the long-run equilibrium policy solution for a dynamic sequence of short-run disequilibrium positions.

For example, the authorities might opt for the vertical path lying completely to the left of the steady-state Phillips curve. This path corresponds to a policy decision to adhere to a low-unemployment target, fully accepting the accompanying risks of

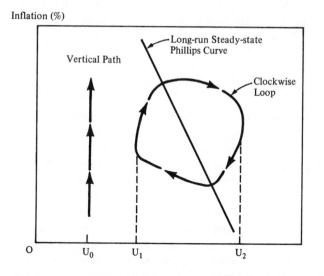

CHART 11 ALTERNATIVE DYNAMIC DISEQUILIBRIUM PATHS. Policymakers may elect to travel a path off the long-run Phillips curve instead of occupying a point on the curve. If they choose the vertical path at the left, they will hold unemployment at U_0 and hope that inflation will not accelerate too rapidly. If they choose the clockwise loop, they will be willing to let unemployment fluctuate within the range U_1 to U_2. Unemployment will be raised when inflationary expectations develop and lowered when they subside.

inflation. These risks, advocates argue, might not be as great as commonly believed. It all depends on how fast the path would unfold in the direction of higher inflation. If acceleration proved to be slow, then significant output and employment gains could be obtained before inflation began to approach socially intolerable levels. Moreover, future leftward shifts in the steady-state Phillips curve, owing to structural improvements in labor and product markets, might further reduce the danger of runaway inflation by lowering the ceiling toward which the path ultimately tends. Less sanguine observers, however, contend that the vertical path is too risky to be a practical alternative.

Another type of path the policymakers might consider takes the form of a dynamic loop or cycle around the steady-state curve. This type of path results when policymakers permit fluctuations to occur in the economy. Instead of maintaining a continually high-pressure economy with its attendant risks of accelerating inflation, the authorities would rely on periodic, controlled variations in economic activity and employment to contain inflation and keep expectations in check. Growth would be slowed and unemployment raised via contractive monetary-fiscal policy when inflationary expectations needed to be subdued. Later, with inflation quelled and price expectations dormant, fast growth could be resumed. After a period of slack the economy could move to a position of low unemployment with low inflation. Over the complete policy cycle the economy would move around dynamic clockwise loops.

Inflexible Price Expectations (Chart 12)

The stop-go policy solution would indeed be an attractive alternative if inflationary expectations tended to fade quickly in downswings and build up slowly in upswings. Then, contractions could be kept short and expansions long. The trouble is, however, that things do not always go that smoothly. As we learned in the late 1960's and early 1970's, inflationary expectations can build up rapidly, thereby leading to swift acceleration in the pace of inflation. Moreover, these expectations may become so firmly entrenched and downwardly inflexible as to be resistant to all but the most protracted sieges of severe unemployment. In such cases stop-go could become a nightmare of long, painful contractions punctuated by brief but inflationary expansions.

In situations like these it might be necessary to supplement monetary-fiscal policy with wage-price freezes, guideposts, and similar controls. The purpose of such controls is two-fold: first, to break and quickly dispel price expectations, thereby shortening the period of slack needed for inflation to decline to acceptable levels; second, to stabilize (deactivate) inflationary expectations so that they will not intervene early to check a vigorous recovery.

The reversal and stabilization of inflationary expectations was a principal rationale for the wage-price controls imposed after mid-1971. In the preceding year, policymakers had thought that the high inflation rates built up in the late 1960's could be brought down to acceptable levels via a temporary period of slack. By 1971, however, inflation had declined only slightly even though unemployment had increased

Inflation (%)

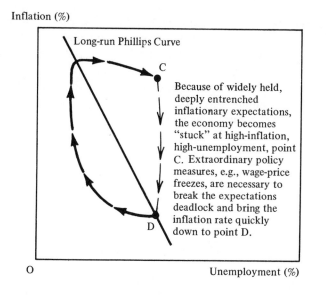

Long-run Phillips Curve

C

Because of widely held,
deeply entrenched
inflationary expectations,
the economy becomes
"stuck" at high-inflation,
high-unemployment, point
C. Extraordinary policy
measures, e.g., wage-price
freezes, are necessary to
break the expectations
deadlock and bring the
inflation rate quickly
down to point D.

D

O   Unemployment (%)

CHART 12 INFLEXIBLE PRICE EXPECTATIONS. If inflationary expectations are deeply entrenched and downwardly inflexible, inflation may be resistant to all but the most protracted sieges of severe unemployment. In such cases the economy may be trapped in a deadlock like point C, where both high inflation and high unemployment persist interminably. Here wage-price freezes and similar controls may be used to break up and dispel the inflationary expectations, thereby shortening the period of high unemployment needed for inflation to decline to acceptable levels like point D.

by almost a full percentage point to a level of roughly 6 percent. Moreover, computer forecasts were indicating that it might take as long as four or five years—with unemployment maintained at 6 percent—to bring the inflation rate down to acceptable levels. This contraction would have been too long. So the initial plan of de-escalating inflation via the unemployment route was scrapped, and wage-price controls were instituted.

The preceding discussion has described three alternative strategies for policymakers confronted with an unfavorable long-run trade-off: namely, (1) stay on the curve, (2) hold unemployment down and let inflation go, and (3) follow a path of controlled loops around the curve. None of these solutions, however, is ideal. Perhaps the best solution, most analysts agree, would be to engineer a leftward shift of the curve by adopting policies to improve the structure and performance of labor and product markets. A host of measures could be used to this end, including job-retraining programs; job-information and job-counseling services; vocational training and similar policies that would improve the coordination of labor force skill characteristics with the economy's skill requirements; provision of relocation subsidies; reduction of discrimination in hiring; and the elimination or reduction of minimum wage laws, agricultural price supports, quotas, and tariffs. Whether the long-run Phillips curve is vertical or downward-sloping, moving it into close proximity of the origin would enable the economy to realize both high employment and reasonable price stability. In this happy state of affairs, the debate between accelerationists and non-accelerationists would become a purely academic issue, having no practical importance.

II

EMPIRICAL EVIDENCE

Most economists would contend that theoretical analysis can find useful application only when it is enriched by empirical measurement. Monetary economics has provided a major avenue for quantitative research. Both Keynesians and Monetarists in recent years have engaged in efforts to estimate the structural relations and implications of their models. In this section we focus on two models that are somewhat representative of Keynesian and Monetarist views—the Federal Reserve Board-MIT econometric model and the econometric model of the Federal Reserve Bank of St. Louis. We chose these two models because each features a well-developed monetary sector, each is fairly well seasoned as econometric models go, each has been widely debated, tested, and applied, particularly in the policy arena and each is representative of a particular view of the transmission mechanism, discussed in detail in the Park, Spencer and Fand articles in the preceding section.

We begin this section with a straightforward overview of the two models by Joseph M. Crews. Crews discusses clearly the channels in each model through which monetary impulses affect the economy.

The second article by Frank de Leeuw and Edward M. Gramlich estimates the importance of the channels in the FRB-MIT model. De Leeuw and Gramlich conclude that while in the FRB-MIT model

monetary policy has an effect similar to its effect in the St. Louis model
(though the timing patterns differ somewhat), the impact of fiscal policy is much greater in the FRB–MIT model.

The article that follows by Leonall C. Andersen and Keith M. Carlson presents the St. Louis model in detail, including an appendix that
reports estimates of its structural relations. Andersen and Carlson
evaluate the successes and failures of the model using recent data.

In his article, the fourth in this section, Dan M. Bechter provides a
comparison of the manner in which changes in the rate of growth of
the money supply affects the rate of price inflation in the St. Louis
model and the SMP (Social Science Research Council–MIT–Pennsylvania) update of the FRB–MIT model. Bechter concludes that both
models underline the importance of monetary policy for long-run price
stability, but because of the lag in its effect monetary policy can do
little to slow inflation quickly.

In recent years many analysts in predicting output and price-level
movements have eschewed the use of fairly complete, multiequation
models of the economy. Some economists have instead used single-
equation, "reduced-form" estimates of the effect of measures of fiscal
and monetary policy on economic activity. A good example of this
approach is reported in the fifth article by David I. Fand. When the
single-equation approach was first used by economists at the Federal
Reserve Bank of St. Louis, it elicited considerable criticism. The kernel
of the criticism, as discussed in the Park article in the preceding section, was that the estimated coefficients of the single, reduced-form
equation should not be presumed to represent the one-way effect of
monetary and fiscal measures on output but could also reflect the opposite effect—of output, and hence aggregate demand, on the supposedly explanatory monetary and fiscal variables. It is necessary that
these explanatory variables be specified in such a way that they are not
sensitive to the endogenous variables. In the sixth reading Raymond E.
Lombra and Raymond G. Torto provide a succinct update of this
"reverse-causation" problem. The authors demonstrate a procedure
for specifying the explanatory monetary variable (the monetary base)
in such a way that it is realistically corrected for "reverse causation."
The authors show that their adjustment has considerable effect on the
relative strength of fiscal and monetary actions.

The closing reading in this section by Michael J. Hamburger surveys
recent opinion and evidence on the lag in the effect of monetary policy
on the economy. Of the three factors considered that might account for
the lag, Hamburger concludes that the most important is the specification of the explanatory monetary variable; the other two factors, the
type of statistical model employed and the seasonal adjustment procedure, are less important.

11
Econometric Models: The Monetarist and Non-Monetarist Views Compared

Joseph M. Crews

The Non-Monetarist View

Two fundamentally different views of the role of money in economic activity underlie current econometric models. The Monetarist view is formulated as an econometric model by the Federal Reserve Bank of St. Louis. The non-Monetarist view, based largely on a disaggregated Keynesian approach to monetary analysis, has given rise to several large-scale econometric models containing up to several hundred equations. The approach is illustrated in this article by the so-called FRB-MIT model.[1]

The Historical Setting

Prior to the Depression of the 1930's, conventional economic theory considered the economy basically stable over the long run and tending toward full employment. The main theme of theoretical analysis was toward long-run equilibrium relationships,

Reprinted with deletions from the Federal Reserve Bank of Richmond, *Monthly Review* (February, 1973), pp. 3-12, by permission of the publisher and the author. The footnotes have been renumbered to follow the abridged article.

[1]Frank de Leeuw and Edward M. Gramlich, "The Channels of Monetary Policy: A Further Report on the Federal Reserve-MIT Model," *Journal of Finance*, 24 (May 1969), 265-90; and Leonall C. Andersen and Keith M. Carlson, "A Monetarist Model for Economic Stabilization," *Review*, Federal Reserve Bank of St. Louis, 52 (April 1970), 7-25.[The De Leeuw-Gramlich article and a more recent update of the Anderson-Carlson article are reprinted in this book.—Ed.]

with little attention devoted to the short-run process through which long-run equilibrium was attained. In this context, the quantity of money, together with the level of output, was viewed as determining the level of prices, but having little to do with long-run real productive growth. This *quantity theory* was brought into serious question as a result of the Depression. The development of an alternative theory of money, interest, and output was initiated by the British economist John Maynard Keynes.

Neo-Keynesian Theory

The approach to macroeconomics developed by Keynes and those who refined his work is known as the income-expenditure approach. Its basic characteristics may be summarized briefly. First, the economy is viewed as consisting of a number of sectors, e.g., the consumption, investment, and government sectors. Demand in each sector is determined by factors peculiar to the sector. Then, all sectoral demands are added together to determine aggregate demand, measured by gross national product, GNP. This process is illustrated in Exhibit 1, where equations 1 and 2 determine consumption and investment demand; government demand is exogenous. Aggregate demand is added together in equation 4. With larger, more complex models, each of these major components of aggregate demand is disaggregated. Consumption may be divided into expenditures for durables, nondurables, and services; in some cases, automobile demand is explained separately. Investment may be broken down into expenditures for producers' equipment, producers' structures, residential construction, and inventory changes. Government spending may be classified as Federal or state and local, with Federal expenditures further subdivided as defense or nondefense. This disaggregation procedure can be carried to any practical degree of detail, limited, of course, by the availability of appropriate data.

A second characteristic of neo-Keynesian models is a built-in policy transmission mechanism that deemphasizes the role of money. For the most part, this mechanism involves the *indirect* linkage of money with aggregate demand *via* interest rates. In its simplest form, it may be stated symbolically as:

$$OMO \rightarrow R \rightarrow M \rightarrow i \rightarrow I \rightarrow GNP.$$

An open market purchase of Government securities by the Federal Reserve, OMO, increases commercial bank reserves, R, and raises the banks' reserves-earning assets ratio. Banks operate to restore their desired ratios by extending new loans or by expanding bank credit in other ways. New loans create new demand deposits, thereby increasing the money supply, M. Given the public's liquidity preferences, a rising money supply causes the general level of interest rates, i, to decline. Given businessmen's "expected profits," expressed by Keynes as the *marginal efficiency of investment,* falling interest rates, i.e., reduced capital costs, induce expanded investment expenditures, I. Finally, increased investment spending causes successive

$$(1) \quad C_t = a_0 + a_1 Y_t + a_2 C_{t-1}$$

$$(2) \quad I_t = b_0 + b_1 P_t + b_2 K_{t-1}$$

$$(3) \quad W_t = c_0 + c_1 Y_t + c_2 t$$

$$(4) \quad Y_t = C_t + I_t + G_t$$

$$(5) \quad P_t = Y_t - W_t$$

$$(6) \quad K_t = K_{t-1} + I_t$$

where C = consumption

$\quad Y$ = income

$\quad W$ = wage income

$\quad P$ = nonwage income

$\quad I$ = net investment

$\quad K$ = capital stock at end of period

$\quad G$ = government expenditures on goods and services

$\quad t$ = time

EXHIBIT 1   AN ILLUSTRATIVE MODEL

Source: Adapted from a similar model presented in M. Liebenberg, A. Hirsch, and J. Popkin, "A Quarterly Econometric Model of the United States: A Progress Report," *Survey of Current Business,* 46 (May 1966), 13-16.

rounds of new final demand spending, causing GNP to rise by a multiple of the initial change in investment.[2]

A number of refinements to this process have been made by later economists. For example, this transmission process involves Keynes's liquidity preference trade-off of money and financial assets. In more sophisticated versions, this trade-off is generalized to better approximate a real world of "numerous financial assets, hence numerous interest rates on . . . different securities. Different types of investment spending are most sensitive to particular interest rates, e.g., plant and equipment investment to the corporate bond rate, residential construction to the mortgage rate, and inventory investment to the bankloan rate."[3] Policy-induced changes in bank reserves cause portfolio adjustments over a wide range of financial and real assets, eventually influencing the components of final demand spending.

In further refinement of the Keynesian theory, a number of writers now argue that

[2]William L. Silber, "Monetary Channels and the Relative Importance of Money Supply and Bank Portfolios," *Journal of Finance,* 24 (March 1969), 81-82.

[3]*Ibid.,* pp. 84-85.

changes in the money supply have direct wealth effects on consumption spending, in addition to the indirect wealth effects operating via interest rate changes, described above.

Two other characteristics of neo-Keynesian models are important as points of comparison with Monetarist models. First, the money supply, in the process described above, is an endogenous variable, whereas Monetarists consider it exogenous. Second, the basic Keynesian model treats the price level as independent of monetary forces. Large-scale neo-Keynesian econometric models, which generally encompass nonmonetary theories of price level determination, are consistent with this treatment. These two points will be clarified at appropriate points in the discussion below.

The FRB–MIT Model

The generalized neo-Keynesian approach to model building may be illustrated by the FRB-MIT model, which is a large-scale model of the U.S. economy constructed by the Board of Governors of the Federal Reserve System and the Economics Department of the Massachusetts Institute of Technology. Its stated purpose is to quantify the monetary policy process and its impact on the economy.[4] The model consists of 10 sectors, the most important of which are the financial, investment, and consumption/inventory sectors. The financial sector is displayed in Exhibit 2 and the real sector in Exhibit 3.

THE FINANCIAL SECTOR

The purpose of the financial sector is to establish the linkage between the instruments of monetary policy and the financial variables that are important in the real sector of the economy. Several types of variables appear in this sector. First, the instruments of monetary policy are nonborrowed reserves and the Federal Reserve discount rate. Nonborrowed reserves serve as a proxy for open market operations. Second, demands for short-term financial assets are explained. These assets include free reserves, demand deposits, currency, commercial loans, and time deposits held by banks, savings and loan associations, and mutual savings banks. Supply, i.e., rate-setting, equations explain interest rates on Treasury bills, commercial loans, commercial paper, mortgages, industrial bonds, and state and local bonds. Other rate-setting equations determine the stock market yield and rates on time deposits held by banks, savings and loan associations, and mutual savings banks. A term-structure equation relates the corporate bond rate to the commercial paper rate.

The workings of the financial sector may be illustrated by tracing the effects of a Federal Reserve purchase of Government securities, represented in the model as an increase in nonborrowed reserves, RU. As shown in Exhibit 2, this purchase causes a rise in free reserves, RF, and a rise in the price of Treasury bills, represented by a fall in the bill rate, RTB. Commercial banks are assumed to have, under given market conditions, a desired proportion of earning to nonearning assets (reserves). An in-

---

[4]See de Leeuw and Gramlich, *op cit.*, p. 266.

crease in nonborrowed reserves lowers the proportion of earning assets in the banks' portfolios below the desired level. In attempting to restore this ratio, banks attempt to purchase similar fixed coupon, short-term financial assets, increase their loan offerings, and increase their demands for commercial paper. The declining Treasury bill rate represents not only a decline in the yield on short-term Government securities but also a decline in short rates generally, for which RTB is a proxy. Other short rates, the commercial paper rate, RCP, and the rate on commercial loans, RCL, follow RTB downward. There follows a complex adjustment process serving to re-

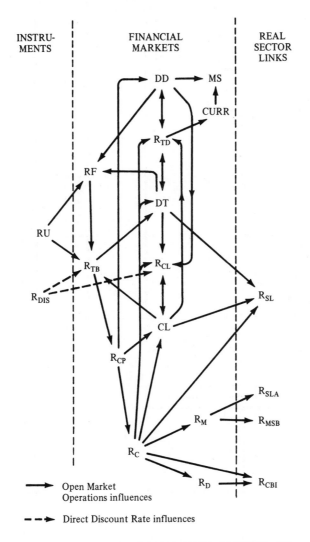

EXHIBIT 2 THE MONETARY POLICY PROCESS OF THE FRB–MIT MODEL

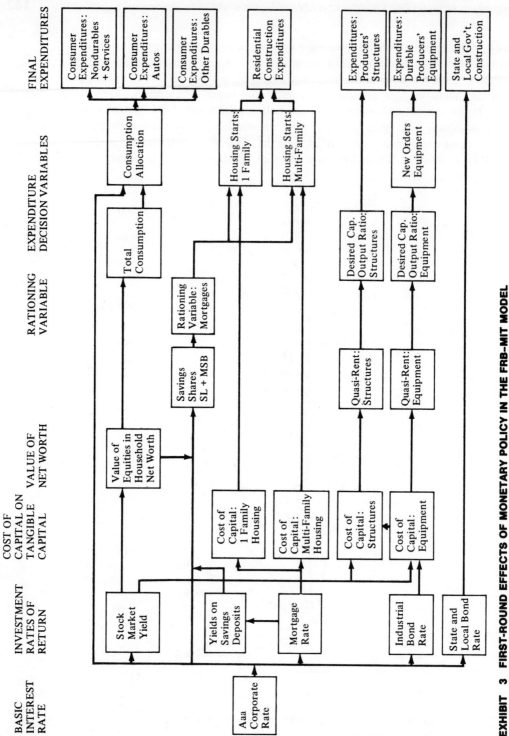

EXHIBIT 3 FIRST-ROUND EFFECTS OF MONETARY POLICY IN THE FRB-MIT MODEL

Source: Frank de Leeuw and Edward M. Gramlich, "The Channels of Monetary Policy," *Journal of Finance*, 24 (May 1969), 281.

store portfolio balance to the commercial banking market. This process is expressed primarily in the equations that determine the time deposit rate and the commercial loan rate.[5]

Part of the adjustment involves acquisition of longer-term financial assets, represented by a term-structure relationship linking the commercial paper rate and the corporate bond rate, RC. The corporate bond rate influences other long-term rates, the mortgage rate, RM, and the stock market yield, RD. These rates pass the monetary stimulus to the real sector by way of the industrial bond rate, RCBI; the state and local government bond rate, RSL; and the deposit rates of nonbank savings institutions, RSLA and RMSB.

THE FINANCIAL-REAL SECTOR LINKAGE

Monetary effects spread through the economy by way of three separate channels: the cost of capital, the net worth of households, and the availability of credit to the household sector. Continuing the above illustration, the impact of lower interest rates may be traced in Exhibit 3. The cost-of-capital channel captures the effect of three long-term interest rates—the corporate bond rate, the mortgage rate, and the stock market yield—on investment expenditures for plant and equipment, expenditures for consumer durables, expenditures for single-and multiple-family housing, and state and local Government construction spending.[6]

The net worth channel passes the effect of changing rates of return on bonds to the stock yield, to equity values in the net worth of households, and to consumption expenditures.

Finally, credit rationing, the third channel, is found to be important in the housing sector. Savings institutions experience large fluctuations in their deposit flows, because of the sluggishness of their lending and deposit rates. In addition, their portfolios usually include a high proportion of long-term, low turnover mortgages. In times of rising interest rates, these institutions are forced to restrict mortgage lending. This nonprice rationing of credit influences the residential construction component of final demand.

The FRB-MIT model thus illustrates two basic characteristics of neo-Keynesian models: (1) a highly detailed sector-by-sector buildup of aggregate demand and (2) a detailed specification of the portfolio adjustment process that attaches a central role to interest rates as an indirect link between monetary policy and final demand.

---

[5]This process is simplified in two ways for presentation in Exhibit 2. First, the portfolio balance terms are commercial loan-to-deposit ratios, which serve as measures of portfolio composition in determining each financial institution's desired deposit or loan rate. The actual market rate is a function of the discrepancy between the lagged actual rate and the desired rate. For simplicity, in Exhibit 2 each separate component of these ratios is shown rather than the full ratio. For example, rather than showing the ratio: CL/DD + DT, each component—commercial loans, CL; demand deposits, DD; and time deposits, DT—is shown separately. Second, in order to simplify the chart and to emphasize financial market interaction, no real sector feedback variables appear. These variables, such as GNP or net worth, enter the several asset demand equations as transactions or scaling variables. For further discussion of these points, see de Leeuw and Gramlich, *op. cit.,* pp. 267-80.

[6]For a more detailed description of the cost-of-capital channel, see de Leeuw and Gramlich, *loc. cit.*

As a point of comparison with Monetarist models, one further characteristic of the FRB–MIT model should be mentioned. Prices are determined in this model by real sector forces, that is, by a variable markup over wage costs.[7] Factors influencing the size of this markup include a productivity trend variable, which allows producers to maintain profit shares even though wages rise faster than prices. Demand shifts and nonlabor cost-push forces are other factors involved in this essentially nonmonetary theory of the price level.

The Monetarist View

Although the quantity theory was in eclipse during the period of neo-Keynesian preeminence, a group of economists, led by Professor Milton Friedman at the University of Chicago, continued to develop the Monetarist approach, restructuring the theory and gathering supporting statistical evidence. With the problems of increasing inflation in the late 1960's and the questionable effectiveness of the 1968 tax surcharge in dampening inflationary pressures, the policy prescriptions and forecasts of neo-Keynesian economists became increasingly subject to question.[8] The Monetarist view gained increased respect among academic economists and policymakers.

Monetarist Theory

Modern Monetarists consider the economy basically stable, with most elements of instability the product of faulty monetary arrangements or improper policy. The reasoning behind this may be briefly summarized. First, there is a stable, but not precise, relationship between the growth rates of money and nominal, i.e., current dollar, national income or GNP. If money balances grow more rapidly in relation to income than people wish, they will attempt to spend the excess, causing prices to rise. On the other hand, if money grows too slowly in relation to income, people will try to build up their cash balances by reducing spending, which would result in a slowing of income growth and rising unemployment.[9] Changes in money and income do not occur simultaneously. On the average, a change in monetary growth will result in a change in real output growth six to nine months later, followed by changes in prices in another six to nine months, according to Friedman's estimates.[10]

[7]See de Leeuw and Gramlich, *op cit.*, Appendix, pp. A15-16.

[8]There is some debate concerning the effectiveness of the 1968 tax surcharge. See, for example, Robert Eisner, "Fiscal and Monetary Policy Reconsidered," *American Economic Review,* 59 (December 1969), 897-905; and the subsequent comments and reply in *American Economic Review,* 61 (June 1971), 444-61. See also, Milton Friedman, "The Counter-Revolution in Monetary Theory." *Occasional Paper No. 33* (London: The Institute of Economic Affairs, 1970), pp. 19-20, and Arthur M. Okun, "The Personal Tax Surcharge and Consumer Demand, 1968-70." *Brookings Papers on Economic Activity* (January 1971), pp. 167-213.

[9]William N. Cox, III, "The Money Supply Controversy," *Monthly Review,* Federal Reserve Bank of Atlanta, 54 (June 1969), 73.

[10]Friedman, *op. cit.,* p. 22.

Carrying this logic further, the Monetarists consider fiscal policy, when not accompanied by changes in the money supply, to be an unlikely source of economic change. For example, increased Government spending, if not accompanied by monetary expansion, will tend to "crowd out" some private spending and have minimal impact on aggregate demand.[11] Fiscal policy distributes income between the private and public sectors but has little impact on price level changes.[12] Thus, short-run variations in prices, output, and employment are thought to be dominated by movements in a policy-determined money supply.[13]

Long-run real economic growth, on the other hand, is thought to be independent of monetary change, being determined by basic growth factors such as expanding productive capacity, population growth, advancing technology, and natural resources. In the long run, monetary change affects only the price level. Accordingly, the basic objective of monetary policy is to "prevent money itself from being a major source of economic disturbance."[14] It follows that stabilization policy should seek a growth rate of money that closely approximates the long-term rate of growth of real productive capacity.

The Monetarist view of the role of interest rates in the policy transmission process may be summarized in the following way:

> . . . Monetary impulses are . . . transmitted by the play of interest rates over a vast array of assets. Variations in interest rates change relative prices of existing assets, relative to both yields and the supply prices of new production. Acceleration or deceleration of monetary impulses are thus converted by the variation of relative prices, or interest rates, into increased or reduced production, and subsequent revisions in supply prices of current output.[15]

Further, while interest rates serve to facilitate real and financial asset adjustments, "the impact of changes in money on any specific interest rate is both too brief and too weak to be either captured statistically or identified as a strategic variable in the transmission process."[16] Therefore, the Monetarists view the *money supply as the strategic variable,* affecting income directly. This view may be represented schematically as:

$$\text{OMO} \rightarrow \text{M} \rightarrow \text{SPENDING} \rightarrow \text{GNP.}$$

A comparison of this description with the generalized neo-Keynesian portfolio

[11]Andersen and Carlson, *op. cit.,* p. 8.
[12]Friedman, *op. cit.,* p. 24.
[13]Ronald L. Teigen, "A Critical Look at Monetarist Economics," *Review,* Federal Reserve Bank of St. Louis, 54 (January 1972), 13.
[14]Milton Friedman, "The Role of Monetary Policy," *American Economic Review,* 58 (March 1968), 12.
[15]Karl Brunner, "The Role of Money and Monetary Policy," *Review,* Federal Reserve Bank of St. Louis, 50 (July 1969), 18.
[16]W. E. Gibson and G. C. Kaufman, "The Relative Impact of Money and Income on Interest Rates: An Empirical Investigation," *Staff Economic Studies* (Washington, D. C. : Board of Governors of the Federal Reserve System, 1966), p. 3.

adjustment process, as illustrated by the FRB-MIT model, focuses on two crucial points at issue: the range of assets involved in the adjustment process and the response patterns of interest rates and prices. Concerning the former, Friedman argues that the spectrum of assets and rates of return influenced by monetary action is extremely broad, including many implicit rates, which are not recorded.[17]

Friedman further argues that recorded rates do not reflect the real cost of capital but rather include anticipated rates of inflation. Moreover, monetary policy may be routed through as yet undiscovered channels. In short, the transmission process is too complicated to be captured by statistical models. The standard practice of using recorded interest rates both underestimates the full impact of monetary actions and narrows the scope of the transmission process to only a relatively few channels. Therefore, Friedman concludes, even the most complex econometric model cannot adequately represent the monetary process.[18]

Monetarists also question the response patterns of interest rates and prices in neo-Keynesian models. They regard the fall in interest rates in response to monetary expansion as a temporary effect. In a longer view, monetary expansion, whether via interest rate effects or direct spending effects, causes rising income and expenditures. The Monetarists are careful to distinguish nominal from real changes. When the economy is operating below the full-employment level, changes in nominal money may significantly affect real economic variables—output and employment—rather than rising prices. As the economy approaches full employment, however, quantities become less responsive, and prices begin to rise. The real value of money balances grows more slowly, or declines, causing a reversal of the initial interest rate effect.[19] Thus, changes in interest rates may be only a result of the adjustment process, rather than a crucial link; and may be directly, rather than inversely, related to changes in money.

Prices, in this process, are a function of "demand pressure"—determined by how close to full employment the economy is operating. In addition, an accumulation of price changes over time tends to generate "price expectations," which serve as a separate influence in future price movements. Thus, the long-run insensitivity of real variables to changes in the money supply and the predominant short-run influence of money on real output and employment are consistent.

The St. Louis Model

The process described above has recently been incorporated into an econometric model by the Federal Reserve Bank of St. Louis.[20] The model makes no attempt to

[17]Friedman, *Occasional Paper No. 33*, p. 25.
[18]Yung C. Park, "Some Current Issues on the Transmission Process of Monetary Policy," *IMF Staff Papers*, 19 (March 1972), 24-26.
[19]For similar, but more detailed, expositions see Friedman, "The Role of Monetary Policy," *American Economic Review*, 58 (March 1968), 6; and David I. Fand, "A Monetarist Model of the Monetary Process," *Journal of Finance*, 25 (May 1970), 279-83.
[20]For a more detailed development, see Andersen and Carlson, *op. cit.*, pp. 8-11.

specify the structure of the economy; rather, it explains such broad measures as total spending, prices, and unemployment in terms of changes in money, Government expenditures, potential output, and price expectations.

The process by which monetary action predominates short-run changes in total spending can be seen by tracing through the flow chart, Exhibit 4. The responses in the actual model accumulate over a number of periods, but no lags except price changes appear in the chart. Total spending, measured by GNP, responds more strongly to money supply changes than to changes in the full-employment budget. The latter actually has a negative impact after three quarters, reflecting the Monetarists' "crowding-out" hypothesis.

Potential output is determined by underlying factors such as growth of natural resources, technology, labor force, and productive capacity. Total spending and potential output together determine the amount of "demand pressure" existing in the economy in the short-run. Demand pressure, a measure of short-run market conditions, combines with long-run price expectations to determine the current change in the price level. Price expectations, measured by a five-quarter weighted average of past price level changes, enter price determination as a separate influence.

The model thus determines changes in total spending and prices separately. Short-run changes in real output are then calculated as a residual by subtracting the price factor from changes in total spending.

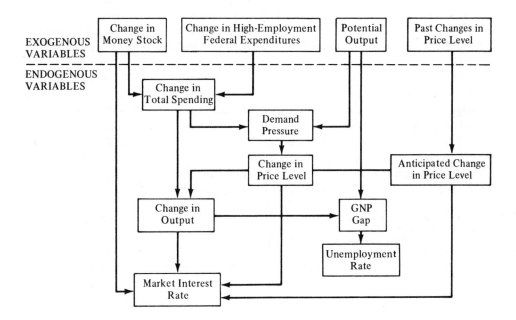

EXHIBIT 4   FLOW DIAGRAM OF THE ST. LOUIS MODEL

Source: Leonall G. Andersen and Keith M. Carlson, "A Monetarist Model for Economic Stabilization," *Review,* Federal Reserve Bank of St. Louis, 52 (April 1970), 10.

Changes in output are subtracted from changes in potential output to determine the GNP gap, a measure of productive slack in the economy. The unemployment rate is directly related to current and past levels of the GNP gap. Changes in output combine with changes in money supply, current and past changes in price levels, and price expectations to determine the level of interest rates. Market interest rates are a result of market interaction, not a crucial link in the transmission process as in the Keynesian view.

In sum, the St. Louis model is a direct formulation of the Monetarist view that monetary changes predominate short-run changes in the real economy, while in the long run money affects only nominal quantities. The model also reflects the contention that the full transmission mechanism cannot be captured by econometric models. The stable relationship found between money and total spending becomes the basis for a small, simple model that explains changes in broad economic aggregates in terms of changes in the money supply.

Summary

This article has examined the econometric implications of two alternative theories of the monetary process. Both the neo-Keynesians and the Monetarists see a general portfolio balance mechanism at work in the economy, but agreement seems to stop there. Their divergent views concerning the importance of interest rates, the direction of effect of money on interest rates, the nature of price determination, and the feasibility of representing the adjustment process econometrically have been discussed above.

Although the two models presented here are representative of current thinking, some preliminary movement toward synthesis is evident. Recent analytical work has introduced prices into Keynesian models as endogenous variables.[21] Later unpublished versions of the FRB-MIT model are structured so that either the money supply or reserves may be used as a policy variable.[22] Recent unpublished Monetarist work specifies structural detail more than in the past.[23] The problem of implicit interest rates remains unresolved. The resolution of this problem and the thrust of current research point in the direction of larger, more detailed econometric models.

[21]Arthur Benavie, "Prices and Wages in the Complete Keynesian Model," *Southern Economic Journal,* 38 (April 1972), 468–77; Teigen, *op. cit.,* p. 15 and footnote 27.

[22]"FRB-MIT-PENN Econometric Model," unpublished staff paper, Federal Reserve Board of Governors, July 13, 1971.

[23]Leonall C. Andersen, "Influence of Monetary and Financial Actions in a Financially Constrained Economy," unpublished paper, May 1971, p. 40.

12

The Channels of Monetary Policy: A Further Report on the Federal Reserve–MIT Model

Frank de Leeuw and
*Edward M. Gramlich**

Introduction

One of the most perplexing questions in macroeconomics has long been the importance of financial variables in influencing the real economy. Opinions on this question have varied greatly from decade to decade and still today vary greatly from economist to economist. Whereas classical economists felt that monetary forces were quite important, indeed the only long-run determinant of the price level, the standard Keynesian view during and after the Great Depression tended to deemphasize the role of money. The postwar period has seen a definite revival of interest in monetary phenomena, but this revival has by no means generated a consensus on the importance of money in influencing GNP.

A basic reason for differences of opinion on the importance of money has been the difficulty in obtaining convincing empirical evidence concerning the sensitivity of aggregate demand to exogenous monetary and fiscal forces. Historical evidence sug-

Reprinted with deletions from the *Journal of Finance,* Vol. 24, No. 2 (May, 1969), pp. 265-290, by permission of the American Finance Association and the authors. The footnotes have been renumbered to follow the abridged article.

* While we take full responsibility for statements in this paper, we stress that credit for the ideas it contains belongs to the entire Federal Reserve-MIT group of which we are only two members. Franco Modigliani, Albert Ando, Charles Bischoff, George de Menil, Dwight Jaffee, and Enid Miller have made especially important contributions to the results reported here; many others have made important contributions to other aspects of the model.

gests that autonomous monetary forces such as gold discoveries and reserve requirement decisions played an important role in such major economic swings as the inflation of 1900-1910, the Great Depression, and the contraction of 1936-1937. These findings are buttressed by the studies of Friedman-Meiselman, the staff of the Federal Reserve Bank of St. Louis, and others who find monetary variables to be much more important than fiscal variables in explaining subsequent movements in GNP. On the other hand, the evidence from several of the large econometric models—the Wharton School model, the OBE model, the Michigan model, and to a lesser extent the Brookings model—is that monetary forces are rather unimportant in influencing total demand.

Behind different assessments of the role of monetary factors lie differences of opinion regarding the number and significance of the channels through which monetary forces operate. Many econometric models include only one channel: namely, the effects of financial yields on the opportunity cost of holding durable goods and structures, which in turn influences tangible investment. Even within this one channel there is room for a wide range of empirical estimates of the strength of the forces at work, and further research is still urgently needed. At the same time, however, the possibility should be investigated that the conflict stems partly from the existence of other channels through which monetary forces work, channels which have either been inadequately treated or completely ignored in previous econometric work.

The Federal Reserve-MIT econometric model project was motivated by a desire to examine these ideas. Our aim was to build a model which, though not necessarily larger than most other existing models, would focus more intensively on monetary forces and the way they affect the economy. The format of an econometric model was chosen because it seemed to be the ideal way to take advantage of recent work in areas such as household and producer behavior, financial behavior, and price-wage determination; of recent econometric advances in techniques for dealing with distributed lags, autocorrelation, and constraints on parameters; and of advances in computer technology making possible rapid estimation and solution of large nonlinear systems. It was also felt that only through a model could one surmount problems having to do with the large number of exogenous monetary and fiscal variables, variable policy multipliers and time lags, and other difficulties which the one-equation approach to explaining GNP necessarily oversimplifies or ignores.

We will concentrate on this central theme—the channels through which monetary forces influence the real economy. Previous reports have dealt with other aspects of the model—its overall structure, its theoretical innovations, the characteristics of its multiplier-accelerator mechanism—and we will touch on these points only to the extent necessary to understand this paper.[1] For those interested, we will provide an Appendix giving a current listing of the model along with mention of the equations which have been altered since our report of one year ago.*

[1]See [6], [11], [14], and [2].

* The Appendix was not published with this article.—Ed.

The first portion of the paper sets out the theoretical and institutional basis for the three channels of monetary policy currently represented in the model.* Cost-of-capital influences constitute one channel, affecting single- and multi-family housing, plant and equipment, state and local construction, and investment in consumer durable goods. The transmission of rates of return on bonds to the value of wealth held in the form of equities constitutes a second channel, affecting household net worth and consumption. Finally, credit rationing constitutes a third channel, which we have so far found to be important only in the housing market. As yet, we have not found either the cost of capital or credit rationing to be important for inventory investment, though we have tested these possibilities extensively.

The second portion of the paper presents estimates of the quantitative importance of each channel. Simulation of different groups of equations of the model and of the full model under varying sets of initial conditions illustrate direct effects and complete-system effects of monetary policies alone and in comparison with fiscal policies. The results of these simulations are still subject to large uncertainties, and we will no doubt be making changes as work on the model continues. For what they are worth, however, the current results imply one- or two-year fiscal policy effects roughly comparable to results for other models and monetary policy effects appreciably larger than results of other models, though smaller that what a simple quantity theory of money would imply. Financial variables are seen to operate with a somewhat longer lag than fiscal variables, and both monetary and fiscal multipliers vary depending on the initial state of the economy.

Chart 1 exhibits the direct effects of monetary policy. As can be seen, financial yields shown at the left affect the various categories of final demand on the right through the three channels described above. Cost-of-capital variables affect all categories of expenditure listed on the right. The combination of these cost-of-capital linkages, the effect of financial yields on net worth and consumption, and the effect of the credit rationing variable in housing, cause for the entire model a very complicated response to monetary forces. Estimating the quantitative importance and timing pattern of this response by simulation experiments is the function of the next section.

Some Empirical Results

For this report we are using a version of the Federal Reserve-MIT econometric model which contains 75 behavioral equations, identities for 35 other endogenous variables, and 70 exogenous variables. Many of the equations are nonlinear, many depend importantly on initial conditions, and many groups of equations have com-

---

* This portion of the paper has not been included here. A discussion of the real and financial sectors of the FRB-MIT model may be found in reading 11 by Joseph M. Crews. Rather thorough examination of the view of the transmission process that underlies the FRB-MIT model is done in Part I in reading 5 by Yung Chul Park and in reading 7 by Roger W. Spencer.—Ed.

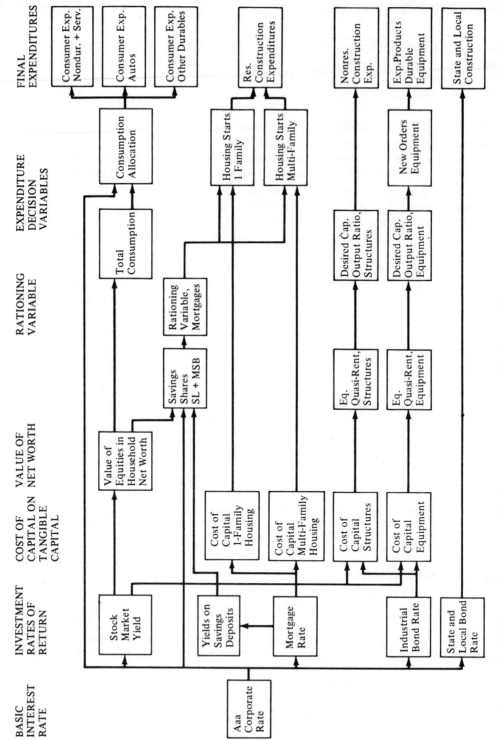

CHART 1   FIRST ROUND EFFECTS OF MONETARY POLICY: FRB–MIT ECONOMETRIC MODEL

plicated internal dynamics. The response patterns of the entire model are thus quite complex, with a great many oscillatory and nonoscillatory mechanisms superimposed on each other. The following results are designed to illustrate just the essential elements of the response of aggregate demand to monetary and fiscal policy measures.

The properties of a model this large and complicated are best illustrated by simulation experiments. In this paper we present a series of such experiments measuring the effects of step changes in key policy variables by computing differences between two simulation runs. The first run in every case is a dynamic simulation of the model over some time period. By dynamic we mean that while we use actual values for all current and lagged exogenous variables, we use only initial actual values for endogenous variables. The model generates solutions for the endogenous variables during the first simulation period, then uses these in generating solutions for the second period, and so forth for each succeeding period. The second run in each experiment is another dynamic simulation identical to the first in all respects except that one of the policy variables is altered by a specified amount beginning in a specified quarter and continuing for all subsequent quarters of the simulation period. The final step, computing differences between the control and experimental simulations, gives the response of endogenous variables in the model to the specified maintained change in the policy variable.

A. Monetary Policy Simulations

1. DIRECT EFFECTS OF MONETARY POLICY

We measure the effect of our central monetary policy instrument, unborrowed reserves, by examining the response of the model to a maintained reserve increase of $1 billion. That is, we assume that the Federal Reserve made $1 billion more unborrowed reserves available than the actual historical amount in the initial quarter and maintained the billion-dollar excess over historical amounts in each succeeding quarter. While actual monetary policy changes rarely follow this step-change pattern, we nevertheless find this a useful experiment because it enables us to compute the multiplier over time for this policy change.

We first conduct this experiment for a subset of the equations of the model including only the financial sector and demand equations for categories of goods and services affected directly by monetary policy. This simulation gives us only the direct effects of monetary policy on financial markets and, through financial markets, on final spending, uncomplicated by feedbacks of output and prices back to the financial sector, or by multiplier-accelerator responses within nonfinancial markets. The results are presented in Chart 2 and summarized in Table 1.

We see from the table that the direct effect of the $1 billion open market operations is to stimulate final demand by $3.5 billion by the end of the year, by $5.4 billion after two years, and on up to $7.0 billion after four years. These numbers are appreciably smaller than the total effect over the first few years including the multi-

Direct Effects on Final Demand of a Billion-Dollar Step Increase in Unborrowed Reserves, Initial
Conditions of 1964 I

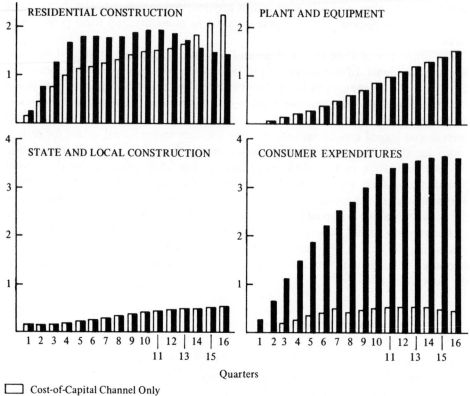

CHART 2 THE THREE CHANNELS OF MONETARY POLICY: FEDERAL RESERVE-MIT MODEL

plier-accelerator mechanism and the feedback from the real sector to the financial
sector.

The bottom panel of the table shows that while residential construction is responsible for much of the early effect, its importance gradually declines over time. This
pattern can be attributed largely to the rationing channel. In periods immediately
following the policy change, market rates of interest fall relative to the sluggish
deposit rates of savings institutions. There follows a sharp rise in savings deposit
inflows, which in turn stimulates housing starts and expenditures. Thus the credit
rationing channel alone comprises 17 percent of the total direct monetary effect by
the end of four quarters. But as time goes on, the normal relation between deposit
rates and market rates is restored and savings inflows fall relative to their recent high
levels. As this happens, the importance of rationing is reduced. In fact, by the end of

Table 1. Direct Effects of a Billion-Dollar Step Increase in Unborrowed Reserves
(Initial Conditions of 1964 I)

a. Billions of Current Dollars

Quarter	Personal Consumption Expenditures			Residential Construction Expenditures			Plant and Equip.	State & Local Con-struction	Total			
	Cost of Capital	Wealth	Total	Cost of Capital	Credit Rationing	Total	Cost of Capital	Cost of Capital	Cost of Capital	Wealth	Credit Rationing	Total
4	.3	1.2	1.5	1.0	.6	1.6	.2	.2	1.7	1.2	.6	3.5
8	.4	2.3	2.7	1.3	.5	1.8	.6	.3	2.6	2.3	.5	5.4
12	.5	3.0	3.5	1.5	.3	1.8	1.1	.4	3.5	3.0	.3	6.8
16	.4	3.2	3.6	2.2	− .8	1.4	1.5	.5	4.6	3.2	− .8	7.0

b. Percentages of the Total Effect

Quarter	Consumption	Residential Construction	Plant & Equip.	State and Local	Channel 1 Cost of Capital	Channel 2 Wealth	Channel 3 Credit Rationing
4	43	45	6	6	49	34	17
8	50	33	11	6	48	43	9
12	51	26	16	7	51	44	5
16	51	20	21	8	66	45	− 11

Note: As explained in the text, the results shown in this table describe only the effect of unborrowed reserves in financial markets and, through financial markets, on final demand for goods and services. They do not include multiplier-accelerator interactions or feedbacks from goods markets to financial markets.

four years deposit rates have adjusted completely, savings funds are returning to their pre–policy-change allocation, and a reverse credit rationing process is at work. In the longer run this process too dies out as deposit inflows settle down to a steady-state rate of growth.

The cost-of-capital channel operates strongly throughout the four-year simulation period. Initial effects are important for housing and ultimate effects both for housing and for plant and equipment. As mentioned in the first section of this paper, cost-of-capital effects on expenditures last only until actual capital stocks have reached their desired levels; but in the model this process is not complete by the end of four years. One reason for this long lag is the time it takes short-term market interest rates to affect long-term rates. The simulations in Table 1 are not carried on for a long enough period to see expenditures induced by changes in the cost of capital recede toward zero. The beginnings of this pattern are visible for consumer durables, but investment in plant and equipment, multi-family housing, and state and local construction is still building up after four years.

The wealth effect also operates strongly throughout the period. Since the change in wealth affects consumption promptly this wealth effect accounts for 35 percent of the total effect by the end of the first year. It builds up gradually to 45 percent by the end of four years, and in the very long run when the other channels fade out of the picture (aside from the permanent replacement effect of the cost of capital) the wealth effect would comprise the entire direct monetary effect.

2. FULL MODEL EFFECTS OF MONETARY POLICY

We turn now to the full model effects of a change in unborrowed reserves. These are different from the direct effects we have described above because we now allow these direct effects to set in motion a multiplier-accelerator process and because we also permit the real sector to feed back into the monetary sector. The former inclusion expands the effects of monetary policy changes in early years while the latter inclusion, by allowing the rise in money income to increase interest rates and partially reverse initial rate movements, gradually dampens the long-run effects.

The results of the full model simulation beginning in 1964 I are shown in Table 2. Here the effects on real GNP build up to $5.4 billion by one year and $10.0 billion by two years, but after that they decline rapidly so that by the end of four years there is scarcely any effect on real income. The four-year effect of the monetary change on money GNP is thus almost entirely in the form of higher prices. For the first two years the full system response for real GNP is much larger than the direct effect shown in Table 1 because of the multiplier-accelerator mechanism. But after that the full system real response dies out because of the oscillations inherent in the accelerator system as well as because of the rises in interest rates stimulated by the rise in money GNP. By way of illustration of this interest-rate feedback, in the direct-effect

Table 2. Effects of a Billion-Dollar Step Increase in Unborrowed Reserves, Full Model Effects
(Initial Conditions of 1964 I)

Quarter	Real GNP (billions 1958 dollars)	GNP Deflator (percentage points)	Money GNP (billions current dollars)	Corporate Aaa Bond Rate (percentage points)	Unemployment Rate (percentage points)
1	.7	—	.8	− .27	—
2	2.0	—	2.3	− .14	− .1
3	3.6	.1	4.3	− .12	− .2
4	5.4	.1	6.6	− .16	− .3
5	7.0	.2	8.9	− .19	− .4
6	8.3	.3	11.1	− .22	− .5
7	9.3	.4	13.2	− .22	− .6
8	10.0	.6	15.1	− .24	− .6
9	10.5	.8	16.9	− .25	− .7
10	10.7	.9	18.6	− .26	− .7
11	10.3	1.2	19.9	− .24	− .7
12	9.4	1.4	20.6	− .25	− .6
13	7.9	1.7	20.6	− .25	− .6
14	6.1	1.9	20.1	− .23	− .5
15	3.9	2.1	19.0	− .23	− .3
16	1.4	2.2	17.2	− .23	− .2

simulations underlying Table 1 the corporate Aaa rate declined by 46 basis points after four years while in the full model simulations underlying Table 2 the corporate rate declined by only 23 basis points.

3. EFFECT OF INITIAL CONDITIONS

We now compare full model multipliers for different initial conditions and different directions of policy change. For one set of simulations we start in 1964 I and raise unborrowed reserves (these are the simulations described already) and for the other set we begin in 1958 II and lower unborrowed reserves.

The obvious difference between these two initial periods is the difference in inflationary potential. The quarters during and after 1964 were ones of fairly high resource utilization, and the expansion of reserves at this time would be expected to stimulate price increases promptly. On the other hand, there was substantial excess capacity in 1958 and the decrease in reserves at that time could be expected to have a minimal short-run effect on prices. The appendix includes a discussion and listing of the non-linear "Phillips curve" equation which largely accounts for this result in the model.*

Another, perhaps less obvious difference between the two periods which affects the simulation results is the difference in initial stock market conditions. . . . The value of common stock in net worth is given by the capitalization identity $ST = 100 \ (Y_{CD}/R_D)$. The response of stock prices to a unit change in R_D, it follows, is equal to $-(ST/R_D)$. If the dividend-price ratio changes by a constant absolute amount, therefore, the absolute change in the value of stock, and hence net worth and consumption, will be greater the lower is the initial level of this dividend-price ratio, and the higher the initial level of stock prices. In a sense, the dividend-price ratio has greater leverage the lower it is. In 1958 the dividend-price ratio was 4.1 percent, and the first-year rise of 14 basis points induced by the restrictive monetary change reduced the value of common stock equities by only $14 billion. But by 1964 the dividend-price ratio had fallen to 3.0 percent, stock values had more than doubled, and the decline induced by the monetary expansion (again 14 basis points) increased the value of common stock by $37 billion. Since the coefficient of net worth in the consumption function is .04, this difference alone directly stimulated almost $1 billion of added consumption.

These differences are illustrated by Tables 2 and 3. We see that initial real income effects in the 1964 simulation are moderately larger than in the 1958 simulation, mainly because of the greater impact of the dividend-price ratio. The price response is substantially higher in 1964, even allowing for the bigger initial real income response, because of the lower initial unemployment rate. But it is interesting to note that the much higher 1964 money GNP response leads to a greater reversal of initial interest rate movements which means that by the end of four years the real GNP response is much less in the 1964 simulations. In the very long run of, say, fifteen or twenty years, the real GNP response would die out in both cases—but this happens more quickly the faster prices respond.

* The Appendix is not reprinted in this book.—Ed.

Table 3. Effects of a Billion-Dollar Step Decrease in Unborrowed Reserves, Full Model Effects
(Initial Conditions of 1958 II)

Quarter	Real GNP (billions 1958 dollars)	GNP Deflator (percentage points)	Money GNP (billions current dollars)	Corporate Aaa Bond Rate (percentage points)	Unemployment Rate (percentage points)
1	− .5	—	− .5	.27	—
2	− 1.3	− .1	− 1.5	.14	.1
3	− 2.7	− .1	− 2.9	.13	.2
4	− 4.2	− .1	− 4.6	.17	.3
5	− 5.4	− .2	− 6.1	.20	.4
6	− 6.5	− .2	− 7.5	.24	.5
7	− 7.3	− .3	− 8.8	.27	.6
8	− 7.9	− .4	− 9.8	.28	.7
9	− 8.3	− .5	− 10.7	.29	.7
10	− 8.5	− .6	− 11.5	.29	.7
11	− 8.6	− .7	− 12.1	.29	.7
12	− 8.4	− .8	− 12.5	.30	.7
13	− 8.1	− .9	− 12.8	.30	.7
14	− 7.7	− 1.0	− 13.1	.30	.7
15	− 7.2	− 1.1	− 13.2	.30	.6
16	− 6.6	− 1.2	− 13.4	.29	.6

B. Comparison of Monetary and Fiscal Policy Multipliers

We conclude the section by comparing these monetary policy multipliers with multipliers for common fiscal policy stabilization tools. The comparisons are given in Table 4, which shows the full model response to a $1 billion increase in unborrowed reserves, a $5 billion increase in real Federal compensation of employees, a .02 decrease in the personal income tax rate. The latter implies an initial revenue loss of $4.5 billion at 1964 I levels.

The size of these policy changes, and hence of the real GNP and price results, is arbitrary; there is nothing "natural" about comparing a $1 billion reserve change with a $5 billion expenditure change or any other specific amount. What are of interest are the dynamic paths, which show a much more rapid approach to peak real GNP effects for Federal spending than for monetary policy, with tax rates in between the two. We have noted before that these findings imply that it is difficult for monetary and fiscal authorities to conduct "fine-tuning" stabilization policy operations, though stabilization operations could be successful against more persistent exogenous swings.[2]

Monetary policy works more slowly than fiscal policy in our model because it takes time for the open market operations to be reflected in changes in long-term

[2][6] page 27.

Table 4. Effects of Three Expansionary Policies
(Initial Conditions of 1964 I)

Quarter	Real GNP (billions 1958 dollars)			GNP Deflator (percentage points)			Money GNP (billions current dollars)			Corporate Aaa Rate (percentage points)			Unemployment Rate (percentage points)		
	A	B	C	A	B	C	A	B	C	A	B	C	A	B	C
1	.7	6.6	1.4	—	—	—	.8	7.3	1.6	− .27	.06	.03	—	− .2	—
2	2.0	8.3	2.9	—	—	—	2.3	9.4	3.4	− .14	.05	.02	− .1	− .5	− .2
3	3.6	8.7	3.6	.1	.2	.1	4.3	10.3	4.4	− .12	.05	.02	− .2	− .6	− .2
4	5.4	8.9	4.0	.1	.2	.1	6.6	11.2	5.2	− .16	.06	.03	− .3	− .6	− .3
5	7.0	9.0	4.5	.2	.4	.2	8.9	12.0	6.1	− .19	.08	.04	− .4	− .6	− .3
6	8.3	8.7	4.8	.3	.4	.2	11.1	12.4	6.8	− .22	.09	.05	− .5	− .6	− .3
7	9.3	8.0	5.0	.4	.6	.3	13.2	12.6	7.6	− .23	.10	.06	− .6	− .6	− .3
8	10.0	7.9	5.2	.6	.7	.4	15.1	13.5	8.5	− .24	.12	.07	− .6	− .6	− .3
9	10.4	7.6	5.3	.8	.9	.5	16.9	14.1	9.3	− .25	.14	.09	− .7	− .5	− .4
10	10.7	6.8	5.4	.9	1.0	.6	18.6	14.3	10.1	− .26	.16	.10	− .7	− .5	− .4
11	10.3	6.1	5.4	1.2	1.1	.7	19.9	14.5	10.9	− .24	.17	.12	− .7	− .4	− .4
12	9.4	5.6	5.2	1.4	1.3	.8	20.6	15.2	11.6	− .25	.19	.14	− .6	− .4	− .3
13	7.9	5.8	4.7	1.7	1.4	.9	20.6	16.5	11.8	− .25	.20	.14	− .6	− .4	− .3
14	6.1	6.2	3.9	1.9	1.6	1.1	20.1	18.2	11.7	− .23	.22	.15	− .5	− .4	− .3
15	3.9	5.7	2.8	2.1	1.8	1.2	19.0	18.8	11.3	− .23	.24	.16	− .3	− .4	− .2
16	1.4	5.0	1.6	2.2	1.9	1.2	17.2	19.2	10.6	− .23	.25	.18	− .2	− .3	− .2

A—Step increase in unborrowed reserves of $1 billion.
B—Step increase in real Federal wage payments of $5 billion.
C—Step decrease in personal tax rate of .02 (about $4.5 billion in revenue).

interest rates, and even more time for these rate changes to be reflected in investment decisions. The latter delay can be attributed to the putty-clay behavior of equipment investment expenditures and the long decision lag for producers' and state and local construction expenditures. If we had found these decision lags to be shorter, or if we had found the more quickly acting credit rationing and wealth effects of monetary policy to be more important in the first year, the model would have implied a more rapid operation of monetary policy.

Comparisons of these results with other models reveal a mixture of similarities and differences. Although the fiscal policy multipliers in Table 4 roughly agree with those of other econometric models, the monetary multipliers are much larger. On the other hand, the monetary multipliers have about the same ultimate effect as these obtained by the Staff of the St. Louis Federal Reserve Bank recently in a regression of GNP on monetary and fiscal variables,* though the timing patterns and the effect of fiscal policy computed by the two studies are radically different.[3] Our monetary multipliers are smaller than what a simple quantity theory of money would imply.

We would like, in conclusion, to encourage the use of the Federal Reserve–MIT model as a framework for resolving these puzzling differences among estimates of

[3] See [1], particularly equation 4.
* The David Fand article in this section contains a good example of this type of regression. —Ed.

monetary and fiscal policy effects. Most of the estimates suggest properties of the economy which can be translated into assertions about equations and parameters in our model. The structure of the model is flexible enough to permit monetary policy to be either a dominant or a rather minor force and to permit the income-expenditure approach with its implication of important fiscal policy effects to be either completely overshadowed or largely valid. Monetary policy is permitted to work through a number of channels, including carefully developed measures of the cost of capital, wealth effects, and credit rationing. We have presented one set of estimates of the model in this paper, suggesting important roles for a wide range of policy instruments. Further work on the specification and estimation of the model should be a useful way to analyze and ultimately reconcile different views about how our major fiscal and monetary policy tools operate.

REFERENCES

1. L. ANDERSEN and J. JORDAN. "Monetary and Fiscal Actions: A Test of Their Relative Importance in Economic Stabilization," *Federal Reserve Bank of St. Louis Monthly Review,* November 1968.

2. A. ANDO and F. MODIGLIANI. "Econometric Analysis of Stabilization Policies," paper to be presented at the December 1968 meetings of the American Economic Association.

3. A. ANDO and F. MODIGLIANI. "The Life Cycle Hypothesis of Saving: Aggregate Implications and Tests," *American Economic Review,* May 1963.

4. C. W. BISCHOFF. *A Study of Distributed Lags and Business Fixed Investment,* Doctoral Dissertation, Massachusetts Institute of Technology, 1968.

5. R. BRUMBERG and F. MODIGLIANI. "Utility Analysis and the Consumption Function: An Interpretation of Cross-Section Data," in *Post-Keynesian Economics,* K. Kurihara, ed., 1955.

6. F. DE LEEUW and E. GRAMLICH. "The Federal Reserve-MIT Econometric Model," *Federal Reserve Bulletin,* January 1968.

7. D. JAFFEE. *Credit Rationing and the Commercial Loan Market,* Doctoral Dissertation, Massachusetts Institute of Technology, 1968.

8. D. JAFFEE and F. MODIGLIANI. "A Theory and Test of Credit Rationing," forthcoming.

9. D. JORGENSON. "Anticipations and Investment Behavior," in *The Brookings Quarterly Econometric Model of the United States,* Duesenberry *et al.,* eds., Rand McNally, 1965.

10. J. LINTNER. "Distribution of Incomes of Corporations Among Dividends, Retained Earnings, and Taxes," *American Economic Review,* May 1956.

11. F. MODIGLIANI. "Econometric Models of Stabilization Policy," presented at the Far Eastern Meeting of the Econometric Society, June 1968.

12. F. MODIGLIANI and R. SUTCH. "Innovations in Interest Rate Policies," *American Economic Review,* May 1966.

13. J. MUTH. "The Demand for Non-Farm Housing," in *The Demand for Durable Goods,* Harberger, ed., University of Chicago Press, 1960.

14. R. RASCHE and H. SHAPIRO. "The FRB-MIT Model: Its Special Features," *American Economic Review,* May 1968.

15. M. REID. *Housing and Income,* University of Chicago Press, 1962.

13

St. Louis Model Revisited

Leonall C. Andersen and
Keith M. Carlson

During the early 1960's a framework of economic analysis stressing the role of monetary aggregates was developed at the Federal Reserve Bank of St. Louis. Originally this framework depended on the "chart" as a tool of analysis, but by the late 1960's efforts had been directed toward the addition of the use of regression techniques in the analysis of economic data. Some of these quantitative research efforts were consolidated in 1970 with the publication of what has come to be known as the "St. Louis model" [4].

1. Origin and Development of St. Louis Model

1.1. Purpose of the Model

The purpose of publishing research results in the form of an empirically estimated model was threefold. First, and foremost, a model with a monetarist foundation was sought for purposes of assisting in the development and evaluation of stabilization policies. Second, there was a desire to add a monetarist model to the existing set of

Reprinted from the *International Economic Review*, Vol. 15, No. 2 (June, 1974), pp. 305-327, by permission of the International Economic Association and the authors.

Keynesian econometric models. Third, the model was offered as a challenge to other monetarists to produce empirical statements of their views.

The purposes of the model can be emphasized by noting some of the purposes for which it was *not* designed. First, the model was not designed for exact quarter-to-quarter forecasting. Its purpose, rather, was to indicate the general nature of the differential response of certain key economic variables to alternative courses of monetary and fiscal action. Second, the model was not offered as a substitute for existing macroeconometric models, though to the extent that it differed in methodology and carried different implications it was offered as a challenge to the models of others. Third, the model was not designed to provide information on allocative detail, which was a reflection of the belief that aggregative behavior can be analyzed quite independently of the behavior of individual sectors.

1.2. Theoretical Foundation

The primary theoretical consideration underlying the development of the model was the modern quantity theory of money.[1] The focus of the modern quantity theory is on the behavior of economic units in response to changes in the money stock. Money is an asset which provides services to its holder as do all other assets. Furthermore, the existing stock of money must be held by someone. As a result, a change in the stock of money will induce a discrepancy between actual and desired holdings of money, which will cause shuffling of the wealth portfolio. Included in this adjustment is a change in spending on goods and services.

A second theoretical consideration which was implicit in the construction of the model, though not explicitly recognized by the model builders at the time, was the effect of search and information costs on economic behavior.[2] Information about equilibrium prices is not costless to gather, and thus economic units must search for equilibrium prices by sampling the market. As a result, prices do not necessarily adjust instantaneously to their new equilibrium level in response to a change in the pace of total spending.

As a result of these theoretical considerations, the relative impact of monetary and fiscal actions requires a careful assessment. This assessment includes differentiating between short-run effects and long-run effects, as well as paying special attention to the method of financing government expenditures.

1.3. Research Strategy

Construction of the St. Louis model was guided by four major principles. As always, an underlying theoretical foundation was considered essential. For the most part, this theoretical frame of reference was the quantity theory as it had been applied by the

---

[1]See [13] and [19].

[2]As a general reference, see [18]. For a specific interpretation of the St. Louis model from the viewpoint of information costs, see [8]. More recent research results at the Federal Reserve Bank of St. Louis, which take into account information costs, are summarized in [7].

St. Louis Bank over the years to the analysis of economic developments. Furthermore, analysis relating to the timing of response of economic variables like prices and output to monetary and fiscal actions was consistent with the theory of search and information costs.

A second principle, reflecting the objectives of the model builder, was that the model have primarily a policy orientation. With this primary interest in economic stabilization, the aim was not to forecast economic events but, rather, to assess the impact of alternative monetary and fiscal policies. Though considerations of forecasting could not be ignored, the emphasis was on capturing the timing and magnitude of the effect of monetary and fiscal actions. As has been demonstrated with other models, a model need not contain policy variables in order to forecast well.[3] Such forecasting models, almost by definition, are of little direct use to policymakers.

A third principle, which might be considered a subprinciple of the policy-orientation principle, is the use of a reduced-form approach. The impact of monetary and fiscal actions cannot be accurately gauged by assuming that such actions affect economic activity via only certain assumed channels. The choice of appropriate monetary policy cannot be formulated by examining only its effect on the economy through, say, interest rate changes or wealth effects. A reduced-form approach is not without its dangers, but the results based on this approach represent an important addition to the results of existing models.

Finally, a small model approach serves as the fourth guiding principle. For purposes of policy formulation, primary interest is focused on a few key economic variables. By keeping the model small and limited in scope, research resources can be concentrated on a few important relationships. Underlying this small model methodology is the belief that sectoral detail is not required to produce an accurate assessment of the aggregative impact of monetary and fiscal actions.

2. Summary of Model

This section summarizes the model and some of its properties. The algebraic form of the model has not changed since the model was published in 1970. This is not to say that some changes in specification would not have been appropriate, but with the initial development of the model, a trial period was considered necessary in order to gain a better understanding of the performance of the model in light of its original purposes.

2.1. Equations of the Model

The model is summarized in algebraic form in Table 1. This summary provides only the essential features of the model, ignoring problems of dimensionality and lag

---

[3]For further discussion of this point, see [11]. For a comparison of the St. Louis model with a forecasting model which places little emphasis on policy variables, see [15].

Table 1.   Algebraic Form of St. Louis Model

---

(1)   Total Spending Equation
$$\Delta Y_t = f_1(\Delta M_t \cdots \Delta M_{t-n}, \Delta E_t \cdots \Delta E_{t-n})$$

(2)   Price Equation
$$\Delta P_t = f_2(D_t \cdots D_{t-n}, \Delta P_t^A)$$

(3)   Demand Pressure Identity
$$D_t = \Delta Y_t - (X_t^F - X_{t-1})$$

(4)   Total Spending Identity
$$\Delta Y_t = \Delta P_t + \Delta X_t$$

(5)   Interest Rate Equation
$$R_t = f_3(\Delta M_t, \Delta X_t \cdots \Delta X_{t-n}, \Delta P_t, \Delta P_t^A)$$

(6)   Anticipated Price Equation
$$\Delta P_t^A = f_4(\Delta P_{t-1} \cdots \Delta P_{t-n})$$

(7)   Unemployment Rate Equation
$$U_t = f_5(G_t, G_{t-1})$$

(8)   GNP Gap Identity
$$G_t = \frac{X_t^F - X_t}{X_t^F}$$

Notation:
   Endogenous Variables
     ΔY_t = change in total spending (nominal GNP)
     ΔP_t = change in price level (GNP price deflator)
     D_t = demand pressure
     ΔX_t = change in output (real GNP)
     R_t = market interest rate
     ΔP_t^A = anticipated change in price level
     U_t = unemployment rate
     G_t = GNP gap
   Exogenous Variables*
     ΔM_t = change in money stock
     ΔE_t = change in high-employment Federal expenditures
     X_t^F = potential (full-employment) output
*Other than lagged variables

length. The exact form of the equations and two sets of statistical estimates of coefficients are given in the Appendix. One set of coefficients is for the sample period ending fourth quarter 1968 and the other is based on data through second quarter 1973.

Equation (1) in Table 1 is the total spending (nominal GNP) equation. The quarterly change in total spending (ΔY) is specified as a function of current and past changes in money stock (ΔM) and current and past changes in high-employment Federal expenditures (ΔE).

Equation (2) specifies the quarterly change in the price level (ΔP) as a function of current and past demand pressures (D) and anticipated price changes (ΔP^A).[4] Demand pressure is defined in equation (3) as the change in total spending minus the potential increase in output ($X^F - X$). This price equation is essentially a short-run Phillips curve extended to include changes in total spending and anticipated prices.[5]

Equation (4) is a definition of changes in total spending in terms of its components. With ΔY determined by equation (1), and ΔP by equation (2), ΔX can be derived from equation (4).

Equation (5) gives the market rate of interest (R) as a function of current changes in the money stock (ΔM), current and past changes in output (ΔX), current price change (ΔP), and anticipated price change (ΔP^A). Anticipated price change is assumed to depend on past price changes.

Equation (7) is the unemployment rate equation and is a transformation of the GNP gap (G), as defined in equation (8), into a measure of unemployment relative to the labor force. This transformation is based on "Okun's Law."[6]

2.2. Workings of the Model

The St. Louis model is described as a reduced-form model, but such a description is not completely accurate in describing each of the equations of the model. However, due to the recursive nature of the model, the reduced-form label is accurate as a general label.

The fundamental relationship of the model is the total spending equation. Total spending is determined by monetary and fiscal (federal spending financed by taxes or borrowing from the public) actions, though no direct information is provided as to how such actions affect spending.

The change in total spending is combined with an estimate of potential output to provide a measure of demand pressure. An estimate of anticipated price change (with the weights on past price changes taken from the long-term interest rate equation) is combined with demand pressure to determine the change in the price level.

The total spending identity provides the determination of the change in output, given the change in total spending and the change in prices. This procedure differs from standard practice in other econometric models, where output and prices are determined separately, then combined to determine total spending.

The changes in output, prices, and anticipated prices and in the money stock determine market interest rates. Interest rates do not exercise a direct role in the model in the determination of spending, output, and prices.

To determine the unemployment rate, the change in output is first combined with the estimate of potential output to determine the GNP gap. The GNP gap is then transformed into the unemployment rate.

[4]For a critique of this price equation, see [14].
[5]For a discussion of the St. Louis model in the context of the Phillips curve controversy, see [5].
[6]See [16].

2.3. Properties of the Model

To describe the model, its characteristics are summarized in relation to four key monetarist propositions.[7] These propositions are:

1. Monetary actions are the dominant factor contributing to economic fluctuations.
2. Monetary actions have little, if any, lasting effect on real variables, with lasting effects on only nominal variables.
3. Fiscal actions, defined as changes in Federal spending with a given money stock, have only a transitory impact on economic activity.
4. The private economy is inherently stable.

MONETARY ACTIONS AS DOMINANT IMPULSE

The St. Louis model, as designed and estimated, is consistent with the proposition that monetary actions are the major factor contributing to economic fluctuations. Though not designed as a model depicting the cyclical movements of the economy, operating via the total spending equation, a change in the growth rate of money gives rise to cyclical variation in real GNP and unemployment. The total spending equation does not permit forces other than monetary and fiscal actions to change the growth in total spending, but analysis of the error term in that equation indicates that such a specification is not unwarranted.[8]

The model does not provide direct evidence disconfirming the hypothesis that nonpolicy influences are instrumental in causing economic fluctuations. However, direct evidence is provided relating to the contribution of monetary as opposed to fiscal actions as a factor contributing to cyclical movements in economic activity.

MONETARY IMPACT ON NOMINAL VARIABLES

Simulations of the St. Louis model indicate that after a considerable period of time a change in the rate of monetary expansion influences only nominal magnitudes, namely, total spending (GNP), the price level, and nominal interest rates. Real magnitudes, notably the growth of output and employment, are unaffected. Following short-run responses to a change in monetary growth, total spending and the price level grow at rates determined by the rate of increase in the money stock. Output and employment grow at rates determined by growth of natural resources, capital stock, labor force, and productivity.

TRANSITORY IMPACT OF FISCAL ACTIONS

Fiscal actions are measured by the change in high-employment Federal expenditures. This choice for a fiscal variable is designed to capture the effects of changes in Federal spending when financed by borrowing or taxation. According to the model,

[7]For further discussion of these propositions, see [1] and [9].
[8]See the appendix to [6].

fiscal actions have short-run effects, but for periods of a year of more, the net effect is much smaller. When first estimated, the long-run fiscal multiplier on nominal GNP was about zero. Estimated with data through second quarter 1973, the value of the multiplier is about 0.5, but still not significantly different from zero.

INHERENT STABILITY OF THE ECONOMY

The St. Louis model does not provide evidence on the proposition that the economy is inherently stable in the sense of Brunner [9]. However, simulations of the St. Louis model demonstrate properties which are consistent with a corollary to the inherent stability proposition, that monetary and fiscal actions are a source of instability.[9] When the model is shocked by changing any one of the three exogenous variables (change in money stock, change in high-employment Federal expenditures, and potential output), simulations indicate an initial period of oscillation followed by a return to a steady long-run, growth path.[10]

3. Evaluation of Model

The St. Louis model was developed in various stages over the period 1968 to 1970. Once published in 1970, its basic form was kept unchanged so as to permit more accurate assessment of its usefulness and validity than if frequent changes in specification were made. Though the fundamental specification of the model has been kept unchanged, the model has been reestimated as new data have become available. Consequently, despite unchanged form, the nature and properties of the model have changed somewhat since first published in 1970.

This section gives a summary of the projection record of the model. This summary is based on simulations of the model outside the sample period. Then some observations are made about the model in the form of apparent "successes" and "failures" of the model to date.

3.1. Projection Record

The projection record for the key economic variables in the St. Louis model is given in Tables 2 to 7. These projections, even though they are beyond the sample period, can be described as *ex post* because they are generated using known values for the exogenous variables as they existed in late 1973. The projections do *not* include intercept adjustments, add factors, or tender loving care, except to the extent that mechanical reestimation with most recent data is given such an interpretation. Furthermore, strike variables are not used, nor is there any use of autoregression in the residuals.

[9] For results of a similar exercise with a large econometric model, the Data Resources Model, see [12].

[10] For a summary of these simulations as well as further discussion of the properties of the model, see [2]. For further discussion of the inherent stability issue and a contrasting interpretation of the St. Louis model, see [17].

Table 2
St. Louis Model Projections* Compared With Actual
NOMINAL GNP
(Annual Rates of Change from Initial Quarter to Terminal Quarter)

Initial Quarter

Terminal quarter	4-68		1-69		2-69		3-69		4-69		1-70		2-70		3-70		4-70		1-71		2-71		3-71		4-71		1-72		2-72		3-72		4-72		1-73		2-73	
	Act.	Proj.	Act.	Proj.	Act.	Proj.	Act.	Proj.	Act.	Proj.	Act.	Proj.	Act.	Proj.	Act.	Proj.	Act.	Proj.	Act.	Proj.	Act.	Proj.	Act.	Proj.	Act.	Proj.	Act.	Proj.	Act.	Proj.	Act.	Proj.	Act.	Proj.	Act.	Proj.	Act.	Proj.
1-69	7.8	8.1																																				
2-69	7.6	7.8	7.5	7.3																																		
3-69	7.8	7.5	7.8	7.1	8.1	7.0																																
4-69	6.6	7.2	6.2	6.8	5.6	6.5	3.1	6.2																														
1-70	6.1	6.9	5.7	6.5	5.1	6.3	3.6	6.1	4.1	5.6																												
2-70	5.9	7.1	5.6	6.8	5.1	6.7	4.1	6.7	4.6	6.7	5.1	7.7																										
3-70	6.1	7.1	5.8	6.9	5.5	6.9	4.9	6.9	5.4	7.0	6.1	7.6	7.1	7.7																								
4-70	5.6	7.1	5.2	6.9	4.9	6.9	4.2	6.9	4.5	7.0	4.7	7.4	4.4	7.5	1.8	7.2																						
1-71	6.6	7.1	6.4	6.9	6.3	6.8	6.0	6.9	6.5	6.9	7.2	7.3	7.8	7.2	8.2	6.9	15.1	6.6																				
2-71	6.7	7.3	6.6	7.2	6.5	7.2	6.2	7.3	6.8	7.4	7.3	7.7	7.9	7.6	8.1	7.6	11.4	8.0	7.9	10.7																		
3-71	6.7	7.8	6.6	7.7	6.5	7.8	6.3	7.9	6.7	8.1	7.2	8.5	7.6	8.6	7.7	8.7	9.8	9.2	7.2	11.1	6.5	11.7																
4-71	6.8	7.9	6.7	7.9	6.6	7.9	6.5	8.1	6.9	8.2	7.3	8.6	7.7	8.7	7.8	8.9	9.3	9.1	7.5	10.4	7.3	10.4	8.0	8.6														
1-72	7.1	7.9	7.0	7.8	7.0	7.9	6.9	8.1	7.3	8.2	7.7	8.5	8.1	8.5	8.3	8.6	9.6	8.8	8.3	9.8	8.4	9.6	9.4	8.2	10.9	7.7												
2-72	7.4	7.9	7.4	7.9	7.3	7.9	7.3	8.1	7.7	8.1	8.1	8.4	8.5	8.3	8.7	8.4	9.9	8.6	8.9	9.5	9.1	9.1	10.0	8.0	11.0	7.7	11.2	8.0										
3-72	7.5	7.9	7.5	7.8	7.5	7.9	7.4	8.0	7.8	8.1	8.2	8.3	8.5	8.3	8.7	8.3	9.7	8.3	8.8	9.0	9.0	8.7	9.7	7.5	10.2	7.1	9.9	6.8	8.7	5.9								
4-72	7.7	8.0	7.7	8.0	7.7	8.1	7.7	8.2	8.1	8.3	8.5	8.5	8.8	8.4	9.0	8.5	10.0	8.6	9.2	9.3	9.5	9.0	10.1	8.2	10.6	8.1	10.5	8.3	10.2	8.5	11.7	10.3						
1-73	8.2	8.1	8.2	8.1	8.2	8.2	8.2	8.3	8.6	8.3	9.0	8.5	9.4	8.5	9.6	8.6	10.5	8.7	10.0	10.0	10.3	9.3	10.9	8.3	11.5	8.2	11.7	8.5	11.9	8.8	13.5	9.7	15.2	9.3				
2-73	8.3	8.1	8.3	8.1	8.3	8.2	8.3	8.3	8.7	8.3	9.1	8.5	9.4	8.5	9.6	8.6	10.5	8.6	10.0	10.0	10.2	9.2	10.8	8.2	11.3	8.3	11.3	8.3	11.3	8.3	12.2	8.5	12.5	8.6	9.8	8.0		
3-73p	8.4	8.0	8.4	8.0	8.5	8.1	8.5	8.2	8.8	8.2	9.2	8.3	9.5	8.3	9.7	8.4	10.5	8.3	10.0	8.8	10.3	8.8	10.7	7.8	11.1	7.7	11.2	7.8	11.2	8.0	11.8	8.5	11.8	7.9	10.1	7.2	10.4	6.4

*Projections in each column are based on regressions using actual data through the quarter heading each column, assuming subsequent actual changes in money and high-employment expenditures. The figures in each column are compounded annual rates of change from the initial quarter to the terminal quarter.
p—3-73 actual is preliminary.

Table 3
St. Louis Model Projections* Compared With Actual
GNP PRICE DEFLATOR
(Annual Rates of Change from Initial Quarter to Terminal Quarter)

Initial Quarter

Terminal quarter	4-68 Act.	4-68 Proj.	1-69 Act.	1-69 Proj.	2-69 Act.	2-69 Proj.	3-69 Act.	3-69 Proj.	4-69 Act.	4-69 Proj.	1-70 Act.	1-70 Proj.	2-70 Act.	2-70 Proj.	3-70 Act.	3-70 Proj.	4-70 Act.	4-70 Proj.	1-71 Act.	1-71 Proj.	2-71 Act.	2-71 Proj.	3-71 Act.	3-71 Proj.	4-71 Act.	4-71 Proj.	1-72 Act.	1-72 Proj.	2-72 Act.	2-72 Proj.	3-72 Act.	3-72 Proj.	4-72 Act.	4-72 Proj.	1-73 Act.	1-73 Proj.	2-73 Act.	2-73 Proj.
1-69	4.2	4.4																																				
2-69	4.9	4.4	5.5	4.4																																		
3-69	5.3	4.4	5.8	4.5	6.1	4.8																																
4-69	5.3	4.5	5.7	4.5	5.8	4.8	5.5	5.2																														
1-70	5.5	4.5	5.9	4.5	6.0	4.8	5.9	5.2	6.3	5.3																												
2-70	5.4	4.5	5.6	4.5	5.6	4.8	5.5	5.2	5.5	5.2	4.6	5.5																										
3-70	5.2	4.5	5.4	4.5	5.3	4.8	5.1	5.2	5.0	5.2	4.3	5.5	4.1	5.2																								
4-70	5.3	4.4	5.5	4.4	5.5	4.7	5.4	5.2	5.3	5.2	5.0	5.5	5.2	5.1	6.4	4.8																						
1-71	5.4	4.4	5.5	4.4	5.4	4.7	5.3	5.2	5.4	5.2	5.1	5.4	5.3	5.1	5.9	4.7	5.5	4.9																				
2-71	5.3	4.4	5.4	4.4	5.1	4.7	5.0	5.2	5.3	5.1	5.1	5.4	5.2	5.0	5.6	4.7	5.2	4.8	4.9	5.2																		
3-71	5.1	4.4	5.2	4.4	4.7	4.7	4.9	5.2	4.9	5.1	4.7	5.4	4.7	5.0	4.9	4.7	4.4	4.8	3.8	5.2	2.8	5.1																
4-71	4.8	4.4	4.8	4.3	4.8	4.7	4.5	5.1	4.5	5.1	4.2	5.4	4.1	5.0	4.2	4.7	3.6	4.8	3.0	5.2	2.1	5.1	1.3	4.4														
1-72	4.8	4.3	4.9	4.3	4.6	4.6	4.7	5.2	4.6	5.1	4.4	5.3	4.4	5.0	4.4	4.6	4.0	4.7	3.7	5.2	3.3	5.1	3.5	4.4	5.7	3.6												
2-72	4.6	4.3	4.6	4.3	4.6	4.6	4.4	5.1	4.3	5.1	4.1	5.3	4.0	4.9	4.0	4.6	3.6	4.7	3.2	5.2	2.8	5.0	2.8	4.3	3.6	3.5	1.6	3.9										
3-72	4.5	4.3	4.5	4.3	4.4	4.6	4.3	5.1	4.2	5.0	3.9	5.3	3.9	4.9	3.8	4.5	3.5	4.6	3.2	5.1	2.8	4.9	2.8	4.2	3.3	3.4	2.2	3.8	2.8	3.4								
4-72	4.4	4.3	4.4	4.3	4.3	4.6	4.2	5.1	4.1	5.0	3.9	5.2	3.8	4.8	3.8	4.5	3.5	4.5	3.2	5.1	2.9	4.9	2.9	4.1	3.3	3.3	2.6	3.7	3.1	3.4	3.3	3.3						
1-73	4.5	4.3	4.5	4.2	4.5	4.6	4.3	5.0	4.2	4.9	4.1	5.1	4.0	4.7	4.0	4.4	3.8	4.4	3.5	5.0	3.4	4.8	3.4	4.0	3.9	3.2	3.4	3.7	4.0	3.3	4.7	3.3	6.0	3.3				
2-73	4.6	4.3	4.7	4.2	4.6	4.5	4.5	5.0	4.5	4.9	4.3	5.1	4.3	4.6	4.3	4.3	4.1	4.3	4.0	4.9	3.8	4.7	4.0	3.8	4.4	3.2	4.2	3.6	4.8	3.3	5.5	3.2	6.7	3.3	7.3	3.8		
3-73p	4.8	4.2	4.8	4.2	4.7	4.5	4.7	4.9	4.6	4.8	4.5	5.0	4.5	4.6	4.5	4.3	4.5	4.3	4.2	4.8	4.1	4.6	4.3	3.7	4.8	3.1	4.6	3.5	5.2	3.2	5.8	3.2	6.7	3.2	7.0	3.7	6.7	4.0

*Projections in each column are based on regressions using actual data through the quarter heading each column, assuming subsequent actual changes in money and high-employment expenditures. The figures in each column are compounded annual rates of change from the initial quarter to the terminal quarter.

p—3-73 actual is preliminary.

211

The interpretation of Tables 2 to 7 is as follows: the numbers along the main diagonal indicate actual (act.) and projected (proj.) values one quarter ahead; the projections are based on coefficients estimated with data through the quarter heading each column. Similarly, the second diagonal represents the actual average and the average of the projection for two quarters ahead, the third diagonal for three quarters ahead, etc.

With respect to the variables of the model, primary interest is focused on the average projection for several quarters ahead. Experience with the St. Louis model indicates that it is not suitable for exact quarter-to-quarter forecasting, or even for periods of two or three quarters. The projection record, as summarized in these tables, provides a basis for attempting to determine what horizon is appropriate for this model. Any conclusions, however, are subject to the usual warnings, in that they reflect the peculiarities of the particular period under review. With a small model, however, continual monitoring of the model's performance is possible with a relatively small amount of effort.

Tables 2 to 7 are based on full model simulations rather than equation-by-equation estimates. Because of the recursive nature of the model, total spending projections would be the same in either case. Before summarizing these results by calculating mean absolute errors along the diagonal for each of the variables, a few comments are offered relating to each of the variables.

TOTAL SPENDING

The results in Table 2 for total spending indicate that for the full nineteen-quarter-ahead period from 1968 to 1973, the projected average annual rate of increase for GNP was in error by 0.4 of a percentage point. The period as a whole consisted of two subperiods which tended to offset each other. The first subperiod, from fourth quarter 1968 to fourth quarter 1971, consisted of an overestimate of 1.1 percentage point, while the second subperiod, from fourth quarter 1971 to third quarter 1973, was an underestimate of 3.4 percentage points. In fact, for each of the last seven quarters the model underestimated the increase in GNP. By comparison only three of the previous 12 quarters were underestimated, and one of those was a post-strike quarter. The problem with the total spending equation is one of capturing the changes in velocity during the period, though for the full period the average increase in velocity was apparently captured with a fair degree of accuracy.

PRICES

The price projections reflect to some extent the errors in the projection of GNP, though the lag structure of the model is such that total spending error is reflected more in real GNP projections. The price equation has long lags because of the anticipated price term, so quarter-to-quarter errors are to be expected given the nature of quarter-to-quarter variation in prices as measured by the GNP deflator and the treatment of government pay increases in the national income accounts. In addition, governmental interference with the operation of the price system and worldwide economic conditions are factors to be considered in interpreting Table 3.

Looking at the period before wage-price controls, from fourth quarter 1968 to second quarter 1971, the model projected inflation at a 4.4 percent average annual rate; the actual increase was at a 5.3 percent average rate. However, the price equation is a learning equation in the sense that reestimation with most recent data quickly captured the inflation experience of the period. For example, for the last year prior to the controls the model projected price advances at a 5.0 percent increase which compared with an actual increase of 5.2 percent.

Despite the inapplicability of the price equation during the period of controls, actual experience did not depart substantially from what the model projected. From second quarter 1971 to third quarter 1973 the model projected a 4.6 percent average annual rate compared to the actual increase of 4.1 percent. And it could be that the general price level has not yet fully adjusted to a level consistent with the long-run trend of monetary growth.

OUTPUT

Given the nature of the price equation, that is, a long lag on past price change and a sticky response to changes in aggregate demand, projections of output tend to mirror projections of total spending. Table 4 indicates that on a quarter-to-quarter basis the pattern of error for output is essentially the same as for total spending—overestimating in the early part of the period and underestimating in the later part.

Over the full period there are some differences. In particular, for the period as a whole output was overestimated while total spending was underestimated. Given the construction of the model, output projections are residually determined and thus reflect fully errors in the projections of total spending and prices.

UNEMPLOYMENT

Projections of unemployment display the property of greater accuracy over short periods than for long periods (Table 5). Relevant to the assessment of the model's performance in connection with unemployment is that the period contained a recession followed by a slow recovery. As a result, a tendency to underestimate the rise in unemployment during recession shows up as a continuing error on an average basis as long as the unemployment rate does not quickly return to its pre-recession level. The estimates for unemployment reflect the learning characteristics of the price equation; that is, the price equation is important because it is the key factor in determining how much total spending is reflected in real output growth, which is the chief determinant of unemployment.

INTEREST RATES

Interest rate projections are especially difficult to interpret as a part of full model simulations because they represent the end of the recursive chain, though this could mean that offsetting errors in the arguments can work to provide an accurate projection on average. Accuracy on average seems to be the case for interest rates in the model (Tables 6 and 7). Projections of the average commercial paper rate for the full

Table 4
St. Louis Model Projections* Compared With Actual
REAL GNP
(Annual Rates of Change from Initial Quarter to Terminal Quarter)

Initial Quarter

Terminal quarter	4-68 Act.	4-68 Proj.	1-69 Act.	1-69 Proj.	2-69 Act.	2-69 Proj.	3-69 Act.	3-69 Proj.	4-69 Act.	4-69 Proj.	1-70 Act.	1-70 Proj.	2-70 Act.	2-70 Proj.	3-70 Act.	3-70 Proj.	4-70 Act.	4-70 Proj.	1-71 Act.	1-71 Proj.	2-71 Act.	2-71 Proj.	3-71 Act.	3-71 Proj.	4-71 Act.	4-71 Proj.	1-72 Act.	1-72 Proj.	2-72 Act.	2-72 Proj.	3-72 Act.	3-72 Proj.	4-72 Act.	4-72 Proj.	1-73 Act.	1-73 Proj.	2-73 Act.	2-73 Proj.
1-69	3.3	3.7																																				
2-69	2.6	3.3	1.9	2.8																																		
3-69	2.4	3.0	1.9	2.6	1.9	2.1																																
4-69	1.2	2.6	0.5	2.2	-0.2	1.7	-2.2	1.0																														
1-70	0.5	2.3	-0.2	2.0	-0.8	1.4	-2.2	0.8	2.1	0.3																												
2-70	0.5	2.5	0.0	2.3	-0.5	1.8	-1.3	1.4	0.8	1.4	0.5	2.1																										
3-70	0.9	2.6	0.4	2.4	0.2	2.0	-0.3	1.6	0.4	1.7	1.7	2.1	2.9	2.4																								
4-70	0.2	2.6	-0.2	2.4	0.6	2.0	0.5	1.6	0.8	1.7	0.4	1.9	2.5	2.5	-4.3	2.3																						
1-71	1.1	2.6	0.9	2.4	0.7	2.0	0.9	2.0	1.1	1.7	1.9	1.8	2.4	2.1	2.2	2.1	9.1	1.6																				
2-71	1.3	2.9	1.1	2.8	1.0	2.4	1.2	2.6	1.4	2.2	2.1	2.2	2.5	2.5	2.4	2.8	6.0	3.1	2.9	5.3																		
3-71	1.5	3.3	1.3	3.3	1.3	3.0	1.8	2.8	1.7	2.9	2.4	3.0	2.7	3.4	2.7	3.9	5.1	4.3	3.2	5.7	3.6	6.3																
4-71	1.9	3.4	1.8	3.4	1.8	3.1	2.1	2.8	2.3	3.0	3.0	3.1	3.4	3.6	3.5	4.1	5.5	4.2	4.4	5.0	5.1	5.1	4.8	4.0														
1-72	2.2	3.4	2.1	3.4	2.1	3.1	2.6	2.8	2.6	3.0	3.2	3.0	3.6	3.4	3.7	3.9	5.4	4.0	4.5	4.4	5.0	4.3	6.6	4.1	4.8	4.0												
2-72	2.7	3.5	2.6	3.5	2.7	3.2	3.0	2.8	3.3	3.0	3.9	2.9	4.3	3.3	3.7	3.9	6.1	3.8	5.5	4.1	6.0	3.9	5.7	3.7	7.1	4.1	9.5	4.0										
3-72	2.9	3.5	2.8	3.4	2.9	3.2	3.4	3.0	3.5	2.9	4.1	2.9	4.5	3.3	4.5	3.7	6.0	3.6	5.5	3.7	6.1	3.9	7.0	3.6	6.7	3.6	7.6	2.9	5.8	2.5								
4-72	3.2	3.6	3.2	3.6	3.3	3.4	3.7	3.1	3.9	3.2	4.4	3.1	4.8	3.6	4.7	3.6	6.3	4.0	5.9	4.1	6.0	3.6	6.7	3.2	7.0	4.6	7.8	4.4	6.9	5.0	8.1	6.8						
1-73	3.5	3.7	3.5	3.7	3.6	3.5	3.7	3.2	4.2	3.3	4.8	3.3	5.2	3.7	5.4	4.0	6.5	4.1	6.2	4.2	6.4	4.0	7.2	4.3	7.3	4.9	8.0	4.8	7.5	5.3	8.4	6.3	8.6	5.9				
2-73	3.4	3.8	3.4	3.8	3.5	3.5	3.6	3.1	4.1	3.4	4.6	3.3	4.9	3.7	5.1	4.1	6.1	4.1	5.8	4.1	6.2	4.1	6.5	4.2	8.0	4.8	6.8	4.6	6.2	5.1	6.3	5.8	5.5	5.2	2.4	4.1		
3-73p	3.4	3.7	3.5	3.7	3.5	3.5	3.6	3.1	4.1	3.3	4.5	3.2	4.8	3.7	5.0	4.0	5.9	4.0	5.6	3.9	5.9	3.9	6.2	4.0	6.1	4.5	6.3	4.5	5.7	4.6	5.6	5.2	4.8	4.6	3.0	3.4	3.5	2.3

*Projections in each column are based on regressions using actual data through the quarter heading each column, assuming subsequent actual changes in money and high-employment expenditures. The figures in each column are compounded annual rates of change from the initial quarter to the terminal quarter.

p—3-73 actual is preliminary.

214

Table 5
St. Louis Model Projections* Compared With Actual
UNEMPLOYMENT RATE
(Average Level from Initial Quarter to Terminal Quarter)

Initial Quarter

Terminal quarter	1-69		2-69		3-69		4-69		1-70		2-70		3-70		4-70		1-71		2-71		3-71		4-71		1-72		2-72		3-72		4-72		1-73		2-73		3-73	
	Act.	Proj.	Act.	Proj.	Act.	Proj.	Act.	Proj.	Act.	Proj.	Act.	Proj.	Act.	Proj.	Act.	Proj.	Act.	Proj.	Act.	Proj.	Act.	Proj.	Act.	Proj.	Act.	Proj.	Act.	Proj.	Act.	Proj.	Act.	Proj.	Act.	Proj.	Act.	Proj.	Act.	Proj.
1-69	3.4	3.7																																			
2-69	3.4	3.7	3.4	3.7																																	
3-69	3.5	3.7	3.5	3.8	3.6	3.9																															
4-69	3.5	3.8	3.5	3.8	3.6	4.0	3.6	4.0																													
1-70	3.6	3.8	3.7	3.9	3.8	4.1	3.9	4.2	4.2	4.5																											
2-70	3.8	3.9	3.9	4.0	4.0	4.2	4.2	4.3	4.5	4.7	4.8	5.0																									
3-70	4.0	4.0	4.1	4.1	4.3	4.3	4.4	4.4	4.7	4.8	5.0	5.1	5.2	5.3																							
4-70	4.2	4.1	4.4	4.1	4.5	4.3	4.7	4.5	5.0	4.8	5.3	5.2	5.5	5.3	5.8	5.4																					
1-71	4.4	4.1	4.6	4.2	4.7	4.4	4.9	4.6	5.2	4.9	5.4	5.3	5.7	5.4	5.9	5.5	6.0	6.1																			
2-71	4.6	4.2	4.7	4.3	4.9	4.5	5.1	4.7	5.3	5.0	5.5	5.4	5.7	5.5	5.9	5.5	5.9	6.1	5.9	5.7																	
3-71	4.7	4.2	4.8	4.3	5.0	4.5	5.2	4.7	5.4	5.1	5.6	5.4	5.8	5.6	5.8	5.6	5.9	6.2	5.9	5.7	6.0	5.8															
4-71	4.8	4.2	4.9	4.3	5.1	4.6	5.3	4.8	5.5	5.1	5.7	5.4	5.8	5.6	5.9	5.6	6.0	6.1	5.9	5.6	6.0	5.7	6.0	5.9													
1-72	4.9	4.3	5.0	4.3	5.2	4.6	5.3	4.8	5.5	5.1	5.7	5.5	5.8	5.6	5.9	5.6	5.9	6.1	5.9	5.6	5.9	5.7	5.9	5.9	5.9	5.7											
2-72	5.0	4.3	5.1	4.3	5.2	4.6	5.4	4.8	5.5	5.2	5.7	5.5	5.8	5.6	5.9	5.6	5.9	6.1	5.9	5.6	5.9	5.8	5.8	5.9	5.8	5.7	5.7	5.7									
3-72	5.0	4.3	5.1	4.4	5.2	4.6	5.4	4.9	5.5	5.2	5.7	5.6	5.7	5.7	5.8	5.6	5.8	6.2	5.8	5.7	5.8	5.8	5.8	6.0	5.7	5.7	5.6	5.7	5.6	5.3								
4-72	5.0	4.3	5.1	4.4	5.2	4.6	5.4	4.9	5.5	5.2	5.6	5.6	5.7	5.7	5.8	5.6	5.8	6.2	5.7	5.7	5.7	5.8	5.7	6.0	5.6	5.8	5.5	5.8	5.4	5.4	5.3	5.2						
1-73	5.0	4.3	5.1	4.4	5.2	4.6	5.3	4.9	5.5	5.3	5.6	5.6	5.7	5.7	5.7	5.6	5.7	6.2	5.7	5.7	5.6	5.9	5.6	6.0	5.5	5.7	5.4	5.7	5.3	5.3	5.2	5.1	5.0	4.9				
2-73	5.0	4.3	5.1	4.4	5.2	4.7	5.3	5.0	5.4	5.3	5.5	5.6	5.6	5.7	5.6	5.7	5.6	6.2	5.6	5.7	5.5	5.9	5.5	6.0	5.4	5.7	5.3	5.7	5.2	5.3	5.1	5.0	5.0	4.9	4.9	4.6		
3-73p	5.0	4.3	5.1	4.4	5.2	4.7	5.3	5.0	5.4	5.3	5.5	5.7	5.5	5.7	5.6	5.6	5.5	6.2	5.5	5.7	5.5	5.9	5.4	6.0	5.3	5.7	5.2	5.7	5.1	5.2	5.0	5.0	4.9	4.8	4.9	4.6	4.8	4.7

*Projections in each column are based on regressions using actual data through the quarter heading each column, assuming subsequent actual changes in money and high-employment expenditures. The figures in each column are averages of the rates from the initial quarter to the terminal quarter inclusive.

p—3-73 actual is preliminary.

215

Table 6
St. Louis Model Projections* Compared With Actual
CORPORATE AAA RATE
(Average Level from Initial Quarter to Terminal Quarter)

Initial Quarter

Terminal quarter	1-69 Act.	1-69 Proj.	2-69 Act.	2-69 Proj.	3-69 Act.	3-69 Proj.	4-69 Act.	4-69 Proj.	1-70 Act.	1-70 Proj.	2-70 Act.	2-70 Proj.	3-70 Act.	3-70 Proj.	4-70 Act.	4-70 Proj.	1-71 Act.	1-71 Proj.	2-71 Act.	2-71 Proj.	3-71 Act.	3-71 Proj.	4-71 Act.	4-71 Proj.	1-72 Act.	1-72 Proj.	2-72 Act.	2-72 Proj.	3-72 Act.	3-72 Proj.	4-72 Act.	4-72 Proj.	1-73 Act.	1-73 Proj.	2-73 Act.	2-73 Proj.	3-73 Act.	3-73 Proj.
1-69	6.7	6.5																																				
2-69	6.8	6.7	6.9	6.9																																		
3-69	6.9	6.8	7.0	7.0	7.1	7.2																																
4-69	7.0	6.9	7.1	7.1	7.3	7.2	7.5	7.3																														
1-70	7.2	7.0	7.3	7.1	7.5	7.3	7.7	7.3	7.9	7.3																												
2-70	7.4	7.0	7.5	7.1	7.6	7.3	7.8	7.4	8.0	7.4	8.1	7.5																										
3-70	7.5	7.0	7.6	7.2	7.8	7.3	7.9	7.4	8.1	7.4	8.2	7.6	8.2	7.8																								
4-70	7.5	7.1	7.7	7.2	7.8	7.3	7.9	7.4	8.0	7.5	8.1	7.6	8.1	7.8	7.9	7.9																						
1-71	7.5	7.1	7.6	7.2	7.7	7.3	7.8	7.5	7.9	7.5	7.9	7.7	7.8	7.8	7.6	7.9	7.2	7.9																				
2-71	7.5	7.1	7.6	7.2	7.7	7.3	7.8	7.5	7.8	7.5	7.8	7.7	7.7	7.8	7.5	7.9	7.3	7.8	7.5	7.8																		
3-71	7.5	7.1	7.6	7.2	7.7	7.4	7.7	7.5	7.8	7.5	7.8	7.7	7.7	7.8	7.5	7.9	7.3	7.8	7.5	7.9	7.6	7.9																
4-71	7.5	7.1	7.6	7.3	7.7	7.6	7.7	7.6	7.7	7.6	7.7	7.8	7.6	7.9	7.5	8.0	7.4	7.9	7.4	8.0	7.4	8.0	7.3	7.9														
1-72	7.5	7.2	7.5	7.3	7.6	7.4	7.6	7.6	7.7	7.6	7.6	7.8	7.6	7.9	7.4	8.0	7.4	7.9	7.4	8.0	7.4	8.0	7.3	7.8	7.2	7.5												
2-72	7.5	7.2	7.5	7.3	7.5	7.4	7.6	7.6	7.6	7.6	7.6	7.8	7.5	7.9	7.4	7.9	7.3	7.9	7.4	7.9	7.3	7.9	7.3	7.6	7.3	7.3	7.3	7.2										
3-72	7.5	7.2	7.5	7.4	7.5	7.4	7.5	7.6	7.6	7.6	7.6	7.8	7.5	7.8	7.4	7.9	7.3	7.8	7.3	7.9	7.3	7.8	7.3	7.5	7.2	7.2	7.2	7.1	7.2	7.0								
4-72	7.4	7.1	7.5	7.2	7.5	7.4	7.5	7.6	7.5	7.5	7.5	7.7	7.5	7.8	7.4	7.8	7.3	7.7	7.3	7.8	7.3	7.7	7.2	7.4	7.2	7.1	7.2	7.0	7.2	7.0	7.1	6.9						
1-73	7.4	7.1	7.5	7.2	7.5	7.4	7.5	7.6	7.5	7.5	7.5	7.7	7.4	7.7	7.3	7.7	7.3	7.7	7.3	7.8	7.3	7.6	7.2	7.3	7.2	7.0	7.2	7.0	7.2	6.9	7.2	6.8	7.2	6.9				
2-73	7.4	7.1	7.4	7.2	7.4	7.2	7.5	7.5	7.5	7.5	7.5	7.7	7.4	7.7	7.3	7.7	7.3	7.6	7.3	7.7	7.3	7.6	7.2	7.2	7.2	6.9	7.2	6.9	7.2	6.8	7.2	6.7	7.3	6.7	7.3	6.7		
3-73p	7.4	7.1	7.4	7.2	7.5	7.3	7.5	7.5	7.5	7.5	7.5	7.6	7.4	7.6	7.4	7.6	7.3	7.5	7.3	7.6	7.3	7.5	7.3	7.1	7.3	6.8	7.3	6.8	7.2	6.7	7.3	6.7	7.4	6.6	7.4	6.7	7.6	6.7

*Projections in each column are based on regressions using actual data through the period *preceding* the quarter heading each column, assuming subsequent actual changes in money and high-employment expenditures. The figures in each column are averages of the rates from the initial quarter to the terminal quarter inclusive.

p—3-73 actual is preliminary.

216

Table 7
St. Louis Model Projections* Compared With Actual
COMMERCIAL PAPER RATE
(Average Level from Initial Quarter to Terminal Quarter)

Initial Quarter

Terminal quarter	1-69		2-69		3-69		4-69		1-70		2-70		3-70		4-70		1-71		2-71		3-71		4-71		1-72		2-72		3-72		4-72		1-73		2-73		3-73	
	Act.	Proj.	Act.	Proj.	Act.	Proj.	Act.	Proj.	Act.	Proj.	Act.	Proj.	Act.	Proj.	Act.	Proj.	Act.	Proj.	Act.	Proj.	Act.	Proj.	Act.	Proj.	Act.	Proj.	Act.	Proj.	Act.	Proj.	Act.	Proj.	Act.	Proj.	Act.	Proj.	Act.	Proj.
1-69	6.7	5.7																																				
2-69	7.1	5.9	7.5	6.3																																		
3-69	7.6	6.2	8.0	6.6	8.5	7.0																																
4-69	8.0	6.4	8.2	6.7	8.6	7.1	8.6	7.6																														
1-70	8.0	6.4	8.3	6.7	8.6	7.1	8.6	7.5	8.6	7.4																												
2-70	8.0	6.4	8.3	6.7	8.5	7.0	8.4	7.4	8.4	7.2	8.2	7.2																										
3-70	8.0	6.4	8.2	6.6	8.3	7.0	8.2	7.4	8.2	7.3	8.0	7.3	7.8	7.5																								
4-70	7.8	6.4	7.9	6.6	8.0	6.9	7.9	7.3	7.7	7.2	7.4	7.3	7.1	7.4	6.3	7.5																						
1-71	7.4	6.3	7.5	6.5	7.5	6.8	7.5	7.2	7.1	7.2	7.1	7.2	6.2	7.3	5.4	7.3	4.6	6.5																				
2-71	7.2	6.2	7.2	6.4	7.2	6.7	7.2	7.1	6.7	7.0	6.7	7.2	5.9	7.0	5.3	6.9	4.8	6.1	5.0	5.9																		
3-71	7.0	6.2	7.1	6.4	7.0	6.7	6.9	7.1	6.6	6.9	6.4	7.0	5.9	7.0	5.4	6.9	5.1	6.1	5.4	6.3	5.7	6.3																
4-71	6.9	6.2	6.9	6.4	6.8	6.7	6.7	7.1	6.4	7.0	6.3	7.0	5.8	7.1	5.3	7.0	5.1	6.3	5.3	6.6	5.4	6.6	5.1	6.6														
1-72	6.7	6.2	6.7	6.4	6.6	6.7	6.4	7.1	6.2	7.0	6.1	7.1	5.5	7.0	5.1	6.9	4.9	6.3	5.1	6.3	5.0	6.5	4.6	6.2	4.1	5.5												
2-72	6.5	6.2	6.5	6.4	6.4	6.6	6.2	7.0	5.9	7.1	5.9	7.1	5.4	6.9	5.1	6.8	4.8	6.1	4.9	6.4	5.0	6.5	4.6	5.8	4.3	5.2	4.6	5.0										
3-72	6.4	6.2	6.4	6.3	6.3	6.6	6.1	6.9	5.7	6.9	5.7	6.9	5.3	6.7	5.0	6.8	4.9	5.9	4.9	6.3	4.9	6.4	4.7	5.5	4.5	5.0	4.8	4.9	4.9	5.0								
4-72	6.3	6.2	6.3	6.3	6.2	6.5	6.1	6.9	5.6	6.8	5.6	6.8	5.3	6.6	5.1	6.5	4.9	5.9	5.0	6.3	4.9	6.3	4.8	5.4	4.7	5.0	4.9	5.0	5.1	5.1	5.3	5.3						
1-73	6.3	6.2	6.3	6.4	6.2	6.6	6.1	6.9	5.8	6.7	5.7	6.7	5.4	6.6	5.2	6.5	4.9	5.9	5.1	6.3	5.0	6.3	5.0	5.5	5.0	5.0	5.3	5.1	5.5	5.3	5.8	5.5	6.3	5.8				
2-73	6.4	6.2	6.4	6.4	6.3	6.5	6.2	6.8	6.0	6.7	5.8	6.7	5.6	6.6	5.4	6.5	5.3	5.8	5.4	6.3	5.4	6.3	5.4	5.4	5.4	5.0	5.7	5.1	6.0	5.3	6.4	5.4	6.9	5.6	7.5	7.5		
3-73p	6.6	6.2	6.6	6.4	6.5	6.5	6.4	6.8	6.3	6.6	6.1	6.6	5.9	6.5	5.8	6.4	5.7	5.8	5.8	6.3	5.8	6.3	5.9	5.4	6.1	5.0	6.4	5.1	6.8	5.3	7.2	5.5	7.9	5.6	8.7	7.5	9.9	6.4

*Projections in each column are based on regressions using actual data through the period *preceding* the quarter heading each column, assuming subsequent actual changes in money and high-employment expenditures. The figures in each column are averages of the rates from the initial quarter to the terminal quarter inclusive.

p—3-73 actual is preliminary.

period are in error by 0.4 of a percentage point. Projections of the corporate bond rate are even closer, showing an error of 0.3 of a percentage point for the full period.

SUMMARY

Table 8 gives the mean absolute error for each of the diagonals in Tables 2 through 7. The mean absolute errors are not adjusted for the number of differences used in the calculation, yet the inverse relationship between the number of observations and the number of the diagonal is relevant for interpreting Table 8. The calculation of mean absolute error for the main diagonal is based on 19 observations whereas the 19th diagonal represents only one observation. In other words, there are 19 one-quarter-ahead projections and one 19-quarters-ahead projection.

For the variables which are projected in rate of change form (nominal GNP, GNP deflator, and real GNP), the mean absolute error declines sharply as you initially move to higher numbered diagonals. But the extent of decline for these rate of change variables tends to fall off after the 3rd or 4th diagonal. Even though the mean absolute error reaches a minimum along the 15th to 17th diagonal, this result does not imply that 15 to 17 quarters ahead represents the optimal projection horizon. These results are based only on this particular sequence of economic events. Repeated experiments would be required to shed light on the best projection horizon.

Table 8. Mean Absolute Error
(Average Absolute Difference of Percents in Tables 2–7)

Diagonal	Nominal GNP	GNP Price Deflator	Real GNP	Unemployment Rate	Commercial Paper Rate	Corporate AAA Rate
Main	2.85	1.46	2.49	0.21	1.01	0.35
2nd	2.37	1.23	1.77	0.20	1.01	0.36
3rd	1.89	1.12	1.55	0.19	1.07	0.35
4th	1.54	0.91	1.61	0.18	1.04	0.35
5th	1.47	0.89	1.63	0.19	1.03	0.37
6th	1.40	0.90	1.61	0.23	1.03	0.39
7th	1.27	0.89	1.52	0.28	0.96	0.36
8th	1.11	0.83	1.53	0.32	0.94	0.33
9th	0.93	0.76	1.43	0.34	0.84	0.29
10th	0.92	0.66	1.34	0.32	0.82	0.25
11th	0.93	0.54	1.20	0.37	0.74	0.22
12th	0.75	0.53	0.99	0.35	0.69	0.19
13th	0.61	0.50	0.87	0.43	0.57	0.16
14th	0.43	0.40	0.68	0.45	0.45	0.15
15th	0.26	0.22	0.48	0.48	0.30	0.12
16th	0.20	0.18	0.28	0.55	0.27	0.18
17th	0.23	0.30	0.20	0.63	0.03	0.23
18th	0.30	0.45	0.30	0.70	0.20	0.25
19th	0.40	0.60	0.30	0.70	0.40	0.30

What seems to be clear with respect to the rate of change variables is that projections several quarters ahead are more reliable than those only one or two quarters ahead. Smoothing the data on rates of change brings them in line with the averaging process implicit in ordinary least squares regression techniques.

Mean absolute errors calculated for variables expressed in level form (unemployment and interest rates) show a substantially different pattern as you move to higher numbered diagonals. These results suggest that projection errors for "level" variables cannot be interpreted in the same way as those for rate of change variables. In the case of the unemployment rate, the minimum mean absolute error for this period was along the 4th diagonal, though this error was essentially unchanged for the first five diagonals. In the case of interest rates, the error was essentially unchanged for the first six or seven diagonals and then declined to a minimum along the 15th to 17th diagonal.

Conclusions regarding these calculations of mean absolute error for the St. Louis model are mixed. The characteristics of the time series of each variable, as well as the distinction between levels and rates of change, have to be considered in an attempt to judge what horizon is appropriate for the model. Each variable requires analysis both in isolation and in the broader context of the model as a whole.

3.2. A Checklist of Successes and Failures

These calculations for the St. Louis model indicate that projections have to be carefully interpreted. Since the model was not formulated primarily as a forecasting device, it should not be judged solely on this basis. Yet, significant departures from experience raise questions about the validity of the model's application for whatever purposes it was designed. In this general spirit, the model is evaluated in a judgmental fashion, giving emphasis on its possible influence on economic thinking and its possible role in the formulation of stabilization policy. The listing is in terms of successes and failures, but it should be emphasized that this checklist is highly subjective in character.

SUCCESSES

With respect to "successes," there is no way of knowing whether these developments would have occurred in the absence of the formulation of the St. Louis model. So the following list is more representative of consistencies with trends in economic thinking than of definite contributions to those trends.

1. Demonstrated short-run vs. long-run effects of stabilization policy.

   The St. Louis model yielded short-run properties which differed substantially from its long-run properties. These varying properties are reflected mainly in the short-run vs. long-run response of real product, prices, unemployment and interest rates.

2. Demonstrated the importance of monetary actions in determination of movements in economic activity.

(i) The reduced-form approach to estimating the impact of monetary actions provoked consideration of the limitations of standard models which, until quite recently, restricted the channel of monetary influence to interest rates. Some standard models have moved more recently in the direction of including real balance effects in spending functions.

(ii) The direct approach to estimating the impact of monetary actions has been associated with a change in thinking about the quickness of response of GNP. Until recently the estimated lag in the effect of monetary actions was very long, reflecting in part the restriction of channels of influence to interest rates.

3. Demonstrated indirectly the role of costs of information in stabilization analysis.

The results of the St. Louis model were consistent with the notion that changes in total demand are reflected initially in real product and only later in prices. The model traces the process whereby there is a short-run trade-off between inflation and unemployment which vanishes in the long run. These results are consistent with the developing literature on costs of information and search.

4. Called attention to an alternative framework of analysis.

Prior to 1968 there were virtually no empirically estimated alternatives to the econometric model constructed on a Keynesian foundation. With a substantially different framework of analysis, many of the conventional results relating to the impact of policy actions were differently analyzed.

5. Demonstrated the usefulness of small models in capturing the aggregative impact of stabilization actions.

Prior to 1968 the trend was toward greater sectoral detail in econometric model building. Now there is a question in the minds of some people whether it is necessary to build a large model with allocative detail in order to gain some notion about the general course of economic developments.

FAILURES

Similarly, the "failures," or shortcomings of the model can be assessed in a subjective manner.

1. Failed to educate policymakers on the long-run effects of their short-run decisions.

One of the purposes of the model, given its properties of varying effects for the short-run compared to the long-run, was to show the longer-run consequences of short-run actions. The recent experience of the U.S. economy with recession, inflation and experiments with price controls serves as ample evidence indicating that the model has failed in this objective.

2. Failed to capture short-run movements in velocity.

   One of the shortcomings of the model, as indicated in Table 2, is that short-run movements in velocity are not successfully captured by the model. This remains an area of further research.

3. Failed to shed light on price developments during periods of governmental controls and worldwide inflation.

   The St. Louis model was in no way able to predict the actions of the Cost of Living Council during the period of controls beginning in third quarter 1971. Similarly, there are exogenous factors which affect economic activity in the short run, and the model is limited in the information it can provide on the consequences of these factors.

4. Failed to cope successfully with large variations in government spending and in the money stock and to anticipate revisions in the money stock data.

   With the monetary and fiscal variables fundamental in their role for the model, any variation beyond historical experience or revisions in the data can give rise to large errors in the short run. It is this inability to anticipate variations in monetary growth or revisions in the data which accounts for the procedure of giving model projections in terms of assumed steady growth rates of money. Since such steady growth rates are seldom, if ever, realized, projections of the model based on this assumption should not be interpreted as forecasts in the same sense as in other models.[11]

4. Conclusions and Future Research

The course of action for the St. Louis model is indicated by the list of failures. Some considerations are beyond the purview of the model, but such a list serves as a set of guidelines. For example, the problem of velocity as well as the timing of economic response to monetary and fiscal actions are continuing topics of study at the Federal Reserve Bank of St. Louis.[12]

Another direction expected for research relating to the model is toward the formulation and testing of hypotheses. Propositions have been developed and tested relating to magnitude and timing of the impact of monetary and fiscal actions, but little has been done on testing propositions relating to the *modus operandi* of monetary and fiscal actions.[13] Development of results along these theoretical lines would help in clarifying an understanding of the foundations of the monetarist propositions, which, in turn, would provide a firmer foundation for policy formulation.

[11]For a full discussion and interpretation of the sources of projection error in the St. Louis model, see [3] and [10].

[12]See [7].

[13]For further discussion, see [11].

APPENDIX

Estimated Equations of the St. Louis Model*

I. Total Spending Equation

   A. Sample period: I/1953 − IV/1968

$$\Delta Y_t = 2.30 + 5.35 \ \Delta M_{t-i} + .05 \ \Delta E_{t-i}$$
$$\qquad\quad (2.69) \quad (6.69) \qquad\quad (.15)$$

                                                  $R^2 = .632$
  S.E. = 3.948
  D-W = 1.741

   B. Sample period: I/1953 − II/1973

$$\Delta Y_t = 1.52 + 5.30 \ \Delta M_{t-i} + \ .54 \ \Delta E_{t-i}$$
$$\qquad\quad (1.59) \quad (8.10) \qquad\quad (1.36)$$

  $R^2 = .683$
  S.E. = 5.169
  D-W = 1.894

II. Price Equation

   A. Sample period: I/1955 − IV/1968

$$\Delta P_t = 2.95 + \ .09 \ D_{t-i} + \ .73 \ \Delta P_t^A$$
$$\qquad\quad (6.60) \quad (9.18) \qquad\quad (5.01)$$

  $R^2 = .788$
  S.E. = 1.072
  D.E. = 1.415

   B. Sample period: I/1955 − II/1973

$$\Delta P_t = 2.46 + \ .09 \ D_{t-i} + \ .96 \ \Delta P_t^A$$
$$\qquad\quad (5.03) \quad (6.00) \qquad\quad (12.92)$$

  $R^2 = .748$
  S.E. = 2.350
  D-W = 1.408

III. Unemployment Rate Equation

   A. Sample period: I/1955 − IV/1968

$$U_t = \ 3.94 + \ .06 \ G_t + \ .26 \ G_{t-i}$$
$$\qquad\ \ (67.42) \quad (1.33) \qquad (6.15)$$

  $R^2 = .915$
  S.E. = .307
  D-W = .596

   B. Sample period: I/1955 − II/1973

$$U_t = \ 3.90 + \ .04 \ G_t + \ .29 \ G_{t-i}$$
$$\qquad\ \ (77.00) \quad (1.00) \qquad (8.20)$$

  $R^2 = .918$
  S.E. = .293
  D-W = .647

IV. Long-Term Interest Rate

   A. Sample period: I/1955 − IV/1968

$$R_t^L = \ 1.28 \ − .05 \ \dot{M}_t + 1.39 \ Z_t + \ .20 \ \dot{X}_{t-i} + \ .97 \ \dot{P}/(U/4)_{t-i}$$
$$\qquad\ (4.63)\ (-2.40) \qquad (8.22) \quad (2.55) \qquad (11.96)$$

  $R^2 = .854$
  S.E. = .306
  D-W = .564

   B. Sample period: I/1955 − II/1973

$$R_t^L = \ 1.44 \ − .04 \ \dot{M}_t + \ 1.50 \ Z_t + \ .12 \ \dot{X}_{t-i} + \ .99 \ \dot{P}/(U/4)_{t-i}$$
$$\qquad\ (5.46)\ (-2.11) \qquad (12.03) \quad (1.67) \qquad (21.81)$$

  $R^2 = .954$
  S.E. = .320
  D-W = .652

V. Short-Term Interest Rate Equation

   A. Sample period: I/1955 − IV/1968

$$R_t^S = \ − .84 \ − .11 \ \dot{M}_t + \ .50 \ Z_t + \ .75 \ \dot{X}_{t-i} + \ 1.06 \ \dot{P}/(U/4)_{t-i}$$
$$\qquad\ (-2.43)\ (-3.72) \qquad (2.78) \quad (9.28) \qquad (12.24)$$

  $R^2 = .839$
  S.E. = .443
  D-W = .593

   B. Sample period: I/1955 − II/1973

$$R_t^S = \ − .44 \ − .12 \ \dot{M}_t + \ .89 \ Z_t + \ .54 \ \dot{X}_{t-i} + \ 1.16 \ \dot{P}/(U/4)_{t-i}$$
$$\qquad\ (-1.02)\ (-3.23) \qquad (3.66) \quad (5.18) \qquad (13.23)$$

  $R^2 = .827$
  S.E. = .679
  D-W = .495

Symbols are defined as:

    ΔY = dollar change in total spending (GNP in current prices)

    ΔM = dollar change in money stock

    ΔE = dollar change in high-employment Federal expenditures

   *Constraints and lag structures correspond to those set forth in the original article discussing the St. Louis model. See Andersen and Carlson, [4]. Coefficient values on lagged variables (subscripted "$t - i$") are sums of the coefficients for current and lagged quarters. Figures enclosed by parentheses under the coefficients are "t" statistics.

ΔP = dollar change in total spending (GNP in current prices) due to price change

$D = Y - (X^F - X)$

X^F = potential output

X = output (GNP in 1958 prices)

ΔP^A = anticipated price change (scaled in dollar units)

U = unemployment as a percent of labor force

$G = ((X^F - X)/X^F) \times 100$

R^L = Moody's seasoned corporate AAA bond rate

$\dot{M}$ = annual rate of change in money stock

Z = dummy variable (0 for I/1955 – IV/1960) and (1 for I/1961 – end of regression period)

$\dot{X}$ = annual rate of change in output (GNP in 1958 prices)

$\dot{P}$ = annual rate of change in GNP price deflator (1958 = 100)

$U/4$ = index of unemployment as a percent of labor force (base = 4.0)

R^S = four- to six-month prime commercial paper rate

REFERENCES

1. ANDERSEN, L., "A Monetarist View of Demand Management: The United States Experience," Federal Reserve Bank of St. Louis *Review* LIII (September, 1971), 3-11.

2. ———, "Properties of a Monetarist Model for Economic Stabilization," in Proceedings of the First Konstanzer Seminar, *Kredit und Kapital,* Beiheft 1 (1972).

3. ———, "The St. Louis Model Revisited," Paper given at the Economic Outlook at Midyear Conference of the Chicago Chapter of the American Statistical Association, Chicago, Illinois (June 7, 1973).

4. ——— and K. CARLSON, "A Monetarist Model for Economic Stabilization," Federal Reserve Bank of St. Louis *Review,* LII (April, 1970), 7-25.

5. ——— and ———, "An Econometric Analysis of the Relation of Monetary Variables to the Behavior of Prices and Unemployment," in O. Eckstein, ed., *The Econometrics of Price Determination,* Conference sponsored by Board of Governors of the Federal Reserve System and Social Science Research Council, Washington, D.C. (October 30-31, 1970), 166-183.

6. ——— and J. JORDAN, "Monetary and Fiscal Actions: A Test of Their Relative Importance in Economic Stabilization," Federal Reserve Bank of St. Louis *Review,* L (November, 1968), 11-24.

7. ——— and D. KARNOSKY, "The Appropriate Time Frame for Controlling Monetary Aggregates: The St. Louis Evidence," in *Controlling Monetary Aggregates II: The Interpretation,* Conference sponsored by Federal Reserve Bank of Boston, Melvin Village, New Hampshire (September, 1972), 147-177.

8. BAIRD, C., *Macroeconomics: An Integration of Monetary, Search, and Income Theories* (Chicago: Science Research Associates, 1973).

9. BRUNNER, K., "Review of B. Hickman, ed., *Econometric Models of Cyclical Behavior,*" *Journal of Economic Literature,* XI (September, 1973), 927-933.

10. CARLSON, K., "Projecting with the St. Louis Model: A Progress Report," Federal Reserve Bank of St. Louis *Review,* LIV (February, 1972), 20-27.

11. ———, "Monetary and Fiscal Actions in Macroeconomic Models: Towards a Clarification of the Issues," Paper presented at the Fourth Annual Konstanzer Conference on Monetary Theory and Policy, Konstanz, West Germany (June, 1973).

12. ECKSTEIN, O., "Instability in the Private and Public Sectors: Some Model Simulations," *Swedish Journal of Economics,* LXXV (March, 1973), 19-26.

13. FRIEDMAN, M., *The Optimum Quantity of Money and Other Essays* (Chicago: Aldine Publishing Company, 1969).

14. GORDON, R., "Discussion of Papers in Session II," in O. Eckstein, ed., *The Econometrics of Price Determination,* Conference sponsored by Board of Governors of the Federal Reserve System and Social Science Research Council, Washington, D.C. (October 30-31, 1970), 202-211.

15. MCNEES, S., "A Comparison of the GNP Forecasting Accuracy of the Fair and St. Louis Econometric Models," Federal Reserve Bank of Boston *New England Economic Review* (September/October, 1973), 29-34.

16. OKUN, A., "Potential GNP: Its Measurement and Significance," *1962 Proceedings of the Business and Economic Statistics Section of the American Statistical Association,* 98-104.

17. ———, "Fiscal-Monetary Activism: Some Analytical Issues," *Brookings Papers on Economic Activity,* 1 (1972), 123-163.

18. PHELPS, E., *et al., Microeconomic Foundations of Employment and Inflation Theory* (New York: W.W. Norton and Company, Inc., 1970).

19. WARBURTON, C., *Depression, Inflation and Monetary Policies, Selected Papers 1945-53* (Baltimore: Johns Hopkins University Press, 1969).

14

Money and Inflation

Dan M. Bechter

Rising prices are worrying consumers and businessmen. The public increasingly wonders why the country is experiencing inflation, and what can be done about it. Much attention is being given to the connection between the rate of growth of the money supply and the rate of increase in the general level of prices. This article is devoted to the question: How much will the rate of inflation in the next two years depend on the rate of growth of money over that period?

The patterns of past economic history cannot be counted on to repeat themselves, but they do aid in the evaluation of policy alternatives. One useful way of using past history is to summarize its lessons in statistical relationships interrelated within an econometric model. Such a model can then be used to stimulate economic behavior under a variety of conditions, and, therefore, to project the consequences of alternative policy choices.

Two well-established econometric models are used in this article to simulate future inflation under alternative growth rates of the money supply. Both of these models contain other variables, besides money, whose future values must be estimated independently before simulation. In order to concentrate on the relationship between money and prices, estimates of the values of these other independent variables are

Reprinted from the Federal Reserve Bank of Kansas City, *Monthly Review* (July-August, 1973), pp. 3-6, by permission of the publisher.

kept the same in all simulations. These estimates, such as of Federal Government expenditures, are considered reasonably likely outcomes at this time. However, forecasting is not the intent of this article. Thus, in what follows, not much should be made of the specific rate of inflation that a simulation associates with a particular rate of growth of the money supply. Nor should much importance be attached to the differences between the results of the two models. Instead, careful note should be made of the finding common to both models, namely, that differential growth rates in the money supply have little immediate impact, but pronounced long-run effects, on the rate of inflation.

Price Determination in Two Models

Two quarterly econometric models of the United States economy were used to generate the simulations summarized in this article: The SSRC-MIT-PENN[1] (SMP) model, and the Federal Reserve Bank of St. Louis (StL) model.

The StL model consists of a small number of equations relating a few key economic aggregates. Economists at the Federal Reserve Bank of St. Louis built their model around their earlier work which gave empirical support to the monetarist view that monetary actions are much more important than fiscal actions in influencing total spending in the economy. Although the StL model is small, and its equations are necessarily expressed in reduced (summary) forms which give little insight into economic behavior, it has performed well.[2]

As models go, the SMP is a big one, containing over 300 variables and equations. It has been developed over the last seven years by economists at the Massachusetts Institute of Technology, at the University of Pennsylvania, and at the Board of Governors of the Federal Reserve System, primarily to help determine the effects of monetary policy on the economy. Its large size partly reflects its structural character—inclusion of equations that are based on economic analyses of behavior, thereby incorporating logical "whys" in their specifications of how variables are interrelated in the economy.[3]

[1]Social Science Research Council, Massachusetts Institute of Technology, and the University of Pennsylvania.

[2]Leonall Andersen and Keith M. Carlson, "A Monetarist Model for Economic Stabilization," *Review* (Federal Reserve Bank of St. Louis, April 1970), pp. 7-25. Also, by the same authors, "An Econometric Analysis of the Relation of Monetary Variables to the Behavior of Prices and Unemployment," in *The Econometrics of Price Determination* (Washington: Social Science Research Council, 1971), pp. 166-83.

[3]Among the earliest progress reports on the SMP model were Frank de Leeuw and Edward Gramlich, "The Federal Reserve-MIT Econometric Model," *Federal Reserve Bulletin* (January 1968), pp. 11-40; and Robert H. Rasche and Harold T. Shapiro, "The FRB-MIT Econometric Model: Its Special Features," *American Economic Review* (May 1968), pp. 123-49. The SMP model has undergone extensive revision since that time. For particular relevance to this article, see George de Menil and Jared J. Enzler, "Prices and Wages in the FR-MIT-PENN Econometric Model," in *The Econometrics of Price Determination* (cited above), pp. 277-308.

Inflation in the StL Model

In the StL model, two forces determine changes in the price level: demand pressure and price expectations.

Demand inflation occurs when aggregate demand is rising faster than aggregate supply ("too much money chasing too few goods"), and is usually identified with full-employment conditions. However, even when the economy is producing at less than capacity, its ability to expand output quickly is limited. Thus, in the StL model, demand pressure is defined and measured in a way that gives an upward push to prices when demand jumps, under any circumstances. This pressure is greater the bigger the increase in demand and the closer the economy is to full employment.

Price expectations, or anticipated changes in the price level, are measured by assuming that people expect inflation to continue at about the rate it has averaged over the previous four years or so. Allowance is made for the effects of current economic conditions on price expectations by adjusting this measure upward for lower rates of unemployment, and by giving greater weight to price behavior in the immediate past when the unemployment rate is falling.

Changes in the price level will tend to turn out as expected if economic units make market decisions based on these expectations, and there is ample evidence that they do. Expectations of increases in the cost of living surely add to union wage demands, and labor costs are an important determinant of prices. The cost of capital also rises as long-term interest rates come to reflect the inflationary expectations of borrowers and lenders.

What are the effects of a change in the money supply in the StL model? The ultimate effect is on the price level and on the price level alone, but, in the short run, changes in the stock of money do influence the level of economic activity by directly determining changes in total spending. These changes, in turn, affect the price level by way of the demand pressure variable described earlier, as well as indirectly through the price expectations variable. However, monetary expansion affects total spending only after a lag, and still another lag must be allowed for between a change in total spending and its influence on the price level.

Following the suggestion of the authors of the StL model, an alternative price equation was used in a separate set of simulations. In this alternative equation, past changes in the supply of money were used instead of the price expectations variable in determining the change in the price level. This reduced-form specification captures both the direct and indirect effects of money on prices, and is probably more appealing to those who are persuaded that such a more direct one-to-one relationship exists.[4]

Inflation in the SMP Model

The SMP model contains a whole set of equations relating prices and wages to productive activity in the economy. Fortunately, one can get a good idea of price

[4]Andersen and Carlson, *Review,* p. 24.

determination in this model from a brief summary of the hypothesis underlying the price-wage sector.

In keeping with its structural character, the model derives the price level by explaining the pricing behavior of private businesses, who are assumed to follow a markup-over-cost rule. The size of this markup is made to depend on demand pressure, being reduced when business is bad, and being limited when business is good by a desire to prevent the entry of new competitors. By making cost a primary determinant of price, the SMP markup formulation focuses on the rental rate on capital and the wage rate. Because labor costs matter so much, the wage relationship is of key importance.

Wages are assumed to increase faster as the unemployment rate falls and as the cost of living rises. The inclusion of the unemployment rate directly associates wage (and thereby price) movements with the level of real output. As a result, built into the SMP model is the assumption of the existence of a long-run trade-off between the rate of inflation and the level of unemployment. This piece of conventional wisdom, known as the Phillips curve, has lost some favor in recent years, but remains a part of most major econometric models.

In the SMP model, as in the StL model, changes in the supply of money affect the price level indirectly through effects on aggregate demand. But where the StL model summarizes these effects in a reduced-form equation, the SMP model traces them through.[5] Monetary expansion, by increasing aggregate demand, increases the demand for labor. Interaction with supply in the labor market determines a level of unemployment which, along with past price changes, determines a rate of increase in wages. As labor expenses go up, private businesses raise prices, and the price level rises. As implied, the connection between money and prices involves many long and variable lags.

Results of Simulations

If these two econometric models are any guide, the rate of inflation in the next few months will depend little on the *current* rate of monetary expansion (Table 1). While the three monetary growth rates used in the simulations are primarily illustrative, their range includes the various rates considered likely in the financial press. Since modified versions of both the SMP model and the StL model were used in the simulations, the results should not be attributed to the models' originators. However, the insensitivity of the price level to the rate of increase in money supply in the short run does fairly reflect the lags in the two models.[6]

[5]Frank de Leeuw and Edward M. Gramlich, "The Channels of Monetary Policy," *Federal Reserve Bulletin* (June 1969), pp. 472–91.

[6]The irregular ups and downs in the quarterly paths of inflation in the SMP model stem from the indirect ways the price level is determined in this model, and the influence of special factors, such as scheduled changes in the minimum wage law and in social security taxes.

Table 1. Simulated Inflation in Two Models of the U.S. Economy

Projected Annual Rates of Change of the Price Level

	1973 I–1974 I	1974 I–1975 I	1973 II	1973 III	1973 IV	1974 I	1974 II	1974 III	1974 IV	1975 I
SMP MODEL Assumed Annual Rates of Growth of M1*										
3%	5.0	4.5	5.0	4.5	4.8	5.9	4.6	4.6	4.4	4.5
5%	5.1	5.0	5.0	4.5	4.9	6.0	4.9	5.0	4.9	5.1
7%	5.2	5.6	5.0	4.6	5.0	6.3	5.2	5.5	5.7	6.0
StL MODEL Assumed Annual Rates of Growth of M1										
3%	3.3	2.3	3.6	3.4	3.2	2.9	2.6	2.4	2.1	1.9
5%	3.4	2.7	3.6	3.5	3.3	3.1	2.9	2.7	2.6	2.6
7%	3.5	3.1	3.6	3.5	3.4	3.3	3.2	3.1	3.1	3.2
Alternative StL MODEL Assumed Annual Rates of Growth of M1										
3%	4.8	3.2	5.3	5.0	4.5	4.2	3.9	3.4	2.9	2.5
5%	5.1	4.4	5.4	5.2	5.0	4.8	4.7	4.5	4.2	4.0
7%	5.5	5.5	5.5	5.5	5.4	5.5	5.6	5.6	5.5	5.4

*M 1 identifies the narrowly defined money supply as currency plus demand deposits.

In both the SMP model and the StL model, the rate of inflation is but .2 percent slower over the first year with a 3 percent instead of a 7 percent rate of increase in the money supply. Even in the alternative StL model, which is intended here as an extreme version that shows a very quick response of prices to money, the difference is but .7 percent. Why this slow reaction? Because, in these two models, rates of inflation for the next few months have been determined already, by *past* rates of monetary expansion, and other factors. One factor in particular affects the results—starting the simulations with inflation already going strong. Further into the future, the models show increasing sensitivity to the current rate of growth of money. By the first quarter of 1975, the simulated rate of inflation is substantially slower with slower monetary expansion. Projections further ahead would show even greater differences.

While any progress in reducing inflation would be welcome, both models also project higher unemployment rates (not shown) accompanying lower rates of monetary expansion. For example, by the end of the first quarter of 1975, the models project an unemployment rate at least one full percentage point higher with a constant 3 percent vs. a constant 7 percent rate of monetary growth. This apparent trade-off between unemployment and inflation is one of the dilemmas that haunts makers of economic policy.

Summary and Conclusions

Two econometric models were used to study the response of the rate of inflation to the rate of increase in the money supply: the large, structural SMP model, and the small, monetarist StL model. Both models exhibit a strong "money really matters" character, and in both models, the price level is determined by monetary forces in the long run. Thus, these models underline the importance of monetary policy decisions for long-run price stability. At the same time, however, the lags between changes in the money supply and changes in the price level which are built into both models suggest that there is little that monetary policy can do to slow inflation quickly. It can be pointed out that recent economic behavior—the coexistence of inflation and unemployment, high interest rates, and the rapid rate of increase in the money supply during 1972—is outside the range of historical experience. This implies that some lack of validity might be attached to results coming from econometric models. Still, unless evidence appears that shows monetary policy affecting economic activity with significantly shorter lags and unless a significantly less critical trade-off between unemployment and inflation can be demonstrated, changes in the rate of growth of the money supply appear to be of limited usefulness as a short-run weapon in the battle against inflation.*

* In the final article in this section Michael Hamburger surveys recent evidence on the lag in the effect of monetary policy. —Ed.

15

Some Issues in Monetary Economics: Fiscal Policy Assumptions and Related Multipliers

David I. Fand

The theory of fiscal policy highlights the direct income-generating effects of government deficits and surpluses and the stabilization aspects of the cumulative multiplier expansion process; but the theory often ignores the interest rate or capital market effects and invariably abstracts from any associated money stock effects. The simplest presentation may be summarized as follows: an increase in government spending is viewed as a *direct* demand for goods and services; reductions in tax rates are viewed as *directly* affecting consumer spending, investment, and aggregate demand; and the initial increase in spending is viewed as setting off a cumulative expansion as given by the multiplier process.[1] More advanced discussions go beyond the 45° diagram, introduce the Hicksian *IS-LM* analysis to account for the capital market effects of changes in fiscal policy; but even this more advanced analysis typically abstracts from the money creation aspects that may be associated with a cumulative expansion.

Reprinted from the Federal Reserve Bank of St. Louis, *Review* (January 1970), pp. 23–27, by permission of the publisher and the author.
[1]The volume of readings, *American Fiscal Policy: Experiment for Prosperity* (Prentice-Hall, 1967), edited by L. Thurow, is a good example. With very few exceptions, the individual papers either abstract from, or ignore, monetary factors, and do not cite any empirical evidence to justify the strategic role assigned to discretionary changes in the full-employment surplus. It appears that such justification was not felt necessary, because the very substantial growth in GNP since 1964 was widely interpreted as the result of the 1964 tax cut and reduction in the full-employment surplus.

A widely quoted statement describing the "Workings of the Multiplier" in the *Economic Report of the President for 1963* illustrates this tendency to omit the capital market and money creation aspects.[2] The direct income-generating effects of the deficit are stressed, but no indication is given whether the rise in income requires stable interest rates, an elastic monetary policy, or a deficit financed through the banking system. Thus, the case for a discretionary tax cut and a reduction in the full-employment surplus, as presented by the Council of Economic Advisers (CEA) in 1963, does not bring in any explicit discussion of the method in which the deficit is financed. Their position is stated as follows:

> Tax reduction will directly increase the disposable income and purchasing power of consumers and business, strengthen incentives and expectations, and raise the net returns on new capital investment. This will lead to initial increases in private consumption and investment expenditures. These increases in spending will set off a cumulative expansion, generating further increases in consumption and investment spending and a general rise in production, income and employment.

The analysis of the 1964 tax cut presented by Arthur Okun in 1965 explicitly justifies the omission of any capital market or monetary effects.[3] Although Okun accepts the view that significant changes in the cost or availability of credit would have an important influence on business investment, he does not make allowance for these factors in his quantitative estimates of the multiplier. He rationalizes his procedure as follows:

> ... in practice, dealing with the period of the last year and a half, I cannot believe that the omission of monetary variables can make a serious difference. By any measure of interest rates or credit conditions I know, there have been no significant monetary changes that would have either stimulated or restrained investment to a major degree.

He does concede that "the maintenance of stable interest rates and stable credit conditions requires monetary action" and that at least to this extent, "monetary policies have made a major contribution to the advance." But in his view, "that contribution is appropriately viewed as permissive rather than causal." Okun's analysis, presented in August 1965, attributing the GNP expansion to the tax-cut multiplier, was a strict fiscal policy interpretation, in contrast to other (monetary and eclectic) interpretations that were presented at that time.[4] His analysis was not modified when it was published in 1968.[5]

[2]See the section, "Workings of the Multiplier" in the *Economic Report of the President for 1963.* This is reprinted in A. M. Okun (ed.), *The Battle Against Unemployment* (Norton, 1965), pp. 88-97.

[3]Okun's analysis of the 1964 tax cut was presented at the 1965 meetings of the American Statistical Association. His paper, "Measuring the Impact of the 1964 Tax Reduction" has been published in W. Heller (ed.), *Perspectives on Economic Growth* (Random House, 1968), pp. 25-51.

[4]See D. I. Fand, "Three Views on the Current Expansion" in G. Horwich (ed.), *Monetary Process and Policy: A Symposium* (Irwin, 1967), analyzing the views of the fiscal proponents, the monetary proponents, and those who take an eclectic position. See also A. F. Burns, *The Management of Prosperity* (Columbia University Press, 1966); M. Friedman, "The Monetary Studies of the National Bureau," reprinted as chapter 12 in his *The Optimum Quantity of Money,* pp. 261-284; B. Sprinkel, "An Evaluation of Recent Federal Reserve Policy" in the *Financial Analysts Journal,* August 1965; and G. Morrison, "The Influence of Money on Economic Activity," in the 1965 *Proceedings* volume of the American Statistical Association.

[5]Okun, in a note added in June 1967 to his 1965 analysis of the tax cut, does concede that "any analysis

If the fiscal approach, with its multiplier analysis, emphasizes the deficit or surplus and relegates both the interest rate and the money creation aspects to a secondary role, the monetary approach emphasizes the money stock effects. To the monetarist, the impact of fiscal actions will depend crucially on *how the government deficit is financed:* expenditures financed either by taxing or borrowing involve a transfer of resources (from the public to the government), with both interest rates and wealth effects on private portfolios, but the net effect of a temporary change in fiscal policy on spending may be ambiguous. Similarly, the effect of a reduction in taxes on private demand, financed through borrowing, will depend on (1) the extent to which it is viewed as a permanent, or temporary, tax cut and (2) its effect on market interest rates. Accordingly, the direct income-generating effects of a deficit—the pure fiscal effect—may be quite small and uncertain. On the other hand, if the deficit is financed through money creation by the banking system—if the deficit is monetized—the effect is unambiguously expansionary.

Many income theorists recognized that the multiplier analysis based on the 45° diagram was inadequate, and modified their analysis to take account of interest rate effects through the Hicksian *IS-LM* framework. But even this modification, while a step in the right direction, does not really make allowance for the money creation aspects of deficits. What is needed is a macroeconomic model, where the monetary effects of the deficit are taken up by introducing an explicit government budget restraint. Recent studies along these lines suggest many of the standard propositions about the multiplier need to be revised.[6]

Aside from these theoretical reasons, the need to separate out the monetary effects from the fiscal effects has been highlighted by the recent Andersen-Jordan study, testing the relative effectiveness of monetary and fiscal actions in stabilization.[7] Their

---

of fiscal impact that covered the more recent period could no longer treat monetary policy as a passive supporting force, nor could it continue to ignore the influence of higher levels of aggregate demand on prices." See W. W. Heller (ed.), *op. cit.,* pp. 27-28.

[6]See L. S. Ritter, "Some Monetary Aspects of Multiplier Theory and Fiscal Policy," *Review of Economic Studies,* February 1956; C. Christ, "A Simple Macroeconomic Model with a Government Budget Restraint," *Journal of Political Economy,* January 1968; and J. M. Culbertson, *Macroeconomic Theory and Stabilization Policy* (McGraw-Hill, 1968), pp. 462-464.

See also K. M. Carlson and D. S. Karnosky, "The Influence of Fiscal and Monetary Actions on Aggregate Demand: A Quantitative Appraisal," *Working Paper No. 4,* March 1969, Federal Reserve Bank of St. Louis; and K. M. Carlson, "Monetary and Fiscal Actions in Macroeconomic Models: A Balance Sheet Analysis," an unpublished manuscript, for an interesting attempt to define and estimate the monetary effects of fiscal policy actions.

[7]The Andersen-Jordan results are presented in "Monetary and Fiscal Actions: A Test of their Relative Importance in Economic Stabilization," Federal Reserve Bank of St. Louis *Review,* November 1968. See also the "Comments" of de Leeuw and F. S. Kalchbrenner, Federal Reserve Bank of St. Louis *Review,* April 1969, and the *Reply* by Andersen and Jordan, Federal Reserve Bank of St. Louis *Review,* April 1969; and R. G. Davis, "How Much Does Money Matter: A Look at Some Recent Evidence," Federal Reserve Bank of New York *Monthly Review,* June 1969, pp. 119-133; the earlier study by M. Friedman and D. Meiselman on "The Relative Stability of Monetary Velocity and the Investment Multiplier in the United

results, while preliminary and subject to further testing, do suggest that the theory of fiscal policy (in the income-expenditure framework), with its emphasis on discretionary changes in the full-employment surplus as the key stabilization instrument, may be incorrect or only partially correct. Their findings also suggest that the tax and expenditure multipliers, as estimated in many income models, tend to confound a *ceteris paribus* fiscal action (excluding money stock effects), with a *mutatis mutandis* fiscal action (incorporating both monetary and fiscal effects).

The need to revise the standard multiplier theory and to develop more discriminating empirical tests of the relative effectiveness of monetary and fiscal actions is recognized even among fiscal policy advocates. There is a significant modification of the multiplier theory in the *Economic Report of the President for 1969,* stressing two points in particular: (1) "the results of the multiplier process are affected by the amount of unused resources available in the economy" and (2) monetary policy does affect the magnitude of the multiplier:

> Developments in financial markets may influence the magnitude of the multiplier. Increases in demands for goods and services will tend to enlarge credit demands. Unless monetary policy permits supplies of funds to expand correspondingly, interest rates will rise and credit will become less readily available. In that event, some offsetting reduction is likely to take place in residential construction and other credit-sensitive expenditures. Generally this will be a partial offset, varying according to how much the supply of credit is permitted to expand.[8]

There is, therefore, a growing consensus that multiplier theory needs to separate out the monetary effects from the pure fiscal effects, in order to develop meaningful tests of the relative contribution of monetary and fiscal policy in stabilization. In particular, we need to define and measure monetary variables so as to separate out exogenous changes in the money stock, resulting from actions taken by the monetary authorities—from endogenous money stock changes—resulting from shifts in the demand for money, so as to remove the identification problem in a manner that is acceptable to the income-expenditure theorists. We also need to define a pure *ceteris paribus* fiscal action with restrictions on the growth rate for the monetary aggregates that is acceptable to the *monetarists.* A revision of multiplier theory along these lines would enable us to distinguish analytically, and estimate, *ceteris paribus* fiscal and monetary multipliers and thus bridge some of the gap between the income-expenditure theory and the quantity theory. But it requires that we find an acceptable method to separate out endogenous and exogenous changes in the money stock and to estimate empirically the money stock effects of deficits and surpluses.

Fiscal deficits are obviously often associated with, if not directly responsible for, substantial increases in the monetary aggregates. Our recent experience reminds us

---

States, 1897-1958" in *Stabilization Policies* (Prentice Hall, 1963), and the subsequent discussion of this study by F. Modigliani and A. Ando, and by T. Mayer and M. DePrano in *American Economic Review,* September 1963.

[8]See *The Economic Report of the President for 1969,* p. 72.

once again that a fiscal deficit, financed by the banking system, will tend to accelerate the growth in the money stock; while a fiscal surplus, whether impounded or used to retire debt, will tend to accelerate the money stock growth. And if the fiscal deficit is financed in part through accelerated monetary expansion, as was the case since the Vietnam escalation in 1965, the growth in GNP reflects the combined effects of fiscal and monetary action.

Monetary policy, measured in terms of the money stock, typically changes in the same direction as fiscal policy. Accordingly, what we observe in most periods (like the 1964 tax cut) is the effect of a combined action incorporating both monetary and fiscal elements. It is therefore fortunate for the development of stabilization theory that they were working in opposite directions on two occasions in recent years—thus providing an interesting test case. In 1966 a sharp increase in the deficit was matched by a very substantial tightening in monetary policy; and the crunch in the latter half of 1966 and the mini-recession in early 1967 clearly demonstrate the power of monetary policy. Similarly in 1968, the very substantial increase in the full-employment surplus enacted in the June 1968 Revenue and Expenditure Control Act (and giving rise to widespread fear of *overkill*) was apparently offset by the preceding and subsequent growth in the monetary aggregates. In these cases, the monetary forces seem to have been the stronger ones, not relatively minor (or permissive) factors that can only accommodate (or validate) fiscal policy actions. Hence, there has been renewed interest in their relative contribution to stabilization.

Table 1. Impact of Fiscal Influences (ΔE) on Economic Activity (ΔY)
$$\Delta Y = f_0 + f_1 \Delta E$$
(First Differences—Billions of Dollars)

	Lags*	f_0	$f_1 \Delta E$ (sum)	$R^2 / D\text{-}W$
II/1919–I/1969	t-6	3.83 (5.16)	.81 (3.01)	.13 .96
II/1919–II/1929	t-7	1.73 (2.44)	3.27 (2.78)	.41 1.58
III/1929–II/1939	t-10	−3.45 (−2.25)	18.28 (2.18)	.14 1.49
III/1939–IV/1946	t-4	4.29 (2.91)	.53 (2.11)	.61 1.43
I/1947–IV/1952	t-4	9.38 (3.91)	−1.49 (−1.76)	.09 .81
I/1953–II/1969	t-3	6.08 (2.95)	1.71 (2.15)	.08 1.13

Note: Regression coefficients are the top figures; their "t" values appear below each coefficient, enclosed by parentheses. R^2 is the percent of variations in the dependent variable which is explained by variations in the independent variable. D-W is the Durbin-Watson statistic.

*Selected on the basis of minimum standard error of estimate, adjusted for degrees of freedom.

This, then, brings us to our first question: How do we define the *ceteris paribus* fiscal action if monetary policy and fiscal policy often move in the same direction? The income-expenditure theorists, who define this as a fiscal action with interest rates held constant, are calibrating monetary policy in a manner which is consistent with their view of the transmission mechanism. On this definition, a *ceteris paribus* fiscal deficit may require a very substantial increase in the stock of money and appears to the *monetarist* as a *mutatis mutandis* effect. To the *monetarist*, a *ceteris paribus* deficit requires a given money stock growth rate, which may lead to a rise in the interest rate; and to fiscal policy advocates, this appears as an *offsetting action* since the rise in interest rates (which they use to calibrate the posture of monetary policy) is restrictive and tends to offset the income-generating effects of the deficit. The *ceteris paribus* effect for deficits or surpluses, as defined by the *monetarist*, will necessarily differ from the definition adopted by the fiscal policy advocates. This point is illustrated in a recent study of monetary and fiscal influences on economic activity for the period 1919-1969.[9] The evidence summarized in Table 1 indicates that when we regress economic activity on fiscal policy, the relation is fairly good. If,

Table 2. Indicators of Monetary (ΔM) and Fiscal (ΔE) Influences on Economic Activity (ΔY)
$$\Delta Y = a_0 + a_1 \Delta M + a_2 \Delta E$$

(Quarterly First Differences—Billions of Dollars)

Time Periods	Lags*	a_0	$a_1 \Delta M$ (sum)	$a_2 \Delta E$ (sum)	R^2 D-W
II/1919–I/69	t-6	1.92 (2.34)	2.89 (4.31)	− .07 (− .28)	.32 1.15
II/1919–II/29	t-3	.36 (.51)	5.62 (3.16)	**	.35 1.58
III/1929–II/39	t-5	− .51 (− .54)	5.40 (3.41)	− 7.97 (− 1.95)	.39 1.86
III/1939–IV/46	t-5	6.32 (1.39)	− 1.21 (− .59)	.35 (.81)	.66 1.60
I/1947–IV/52	t-10	3.65 (.84)	13.82 (3.51)	− 3.37 (− 4.12)	.72 2.74
I/1953–I/69	t-4	1.42 (.74)	8.85 (4.70)	− .84 (− 1.07)	.47 1.71

Note: Regression coefficients are the top figures; their "*t*" statistics appear below each coefficient, enclosed by parentheses. R^2 is the percent of variations in the dependent variable which is explained by variations in the independent variable. *D-W* is the Durbin-Watson statistic.

*Lags are selected on the basis of minimum standard error, adjusted for degrees of freedom.

**Fiscal variable omitted for 1919-1929 because it increased the standard error of the estimate.

[9]Michael Keran, "Monetary and Fiscal Influences on Economic Activity—The Historical Evidence" in the November 1969 issue of this *Review*.

however, we include a monetary aggregate variable in the regression, we find, as shown in Table 2, that the *ceteris paribus* fiscal effect, as defined by the *monetarist,* is either statistically insignificant or has the wrong sign. The evidence summarized in Tables 1 and 2 illustrates the problem of separating out the fiscal effect from the effect due to the monetary aggregate.

This difference in concepts helps explain the existence of a fairly pronounced communications gap. What a monetarist regards as a *ceteris paribus* deficit may entail a rise in interest rates, and will therefore appear as an *offsetting* action to the fiscal advocate; what a fiscal advocate regards as a *ceteris paribus* fiscal effect may entail accelerated growth in the money stock, and will therefore appear as a *mutatis mutandis* monetary effect to the monetarist. This applies especially to the analysis of the 1964 tax cut.

The money stock effects of deficits and surpluses need to be quantified if we are to obtain a realistic formulation of the government budget restraint. Once this is done we may be able to estimate the differential effects of nonmonetized and monetized deficits, and obtain acceptable estimates of fiscal multipliers—for the *ceteris paribus* and for the *mutatis mutandis* cases. We would also like to derive such estimates for the *monetarist* who calibrates monetary actions in terms of the money stock growth and for the fiscal advocates who calibrate monetary policy in terms of interest rates. Once this is done, we may be able to translate the results obtained in these two frameworks. This should help bridge the communication gap, and it may also help reconcile the two opposing points of view.[10]

[10]A technique that enabled us to separate out exogenous changes in the money stock due to monetary policy from endogenous changes induced by the real sector would also enable us to estimate a *ceteris paribus* fiscal action in terms of exogenous money stock behavior. This approach would, in principle, be acceptable to the fiscal advocates. See K. M. Carlson and D. S. Karnosky, *op. cit.*

The full-employment surplus (or deficit) is generally accepted as the best measure of fiscal policy, in preference to the actual surplus (or deficit), which is affected by the level of activity and behaves therefore more nearly like an endogenous variable. But the full-employment surplus is available only for the income and product budget and is tied to an income-expenditure framework. It may be desirable to experiment with "similar" concepts (separating out endogenous effects) for the cash budget and the new, and comprehensive, liquidity budget, to determine which of these budgets provides the most useful measure of fiscal policy.

16

Measuring the Impact of Monetary and Fiscal Actions: A New Look at the Specification Problem

Raymond E. Lombra and
*Raymond G. Torto**

The now well-known 1968 article by Andersen and Jordan (hereafter, A-J) generated considerable interest when the study concluded that the response of economic activity to monetary actions was substantial while the response to fiscal actions was negligible. The major critiques of the A-J work centered on the characteristics of the reduced-form, single-equation approach they employed. De Leeuw and Kalchbrenner (hereafter, D-K) stated: "The art of learning something from single equation regressions of the St. Louis type consists in devising variables which can be manipulated by policymakers but which have been adjusted in such a way that they are not terribly sensitive to current movements in the endogenous variables" (1969, p. 7). In most criticisms of the A-J article, the key issue has most always been the second requirement in the above quotation. This charge of simultaneous equation bias has been labeled the reverse-causation argument and as D-K have said: "Only if we can devise fiscal and monetary policy representations which get around this second prob-

Reprinted from *The Review of Economics and Statistics,* Vol. 56, No. 1 (February, 1974), pp. 104–107, by permission of the Harvard University Press and the authors.

* We would like to thank Edward Kane and Will Mason for stimulating our work in this area, and William Beeman, Herbert Kaufman and an anonymous referee who made helpful comments on an earlier draft. The opinions expressed and errors remaining are those of the authors and do not necessarily represent the views of their respective institutions.

lem will the single equation approach be able to tell us something about the effects of macro-economic policies" (1969, p. 7).*

In order to construct fiscal and monetary variables which were not terribly sensitive to current movements in the endogenous variables, authors such as D-K and Gramlich (1971) subtracted out components of the monetary base which they believed to be influenced by economic activity and, therefore, to be endogenous. In this way there is, in theory, a mitigation of the influence of economic activity on the monetary base. Once adjusted, the newly constructed monetary and fiscal variables were employed in A-J-type, single-equation models. The resulting tests raised serious doubts about the validity of the A-J conclusions.[1] In criticism of such approaches A-J said: "Their process of 'peeling' the monetary base (first subtracting borrowing from Reserve Banks and then currency held by others than banks) in arriving at the concept 'unborrowed reserves' may make sense statistically under special conditions, but this process has no economic relevance within the context of the customary body of economic theory which has evolved around the monetary base" (1969, p. 13).**

In further work on this topic Andersen (1969) concluded that if there is any reverse causation, the only way it can be measured is through the actions of the Federal Reserve System rather than through the behavior of the public. More recently, in an insightful and rigorous treatment of problems generated by endogenous stabilization policies, Goldfeld and Blinder argued: "If, during the period [the model-builder] is studying the stabilization authorities were reacting endogenously to the course of the economy, it may be crucial for him to estimate any systematic reaction patterns that existed and append these equations to his econometric model. Otherwise, he may get a very misleading picture of the way fiscal and monetary policies have worked in the past" (1972, p. 586). This suggestion, to take explicit account of the behavior of the Federal Reserve, is the focus of this note. We believe our measure of reverse causation makes both statistical sense (which D-K and Goldfeld-Blinder emphasize) and has "economic relevance" vis-à-vis the received theory evolving around the monetary base (which A-J find paramount).

Our argument is based on the realization that the supply and demand for money are interdependent and that this interdependence provides an avenue for the reverse influence of the business cycle on money. This point is argued at length in another paper (Lombra-Torto, 1973) where it is shown that Federal Reserve open-market operations (hereafter, OMO) are predominantly "defensive" in nature.[2] These "de-

---

* While it was not practicable to reprint the original Andersen-Jordan and de Leeuw-Kalchbrenner articles here, this article is preceded by an excerpt from an article by David I. Fand that is exemplary of the single-equation, reduced-form approach.—Ed.

[1]Silber's recent paper (1971) in this *Review* also raised some doubts about the St. Louis results by uncovering considerable instability in the estimated impact multipliers over the postwar period. Most recently, Waud (1972), using disaggregated data, some different measures of policy actions, and the same basic reduced-form approach, reached conclusions in sharp contrast to those of A-J.

** By this A-J mean that the Federal Reserve controls only (some of) the *sources* of the monetary base; currency in circulation is a *use* of the monetary base determined by the nonbank public and subtracting it out leaves a magnitude (reserves) which cannot be presumed to be so readily controlled by the Federal Reserve.—Ed.

[2]Our study draws heavily on the path-breaking work of John Wood (1967). Following Wood, we derived our reaction function within the framework of a formal optimization scheme.

fensive" operations are characterized by both *offsetting* and *accommodating* actions designed to moderate variations in money market conditions.[3] We have shown that "defensive" actions by the Federal Reserve include accommodation of changes in both the demand for deposits and the demand for currency (1973, pp. 50–51).[4] It is important to note that such accommodating behavior via "defensive" OMO leads, *ceteris paribus*, to changes in the monetary base (i.e., supply responds to demand).[5] Such accommodated changes in the monetary base in response to changes in the demand for money clearly indicate that the supply of and demand for money are interdependent and that the monetary base is an endogenously determined variable. Furthermore, it implies that anyone assuming changes in the monetary base are the result of *only* "dynamic" OMO (i.e., conscious counter-cyclical stabilization actions) might incorrectly overestimate the contribution of, or importance of, changes in the monetary base on GNP. Goldfeld and Blinder make the same point: "If the stabilization authorities are behaving in a procyclical manner, reduced-form estimates of policy multipliers are likely to be biased upward" (1972, p. 608).

The identity for the monetary base can be expressed as ($\Delta MB = \Delta G' + \Delta G'' + \Delta A$), where ΔMB is the change in the monetary base, $\Delta G'$ is that component of OMO we consider "defensive," $\Delta G''$ is "dynamic," and ΔA is the net change in all other factors that comprise the source side of the monetary base equation.*

We have briefly argued above and demonstrated elsewhere (1973, pp. 51–53) that movements in $\Delta G'$, especially those explained by the accommodating behavior of the Federal Reserve, bring about changes in *MB*. These changes in *MB*, due to "defen-.

---

[3]Offsetting actions are those adjustments in the Federal Reserve's holdings of government securities undertaken to offset changes in operating transactions (i.e., factors affecting reserves), or equivalently, to offset changes in the sources of the monetary base. For example, an increase in float, *ceteris paribus*, would increase free reserves (and the monetary base). In response, the Federal Reserve sells securities to offset the increase. Accommodating actions are those adjustments in the Federal Reserve's holdings of government securities undertaken to accommodate changes in required reserves. These actions are tantamount to accommodating changes in the demand for deposits (see Guttentag, 1966, pp. 9–11, and Lombra-Torto, 1973, pp. 49–51). In the language of contemporary optimizing theory one can view these actions as implying (or "revealing") that the Federal Reserve's objective function contains independent money market arguments such as the level, and, or variance of free reserves and interest rates.

[4]An increase in required reserves (total reserves constant) would lower excess reserves and, therefore, free reserves (member-bank borrowings constant). Maintaining the level of free reserves would call for supplying (i.e., accommodating) the increase in required reserves. Of course, the increased supply of reserves as a result of the Federal Reserve's action should also moderate any upward movement in money market interest rates.

[5]Most studies of Federal Reserve behavior to date have defined "defensive" operations narrowly as the offsetting of changes in operating transactions (i.e., factors affecting reserves) or equivalently, as offsetting changes in the sources of the monetary base. Like Guttentag (1966), we have broadened the concept of "defensive" OMO to include accommodating actions. In the extreme case one could argue that the monetary authorities perfectly offset (on a dollar-for-dollar basis) changes in the sources of the monetary base (which are functionally related to economic activity), thereby not allowing economic activity to affect the sources.

* For a detailed discussion of the sources and uses of the monetary base see the article by Jerry L. Jordan in the next section.—Ed.

sive" actions, are then a measure of the reverse influence of economic activity of the monetary base. If we neutralize[6] the monetary base (i.e., purge it of this reverse influence or feedback) by subtracting $\Delta G'$ from ΔMB we have a variable that can be "manipulated by policymakers . . . [and is] not terribly sensitive to current movements in the endogenous variables" (D-K, 1969, p. 7). In this way, more light might be shed on the issues that A-J sought to test, with consideration given to the major drawback of the single-equation approach—the reverse-causation argument.

Using the results of a previous study, we have constructed a neutralized monetary base measure ($\Delta MB^* = \Delta MB - \Delta G'$)[7] and have employed this variable in a single-equation model of the A-J prototype with the lag structure estimated with the use of the Almon technique (1965). The only difference in our equations aside from that which is described above is that we found no reason to assume that the impact lag for both monetary and fiscal policy should be of equal length. We regressed the quarterly change in GNP (ΔY) on quarterly changes in the monetary base (ΔMB) and high-employment expenditures (ΔHEE).[8] Presented below are the results for the

[6]We use this term as does Patric Hendershott (1968), i.e., we want to construct a monetary variable dominated by Federal Reserve "dynamic" actions and not directly influenced by actions of the private sector of the economy. Unlike Hendershott, however, we neutralize from the supply side and not the demand side.

[7]Estimates for $\Delta G'$ were obtained by regressing ΔG on those variables which measure the offsetting and accommodating behavior of the monetary authorities. Specifically, ΔG was regressed on changes in the other sources of the non-borrowed monetary base (ΔA), changes in member-bank borrowing (ΔB), changes in required reserves (ΔRR), and changes in currency holdings of the nonbank public (ΔC). This equation was part of a modification of Stephen Goldfeld's econometric model (Lombra-Torto, 1971) in which we treated the Federal Reserve endogenously. Estimation was by two-stage least squares since member-bank borrowing, required reserves, and currency are all endogenous variables. A more detailed explanation of this specific equation is available in (Lombra-Torto, 1973). The results for 1952 I-1968 II were:

$$\Delta G = -.4091 \Delta A - 1.2100 \Delta B + 1.0649 \Delta RR + .8102 \Delta C$$
$$(.070) \quad (.3528) \quad (.2721) \quad (.1655)$$
$$t = 5.81 \quad t = 3.43 \quad t = 3.91 \quad t = 4.90$$
$$R^2 = .8014$$
$$\text{D.W.} = 2.16$$
$$\text{S.E.} = .392$$

One could neutralize other popular measures of monetary policy such as free reserves (FR) or nonborrowed reserves (NBR) by utilizing the following identities ($FR = A + G - C - RR$ and $NBR = FR + RR$) and substituting our estimates of G' into each. Further, one can relate ΔMB^* to ΔFR. For example, $\Delta MB^* = \Delta FR + \Delta RR + \Delta B + \Delta C - \Delta G'$, and $\Delta MB^* = \Delta FR$ only if $\Delta G' = \Delta RR + \Delta B + \Delta C$. It should be emphasized that this study deals only with the 1953-1968 period and extension of the analysis to the present is a subject for future research.

[8]The variables ΔY and ΔHEE are quarterly changes in billions of dollars measured at annual rates,

[8]The variables ΔY and ΔHEE are quarterly changes in billions of dollars measured at annual rates, while ΔMB is measured as the change in billions of dollars of monthly averages over the last month of each quarter. The variables ΔY and ΔHEE are exactly what A-J (and D-K) employed. The base variable is, however, not seasonally adjusted, or adjusted for reserve requirement changes. The results presented here were not affected when experiments with seasonally adjusted data for the monetary base were performed.

summed distributed lag weights using first the base, equation (1), and then the neutralized base, equation (2), for 1952 I to 1968 II.[9]

$$\Delta Y = 5.27 + \sum_{i=0}^{4} 9.40\ \Delta MB_{t-i} + \sum_{i=0}^{9} 0.41\ \Delta HEE_{t-i} \qquad \begin{matrix} \bar{R}^2 = .44 \\ \text{S.E.} = 4.59 \end{matrix}$$
$$t = 5.75 \qquad t = 4.50 \qquad\quad t = 0.73 \qquad\qquad \text{D.W.} = 1.63 \quad (1)$$

$$\Delta Y = 5.08 + \sum_{i=0}^{4} 7.80\ \Delta MB^{*}_{t-i} + \sum_{i=0}^{9} 2.78\ \Delta HEE_{t-i} \qquad \begin{matrix} \bar{R}^2 = .34 \\ \text{S.E.} = 4.99 \end{matrix}$$
$$t = 5.06 \qquad t = 2.81 \qquad\quad t = 5.35 \qquad\qquad \text{D.W.} = 1.31 \quad (2)$$

If our hypothesis is correct, neutralization of the monetary base should reduce the impact of the monetary variable on GNP. This does occur in equation (2) with both a fall in the size of the coefficient and a drop in its statistical significance. At the same time the fiscal policy multiplier becomes larger and is now statistically significant. However, we find that over four quarters the monetary base multiplier is almost three times the fiscal expenditure multiplier summed over nine quarters.[10] Thus, after correcting for the endogeneity of the monetary base we still find that money matters, and significantly so, but at the same time, so does fiscal policy.[11]

This note has taken a new look at the specification error associated with measuring the impact of monetary and fiscal policy in a reduced-form, single-equation model, and has demonstrated a procedure for correcting the error. Specifically, it has been shown that the failure to incorporate explicitly the behavior of the Federal Reserve into the model has a considerable effect on the conclusions reached on the relative strength of monetary and fiscal actions. Furthermore, the biases are resolved in the direction expected by us and Goldfeld-Blinder.

We would prefer however, not to enter a "correlation derby" on this matter, but rather suggest to all model-builders that further explicit modeling on the behavior of monetary policymakers (and fiscal policymakers) is necessary in macro-econometric models in order to insure against suppression of information on the policy process.

[9]As in the A-J study (1968), the distributed lag weights were estimated with fourth degree polynomials constrained to zero at the end points. The lag pattern finally selected for equation (2) was chosen after considerable variation of the length of lags and type of constraints employed in order to minimize the standard error of the equation. We then imposed that lag structure on equation (1) in order to facilitate strict comparability. However, independent experiments with the lag structure for equation (1) were performed and suggested the lag structure on ΔMB was identical to the one we (and A-J) imposed on it, while the sum of the distributed lag weights on HEE in equation (1) was relatively insensitive to lengthening the lag from 4 to 9 quarters.

[10]We might note that if one prefers to use the money supply as a measure of monetary actions, and if the relationship between the monetary base and the money supply is of the order of 1:2.5 then the monetary and fiscal policy multipliers approach equality.

[11]As a partial test of our adjustment of the base we regressed ΔMB^{*} on ΔY. If our procedure has removed some of the feedback of GNP on the base the coefficient on ΔY should be lower when ΔMB^{*} is the regressand than when ΔMB is the regressand. The test, a variant of one proposed by Andersen (1969), confirms our hypothesis and the results are available from the authors.

Such an inference seems only logical in light of the sizable differences in the policy impact multipliers demonstrated in equations (1) and (2) in this note.

REFERENCES

ALMON, S., "The Distributed Lag between Capital Appropriations and Expenditures," *Econometrica*, 33 (Jan. 1965), 178-196.

ANDERSEN, L. C., "Additional Empirical Evidence on the Reverse-Causation Argument," *Review* (Federal Reserve Bank of St. Louis, Aug. 1969), 19-23.

———, and J. JORDAN, "Monetary and Fiscal Actions: A Test of Their Relative Importance in Economic Stabilization," *Review* (Federal Reserve Bank of St. Louis, Nov. 1968), 11-24.

———, and ———, "Reply," *Review* (Federal Reserve Bank of St. Louis, Apr. 1969), 12-16.

DE LEEUW, F., and J. KALCHBRENNER, "Monetary and Fiscal Actions: A Test of Their Relative Importance in Economic Stabilization—Comment," *Review* (Federal Reserve Bank of St. Louis, Apr. 1969), 6-11.

GOLDFELD, S., and A. BLINDER, "Some Implications of Endogenous Stabilization Policy," *Brookings Papers on Economic Activity* (3:1972), 585-640.

GRAMLICH, E., "The Usefulness of Monetary and Fiscal Policy as Discretionary Stabilization Tools," *Journal of Money, Credit and Banking*, 3 (May 1971), 506-532.

GUTTENTAG, J., "The Strategy of Open-Market Operations," *Quarterly Journal of Economics*, 80 (Feb. 1966), 1-30.

HENDERSHOTT, P., *The Neutralized Money Stock: An Unbiased Measure of Federal Reserve Policy Actions* (Homewood, Ill.: Richard D. Irwin), 1968.

LOMBRA, R. E., and R. G. TORTO, "Endogenous Federal Reserve Open Market Operations in a Macro-Econometric Model: A First Report." Presented at the Winter Meeting of the Econometric Society, 1971.

———, and ———, "Federal Reserve 'Defensive' Behavior and the Reserve Causation Argument," *Southern Economic Journal*, 40 (July 1973), 47-55, and *Staff Economic Studies*, no. 75 (Board of Governors of the Federal Reserve System), 1972.

SILBER, W., "The St. Louis Equation: 'Democratic' and 'Republican' Versions and Other Experiments," this REVIEW, 53 (Nov. 1971) 362-367.

WAUD, R., "Monetary and Fiscal Effects on Economic Activity." Presented at the Winter Meeting of the Econometric Society, 1972.

WOOD, J., "A Model of Federal Reserve Behavior," in George Horwich (ed.), *Monetary Process and Policy* (Homewood, Ill.: Richard D. Irwin), 1967, 135-166.

The Lag in the Effect of Monetary Policy: A Survey of Recent Literature

*Michael J. Hamburger**

During the last ten years the views of economists—both monetarists and nonmonetarists—on the lag in the effect of monetary policy on the economy have changed considerably. This article examines some of the recent evidence which has served as the basis for these changes.

Prior to 1960, quantitative estimates of the lag in the effect of monetary policy were rare. While there had always been disagreement on the effectiveness of monetary policy, a substantial number of economists seemed to accept the proposition that there was sufficient impact in the reasonably short run for monetary policy to be used as a device for economic stabilization. Although this view did not go unquestioned— see, for example, Mayer [26] and Smith [29][1]—the main challenge to the conventional thinking came from Milton Friedman. He argued that monetary policy acts with so long and variable a lag that attempts to pursue a contracyclical monetary policy might aggrevate, rather than ameliorate, economic fluctuations. In summarizing work done in collaboration with Anna Schwartz, he wrote [16]: "We have found

Reprinted from the Federal Reserve Bank of New York, *Monetary Aggregates and Monetary Policy* (1974), pp. 104–113, by permission of the publisher.

* The author wishes to acknowledge the helpful comments of Richard G. Davis, David H. Kopf, Robert G. Link, and other colleagues at the Federal Reserve Bank of New York. In addition, the excellent research assistance of Susan Skinner and Rona Stein is gratefully acknowledged. The views expressed in this paper are the author's alone and do not necessarily reflect those of the individuals noted above or the Federal Reserve Bank of New York.

[1]The numbers in brackets refer to the works cited at the end of this article.

that, on the average of 18 cycles, peaks in the rate of change in the stock of money tend to precede peaks in general business by about 16 months and troughs in the rate of change in the stock of money precede troughs in general business by about 12 months. . . . For individual cycles, the recorded lead has varied between 6 and 29 months at peaks and between 4 and 22 months at troughs."

Many economists were simply not prepared to believe Friedman's estimates of either the length or the variability of the lag. As Culbertson [11] put it, "if we assume that government stabilization policies . . . act with so long and variable a lag, how do we set about explaining the surprising moderateness of the economic fluctuations that we have suffered in the past decade?" Culbertson's own conclusion was that "the broad record of experience support[s] the view that [contracyclical] monetary, debt-management, and fiscal adjustments can be counted on to have their predominant direct effects within three to six months, soon enough that if they are undertaken moderately early in a cyclical phase they will not be destabilizing."

Kareken and Solow [5] also appear to have been unwilling to accept Friedman's estimates. They summarized their results as follows: "Monetary policy works neither so slowly as Friedman thinks, nor as quickly and surely as the Federal Reserve itself seems to believe. . . . Though the *full* results of policy changes on the flow of expenditures may be a long time coming, nevertheless the chain of effects is spread out over a fairly wide interval. This means that *some* effect comes reasonably quickly, and that the effects build up over time so that some substantial stabilizing power results after a lapse of time of the order of six or nine months."

However, as Mayer [27] pointed out, this statement is inconsistent with the evidence presented by Karenken and Solow. They reported estimates of the complete lag in the effect of monetary policy on the flow of expenditures for only one component of gross national product (GNP), namely, inventory investment, and this lag is much longer than Friedman's lag. For another sector—producers' durable equipment—they provided data for only part of the lag, but even this is longer than Friedman's lag. Thus, Mayer noted that Karenken and Solow "should have criticized Friedman, not for overestimating, but for underestimating the lag."

More recently, it is the *monetarists* who have taken the view that the lag in the effect of monetary policy is relatively short and the nonmonetarists who seem to be claiming longer lags. This showed up in the reaction to the St. Louis (Andersen and Jordan) equation [4]. According to this equation, the total response of GNP to changes in the money supply is completed within a year.

In his review of the Andersen and Jordan article, Davis [12] wrote "the most surprising thing about the world of the St. Louis equation is not so much the force, but rather the speed with which money begins to act on the economy." If the level of the money supply undergoes a $1 billion once-and-for-all rise in a given quarter, it will (according to the St. Louis equation) raise GNP by $1.6 billion in that quarter and by $6.6 billion during four quarters. In contrast, Davis found that in the Federal Reserve Board–Massachusetts Institute of Technology model—which was estimated by assuming nonborrowed reserves to be the basic monetary policy variable—a once-and-for-all increase in the money supply of $1 billion in a given quarter has almost no effect on GNP in that quarter and, even after four quarters, the level of GNP is only about $400 million higher than it otherwise would be. Thus, he concluded, "what is at stake in the case of the St. Louis equation is not merely a 'shade of difference' but a strikingly contrasting view of the world—at least relative to what is normally taken as the orthodox view roughly replicated and confirmed both in methods and in result by the Board-MIT model."[2]

The Federal Reserve Board-MIT model (henceforth called the FRB-MIT model) is not the only econometric model suggesting that monetary policy operates with a long distributed lag. Indeed, practically every *structural* model of the United States economy which has been addressed to this question has arrived at essentially the same answer.[3]

The most recent advocates of short lags are Arthur Laffer and R. David Ranson [25]. They have argued that: "Monetary policy, as represented by changes in the conventionally defined money supply [demand deposits plus currency], has an immediate and permanent impact on the level of GNP. For every dollar increase in the money supply, GNP will rise by about $4.00 or $5.00 in the current quarter, and not fall back [or rise any further] in the future. Alternatively, every 1 percent change in the money supply is associated with a 1 percent change in GNP."

This article reviews some of the recent professional literature on the lag in the effect of monetary policy, with the objective of examining the factors which account for differences in the results. Among the factors considered are: (1) the type of statistical estimating model, i.e., structural versus reduced-form equations; (2) the specification of the monetary policy variable; and (3) the influence of the seasonal adjustment procedure. For the most part, the analysis is confined to the results obtained by others. New estimation is undertaken only in those instances where it is considered necessary to reconcile different sets of results.

Structural versus Reduced-Form Models

We turn first to the question of whether it is more appropriate to use structural or reduced-form models to estimate the effects of stabilization policy on the economy. A structural model of the economy attempts to set forth in equation form what are considered to be the underlying or basic economic relationships in the economy. Although many mathematical and statistical complications may arise such a set of equations can, in principle, be "reduced" (solved). In this way key economic vari-

---

[2]The properties of the Federal Reserve-MIT model are discussed by de Leeuw and Gramlich [13, 14] and by Ando and Modigliani [6].
[3]See Hamburger [21] and Mayer [27]. For a recent discussion of why the lag should be long, see Davis [12], Gramlich [19], and Pierce [28]. The alternative view is presented by White [31], who also gives reasons for believing that the procedures used to estimate the parameters of large-scale econometric models, particularly the FRB-MIT model, may yield "greatly exaggerated" estimates of the length of the lag.

ables, such as GNP, can be expressed directly as functions of policy variables and other forces exogenous to the economy. While the difference between a structural model and a reduced-form model is largely mathematical and does not necessarily involve different assumptions about the workings of the economy, a lively debate has developed over the advantages and disadvantages of these two approaches.

Users of structural models stress the importance of tracing the paths by which changes in monetary policy are assumed to influence the economy. Another advantage often claimed for the structural approach is that it permits one to incorporate *a priori* knowledge about the economy, for example, knowledge about identities, lags, the mathematical forms of relationships, and what variables should or should not be included in various equations (Gramlich [20]).

On the other hand those who prefer the reduced-form approach contend that, if one is primarily interested in explaining the behavior of a few key variables, such as GNP, prices, and unemployment, it is unnecessary to estimate all the parameters of a large-scale model. In addition it is argued that, if the economy is very complicated, it may be too difficult to study even with a very complicated model. Hence, it may be useful simply to examine the relationship between inputs such as monetary and fiscal policy and outputs such as GNP.

Considering the heat of the debate, it is surprising that very little evidence has been presented to support either position. The only studies of which I am aware come from two sources: simulations with the FRB-MIT model, reported by de Leeuw and Gramlich [13, 14], and the separate work of de Leeuw and Kalchbrenner [15]. The latter study reported the estimates of a reduced form equation for GNP, using monetary and fiscal policy variables similar to those in the FRB-MIT model. The form of the equation is:

Equation 1

$$\Delta Y_t = a + \sum_{i=0}^{7} b_i \Delta NBR_{t-i} + \sum_{i=0}^{7} c_i \Delta E_{t-i} + \sum_{i=0}^{7} d_i \Delta RA_{t-i} + u_t$$

where

ΔY = Quarterly change in GNP, current dollars.

ΔNBR = Quarterly change in nonborrowed reserves adjusted for reserve requirement changes.

ΔE = Quarterly change in high-employment expenditures of the Federal Government, current dollars.

ΔRA = Quarterly change in high-employment receipts of the Federal Government in current-period prices.

u = Random error term.

All variables are adjusted for seasonal variation, and the lag structures are estimated by using the Almon distributed lag technique.[4]

Chart 1 illustrates the lag distributions of the effect on GNP of nonborrowed reserves—the principal monetary variable used in the studies just mentioned. The chart shows the cumulative effects of a one-dollar change in nonborrowed reserves on the level of GNP as illustrated by four experiments, the reduced-form equation of de Leeuw and Kalchbrenner, and three versions of the FRB–MIT model. The heavy broken line traces the sum of the regression coefficients for the current and lagged values of nonborrowed reserves in the de Leeuw-Kalchbrenner equation (i.e., the sum of the b_i's). The other lines show the results obtained from simulations of the FRB–MIT model; FRB–MIT 1969(a) and FRB–MIT 1969(b) represent simulations of the 1969 version of the model, with two different sets of initial conditions.[5] FRB–MIT 1968 gives the simulation results for an earlier version of the model.

Although there are some large short-run differences in the simulation results, these three experiments suggest similar long-run effects of nonborrowed reserves on income. Such a finding is not very surprising; what is significant, in view of the debate between those who prefer structural models and those who prefer reduced forms, is that after the first three or four quarters the de Leeuw-Kalchbrenner results lie well within the range of the simulation results.[6]

Thus, we find that when nonborrowed reserves are chosen as the exogenous monetary policy variable, i.e., the variable used in *estimating* the parameters of the model, it makes very little difference whether the lag in the effect of policy is determined by a structural or a reduced-form model. There is, to be sure, no assurance that similar results would be obtained with other monetary variables or with other structural models (including more recent versions of the FRB–MIT model). In the present case,

---

[4]Use of the Almon [1] procedure has become quite popular in recent years as it imposes very little *a priori* restriction on the shape of the lag structure, requiring merely that it can be approximated by a polynomial. In the applications discussed in this article, it is generally assumed that a second- or a fourth-degree polynomial is sufficiently flexible to reproduce closely the true lag structure.

[5]For the FRB–MIT 1969(a) simulation, the values of all exogenous variables in the model, except nonborrowed reserves, are set equal to their actual values starting in the first quarter of 1964. For the FRB–MIT 1969(b) simulation, the starting values for these variables are their actual values in the second quarter of 1958. The obvious difference between these two sets of initial conditions is the difference in inflationary potential. The quarters during and after 1964 were ones of high resource utilization, and an expansion of reserves at such a time might be expected to stimulate price increases promptly. On the other hand, there was substantial excess capacity in 1958 and a change in reserves under such conditions would be expected to have a minimal short-run effect on prices. The difference in these price effects is significant since it is movements in *current*-dollar GNP which are being explained.

[6]De Leeuw and Kalchbrenner do not estimate lags longer than seven quarters. While it is conceivable that the curve representing their results could flatten out (or decline) after period t-7, the shape of the curve up to that point and the results obtained by others, such as those shown in Chart 2, make this possibility seem highly unlikely. The initial negative values for the de Leeuw-Kalchbrenner curve arise because of the large negative estimate of b_0 in equation 1; the estimates for all other b's are positive. As de Leeuw and Kalchbrenner pointed out, it is difficult to provide an economic explanation for changes in nonborrowed reserves having a negative effect on GNP in the current quarter. It seems more reasonable, therefore, that the result reflects "reverse causation," running from GNP to nonborrowed reserves—that is, the Federal Reserve's attempt to pursue a contracyclical monetary policy. This point is discussed at greater length in Hamburger [22].

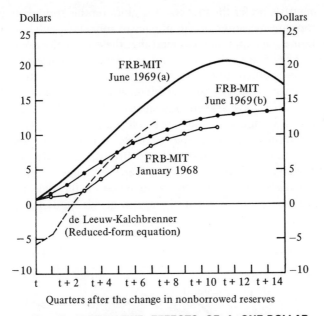

Dollars

25
20   FRB-MIT
     June 1969(a)
              FRB-MIT
15   June 1969(b)

10

5   FRB-MIT
     January 1968

0

     de Leeuw-Kalchbrenner
     (Reduced-form equation)
-5

-10

t   t + 2   t + 4   t + 6   t + 8   t + 10 t + 12 t + 14

Quarters after the change in nonborrowed reserves

CHART 1 CUMULATIVE EFFECTS OF A ONE-DOLLAR CHANGE IN NONBORROWED RESERVES ON GNP

Note: FRB-MIT = Federal Reserve Board-Massachusetts Institute of Technology econometric model.

however, the use of reduced-form equations does not lead to estimates of the effects of monetary policy on the economy that differ from those obtained from a structural model. For the purposes of our analysis, this finding implies that the type of statistical model employed to estimate the lag in the effect of monetary policy may be less important than other factors in explaining the differences in the results that have been reported in the literature.

Specification of the Monetary Policy Variable

Another important difference among the various studies of the lag is the variable used to represent monetary policy. The aim of this section is not to contribute to the controversy about the most appropriate variable, but rather to summarize the arguments and spell out the implications of the choice for the estimate of the lag in the effect of policy.

In recent years three of the most popular indicators of the thrust of monetary policy have been the money supply, the monetary base, and effective nonborrowed reserves.[7] Monetarists prefer the first two variables on the grounds that they provide the most appropriate measures of the impact of monetary policy on the economy. Critics of the monetarist approach contend that these variables are deficient because they reflect the effects of both policy and nonpolicy influences and hence do not provide reliable (i.e., statistically unbiased) measures of Federal Reserve actions. The variable most often suggested by these economists is effective nonborrowed reserves.[8] In reply the monetarists have argued that, since the Federal Reserve has the power to offset the effects of all nonpolicy influences on the money supply (or the monetary base), it is the movements in the money variable and not the reasons for the movements which are important (Brunner [7] and Brunner and Meltzer [8]). However, this sidesteps the statistical question of whether the money supply or the monetary base qualify as exogenous variables to be included on the right-hand side of a reduced-form equation. (For a further discussion, see Gramlich [20] and Hamburger[22].)*

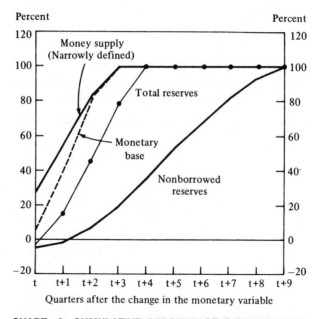

CHART 2 CUMULATIVE PERCENTAGE DISTRIBUTIONS OF THE EFFECTS OF VARIOUS MONETARY AGGREGATES ON GNP

Sources: See footnote 9.

[7]Nonborrowed reserves adjusted for changes in reserve requirements. A similar adjustment is made in computing the monetary base, which is defined as total member bank reserves plus the currency holdings of nonmember banks and the nonbank public. The reserve figure included in the base is also adjusted to neutralize the effects of changes in the ratio of demand deposits to time deposits and changes in the distribution of deposits among banks subject to different reserve requirements.

[8]Among others, see de Leeuw and Kalchbrenner [15], Gramely [18], and Hendershott [23].

* See the preceding article by Lombra and Torto for an interesting attempt to resolve this issue.—Ed.

Chart 2 presents the cumulative percentage distributions of the effects of various monetary variables on nominal GNP, as implied by the parameter estimates for equations similar to equation 1, that is, reduced-form equations relating quarterly changes in GNP to quarterly changes in monetary and fiscal policy variables. The monetary variables are effective nonborrowed reserves, the monetary base, the narrowly defined money supply (private holdings of currency and demand deposits), and total reserves. The latter is defined as effective nonborrowed reserves plus member bank borrowings from the Federal Reserve. It is also approximately equal to the monetary base less the currency holdings of nonmember banks and of the nonbank public. Once again, the lag structures for the monetary and fiscal policy variables are estimated using the Almon distributed lag technique. In all cases, with the possible exception of the monetary base, the lags chosen are those which maximize the $\bar{R}^2$ (coefficient of determination adjusted for degrees of freedom) of the equation. Percentage distributions are used to highlight the distribution of the effects over time as opposed to their dollar magnitudes.[9]

The results indicate that the choice of the exogenous monetary policy variable has a significant effect on the estimate of the lag in the effect of policy. If the money supply, the monetary base, or total reserves are taken as the monetary variable, the results suggest that the total response of GNP to a change in policy is completed within four or five quarters. On the other hand, those who consider nonborrowed reserves to be the appropriate variable would conclude that less than 40 percent of the effect occurs in five quarters and that the full effect is distributed over two and a half years.[10]

Thus, the evidence suggests that the relatively short lags that have been found by the monetarists in recent years depend more on their specification of the monetary policy variable than on the use of a reduced-form equation. Whether or not these estimates understate the true length of the lag, they seem roughly consistent with the prevailing view among economists in the early 1960's. They are, for example, essentially identical with Mayer's [26] results which suggested that most of the effect of a change in policy occurs within five quarters. As indicated above, wide acceptance of the proposition that monetary policy operates with a long lag—i.e., a substantial portion of the impact of a policy change does not take place until a year or more later—is of relatively recent vintage and appears to have been heavily influenced by

[9]The estimates shown in Chart 2 are derived from the equations reported by Corrigan [10] and by Andersen and Jordan [4]. Corrigan's results are used for the nonborrowed reserves, total reserves, and money supply curves (the nonborrowed reserves equation is not shown in his article but is available on request). He did not estimate an equation for the monetary base. The fiscal policies variables used in all three equations are the changes in the Government spending and tax components of the "initial stimulus" measure of fiscal policy. The monetary base curve is derived from the Andersen and Jordan results. The fiscal measures used in this study are the Government expenditure and receipt components of the high-employment budget. The criterion used by Andersen and Jordan to select their lag structures is described by Keran [24].

[10]A similar conclusion was reached by Andersen [2], who found even longer lags when nonborrowed reserves are used as the monetary policy variable.

the results of those who do not consider the money supply to be an appropriate measure of monetary policy impulses.

The Seasonal Adjustment Problem

One of the most recent investigations of the effects of monetary and fiscal policy on the economy is that conducted by Laffer and Ranson for the Office of Management and Budget [25]. Perhaps the most striking finding of this study is that every change in the money supply has virtually all its effect on the level of GNP in the quarter in which it occurs. Or, to put this differently, there is little evidence of a lag in the effect of monetary policy. This finding which stands at odds with most other evidence, both theoretical and empirical, is attributed by Laffer and Ranson largely to their use of data that are *not* adjusted for seasonal variation.[11] They contend that the averaging (or smoothing) properties of most seasonal adjustment procedures tend to distort the timing of statistical relationships. Hence, specious lag structures may be introduced into the results.

As shown below, however, the results reported by Laffer and Ranson are much more dependent on their choice of time period (1948-69) than on the use of seasonally unadjusted data. For, if their nominal GNP equation is reestimated for the period 1953-1969 (the period employed in the current version of the St. Louis model [3] and in most other recent investigations), it makes very little difference whether one uses seasonally adjusted or unadjusted data. They both indicate that a significant portion of the effect of a change in money does not occur for at least two quarters.

The equation selected by Laffer and Ranson to explain the percentage change in nominal GNP is:[12]

Equation 2

$$\%\Delta Y = 3.21 + 1.10\%\Delta M_1 + .136\%\Delta G - .069\%\Delta G_{-1}$$
$$(4.9) \quad (5.5) \quad\quad (6.9) \quad\quad (3.3)$$

$$- .039\%\Delta G_{-2} - .024\%\Delta G_{-3} - .046\Delta SH$$
$$(1.9) \quad\quad (1.2) \quad\quad (3.7)$$

$$+ .068\%\Delta S\&P_{-1} - 9.8\ D_1 + 2.5\ D_2 - 3.0\ D_3$$
$$(2.2) \quad\quad (12.1) \quad (2.6) \quad (4.1)$$

$$\bar{R}^2 = .958 \quad SE = 1.31 \quad \text{Interval: 1948-I to 1969-IV}$$

[11]Other studies which find very short lags in the effect of monetary policy are cited by Laffer and Ranson [25].

[12]The numbers in parentheses are t-statistics for the regression coefficients. SE is the standard error of estimate of the regression. A subscript preceded by a minus sign indicates that the variable is lagged that many quarters. In estimating their model, Laffer and Ranson use quarterly changes in the natural logarithms of the variables. This is roughly equivalent to using quarter-to-quarter percentage changes.

where

$\%\Delta Y$ = Quarterly percentage change in nominal GNP.
$\%\Delta M_1$ = Quarterly percentage change in M_1 (the narrowly defined money supply).
$\%\Delta G$ = Quarterly percentage change in Federal Government purchases of goods and services.
ΔSH = Quarterly change in a measure of industrial man-hours lost due to strikes.
$\%\Delta S\&P$ = Quarterly percentage change in Standard and Poor's Composite Index of Common Stock Prices (the "S&P 500").
D_1 = Seasonal dummy variable for the first quarter.
D_2 = Seasonal dummy variable for the second quarter.
D_3 = Seasonal dummy variable for the third quarter.

All data used in the calculations are unadjusted for seasonal variation. The three dummy variables (D_1, D_2, and D_3) are introduced to allow for such variation and to permit estimation of the seasonal factors. In principle, joint estimation of the seasonal factors and the economic parameters of a model is preferable to the use of data generated by the standard type of seasonal adjustment procedure. However, in having only three dummy variables, Laffer and Ransom assume that the seasonal pattern in income is constant over the entire sample period. If this assumption is not correct, it becomes a purely empirical question as to whether their procedure is any better or worse than the use of seasonally adjusted data.

Stock market prices are included in the equation on the assumption that the current market value of equities provides an efficient forecast of future income. The variable representing the percentage of manhours lost due to strikes (SH) is included for institutional reasons.

Aside from these factors, the Laffer-Ranson equation is quite similar to the St. Louis equation. The most important difference is that the former contains only the current-quarter value of money. This implies that a change in the money supply has a once-and-for-all effect on the level of income. Equation 3 shows the results obtained when four lagged values of the percentage change in M_1 are included in the model. Only the coefficients of the money variables are shown below; the rest of the results for this equation as well as those for equation 2 are reproduced in the first portion of Table 1.

Equation 3

$$\%\Delta Y = 3.36 + 1.03\%\Delta M_1 - .41\%\Delta M_{1-1} + .49\%\Delta M_{1-2}$$
$$\quad (3.9) \quad (4.4) \qquad\quad (1.7) \qquad\qquad (2.1)$$

$$\qquad - .31\%\Delta M_{1-3} + .30\%\Delta M_{1-4} \dots$$
$$\qquad\quad (1.3) \qquad\qquad (1.3)$$

$$\bar{R}^{-2} = .961 \quad SE = 1.26 \quad \text{Interval: 1948-I to 1969-IV}$$

Table 1. Regressions Explaining the Percentage Change in Gross National Product
(Quarterly seasonally unadjusted data)

Equation	Constant	%ΔM₁	%ΔM₁₋₁	%ΔM₁₋₂	%ΔM₁₋₃	%ΔM₁₋₄	%ΔG	%ΔG₋₁	%ΔG₋₂	%ΔG₋₃	ΔSH	%ΔS&P₋₁	D₁	D₂	D₃	R̃² SE
						1948–I to 1969–IV										
2	3.21 (4.9)	1.10 (5.5)					.136 (6.9)	− .069 (3.3)	− .039 (1.9)	− .024 (1.2)	− .046 (3.7)	.068 (2.2)	− 9.8 (12.1)	2.5 (2.6)	− 3.0 (4.1)	.958 1.31
3	3.36 (3.9)	1.03 (4.4)	− .41 (1.7)	.49 (2.1)	− .31 (1.3)	.30 (1.3)	.136 (7.1)	− .073 (3.7)	− .034 (1.7)	− .024 (1.3)	− .045 (3.6)	.095 (2.9)	− 9.5 (7.6)	1.3 (0.9)	− 2.9 (2.4)	.961 1.26
						1948–I to 1952–IV										
2a	5.05 (4.8)	.61 (1.6)					.125 (5.7)	− .119 (5.6)	− .022 (1.2)	− .015 (0.6)	− .050 (3.3)	.221 (3.2)	− 11.0 (8.8)	− 1.5 (0.8)	− 2.7 (2.3)	.983 0.86
3a	2.38 (1.06)	1.11 (2.0)	− .29 (.5)	− .18 (.2)	− .24 (.3)	.66 (1.4)	.121 (3.7)	− .122 (4.0)	− .024 (.9)	− .030 (.9)	− .036 (1.9)	.171 (2.0)	− 7.2 (2.3)	3.7 (.8)	1.0 (.3)	.983 0.86
						1953–I to 1969–IV										
2b	4.16 (5.1)	.73 (3.1)					.143 (3.8)	− .008 (0.2)	− .042 (1.1)	− .048 (1.3)	− .022 (1.4)	.061 (1.8)	− 11.2 (10.2)	1.8 (1.6)	− 4.2 (4.2)	.964 1.20
3b	5.18 (5.1)	.64 (2.4)	− .40 (1.3)	.88 (3.1)	− .07 (.3)	− .05 (.2)	.160 (4.4)	.002 (.1)	− .044 (1.2)	− .068 (1.9)	− .026 (1.7)	.079 (2.1)	− 11.6 (7.8)	− 1.8 (1.0)	− 5.2 (3.6)	.968 1.13

Note: Values of "t" statistics are indicated in parentheses. For explanation of the symbols other than those shown below, see equation 2 above.

R̃² = Coefficient of determination (adjusted for degrees of freedom).

SE = Standard error of estimate of the regression.

Following Laffer and Ranson, the coefficients of this equation are estimated without the use of the Almon distributed lag technique. Although some of the lagged money coefficients approach statistical significance, equation 3—like equation 2—implies that the current and long-run effects of money on income are, for all practical purposes, the same. An increase of 1 percent in M_1 is associated with a roughly 1 percent rise in income in the current quarter and a 1.1 percent rise in the long run.

To test the hypothesis, suggested above, that it is the time interval used by Laffer and Ranson which is largely responsible for this result equations 2 and 3 were reestimated for the subperiods 1948-I to 1952-IV and 1953-I to 1969-IV. The results (see the two lower sections of Table 1) show that (a) the relationship between money and income in the 1948-1952 period is not statistically significant (equations 2a and 3a)[13] and (b) there is a significant lag in the effect of money on income during the

[13]The contribution of the five money variables to the explanatory power of equation 3a may be evaluated by using the statistical procedure known as the F-test. When this is done, we find that the relationship between money and income is not significant even at the .20 confidence level. It should also be noted that the poor showing of the money variables in the 1948-1952 period cannot be attributed simply to the shortness of the period and hence the limited number of degrees of freedom. These conditions do not prevent us from finding statistically significant relationships for most of the other variables included in equations 2a and 3a.

more recent period. Indeed, the largest single change in income as a result of a change in money during this period occurs after a lag of two quarters (equation 3b).[14]

Perhaps the most interesting feature of the results is the similarity between the "money coefficients" for the period 1953-1969 (equation 3b) and those which have been obtained by other researchers using seasonally adjusted data for the same period. To demonstrate this, equation 3b was reestimated with seasonally adjusted data for M_1, GNP, and G. The coefficients for the current and lagged money variables for this equation (3b′) and for equations 3 and 3b are reported in Table 2. Once again the equations are estimated *without* the use of the Almon distributed lag technique. Chart 3 shows the cumulative percentage distribution of the effects of money on income as implied by these equations. It is clear from the chart that it is the time

Table 2. Selected Regression Results for Equations Explaining the Percentage Change in Gross National Product

(Quarterly data)

Equation	Time Period	Data	\multicolumn{5}{c}{Regression Coefficients}	$\bar{R}^2$ SE
			$\%\Delta M_1$	$\%\Delta M_{1-1}$	$\%\Delta M_{1-2}$	$\%\Delta M_{1-3}$	$\%\Delta M_{1-4}$	
3	1948-I to 1969-IV	NSA	1.03 (4.4)	− .41 (1.7)	.49 (2.1)	− .31 (1.3)	− .30 (1.3)	.961 1.26
3b	1953-I to 1969-IV	NSA	.64 (2.4)	− .40 (1.3)	.88 (3.1)	− .07 (0.3)	− .05 (0.2)	.968 1.13
3b′	1953-I to 1969-IV	SA	.37 (1.8)	− .08 (0.3)	.53 (1.9)	.32 (1.2)	− .21 (1.1)	.541 0.71

Note: Values of "t" statistics are indicated in parenthesis. For explanation of the symbols other than those shown below, see equation 2.

$\bar{R}^2$ = Coefficient of determination (adjusted for degrees of freedom).
SE = Standard error of estimate of the regression.
NSA = Not seasonally adjusted.
SA = Seasonally adjusted data are used for M_1, GNP, and G.

[14]In fairness to Laffer and Ranson, it should be noted that even for equation 3b we are unable to reject the hypothesis (at the .05 confidence level) that the current-quarter money coefficient is less than 1.0. However, there appears to be no necessary reason why the current-quarter effect should be singled out for special consideration. Thus, equation 3b also implies that after six months the cumulative effect of money on income is not significantly different from zero.

The hypothesis that the same regression model fits the entire Laffer-Ranson sample period (1948-1969) may be evaluated by means of a procedure developed by Chow [9]. Doing this, we find that the hypothesis may be rejected at the .01 confidence level, that is, the differences in the parameter estimates of equations 2a and 2b and equations 3a and 3b are statistically significant.

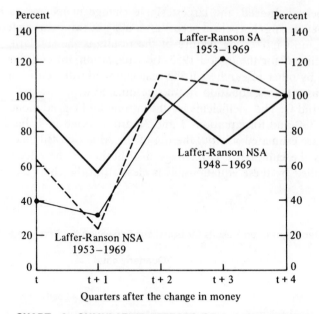

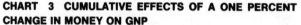

CHART 3 CUMULATIVE EFFECTS OF A ONE PERCENT CHANGE IN MONEY ON GNP

Note: NSA = not seasonally adjusted; SA = seasonally adjusted.

period chosen by Laffer and Ranson which is largely responsible for their controversial result rather than the use of seasonally unadjusted data. This shows up even more dramatically when the equations are estimated with the Almon procedure. When this is done, there is very little difference between the distributed lag implied by the Laffer-Ranson equations (using seasonally unadjusted data but fitted to the 1953-1969 period) and that implied by the St. Louis equation [3], see Chart 4.[15] Thus, once the period through the Korean war is eliminated from the analysis, it makes no difference at all whether the relationship between money and income is estimated with seasonally adjusted data or unadjusted data and dummy variables. Both procedures yield a relatively short, but nevertheless positive, lag in the effect of monetary policy.[16]

[15]For comparative purposes, the constraints imposed in estimating the Laffer-Ranson equations with the Almon procedure are the same as those used in the St. Louis equation, i.e., a fourth-degree polynomial with the t + 1 and t − 5 values of the money coefficients set equal to zero.

[16]An almost identical conclusion is reached in a paper by Johnson [23a]. Laffer and Ranson provide an alternative explanation of the difference between their own lag results—shown in equation 3—and the St. Louis results. However, there is no mention in their article that the time period employed to estimate their equations is considerably different from that used in the St. Louis model and most other recent studies.

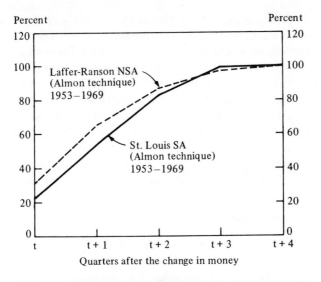

CHART 4 CUMULATIVE PERCENTAGE DISTRIBUTION OF THE EFFECTS OF MONEY ON GNP

Note: NSA = not seasonally adjusted; SA = seasonally adjusted.

The Almon Lag Technique

Finally, it seems worthwhile to say a few words about the use of the Almon technique and its effect on the estimates of the structure (or distribution) of the lag. As noted earlier, this procedure has become quite popular in recent years. It tends to smooth out the pattern of the lag coefficients and makes them easier to rationalize. However, the extent of the differences in the estimates obtained for individual lag coefficients, with and without the use of the technique, provides some reason for concern.

For example, in his experiments with the St. Louis equation, Davis found that either 29 percent or 46 percent of the ultimate effect of money on income could be attributed to the current quarter. The lower number was obtained when the equation was estimated using the Almon technique, while the higher value occurred when the Almon constraint was not imposed on the equation. The explanatory power of the equation was essentially the same in both cases.[17] In the Laffer-Ranson model as well, substantially different estimates of the lag structure are consistent with about the same $\bar{R}^2$. In this model the estimates of the current-quarter effect of money on income are 31 percent with the Almon technique and 64 percent with unconstrained

[17]See Davis [12]. The estimates of $\bar{R}^2$ are .46 and .47, respectively. The period used to estimate the equation was 1952-I to 1968-II.

lags (compare the Laffer-Ranson NSA curves for the 1953-1969 period in Charts 3 and 4). On the other hand, over the first six months it is the *Almon* technique which yields a faster response of income to money, for both the Davis experiments and the Laffer-Ranson model, than is obtained with unconstrained lags.

The wide divergence in these estimates of the impact of monetary variables over short periods, depending on the nature of the estimating procedure employed, suggests that existing estimates of the underlying lag structure are not very precise. One reason for this may be that the pattern of the lag varies over time.[18] In any event, the uncertainties surrounding the structure (distribution) of the lag are not eliminated by the Almon technique. Thus, use of any existing estimates of the lag structure as a firm basis for short-run policy making would seem rather hazardous at this time.

Concluding Comments

One finding stands out from the results presented above, namely, that there is a lag in the effect of monetary policy. Nevertheless, estimates of the length of the lag differ considerably. Of the three factors considered in this paper that might account for these differences, the most important is the specification of the appropriate monetary policy variable (or variables) in the construction of econometric models. Use of nonborrowed reserves as the exogenous monetary variable suggests that less than 40 percent of the impact of a monetary action occurs within five quarters and that the full effect is distributed over two and a half years. On the other hand, use of the money supply, the monetary base, or total reserves suggests that most of the effect occurs within four or five quarters. The latter estimate of the lag may appear to be relatively short. However, it does not seem to be grossly out of line with the view held by the majority of economists in the early 1960's.

The two other factors considered and found to be less important in explaining the differences in the estimates of the length of the lag are (1) the type of statistical estimating model (structural versus reduced-form equations) and (2) the seasonal adjustment procedure. In both of these instances, though, there is not enough evidence available to draw very firm conclusions; hence further work might prove fruitful.

Finally, more work is also needed to help refine estimates of the distribution of the lag. Existing estimates of the lag structure do not appear to be sufficiently precise to justify large or frequent short-run adjustments in the growth rates of monetary aggregates.

REFERENCES

1. ALMON, S. "The Distributed Lag between Capital Appropriations and Expenditures." *Econometrica* (January 1965), pp. 178-96.

[18]Some support for this hypothesis is provided by the simulation results for the FRB-MIT model shown in Chart 1 as well as the results obtained by Warburton [30] and Friedman and Schwartz [17] in their analyses of the timing relations between the upswings and downswings in money and economic activity.

2. ANDERSEN, L. C. "An Evaluation of the Impacts of Monetary and Fiscal Policy on Economic Activity." In *1969 Proceedings of the Business and Economic Statistics Section* (Washington, D.C.: American Statistical Association, 1969), pp. 233-40.

3. ANDERSEN, L. C., and CARLSON, K. M. "A Monetarist Model for Economic Stabilization." *Review* (Federal Reserve Bank of St. Louis, April 1970), pp. 7-27 (especially p. 11).

4. ANDERSEN, L. C., and JORDAN, J. "Monetary and Fiscal Actions: A Test of Their Relative Importance in Economic Stabilization." *Review* (Federal Reserve Bank of St. Louis, November 1968), pp. 11-24.

5. ANDO, A., BROWN, E. C., SOLOW, R., and KAREKEN J. "Lags in Fiscal and Monetary Policy." In Commission on Money and Credit, *Stabilization Policies* (Englewood Cliffs, N.J.: Prentice Hall, Inc., 1963), pp. 1-163 (especially p. 2).

6. ANDO, A., and MODIGLIANI, F. "Econometric Analysis of Stabilization Policies." *American Economic Review* (May 1968), pp. 296-314.

7. BRUNNER, K. "The Role of Money and Monetary Policy." *Review* (Federal Reserve Bank of St. Louis, July 1968), pp. 8-24.

8. BRUNNER, K., and MELTZER, A. H. "Money, Debt, and Economic Activity." *Journal of Political Economy,* (September/October 1972), pp. 951-77.

9. CHOW, G. "Tests of Equality between Two Sets of Coefficients in Two Linear Regressions." *Econometrica* (July 160), pp. 591-605.

10. CORRIGAN, E. G. "The Measurement and Importance of Fiscal Policy Changes." *Monthly Review* (Federal Reserve Bank of New York, June 1970), pp. 133-45.

11. CULBERTSON, J. M. "Friedman on the Lag in Effect of Monetary Policy." *Journal of Political Economy* (December 1960), pp. 617-21 (especially p. 621).

12. DAVIS, R. G. "How Much Does Money Matter? A Look at Some Recent Evidence." *Monthly Review* (Federal Reserve Bank of New York, June 1969), pp. 119-31 (especially pp. 122-24).

13. DE LEEUW, F., and GRAMLICH, E. M. "The Channels of Monetary Policy." *Federal Reserve Bulletin* (June 1969), pp. 472-91.

14. DE LEEUW, F., and GRAMLICH, E. M. "The Federal Reserve-MIT Econometric Model." *Federal Reserve Bulletin* (January 1968), pp. 11-40.

15. DE LEEUW, F., and KALCHBRENNER, J. "Monetary and Fiscal Actions: A Test of Their Relative Importance in Economic Stabilization—Comment." *Review* (Federal Reserve Bank of St. Louis, April 1969), pp. 6-11.

16. FRIEDMAN, M. *A Program for Monetary Stability* (New York: Fordham University Press, 1960), especially p. 87.

17. FRIEDMAN, M., and SCHWARTZ, A. J. *A Monetary History of the United States, 1867-1960* (Princeton: Princeton University Press, 1963).

18. GRAMLEY, L. E. "Guidelines for Monetary Policy—The Case Against Simple Rules." A paper presented at the Financial Conference of the National Industrial Conference Board, New York, February 21, 1969. Reprinted in W. L. Smith and R. L. Teigen (eds.) *Readings in Money, National Income, and Stabilization Policy* (Homewood, Ill.: Richard D. Irwin, Inc., 1970), pp. 488-95.

19. GRAMLICH, E. M. "The Role of Money in Economic Activity: Complicated or Simple?" *Business Economics* (September 1969), pp. 21-26.

20. GRAMLICH, E. M. "The Usefulness of Monetary and Fiscal Policy as Discretionary Stabilization Tools." *Journal of Money, Credit and Banking* (May 1971, Part 2), pp. 20, 506-32 (especially p. 514).

21. HAMBURGER, M. J. "The Impact of Monetary Variables: A Survey of Recent Econometric Literature." In *Essays in Domestic and International Finance* (New York: Federal Reserve Bank of New York, 1969), pp 37–49.

22. HAMBURGER, M. J. "Indicators of Monetary Policy: The Arguments and the Evidence." *American Economic Review* (May 1970), pp. 32–39.

23. HENDERSHOTT, P. H. "A Quality Theory of Money." *Nebraska Journal of Economics and Business* (Autumn 1969), pp. 28–37.

23a. JOHNSON, D. D. "Properties of Alternative Seasonal Adjustment Techniques, A Comment on the OMB Model." *Journal of Business* (April 1973), pp. 284–303.

24. KERAN, M. W. "Monetary and Fiscal Influences on Economic Activity—The Historical Evidence." *Review* (Federal Reserve Bank of St. Louis, November 1968), pp. 5–24 (especially p. 18, footnote 22).

25. LAFFER, A. B., and RANSON, R.D. "A Formal Model of the Economy." *Journal of Business* (July 1971), pp. 247–70 (especially pp. 257–59).

26. MAYER, T. "The Inflexibility of Monetary Policy." *Review of Economics and Statistics* (November 1958), pp. 358–74.

27. MAYER, T. "The Lag in Effect of Monetary Policy: Some Criticisms." *Western Economic Journal* (September 1967), pp. 324–42 (especially pp. 326 and 328).

28. PIERCE, J. L. "Critique of 'A Formal Model of the Economy for the Office of Management and Budget' by Arthur B. Laffer and R. David Ranson." In United States Congress, Joint Economic Committee, *The 1971 Economic Report of the President, Hearings,* Part I (February 1971), pp. 300–12.

29. SMITH, W. L. "On the Effectiveness of Monetary Policy." *American Economic Review* (September 1956), pp. 588–606.

30. WARBURTON, C. "Variability of the Lag in the Effect of Monetary Policy, 1919–1965." *Western Economic Journal* (June 1971), pp. 115–33.

31. WHITE, W. H. "The Timeliness of the Effects of Monetary Policy: The New Evidence from Econometric Models." *Banca Nazionale del Lavoro Quarterly Review* (September 1968), pp. 276–303.

III

MONEY SUPPLY, MONEY DEMAND, AND INTEREST RATES

A. Money Supply

The articles in Section II indicate that monetary aggregates have an effect on the performance of the economy. The articles in this section consider the relationships among these aggregates. The opening piece by Jerry L. Jordan is a simple exposition of a linear framework for the determination of the money supply. Jordan shows how the money supply depends on the monetary base as well as the behavioral parameters of the "money multiplier." The following article by Jane Anderson and Thomas M. Humphrey uses the same framework to examine how historical data on changes in the monetary base and in the parameters of the money multiplier have contributed to changes in the money stock.

Next, David I. Fand extends the Jordan framework by outlining, in general rather than linear notation, more sophisticated money supply theories. Some empirical estimation of the implications of these theories has taken place and an impressive amount of it is reviewed in the final article in this section by Robert H. Rasche. Rasche compares and contrasts different empirical estimates of the effect of various interest rates on the money stock.

Elements of Money Stock Determination

Jerry L. Jordan

Recent discussion of the role of money in stabilization policy has culminated in two central issues. The first involves the strength and reliability of the relation between changes in money and changes in total spending. If this relation is sufficiently strong and reliable, changes in the money stock can be used as an indicator of the influence of monetary stabilization actions on the economy.[1] The second issue centers on whether or not the monetary authorities can determine the growth of the money stock with sufficient precision, if it is deemed desirable to do so.

This article is concerned primarily with the second issue—determination of the money stock.[2] A framework describing the factors which influence the monetary authorities' ability to determine the money stock is presented, and the behavior of these factors in recent years is illustrated. In addition, examples of ways in which these factors influence the money stock are discussed.

Factors Influencing the Money Stock

The following sections present essential elements and concepts which are used to construct a "money supply model" for the U.S. economy. First, the necessary infor-

Reprinted from the Reserve Bank of St. Louis, *Review* (October, 1969), pp. 10-19, by permission of the publisher.

[1]Leonall C. Andersen and Jerry L. Jordan, "Monetary and Fiscal Actions: A Test of Their Relative Importance in Economic Stabilization," this *Review,* November 1968.

[2]Private demand deposits plus currency in the hands of the public.

mation regarding institutional aspects of the U.S. banking system are summarized. Then, the main elements of the model—the monetary base, the member bank reserve-to-deposit ratio, the currency-to-demand deposit ratio, the time deposit-to-demand deposit ratio, and the U.S. Government deposit-to-demand deposit ratio—are discussed.

Institutional Aspects of the U.S. Banking System

Students of money and banking are taught that if commercial bank reserve requirements are less than 100 percent, the reserves of the banking system can support a "multiple" of deposits. In fact it is often said that under a fractional reserve system the banking system "creates" deposits. The familiar textbook exposition tells us that the amount of deposits (D) in the system is equal to the reciprocal of the reserve requirement ratio (r) times the amount of reserves (R):

$$D = \frac{1}{r} \times R.$$

Thus if the banking system has $100 of reserves, and the reserve requirement ratio is 20 percent (.2), deposits will be $100/.2 or $500. If the banks acquire an additional $1 in reserves (for instance from the Federal Reserve), deposits will increase by $5.

There are many simplifying assumptions underlying this elementary deposit-expansion relation. First, it is assumed that all bank deposits are subject to the same reserve requirement. Second, all banks are subject to the same regulations; in other words, all banks are members of the Federal Reserve System, and the Federal Reserve does not differentiate among classes of banks. Third, banks do not hold excess reserves; they are always "loaned up." And finally, there is no "cash drain." The public desires to hold a fixed quantity of currency, and their desires for currency are not influenced by the existence of more or less deposits.

Since the above assumptions are not true, the accuracy with which a monetary analyst can estimate how many deposits will be "created" by an addition of $1 in reserves to the banking system, depends on his ability to determine:

1. how the deposits will be distributed between member and nonmember banks;
2. how the deposits will be distributed between reserve city and country banks, which are subject to different reserve requirements;
3. how the deposits will be distributed among private demand deposits, Government demand deposits, and the subclasses of time deposits, all of which are subject to different reserve requirements;
4. how the change in deposits will affect banks' desired ratio of excess reserves to total deposits; and
5. how a change in deposits will affect the public's desired ratio of currency to demand deposits.

These questions can be answered best within the context of a "money supply model" which is constructed to include the institutional realities of the U.S. banking system, and which does not require the special assumptions of the simple deposit expansion equation. A thoroughly developed and tested money supply model has been advanced by Professors Brunner and Meltzer.[3] The following sections present the general form and essential features of this model.

The Monetary Base

A useful concept for monetary analysis is provided by the "monetary base" or "high-powered money."[4] The monetary base is defined as the net monetary liabilities of the Government (U.S. Treasury and Federal Reserve System) held by the public (commercial banks and nonbank public). More specifically, the monetary base is derived from a consolidated balance sheet of the Treasury and Federal Reserve "monetary" accounts. This consolidated monetary base balance sheet is illustrated in Table 1, and monthly data for the monetary base (B) are shown in Chart 1.

The growth of the monetary base, that is, "base money," is determined primarily by Federal Reserve holdings of U.S. Government securities, the dominant asset or source component of the base.[5] In recent decades changes in other sources either have been small or have been offset by changes in security holdings. A change in the Treasury's gold holdings is potentially an important source of increase or decrease in the base. However, since March 1968 the size of the gold stock has been changing only by small increments. In the postwar period the influence of changes in the gold stock were generally offset by compensating changes in Federal Reserve holdings of U.S. Government securities.

The liabilities or uses of the monetary base, or net monetary liabilities of the Federal Reserve and Treasury, are shown in Table 1 to be currency in circulation plus member bank deposits at the Federal Reserve. Part of the currency in circulation is held by the public, part is held as legal reserves by member banks, and another part is held as desired contingency reserves by nonmember commercial banks. In order to relate the uses of the base to the money stock, the uses are regrouped from the *uses* side of Table 1 as currency held by the nonbank public plus reserves of all commercial banks, shown in Table 2.

[3]Karl Brunner and Allan Meltzer, "Liquidity Traps for Money, Bank Credit, and Interest Rates," *Journal of Political Economy,* Vol. 76, January/February 1968. Also see Albert E. Burger, *An Analysis of the Brunner-Meltzer Non-Linear Money Supply Hypothesis,* Working Paper No. 7, Federal Reserve Bank of St. Louis, May 1969.

[4]For further discussion of this concept, see Leonall C. Andersen and Jerry L. Jordan, "The Monetary Base: Explanation and Analytical Use," this *Review,* August 1968.

[5]For a discussion of the statistical relation among source components of the base, see Michael W. Keran and Christopher Babb, "An Explanation of Federal Reserve Actions (1933-68)," this *Review,* July 1969.

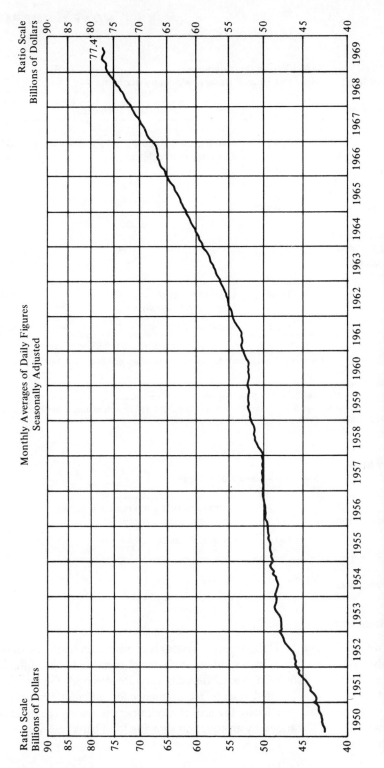

Ratio Scale
Billions of Dollars

Monthly Averages of Daily Figures
Seasonally Adjusted

Ratio Scale
Billions of Dollars

CHART 1 MONETARY BASE* MONTHLY AVERAGES OF DAILY FIGURES SEASONALLY ADJUSTED

*Uses of the monetary base are member bank reserves and currency held by the public and nonmember banks. Adjustments are made for reserve requirement changes and shifts in deposits among classes of banks.
Data are compiled by this bank.
Latest data plotted, September [1969]

Table 1. Monetary Base

(July 1969—billions of dollars)

Consolidated Treasury and Federal Reserve Monetary Accounts

Sources of the Base		Uses of the Base	
Federal Reserve Credit:			
Holdings of securities[a]	$54.3	Member bank deposits at Federal Reserve	$22.3
Discounts and advances	1.2	Currency in circulation	51.3
Float	2.7		
Other Federal Reserve assets	2.7		
Gold stock	10.4		
Treasury currency outstanding	6.7		
Treasury cash holdings	− .7		
Treasury deposits at Federal Reserve	− 1.1		
Foreign deposits at Federal Reserve	− .1		
Other liabilities and capital accounts	− 2.0		
Other Federal Reserve deposits	− .5		
Sources of the base	$73.6	Uses of the base	$73.6
Reserve adjustment[b]	3.9	Reserve Adjustment[b]	3.9
Monetary base	$77.5	Monetary base	$77.5

Note: Data are not seasonally adjusted. Member bank deposits at Federal Reserve plus currency held by member banks equals total reserves (required reserves plus excess reserves).

[a]Includes acceptances not shown separately.

[b]Leonall C. Andersen and Jerry L. Jordan, "The Monetary Base: Explanation and Analytical Use," this *Review,* August 1968.

Source: "Member Bank Reserves, Federal Reserve Bank Credit, and Related Items," the first table appearing in the Financial and Business Statistics section of the Federal Reserve *Bulletin.*

Table 2. Uses of Monetary Base

(July 1969—billions of dollars)

Currency in circulation	$51.3	Currency held by the nonbank public	$45.1
Member bank deposits at Federal Reserve	22.3	Commercial bank reserves*	28.5
Uses of the base	$73.6	Uses of the base	$73.6

Note: Not seasonally adjusted data.

*Includes vault cash of nonmember banks.

Uses of Reserves

As noted above, analysis of the U.S. monetary system is complicated by the existence of both member and nonmember banks, different classes of member banks, different reserve requirements on different types of deposits (private demand, Government demand, and time), and graduated reserve requirements for different amounts of deposits. It is thus necessary to allocate the uses of bank reserves among the different types of deposits. This is illustrated by an equation showing total bank reserves (R) in terms of their uses:

$$R = RR_m + ER_m + VC_n,$$

where

RR_m = required reserves of member banks,
ER_m = excess reserves of member banks,
VC_n = vault cash of nonmember banks.

In turn, required reserves of member banks are decomposed as:

$$RR_m = R^d + R^t,$$

where

R^d = required reserves behind demand deposits at member banks,
R^t = required reserves behind time deposits at member banks.

In turn, required reserves behind demand deposits at member banks are the sum of the amount of reserves required behind demand deposits over and under $5 million at each reserve city and country bank, and similarly for time and savings deposits.[6] Present required reserve ratios for each deposit category are shown in Table 3.

Table 3. Reserve Requirements of Member Banks
(In effect September 30, 1969)

Type of Deposit	Percentage Requirement
Net Demand deposits:*	
Reserve city banks:	
Under $5 million	17.0%
Over $5 million	17.5
Country banks:	
Under $5 million	12.5
Over $5 million	13.0
Time deposits (all classes of banks):	
Savings deposits	3.0
Other Time Deposits:	
Under $5 million	3.0
Over $5 million	6.0

*Demand deposits subject to reserve requirements are gross demand deposits minus cash items in the process of collection and demand balances due from domestic banks.
Source: Federal Reserve *Bulletin.*

[6]Expanding the equation for total bank reserves,

$$R = R^d + R^t + ER_m + VC_n.$$

And since R^d, for instance, is the appropriate required reserve ratio times the amount of deposits in each reserve requirement classification, the above expression is rewritten in terms of weighted average reserve ratios and deposits. See footnote 7.

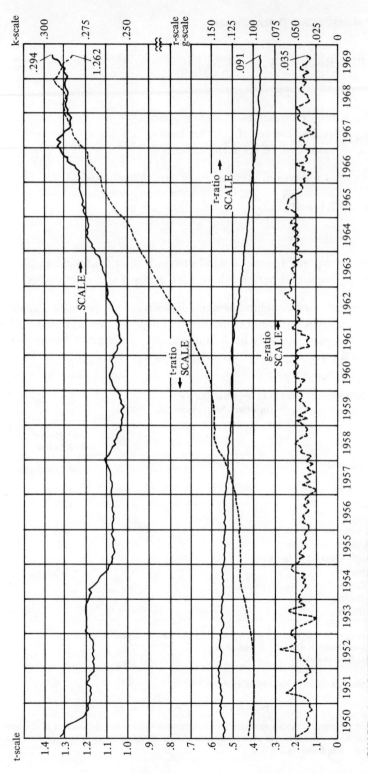

CHART 2 MONETARY MULTIPLIER RATIOS

Latest data plotted: September, 1969

Alternatively, the total amount of commercial bank reserves can be expressed as a proportion (r) of total bank deposits:

$$R = r (D + T + G).$$

where

D = private demand deposits,
T = time deposits,
G = U.S. Government (Treasury) deposits at commercial banks.

The "r-ratio" is defined to be a weighted-average reserve ratio against all bank deposits, but is computed directly by dividing total reserves by total deposits.[7] The trend of the r-ratio in the postwar period is shown in Chart 2. An important factor contributing to the gradual downward trend of the r-ratio is the relatively more rapid growth of time deposits (which are subject to lower reserve requirements) than demand deposits.

Currency Held by the Public

One of the important factors influencing the amount of money the banking system can create, given an increase in monetary base, is the proportion of currency to demand deposits the public desires to hold. For example, if the public held a fixed total *amount* of currency, all changes in the supply of base money by the Federal Reserve would remain in the banking system as reserves and would be reflected entirely in changes in deposits, the amount depending on the reserve requirement ratios for different classes and types of deposit. On the other hand, if the public always desired to hold a fixed *ratio* of currency to demand deposits (for example exactly \$.25 in currency for every \$.75 of demand deposits), the deposit creating potential of the banking system would be substantially less. Clearly the "currency drain" associated with an increase in the base must be taken into account in deter-

---

[7]For the interested reader,

$$r = a \, \delta r^d + (1 - a) \, \tau \, r^t + e + v,$$

where

a = the proportion of member bank demand deposits to total deposits,
δ = the proportion of net demand deposits of member banks to total demand deposits,
r^d = a weighted-average reserve requirement ratio for member bank demand deposits,
τ = the proportion of net time deposits of member banks to total time deposits,
r^t = a weighted average reserve requirement ratio for member bank time deposits,
e = ratio of excess reserves to total bank deposits,
v = ratio of nonmember bank vault cash to total bank deposits.

This definition is altered somewhat by the recently instituted lagged-reserve-requirement provisions of the Federal Reserve. It is worth emphasizing that some of the above ratios are determined by the behavior of commercial banks and the public, and others are determined primarily by the Federal Reserve. The fact that these ratios are not fixed does not impair the usefulness of the analysis.

mining how much base money must be supplied to achieve a desired increase in the money stock. Currency (C) can be expressed as a proportion (k) of demand deposits (D), that is:

$$C = k\,D,$$
$$\text{or}$$
$$k = C/D.$$

Changes in the level of the "k-ratio" over time are influenced by such factors as income levels, utilization of credit cards, and uncertainties regarding general economic stability. The trend of the k-ratio is shown in Chart 2.[8]

Time Deposits

Time deposits are not included in the definition of the money stock discussed in this article. Nevertheless, since member banks are required to hold reserves behind time deposits, information regarding the public's desired holdings of time to demand deposits is necessary in order to determine how much the stock of money will change following a change in the stock of monetary base.

Reserve requirements are much lower against time deposits than against demand deposits as shown in Table 3; consequently a given amount of reserves would allow more time deposits to be supported than demand deposits. Time deposits (T) can be expressed as a proportion (t) of demand deposits (D), that is:

$$T = t\,D,$$
$$\text{or}$$
$$t = T/D.$$

The trend of the "t-ratio" is shown in Chart 2.

The factors influencing the t-ratio are more complex to analyze than those affecting the k-ratio. Commercial banks are permitted to pay interest on time deposits up to ceiling rates set by the Federal Reserve and the Federal Deposit Insurance Corporation (see Table 4). Consequently, the growth of time deposits over time is influenced by competition among banks for individual and business savings within the limits permitted by the legal interest rate ceilings.

The interest rates which banks are willing to offer on time deposits (below the ceilings) are determined primarily by opportunities that are available for profitable investment of the funds in loans or securities. Similarly, the decisions by individuals and businesses to deposit their funds in banks are influenced by the interest rates available from alternative earning assets such as savings and loan shares, mutual

---

[8]For a detailed examination of the behavior of the currency to demand deposit ratio, see Phillip Cagan, *Determinants and Effects of Changes in the U.S. Money Stock, 1875-1960* (New York: National Bureau of Economic Research, 1965), chapter 4.

Table 4. Maximum Interest Rates Payable on Time and Savings Deposits
(Effective April 19, 1968)

Type of Deposit	Percent Per Annum
Savings deposits	4.00%
Other time deposits:	
Multiple maturity*:	
90 days or more	5.00
Less than 90 days (30–89 days)	4.00
Single maturity:	
Less than $100,000	5.00
$100,000 or more:	
30–59 days	5.50
60–89 days	5.75
90–179 days	6.00
180 days and over	6.25

*Multiple maturity time deposits include deposits that are automatically renewable at maturity without action by the depositor and deposits that are payable after written notice of withdrawal.

Source: Federal Reserve *Bulletin.*

savings bank deposits, bonds, stocks, commercial paper, and direct investments in real assets.[9] If the interest returns from these other assets are sufficiently high that the interest rate ceilings on time deposits prevent banks from effectively competing for the public's savings, then time deposits may not grow (or may even decline) and all increases in commercial bank reserves can be used to support demand deposits. This point will be discussed in more detail below.

U.S. Government Deposits

Commercial banks are required to hold the same proportion of reserves against Federal Government demand deposits as against private demand deposits. Therefore, even though Government deposits are *not* included in the definition of the money stock, changes in the amount of Government deposits influence the amount of private deposits the banking system can support with a given amount of base money or reserves. Government deposits (G) can be expressed as a proportion (g) of private demand deposits (D), that is:

$$G = g\,D,$$
$$\text{or}$$
$$g = G/D.$$

[9]Jerry L. Jordan, *The Market for Deposit-Type Financial Assets,* Working Paper No. 8, Federal Reserve Bank of St. Louis, March 1969.

The amount of Government deposits in commercial banks is determined by the flow of Treasury receipts (primarily from taxes) relative to Treasury expenditures and by the Treasury's discretion about what proportion of its balances to keep with commercial banks rather than at the Federal Reserve. Thus, short-run fluctuations in the "g-ratio" are primarily the result of actions by the U.S. Treasury. The Federal Reserve must assess, from past experience and information available from the Treasury, what will happen to Treasury balances in an impending period in order to determine the influence of changes in Treasury balances in the money stock. The monthly pattern of the g-ratio is shown in Chart 2.

The Monetary Multiplier

All of the essential elements for determination of the money stock have now been discussed. The definitional relations are as follows:

$$M = D + C \tag{1}$$

$$B = R + C \tag{2}$$

$$R = r\,(D + T + G) \tag{3}$$

$$C = k\,D \tag{4}$$

$$T = t\,D \tag{5}$$

$$G = g\,D \tag{6}$$

By substituting (3) and (4) into (2), we get:

$$B = r\,(D + T + G) + kD, \tag{7}$$

that is, we express the monetary base solely in terms of the various deposits. Substituting (5) and (6) into (7), we get:

$$B = r\,(D + t\,D + g\,D) + kD, \tag{8}$$

that is, we express the base solely in terms of private demand deposits to reduce the number of variables. Simplifying, we write (8) as:

$$B = [r\,(1 + t + g) + k] \times D, \tag{8$'$}$$

from which, by simple manipulation, we can express deposits in terms of the base as follows:

$$D = \frac{1}{r\,(1 + t + g) + k} \times B. \tag{9}$$

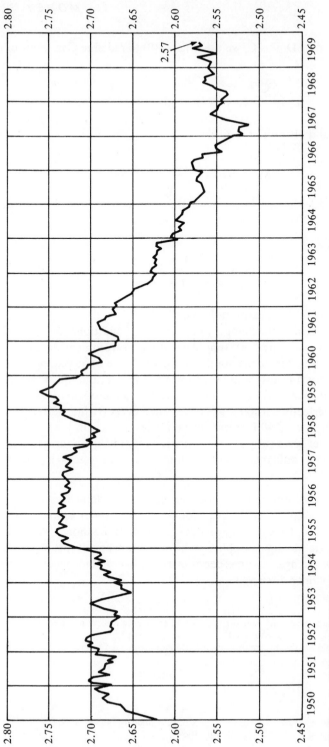

CHART 3 MONETARY MULTIPLIER

Latest data plotted: September.

Since we want to find D plus C, we use (4) and (9) to redefine C in terms of the base:

$$C = \frac{k}{r(1 + t + g) + k} \times B. \qquad (10)$$

Substituting (9) and (10) into (1) gives:

$$M = \frac{1 + k}{r(1 + t + g) + k} \times B, \qquad (1')$$

or the money stock defined in terms of the monetary base.[10] We can denote the quotient as:

$$m = \frac{1 + k}{r(1 + t + g) + k},$$

where m is called the "monetary multiplier."[11]

The factors that can cause changes in the monetary multiplier are all of the factors which influence the currency (k), time deposit (t), Government deposit (g), and reserve (r) ratios, that is, the "behavioral parameters." The observed monthly values of these ratios in the past twenty years are shown in Chart 2, and the monthly values for the monetary multiplier (m) are shown in Chart 3. Quite obviously, if the monetary multiplier were perfectly constant, at say 2.5, then every $1 increase in the monetary base would result in a $2.50 increase in the money stock. On the other hand, if the monetary multiplier were subject to substantial unpredictable variation, the Federal Reserve would have difficulty in determining the money stock by controlling the base.

Since the monetary multiplier is not constant, the Federal Reserve must predict the value of the multiplier for the impending month in order to know how much to increase the monetary base to achieve a desired level of the money stock. Techniques for predicting the monetary multiplier go beyond the scope of this paper.[12] However, examples of how changes in time deposits and Government deposits influence the stock of money will be discussed.

---

[10]Since the monetary base is adjusted for the effect of changes in reserve requirements, a corresponding adjustment is made to the reserve ratio (r).

[11]The reader should be able to demonstrate that if money is defined to include time deposits (M_2 = D + C + T), then

$$m_2 = \frac{1 + k + t}{r(1 + t + g) + k}.$$

[12]For one straight-forward approach, see Lyle Kalish, *A Study of Money Stock Control,* Working Paper No. 11, Federal Reserve Bank of St. Louis, July 1969.

The Influence of Two Factors on the Money Stock

The following sections present examples of the ways changes in the growth of time deposits and U.S. Government deposits influence the money creation process. The effects are illustrated both by changes in the ratios in the monetary .multiplier and with the use of commercial bank balance sheet "T-Accounts."

Changes in Time Deposits

The growth of time deposits relative to demand deposits is determined by many factors, including those which influence the interest rates offered by commercial banks on such deposits and those which influence the quantity of time deposits demanded by the public at each interest rate. Both the banks' supply of time deposits and the public's demand for them are a function of relative costs and returns of alternative sources of funds and earning assets. Thus, accuracy of predictions of the t-ratio (time deposits to demand deposits) for a future period is influenced by the ability of the forecasters to anticipate the banks' and public's behavior. Experience has shown that changes in this ratio tend to be dominated by rather long-run trends, with exceptions occurring at those times when interest rate ceilings imposed by the monetary authorities prevent banks from effectively competing for deposits. It is these special cases that will be discussed.

When market interest rates rise above the ceiling rates banks are permitted to offer on time deposits, some individuals and businesses who might otherwise hold time deposits decide to buy bonds or other earning assets instead. This effect has been most pronounced on the banks' class of time deposits called "large negotiable certificates of deposit" (CD's). To depositors, these are highly liquid assets which are considered by the purchasers to be close substitutes for Treasury bills and commercial paper.[13] On at least four occasions since 1965 the yields on these substitute assets have risen above the rates banks were permitted to offer on CD's, causing the growth of CD's to slow sharply or even become negative.

To illustrate the effect on the money stock of a rise in market interest rates above Regulation Q ceilings, assume that the growth of time deposits ceases, and banks hold the same total amount of time deposits while demand deposits continue to grow. In the money supply model this is reflected in a decline in the t-ratio (time deposits divided by demand deposits), and since the t-ratio appears in the denominator of the multiplier, the multiplier would get larger as the t-ratio gets smaller.

For example, assume the following initial values for the monetary base and the parameters of the multiplier:

$$B = \$75 \text{ billion}$$
$$t = 1.3$$

---

[13]Jordan, *Deposit-Type Financial Assets,* chapter 4.

$$g = .04$$
$$k = .3$$
$$r = .1$$

since

$$M = \frac{1 + k}{r(1 + t + g) + k} \times B,$$

we can solve to find M = $182.6 billion.

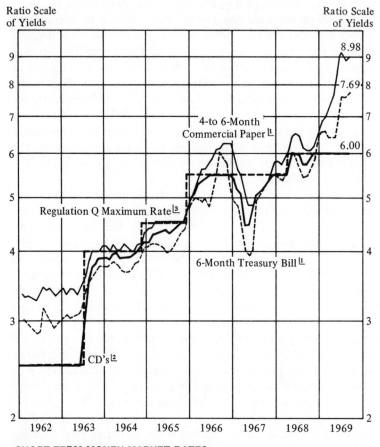

SHORT-TERM MONEY MARKET RATES

[1]Market yields converted from discount to bond equivalent basis.

[2]Average new issue rates on six month certificates of deposit of $100,000 or more. Data are estimated by the Federal Reserve Bank of St. Louis from guide rates published in the Bond Buyer and are monthly averages of Wednesday figures.

[3]Rate on deposits in amounts of $100,000 or more maturing in 90-179 days.

Latest data plotted: September.

Now suppose that in the course of several months the base increases by $1 billion, but time deposits do not grow at all as a result of the high market rates of interest relative to Regulation Q ceilings. If all of the ratios in the multiplier (including the t-ratio) had remained unchanged in this period, the money stock would have increased by about $2.4 billion to $185 billion. But since time deposits did not change while demand deposits continued to grow, the t-ratio would fall, to 1.28, for example, which causes the multiplier to increase (still assuming the other behavioral parameters remain the same).[14]

The reader should be careful not to interpret this greater increase in money (especially demand deposits) to mean that the banks can extend more credit than otherwise. Since the reserve requirements on demand deposits are greater than on time deposits, the $1 billion increase in monetary base would have supported a greater amount of *total* deposits (demand plus time) if time deposits grew proportionally to demand deposits, rather than only demand deposits increasing. With the assumed initial values for the parameters of the multiplier and the postulated $1 billion increase in the monetary base, money plus time deposits would have increased by almost $4.8 billion, almost twice as much as money.

To interpret the effects of this increase in money on the economy, it is necessary to analyze the increase in the supply of money compared to the demand for money to hold, and the supplies of and demands for other assets. We postulated above that market interest rates rose above the ceiling rates banks are permitted to pay on time deposits (especially CD's). In such a situation the volume of CD's (quantity *supplied*) is any amount depositors wish at the ceiling rates. Since the yields on good substitutes become more attractive than CD's, the *demand* for CD's declines, resulting in a decline in the outstanding volume of CD's or a slowing in the growth rate. In other words, a change in the relative yields on substitute assets causes a shift in the demand for CD's (negative), which causes a decline in the volume.

Disintermediation

We noted above that *total* deposits of banks may decline as a result of this "disintermediation" of time deposits. This means that banks must contract their assets, either loans or security holdings, as deposits decline. An understanding of the actions of banks in the face of a deposit drain and actions of those who withdraw their deposits is important information in assessing the effects of the disintermediation caused by the interest rate ceilings.

To illustrate two possible effects of disintermediation, we will use highly simplified examples and T-accounts (commercial bank balance sheets). Account 1 shows the banking system in its initial condition having total reserves (TR) = $25, required reserves (RR) = $25 and excess reserves (ER) = 0, security holdings (S) = $100 and loans outstanding (L) = $175. Bank liabilities are demand deposits (DD) = $100

[14]In practice, as the t-ratio falls from 1.3 to 1.28, demand deposits grow and time deposits do not, and the average reserve requirement ratio (r) will rise. This will slightly attenuate the increase in the multiplier and the money stock.

Account 1. Banking System

Assets				Liabilities	
TR			$ 25	DD	$100
	RR	$25		TD	200
	ER	0			
S			100		
L			175		
Total			$300	Total	$300

Account 2. Banking System

Assets				Liabilities	
TR			$ 25	DD	$100
	RR	$24		TD	180
	ER	1			
S			80		
L			175		
Total			$280	Total	$280

and time deposits (TD) = $200. We have assumed that reserve requirements against demand deposits are 15 percent and reserve requirements against time deposits are 5 percent.

Account 2 shows the effect of a corporation reducing its holdings of time deposits by $20 and buying $20 in securities from the banks because of the higher return available on the latter. The immediate effect is that the ownership of the securities is changed—the corporation directly holds the securities instead of having a deposit in a bank which owns the securities, hence the term "disintermediation"—and the banks are left with $1 of excess reserves. The banking system can create loans (or buy some securities), based on the dollar of excess reserves, and increase demand deposits by a multiple of $1. In this simplified example, the effect of disintermediation resulting from relatively low interest rate ceilings is potentially expansionary on total loans, even though total deposits decrease.

For the second example, a bank, in its usual role as an intermediary, sells CD's to a corporation which wishes to invest short-term funds. With the proceeds of the sale of the CD's, the bank lends to another corporation (less the amount the bank must hold as required reserves, of course). Another simplified example of the potential effects of disintermediation on the banking system and total credit is illustrated in Account 3. For exposition, assume that the one-bank holding companies of commercial banks establish subsidiaries for the purpose of buying and selling commercial paper.

Account 3. Banking System

Assets				Liabilities	
TR			$ 25	DD	$100
	RR	$24		TD	180
	ER	1			
S			100		
L			155		
Total			$280	Total	$280

Account 4. Subsidiary of One-Bank Holding Company

Assets		Liabilities	
Commercial paper held	$20	Commercial paper outstanding	$20

For our example, assume the first corporation does not wish to renew $20 of its CD holdings when they reach maturity, but rather, because of generally rising short-term market interest rates, seeks a yield greater than the bank is permitted to pay. Our hypothetical subsidiary of the one-bank holding company can offer to sell its own commercial paper (I.O.U.) to the first corporation at competitive market interest rates (Account 4).

We assume the corporation buys the subsidiary's commercial paper. As a result of their reduced deposits, the banks are forced to contract assets proportionately (as a first step in a partial analysis). Instead of selling securities, as in our previous example, the banks can contract loans outstanding by $20, as shown in Account 3 (as compared to Account 1). The subsidiary can in turn use the proceeds of its sale of commercial paper to purchase the paper of another corporation which seeks to borrow short-term money, possibly a corporation which was having difficulty getting a bank loan since bank assets and liabilities were contracting.

We find that the initial effect of the disintermediation is that the total of bank loans plus commercial paper debts of borrowing corporations is the same as the initial amount of bank loans outstanding and that the total of time deposits plus commercial paper assets of lending corporations is the same as the initial amount of time deposits at banks. However, we also find that banks have acquired an additional $1 of excess reserves which they can lend and thereby increase demand deposits.

In summary, both of the examples of the disintermediation of time deposits caused by the interest rate ceilings show that the same initial amount of reserves in the banking system can, under certain circumstances, support a larger amount of demand deposits (and therefore money stock). In other words, if the disintermediation means only that some funds flow through channels which are not subject to reserve requirements and interest rate ceilings, the effects of the relatively low interest rate ceilings on commercial bank time deposits are potentially expansionary on total loans.

U.S. Government Deposits and Money

As previously discussed, the monetary base summarizes all of the actions of the Federal Reserve which influence the money stock. However, the Treasury cannot be overlooked as an agency which can influence the money stock over at least short periods. In the money supply model, the influence of changes in the amount of Government deposits is reflected in movements in the g-ratio (Government deposits divided by private demand deposits) in the monetary multiplier.

In recent years the Government's balances at commercial banks have fluctuated from $3 billion to $9 billion within a few months time. Private demand deposits averaged about $150 billion in mid-1969. The g-ratio is therefore quite small, ranging from about .02 to about .06, but frequently doubles or falls by half over the course of a month or two.

Similar to the effect of changes in the t-ratio, increases in the g-ratio result in a fall in the multiplier since the ratio appears in the denominator. Using again the initial values we assumed for the base and multiplier, we have:

$$M = \frac{1 + .3}{.1 \, (1 + 1.3 + .04) + .3} \times \$75 \text{ billion} = \$182.6 \text{ billion},$$

where .04 is the value of the g-ratio. These values imply that demand deposits (D) are about $140.5 billion and Government deposits (G) are $5.6 billion. Now suppose that individuals and businesses pay taxes of $1 billion by writing checks which draw down (D) to $139.5 billion and Government balances rise to $6.6 billion. Assuming no change in time deposits or currency held by the public and no change in the base, we would find that the g-ratio rises to .047 (and the k- and t-ratios rise slightly) to give us:

$$M = \frac{1 + .302}{.1 \, (1 + 1.309 + .047) + .302} \times \$75 \text{ billion} = \$181.6 \text{ billion}.$$

A similar example of the effects on the money stock of an increase in Government deposits at commercial banks which is associated with a change in time deposits (people pay taxes by reducing their savings or holdings of CD's) would be somewhat more complicated. In the above example, taxes were paid out of demand deposits, and the reserve ratio (r) was not changed, which implies that the distribution of the increment in Government deposits among reserve city, country, and nonmember banks was the same as the distribution of the $1 billion reduction in private demand deposits.

When taxes are paid out of time deposits, the r-ratio rises, since reserve requirements against Government deposits are approximately three times the reserve requirements against time deposits. These movements are very small, and any accompanying reduction in the excess reserve ratio would attenuate the effect. Nonetheless, the effect on money is a combination of small changes in the k-, r-, t-, and g-ratios.

Summary

The behavioral parameters of the money supply framework presented here are the currency (k), reserve (r), time deposit (t), and Government deposit (g) ratios. The changes in these ratios reflect the actions of the Treasury, banks, and nonbank public which influence the money stock. The k-ratio is determined by the public's preferences for currency versus demand deposits; the t-ratio reflects the interaction of the banks' supply of and the public's demand for time deposits as compared to the supply of and demand for demand deposits; and the g-ratio is dominated by changes in Government balances at commercial banks. The r-ratio is the least volatile of the behavioral parameters, although it is influenced by the banks' desired holdings of excess reserves and the distribution of total deposits among all the subclasses of deposits in the various classes of banks, which are subject to a large array of reserve requirements.

The main policy actions of the monetary authorities—open market operations, changes in reserve requirements, and administration of the discount window—are summarized by the monetary base. The growth of the base summarizes the *influence* of the monetary authorities' defensive and dynamic *actions* on the growth of the money stock, regardless of the *intent* of these actions. The degree of accuracy that can be achieved by the monetary authorities in controlling the money stock is a function of their ability to determine the monetary base, and to predict the net influence of the public's and banks' behavior as summarized by changes in the money supply multiplier.

Determinants of Change in the Money Stock: 1960–1970

*Jane Anderson and
Thomas M. Humphrey*

This article presents data showing the relative contributions of the multiplier and the base to changes in the stock of money over the decade of the 1960's. It also develops numerical estimates of the relative contribution of each of the constituent ratios of the multiplier to changes in the multiplier and the money stock. However, the reader should be forewarned of the limitations of the analysis presented in the following paragraphs. Although the monetary base and the money multiplier ratios will be treated as separate, mutually independent determinants of money stock change, these entities, in actuality, are not independent of each other. Changes in one of the determinants will induce changes in the others. Alterations in the monetary base wrought by the Federal Reserve will induce responses by banks and individuals that will alter the multiplier ratios. Consider, for example, the effects of an increase in the monetary base on the time deposit ratio. To achieve an increase in the base, the Federal Reserve may purchase Treasury bills on the open market. The increased demand for these securities raises their price and lowers their yield. The decline in Treasury bill yields is transmitted to other short-term assets—commercial paper, savings and loan shares, etc.—that compete with time deposits in individuals' portfolios. As the yields on these alternative short-term assets decline relative to the yield on time deposits, wealth-holders switch from the former assets to the latter, thereby

Reprinted, with deletions, from the Federal Reserve Bank of Richmond, *Monthly Review* (March, 1972), pp. 3-7, by permission of the publisher and the authors.

raising the time deposit ratio. The reserve ratio, too, may rise if banks respond to the decline in short-term yields by holding a larger proportion of bank assets in the form of excess reserves.

Similarly, interrelationships also exist among the constituent ratios of the multiplier since they are mechanically linked to each other in an accounting or definitional sense. For example, the reserve ratio, *r,* a weighted average of the excess and legal required reserve ratios associated with demand, time, and government deposits, will fall when the proportion of time to demand deposits rises. A rise in the *t* ratio alters the composition of the weights in favor of the relatively low required reserve ratio for time deposits, thereby pulling down the weighted average. Because of such interdependencies, estimates of the proportion of money stock change attributable to each determinant will be subject to error. For example, suppose 10 percent of the money stock change is estimated to be attributable to changes in the time deposit ratio, and 30 percent to changes in the reserve ratio. These estimates may understate the contribution of the time deposit ratio to money stock change if part of the change in the

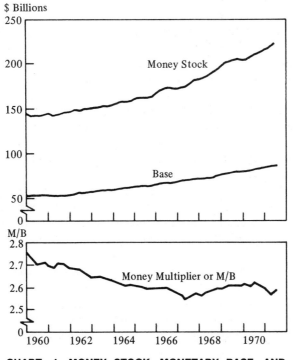

CHART 1 MONEY STOCK, MONETARY BASE, AND MONEY MULTIPLIER: 1960–1971

Source: Federal Reserve Bank of St. Louis.

reserve ratio was induced by changes in the time deposit ratio. Thus, the estimates presented below should be interpreted as rough approximations only.

Contributions of Variation in the Base and the Multiplier to Changes in the Money Stock

In order to investigate the relative importance of the base and multiplier components as sources of money stock change, it is convenient to state relationships among these variables in terms of percentage rates of change. Then, the percentage change in the money stock is approximately equal to the sum of the percentage changes in the base and the multiplier.[1]

Over the span from 1960 to 1970 the money stock, base, and multiplier exhibited average annual growth rates of 4 percent, 4.5 percent and −0.5 percent respectively. Note that the base and the multiplier moved in opposite directions. The growth rate of the money supply reflected both the upward pull of the base and the downward pull of the multiplier. Because of the latter, the money stock growth rate was only eight-ninths that of the base. But the 4 percent growth rate of the money supply clearly reflected the dominant numerical influence of the base. In terms of the $M = mB$ identity, if the base had remained constant while the multiplier fell, the money stock would have declined by 0.5 percent per annum. If the multiplier had remained constant while the base rose, the money supply would have risen 4.5 percent per year.

Even over the period spanning the last four years of the decade, when the multiplier exhibited a positive growth rate, the base accounted for 91 percent of the growth of the money stock. The picture is roughly the same if monthly instead of yearly data are used and if initial and terminal dates of January 1960 and September 1971 are chosen over which to calculate growth rates. Over that 139-month interval, the growth contributions of the base and multiplier were 110 percent and −7 percent, respectively, of the total growth of the money supply. This evidence indicates that, over the long run, changes in the monetary base were definitely the dominant determinant of money stock change, and that changes in the multiplier played only a minor role.

Over shorter periods of time, however, variations in the multiplier have exerted greater influence on money stock changes than in the long run. This is indicated in Table 1, which shows that on a yearly basis the multiplier sometimes accounted for fairly significant proportions of total changes in the money supply. The small *average* value of the relative contribution of the multiplier to money stock change is mislead-

---

[1]More precisely, the percentage change in the money stock measured over discrete intervals of time, such as a quarter or a year, is equal to the percentage change in the base *plus* the percentage change in the multiplier *plus* the product of the percentage changes in the base and the multiplier, respectively. This last factor, however, is usually small enough to disregard and is ignored in the discussion of the text.

Table 1. Contribution of Monetary Base and Money Multiplier to Change of Money Supply

Year	Percentage Change of			Relative Contribution[1] of		
	Money Stock	Base	Multiplier	Total[2]	Base	Multiplier
1960	− 1.17	0.38	− 1.54	100	− 32.6	131.4
1961	1.65	2.16	− 0.51	100	130.9	− 30.5
1962	2.13	3.40	− 1.22	100	159.4	− 57.2
1963	2.91	4.00	− 1.05	100	137.4	− 36.0
1964	3.92	4.87	− 0.90	100	124.1	− 23.0
1965	4.19	4.92	− 0.71	100	117.4	− 16.9
1966	4.42	4.99	− 0.53	100	112.9	− 12.0
1967	3.94	4.76	− 0.80	100	120.9	− 20.4
1968	7.12	6.13	0.94	100	86.0	13.1
1969	5.96	4.86	1.05	100	81.6	17.6
1970	4.06	4.50	− 0.41	100	110.7	− 10.0
Mean Value of Yearly Figures	3.56	4.09	− 0.52	100	104.4	− 4.0

[1] A negative relative contribution signifies that the determinant exerted an influence opposite to the direction of change of the money supply.

[2] Sum of relative contributions may not exactly equal 100 because of rounding and approximation error.

ing because in each year the multiplier's contribution deviated markedly from its 11-year average. In fact, the *standard deviation* (a statistical measure of variation about the mean) of the relative contribution of the multiplier was practically the same as the standard deviation of the base's contribution. The measured magnitude and variability of the multiplier on a year-to-year basis adds support to the nonmonetarists' claim that instability of the multiplier may create difficulties for monetary control in the short run. The short-run importance of multiplier movements as a source of money stock change would have been even more manifest if quarterly and monthly changes had been examined.

Sources of Change in the Multiplier

In the preceding section, changes in the money supply were attributed to changes in the base and changes in the multiplier. This was a convenient first approximation. Because the money multiplier itself embodies several determinants of the money stock, however, a better understanding of changes in the money supply requires specification of the factors contributing to changes in the multiplier.

As previously mentioned, the money multiplier is composed of several ratios reflecting the portfolio composition decisions of bankers and nonbank individuals. It is changes in these ratios that cause changes in the multiplier. For example, assuming all other factors constant, a rise in the ratio of currency to deposits, *k*, will reduce the size of the multiplier. The multiplier relation between the money stock and monetary

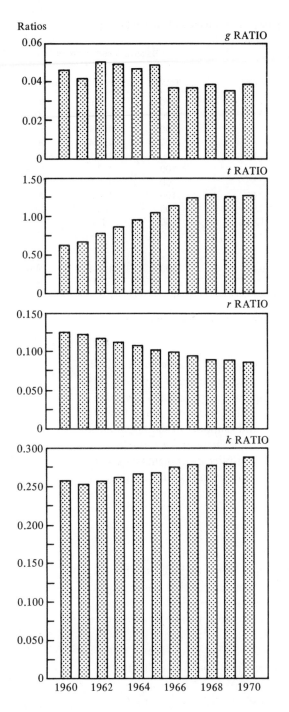

CHART 2 VALUES OF CONSTITUENT RATIOS OF THE MONEY MULTIPLIER: 1960–1970
(Annual Average Values)

Source: Federal Reserve Bank of St. Louis.

base falls because the rising k ratio reduces the proportion of the base that banks are able to acquire as reserves to support demand deposits equal to some multiple of reserves. Changes in the other ratios also act to alter the size of the multiplier. Increases in the time, t, and government, g, deposit ratios cause the multiplier to fall by reducing the share of total reserves available to support the money supply. Time and government deposits (not counted as part of the money supply) must be backed by legal reserves. Growth of these deposits relative to private demand deposits means that a larger portion of total reserves are absorbed to support nonmonetary liabilities. In short, the immobilization of a growing portion of the base, as backing behind nonmonetary deposits, lowers the money-creating leverage of the base. In contrast, a fall in the reserve, r, ratio acts to increase the multiplier because it permits a greater amount of money to be created per dollar of reserves.

The yearly average values of the multiplier ratios are shown in Chart 2. The trends of both the time deposit and currency ratios have been upward, the former ratio exhibiting substantial year-to-year growth and the latter registering more moderate gains. The reserve ratio, on the other hand, has declined gradually but persistently. Only the government deposit ratio has shown no perceptible trend.

Table 2 shows the contribution of changes in each of the ratios to year-to-year percentage changes in the multiplier. The method used to derive the estimates ap-

Table 2. Contributions of Multiplier Ratios to Changes in the Money Multiplier

Year	Percentage Change in Multiplier	Attributable to Changes in[1,2]				Total Contribution	Relative Contribution of Changes in[3,4]			
		Currency Ratio	Reserve Ratio	Time Deposit Ratio	Government Deposit Ratio		Currency Ratio	Reserve Ratio	Time Deposit Ratio	Government Deposit Ratio
1960	− 1.6	− 0.60	0.00	− 0.84	− 0.16	100	37.5	0.0	52.5	10.0
1961	− 0.5	0.63	0.83	− 2.08	0.13	100	− 125.0	− 166.7	416.7	− 25.0
1962	− 1.2	− 0.48	1.75	− 2.26	− 0.21	100	40.0	− 145.7	188.6	17.1
1963	− 1.0	− 1.00	3.01	− 3.10	0.05	100	95.5	− 286.4	295.5	− 4.5
1964	− 0.9	− 1.16	2.31	− 2.14	0.09	100	128.6	− 257.1	238.1	− 9.5
1965	− 0.7	− 0.27	1.18	− 1.59	− 0.03	100	38.5	− 169.2	226.9	3.8
1966	− 0.5	− 0.73	1.50	− 1.47	0.20	100	146.7	− 300.0	293.3	− 40.0
1967	− 0.8	− 0.55	2.83	− 3.08	0.00	100	69.2	− 353.8	384.6	0.0
1968	0.9	0.09	− 1.49	0.65	0.03	100	10.3	165.5	− 72.4	− 3.4
1969	1.0	− 0.29	0.57	0.67	0.05	100	− 28.6	57.1	66.7	4.8
1970	− 0.4	− 0.89	0.74	− 0.22	− 0.03	100	223.1	− 184.6	53.8	7.7
Mean Value of Yearly Figures	− 0.52	− 0.31	1.20	− 1.41	0.01	100	57.8	− 149.2	194.9	− 3.5

[1] Sum of contributions of changes in the multiplier ratios may not exactly equal to percentage change of multiplier because of rounding and approximation error.

[2] If changes of ratio and multiplier are of opposite sign, then that ratio change exerted an influence on the multiplier opposite to the direction of actual change of multiplier.

[3] Sum of contributions may not exactly equal to 100 because of rounding and approximation error.

[4] A negative relative contribution signifies that the particular ratio exerted an influence on the multiplier opposite to the direction of actual change of multiplier.

pearing in the table is described in the appendix to this article.* Roughly, the separate influence exerted by the change in each ratio was calculated by (1) estimating
the percentage change in the multiplier resulting from a small unit change in the
ratio, the other ratios being assumed constant, and (2) multiplying this figure by the
actual number of units that the ratio changed over the year. For example, if, in a
given year, the multiplier tended to decrease by one-fourth of 1 percent for every one
percentage point rise in the currency ratio, then a yearly rise of five percentage points
in the currency ratio would, by itself, cause a 1¼ fall in the multiplier. The separate
contribution of each determinant is calculated similarly, and the total of all the
separate contributions equals the percentage change in the multiplier.

It is evident from the table that changes in the time deposit ratio had the greatest
single impact on the multiplier, with reserve ratio changes a close second. Taken
together, however, the *combined* influence of the time deposit and reserve ratio
changes usually was not great. During the 1960's the reserve ratio was falling, while
the time deposit ratio was rising. Thus, the two ratios exerted opposite influences on
the multiplier. In most years the falling reserve ratio partially offset the influence of
the rising time deposit ratio. The offset, however, was incomplete, and the influence
of time deposit ratio dominated. Together with the rising currency ratio, then, the
rising time deposit ratio contributed more than enough to offset the influence of
reserve ratio changes that tended to raise the multiplier. In short, the main factors
accounting for the negative growth rate of the multiplier were changes in the currency and time deposit ratios.

Table 3. Relative Contribution of Each Determinant to Total Percentage Change in Money Stock

Year	Total Contribution[1]	Base	Currency Ratio	Reserve Ratio	Time Deposit Ratio	Government Deposit Ratio
1960	100	− 32.6	49.3	0.0	68.9	13.1
1961	100	130.9	38.1	50.8	− 127.1	7.6
1962	100	159.4	− 22.9	83.3	− 107.9	− 9.8
1963	100	137.4	− 34.4	103.1	− 106.4	1.6
1964	100	124.1	− 29.6	59.1	− 54.7	2.2
1965	100	117.4	− 6.5	28.6	− 38.3	0.6
1966	100	112.9	− 17.6	36.0	− 35.2	4.8
1967	100	120.9	− 14.1	72.2	− 78.4	0.0
1968	100	86.0	1.3	21.7	− 9.5	− 4.4
1969	100	81.6	− 5.0	10.0	11.7	0.8
1970	100	110.7	− 22.3	18.4	− 5.4	− 0.8
Mean Value of Yearly Figures	100	104.4	− 5.8	43.9	− 43.8	1.3

Contributions[2] (percentage of total) of changes in

[1] Sum of contributions may not exactly equal to 100 because of rounding and approximation error.
[2] A negative relative contribution signifies that the particular ratio exerted an influence opposite to the direction of change of the money supply.

* The Appendix is not reprinted in this book.—Ed.

Conclusion

The relative contributions of each of the money stock determinants to yearly changes in the money supply are summarized in Table 3. The table indicates that although the base was the dominant determinant of money stock change, the reserve, time deposit, and currency ratios played significant roles. Generally, the positive relative contributions of the rising monetary base and the falling reserve ratio more than offset the negative relative contributions of the rising currency and time deposit ratios. Numerically, the main contributors to the positive growth rate of the money stock were changes in the base and the reserve ratio.

20

Can the Central Bank Control the Money Stock?

David I. Fand

The money stock at any moment in time is the result of portfolio decisions by the central bank, by the commercial banks, and by the public (including the nonbank intermediaries):[1] the central bank determines the amount of high-powered money or monetary base, that is, currency plus bank reserves, that it will supply;[2] the commercial banks determine the volume of loans and other assets that they will acquire and the quantity of reserves they will hold as excess (and free) reserves; and the public determines how to allocate their holdings of monetary wealth among currency, de-

Reprinted from the Federal Reserve Bank of St. Louis *Review* (January, 1970), pp. 12–16, by permission of the publisher and the author.

[1]For a discussion of the determinants of the money stock see M. Friedman and A. Schwartz, *A Monetary History of the U.S. 1867–1960* (Princeton, 1963), Appendix B on "Proximate Determinants of the Nominal Stock of Money"; P. Cagan, *Determinants and Effects of Changes in the Stock of Money 1875–1960* (Columbia, 1965), Chapter I on "The Money Stock and Its Three Determinants"; K. Brunner, "A Schema for the Supply Theory of Money," *International Economic Review*, January 1961; D. Fand, "Some Implications of Money Supply Analysis," *American Economic Review*, May 1967.

[2]The high-powered money concept used by M. Friedman, A. Schwartz, and P. Cagan is essentially the monetary base concept used by K. Brunner, A. Meltzer, and others. The monetary base may be defined either in terms of the sources (Federal Reserve credit, gold stock, Treasury items, etc.) or *uses* (member bank reserves and currency). To compare movements in the monetary base over time, we need to make a correction for changes in reserve requirements. As used here, the monetary base includes a reserve adjustment; that is, it is equal to the source base plus the reserve adjustment.

For a very clear exposition see L. Andersen and J. Jordan, "The Monetary Base—Explanations and Analytical Use" in the August 1968 issue of the St. Louis Federal Reserve Bank *Review*.

mand, time and savings deposits, CD's, intermediary claims, and other financial assets. The money stock that emerges reflects all these decisions.

It is a natural question to consider whether the central bank, by controlling the monetary base, can actually achieve fairly precise control over the money stock. This depends on whether the link between the monetary base and bank reserves, and between bank reserves and the money stock (the *monetary base-bank reserves-money stock* linkage) is fairly tight and therefore predictable. If there is a tight linkage the monetary authorities can formulate their policies and achieve any particular target for the money stock; on the other hand, if there is significant and unpredictable slippage, and the central bank control over the money stock is not sufficiently precise to achieve a given target, it will necessarily have to formulate its policies in terms of other variables that it can control. The variable used to express (or define) the central bank's objective, or to implement its policy decisions, must therefore be one that it can control within reasonable limits.[3]

The recently recurring idea that the money stock is perhaps best viewed as an endogenous variable, although not a new idea (it would have been acceptable to "real bill" theorists), has received new and powerful support from those who follow the "New View" approach in monetary economics.[4] New View theorists have questioned the validity of much of classical monetary theory concerning the importance of money relative to other liquid assets, the uniqueness of commercial banks relative to other intermediaries, and the extent to which the central bank can control the nominal money stock.[5] They argue that the central bank can control its instruments (open market operations, reserve requirements, discount rate) and some money mar-

---

[3]It is presumably for this reason that some models treat unborrowed reserves as the policy variable (the practice followed in the FRB-MIT model and other econometric models). These model builders believe that some components of the monetary base, and perhaps the entire base, behave as endogenous variables—as the variables that respond to income changes, and are not directly (or completely) under the control of the central bank. They do believe that the Federal Reserve can control the volume of unborrowed reserves.

[4]For the development of the New View, see J. Gurley and E. Shaw, *Money in a Theory of Finance* (Brookings, 1959); D. Fand, "Intermediary Claims and the Adequacy of Our Monetary Controls," and J. Tobin, "Commercial Banks as Creators of 'Money,'" in D. Carson (ed), *Banking and Monetary Studies* (Irwin, 1963); H. Johnson, *Essays in Monetary Economics* (Allen and Unwin, 1967), Chapters 1 and 2; W. Brainard, "Financial Intermediaries and a Theory of Monetary Control," in D. Hester and J. Tobin (eds.), *Financial Markets and Economic Activity* (Wiley, 1967); and K. Brunner, "The Role of Money and Monetary Policy," in the July 1968 issue of the St. Louis Federal Reserve Bank *Review*.

[5]Tobin offers the following description of the New View: "A more recent development in monetary economics tends to blur the sharp traditional distinctions between money and other assets and between commercial banks and other financial intermediaries; to focus on demands for and supplies of the whole spectrum of assets rather than on the quantity and velocity of 'money'; and to regard the structure of interest rates, asset yields, and credit availabilities rather than the quantity of money as the linkage between monetary and financial institutions and policies on the one hand and the real economy on the other."

He also suggests that this general equilibrium approach to the financial sector tends to question the presumed uniqueness of commercial banks: "Neither individually nor collectively do commercial banks possess a widow's cruse. Quite apart from legal reserve requirements, commercial banks are limited in scale by the same kinds of economic processes that determine the aggregate size of other intermediaries."

J. Tobin, "Commercial Banks as Creators of 'Money,'" *op. cit.*, pp. 410-412.

ket variables (free reserves, Treasury bill rate); that the commercial banks supply deposits at a fixed rate; and that the stock of money and liquid assets which emerge—at least in the short run—largely reflect the public's preference for demand and time deposits, intermediary claims, and other financial assets.[6]

Two schools of monetary economics differ on the use of the money stock as an indicator or target variable and on the extent to which it is an endogenous variable and therefore not available to the monetary authorities as a stabilization instrument. The *nonmonetarists* believe that the central bank should formulate its policies in terms of money market variables and implement them through operations on the instrument variables. They view the money stock as (in part) an endogenous variable, and do not conceive of it as a proper instrument or target variable. The *monetarists* believe that the central bank can, and should, define its objectives and implement its policies in terms of the money stock. Indeed, these two conceptions of the money stock and its role in monetary policy decisions summarize some important substantive differences that have emerged in monetary economics:

1. between the *monetarist* view that changes in the nominal money stock may be a causal, active, and independent factor in influencing aggregate demand and the price level and the *nonmonetarist* views ranging from (a) the older "real bills" doctrine that the money stock responds primarily to changes in the real economy; (b) the Income-Expenditure theories (associated with the 45° diagram) which view money as an accommodating factor; and (c) the more recent New View doctrine that the money stock is best viewed as one of several endogenous liquidity aggregates;

2. between the monetarist view that the money stock—using either the conventional or the broader definition—is a reasonably well-behaved quantity and the Radcliffe-type view that rejects these measures as narrow and inappropriate and argues for a broader liquidity aggregate; and

3. between the monetarist view that the monetary policy posture should be gauged by the behavior of a monetary aggregate and the Income-Expenditure theories viewing market interest rates as the proper indicator variable.

Many who question the advisability of operating monetary policy in terms of money stock guidelines also question whether the central bank control is precise enough to comply with the guideline requirements. The extent of this control is therefore a key question. Is the money stock best viewed as an endogenous variable—determined by the interaction of the financial and real sectors—and outside the direct control of the central bank? Or is it more nearly correct to view it as an exogenous variable—as a policy instrument—that the authorities can control and whose behavior can be made to conform to the stabilization guidelines?

[6]Some monetary theorists have argued that while a skillfull central bank can manipulate its controls to keep the nominal money stock (M) on target, it is preferable nevertheless to think of (M) as an endogenous variable. They argue that a "theory which takes as data the instruments of control rather than M, will not break down if and when there are changes in the targets or the marksmanship of the authorities." See J. Tobin, "Money, Capital and Other Stores of Value," *American Economic Review,* May 1961.

This issue is essentially an empirical one: Does control over the monetary base and other instruments provide the central bank with sufficient powers to fit the behavior of the money stock into a given stabilization program? The *monetarists,* in assigning an important role for the money stock in stabilization policy, assume that the central bank can engineer the desired behavior of the money stock. The substantive issue can be reformulated in terms of an empirically refutable hypothesis, as follows: Do changes in commercial bank free reserve behavior, and do portfolio shifts by the public involving currency, demand and time deposits, and other financial assets introduce enough variability and enough "noise" to break the *monetary base-bank reserves-money stock* linkage and justify treating the money stock as an endogenous variable—and essentially outside the control of the central bank?

The empirical examination of this issue fits in naturally to a framework of money supply analysis which I have described in an earlier article.[7] The analysis developed there defines four money supply functions which incorporate alternative assumptions concerning portfolio adjustments.

If we let

M = the nominal money stock

X = a vector of Federal Reserve (monetary policy) instruments variables (the monetary base, reserve requirements, discount rate, Regulation Q)

r_b = a vector of endogenous financial variables (e.g., the Treasury bill rate, the Federal funds rate, the Eurodollar rate, the rate on time deposits and other intermediary claims)

T, C = time deposits, currency, shares, and other financial assets that are close substitutes for demand deposits

Y = a vector of real sector variables (*GNP*, business investment, durables, etc.)

a money supply (*M.S.*) function may be written as:

$$M = f(X, r_b; T, C: Y).$$

The four *M.S.* functions that follow reflect alternative *ceteris paribus* conditions changing the portfolio adjustments that we permit for both the banks and the public:

1. *M.S.*(I) is a short-run supply concept. It gives the money supply response to a change in reserves on the assumption that while banks may choose to adjust their free reserves, the public can only carry out a limited adjustment with respect to currency, time deposits, and other financial assets. There are several

[7]See D. Fand, "Some Implications of Money Supply Analysis," *American Economic Review,* May 1967.

ways to impose *certeris paribus* conditions on the public's holdings of currency, time deposits, and other financial assets. Some investigators hold *levels* of these assets constant, others hold *ratios* constant, and different investigators impose this *ceteris paribus* condition in a manner most compatible with their model. M.S.(I) is of the form $M = f(X, r_b; T, C: Y)$, where T and C specify our assumptions for currency, time deposits, and other close substitutes. To use it as a short-run concept, we assume that all variables in the real sector of the economy, including stocks of real assets and flows such as consumption and investment, are held constant, so that it is primarily a function of the monetary policy instrument variables. Accordingly, if M.S.(I) is fairly stable, it provides some support for the view that the monetary authorities can achieve fairly precise control over the money stock.

2. To construct M.S.(II), we remove some of these portfolio restrictions by permitting the public to adjust their holdings of currency and time deposits, and the terms on which banks supply time deposits to reflect the underlying preferences. This function is of the form $f(X, r_b: Y)$, and does not contain any arbitrary assumptions about currency, time deposits, or the rate paid on time deposits. It is derived by assuming (a) that the banks may adjust their free reserves and the rate paid on time deposits and (b) that the public's holdings of currency and time deposits will be determined by their demand function for these assets. Although M.S.(II) does permit a greater degree of portfolio adjustment, it still is a short-run and restricted function because it assumes that the real sector variables and all other financial assets are held constant.

3. To construct M.S.(III), we permit portfolio adjustments throughout the entire financial sector and solve all the equations in the financial sector simultaneously. The Treasury bill rate and other rates which are endogenous variables in the financial sector will therefore be determined and no longer enter as independent arguments in the money supply function. M.S.(III) is a reduced-form equation of the form $M = g(X:Y)$, where all endogenous financial variables will have values determined by the simultaneous solution of the behavior equations in the financial sector. This function measures the supply response due to a change in the monetary base or some other policy instrument, assuming that all the variables in the financial sector adjust simultaneously.

4. Finally, we define M.S.(IV) in the form of $M = g(X)$, a reduced-form equation which measures the movements in the money stock in response to adjustments in both the real and the financial sector. To derive this money supply, we must solve all the structural equations in the financial and real sectors simultaneously to obtain the reduced form. The real sector variables are no longer treated as exogenous variables, but are now determined simultaneously with all the endogenous financial sector variables. This reduced-form M.S. gives the equilibrium stocks of money as a function of the monetary base and other monetary policy instrument variables. This is the natural M.S. function to construct for those who view the money stock as passive and responding to real

sector developments and for those who view the money stock as an accommodating variable, whose changes may be necessary in order to validate changes in the real economy.[8]

This brief review of the four money supply functions suggests that it is possible to test some of the substantive points that have come up in the recent "control over the money stock" discussions. For example, *M.S.*(I) postulates that we can predict the effect of changes in the monetary base (and other instruments) on the money stock, assuming that the public's portfolio adjustments are restricted; *M.S.*(II) postulates that we can predict the effect of a change in the monetary base (and other instruments) on the money stock, even allowing the public to adjust their currency and holdings of demand and time deposits; while *M.S.*(III) postulates that we can predict the money stock response, even allowing the public to adjust their entire portfolios. These three *M.S.* functions assume that commercial bank free reserve behavior and the public's behavior with respect to currency and demand and time deposits are stable; and that the substitution of intermediary claims and liquid assets for money conforms to behavior that can be incorporated into a stable *M.S.* function. Econometric estimates of these three functions provide some evidence for testing the reliability of the *monetary base-bank reserve-money stock* linkage.[9]

Those who follow the "real bills" view—that the money stock is determined by the real sector variables—or the view in many income-expenditure models—that the money stock is an accommodating or permissive variable—presumably deny the possibility of constructing such functions. In their view these three *M.S.* functions do not allow any changes in fiscal policy or in the real sector variables; they permit only restricted changes in the financial sector variables, and they emphasize the monetary base and the central bank's instrument variables. Accordingly, they should predict that the first three *M.S.* functions highlighting the instrument variables are unstable and lack content; indeed, their approach to monetary theory implies that only *M.S.*(IV), which incorporates changes in the real sector, contains the relevant independent variables.

An analysis of these four money supply functions has implications for the use of the money stock as an independent and major instrument in stabilization. Those who argue that money is, at least in part, an endogenous variable, and who question the precision with which it can be controlled, assume (implicitly perhaps) that no statis-

---

[8]The *M.S.*(IV) function as written implies that an increase in the monetary base will affect the money supply if it induces some real sector changes. A "real bills" proponent might therefore prefer to write it as follows:

$$M = f(Y) \text{ and } X = g(Y),$$

where M and X are both determined by the real sector variables in Y.

[9]A comparison of the three *M.S.* functions enables us to evaluate the quantitative effects of these portfolio shifts on the money stock. Consider a given change in the monetary base, or any other instrument variable, and compare the money stock response in these three functions. The calculated differences reflect the portfolio adjustments that we introduce as we move from *M.S.*(I) to *M.S.*(III)—i.e., shifts among currency, demand and time deposits, and the substitution of intermediary claims for money—and thus provide a measure of these effects on the money stock.

tically significant supply function can be estimated relating the money stock to the monetary base and other instrument variables. Moreover, if such a function is estimated, it would have to be a reduced-form function and a variant of the *M.S.*(IV) concept, incorporating feedbacks from the real sector.

In an earlier study, we compared estimates of the *M.S.* functions calculated from different econometric models. We found that the elasticities and multipliers for the first three *M.S.* functions based primarily on financial variables appear to be stable enough to justify further effort toward their refinement and improvement. We also found that: "There are at present too few studies available to calculate reliable *M.S.*(IV) elasticities. But the available evidence, meager though it may be, does not

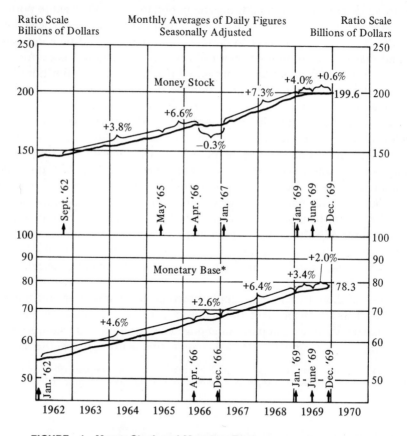

FIGURE 1 Money Stock and Monetary Base

* Uses of the monetary base are member bank reserves and currency held by the public and nonmember banks. Adjustments are made for reserve requirement changes and shifts in deposits among classes of banks. Data are computed by this bank.

Percentages are annual rates of change for periods indicated.

Latest data plotted: December preliminary

Prepared by Federal Reserve Bank of St. Louis

point to any superiority of *M.S.*(IV) over *M.S.*(I), and does not appear to favor a real view over a monetary view. Those who take the view that money is passive, responding primarily to the real economy, have to recognize that this is an assumption rather than a proposition derived from empirical evidence."[10]

Our findings also suggest that the money stock behavior could be made to conform to a specified stabilization program. For example, by controlling movements in the monetary base, monetary authorities can control quite adequately movements in the money stock. Figure 1 illustrates a rather close relationship between the monetary base and the money stock.

While this research is far from conclusive, it is consistent with a number of other findings.[11] It is difficult to maintain the view that the money stock is sufficiently endogenous so that it is outside the *direct* control of the authorities, without getting dangerously close to a "real bills" position. Accordingly, the focus of the "control over the money stock" discussion will shift, in my opinion, to the more interesting question—and the more relevant and less ideological question—concerning the length of the period needed to give the Federal Reserve System sufficient control to achieve a given money stock guideline. Assuming that a "reasonable" degree of precision has been defined, can the particular guideline requirements be achieved in a week? a month? a quarter? Or must we extend the period in order to overcome false signals, "noise," forecasting errors and other disturbances?"[12] It would appear that the degree of precision desired is not independent of the time period required for the execution of policy, and it is reassuring to note that recent discussions have been directed increasingly at these points.

[10]See D. Fand, "Some Implications of Money Supply Analysis," *op. cit.,* p. 392. The calculated elasticities and multipliers suggest that the short-run *M.S.* functions—such as the *M.S.*(I) and *M.S.*(II)—are reasonably stable. These are preliminary findings, derived by using the steady-state solutions to simplify the analysis; they are subject to revision and require the construction of significance tests.

[11]See the references to Andersen, Brunner, Cagan, Friedman and Schwartz, and Meltzer in footnotes 1, 2 and 4.

[12]This formulation of the problem has come up in several recent papers. Governor Maisel emphasizes this point as follows: "This growth of money supply in any period is the result of actions taken by the Federal Reserve, the Treasury, the commercial banks, and the public. Over a longer period, the Fed may play a paramount role, but this is definitely not the case in the short run. To the best of my knowledge, the Fed has not and probably would have great difficulties controlling within rather wide limits the growth of the narrowly defined money supply in any week or month."

See Sherman J. Maisel, "Controlling Monetary Aggregates," in *Controlling Monetary Aggregates* (Boston: Federal Reserve Bank of Boston, 1969). For some other discussions of this issue, see A. J. Meigs, "The Case for Simple Rules," *op. cit.*; L. Gramley, "Guidelines for Monetary Policy—The Case Against Simple Rules," *op. cit.*; the Hearings on Standards for Guiding Monetary Action, *op. cit.*; A. Meltzer, "Controlling Money," *Controlling Monetary Aggregates* (Boston: Federal Reserve Bank, 1969). See also L. Kallish, "A Study of Money Stock Control," *Working Paper No. 11,* Federal Reserve Bank of St. Louis, for an interesting attempt to develop confidence limits for measuring the money managers' success in controlling the money stock.

21

A Review of Empirical Studies of the Money Supply Mechanism

Robert H. Rasche

In recent years there has been considerable discussion concerning techniques for conducting monetary policy. The traditional practitioners of the art of policymaking have argued for the use of operating procedures which focus on "money market conditions." At various times this has been construed to mean free reserves, the Treasury bill rate, the Federal funds rate, or a combination of these.[1] Alternatively, it has been argued that the target of monetary policy actions should be a monetary aggregate and that this target can be achieved by control of some reserve aggregate concept such as the monetary base.[2]

This article surveys the accumulated empirical evidence on the interest sensitivity of some reserve multipliers. If these multipliers are highly sensitive to interest rate changes, then it may be difficult to implement monetary control through the control of reserve aggregates. The available evidence consistently indicates, however, that

Reprinted from the Federal Reserve Bank of St. Louis, *Review* (July, 1972), pp. 11-19, by permission of the publisher and the author.

[1]Stephen H. Axilrod, "The FOMC Directive as Structured in the Late 1960's: Theory and Appraisal," in *Open Market Policies and Operating Procedures—Staff Studies* (Washington, D.C.: Board of Governors of the Federal Reserve System, 1971), pp. 1-36.

[2]For example, see Albert E. Burger, Lionel Kalish III, and Christopher T. Babb, "Money Stock Control and Its Implications for Monetary Policy," this *Review* (October 1971), pp. 6-22.

the interest sensitivity of various multiplier concepts is extremely low. This suggests that control of monetary aggregates through reserve control should not be very difficult to implement.[3]

Conditions Inhibiting Control of the Money Stock

The issue examined here is the feasibility of control of a monetary aggregate such as the narrowly defined money stock (M_1), given control of some reserve aggregate concept. The problem can be illustrated by the equation

$$M = mR$$

where "M" is the money stock, "R" is some reserve aggregate concept, and "m" is the appropriate reserve multiplier.[4] Two sources of difficulty can arise in such a control procedure.

First, there can be systematic feedbacks on "m" through market forces which tend to offset the expected effect of a change in the reserve aggregate on the money stock. This influence of the behavior of reserves on the value of the multiplier can be stated as

$$m = f(R).$$

The sources of feedback from changes in "R" to changes in "m" will vary depending on the choice of a reserve aggregate concept. If the net source base concept is used for "R", the associated multiplier (m) is

$$m = \frac{1 + k}{(r - b)(1 + t + d) + k}$$

where "r" and "b" are the ratios of bank reserves and member bank borrowings to commercial bank deposits, respectively, "t", "k" and "d", respectively, are the ratios of time deposits, currency held by the public, and U.S. Government deposits at commercial banks to the demand deposit component of the money supply. Therefore, the important behavioral relationships influencing the stability of the multiplier

---

[3]If, however, these multipliers *are* highly sensitive to interest rate changes, then accurate monetary control through a reserve control procedure requires a precise estimate of the impact of reserve changes on interest rates, in addition to a precise estimate of the interest elasticity of the reserve multiplier.

[4]A number of candidates have been proposed for "R" including the monetary base, unborrowed reserves plus currency, total reserves, unborrowed reserves, and reserves available to support private deposits. For a discussion of the relative virtues of many of these, see Richard Davis, "Short-Run Targets for Open Market Operations," in *Open Market Policies and Operating Procedures—Staff Studies* (Washington, D.C.: Board of Governors of the Federal Reserve System, 1971), pp. 37-45.

in the presence of reserve changes are the public's demand for currency and time deposits, banks' demand for excess reserves and borrowings, and the supply of time deposits.[5]

An example of a feedback effect on "m" would be where there exists a sizable short-run interest elasticity of demand for excess reserves by commercial banks. In order to force additional reserves into the banking system to expand the money stock, the Federal Reserve would have to buy Government securities, thus pushing short-term interest rates down. If the amount of excess reserves demanded by banks is very sensitive to changes in short-term interest rates, this interest rate movement would induce banks to hold larger quantities of excess reserves. This portfolio shift then offsets the policy to increase the money stock.

The existence of strong feedback effects on the reserve multiplier does not mean that monetary control through reserve aggregates is impossible. The stronger the feedback, the larger the necessary magnitude of the open market operation required to achieve a given change in the money stock and the larger the associated variance in short-term interest rates.

The second source of difficulty in this type of monetary control procedure is that the relationship between the reserve aggregate and the money stock is subject to random fluctuation. Specifically, we can write

$$m_t = f(R_t) + \varepsilon_t$$

where "ε_t" is an unknown random disturbance to "m_t". If such fluctuations are truly random, then in the long run policymakers should be able to hit the desired average stock of money quite closely. If this random component is large, then in a short time period, such as one or two months, the average "m" could deviate considerably from the forecast "m" and cause a large average error around the desired path of the money stock.

It can be shown that for a given variance of "ε_t", under a control procedure such as that recently proposed by Burger, Kalish, and Babb, the variance of the actual path of the money stock around the desired path will depend on the sensitivity of the reserve multiplier (m) to changes in the reserve aggregate.[6] The smaller the sensitivity of the multiplier, the smaller will be the variance of the actual money stock around the desired money stock.

---

[5]For a detailed discussion of the functional relationship of the multiplier expression to asset holdings of the nonbank public, the banking system, and the Treasury, see Albert E. Burger, *The Money Supply Process* (Belmont, California: Wadsworth, 1971), especially chaps. 4-5, and Karl Brunner and Allan H. Meltzer, "Liquidity Traps for Money, Bank Credit, and Interest Rates, *Journal of Political Economy* (January/February 1968), pp. 1-37.

[6]Burger, Kalish, and Babb, "Money Stock Control."

The Nature of Available Evidence on Multiplier Sensitivity

Over the past decade there has been considerable empirical research directed at measuring the relationship between the money stock and various reserve aggregates. This work has evolved primarily from attempts to construct econometric models of basic financial relationships in the U.S. economy. As a by-product, these studies provide information on the interest elasticities of the behavioral parameters of the reserve multiplier, the existence of which cause feedbacks against policy actions as discussed above.

Most of the more detailed studies have worked with quarterly data, which may be too highly aggregated in time to provide information that policymakers desire if the reactions of the banking system and the public are distributed over time. However, studies using shorter time horizons do exist for some components of the money supply mechanism, and these can be used to obtain information on how the estimated elasticities are likely to change as the horizon becomes shorter.

There are several potential sources of feedback which will offset the expected impact of a change in reserve aggregates on the change in the money stock. Some of the feedback, such as a change in the demand for currency and time deposits by the nonbank public as a result of increased economic activity, has been shown to occur only slowly, and does not cause difficulties for short-run control.[7]

The troublesome source of changes in the multiplier relationship is the impact of changes in interest rates on the behavioral parameters in the multiplier. Changes in market interest rates and changes in reserves available to the banking system cannot be controlled simultaneously by the Federal Reserve System. When the Federal Reserve follows a reserve aggregate operating procedure, interest rates are affected by changes in reserves. Under a money market conditions operating strategy, changes in reserve aggregates come about as a result of the attempt to achieve certain levels of interest rates. Hence, if the goal is to control money through changes in reserve aggregates, the major issue is the interest elasticity of the relationship between the money stock and reserve aggregates.

It will be necessary to distinguish between short-run, or impact, elasticities of the reserve multiplier and long-run, or equilibrium, elasticities. The former include only the impact which comes from the adjustment of economic units to a change in interest rates within one period of time. Many studies, however, have indicated that economic units respond to such changes with a distributed lag; that is, part of the response takes place in the same period, and the remainder of the response takes place over several periods following a change in interest rates. The impact, or short-run, interest elasticity is the percentage change in the reserve multiplier with respect to a percentage change in interest rates within the time period in which the interest

---

[7]See David I. Fand, "Some Implications of Money Supply Analysis," *American Economic Review* (May 1967), pp. 380-400.

rate changes. The equilibrium, or long-run, elasticity is the total response of the reserve multiplier after economic units have had sufficient time to adjust to a new portfolio equilibrium.[8]

In the studies cited below, estimates have been obtained for the interest elasticity of the money stock for given values of various reserve aggregates. Thus, the money stock elasticities computed are the interest elasticities of the reserve multiplier.

Interest Elasticity Estimates from Data Prior to 1965

Teigen I

An early econometric investigation of the money supply relationship was that of Ronald Teigen.[9] His study does not develop the detailed specifications which are characteristic of more recent studies. In particular, the stocks of currency in the hands of the public and demand deposits at nonmember banks are assumed exogenous.[10] In addition, Teigen takes the quantity of time deposits at member banks and government deposits at member banks as exogenous variables.[11]

Teigen tests the hypothesis that the banking system takes more than one period to respond to changes in interest rates, but this hypothesis is rejected for the post-war data. Thus his impact and equilibrium interest elasticities of the money supply relationship are equal. His estimated coefficients of elasticity are 0.1950 for the commercial paper rate and −0.1695 for the discount rate.[12]

[8]For a discussion of impact versus long-run responses, see Arthur S. Goldberger, *Impact Multipliers and Dynamic Properties of the Klein-Goldberger Model* (Amsterdam: North-Holland, 1959).

[9]Ronald L. Teigen, "Demand and Supply Functions for Money in the United States: Some Structural Estimates," *Econometrica* (October 1964), pp. 476–509.

[10]It is necessary to distinguish here between the construction of the model from historical data and the use of the model to determine interest elasticities. In the construction of the model, the ratio of currency to demand deposits at member banks and the ratio of demand deposits at nonmember banks to those at member banks are, in fact, exogenous variables which vary from one observation to the next. In determining the value of the elasticity of the relationship, these exogenous variables are kept fixed at some point, conventionally their mean value for the sample period. Hence, the computations implicitly assume positive interest rate responses for the public's currency demand and the supply of demand deposits by nonmember banks, which are equal to the interest rate response of demand deposits supplied by member banks. For nonmember banks, the assumption probably does not seriously affect the analysis. On the other hand, the public's currency demand is usually found to have a zero, or slightly negative, interest elasticity, at least in the long run. If the true interest elasticity of currency demand is zero, then the bias introduced by the constant ratio of currency to money stock is indeterminate. On the one hand, the *direct* effect of increased currency in the hands of the public as demand deposits supplied by banks increase biases the interest elasticity of the money supply upward. On the other hand, the *indirect* effect that the assumed increase in currency withdraws reserves from the banking system causes the model to understate the desired amount of deposit expansion. Since the magnitudes involved are small, the net bias should not be substantial.

[11]These variables do not explicitly appear in his model. However, the reserve aggregate which he uses is unborrowed reserves available to support private demand deposits. Later studies use more broadly defined aggregates such as unborrowed reserves, or unborrowed reserves plus currency. To make the studies comparable, the model must be reformulated with time deposits at member banks and government deposits at member banks explicitly appearing as exogenous variables.

[12]Teigen, "Demand and Supply Functions," p. 502.

De Leeuw I

Frank de Leeuw attempted to obtain more detailed numerical estimates of behavior in important financial markets than did Teigen.[13] In particular, de Leeuw separates bank borrowing and excess reserve behavior, and explicity estimates functions for currency demand and time deposit demand at commercial banks by the nonbank public.

The interest elasticity estimates from this study are summarized in Table 1. In all cases the absolute value of the long-run elasticities are less than one, and the short-run elasticities never exceed 0.2 in absolute value. The available data do not permit reconstruction of the interest elasticities of excess reserves. However, de Leeuw did publish the results of a computation of the implicit interest elasticities of the money-reserve relationship derived from the estimated borrowings and excess reserves functions. In this computation, he takes the ratios of currency, time deposits, U.S. Government deposits, and nonmember bank demand deposits to money stock as constant. Thus the biases which were introduced into Teigen's computations are again present here. De Leeuw's reserve aggregate is nonborrowed reserves plus currency in the hands of the public. His estimated long-run elasticities, valued at the sample means, are 0.172 and −0.214 for the Treasury bill rate and the discount rate, respec-

Table 1. Interest Elasticities of Various Functions in de Leeuw's Original Brookings Model

Specification	Impact*	Equilibrium*
Currency Demand		
Private Securities Rate	− 0.032	− 0.364
Time Deposit Rate	− 0.012	− 0.136
Time Deposit Demand		
Treasury Bill Rate	− 0.038	− 0.374
Time Deposit Rate	0.070	0.683
Bank Borrowings		
Treasury Bill Rate	0.134	0.50
Discount Rate	− 0.186	− 0.70
Excess Reserves		
Treasury Bill Rate	n.a.	n.a.
Discount Rate	n.a.	n.a.

*Impact elasticities are calculated by using the respective equilibrium elasticities and regression coefficients of the lagged dependent variables from various tables in the source cited below. The equilibrium elasticities for currency and time deposit demand are from p. 493, and for bank borrowings from p. 512. The respective regression coefficients used in calculating the impact elasticities can be found in Tables 13.2, 13.4, and 13.12.

Source: Frank de Leeuw, "A Model of Financial Behavior," in *The Brookings Quarterly Econometric Model of the United States,* ed. James S. Duesenberry et al. (Chicago: Rand McNally, 1965), chap. 13.

[13]Frank de Leeuw, "A Model of Financial Behavior," in *The Brookings Quarterly Econometric Model of the United States,* ed. James S. Duesenberry et al. (Chicago: Rand McNally, 1965), chap. 13.

tively. When valued in 1962 (the end of his sample period) these elasticities are 0.245 and −0.348, respectively.[14]

These numbers seem quite compatible with those obtained by Teigen for approximately the same sample period. However, de Leeuw finds that the entire adjustment of banks to portfolio changes takes place only gradually over time, and his impact elasticities for borrowings are only about one-fourth of the equilibrium values. This suggests that if the data were available to compute the short-run elasticity for the money supply relationship, the estimates over a one-quarter period would be considerably lower than those obtained by Teigen.

The currency and time deposit demand equations which de Leeuw incorporates into the above computations are almost completely insensitive to interest rate changes over a one-quarter horizon. This implies that over a one-quarter horizon changes in reserves available to support private demand deposits, which are caused by interest induced changes in currency and time deposit demand, are negligible. Thus, it is highly probable that the assumptions of constant currency/money stock or time deposit/money stock ratios result in a net upward bias in the computed interest elasticity of the money supply relationship.

De Leeuw II

In a subsequent study for the Brookings model de Leeuw produced a condensed model of financial behavior in which the excess reserve and borrowings equations were aggregated into a single function to explain free reserves.[15] In that study estimates of the interest elasticity of the money supply relationship are not provided. However, using the free reserve-interest rate coefficient estimates and information given in the earlier study it is possible to replicate the computations of the larger model.[16]

The estimated impact elasticities at the sample means are 0.037 for the Treasury bill rate, and −0.046 for the discount rate.[17] The corresponding long-run elasticities are 0.096 and −0.118 respectively. The absolute values are lower by a factor of almost fifty percent from the values obtained in the earlier study, even though the data and the sample period have remained essentially unchanged.

It is likely that some downward bias has been introduced into these estimates by aggregating excess reserves and borrowings into free reserves in the estimation of the model. From the information presented in the first study, it is not possible to aggregate the interest elasticities of these two components. However, the early work suggests that the response of banks to a disequilibrium in borrowings from the Federal Reserve is much faster than the response to a similar situation with respect to excess reserves.

[14]Ibid., p. 518.

[15]Frank de Leeuw, "A Condensed Model of Financial Behavior," in *The Brookings Model: Some Further Results,* ed. James S. Duesenberry et al. (Chicago: Rand McNally, 1969), pp. 270-315.

[16]De Leeuw, "A Model of Financial Behavior."

[17]Unless otherwise stated, data cited have been computed by this author.

Goldfeld

The most detailed study of financial markets is found in the work of Stephen Gold-feld.[18] In this study, equations are specified for both the demand for excess reserves and the demand for borrowings from the Federal Reserve System. Separate equations are estimated for country banks and city banks.

The Goldfeld results suggest very large (in absolute value) interest elasticities for the borrowings equations relative to those found by de Leeuw. There do not appear to be large differences in the impact elasticities of borrowings across the bank classes, but the speed of adjustment to interest rate changes is much slower for borrowings by country banks than for city banks. This is reflected in the lower impact elasticities and the higher equilibrium elasticities for the country banks than the corresponding numbers for the city banks.

The excess reserve interest elasticities reported by Goldfeld are negligible, particularly when compared with the borrowings elasticities. In addition, he finds that banks respond quite quickly to disequilibrium in excess reserve holdings. Thus, the long-run elasticities for excess reserve demand are not much different from the impact elasticities, particularly for city banks. This result is similar to that of the Teigen study where no evidence of a distributed lag in bank response was found.

Goldfeld reports interest elasticities of a money supply relationship comparable to that derived by both Teigen and de Leeuw. The impact elasticities, with respect to the Treasury bill rate and the discount rate in this function, 0.042 and −0.029, respectively, are derived from the elasticities reported in Table 2. The corresponding long-run elasticities are 0.222 and −0.076.[19] These results are quite close to the values reported by both Teigen and de Leeuw for the Treasury bill rate, but considerably below the estimates for the discount rate in the other studies.

The sources of the differences are fairly conspicuous. In Teigen's study, where there is no disaggregation of excess reserves from borrowings, the Treasury bill rate and the discount rate appear only as the differential between the two rates. Hence the regression coefficient of the discount rate is constrained to have the same absolute value, but with the opposite sign from that of the bill rate. Since the mean of the discount rate for the sample period is slightly larger than that of the bill rate, the computed coefficient of elasticity of the discount rate is, in effect, constrained to be slightly smaller in absolute value than that of the bill rate. De Leeuw constrains this excess reserve specification to include only the differential between the bill rate and the discount rate. With the constraints that are imposed in the estimation of the Teigen and de Leeuw studies, it would seem reasonable to conclude that the Gold-feld estimate of the response of the money supply relationship to discount rate changes is more reliable for this period.

There seem to be no major discrepancies in the estimated long-run responsiveness of the money supply to changes in the bill rate, but considerable variance exists

---

[18]Stephen M. Goldfeld, *Commercial Bank Behavior and Economic Activity* (Amsterdam: North-Holland, 1966).
[19]Ibid., p. 191.

Table 2. Interest Elasticities of Various Functions in the Goldfeld Model

Specification	Impact*	Equilibrium*
Currency Demand		
Treasury Bill Rate	− 0.008	− 0.07
Time Deposit Rate	− 0.015	− 0.14
Time Deposit Demand		
Time Deposit Rate	0.028	0.37
Long-Term Government Rate	− 0.125	− 1.62
Bank Borrowings		
City Banks		
Discount Rate	− 0.98	− 2.382
Treasury Bill Rate	0.88	2.134
Country Banks		
Discount Rate	− 0.88	− 2.926
Treasury Bill Rate	0.79	2.625
Excess Reserves		
City Banks		
Treasury Bill Rate	− 0.38	− 0.35
Country Banks		
Treasury Bill Rate	− 0.15	− 0.25

*The equilibrium elasticities for currency and time deposit demand are found on p. 160 of the source cited below. The corresponding impact elasticities are calculated by using the equilibrium elasticities and regression coefficients of the lagged dependent variables from Tables 5.7 and 5.9, respectively. Both equilibrium and impact elasticities for bank borrowings and excess reserves are found on pp. 150 and 149, respectively.

Source: Stephen M. Goldfeld, *Commercial Bank Behavior and Economic Activity* (Amsterdam: North-Holland, 1966).

among the short-run elasticity estimates. The most uncertain issue, on the basis of the evidence reviewed so far, is the source of the interest elasticity. Goldfeld suggests that the source is bank borrowing behavior, de Leeuw suggests that it is bank behavior with respect to excess reserves, and Teigen does not attempt to discriminate between the two.

Goldfeld and Kane

There exists an additional study by Goldfeld and Kane which provides some independent information on the question of the interest elasticity of bank borrowings from the Federal Reserve.[20] This study is based on weekly data from the period July 1953 to December 1963 and disaggregates banks into four classes—New York City, Chicago, Other Reserve City, and Country banks. They find that the estimated short-run (one week) Treasury bill rate elasticities range from a high of 0.56 for New York

[20]Stephen M. Goldfeld and Edward J. Kane, "The Determinants of Member-Bank Borrowing: An Econometric Study," *Journal of Finance* (September 1966), pp. 499–514, and Stephen M. Goldfeld, "An Extension of the Monetary Sector," in *The Brookings Model: Some Further Results,* ed. James S. Duesenberry et al. (Chicago: Rand McNally, 1969), pp. 317–360.

City banks to a low of 0.08 for Chicago banks. When aggregated over all classes of banks, the short-run interest elasticity for the banking system as a whole is found to be 0.21. Their reported long-run interest elasticities of borrowings range from 2.8 to 3.9.[21]

These estimates seem consistent with the results of the quarterly study by Goldfeld and tend to add to the uncertainty of the high excess reserve and low borrowings elasticities reported by de Leeuw. The only difficulty in reconciling the weekly estimates with the quarterly work of Goldfeld is the implied definition of long run. In the quarterly study, the long run is achieved only after several quarters have elapsed. In the weekly study, the implied long run is a period of several weeks. The possibility remains that long run in the two studies has two different meanings. However, it seems safe to conclude that borrowing behavior of banks is an important source of interest elasticity of the money supply relationship when the Treasury bill rate changes and the discount rate remains constant.

Teigen II

A quarterly study which deals with the period of the 1950s through the early 1960s is that of Teigen.[22] The study contains supply elasticities only for the demand deposit component of the money supply. The results for the elasticity of the discount rate are not very different from those reported by Goldfeld, but the elasticity of the Treasury bill rate is considerably lower than the results obtained by Goldfeld, de Leeuw, and Teigen's earlier results.

Brunner and Meltzer

Karl Brunner and Allan Meltzer have estimated the interest elasticity of the money supply relationship using annual data over a sample period including the interwar and postwar periods.[23] In the two-stage least-squares estimates of their "nonlinear" money supply hypothesis, they find that the elasticity of the money supply function with respect to the adjusted monetary base is insignificantly different from one. Therefore, the interest elasticities of this function can be interpreted as interest elasticities of the reserve multiplier. Their estimate of the Treasury bill rate elasticity is 0.66 and the estimate of the discount rate elasticity is -0.31.[24] Since there are no lagged variables in the equation, these estimates can be compared with the equilibrium elasticities derived from the studies which used shorter time intervals. Both

---

[21]Goldfeld and Kane, "The Determinants of Member-Bank Borrowing: An Econometric Study," p. 512.

[22]Ronald L. Teigen, "An Aggregated Quarterly Model of the U.S. Monetary Sector, 1953-1964," in *Targets and Indicators of Monetary Policy,* ed. Karl Brunner (San Francisco: Chandler Publishing Company, 1969), pp. 175-218.

[23]Karl Brunner and Allan H. Meltzer, "Some Further Investigations of Demand and Supply Functions for Money," *Journal of Finance* (May 1964), pp. 240-283.

[24]Ibid., p. 277.

elasticities appear to differ from the implied equilibrium values of the quarterly studies by a factor of over two. Given the many difficulties in estimating distributed lag effects from time series data, such inconsistencies are not surprising.

Estimates from Data Including Post-1965 Period

The shortcoming of the studies discussed so far is that they are based on data generated in the 1950s and early 1960s. During the 1960s there were many changes in the environment in which the banking system operated which could have significantly altered (and presumably increased) the interest elasticity of the money supply relationship. These changes included the evolution of an active market for large negotiable certificates of deposit, the involvement of large banks in the Eurodollar market through borrowings from (or lending to) their foreign subsidiaries, and the entrance of banks into the commercial paper market through parent one-bank holding companies.

Unfortunately, it is difficult to obtain empirical evidence on many of these innovations since they were effectively legislated out of existence before enough data were generated to assess their effects. The impact of the CD market can be assessed, along with the responsiveness of the banking system in terms of free reserves in the 1960s, through the quarterly financial model in the MPS model.[25] In addition, estimates of the interest elasticity of the money supply-reserve relationship on a monthly basis can be obtained from a financial market model developed by Thomas Thomson and James Pierce.[26]

Evaluation of Quarterly Money Supply Elasticities

The quarterly MPS model contains a financial sector which includes detail specifications of the commercial loan market and the mortgage market, as well as specifications dealing with bank and nonbank behavior with respect to holdings of currency, time deposits and free reserves. The estimated elasticities for the latter set of functions are tabulated in Table 3. Both the CD demand and supply functions, which did not exist in the earlier studies, assume that the full response to an interest rate change takes place within one quarter. Thus the impact and equilibrium elasticities are equal.

The CD demand function, in particular, indicates a highly sensitive response to interest rate changes, which is consistent with casual impressions of the nature of the

[25]This model is the publicly available version which developed out of the Federal Reserve-MIT-Pennsylvania econometric model project.

[26]Thomas D. Thomson and James L. Pierce, "A Monthly Econometric Model of the Financial Sector" (a paper presented at the May 1971 meeting of the Federal Reserve System Committee on Financial Analysis).

Table 3. Interest Elasticities of Various Functions in the M.P.S. Model

Specification	Impact Elasticity	Equilibrium Elasticity
Currency Demand		
Treasury Bill Rate	0.0037	0.026
Non-CD Time Deposit Demand		
Time Deposit Rate	0.3	2.9
S&L—Mut. Sav. Bk. Rate	− 0.2	− 2.0
Treasury Bill Rate	− 0.15	− 1.4
CD Demand [1969 Values]		
Treasury Bill Rate	− 6.14	− 6.14
Commercial Paper Rate	− 4.28	− 4.28
CD Rate	11.46	11.46
Free Reserves		
Treasury Bill Rate		
1965 Values	− 2.99	− 6.42
1969 Values	− 3.95	− 8.47
Discount Rate		
1965 Values	3.23	6.93
1969 Values	3.48	7.46
Supply of CDs by Banks [1969 Values]		
CD Rate	− 1.06	− 1.06
Treasury Bill Rate	0.98	0.98

CD market. However, these estimates are drawn from a considerably smaller sample than that for the rest of the specifications, and therefore there is less certainty about the stability of the functions over time.

The estimates for the currency demand equation and the demand equation for non-CD time deposits tend to confirm the de Leeuw and Goldfeld results of extremely low impact elasticities. The time deposit function does suggest higher long-run elasticities than had been previously estimated. This appears attributable, in part, to the evolution of special forms of time deposit accounts, such as small consumer-type CDs, during the late 1960s.[27]

The MPS model does not distinguish between excess reserves and borrowings of member banks, but does estimate a relationship between the Treasury bill rate, the discount rate, and free reserves. No constraints are applied to the coefficients of the two rates. In Table 3 both the impact and the equilibrium elasticities of this function are considerably higher than those estimated in the earlier studies. This is partially due to the fact that the estimated function is linear and therefore the value of the elasticity coefficient is not constant at all points along the function. Evaluation of the

---

[27]The estimated function allows for a change in structure during the early 1960s, which indicates that the interest elasticities in the latter part of the sample period are about fifty percent higher than those estimated for the first part of the sample period.

elasticity coefficient at the very high values of interest rates in 1969 gives estimates of the impact and equilibrium Treasury bill rate elasticities which are 50 and 25 percent higher, respectively, than the values at 1965 interest rate levels. Even after accounting for the higher levels of interest rates in the late 1960s, it appears that differences in specifications and/or differences in sample periods have produced higher interest rate elasticity estimates for the free reserve relationship than had previously been found.

Simulation experiments were performed with the MPS model which permitted relaxation of restrictions under which interest elasticities of the money supply relationship were computed in the studies discussed above. First, in addition to the impact elasticities, the pattern of response of the money stock over time to a maintained change in the Treasury bill rate was computed. The simulations were continued for eight quarters, after which the computed elasticities settled down at close to the equilibrium values.

Second, the response of the demand for currency and the demand for time deposits to the changes in interest rates can be included or excluded from the computation of the elasticities. Time deposit demand is split into large negotiable certificates of deposit and other time deposits. The inclusion of the currency and time deposit responses in the simulation is analogous to a controlled experiment in which the nonbank private sector demand for bank demand deposits is shifted once and maintained in its new position. This shift is allowed to occur without any effect on the demand functions for time deposits or currency. This shift generates an initial change in interest rates. The changes in the money stock, which are observed over time, are the result of the interest rate induced portfolio shifts by banks and the nonbank public, and they trace out the interest elasticity of the money supply relationship over various time intervals. Finally, elasticities are computed for both demand deposits and the M_1 money stock concept.

The estimated elasticities from three sets of simulations are presented in Table 4. These computations are generated under the assumption that the Federal Reserve would not impose a Regulation Q constraint which would prevent banks from offering new CDs at competitive rates.

If such constraints were effective, increases in the Treasury bill rate would cause a shift in the demand for CDs. At the constrained new issue rate for CDs the public would not renew outstanding certificates as they matured. Over time the stock of CDs would decline, and there could be a sizable reduction in the ratio of time deposits to demand deposits. The change in this ratio would, in turn, cause a fluctuation in the reserve multiplier. The observed result would also be highly sensitive to the initial conditions of the Treasury bill rate relative to the Regulation Q ceiling, and the historical pattern of Regulation Q restraint.

In the first section of Table 4, the interest elasticities include the interest rate induced reactions in the public's demand for currency, large certificates of deposit as well as other time deposits, and the interest elasticity of the commercial banking sector's supply function for large certificates of deposit. The interest elasticity of M_1

is consistently smaller than the interest elasticity of the demand deposit component. This is because the model indicates a small negative response of the demand for currency to changes in interest rates. Hence, as interest rates increase and the amount of bank deposits available to the economy expands, there is an offsetting movement in currency balances outstanding.

The exclusion of the nonbank private sector's demand for currency and time deposits other than large certificates of deposit lowers the interest elasticity of the money supply relationship.[28] This is because a rise (fall) in interest rates decreases (increases) the quantity demanded of both of these assets. This relationship is straightforward in the case of currency. For time deposits the expected equilibrium response would be for a large quantity of time deposits to be demanded with higher levels of all interest rates. The model postulates, however, that the rate which banks offer on non-CD time deposits responds quite sluggishly to changes in market interest rates. Thus the short-run effect is for disintermediation away from commercial bank time deposits. If the elasticity patterns were computed over a longer time horizon, the elasticities in the first experiment would eventually become smaller than those for the second experiment. In all cases the impact elasticities are essentially the same size.

These results can be compared with those from earlier empirical studies which do not include the CD market. It appears from section C of Table 4 that when the CD market is operating freely, the estimated interest elasticity of the money supply relationship differs little from the results drawn from studies of earlier periods. If anything, the elasticities reported in this section of the table are generally lower than those discussed above. On the other hand, sections A and B of Table 4 suggest that the net bias involved in computing the interest elasticities with a constant currency/deposit ratio and a constant level of time deposits tends toward zero. That is, the estimates obtained under these assumptions give estimates of elasticities which are too low.

Evaluation of Monthly Money Supply Elasticities

The same type of analysis of the money stock-reserve relationship as that performed with the MPS quarterly econometric model can be carried out on a monthly basis using the financial market model of Pierce and Thompson. The results over an eighteen month period are presented in Table 5. In this model, demand for currency by the public is specified to be completely interest inelastic, so the assumptions underlying the calculations of sections B and C of Table 4 are identical to the assumptions made for the right-hand column of Table 5. The analogy to section A of Table 4 is presented in the left-hand column of Table 5.

---

[28]This exclusion of currency and time deposit demand allows these demand functions to shift in such a way that the quantity demanded at the new Treasury bill rate is exactly equal to the quantity demanded at the original level of the Treasury bill rate.

Table 4. Money Supply Elasticity Computations—MPS Model

A. Currency, Time Deposits, and CDs Included

Quarter	Demand Deposits	M_1
1	0.106	0.083
2	0.175	0.137
3	0.214	0.167
4	0.240	0.188
First-Year Average	0.184	0.144
5	0.279	0.218
6	0.309	0.240
7	0.317	0.247
8	0.337	0.250
Second-Year Average	0.311	0.239

B. Currency, CDs Included; Time Deposits Excluded

Quarter	Demand Deposits	M_1
1	0.099	0.078
2	0.157	0.123
3	0.185	0.145
4	0.204	0.159
First-Year Average	0.161	0.126
5	0.233	0.181
6	0.254	0.196
7	0.256	0.198
8	0.259	0.200
Second-Year Average	0.251	0.194

C. CDs Included; Time Deposits, Currency Excluded

Quarter	Demand Deposits	M_1
1	0.094	0.074
2	0.149	0.118
3	0.173	0.136
4	0.186	0.147
First-Year Average	0.151	0.119
5	0.202	0.159
6	0.211	0.166
7	0.220	0.173
8	0.226	0.177
Second-Year Average	0.215	0.169

Table 5. Money Supply Elasticity Computations
(Monthly Financial Market Model)

Month	Time Deposits Included	Time Deposits Excluded
1	0.138	0.137
2	0.195	0.192
3	0.231	0.226
4	0.250	0.243
5	0.252	0.244
6	0.250	0.243
First 6-Month Average	0.219	0.214
7	0.266	0.256
8	0.272	0.262
9	0.275	0.262
10	0.279	0.269
11	0.284	0.272
12	0.292	0.281
Second 6-Month Average	0.278	0.267
13	0.303	0.290
14	0.311	0.296
15	0.236	0.222
16	0.220	0.202
17	0.233	0.216
18	0.246	0.230
Third 6-Month Average	0.258	0.243

The implication of the monthly model is that the money stock–reserve relationship is slightly more elastic in the short run than the various quarterly estimates imply. The implied impact elasticity (over a one-month period in this case) is about 0.15. The average elasticity over this first twelve months is estimated at about 0.25, or about one-third more than the estimate over the corresponding four-quarter horizon from the MPS model. After eighteen months have elapsed the elasticity values reflect the long-run, or equilibrium, values. This horizon agrees reasonably well with the horizon of the MPS model.

Conclusions

It is difficult to draw a finely defined set of conclusions from the set of studies which have been examined. There exists a range of elasticity estimates among these studies which cannot be reconciled with the information which is readily available at the present time.

However, while a single point cannot be established as the most probable value for the interest elasticity of the money supply, it appears that the studies do provide information which can be of value in policy discussions concerning the control of the money stock. A broad, but valuable conclusion is that the interest elasticity of the money supply during the sample period of these studies appears to be extremely low, It seems appropriate to conclude with almost complete certainty that the long-run elasticity during this period was less than 0.5 and that the impact elasticity (one quarter) was probably no greater than 0.10 to 0.15. All these elasticities are relevant for policy actions which result in changes in the Treasury bill rate, while leaving the discount rate unchanged.

For the class of policy actions which simultaneously alters the Treasury bill rate and the discount rate by the same amount from an initial position where the two are approximately equal, it is the sum of the interest elasticities of the money supply which is relevant. Two of the studies suggest that the elasticity with respect to the discount rate is slightly smaller than that with respect to the bill rate. The estimation of these relationships involves constraints on parameters, and hence, is not a valid test of the hypothesis that the two elasticities are significantly different. In the Goldfeld study, where there are no constraints imposed on the estimated parameters, the estimated coefficient of elasticity for the discount rate is considerably smaller in absolute value than that of the bill rate. Therefore, it would appear that while the interest elasticity of the money supply relationship is likely to be smaller when both rates are changed simultaneously, it is almost certain that the coefficient of elasticity will remain positive. Furthermore, the elasticity under such a policy probably does not exceed one-half to two-thirds of the interest elasticity under a policy of keeping the discount rate fixed.

The available evidence suggests quite conclusively that the short-run feedbacks through interest rate changes, which would be generated by policy changes in reserve aggregates, are very weak and should cause little, if any, difficulty for the implementation of policy actions aimed at controlling the money stock through the control of a reserve aggregate. Of course, the size of random fluctuations in the reserve multiplier remains a major factor in determining the size of deviations of the money stock from its targeted value. An issue which remains to be investigated is the size of the variance of the multipliers associated with various reserve concepts.

B. Money Demand

In Section I most of the articles indicated that one's view of the way monetary impulses affected the economy had important implications for the specification of the monetary demand relation.

In this section John T. Boorman reviews the major formulations of the money demand function. He compares the results of alternative tests of these relations that have been presented in the literature. His survey provides a summary treatment of the current consensus that has been achieved on the elements deemed most important in the determination of the public's demand for money.

The Evidence on the Demand for Money: Theoretical Formulations and Empirical Results

John T. Boorman

Introduction

Numerous theories have been proposed to explain the public's demand for money. Though the range of hypotheses implicit in these theories is extremely broad, there are certain important elements common to all of them. Most significantly, almost all of these theories can be generalized into a proposition about the existence of a stable relationship between a few important economic variables and the stock of money demanded.

While diverse theories often posit similar variables to explain the demand for money, they frequently differ in the specific role assigned to each. For example, in the simplest version of the transactions theory of the demand for money, the stock of money demanded is hypothesized to be strictly proportional to a single variable—the volume of transactions to be facilitated by that money stock. In comparison, the inventory theoretic view, which recognizes the interest rate as an opportunity cost of holding money balances and introduces brokerage fees and other charges as explicit costs of switching wealth between interest-bearing assets and money, denies this proportionality between money and income. In this model the minimization of the

This article was revised especially for this volume. The original article appeared in John T. Boorman and Thomas M. Havrilesky, *Money Supply, Money Demand, and Macroeconomic Models* (Arlington Heights, Ill.: AHM Publishing Corporation, 1972). The author thanks Thomas Havrilesky for helpful comments.

total cost of managing money balances leads to a solution that suggests the possibility of substantial economies of scale in the demand for money.

As another example, in the liquidity preference theories of John Maynard Keynes and James Tobin the role of money as an asset is stressed and the motives for holding money examined. An analysis of the costs (income foregone) and benefits (risks avoided) of holding wealth in the form of money balances suggests a hypothesis in which income and the interest rate on alternative financial assets are suggested as the primary determinants of desired money balances. In comparison, Milton Friedman's "Restatement" of the quantity theory eschews a specific focus on the "roles" of money or on the "motives" of individuals in holding money balances.[1] Instead, Friedman emphasizes the services yielded by money in individual and business portfolios. In this view money is simply one among the many assets—including physical and human assets—held by the public. This leads to the hypothesis that all of the alternatives available to the wealth holder may influence his desired money balances.

These examples of alternative money demand hypotheses suggest some of the major questions that have been the focus of empirical investigation. A more complete list would include the following specific problems:

1. What empirical measure should be used to represent the theoretical concept of "money"?

2. How are empirically testable money demand functions conventionally specified? In this connection it is useful to examine some of the more common formulations that have included either a role for expectations in the determination of desired money balances or a distinction between the long-run equilibrium level and the short-run adjustment pattern by which equilibrium is approached.

3. What is the role of the interest rate in the money demand function? This issue raises several related questions:

   a. If the interest rate is statistically important in the determination of the demand for money, what is the interest elasticity of money balances?

   b. Which one of the alternative interest rate measures available is most relevant to the determination of the demand for money?

   c. Given that the interest rate is important in the money demand function, has evidence been presented that would support the existence (historical or potential) of a "liquidity trap"?

4. What is the relative significance of income, wealth, and other economic variables that have been suggested along with the interest rate as determinants of the demand for money?

[1]M. Friedman, "The Quantity Theory of Money, A Restatement," in Milton Friedman (ed.), *Studies in the Quantity Theory of Money* (Chicago, 1956). See D. Patinkin, "The Chicago Tradition, the Quantity Theory, and Friedman," *Journal of Money, Credit, and Banking,* 1 (February 1969), pp. 46-70.

5. Do money demand functions that include the essential arguments suggested by alternative theories appear to be stable over the postwar period?

These are the major issues raised in the empirical literature on the demand for money. Each of these will be considered in turn.[2]

The Empirical Definition of Money

What assets ought to be included in our measure of "the money stock"? If we focus on those theories that emphasize the transactions motive for holding money, the proper definition of money is not a profound problem. Money should be defined to consist only of those assets that serve as generally acceptable media of exchange. It is widely agreed that only commercial bank demand deposits and currency in circulation provide this service. However, if the public's demand for money is viewed as arising from a speculative motive, the list of assets in the definition of money may be expanded to include at least some assets that are stable in nominal value, i.e., fixed dollar assets whose value is independent of variations in the interest rate. Finally, if the demand for money is approached as part of the general theory of demand, all assets that are close substitutes for the media of exchange (and respond to the same yields in the demand function) should be included in the definition. This approach clearly indicates that the proper definition of money is largely an empirical question.

Allan H. Meltzer has enunciated one possible criterion for selecting the appropriate definition of money.

> The problem is one of defining money so that a stable demand function can be shown to have existed under differing institutional arrangements, changes in social and political environment, and changes in economic conditions, or to explain the effects of such changes on the function.[3]

This criterion focuses on the implications of the definition of money for the degree of control that the monetary authority has over crucial macroeconomic variables.[4] The money stock and interest rates are thought to have a strong effect upon aggregate demand, employment, and the price level in the economy. If the demand for money is unstable (shifts unpredictably), the effect of monetary policy actions on the equilibrium money stock and interest rates will be uncertain. In short, stability of the money demand function and a capability on the part of the monetary authority to influence closely the stock of assets corresponding to the theoretical concept of money employed in that function would seem to be necessary conditions for the successful

---

[2]More general issues, particularly those dealing with econometric problems in the estimation of money demand functions, will be discussed—often in footnotes—at various points of the text.

[3]A. H. Meltzer, "The Demand for Money: The Evidence from the Time Series," *Journal of Political Economy,* 71 (June 1963), p. 222.

[4]There are, of course, additional criteria by which to define a measure of the money stock. George

implementation of monetary policy.[5] These conditions will allow the authorities to exert a predictable influence over the equilibrium stock of money, the interest rate, and other variables in the money demand equation.

Economists traditionally have defined money in the "narrow" sense as the sum of demand deposit liabilities of commercial banks and currency held by the public. However, a number of analysts include time deposits at commercial banks within their measure of the money stock. Milton Friedman, for example, views time deposits as "a temporary abode of purchasing power" and includes them in the "broad" measure of money that he employs in his empirical work. A few researchers go beyond even this "broad" concept to include such things as savings and loan shares, mutual savings bank deposits, and claims against other financial intermediaries in their measure of "money." Conceptually, of course, it is possible to go even further and include still other financial assets (or even some measure of credit availability, such as commercial bank "lines of credit") in a measure of money.[6]

In this survey, evidence on the question of the best definition of money must be satisfied in accord with the Meltzer criterion. David Laidler has suggested an explicit set of conditions by which to evaluate the relative stability of alternative empirical functions. As he expresses it:

> A "more stable demand for money function" may be taken to be one that requires knowledge of fewer variables and their parameters in order to predict the demand for money with a given degree of accuracy or, which amounts to the same thing, one that yields parameter estimates that are less subject to variation when the same arguments are included in the function and hence enable more accurate prediction of the demand for money to be made.[7]

Kaufman, following Milton Friedman and David Meiselman, defines money according to its correlation with income (taking into consideration the possible lead-lag relationship between money and income). In selecting the set of financial assets to be included in the money supply, he employs two criteria originally specified by Friedman and Meiselman: choose that set that (1) has the highest correlation with income and (2) has a higher correlation with income than any of the components separately. This alternative operational approach, unlike the Meltzer criterion, derives from the proposition that the equilibrium nominal money stock can be controlled by the monetary authority and suggests a rather specific theoretical model on which to base monetary policy. The Meltzer criterion is preferred here since it is compatible with a more broadly defined set of money demand functions. See G. G. Kaufman, "More on an Empirical Definition of Money," *American Economic Review*, 59 (March 1969), pp. 78-87, M. Friedman and D. Meiselman, "Relative Stability of Monetary Velocity and the Investment Multiplier in the United States 1897-1957," Commission on Money and Credit, *Stabilization Policies* (Englewood Cliffs, N.J. 1963).

Frederick C. Schadrack, in "An Empirical Approach to the Definition of Money," *Monetary Aggregates and Monetary Policy*. Federal Reserve Bank of New York (1974) pp. 28-34 extends these empirical criteria to include goodness of fit, stability over time and predictive accuracy in regression equations with GNP as a dependent variable and six different monetary aggregates as alternative explanatory variables.

[5]See S. J. Maisel, "Controlling Monetary Aggregates," in *Controlling Monetary Aggregates: Proceedings of the Monetary Conference of the Federal Reserve Bank of Boston* (June 1969), pp. 152-174, and M. J. Hamburger, "The Demand for Money in 1971: Was There a Shift? A Comment," *Journal of Money, Credit and Banking*, 5 (May 1973), pp. 720-725.

[6]See A. B. Laffer, "Trade Credit and the Money Market," *Journal of Political Economy*, 78 (March/April 1970), pp. 239-267.

[7]D. Laidler, "The Definition of Money: Theoretical and Empirical Problems," *The Journal of Money, Credit and Banking*, 1 (August 1968), p. 516.

In an empirical study Laidler (40) contends that the most stable money demand function he has been able to isolate is one employing Friedman's broad definition of money ($M2$). This contrasts with earlier results presented by Karl Brunner and Allan Meltzer (5), in which they found that the narrow measure ($M1$)—demand deposits plus currency—yielded the most satisfactory money demand relation.

What accounts for these contrasting conclusions? First, these two studies specify different explanatory variables in their money demand equations. Second, they use data from different time periods to estimate the parameters of these relations. Finally, they employ different procedures to test their hypotheses. Since the relative performance of alternative measures of the money stock in empirical money demand functions is likely to be highly sensitive to all of these considerations, it is impossible to choose the better measure of money on the basis of these studies alone.

However, an alternative empirical approach is available. The stability of the money demand function is closely linked to the degree of substitutability that exists between money, as it is defined in that function, and other financial assets. For example, if the secular and cyclical changes in the competitive position of financial intermediaries make available substitutes for currency in circulation and demand deposits held by the nonbank public (the narrowly defined money stock), the demand for money, so defined, may shift as these substitutes appear. In such a case a demand function for some broader measure of money, one that includes these close substitutes, would be more stable, i.e., would shift less over time, than a function defined on a narrow money measure.[8] Under these conditions monetary policy actions that concentrate on the narrower measure of money would be focusing on an unstable, shifting target. Policy actions that focus on broader measures of money would be more appropriate.

A substantial body of evidence has now been presented on this issue. Specifically, the question that has been addressed is the following: Are assets such as commercial bank time deposits, savings and loan shares, mutual savings bank deposits, and others that have been suggested for inclusion in a measure of "money" sufficiently close substitutes for commercial bank demand deposits to warrant treating them in a single measure?

In a study on the demand for liquid assets by the public, Edgar Feige (15) mea-

---

[8]Gurley and Shaw, for example, emphasize the substitutability between claims on certain financial intermediaries and demand deposits at commercial banks, and they argue that "money" must be defined so as to include these substitutes. Evidence supporting this position is presented below. See J. G. Gurley and E. S. Shaw, *Money in a Theory of Finance* (Washington, D.C., 1960).

This view is also embodied in the report of the Radcliffe Committee, which views "liquidity" and "the stock of liquid assets" held by the public as the relevant concept on which to focus in monetary theory and policy. In this view only policy actions that change the *total liquidity* of the public—and not simply the composition of the public's stock of liquid assets—are likely to lead to predictable results. This is so because of the high degree of substitutability that exists between the narrowly defined money stock and near-monies. See *The Radcliffe Report,* Committee on the Working of the Monetary System (London, 1959).

sured the cross elasticities of demand between various assets.[9] Using data on the volume of liquid assets held by households in each state of the United States for each year during the period from 1949 to 1959, Feige found that the yields on nonbank intermediary liabilities (savings and loan shares, etc.) did not affect the demand for money. Ownership of each of these assets was found to be highly sensitive only to its "own rate" of interest. In Feige's results there appears to be little substitutability between demand deposits, time deposits, savings and loan shares, or mutual savings bank deposits. In fact, demand deposits were found to be mildly *complementary* with savings and loan shares and mutual savings bank deposits; demand and time deposits at commercial banks were only very weak substitutes for each other. From this and other evidence Feige concludes that the narrow definition of money is the preferred definition when estimating money demand functions and that analysts need not concern themselves with the effects of the activities of other intermediaries on the public's demand for money.[10]

Feige's conclusions are disputed by T. H. Lee (46) and V. K. Chetty (10). Lee's work will be described in detail in connection with our survey of the relevance of alternative interest rate measures in the money demand function. Briefly, Lee suggests that the liabilities of financial intermediaries, particularly savings and loan shares, are indeed very good *substitutes* for money. Rather than supporting Friedman's "broad" definition of money, however, he claims that the definition should be extended to encompass an even broader collection of assets, including as a minimum, shares in savings and loan associations.

Chetty makes a similar proposal. In his work a technique originally developed in production theory to measure the substitutability between capital and labor in the production process is employed to measure the substitutability among assets in the consumer's utility function.[11] Chetty assumes that consumers attempt to maximize

[9]The cross elasticity of demand is the most frequently used measure of substitutability. If we consider two assets X and Y, and the returns on each, i_x and i_y, the cross elasticity of X with respect to Y equals the percentage change in the quantity of X demanded, divided by the percentage change in the return of Y.

$$\eta_{x.y} = \frac{\Delta x / x}{\Delta i_y / i_y}$$

If an increase in the return on asset Y (Δi_y positive) causes a switch in holdings from X to Y, Δx will be negative and the cross elasticity will be negative. In this case the assets X and Y are said to be "substitutes." If $\eta_{x.y}$ is positive, indicating a *direct* relationship between the return on Y and holdings of asset X, these assets are said to be "complements."

[10]Feige's methods in deriving these results are subject to several criticisms. First, there are serious questions as to whether the way in which he measures the rate of return on commercial bank demand deposits reflects the relevant return considered by asset holders in allocating their portfolios. Second, his data measure the assets owned in a state by residents of all states when, in fact, the relevant measure for his purposes should have been the assets owned by the residents of each state. His data probably require the inclusion of rates on out-of-state assets in order to capture the effects of ownership that crosses state lines. These problems detract from Feige's results.

[11]See K. J. Arrow, H. B. Chenery, B. S. Minhas, and R. M. Solow, "Capital-Labor Substitution and Economic Efficiency," *Review of Economics and Statistics*, 63 (August 1961), pp. 225-250.

their utility (subject to the budget constraint) by combining money (demand deposits plus currency in circulation), time deposits, and other assets to produce desired levels of liquidity at the lowest cost. By combining the conditions required for utility maximization with the budget constraint, he derives an equation that contains parameters that, when estimated, yield measures of the partial elasticities of substitution between money and other assets.

On the basis of his estimates, Chetty concludes that while savings and loan shares and mutual savings bank deposits are rather good substitutes for money, time deposits appear to be virtually perfect substitutes. This last finding supports Friedman's use of the "broad" definition of money. Nevertheless, as did Lee, Chetty suggests that an even broader measure of money may be more appropriate and shows how such a measure may be calculated. Employing weights that measure the "moneyness' of assets as implied by their substitutability with demand deposits and currency, he constructs a weighted average of demand deposits and currency (with weights constrained to unity), time deposits (TD), saving and loan shares (SL), and mutual savings bank deposits (MS). The final form of the equation defining this average "money" stock is

$$M_a = DD + C + TD + 0.615SL + 0.88\ MS.$$

Note that the coefficient (unity) on the time deposit variable reflects Chetty's conclusion of perfect substitutability between these deposits and narrowly defined money.[12]

While these findings by Lee and Chetty clearly favor a broader measure of money, an important recent study by Stephen Goldfeld (24), which provides consistent and comparable data on several of the questions addressed in this survey, contains persuasive evidence that focusing on narrow measures of money will yield demand functions with significantly superior predictive capabilities to those that define money in some broader fashion. Goldfeld does not concentrate explicitly on the substitutability of various potential components of "money." Rather, his procedure is to confront various hypotheses with the same set of data and very closely related functional specifications. This has the advantage of limiting the number of factors that can be introduced to explain differing statistical results—the major problem in making comparative judgements on the diverse evidence presented by the authors cited above.

Goldfeld begins by noting that the inclusion of time deposits in the definition of money seems questionable on theoretical grounds "since it constrains the specification . . . of $M1$ (narrow money) and time deposits to be the same" and potentially distorts the influence of interest rates on the component measures. However, he recognizes that these weaknesses could be offset if an empirically more stable de-

---

[12]This evidence also lends support to the broad measure of money used by Lydall in his empirical study of the demand for money in Britain and increases the importance of Lydall's conclusions on the issues discussed below. See H. Lydall, "Income, Assets, and the Demand for Money," *Review of Economics and Statistics,* 40 (February 1958), pp. 1-14.

mand function resulted from this formulation. His results, however, suggest that this "is definitely not the case."[13]

The alternative equations Goldfeld estimated with broad money include a lagged dependent variable, income, and interest rates as arguments. His estimates are such as to make one suspicious of the use of the broad money measure as the dependent variable. First, the time deposit rate appears to have a negligible influence on holdings of broad money. This may be an empirical reflection of the offsetting effects of this rate on demand deposits and time deposits and the loss of information involved in aggregating over those components. Second, the long-run elasticity of broad money is extremely high, exceeding the elasticities estimated separately for each of the components. Both of these results suggest serious problems with a function specified on the broad money measure. Goldfeld's additional statistical tests strengthen the initial suspicion engendered by those results. While the traditional criterion statistics—R^2 and the standard error of the estimate—provide little help choosing between the broad money or narrow money formulation, dynamic simulations and stability tests provide persuasive evidence of the superiority of the narrow money form. The broad money equation yields "ludicrously" large errors in long-run forecasting tests and is easily rejected on the basis of formal stability tests.[14]

Additional tests on the forecasting performance and stability of equations estimated for each of the components of $M2$ (broad money), suggest his general conclusion that

> the simple specification used for $M1$ will not work for time deposits, and . . . even given the questionable time deposit equation, the ex post forecasts of $M2$ obtained from the aggregate equation are inferior to those obtained from adding together the separate component forecasts, thus suggesting that *aggregation is inflicting some positive harm*[15] (emphasis added).

In short, Goldfeld's results suggest that in model building and other work *more* rather than *less* disaggregation of the money demand equation seems to be desirable.[16]

---

[13]S. M. Goldfeld, "The Demand for Money Revisited," *Brookings Papers on Economic Activity* (3:1973), p. 593.

[14]Goldfeld's primary test consists of dynamically simulating his estimated equations. This involves forecasting both within-sample and out-of-sample values for the dependent variable and evaluating the quality of those forecasts by a measure such as the root mean square error. His tests take two general forms: (1) four quarter ex post forecasts made by taking sequentially longer subperiods within the sample from which to derive coefficient estimates and evaluating forecasts for four quarters beyond each successive estimating period and (2) splitting the sample period in half, deriving estimates from the first half data and evaluating the long-run forecasting ability of the equation over the second half of the sample period. In both cases the broad money equation performed substantially worse than the narrow money form. These results were formerly confirmed through the use of the Chow test of stability. See Goldfeld, *op. cit.*, pp. 592-595.

[15]*Ibid.*, p. 595.

[16]Dickson and Starleaf suggest a similar conclusion. Their estimates of various functions that include distributed lags on all arguments suggest that "the Demand Functions for $M1$ and TD (time deposits) appear to be so different as to dictate their separate, rather than combined, analysis." H. D. Dickson and D. R. Starleaf, "Polynomial Distributed Lag Structures in the Demand Function for Money," *Journal of Finance*, 27 (December 1972), p. 1042.

Because of these conflicting results, many economists feel that this issue is still unresolved, and further evidence is sought. In the remainder of this survey, therefore, whenever we are reporting on empirical work, we shall cite the specific definition of money used by a particular author. In several instances, work reported on in connection with other issues will have direct implications for the appropriate empirical definition of money. Let us now turn to an examination of the general form of the money demand functions specified in empirical work and to a review of the evidence on the role of the interest rate in determining the public's demand for money. This latter issue has critical implications for national economic policy.

Conventional Formulations of the Demand for Money Function

In most formulations of the money demand function real money balances are related to "the" interest rate on relevant substitute assets and some scale variable related to economic activity, such as income or wealth. The equation specified is sometimes linear but more often exponential in form. These alternative forms may be specified as follows:

$$\frac{M_d}{P} = m_d = a_1 + a_2 i + a_3 X \tag{1}$$

$$\frac{M_d}{P} = m_d = \alpha i^{\beta_1} X^{\beta_2}, \tag{2}$$

where M_d/P is the stock of real money balances demanded, i is an interest rate, and X represents other variables such as wealth, permanent income, or current income.[17]

---

[17]Money demand functions are generally cast in real terms on the assumption that the price elasticity of nominal money balances is unity. The implication of this assumption is that price-level changes alone will cause no change in the demand for *real* money balances or, alternatively, that the demand for nominal balances is proportional to the price level. This assumption implies that the public is free of money illusion in its demand for real money balances. Let us examine this assumption further. Let X in equation (2) above be a measure of real wealth, W. Then;

$$\frac{M_d}{P} = \alpha \times i^{\beta_1} \cdot W^{\beta_2}.$$

If *nominal* money balances were specified as a function of *nominal* wealth, this equation would be

$$M_d = \alpha \times i^{\beta_1} \times (P \cdot W)^{\beta_2'}.$$

But these two equations are quite different. The first equation implies that the price-level elasticity is unity—the exponent of P equals one—and β_2 is the wealth elasticity of *real* money balances. But in the latter form β_2' is some *average* of the price level and wealth elasticities of nominal money balances. Consequently, if the price level elasticity is really unity, but the true wealth elasticity is not equal to one,

When equation (2) is employed, a logarithmic transformation is made so that the equation is *linear* in the logarithms of the variables and, more importantly, linear in the parameters to be estimated. Taking natural logs of both sides of the equation;

$$ln \frac{M_d}{P} = ln\ m_d = ln\ \alpha + \beta_1\ ln\ i + \beta_2\ ln\ X.^{18} \tag{3}$$

These simple linear (in the coefficients) models may be fitted to empirical observations of variables if, and only if, two additional assumptions are made. First, we must assume that the money market is always in equilibrium so that desired money balances, M_d, equal the actual money stock reported in the statistical series, M. Second, we must assume that there exist exact empirical counterparts to the theoretical variables specified; for example, the average of daily rates quoted by the New York Federal Reserve Bank on U.S. Treasury Bills may be chosen as the empirical measure of "the interest rate." With data on each of the variables specified in the equa-

---

β_2' will be *biased* toward that value and will not be a good estimate of the true wealth elasticity. To avoid that bias, investigators have generally chosen to work with functions cast in real terms.

The validity of this procedure is supported by evidence presented by Allan Meltzer (49). His work indicates that when the price variable is included as a separate argument in a log-linear equation, its coefficient is very close to unity. Furthermore, if nominal wealth is employed in an equation with nominal balances specified as the dependent variable, the wealth elasticity is closer to unity than if these measures are cast in real terms.

Additional evidence on this point has been presented by Harold D. Dickson and Dennis R. Starleaf (13). Employing an equation similar in form to (3) but with distributed lag functions defined on the independent variables, including GNP, they found that the estimated price elasticity of the narrowly defined money stock, $M1$, was not significantly different from unity. On this evidence they concluded that the demand for real money balances is homogenous of degree zero in the price level; therefore, the demand for money is free of money illusion. On this and other evidence the assumed proportionality of nominal money balances to the price level would appear to have a firm basis in empirical analysis.

[18]In this form the coefficients β_1, and β_2 can be directly estimated by linear regression techniques, and those coefficients will be elasticities. This may be shown as follows: Let $\eta_{m \cdot i}$ denote the interest elasticity of money demand (let m in this instance represent real money balances demanded); then,

$$\eta_{m \cdot i} = \frac{\partial m/m}{\partial i/i} = \frac{\partial m}{\partial i} \cdot \frac{i}{m};$$

but, from equation (2),

$$\partial M/\partial i = \beta_1\ (\alpha X^{\beta_2}) \cdot i^{(\beta_1 - 1)};$$

therefore,

$$\eta_{M \cdot i} = \beta_1\ (\alpha X^{\beta_2}) \cdot i^{(\beta_1 - 1)} \cdot \frac{i}{\alpha X^{\beta_2} \cdot i^{\beta_1}} = \frac{\beta_1 \cdot i^{\beta_1}}{i^{\beta_1}} = \beta_1.$$

Consequently, elasticities may be estimated directly by employing the log-linear form of equation (2) in the regression procedure.

tion, multiple regression methods may be employed to derive estimates of the coefficients in these single equation models.[19]

Several modifications can be made to this basic equation to introduce significant additional flexibility into the hypotheses. One of the most important of these is the introduction of the concept of "desired," as opposed to "actual," money balances and the specification of a "partial adjustment" mechanism by which actual holdings adjust to desired levels.

For example, desired real money balances, m_T^*, may be postulated to depend upon the same variables specified in equation (3)

$$ln \ m_T^* = ln \ \alpha + \beta_1 \ ln \ i_T + \beta_2 \ ln \ X_T \qquad (4)$$

and the adjustment process of actual to desired levels of money demand may be specified as follows:

$$(ln \ m_T - ln \ m_{T-1}) = \lambda \ (ln \ m_T^* - ln \ m_{T-1}). \qquad (5)$$

In this form λ, the adjustment coefficient, measures the rate at which adjustments are made to bring *actual* money holdings in line with the current *desired* level. Generally, λ is specified to be between zero and one, indicating that any such process of adjustment is only partially successful during one period. (The magnitude of λ will often be explained in empirical literature as reflecting the cost of adjusting portfolios relative to the cost of not adjusting them).

While m_T^*, the current desired level of real money holdings, is not directly observable or measurable, postulation of the above adjustment process allows derivation of an estimating equation with solely observable quantities. Substituting equation (4) into the adjustment equation (5) and rearranging yields

$$ln \ m_T = \lambda ln \ \alpha + \lambda \beta_1 \ ln \ i_T + \lambda \beta_2 \ ln \ X_T + (1 - \lambda) \ ln \ m_{T-1}. \qquad (6)$$

In this form λ can be calculated from the coefficient estimate of the lagged dependent variable, m_{T-1}, and α, β_1, and β_2 can be calculated from this value and the coefficients estimated for the other terms. If, for example, a coefficient of 0.60 is estimated

[19]Least-squares regression analysis may be defined as a procedure whereby an hypothesized relationship may be confronted with actual data in order to derive numerical estimates of the parameters specified in that relationship. Under specified conditions concerning the nature of the hypothesized relationship and the characteristics of the data employed, these techniques will yield estimates with certain desirable statistical properties. In the models above, for example, data on the size of the money stock, the value of the interest rate, and, say, national wealth may be employed in regression analysis to derive estimates of β_1, the interest elasticity of money demand, and β_2, the wealth elasticity of money demand. For a discussion of the mechanics of least-squares regression and the properties of least-squares estimators, see S. Hymans, *Probability Theory* (Englewood Cliffs, N.J., 1966) Chapter 8, and J. Kmenta, *Elements of Econometrics* (New York, 1971), Chapters 7 and 10.

on the lagged term, then $\lambda = (1 - 0.60) = 0.40$, suggesting that in each period 40 percent of the gap between actual and desired money balances will be closed by the public's actions.[20]

While this form has proved useful in many applications, it has the unfortunate characteristic of restricting the adjustment pattern in the dependent variable to be the same regardless of the source of the initial disturbance. Whether an interest rate change or an income (or wealth) change disturbs the initial (long-run) equilibrium, the adjustment path to a new equilibrium must be the same. There are several plausible theoretical reasons why this is not likely to be the case. In addition, empirical results often suggest implausibly long lags for the adjustment process. These long lags are difficult to explain on the basis of probable costs involved in adjusting financial portfolios.

An alternative, and perhaps superior, rationale for the presence of a significant lagged term in the money demand function derives from the "adaptive expectations" model. In this formulation it is assumed that the public is actually holding its desired level of money balances but that level itself is assumed to depend upon expected values of one or more of the independent variables rather than on current actual values. Thus,

$$ln\ m_T = ln\ \alpha + \beta_1\ ln\ i_T + \beta_2\ ln\ X_T^e, \tag{7}$$

where X_T^e is the value of X expected to prevail in period t. Since X_T^e is not observable some hypothesis must be specified on how expectations are formulated. It may be postulated, for example, that current expectations are formed by modifying previous expectations in the light of current experience. For example:

$$ln\ X_T^e - ln\ X_{T-1}^e = (1 - \lambda)\ (ln\ X_T - ln\ X_{T-1}^e) \tag{8}$$

or equivalently,

$$ln\ X_T^e = (1 - \lambda)\ ln\ X_T + \lambda\ ln\ X_{T-1}^e \qquad 0 \leq \lambda < 1.$$

This formulation depends upon knowledge of X_T in period *t*. An alternative formulation, which avoids this implicit assumption that X_T be known in advance of formu-

---

[20]In this formulation, the long run interest and income (or wealth) elasticities are β_1 and β_2, respectively. The short run elasticities are given by $\lambda\beta_1$ and $\lambda\beta_2$. For example, in steady-state equilibrium, $M_T = M_{T-1} = M_{T-2}\ldots$
Then, from equation (6),

$$ln\ M_T - (1 - \lambda)\ ln\ M_{T-1} = \lambda\ ln\ \alpha + \lambda\ \beta_1\ ln\ i_T + \lambda\ \beta_2\ ln\ X_T$$

$$ln\ M_T\ [1 - 1 + \lambda] = \lambda\ ln\ \alpha + \lambda\ \beta_1\ ln\ i_T + \lambda\ \beta_2\ ln\ X_T$$

$$ln\ M_T = ln\ \alpha + \beta_1\ ln\ i_T + \beta_2\ ln\ X_T$$

as in equation (4). Because of the assumed constraint on λ, short run elasticities will be smaller (in absolute terms) than longer run elasticities.

lating the expectation, makes the revision of expectations dependent upon the most recent error in expectations, assuming data on current period values are not available, i.e.,

$$ln \, X_T^e - ln \, X_{T-1}^e = (1 - \lambda) \, (ln \, X_{T-1} - ln \, X_{T-1}^e). \tag{9}$$

In this form expectations are revised by some fraction of the discrepency between last period's expectations and the actual value of X_{T-1}.

Either of these forms can be employed to derive an estimating equation specified solely in terms of observable values. For example, substituting the basic demand relation (4) into the first of the adaptive expectations models specified above (8) and applying a Koyck transformation yields,[21]

$$ln \, m_T = (1-\lambda) \, ln \, \alpha + (1-\lambda) \, \beta_1 \, ln \, X_T + (1-\lambda) \, \beta_2 \, ln \, i_T + \lambda \, ln \, m_{T-1}. \tag{10}$$

In this formulation the adaptive expectations model is formally the same as the partial adjustment model although the interpretation of the estimated coefficient on the lagged dependent variable and other variables is very different in the two equations. The adaptive expectations model, however, is the starting point for a whole family of models that allow the introduction of a great many alternative hypotheses into the basic structure. In particular, different expectational patterns may be specified for each of the independent variables in the equation or expectations on one or more of the variables may be allowed to adjust in different proportions to two or more of the previous expectations (forecasting) errors.[22] For example,

$$ln \, X_T^e - ln \, X_{T-1}^e = (1 - \lambda_1) \, (ln \, X_T - ln \, X_T^e)$$
$$+ \, (1 - \lambda_2) \, (ln \, X_{T-1} - ln \, X_{T-1}^e), \tag{11}$$

where λ_1 is not restricted to equal λ_2. In addition, the adaptive expectations model may be combined with the partial adjustment model to capture the potential lagged effects generated by each. An example of this will be seen below.

Unfortunately, the capacity to specify new and richer lag structures rather quickly surpasses the econometric ability to derive useful statistical estimates of the included parameters.[23] Because of this limitation, a far more general lag model has gained wide popularity. The Almon distributed lag technique allows estimation of a rather general lag pattern that can be rationalized in any number of ways. Only the length of the lag and the degree of the polynominal along which the weights lie must be

[21]See Kmenta, *op. cit.*, pp. 474 ff.
[22]See Goldfeld, *op. cit.*, p. 600.
[23]See Z. Griliches, "Distributed Lags: A Survey," *Econometrica*, 35 (January 1967).

specified in advance.[24] Perhaps the major advantage of this form over the models specified above is the elimination of the somewhat restrictive assumption that the weights describing the assumed adjustment path lie along a monotonically declining simple geometric lag structure. On the other hand, the method requires less care in the formulation of detailed hypotheses to rationalize the introduction of any lag structure.

Some form of one of the basic models specified above underlies most of the empirical work on the money demand function. We shall now turn to an examination of the results of that work for one of the most important issues in this area—the importance of the interest rate in determining the public's money demand.

The Role of Interest Rate in the Money Demand Function

Single-Equation Estimates

The stimulus for much of the econometric work on the demand for money and for the primary focus of that work on the importance of the interest rate as an argument in the money demand function derives from Keynes' presentation of the liquidity preference theory in *The General Theory of Employment, Interest, and Money* (1936). Although Pigou as early as 1917 had suggested that the interest rate was a potentially important factor determining the public's money holding behavior, it was Keynes full explication of the "speculative" motive for holding "idle" money balances that provided the major impetus for testing this hypothesis. Research has been further encouraged by the work of Milton Friedman (19). Contrary to the findings of most other investigators, he finds little basis for assigning a significant role for the interest rate in determining the demand for money.

One of the earliest studies to address this issue was done by Henry Latané (45). Latané specified and tested three alternative models of the demand for money. In his first test he proposed a constant ratio of total money balances to nominal national income, $M/Y = k$. This hypothesis represented a crude form of the quantity theory. By showing graphically that this ratio was highly variable, fluctuating between a low of 0.26 to a high of 0.50 in the period from 1919 to 1952, Latané rejected this hypothesis.

In his second test Latané proposed a Keynesian-type money demand function, in which the total demand for money balances was specified to be the sum of a transactions component dependent on the level of income and an asset or speculative component dependent on the rate of interest:

$$M = a \left(\frac{1}{i}\right) + bY + c. \qquad (12)$$

[24]See S. Almon, "The Distributed Lag Between Capital Appropriations and Expenditures," *Econometrica,* 33 (January 1965).

Latané showed that this form implies a continually declining ratio of money balances to income as income increases (and the interest rate remains constant).[25] Since empirical evidence indicated that this was not the case, Latané also rejected this form.

Latané's last model proposed that the ratio of nominal money balances to (nominal) aggregate income was dependent upon the rate of interest:

$$\frac{M}{Y} = f(i). \tag{13}$$

In testing this model, he specified a simple linear form, and derived the following regression estimates:

$$\frac{M}{Y} = 0.0074 \left(\frac{1}{i}\right) + 0.1088.$$

This equation was then used to predict values of the dependent variable for dates not included in the original data. The success of these predictions prompted Latané to conclude that he had identified a stable behavioral relation between cash balances, income, and the long-term rate of interest. Specifically, "In the past thirty years, each 1.0 percent change in $(1/i)$ has tended to be associated with a change of 0.8 percent in gross national product held as currency and demand deposits."[26]

One characteristic of Latané's last model, shared by the money demand functions tested by several other authors, should be mentioned. The equation form chosen by Latané to test the interest sensitivity of the cash balance ratio constrains the income elasticity of the demand for money to equal unity.[27] The effects of this arbitrary

[25]This may be seen by dividing both sides of equation (12) by Y:

$$\frac{M}{Y} = \frac{a}{i \cdot Y} + b + \frac{c}{Y}$$

If Y increases, a/Y and c/Y will decline. Thus, with the interest rate constant, the proportion of income held in the form of money balances would decline as income increased.

[26]H. A. Latané, "Cash Balances and the Interest Rate—A Pragmatic Approach," *Review of Economics and Statistics*, 36 (November 1954), p. 460.

[27]This may be shown as follows: Let $\eta_{M \cdot Y}$ denote the income elasticity of money balances. Then,

$$\eta_{M \cdot Y} = \frac{\Delta M/M}{\Delta Y/Y} = \frac{\Delta M}{\Delta Y} \cdot \frac{Y}{M}.$$

But from Latané's basic model (13), we may write

$$\Delta M = f(i) \cdot \Delta Y.$$

Therefore,

$$\eta_{M \cdot Y} = f(i) \cdot \frac{Y}{M} = \frac{f(i) \cdot Y}{f(i) \cdot Y} = 1.$$

restriction on the value of the income elasticity of money balances can only be judged by comparing the results of this model with those derived from models that are not so constrained.

Several investigators, in testing the liquidity preference theory, have attempted to isolate the "asset" or "idle" balance component of the public's total money holdings from money balances held strictly for transactions purposes and to estimate the influence of the interest rate on the former component alone. James Tobin (64), in an early study, and Martin Bronfenbrenner and Thomas Mayer (4), in subsequent work, employed this approach.

In calculating the idle balance component of total money balances, Tobin (like Latané) assumed that desired *transactions* balances are proportional to the level of income. To determine the exact factor of proportionality between transaction balances and income, Tobin further assumed that during periods of very high interest rates and high economic activity, when the ratio of total money holdings to income is at its lowest level, idle balances are zero and the total money stock is held solely for transactions purposes. The minimum value for this ratio was found to occur in 1929. Therefore, Tobin asserted that this 1929 ratio actually measures the constant factor of proportionality between transactions balances and income. This may be seen symbolically. Let

$$M_{total} = M_{idle} + M_{trans} = f(i) + kY,$$

where

$$M_{idle} = f(i) \text{ and } M_{trans} = kY.$$

If $M_{idle} = f(i) = O$, as Tobin asserts for 1929, then in 1929

$$M_{total} = kY \text{ and } \frac{M_{total}}{Y} = k$$

One alternative but equally restrictive approach to the demand for transactions balances is represented by the inventory theoretic model of the Baumol-Tobin type. In this model the demand for money is shown to conform to the familiar "square root law" of inventory analysis, i.e.,

$$M_d = \frac{1}{2}\sqrt{\frac{2bT}{i}} = \frac{1}{2} \cdot \sqrt{2b} \cdot T^{\frac{1}{2}} \cdot i^{-\frac{1}{2}},$$

where T is the volume of expenditures financed in a given period, b is the cost of switching between income earning assets and money, and i is the interest rate. In this case

$$\eta_{M \cdot T} = \frac{\partial M}{\partial T} \cdot \frac{T}{M} = \frac{\frac{1}{2} \cdot \frac{1}{2} \cdot \sqrt{2b} \cdot T^{-\frac{1}{2}} i^{-\frac{1}{2}}}{1} \cdot \frac{T}{\frac{1}{2} \cdot \sqrt{2b} \cdot T^{\frac{1}{2}} \cdot i^{-\frac{1}{2}}} = \frac{1}{2}$$

i.e., the transactions (or income) elasticity of the demand for money balances is one half. In this framework one would expect to find substantial economies of scale in the holding of money balances. These are ruled out in Latané's formulation as they are in the crude form of the quantity theory. See W. Baumol, "The Transactions Demand for Cash: An Inventory Theoretic Approach," *Quarterly Journal of Economics,* 66 (November 1952).

Since k (the reciprocal of the transactions velocity of circulation of money, V_t) was assumed to be a constant, this allowed a calculation of idle balances for other years as

$$(M_{idle})_t = (M_{total})_t - (M_{trans})_t = (M_{total})_t - k_{1929}(Y_t)$$

Tobin plotted idle balances calculated in this manner for each year against interest rates. For the period ending in 1945 he obtained excellent representations of what appeared to be Keynesian liquidity preference functions—the roughly hyperbolic functions generally depicted in the discussion of Keynesian theory. Although the scatter diagrams did not appear to yield such well-behaved relations for subsequent years, it did appear that Tobin had isolated a statistical liquidity preference function.

In their work Bronfenbrenner and Mayer (4) estimated regression coefficients in equations that contained a wealth measure and lagged money balances as explanatory variables, in addition to the interest rate. As the dependent variable, they alternately used total money balances and a measure of idle balances, similar to the one originally defined by Tobin. The equation they estimated in log-linear form was

$$\log (M/P)_t = \alpha_1 + \alpha_2 \log i + \alpha_3 \log W + \alpha_4 \log (M/P)_{t-1}. \qquad (14)$$

This is virtually identical to the basic form derived in the previous section. In the equations employing idle balances as well as in those specifying total money balances as the dependent variable, the coefficient of the interest rate had a negative sign attached to it and was statistically significantly different from zero at the 1 percent level.[28]

In further tests based on equations similar to the one above Bronfenbrenner and Mayer concluded that the liquidity preference hypothesis did a better job of predicting the movement of money balances from year to year than did a "naive" model that assumed that there would be no relation (or a random relation) between movements in the interest rate and money balances. This again appeared as evidence favorable to the liquidity preference hypothesis.

Virtually all work presented since the Bronfenbrenner and Mayer study has wisely avoided the arbitrary classification of money balances into active and idle components. Even earlier authors, such as Latané, felt that such a distinction did not allow for the possible effect of the interest rate on "active balances."[29] Many economists believe that such a dichotomy is unreasonable since total money balances are simply

[28]To say that a coefficient is "statistically significantly different from zero" at the 1 percent level is to imply that there is less than one chance in a hundred that the estimated coefficient differs from zero solely because of random (chance) factors affecting the data from which the estimate was derived. If we cannot judge a coefficient to be significantly different from zero at the 1 percent level or 5 percent level of significance, we generally have little confidence in the hypothesized relation which that coefficient represents.

[29]Latané, *op. cit.*, pp. 456–457.

one of many assets held for the services they provide and cannot be separated into unique components.[30]

Among studies specifying total money balances as the dependent variable are those by Meltzer (49), Brunner and Meltzer (5, 6), Laidler (40, 41), Heller (30), Chow (11) and Goldfeld (24). These studies use different time periods to test their basic hypotheses; they include variables other then the interest rate in the money demand equation; and often they differ in the empirical measure chosen to represent "the interest rate," some specifying the rate on U.S. Treasury Bills or short-term commercial paper, while others employ the rate on long-term government bonds or corporate securities. Yet, in spite of these many differences, these studies, like the ones above, show that the interest rate measure is an important factor in explaining variations in the demand for money. Some of the more important characteristics of these studies are summarized in Table 1.

In addition to the unanimous conclusion that the interest rate is an important determinant of the demand for money, these studies demonstrate a strong consistency in their estimates of the interest elasticity of money balances. (As discussed below, such consistency over different periods of time suggests a rather stable demand for money function.) Those studies employing a long-term rate of interest report elasticities in the range of -0.4 to -0.9. However, the estimates in the lower half of this range occur only when money is defined in a "broad" sense (inclusive of commercial bank time deposits). Considering only those studies that use the narrow measure of money we find that the range of elasticity estimates narrows to -0.7 to -0.9.

When the short-term rate of interest is employed, the estimated elasticities range from -0.07 to -0.50. However, the estimates in the upper part of this range derive from those studies that specify "idle" balances as the dependent variable. If we exclude these results and consider only total money balances as the dependent variable, the elasticity of money balances with respect to the short-term interest rate lies in the range from -0.07 to -0.20. This result holds whether money is defined in the "narrow" or "broad" sense. The difference between the long-rate and the short-rate elasticities may be an indication of the different rates of adjustment by the public to what they consider to be temporary versus long-term movements in financial variables. Statistically, it also reflects the fact that the long-term rate fluctuates far less than the short-term rate. We shall consider this point again below.

Simultaneous-Equation Models

All of the studies reported in Table 1 have one basic characteristic in common: the estimates of interest elasticities are derived from single-equation models. Elementary statistics teaches that in order for estimated coefficients derived by least-squares regression methods to have certain desirable characteristics (unbiasedness, efficiency, etc.), there must be a one-way causation from the independent to the dependent variable, with no direct feedback. Thus, in the single-equation models specified

[30]M. Friedman, "The Demand for Money—Some Theoretical and Empirical Results," *Journal of Political Economy,* 67 (June 1959), pp. 327-351.

above, the interest rate and other explanatory variables must be assumed to influence the stock of money, the dependent variable, but the stock of money must not, in turn, influence these variables.

In contrast, if the conventional aggregate economic model is considered, it is obvious that the causation between interest rates, real factors, and the money stock is not unidirectional. There are simultaneous interrelations between both the supply of and demand for money as well as between monetary and real factors. This leads to what is commonly referred to as an "identification" problem.[31]

---

[31]The source and nature of "simultaneous-equation bias" may be illustrated as follows. Consider the usual supply-demand relationship as drawn in Figure A.

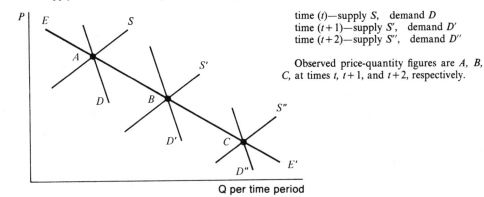

time (*t*)—supply *S*,   demand *D*
time (*t*+1)—supply *S'*,   demand *D'*
time (*t*+2)—supply *S''*,   demand *D''*

Observed price-quantity figures are *A*, *B*, *C*, at times *t*, *t*+1, and *t*+2, respectively.

An attempt to fit a statistical demand or supply curve to empirical observations will not, in fact, yield the desired relationship except in very special circumstances. The usual time series observations of price (P) and quantity (Q) do not correspond to either any one demand curve or any one supply curve. Rather, they are intersection points of various supply and demand curves that are almost continuously shifting either randomly or systematically due to the influence of outside factors.

Attempts to derive single-equation estimates of these curves on the basis of observed data will result in a statistical construct that is neither a supply curve nor a demand curve. For example, the least-squares regression line that could be fit to the data in Figure A would be *EE'*. This line would have a negative slope in the situation drawn here only because of the tendency for the supply curve to shift relatively more than the demand curve. Yet a statistical study of the data involved could easily be misunderstood by the unwary to represent the true demand relation. This would lead one to accept a meaningless estimate of the

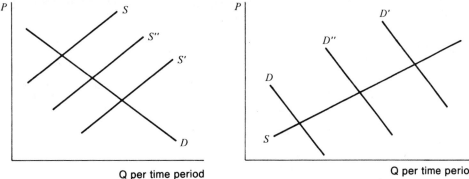

Table 1. The Demand for Money in Single-Equation Studies

Study	Interest Rate Elasticity of M		Interest Rate Measure Employed	Other Variables in M_D Function	Data and Time Period
1. Latané (45)		-0.7 (M1)	R_B	GNP	1919–1952 (A)
2. Bronfenbrenner and	a) -0.3 –	-0.5 (M$_{Idle}$)	R_{4-6}	GNP, Wealth	1919–1956 (A)
Mayer (4)	b) approx.	-0.1 (M1)	R_{4-6}	GNP, Wealth	1919–1956 (A)
3. Meltzer (49)	a) -0.7 –	-0.9 (M1)	$R_{20\,yr}$	Net Nonhuman Wealth	1900–1958 (A)
	b) -0.5 –	-0.6 (M2)	$R_{20\,yr}$	Net Nonhuman Wealth	1900–1958 (A)
	c)	-0.4 (M3)	$R_{20\,yr}$	Net Nonhuman Wealth	1900–1949 (A)
4. Heller (30)	a)	-0.1 (M1)	R_{60-80}	GNP	1947–1958 (Q)
	b)	-0.1 (M2)	R_{60-80}	Private Nonhuman Wealth	1947–1958 (Q)
5. Laidler (40)	a) not available (M1)		R_{4-6}	Permanent Income	1920–1960 (A)
	b) not available (M2)		R_{4-6}	Permanent Income	1892–1960 (A)
6. Laidler (41)	a) -0.18 –	-0.20 (M1)	R_{4-6}	Permanent Income	1919–1960 and subperiods (A)
	b) -0.5 –	-0.8 (M1)	$R_{20\,yr}$	Permanent Income	1919–1960 and subperiods (A)
	c) approx.	-0.15 (M2)	R_{4-6}	Permanent Income	1892–1960 and subperiods (A)
	d) -0.3 –	-0.5 (M2)	$R_{20\,yr}$	Permanent Income	1892–1960 and subperiods (A)
7. Chow (11)	a) approx.	-0.75 (M1)	$R_{20\,yr}$	Permanent Income	1897–1958 (excl. war years) (A)
	b) approx.	-0.79 (M1)	$R_{20\,yr}$	Current Income and Lagged Money Stock	1897–1958 (excl. war years) (A)
8. Goldfeld (25)	a)	-0.07 -0.16 (M1)	R_{4-6} R_{TD}	GNP	1952–1972 (Q)
	b)	-0.07 -0.15 (M1)	R_{4-6} R_{TD}	GNP (Almon lags)	1952–1972 (Q)

Notes: $M1 = DD + C$; $M2 = M1 + TD$; $M3 = M2 +$ Deposits at Mutual Savings Banks and the Postal Savings System; $R_B =$ interest rate on high-grade corporate bonds; $R_{20\,yr} =$ rate on 20-year corporate bonds; $R_{4-6} =$ rate on 4-6 month prime commercial paper; $R_{60-80} =$ rate on 60-80 day commercial paper; $R_{TD} =$ commercial bank time deposit rate; $A =$ annual; $Q =$ quarterly.

Fortunately, a substantial body of empirical work does assume simultaneity either between money supply and money demand or, more generally, between the monetary and the (real) expenditure sectors of the economy. These studies employ statistical techniques designed to correct for the interaction among "dependent" and "independent" variables specified within a single equation and to derive estimates which have certain desirable statistical properties. In these studies the money demand function is estimated as one element in a multiequation model. Some examples of the results of these studies are presented in Table 2.[32]

---

slope and, thus, of the elasticity of the demand curve.

The only way in which such time series data could readily yield true structural estimates of the parameters of either the supply curve or the demand curve would be in the very special circumstances where one of the curves is stable and the shifting of the other curve traces out points along the desired curve. This is pictured in Figure B. To get around this problem, the true interaction of supply-demand relations in determining price-quantity figures must be considered. This may be done by specifying a simultaneous-equation model including both a supply equation and a demand equation and by taking care to observe well defined rules for "identification." See G. Tintner, *Econometrics* (New York, 1962), Chapter 6.

[32]All of the studies reported in Table 2 employ two-stage least squares in the estimating process. For a discussion of the mechanics of this technique and the characteristics of the estimates derived from it, see J. Johnston, *Econometric Methods* (New York, 1963), Chapter 9, or Kmenta, *op. cit.*, Chapter 13.

Table 2. Money and Deposit Demand in Simultaneous-Equation Models

Study	Representative Equation (seasonal dummies omitted where appropriate)	Interest Elasticity	Interest Rate Measure	Data
1. Brunner and Meltzer (6)	$M1 = -18.994\ r^* + 0.201\ W/Pa - 54.72\ Y/Y_p + 0.347P_y$ W/Pa = real public wealth P_y = price index Y/Y_y = ratio of current to permanent income	-0.75	r = bond yield	1930–1959 (A)
	$M2 = -16.806\ r^* + 0.340\ W/Pa - 44.81\ Y/Y_p + 0.290P_y$	-0.42	r = bond yield	1930–1959 (A)
2. Teigen (62)	$\Delta D = 3.101 + 0.0719Y^* - 0.0018r_b^*\ Y^* - 0.0066r_p Y^* - 0.1895\ D_{T-1}$ D = demand deposits adjusted at commercial banks Y = gross national product	-0.10 -0.43	r_b = Treas. bill rate r_p = rate on bank time deposits	1953–1964 (Q)
3. de Leeuw (47)	$\dfrac{\Delta D}{W} = 0.0067 - 0.158 \left(\dfrac{D}{W}\right)_{r-1} - 0.00355r_s^*$ $- 0.0451r_p^* - 0.140\ \dfrac{Inv}{W_{r-1}}$ + other terms W = wealth measure $Inv.$ = bus. investment	-0.35 -0.17	r_s = yield on private securities r_p = rate on bank time deposits	1948–1962 (Q)
4. Goldfeld (24)	$\Delta D = -0.270 - 0.127D_{T-1} + 0.140Y^*$ $- 0.0066r_b^*Y^* - 0.012r_p Y^*$ Y = gross national product	-0.11 -0.18	r_b = Treas. bill rate r_p = rate on bank time deposits	1950–1962 (Q)
5. Dickson and Starleaf (13)	$M1 = ln\ a_o + 0.660\ ln\ Y^a - 0.077\ ln\ R^a_{4-6} - 0.182\ ln\ R^a_{TD} + 1.037\ ln\ P^a$	-0.08 -0.18	R_{4-6} = comm. paper rate R_{TD} = comm. bank time deposit rate	1952–1969 (Q)

Where ^{a} indicates weighted average of current and past values; estimated using Almon distributed lags.

*An asterisk is used to denote an independent variable used in the money (or D) demand function, which is treated as endogenously determined within the multiequation model as a whole. A = annual; Q = quarterly

The results derived from simultaneous-equation models generally confirm the single-equation results reported above. Those studies employing a short-term market rate of interest in the money or demand deposit demand equation, report elasticities in the range of -0.08 to -0.18. This compares with the -0.7 to -0.2 range reported in the single equation studies in Table 1. The elasticity estimates with respect to the rate on commercial bank time deposits is generally -0.17 or -0.18.[33] The elasticity measures based on long-term rates are again substantially higher than the short-term rate elasticities. They range from -0.35 in de Leeuw's work to -0.75 in Brunner and Meltzer's model. Since de Leeuw's measure is a weighted average of rates on private securities of different maturities, and not a long-term rate comparable to the corporate bond yields used in the other studies, these results are not inconsistent with the evidence presented in Table 1.

Most of the equations reported in Table 2 are estimated within an explicitly specified structural model either of the monetary sector or of the monetary and expenditures sectors combined. Several authors, interested primarily in the money demand

[33]This is virtually identical to the result obtained by Goldfeld in his single-equation study. See Table 1.

relation outside the framework of a fully specified multiequation model but cognizant of the potential estimation problems implicit in the single-equation approach, have employed the method of instrumental variables in deriving their estimates of the parameters in the money demand equation. Essentially, this method allows one to act as if he is operating within a fully specified structural model by postulating the exogenous variables that would appear in the model were it to be fully defined. In this way those exogenous variables can be employed as "instruments" in the first stage of a two-stage least-squares estimation process with the predicted values of the "endogenous" or jointly dependent variables from this first-stage estimation being employed in the money demand function in the second stage.

One interesting example of this approach is contained in a recent paper by Harold D. Dickson and Dennis R. Starleaf (13). Their work is all the more interesting because it applies this technique to an equation that contains Almon-estimated distributed lag terms on each of the independent variables—income, the interest rate and the price level. Their results, reported in Table 2, are broadly consistent both with the results of simultaneous-equation models and with the single-equation results presented by Goldfeld, which employ a similar equation form. Using quarterly data for 1952-I through 1969-IV, they obtain estimated interest elasticities of -0.077 and -0.182 for the 4-6 month commercial paper rate and the rate on commercial bank time deposit, respectively.

In summary, it should be emphasized that both those studies based on single-equation models as well as those that employ multiequation estimation techniques appear to support the hypothesis that the interest rate is an important determinant of the demand for money. Furthermore, since the multiequation estimates are less likely to be biased because they take explicit consideration of the simultaneous nature of the relations involved, the similarity of results from those studies with those in single-equation work lends strong support to the single-equation estimates and indicates that, in this case, the identification problem may not be particularly serious.

Alternative Interest Rate Measures in the Money Demand Function

The studies cited in the previous section contain virtually overwhelming evidence that some interest rate should appear in the demand for money function. However, there is still disagreement as to which empirical measure should be used to represent the theoretical argument. Much of the available evidence that attempts to determine which rate best explains the demand for money is inconsistent. Furthermore, tests by different analysts often employ data from different time periods, specify different dependent variables, and include dissimilar constraints within the function, making comparisons among these empirical studies rather tenuous.

The problem may stem partly from the fact that theory provides little guidance on this issue. Some writers, like Brunner and Meltzer, argue that the demand for money should be treated within the broad theory of portfolio selection and suggest that this demand depends on the yield on equities as well as that on bonds. Others, like

Bronfenbrenner and Mayer (4), Laidler (40, 41), and Heller (30), argue that some short-term interest rate is the more relevant argument since it measures the opportunity cost of holding money as the rate of return on what they consider to be money's closest substitutes. Still others, including Gurley and Shaw (26) emphasize the liquidity of money and the minimal risks associated with changes in its nominal value. They argue that the closest substitutes for money are assets with similar characteristics, such as the liabilities of financial intermediaries (e.g., savings and loan associations), and that it is the rates on these assets that are most relevant to the money demand function.[34]

One attempt to present direct evidence on this issue was made by Heller in 1965. In alternative money demand equations Heller compared the performance of the long-term rate of interest as measured by the rate on U.S. government bonds with that of a short-term rate, measured as the yield on 60–90-day commercial paper. Regression coefficients were estimated for equations in log-linear form using quarterly observations for the period 1947–1958. Both $M1$ and $M2$ were tried as dependent variables with the interest rate and current income or nonhuman wealth specified as alternative constraints. In these regressions the long-term rate of interest *never* appeared as a statistically important explanatory variable,[35] while the short-term rate was important in all equations but one. Consequently, Heller concluded,

> The short-term rate is of greater importance (than the long-term rate) in the money function. The closest substitute for money available, a 60 to 90 day commercial paper, is most influential in deciding whether to hold assets in the form of money or not. Long-term interest rates do not influence the quantity of money demanded. . . .[36]

Results presented by Laidler (41) generally support Heller's conclusions. Laidler examines evidence derived from equations fit to annual data for the period 1892–1960 and for subperiods therein. He bases his analysis on the following proposition:

> Given that the interest rate is an important variable in the demand for money, and that movements of various interest rates are related to one another, one would expect almost any rate chosen at random to show some relationship to cash balances . . . however, though all interest rates are interrelated, there is no reason to suppose that the nature of their interrelationship remains unchanged for all time. Thus, if the demand function for money is stable, one would expect the "right" interest rate to show the same relationship to the demand for money in different time periods while the "wrong" one need not.[37]

---

[34]See the first section of this survey for some implications of this view.

[35]The long-term rate was never significant at the 5 percent level, and in some of the equations it appeared with the wrong sign.

[36]H. R. Heller, "The Demand for Money—The Evidence from the Short-Run Data," *Quarterly Journal of Economics,* 79 (May 1965), p. 297.

[37]D. Laidler, "The Rate of Interest and the Demand for Money—Some Empirical Evidence," *Journal of Political Economy,* 74 (December 1966), p. 547.

Laidler uses the rate on 4–6-month commercial paper and the yield on 20-year bonds as his alternative interest rate measures. His equations are in log-linear form and include only permanent income as an additional explanatory variable. When his dependent variable is $M2$, he claims that "there is little question of the superior explanatory power of the shorter interest rate."[38] When the dependent variable is specified as $M1$ his results are somewhat contradictory. When he employs levels of the logarithms of the variables, the long-term rate explains more of the variation in $M1$ for most periods than does the short rate. Nonetheless, he maintains his original conclusion that a short-term rate is the relevant rate measure in the money demand function arguing that "the contradictory conclusions obtained with the narrower definition reflect only the fact that that definition is an unsatisfactory one."[39] The basis for his conclusion on this matter is to be found in our comments on his previous work (40), reported in the first section of this survey.

The conclusions derived from this work by Heller and Laidler are challenged by Michael Hamburger. In his study of the demand for money by households Hamburger (27) concludes that long-term interest rates are the relevant determinants of the demand for money. Employing a model that includes distributed lags to measure the rate of adjustment of households to changed market conditions, he finds that in the household demand for money function "for short-run analysis . . . , it is useful to include two yields—one on debts and one equities—and that the elasticities of the demand for money are approximately the same with respect to both of these rates."[40] His findings show that government bills (short-term securities) may be poorer substitutes for money for the household sector than longer-term securities. Commenting on previous work, Hamburger claims that Heller's conclusions depend on the choice of time period. During the period 1947–1951 the Federal Reserve pegged interest rates distorting more normal market relationships. When Hamburger reruns Heller's regressions excluding these years, he finds that the long-term rate and the short-term rate appear equally important.

Additional evidence has been reported by T. H. Lee (46). Lee criticizes the previous work done by the cited authors because they restrict their comparisons to only two alternative rate measures. Furthermore, he argues that the *differentials* between interest rates and the yield on money, rather than simply interest rate *levels,* are the relevant measures that should appear in money demand functions.

Like Laidler, Lee specifies a Friedman-type permanent income money demand model as the basic framework for his tests. He tries both $M1$ and $M2$ as dependent variables and, in addition to his alternative interest rate measures, either permanent income or permanent income and lagged money balances as explanatory variables. His regression estimates show that "the yield on nonbank intermediary liabilities is the most significant interest rate variable in affirming the demand for money." Spe-

[38]*Ibid.,* p. 547.

[39]*Ibid.,* p. 553.

[40]The rates Hamburger used were Moody's Aaa rate on long-term corporate bonds and Moody's dividend yield. M. J. Hamburger, "The Demand for Money by Households . . . ," *Journal of Political Economy,* 74 (December 1966), p. 608.

cifically, "the yield on savings and loan shares performs the best in terms of R^2 among respective regressions of static or dynamic formulations."[41]

With the exception of Lee's work, the interest rate measure included in the other money demand functions cited was the absolute level of the rate on some asset alternative to money.[42] One implication of this formulation is that the (marginal) rate of return on money is assumed to be zero. Robert S. Barro and Anthony M. Santomero (2) have argued that "at least one component of (narrowly defined) money, demand deposits, bears a form of interest which should be taken into account in determining the opportunity cost of holding money."[43] Their argument rests on the assumption that the provision of services or the remission of charges by banks in accordance with the size of a customer's deposit balance represents an effective interest return on those deposits.

To test this proposition, Barro and Santomero surveyed the largest one hundred commercial banks in the United States to determine "the rates at which they have remitted service charges as a function of demand deposit balances."[44] From the survey results an annual series measuring the imputed marginal rate of return on demand deposits was constructed for 1950-1968. This measure was then employed within the framework of a Baumol-Tobin inventory theoretic model of the demand for money by households.[45] Relating real per capita money balances, (M/PN), real per capita consumption expenditure, (Y/PN), and the differential between the rate on an alternative asset—the dividend rate on savings and loan shares—and the imputed demand deposit rate, the following estimates are derived:

$$\log \left(\frac{M}{PN}\right)_T = -3.96 + 1.044 \log \left(\frac{Y}{PN}\right)_T - 0.549 \log (r_S - r_D)_T.$$

These results support the basic hypothesis: There is a substantial interest elasticity of household money demand with respect to the rate differential $(r_S - r_D)$.

[41]T. H. Lee, "Alternative Interest Rates and the Demand for Money: The Empirical Evidence," *American Economic Review*, 57 (December 1967), p. 1171.

[42]Hamburger later criticized Lee's evidence because his "findings depend critically on the use of interest rate differentials. Once this procedure is abandoned and the yield on money is introduced as a separate variable, there is little evidence that S + L shares are closer substitutes for money (narrowly defined) than other assets. In addition, the demand for money appears to adjust more slowly to changes in yields on S + L shares than to changes in other rates." Hamburger, "Alternative Interest Rates . . . ," *op. cit.*, p. 407.

[43]R. J. Barro and A. M. Santomero, "Household Money Holdings and the Demand Deposit Rate," *Journal of Money, Credit and Banking*, 4 (May 1972), p. 397.

[44]*Ibid.*, p. 399.

[45]An interesting implication of their formulation of the inventory model is that the income elasticity need not be less than one. This contradicts the conventional view that inventory models are necessarily associated with economies of scale as shown on page 330. As they argue; "The key element which is typically neglected is transactions costs. As transaction volume increases, economies of scale are realized only to the extent that transactions costs rise less than transactions volume. Since transaction costs depend largely on value of time, and since value of time may increase even faster than transactions volume, diseconomies of scale (money being a "luxury") is quite compatible with the inventory approach." Barro and Santomero, *op. cit.*, p. 408.

It is important to note that the estimated interest elasticity applies solely to the rate differential. Since that differential (as measured by Barro and Santomero) has been fairly constant over the postwar period, the elasticity with respect to the level of rates may be quite small. The coefficient of real per capita expenditure indicates the expenditure elasticity of money demand is close to unity, suggesting an absence of economies of scale in household demand for money.

The highly tentative nature of these results should now be evident. While Heller and Laidler argue that the short-term rate is the relevant measure in the money demand function, this conclusion is challenged by both Hamburger and Lee. Lee's results further indicate that it may be the differential between the yield on money and the yield on the liabilities of some financial intermediary rather than a market interest rate that is the most appropriate constraint on desired money balances. But this contention is disputed by Hamburger. Barro and Santomero's results suggest the addition of some measure of the return on demand deposits to the equation. Additional work in which a serious attempt is made to make new results comparable to the results of previous investigators will be required before any firm conclusions are possible on this critical empirical issue.

Interest Elasticity and the Liquidity Trap

The evidence reviewed above clearly supports the Keynesian notion of an interest sensitive demand for money or liquidity preference function.[46] However, Keynes went further than merely to posit the interest rate as a determinant of the public's demand for money. In *The General Theory* he also speculated briefly about the shape of the liquidity preference function. Specifically, he noted,

> There is the possibility . . . , that, after the rate of interest has fallen to a certain level, liquidity preference may become virtually absolute in the sense that almost everyone prefers cash to holding a debt which yields so low a rate of interest. In this event the monetary authority would have lost effective control over the rate of interest. But while this limiting case might become practically important in the future, I know of no example of it hitherto.[47]

In spite of Keynes' disclaimer, his suggestion that the liquidity preference curve *may* become perfectly interest elastic at some low level of the interest rate attracted much attention and stimulated a substantial amount of "searching" for this phenomenon. His suggestion is responsible for the shape given the liquidity preference curve in most texts (as shown in Figure 1).

The implication of this hypothesis, is that the interest elasticity of the liquidity

[46]All of the studies cited above employ data from the United States. The evidence employing data from the United Kingdom is somewhat less conclusive on this issue. See, for example, A. A. Walters, "The Radcliffe Report—Ten Years After: A Survey of Empirical Evidence" in O. R. Croome and H. G. Johnson (eds.), *Money in Britain 1959-1969* (Oxford, 1969).

[47]J. M. Keynes, *The General Theory of Employment, Interest, and Money* (London and New York, 1936), p. 207.

FIGURE 1

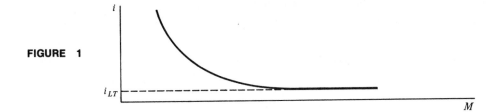

preference function should increase as the interest rate declines. This proposition has been tested by Bronfenbrenner and Mayer (4), by Meltzer (49), by Laidler (41), by Konstas and Khouja (38) and by others.

Bronfenbrenner and Mayer, after examining the relation between the short-term interest rate and the Cambridge k, (M/Y), tested to see if the elasticity of their estimated liquidity functions increased as the interest rate fell. Specifically, they calculated the "rank" correlation coefficient between elasticities and the level of interest rates. This involves ordering the level of interest rates from highest to lowest and comparing the ordering of the elasticities associated with those rates. If the highest rate were associated with the lowest elasticity, the lowest rate with the highest elasticity, and so on for all rates in between, there would be perfect negative rank correlation between these two measures. However, Bronfenbrenner and Mayer calculate a ranks correlation coefficient of + 0.16, which not only is not statistically significant, but is of the wrong sign. They concluded that "the absence of a negative correlation in a period when interest rates were at times quite low, casts doubt on, if not the truth, then at least the relevance of the liquidity trap proposition. . . ."[48]

Other investigators have supported these conclusions. In 1963 Allan Meltzer (49) fit velocity functions for the six decades from 1900 to 1958. As he interprets his results, "The data deny that the interest elasticity of the demand for money or velocity became exceptionally large during that decade (the 1930's). Indeed, the interest elasticity of V_1 was slightly below the average for the (entire) fifty-nine years."[49] This evidence of a lower than average interest elasticity during periods of low interest rates is consistent with Bronfenbrenner and Mayer's positive rank-correlation coefficient.

Meltzer's work with Karl Brunner (5) adds additional support to this position. Using estimates derived from data for the 1930's, they were able to predict the velocity of circulation for the 1950's with sufficiently small mean errors to conclude that the velocity function remained highly stable over these periods of differing inter-

---

[48]M. Bronfenbrenner and T. Mayer, "Liquidity Functions in the American Economy," *Econometrica*, 28 (October 1960), p. 831.

[49]For the purpose of these tests, Meltzer defines income as the return on wealth, i.e., the interest rate or rate of return, r, times the wealth stock, W. The wealth measure used to calculate income in this formula is net nonhuman wealth of the public—the same variable employed in his money demand functions. The measure of money he employs is narrow money ($DD + C$). Meltzer, *op. cit.*, p. 243.

est rate levels. They conclude that "the liquidity trap proposition is denied by the evidence."[50]

    David Laidler (41) has reported evidence from a test somewhat similar to Bronfenbrenner and Mayer's. Employing both the narrow ($M1$) and the broad ($M2$) definitions of money and testing both the long-rate and the short-rate of interest in separate regressions, Laidler divided the observations for the period 1892–1960 into two subsets: those years in which the relevant interest rate was above the mean and those in which it was below the mean. The general equation tested was

$$ln \; M = a + b_1 \; ln \; Y_p + b_2 \; ln \; i,$$

where Y_p is permanent income. Laidler's results, using both logarithms and first differences of logarithms of the variables defined above, demonstrated very little tendency for the interest elasticity (b_2) to be higher (in absolute value) for the low interest rate observations than it was in the equations fitted to the high interest rate observations. As he notes, "the elasticity with respect to the short rate seems to fall a little at low rates of interest, though the elasticity with respect to the long rate rises slightly at low interest rates. . . . Thus, the hypothesis of the liquidity trap, as it is usually presented, appears to be refuted."[51]

An interesting article by Konstas and Khouja reports on statistical tests relevant to this issue. In their study the authors attempt to specify a functional form for the demand for money relation which accurately portrays the characteristics originally suggested by Keynes. In their model,

    In regard to the speculative part of the demand for money, . . . the function which is consistent with Keynesian requirements must be stated in the following manner:

$$M2 = \frac{\beta}{r - \alpha}; \beta > 0, \alpha > 0. \; ^{52}$$

    This formulation quite accurately reflects the properties of the function shown in Figure 1. It allows for a minimum interest rate level, α, and for increasing interest elasticity of money balances as interest rates decline toward α. The authors estimate the parameters of this model using annual observations for the period 1919–1965. In general, the data seem to fit this relationship rather closely.

[50]Brunner and Meltzer, *op. cit.,* p. 350.

[51]Laidler, "The Rate of Interest . . .", *op. cit.,* p. 550.

[52]Konstas and Khouja, *op. cit.,* p. 767. For another study that claims to formulate and test Keynes' original liquidity preference hypothesis more accurately than is done in some of the literature cited above, see D. R. Starleaf and R. Reimer, "The Keynesian Demand Function for Money: Some Statistical Tests," *Journal of Finance,* 22 (March 1967), pp. 71–76. Their work relates primarily to the Keynesian proposition that it is not necessarily the absolute level of the rate of interest that is important in determining the demand for money but the relationship of that current rate to a conceptual "normal" rate. Starleaf and Reimer found no evidence to suggest that the normal rate, as they calculated it, was an important variable in the demand for money.

Konstas and Khouja use their estimated relation to examine the claim that the United States economy was in a liquidity trap in the 1930's. Specifically, they calculate an estimate of the speculative component of total money balances by subtracting estimated transactions balances from (actual) total money balances for each of the years 1919–1965. The pattern indicated in the relation between the long-term interest rate and calculated idle balances fails to confirm the claim that monetary policy was impotent in the 1930's because of the very high interest elasticity of the demand for money. They conclude that their test "does not seem to offer much evidence in support of this claim."[53] These results add to the weight of the evidence reported above.

Most of the individual tests cited in this section approach the question of the liquidity trap indirectly. Furthermore, some of the results of Laidler's tests with the long-term rate of interest could be taken as very weak support for the existence of the low level trap. However, the weight of all these studies together seems sufficient to allow a rather firm judgment against the historical existence of the liquidity trap. In addition, work by Brunner and Meltzer has shown that the necessary and sufficient conditions for the occurrence of a liquidity trap in the demand function for money are extremely restrictive.[54] Consequently, the conclusion on the absence of a liquidity trap would seem warranted by the lack of any falsifying evidence.

An Alternative View: Interest Rates, Permanent Income and Variations in Velocity

One implication of the work surveyed above is that cyclical variations in interest rates are important determinants of the evident cyclical variations in the demand for money and the velocity of circulation of money. This view has been disputed by at least one important analyst, Milton Friedman. Although in his "Restatement" of the quantity theory of money Friedman develops a theoretical money demand function that includes several interest rate terms as explanatory variables, his statistical work leads him to question the empirical significance of the interest rate in determining actual money holdings.

Friedman's empirical work begins with an observation on the behavior of the income velocity of money. He notes that from 1870 to 1954, over long periods of time, the income velocity of circulation (Y/M) moved in a direction opposite to that of real income, but over shorter periods of time, during business cycles, these variables moved in the same direction.[55] He attempts to reconcile these observations by explaining the public's behavior regarding the demand for real money balances.

---

[53]Konstas and Khouja, *op. cit.,* p. 774.

[54]K. Brunner and A. H. Meltzer, "Liquidity Traps for Money, Bank Credit, and Interest Rates," *Journal of Political Economy,* 76 (February 1968), 1–37.

[55]The inverse long-term relation between income and velocity implies more than simply a direct relation between income and money. It implies that as income increases, money increases more than proportionately, so that money may be viewed as a "luxury" good. This long-term relationship has not prevailed in the postwar period, however, as velocity has trended upward rather strongly.

Friedman argues that the *nominal* stock of money in the economy is determined in the first instance on the supply side of the market by the monetary authorities and that "holders of money cannot alter this amount directly." In contrast, however, the holders of money "can make the *real* amount of money anything in the aggregate they want to."[56] For, if individuals find themselves holding too large a stock of nominal money balances, their attempt to decrease these balances by increasing expenditures will reduce the real quantity of money to the desired level by raising money income and prices. Conversely, lowering expenditures to increase money holdings will lower money income and prices, thereby raising the real quantity of money to the desired equilibrium level.

This analysis suggests that since the *nominal* stock of money is predetermined by the monetary authorities, an explanation of the observed behavior of the *real* volume of money balances and the income velocity of money requires an examination of the demand for money.[57] It may be possible to explain the patterns exhibited by velocity through an analysis of the historical behavior of the explanatory variables that enter a stable demand for money function. However, Friedman's attempt to find variables in addition to income that enter the money demand function and that "exert an influence opposite to that of income . . . sufficiently potent to dominate the [cyclical] movement of velocity"[58] is unsuccessful. As he reports,

> . . . the other variables that come first to mind are interest rates, and these display cyclical patterns that seem most unlikely to account for the sizable, highly consistent, and roughly synchronous cyclical pattern in velocity.[59]

As an alternative approach, suggested by his work on the consumption function, Friedman employs the concept of permanent income in the money demand function to reconcile the cyclical and secular behavior of velocity. This attempt starts by viewing "the statistical magnitude called 'real income' as corresponding to a different theoretical construct in the cyclical than in the secular analysis."[60] This reconciliation depends on the relation between measured and permanent income. If permanent income rises less than measured income during cyclical expansions and falls less than measured income in contractions, and if money balances are adapted to permanent income, "they might rise and fall more than in proportion to permanent income, as is required by our secular results, yet less than in proportion to measured income, as is required by our cyclical results."[61]

[56]M. Friedman, "The Demand for Money . . . ," *op. cit.*, p. 330.
[57]Following Fisher in employing the equation of exchange, Friedman often couches his analytical discussion in terms of the velocity of circulation of money rather than the demand function for money balances. But since $V = (Y/M)$, an increase in the demand for nominal balances relative to nominal income will be reflected in a decrease in the income velocity of circulation of money and, conversely, a decrease in the demand for money will be reflected as an increase in velocity.
[58]Friedman, "The Demand for Money . . . ," *op. cit.*, p. 332.
[59]*Ibid.*
[60]*Ibid.*
[61]*Ibid.*, p. 334.

On the basis of this theoretical reconciliation of the conflicting behavior of observed velocity, Friedman turns to an empirical examination of this phenomenon. As he notes, "An interpretation in terms of interest rates can also rationalize the qualitative results; [but] we reject it because it appears likely to be contradicted on a more detailed quantitative level."[62]

In his empirical tests Friedman measures both money balances and permanent income in real (i.e., deflated) per capita form and specifies the following exponential money demand function:

$$\frac{M}{NP} = \alpha \left(\frac{Y_p}{NP}\right)^{\delta}$$

or, in logarithmic form,

$$ln\,\frac{M}{NP} = ln\,\alpha + \delta\,ln\left(\frac{Y_p}{NP}\right), \qquad (15)$$

where P is an index of (permanent) prices, N is population, and Y_p is permanent income.[63]

Friedman fits this function to cycle-average data for the period 1869-1957. His estimate of δ, the permanent income elasticity of real money balances, is 1.8. Using this relationship, he calculates annual within-cycle projections of the velocity of circulation of money and finds that his formulation predicts actual velocity figures fairly well. Most importantly, however, he also finds that *the errors that are evident in these predictions are almost completely unrelated to the level of interest rates.* Thus, he concludes that there is little role for the interest rate, in addition to permanent income, in explaining variations in the velocity of circulation of money or the variation in money balances.[64]

Friedman achieves these results by using some statistical techniques not generally

---

[62]*Ibid.*, p. 335.

[63]Friedman originally derived his permanent income concept in connection with his studies on the consumption function. Permanent income is calculated as a weighted average of past income levels with the weights attached to the income levels of the more distant past declining geometrically. See M. Friedman, *A Theory of the Consumption Function* (Princeton, N.J., 1957), pp. 142-147.

[64]Friedman's conclusion would seem to be supported for the postwar period in evidence presented by Sam Peltzman. Challenging the conventional conclusion, Peltzman argues that his "results do imply strongly that interest rate movements cannot explain the postwar rise in velocity" (p. 134). In Peltzman's work this increase is associated with a secular trend in (unspecified) factors other than income and interest rates. See S. Peltzman, "The Structure of the Money-Expenditure Relationship," *American Economic Review,* 59 (March 1969), pp. 129-137. For a critique of Peltzman's methodology, see D. M. Jaffee, "The Structure of the Money Expenditure Relationship: Comment," *American Economic Review,* 60 (March 1970), pp. 216-219. In view of the serious econometric problems that arise in interpreting Peltzman's use of second differences and Jaffee's use of first differences, the uncertainty surrounding Peltzman's assumption about the public's behavior as regards the formulation of expectations about changes in the money stock, and the fact that Jaffee found some role for the interest rate in Peltzman's "reformulated" model, the overwhelming evidence on this issue from other sources would seem to stand.

used by other investigators. His use of cycle-average data,[65] for example, contrasts with the more common practice of using chronologically determined, annual or quarterly data in regression studies. Also, his use of the broad definition of money is claimed by many to bias his results against finding any role for the interest rate in the determination of money demand.[66] This latter contention may be explained as follows: if demand deposit balances are negatively related to interest rates, but time deposits are positively related to the rate paid on such deposits, a general increase in interest rates will decrease the demand for demand deposits and increase the demand for time deposits. If these two assets are added together in a single measure, these movements will tend to cancel out and the sum, $DD + TD$, may appear to be completely interest-insensitive.

In addition, Laidler (41) has pointed out that over the period covered by Friedman's study there was a slight downward trend in interest rates and that by omitting an interest rate term from his regression equation some of the (trend) influence of the interest rate on money balances was attributed to the trend in the permanent income variable. Since the decline in rates over this period would be expected to cause a relative increase in money balances, the absence of an interest rate term in the equation may help to explain the rather high (1.8) income elasticity estimated in Friedman's tests.

Friedman's results have been even more seriously challenged in the work of other analysts. Several of the studies reported in Table 1 include interest rates along with Friedman's measure of permanent income in log linear money demand functions. For example, Meltzer (49) showed that the long-term rate of interest generally appears as a highly significant variable in his regressions. He suggests that Friedman's use of the permanent income measure combines the influence of income, wealth, and interest rates into a single measure and obscures the separate impact of each on money demand. In addition to demonstrating the significant role of the interest rate when explicitly included in the function, Meltzer derives an estimate of the (permanent) income elasticity that is closer to unity than to Friedman's estimate of 1.8. This would appear to confirm Laidler's contention mentioned above.

Other works by Brunner and Meltzer (5) and by Chow (11) confirm the important role of the interest rate in alternative money demand or velocity functions. However, one important point with respect to these studies must be mentioned in defense of Friedman. These studies employ annual time series data, and these data are not strictly comparable to Friedman's (perhaps more subtle) cycle-average data. Consequently, their results do not represent a satisfactory refutation of his findings. However, Laidler (41), employing cycle-average data for the period 1891-1957, refitted

---

[65]An annual time series of observations on a given variable, X, represents a list of values for that variable for each year over a specified period of time. Cycle-average data on the other hand rely not on calendar years to generate observations, but rather on the cyclical swings in economic activity as defined by the National Bureau of Economic Research. Those who use cycle-average data argue that such a choice of values is economically more meaningful than the arbitrary designation of the calendar (or fiscal) year as the standard measure of time used to generate statistical data.

[66]See the discussion of this problem in connection with some results reported by Goldfeld (25).

Friedman's original equation and compared the results with those obtained when an interest rate term was included in the equation. His results are as follows:

$$\log \frac{M}{NP} = -2.017 + 1.618 \log \left(\frac{Y_p}{NP}\right)$$

$$\log \frac{M}{NP} = -1.403 + 1.430 \log \left(\frac{Y_p}{NP}\right) - 0.158 \log i_e$$

where i_e is the rate on 4-6-month commercial paper.

Laidler used these estimates to predict annual levels of per capita real money balances—a procedure very similar to Friedman's use of his equation to predict annual within-cycle values for the velocity of circulation of money. The mean error of prediction[67] for the equation that includes the interest rate is less than half that for the equation that contains only permanent income. Since the interest rate equation explains the data significantly better than Friedman's original equation, Laidler concludes that "the difference in the intercept and coefficient of the logarithm of permanent income that results from the omission of the interest rate is sufficient to produce misleading results (about the relation between prediction errors and the level of the rate of interest)." It appears that there was indeed "some secular (long-term) correlation between permanent income and [the] interest rate which caused permanent income to pick up part of the effect of interest rates in the regression from which the latter variable was omitted."[68]

As Laidler points out, then, the evidence coming from so many different sources is so persuasive that "it is probably safe to conclude that the rate of interest must be included in the demand function for money."[69] Friedman's results may be attributed in large part to his rather special statistical techniques.

The Scale Factor in Money Demand Functions: Current Income, Permanent Income, or Wealth

The results surveyed above suggest that the performance of any given interest rate measure in an empirical money demand function depends both on the way in which the dependent variable is defined and on the choice of other explanatory variables included in the equation. As already indicated, the other factors most commonly specified as determinants of the demand for money are income and wealth. The use of income—or some other measure of the volume of transactions—as a constraint on the level of money demand is generally related to the role of money as a medium of

---

[67]The mean error of prediction is the arithmetic average of the absolute value of the difference between the actual and predicted values of a given variable for all points for which a prediction is obtained.

[68]D. Laidler, "The Rate of Interest . . . ," *op. cit.*, p. 546.

[69]*Ibid.*

exchange. This is stated explicitly in Keynesian demand function, $M_d = L_1(Y) + L_2(i)$, in the Cambridge equation, $M = k \cdot Y$, and in the inventory theoretic model of money demand, $M_d = 1/2 \sqrt{2bT/i}$, where Y is the level of income and T is a measure of the volume of transactions.

On the other hand, when the role of money as a productive asset or a durable consumer good is stressed, a wealth measure is generally proposed as the relevant explanatory variable in the demand for money function. Attention is focused on "the equilibrium of the balance sheet, the allocation of assets, and the services that money provides." In this view "effecting a volume of transactions is but one of these services."[70]

In statistical work three measures have most frequently been employed as empirical counterparts to these theoretical constraints: current income, proposed as a proxy for the volume of transactions to be effected by the money stock; nonhuman wealth, measured as consolidated net worth in the balance sheet of the public; and Friedman's "permanent income," proposed as a proxy for a wealth concept that includes the present value of future labor income as well as the value of real physical assets. This last measure includes the value of both human and nonhuman wealth.[71]

Meltzer (49) tests all three of these variables in loglinear equations that specify both $M1$ and $M2$ as dependent variables and which include the yield on corporate bonds as the measure of the interest rate. Meltzer's basic model proposes nonhuman wealth (W) as the relevant constraint on money demand. He finds the elasticity of "narrow" money ($M1$) with respect to this measure of wealth to be close to unity. This contrasts with Friedman's finding (reported above) of an elasticity of "broad" money balances with respect to permanent income ("total" wealth) of 1.8.

Meltzer attempts to reconcile these results. His findings, which are confirmed by those of Laidler, suggest that Friedman's use of "broad" money as the dependent variable in his equation and the absence of an interest rate term from that equation are responsible for his very high estimate of this parameter. Meltzer contends that it is time deposits which are highly elastic with respect to wealth and that by including these deposits in his measure of "money" Friedman has overstated the wealth elasticity of money defined as ($DD + C$). More importantly, Meltzer claims that his measure of nonhuman wealth produces an empirical money demand function which explains a slightly higher proportion of the variance of money balances defined either as $M1$ or $M2$ than does Friedman's permanent income measure.[72]

---

[70]Meltzer, *op. cit.*, p. 232.

[71]Permanent income may be interpreted as "reflecting the effect of those factors that the unit regards as determining its capital value or wealth: the nonhuman wealth it owns; the personal attributes of the earners in the unit, such as their training, ability, personality; the attributes of the economic activity of the earners, such as the occupation followed, the location of the economic activity, and so on. It is analogous to the "expected" value of a probability distribution." M. Friedman, *A Theory of the Consumption Function, op. cit.*, p. 21.

[72]Meltzer's basic "wealth" definition includes "total wealth" as estimated by Goldsmith, adjusted to exclude government securities, inventories, public land, and the monetary gold and silver stock and to include the monetary and nonmonetary debt of state, local, and federal governments. R. W. Goldsmith, *A Study of Savings in the United States* (Princeton, N.J., 1956).

Meltzer also finds his wealth measure "superior" to current income in the empirical demand for money function; for when both wealth and income are included in the equation, the income variable appears to play no significant role in explaining the variation in money balances, whereas the wealth variable maintains approximately the same size coefficient (and significance) in all tests. Thus, Meltzer concludes that a nonhuman wealth measure is slightly superior to Friedman's permanent income variable and far more important than current, measured income in explaining variations in the demand for money.

These results are supported in further tests carried out by Brunner and Meltzer (5). Their experiments involved comparisons of the predictions of measured velocity made from various formulations of the money demand function. In their words,

> . . . the tests sharply discriminate between the effects of income and wealth on the demand for money. . . . income appears to play a much smaller role than wealth as a determinant of desired money balances. The evidence from a number of Keynesian-type equations that take income as a constraint and ignore the effect of wealth suggests that, in general, such equations will not predict velocity or desired money balances as well as a "naive" model.[73]

Their tests on human versus nonhuman wealth measures as explanatory variables in the money demand function yield less certain results. They conclude that the relative importance of these two measures remains an "open question" in their work.

Further evidence has been put forward by Heller (30), Laidler (40), Chow (11), and Goldfeld (24). Employing quarterly data for the postwar period, Heller calculates regression coefficients for six alternative relations. Both $M1$ and $M2$ are specified as dependent variables in equations that include income and the short-term rate of interest, wealth and the short-term rate, or both income and wealth and the short-term rate as explanatory variables. The coefficients of both GNP and wealth are statistically significant in all equations in which only one of these variables appears with the short-term interest rate. However, when both of these constraints are included in the same equation, only one of them retains its significance: GNP in the $M1$ equation and wealth in the $M2$ equation.

Heller attributes this result to the fact that time deposits (included in the $M2$ measure) are related positively to wealth and negatively to income. A negative income coefficient results when time deposits are regressed against both income and wealth in a single equation. This indicates a substitution effect between time deposits and demand deposits: i.e., with wealth constant an increase in GNP will cause a fall in the volume of time deposits and a rise in the quantity of currency and demand deposits. Heller interprets this evidence as showing that time deposits and demand deposits are demanded for different reasons: "the transactions motives for cash and demand deposits and the speculative or precautionary motive for time deposits."[74]

---

[73]Brunner and Meltzer, *op. cit.,* p. 350. The "naive" model referred to by the authors is a model that assumes that velocity in any one year will be the same as actual velocity in the previous period.

[74]Heller, *op. cit.,* p. 300.

The results of tests such as those conducted by Heller appear to be quite sensitive to the quarterly time frame in which the data are measured. Sharply contrasting results are derived from annual data. For example, Laidler set out to compare the explanatory power of four alternative money demand hypotheses. These include (1) the textbook equation with current income and an interest rate as constraints, (2) a Friedman-type permanent income formulation, (3) a model that includes permanent income as a proxy for the volume of transactions and a measure of accumulated transitory income and negative transitory consumption to account for the allocation of funds from these sources to money balances, and (4) a model that includes the last factor specified above and a nonhuman wealth measure defined as accumulated savings out of permanent income.

Implicit in Laidler's tests of these hypotheses is a comparison of the explanatory power of current income, permanent income, and his indirect measure of nonhuman wealth (accumulated savings out of Y_p) as explanatory variables in the money demand function. From his regressions, which employ first differences of annual observations, Laidler finds that "though the results are not absolutely decisive, they strongly suggest that permanent income provides a better theory of the demand for money than does either nonhuman wealth or any other set of variables tested."[75]

Laidler's third hypothesis, which includes a measure of transitory income in the money demand equation, performs the least satisfactorily over the period covered by his data. Although both the nonhuman wealth (4) and the permanent income (2) hypotheses explain the variation in the dependent variable quite satisfactorily, Laidler judges the results with permanent income to be marginally superior. More importantly, both wealth and permanent income explain more of the variation in the dependent variable than does current income (1) hypothesis. Furthermore, this last finding obtains regardless of the definition of money employed. Thus, using annual data rather than quarterly figures, Laidler challengers Heller's assertion that current income is the relevant constraint on narrow money balances.

An interesting set of experiments performed by Gregory Chow may shed some light on the apparent inconsistencies in these results. Chow attempts to isolate two different sets of factors influencing money holdings: those that determine the long-run equilibrium demand for money and those that influence the rate at which people will make short-run adjustments to restore equilibrium. These adjustments take place when a discrepancy exists between the long-run desired level of money balances and actual money holdings.

Chow reasons that money may be treated as a consumer durable good. He applies to the analysis of the demand for money a model originally developed to explain the demand for automobiles. In this model the long-run demand for money is posited to depend on some measure of the individual's total assets (a wealth measure) and the opportunity cost of holding those balances, the interest rate. The short-run demand for money, however, will depend on the rate at which individuals try to adjust their

---

[75]D. Laidler, "Some Evidence on the Demand for Money," *Journal of Political Economy,* 74 (February 1966), p. 63.

actual money balances to this long-run desired level. This speed of adjustment in turn depends on the actual size of any discrepancy between actual and desired balances and the rate of change of the individual's total assets (or the rate of savings)— the source from which money balances may be accumulated. Chow summarizes these factors as follows:

> Three sets of factors govern the demand for money. The first set is derived from considering the demand for services from holding money in the long-run. The second is due to time lags in the adjustment of demand to equilibrium. The third is from treating the change in the money stock as a part of saving.[76]

This model reflects both the expectational factors and partial adjustment mechanism described in the second section of this survey.

Like Laidler, Chow tests his hypothesis on annual data. The period covered is 1897-1958. In the long-run equilibrium demand function permanent income always performs far better than current income but, as in Laidler's work, only marginally better than a wealth measure.[77] However, in the short-run functions that attempt to measure the speed of adjustment to equilibrium current income is preferable to either wealth or permanent income.

A word of caution is in order in interpreting these estimates. The use of permanent income as the constraint variable determining the long-run desired level of money balances muddies the results. Permanent income is calculated as a weighted average of past levels of measured income. Consequently, the long-run demand for money function that employs this variable may be written as follows (ignoring interest rates):

$$\left(\frac{M_d}{P}\right)_T = f(Y_p) = b(Y_p)_T = b[\beta_0 \, Y_T + \beta_1 \, Y_{T-1} \ldots \beta_n \, Y_{T-n}].$$

Assuming the weights, β_i, follow a geometrically declining lag function (following Friedman), we may write

$$\left(\frac{M_d}{P}\right)_T = b[\beta_0 \, Y_T + \beta_0 \, (1 - \beta_0) \, Y_{T-1}$$
$$+ \, \beta_0 \, (1 - \beta_0)^2 \, Y_{T-2} \ldots \beta_0 \, (1 - \beta_0)^n \, Y_{T-n}).$$

But if $(1 - \beta_0)^j \to 0$ as $j \to n$, by a Koyck transformation,[78] this can be shown equivalent to

$$\left(\frac{M_d}{P}\right)_T = (1 - \beta_0) \left(\frac{M_d}{P}\right)_{T-1} + b\beta_0 Y_T. \qquad (16)$$

---

[76]Gregory Chow, "On the Short-Run and Long-Run Demand for Money," *Journal of Political Economy,* 74 (April 1966), p. 115.

[77]Chow uses the same measure of net nonhuman wealth as was employed by Meltzer.

[78]The third section of this article explains the Koyck transformation. See also R. J. Wonnacott and T. H. Wonnacott, *Econometrics* (New York; 1970), pp. 145-146.

On the other hand, if the public only partially adjusts its current money holdings to the long-run desired level and this desired level depends on *current measured income*, the following may be specified to describe this behavior:

$$\left(\frac{M}{P}\right)_T - \left(\frac{M}{P}\right)_{T-1} = \lambda\left[\left(\frac{M}{P}\right)_T^* - \left(\frac{M}{P}\right)_{T-1}\right]$$

where $(M/P)_T^*$ is the desired level of money balances and

$$\left(\frac{M}{P}\right)_T^* = a\, Y_r$$

Substituting:

$$\left(\frac{M}{P}\right)_T - \left(\frac{M}{P}\right)_{T-1} = \lambda\left[a\, Y_T - \left(\frac{M}{P}\right)_{T-1}\right]$$

$$\left(\frac{M}{P}\right)_T = (1-\lambda)\left(\frac{M}{P}\right)_{T-1} + \lambda a\, Y_T. \tag{17}$$

But this form (17), derived from a partial adjustment model in which desired money balances depend on current measured income, is indistinguishable from equation (16), which postulates that the demand for money depends on permanent income.

These relationships make unique interpretation of Chow's results impossible. They suggest that in his short-run adjustment relation, from which he concludes that current income is the appropriate explanatory variable in the demand for money function, he may simply have been measuring an equilibrium relation between desired money balances and permanent income. In short, this test is not sufficient to distinguish between a permanent income hypothesis and the hypothesis that the demand for money balances depends on current measured income but that the public is slow to adjust to its long-run desired level.

However, if there is any validity to Chow's results, they suggest a possible reconciliation of the conflict between those obtained by Heller using quarterly data and those presented by Laidler based on annual data. Heller's method may have picked up the influence of short-run adjustment factors which dominate the quarterly figures, but are less important in the longer-run annual observations.

Additional evidence using quarterly data is presented by Goldfeld (25). Within the framework of his basic log-linear model—which includes a lagged dependent variable (derived from a partial adjustment hypothesis) and both the commercial paper rate and the rate on bank time deposits—he compares the relative power of income, net worth, and changes in net worth in explaining holdings of narrow money. His results show that the absence of an income variable reduces the estimated speed of adjustment to an unreasonably low figure. When income and wealth are both included, the latter is insignificant while the former remains important. When the change in wealth is added as a third constraint, "the level effect of net worth is obliterated."[79]

The comparative predictive ability of Goldfeld's wealth equation in dynamic simulations is far inferior to that of his original income-only equation. In addition, though the inclusion of the change in net worth variable "improves the explanatory power of the equation, [it] slightly worsens its predictive ability."[80]

In summary, the bulk of the evidence available from studies employing annual data indicates rather clearly that some measure of wealth rather than measured income is the most relevant constraint on the equilibrium level of the demand for money balances. Whether this constraint is best represented by a permanent income measure that purports to include a human wealth component or by a nonhuman wealth measure, such as those employed by Chow or Meltzer, is much less apparent. At the same time, other evidence certainly suggests that current income may be related to the demand for money through short-run adjustments made to bring *actual* money balances in line with *desired* money holdings. Unfortunately, measurement difficulties with quarterly wealth data make the results of tests employing these measures difficult to interpret. However, this in turn suggests that for pragmatic policy purposes one may wish to choose that variable that performs best when the criteria chosen is predictive and forecasting accuracy. On these grounds, current income, as suggested by Goldfeld's results, is probably the most useful scale factor to employ in short-run money demand functions.

The Stability of the Money Demand Function

Harry Johnson, in his 1962 survey of monetary theory (32), listed three unsettled issues related to the demand for money. These issues included the appropriate empirical definition of money, the choice of arguments to be included in the money demand function, and the stability of the empirical relationship between those arguments and the monetary aggregate. These are not, of course, separable issues. The stability of any empirical function will depend upon the variables included in that function. Likewise, the criteria for choosing the appropriate definition of money has most often been defined in terms of the stability of the demand function for that monetary measure. However, for heuristic purposes, we have attempted to separate these issues in the empirical literature. It is hoped that by this point in the survey the major areas of agreement and of continuing contention on the first two issues have become evident.

[79]Goldfeld, *op. cit.,* p. 614
[80]*Ibid.,* p. 615.

It should be clear, however, that there has been an underlying assumption throughout this discussion that we were in fact dealing with stable relationships. While the diversity of functional forms and data periods employed by the various authors cited has made more difficult the task of reconciling divergent results, the similarity of elasticity estimates over these wide ranging studies would seem to support the essential validity of this assumption. It is worthwhile, however, briefly to consider this stability issue more explicitly.

One serious attack on the apparent stability of postwar money demand functions was presented by William Poole (54). Employing a log-linear money demand function similar to equation (3) above, Poole estimated interest elasticities of real money balances by constraining the values of the income elasticities within a range 0.5 to 3.0. Employing quarterly data for 1947-1969, his results demonstrate a *direct* relation between the constrained income elasticity and the estimated interest elasticity. More importantly, he finds that "the goodness of fit is practically unchanged over an extremely wide range of income elasticities," implying that there is insufficient information in the statistics to permit a choice among these results. On this evidence he makes the very strong assertion that "using postwar data alone, it is impossible to obtain a satisfactory estimate of the demand for money function."[81]

Goldfeld (24) has taken up this issue and persuasively countered Poole's critique. Employing an equation similar to the one specified by Poole but including a lagged dependent variable, he finds that "the interest elasticities display a clear tendency to increase with [the constrained income elasticity] but the rise is not nearly as pronounced as Poole found."[82] While Goldfeld also finds uniformly high R^2's for the various forms of the equations, he claims that this is misleading and convincingly demonstrates this by additional testing on these equations.

Though the R^2's are uniformly high for all equations, they tend to rise slightly with the constrained value of the income elasticity. However, this statistic is not strictly comparable across equations and cannot be used alone as a selection criterion. Goldfeld demonstrates this by constraining the income elasticity to the value first derived in an unconstrained form of the same equation. The constrained form reproduces the results of the unconstrained form except for the R^2, indicating the noncomparability of the R^2's resulting from the use of different dependent variables.[83]

However, there may still be a statistical means by which to choose among these equations. Goldfeld first examines the standard error of the regression and finds it lowest, as it must be, for the value derived from the unconstrained form. He then evaluates the equations by examining the root mean-square error derived from two

---

[81]W. Poole, "Whither Money Demand?" *Brookings Papers on Economic Activity* (3: 1970), pp. 489. Poole's final conclusion is not that we must give up on money demand functions, but rather that since postwar data are unreliable, additional weight must be given to long-run estimates.

[82]Goldfeld, *op. cit.,* p. 585.

[83]The dependent variable is $(ln\ M_T - e\ ln\ Y_T)$, where e is the constrained income elasticity. This variable will differ, of course, for each assumed value of the elasticity constraint.

different types of dynamic simulations on the estimated equations. As he notes, this is a more stringent test of the estimation results and is likely to be more relevant from a forecasting point of view. His results show clearly that the root mean-square errors deteriorate even more rapidly than the standard error of the regression as elasticity values diverge further from the value estimated in the unconstrained equation. He concludes, then, that Poole's rejection of estimates derived from postwar data is unwarranted and that the "income elasticity can be pinned down within a reasonable range of accuracy."[84] The estimate that he derives is 0.68, significantly less than unity and consistent with the proposition that there are economics of scale in holding money balances.

Additional dynamic simulations on his basic equation convince Goldfeld that the relationship underlying his empirical estimates has remained rather stable in the postwar period. Both short-term (out of sample) forecasts four quarters ahead of various defined subsamples of the data period and longer-term simulations over a later part of the sample period based on estimates for an earlier subperiod, suggest reasonable stability. A formal Chow test of stability, carried out by splitting the data sample into two subperiods suggested by the major institutional change brought about by the introduction of certificates of deposits (CD's) in 1961, also fails to deliver evidence upon which to reject the hypothesis of stability.[85]

The evidence on the postwar stability of the money demand relation generally conforms to the results of work that has examined the issue over longer periods with annual data. The work by Brunner and Meltzer (9), Meltzer (49), Laidler (44), and other authors cited directly supports this long-run stability. Recent work by Moshin S. Khan, using a new and more flexible technique to determine whether a regression estimate is stable over a full sample period, adds to the weight of evidence in favor of this conclusion. Using either current income or permanent income along with a long-term rate of interest, his tests over the period 1901–1965 fail to offer any support for the hypothesis that there were significant structural shifts in the money demand relations over that period.[86]

One final piece of evidence is worth citing on this issue. In 1971, both within and outside of the Federal Reserve, it was fairly widely held that, regardless of the historical stability of the money demand function, a substantial shift had occurred in the early part of that year. Even the Council of Economic Advisers in the *Economic Report to the President* in 1972 expressed this view: "In the first half of 1971, the public apparently wanted to hold more money balances at the prevailing level of

[84]Goldfeld, *op. cit.*, p. 589.

[85]For an alternative view of the effect of the creation of the CD market see M. B. Slovin and M. E. Sushka, *"A Financial Market Approach to the Demand for Money and the Implications for Monetary Policy,"* Board of Governors of the Federal Reserve System (1972), manuscript.

[86]Kahn's tests with the short-term rate suggest some instability in the relationship around 1948. This instability appears whether money is defined narrowly or broadly. In this respect Kahn's results conflict with Laidler's conclusion that the most stable demand function is one that includes the short-term rate as an explanatory variable. See M. S. Khan, "The Stability of the Demand for Money Function in the United States, 1901–1965," International Monetary Fund (July 1974).

interest rates and income than past relations among income, interest rates, and money balances suggested."[87]

Hamburger (29) has examined this view in the light of more recent evidence. Fortunately for the conclusions reached in the studies cited above, but unfortunately for our judgment on the ability of monetary economists to recognize short-run fluctuations in money demand, this recent evidence fails to confirm the instability widely assumed over that period.

In the second quarter of 1971 in the face of an increase in interest rates and a decline in the rate of growth of income, contrary to what conventional theory would predict, there was a sharp *increase* in the growth of the narrow money stock. But there is a certain weakness in conventional theory in its simplest form in that it fails to consider delayed reactions ("adjustments") to previous income and interest rate changes. Hamburger suggests that within the framework of the FRB-MIT-PENN Model, once allowance is made for such lagged adjustments even "the evidence that was available in 1971 provided only marginal support for the hypothesis that there was an upward shift in the demand for money" at that time.[88] On the basis of results obtained with more recent versions of the model that incorporate the influence of inflation on money demand, even that marginal support disappears. Perhaps more disturbing, equations developed since that time to explain month-to-month changes in $M1$ have no difficulty "explaining the rapid growth of $M1$ during the second quarter of 1971 *with relationships derived from earlier periods*" (emphasis added).[89]

This episode is reviewed here to point out a continuing dilemma facing policy makers. While it can be shown that the existence of a stable demand for money function is necessary for the conduct of effective monetary policy and while it is widely accepted, on the basis of the evidence surveyed here, that this condition has been met over a long period in the United States, it is another matter entirely for policy makers and their advisers "to make reasonably accurate on-the-spot judgments as to whether changes in the demand for money are occurring at particular points in time."[90] At this point the science of the economist becomes partner to the artistry of the policy maker.

Concluding Comment

The first and most important result of this survey is that the evidence supporting the existence of a reasonably stable demand for money function would seem to be overwhelming. This is true both of long-term evidence covering the last seventy years or so and of the evidence from the postwar period. Second, and perhaps next in importance for the conduct of monetary policy, the vast majority of this same evidence

[87]Council of Economic Advisers, *Economic Report to the President* (January 1972), p. 58.
[88]M. J. Hamburger, "The Demand for Money in 1971 . . . ," *op. cit.,* p. 721.
[89]*Ibid.,* p. 723.
[90]*Ibid.,* p. 724.

supports the hypothesis that the interest rate plays a significant role in the determination of the public's desired money holdings. Furthermore, the range of estimates for the interest elasticity of money balances has been fairly narrowly circumscribed, with the best results suggesting an elasticity of about − 0.2 for the short rate and approximately − 0.7 for the long rate. Unfortunately, it is not yet possible to state confidently which particular interest rate measure yields the most stable money demand relationship. Moreover, this question is so intimately connected with the problem of the "correct" definition of money that judgment must be suspended on this issue pending additional work, including work on the term structure of interest rates.

Third, there appears to be almost no support for the liquidity-trap hypothesis.

Finally, the best evidence to date suggests that, in addition to an interest rate measure, some measure of wealth—either a direct balance sheet measure or a proxy variable such as permanent income—would seem to be most relevant to the public's long-run decision to hold money balances. However, there is a growing body of evidence that short-run movements in money balances, determined by the speed at which people adjust their actual money holdings to a long-run equilibrium level, may be dependent upon the flow of income in this period and in the recent past.

These conclusions rest primarily on the evidence cited in this study. Other important works, many of which are included in the References, could also have been used to support some of these conclusions. The studies reviewed were selected because of their historical importance in the debate on the issues to which we have directed our attention or because they represent the best starting point for students of these problems. In short, no claim is made that this survey, in spite of its length, represents an exhaustive review of all of the literature in this field.

REFERENCES

1. BARRO, ROBERT J., "Inflation, the Payments Period, and the Demand for Money," *Journal of Political Economy*, 78 (November/December 1970), pp. 1228-1263.
2. ———, and ANTHONY M. SANTOMERO, "Household Money Holdings and the Demand Deposit Rate," *Journal of Money, Credit, and Banking*, 4 (May 1972), pp. 397-413.
3. BAUMOL, W., "The Transactions Demand for Cash: An Inventory Theoretic Approach," *Quarterly Journal of Economics, 66* (November 1952), pp. 545-556.
4. BRONFENBRENNER, MARTIN, and THOMAS MAYER, "Liquidity Functions in the American Economy," *Econometrica*, 28 (October 1960), pp. 810-834.
5. BRUNNER, KARL, and ALLAN H. MELTZER, "Predicting Velocity: Implications for Theory and Policy," *Journal of Finance*, 18 (May 1963), pp. 319-354.
6. ———, "Some Further Evidence on Supply and Demand Functions for Money," *Journal of Finance*, 19 (May 1964), pp. 240-283.
7. ———, "Economics of Scale in Cash Balances Reconsidered," *Quarterly Journal of Economics,* 81 (August 1967), pp. 422-436.
8. ———, "Liquidity Traps for Money, Bank Credit, and Interest Rates," *Journal of Political Economy*, 76 (February 1968), pp. 1-37.

9. ——, "Comment on the Long-Run and Short-Run Demand for Money," *Journal of Political Economy,* 76 (November/December 1968), pp. 1234-1239.

10. CHETTY, V. K., "On Measuring the Nearness of Near-Moneys," *American Economic Review,* 59 (June 1969), pp. 270-281.

11. CHOW, GREGORY, "On the Short-Run and Long-Run Demand for Money," *Journal of Political Economy,* 74 (April 1966), pp. 111-131.

12. ——, "Long-Run and Short-Run Demand for Money: Reply and Further Notes," *Journal of Political Economy,* 76 (November/December 1968), pp. 1240-1243.

13. DICKSON, HAROLD D., and DENNIS R. STARLEAF, "Polynomial Distributed Lag Structures in the Demand Function for Money," *Journal of Finance,* 27 (December 1972), pp. 1035-1043.

14. EISNER, ROBERT, "Another Look at Liquidity Preference," *Econometrica,* 31 (July 1963), pp. 531-538.

15. FEIGE, EDGAR, *The Demand for Liquid Assets: A Temporal Cross Section Analysis.* Englewood Cliffs Company, 1964.

16. ——, "Expectations and Adjustments in the Monetary Sector," *American Economic Review,* 57 (May 1967), pp. 462-473.

17. FRIEDMAN, MILTON, *A Theory of the Consumption Function.* Princeton: Princeton University Press, 1957.

18. ——, "The Quantity Theory of Money, A Restatement," in Milton Friedman (ed.), *Studies in the Quantity Theory of Money.* Chicago: University of Chicago Press, 1956.

19. ——, "The Demand for Money—Some Theoretical and Empirical Results," *Journal of Political Economy,* 67 (June 1959), pp. 327-351.

20. ——, and ANNA J. SCHWARTZ, *A Monetary History of the United States, 1867-1960.* Princeton: National Bureau of Economic Research, 1963.

21. ——, and DAVID MEISELMAN, "Relative Stability of Monetary Velocity and the Investment Multiplier in the United States 1897-1957," in Commission on Money and Credit, *Stabilization Policies,* Englewood Cliffs, N.J., Prentice-Hall, 1963.

22. GALPER, HARVEY, "Alternative Interest Rates and the Demand for Money: Comment," *American Economic Review,* 59 (June 1969), pp. 401-407.

23. GOLDFELD, STEPHEN, *Commercial Bank Behavior and Economic Activity.* Amsterdam: North-Holland Publishing Company, 1966.

24. ——, "The Demand for Money Revisited," *Brookings Papers on Economic Activity* (3:1973), pp. 577-638.

25. GRILICHES, ZVI., "Distributed Lags: A Survey," *Econometrica,* 35 (January 1967), pp. 16-49.

26. GURLEY, JOHN G., and EDWARD S. SHAW, *Money in a Theory of Finance.* Washington, D.C.: The Brookings Institution, 1960.

27. HAMBURGER, MICHAEL J., "The Demand for Money by Households, Money Substitutes, and Monetary Policy," *Journal of Political Economy,* 74 (December 1966), pp. 600-623.

28. ——, "Alternative Interest Rates and the Demand for Money: Comment," *American Economic Review,* 59 (June 1969), pp. 407-412.

29. ——, "The Demand for Money in 1971: Was There a Shift? A Comment," *Journal of Money, Credit, and Banking,* 5 (May 1973), pp. 720-725.

30. HELLER, H. R., "The Demand for Money—The Evidence from the Short-Run Data," *Quarterly Journal of Economics,* 79 (June 1965), pp. 291-303.

31. JAFFEE, DWIGHT M., "The Structure of the Money-Expenditure Relationship: Comment," *American Economic Review,* 60 (March 1970), pp. 216-219.

32. JOHNSON, HARRY G., "Monetary Theory and Policy," *American Economic Review,* 52 (June 1962), pp. 335-384.

33. JONES, DAVID, "The Demand for Money: A Review of the Empirical Literature," Staff Economic Studies of the Federal Reserve System, paper presented to the Federal Reserve System Committee on Financial Analysis in St. Louis (October 1965).

34. KAMINOW, I. P., "The Household Demand for Money: An Empirical Study," *Journal of Finance,* 24 (September 1969), pp. 679-696.

35. KARNI, EDI, "The Value of Time and the Demand for Money," *Journal of Money, Credit, and Banking,* 6 (February 1974), pp. 45-64.

36. KAUFMAN, GEORGE G., "More on an Empirical Definition of Money," *American Economic Review,* 59 (March 1969), pp. 78-87.

37. KEYNES, JOHN MAYNARD, *The General Theory of Employment, Interest, and Money.* London and New York: Harcourt, Brace and Company, 1936.

38. KONSTAS, PANOS, and MOHAMAD W. KHOUJA, "The Keynesian Demand-for-Money Function: Another Look and Some Additional Evidence," *Journal of Money, Credit and Banking,* 1 (November 1969), pp. 765-777.

39. LAFFER, ARTHUR B., "Trade Credit and the Money Market," *Journal of Political Economy,* 78 (March/April 1970), pp. 239-267.

40. LAIDLER, DAVID, "Some Evidence on the Demand for Money," *Journal of Political Economy,* 74 (February 1966), pp. 55-68.

41. ———, "The Rate of Interest and the Demand for Money—Some Empirical Evidence," *Journal of Political Economy,* 74 (December 1966), pp. 545-555.

42. ———, *The Demand for Money: Theories and Evidence.* Scranton: International Textbook Company, 1969.

43. ———, "The Definition of Money: Theoretical and Empirical Problems," *Journal of Money, Credit and Banking,* 1 (August 1969), pp. 509-525.

44. ———, "A Survey of Some Current Problems," in G. Clayton, J. C. Gilbert, and R. Sidgewick (eds.), *Monetary Theory and Monetary Policy in the 1970's.* New York: Oxford University Press, 1971.

45. LATANÉ, HENRY A., "Cash Balances and the Interest Rate—A Pragmatic Approach," *Review of Economics and Statistics,* 36 (November 1954), pp. 456-460.

46. LEE, T. H., "Alternative Interest Rates and the Demand for Money: The Empirical Evidence," *American Economic Review,* 57 (December 1967), pp. 1168-1181.

47. DE LEEUW, FRANK, "A Model of Financial Behavior," in James Duesenberry, Gary Fromm, Lawrence Klein, and Edwin Kuh (eds.), *The Brookings Quarterly Econometric Model of the United States.* Chicago: Rand McNally and Company, 1965, pp. 464-530.

48. LYDALL, HAROLD, "Income, Assets, and the Demand for Money," *Review of Economics and Statistics,* 40 (February 1958), pp. 1-14.

49. MELTZER, ALLAN H., "The Demand for Money: The Evidence from the Time Series," *Journal of Political Economy,* 71 (June 1963), pp. 219-246.

50. ———, "The Demand for Money: A Cross Section Study of Business Firms," *Quarterly Journal of Economics,* 77 (August 1963), pp. 405-422.

51. OCHS, J., "The Transaction Demand for Money and Choices Involving Risk," *Journal of Political Economy,* 76 (March/April 1968), pp. 289-291.

52. PATINKIN, DON, "The Chicago Tradition, The Quantity Theory and Friedman," *Journal of Money, Credit and Banking,* 1 (February 1969), pp. 46-70.

53. PELTZMAN, SAM, "The Structure of the Money Expenditure Relationship," *American Economic Review,* 59 (March 1969), pp. 129-137.

54. POOLE, WILLIAM, "Whither Money Demand?" *Brookings Papers on Economic Activity* (3:1970), pp. 485-500.

55. SANTOMERO, ANTHONY M., "A Model of the Demand for Money By Households," *Journal of Finance,* 29 (March, 1974), pp. 89-102.

56. SCHADRACK, FREDERICK C., An Empirical Approach to the Definition of Money," *Monetary Aggregates and Monetary Policy,* Federal Reserve Bank of New York, (1974), pp. 28-34.

57. SHAPIRO, A. A., "Inflation, Lags, and the Demand for Money," *International Economic Review,* 16 (February 1975), pp. 81-96.

58. SHAPIRO, HAROLD, "Distributed Lags, Interest Rate Expectations and the Impact of Monetary Policy: An Econometric Analysis of a Canadian Experience," *American Economic Review,* 57 (May 1967), pp. 444-461.

59. SLOVIN, M. B., and M. E. SUSHKA, "A Financial Market Approach to the Demand for Money and the Implications for Monetary Policy," Board of Governors, Federal Reserve (1972), manuscript.

60. STARLEAF, DENNIS R., and RICHARD REIMER, "The Keynesian Demand Function for Money: Some Statistical Tests," *Journal of Finance,* 22 (March 1967), pp. 71-76.

61. TEIGEN, RONALD, "Demand and Supply Functions for Money in the United States, Some Structural Estimates," *Econometrica,* 32 (October 1964), pp. 477-509.

62. ————, "An Aggregated Quarterly Model of the U.S. Monetary Sector, 1953-1964," unpublished manuscript presented to the Conference on Targets and Indicators of Monetary Policy, University of California at Los Angeles (April 1966).

63. TOBIN, JAMES, "Liquidity Preference and Monetary Policy," *Review of Economics and Statistics,* 29 (May 1947), pp. 124-131.

64. ————, "The Interest Elasticity of Transaction Demand for Cash," *Review of Economics and Statistics,* 38 (August 1956), pp. 241-247.

65. ————, "Liquidity Preference as Behavior Towards Risk," *Review of Economic Studies,* 25 (February 1958), pp. 65-86.

66. TAYLOR, L. D., and J. P. NEWHOUSE, "On the Long-Run and Short-Run Demand for Money: A Comment," *Journal of Political Economy,* 77 (September/October 1969), pp. 851-856.

67. TSIANG, S. C., "The Precautionary Demand for Money: An Inventory Theoretical Analysis," *Journal of Political Economy,* 77 (January/February 1969), pp. 99-117.

68. TURNOVSKY, STEPHEN J., "The Demand for Money and the Determination of the Rate of Interest Under Uncertainty," *Journal of Money, Credit and Banking,* 3 (May 1971), pp. 183-204.

69. WALTERS, ALAN A., "The Demand for Money-The Dynamic Properties of the Multiplier," *Journal of Political Economy,* 75 (June 1967), pp. 293-298.

70. WHALEN, EDWARD L., "A Cross-Section Study of Business Demand for Cash," *Journal of Finance,* 20 (September 1965), pp. 423-443.

71. ZAREMBKA, P., "Functional Form in the Demand for Money," *Journal of the American Statistical Association,* 63 (June 1968), pp. 502-511.

C. Interest Rates

The two essays in this section discuss the major factors determining the structure of interest rates in the economy. The implications of the quantity theory formulation of the demand for money for theories of the determination of the price level and interest rates are explored in a seminal article by Milton Friedman. Friedman's explanation is consistent with the notion discussed in the readings in Section IB, that money affects the economy through a wide spectrum of portfolio adjustments wherein short-run effects on interest rates, especially long-term rates, may be quite small. Benjamin M. Friedman's article reviews the movement of long-term interest rates and maturity structure of interest rates as they are theoretically influenced by risk, liquidity, the supply of securities, expectations, inflation, and intermediation factors. He then relates each of these theoretical outlooks to the movement of interest rates in the real world during 1974.

Factors Affecting the Level of Interest Rates

Milton Friedman

There is a problem in terminology that is worth commenting on at the outset. In all sorts of monetary discussions, there is a tendency to use the word "money" in three different senses. We speak of a man making money when we mean that he is earning income. We speak of a man borrowing money when we mean that he is engaging in a credit transaction. Similarly, we speak of the money market in the sense of a credit market. Finally, we talk about money when we mean those green pieces of paper we carry in our pocket or the deposits to our credit at banks.

Confusion of Credit with Money

Much of the misunderstanding about the relationship between money and interest rates comes from a failure to keep those three senses of the term "money" distinct, in particular to keep "credit" distinct from "quantity of money." In discussing credit, it is natural and correct to say that the interest rate is the price of credit. General price theory tells us that the price of anything will be lowered by an increase in supply and will be raised by a reduction in supply. Therefore, it is natural to say that an increase in credit will reduce the rate of interest. That is correct. A shift to the right of the

Reprinted from the *Proceedings* of the 1968 Conference on Savings and Residential Financing, sponsored by the United States Savings and Loan League (Chicago: The League, 1969), pp. 11-27, by permission of the publisher and the author.

supply curve of loanable funds—that is, an increase in the supply of loanable funds at each interest rate—will, other things being the same, tend to reduce the interest rate. A decrease in supply will tend to raise it.

The tendency to confuse credit with money leads to the further belief that an increase in the quantity of money will tend to reduce interest rates and a reduction in the quantity of money will tend to increase interest rates.

Because of this confusion, there is also a tendency to regard the term "monetary ease" as unambiguous, as meaning either a more rapid increase in the quantity of money or lower interest rates and, similarly, monetary tightness as meaning either a reduction in the quantity of money or higher interest rates.

Interest Rate Price of Credit, Not Money

My main thesis is that this is wrong, that the relation between the quantity of money and the level and movement of interest is much more complicated than the relation that is suggested by the identification of money with credit. It is more complicated because the interest rate is not the price of money. The interest rate is the price of credit. The price level or the inverse of the price level is the price of money. What is to be expected from general price theory is what the quantity theory says, namely, that a rapid increase in the quantity of money means an increase in prices of goods and services, and that a decrease in the quantity of money means a decrease in the price of goods and services. Therefore, to see what effect changes in the quantity of money have on interest rates, it is necessary to look more deeply beneath the surface.

Before going into the detailed analysis, let me prepare the groundwork by discussing some facts. If you ask most economists, or most noneconomists for that matter, certainly if you ask most people at savings and loan institutions or in banks, whether an increased quantity of money will mean higher or lower interest rates, everybody will say lower interest rates; but looking at broad facts shows the reverse.

If I ask in what countries in the world are interest rates high, there will be widespread agreement that they are high in Brazil, Argentina, and Chile. If I say, "I take it that in those countries there are very low rates of increase in the quantity of money and that interest rates are high because money has been tight," you will laugh at me. Those are countries which have had very rapid increase in the quantity of money and inflation.

If I ask in what countries of the world are interest rates low, you will tell me in countries like Switzerland. On the usual view, this would imply that they have been having rapid increased in the quantity of money. Yet we all know that the situation is precisely the reverse. Switzerland is a country which has held down the quantity of money.

Let us turn to the United States. Suppose I said, "What is the period in the United States when interest rates fell most rapidly?" There is not the slightest doubt when that was. It was the period from about 1929 to the mid-1930s. Would you then say, "That must have been the period when the quantity of money was increasing."

Obviously not. We all know that it is the opposite. From 1929 to 1933, the quantity of money fell by one-third and, as I shall proceed later to say, therefore interest rates fell, although in terms of the usual presumptions that economists have and which are enshrined in our elementary textbooks, one would say precisely the opposite.

Similarly, interest rates are high now in the United States in nominal terms. Nominal interest rates are far higher than they were in the mid-'30s, far higher than they were just after the war. Yet, in the past five or six years, the quantity of money has been increasing relatively rapidly.

The point of this crude and rough survey of experience is to bring home that the broadest factual evidence runs precisely contrary to what most of us teach our students and what is accepted almost without question by the Federal Reserve System, by bankers, by the savings and loan business.

So far I have mentioned one set of broad facts, namely, the relation between the level of interest rates and the rate of change in the quantity of money. When the quantity of money has been increasing very rapidly, there is a tendency to have high interest rates; when it has been decreasing very rapidly or increasing slowly, there is a tendency to have low interest rates.

Gibson Paradox: Prices, Interest Rates Move Together

Another empirical regularity, which was pointed out many years ago, exists not between money and interest rates but between prices and interest rates. The Gibson paradox is the observed empirical tendency for prices and interest rates to move together. When prices are rising, interest rates tend to be rising; when prices are falling, interest rates tend to be falling.

This was regarded as a paradox because of the orthodox view I have been questioning. Ordinarily, prices would be expected to be rising because the quantity of money is increasing. If the quantity of money is increasing, the orthodox view is that interest rates should be falling. Yet we find that when prices are rising, interest rates are rising, and when prices are falling, interest rates are falling.

That is another piece of empirical evidence which needs to be interpreted by any theory which tries to explain the relationship between the changes in the quantity of money, on the one hand, and the level or direction of movement in interest rates, on the other hand.

Let me turn from this background to a theoretical analysis of the relationship between money and interest rates. This analysis is one which has been developed over the past few years, and in that period three different empirical pieces of work have been done which I am going to summarize for you. To the best of my knowledge, none is yet published.

The first is some work that Anna Schwartz and I have done in studying the relationships between longer term movements in the quantity of money and in interest rates. The second is some work that Phillip Cagan has done at the National

Bureau on shorter term movements in interest rates within the cycle. Anna's and my work uses as the basic unit a half-cycle, so it has to do with the intercycle movement. Phil Cagan's work has to do with the intracycle movement.

The third is a doctoral dissertation just recently completed at the University of Chicago by William Gibson, who is now at the University of California in Los Angeles, which also deals with the shorter period relationships between money and interest rates.

The new work in this area is an interesting phenomenon because it reflects a very long cycle. Irving Fisher worked on this problem back in the '20s and '30s. What the three of us have done is to redo Fisher and find that he was right after all. While there has been considerable work done in these past three years, it owes a great deal to the much earlier work done by Fisher. This is particularly true of the analysis of the Gibson paradox.

Analysis of Changes in Money, Interest Rates

I should like to present to you what seems to me now to be the correct theoretical analysis of the relationship between changes in the quantity of money and interest rates. I shall argue that there are three sets of effects which have to be distinguished. The first is the liquidity effect. The second is what I shall call the income effect. The third is the price anticipations effect. I shall argue that, of these three effects, the first one works in the direction which has been generally expected, but the second and the third work in the opposite direction. If the effect of monetary change on interest rates is to be understood, all three have to be taken into account.

The liquidity effect in its simplest form is the usual textbook relationship between the quantity of money and the interest rate which says that the larger the quantity of money, the lower the interest rate will have to be to induce people to hold it. I have drawn it in that form in Figure 1, but no one who is careful writes it in that form and this is one of the slips in the analysis. What really should be measured on the

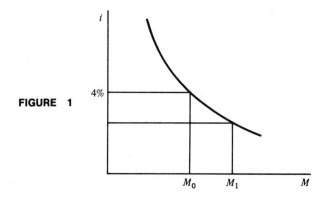

FIGURE 1

horizontal axis is not *M*, the nominal quantity of money, but *M/P*, the real quantity of money.

Part of the story of tracing the effect of a change in money is going from a change in the nominal quantity of money to what happens to the real quantity of money. For the moment, however, let us waive that. We shall come back to it because it is in the second set of effects—the income effect or income-and-price effect. Let us stay here for the moment with the liquidity effect.

Consider now Figure 2, in which time is measured on the horizontal axis. Let us suppose that up to some moment of time, t_0, there has been a constant rate of increase in the quantity of money, say 3 percent per year. At a certain time it suddenly starts increasing at 5 percent a year. Let us suppose that interest rates prior to t_0 have been 4 percent, as shown on Figure 2. What should we expect to be the pattern of behavior of interest rates as a result of this one-shot change in monetary growth as it works itself out through time? That is the central theoretical problem.

The first tendency of any economist, in terms of our present literature, is to stress the fact that in order to get people to hold the large quantity of money, interest rates will have to go down. As shown in Figure 1, people were willing to hold M_0 at a rate of interest of 4 percent. To get them to hold more, there will have to be a movement along the curve to lower interest rates. There is an implicit assumption in that analysis that needs to be brought to the surface. The implicit assumption is that prices are not in the first instance affected by the change in the quantity of money.

Let us suppose that prior to this time, prices were stable. Let us suppose for a moment that 3 percent corresponds to the rate of output increase in the economy and that velocity is constant, just to keep matters simple. None of these assumptions really affects the essence of what I am saying. If, when the quantity of money started increasing at 5 percent per year instead of 3 percent, prices suddenly started increasing at 2 percent per year, you would stay exactly in the same place on the curve in Figure 1 (if the horizontal axis is interpreted as *M/P*), and there would be no tendency for interest rates to go down. The implicit assumption that, in the first instance, the effect is not likely to be on prices, is consistent with much empirical evidence. I should qualify this statement. The implicit assumption seems correct *if* this jump from 3 percent to 5 percent is an unanticipated jump. If it were announced

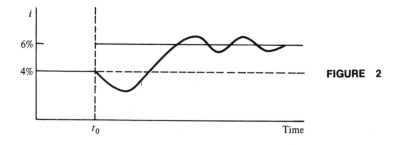

FIGURE 2

that the jump was going to occur, it would be more plausible that it would have an immediate effect on prices.

Liquidity Effect: Price of Securities Up, Interest Rate Down

If this is an unanticipated jump in the rate of monetary increase, it is reasonable to suppose that its first impact will be that people will find the composition of their portfolios disturbed. Holders of cash will find that they have more cash than they planned to have. Their first impulse will be to attempt to readjust the portfolios by replacing cash with other securities. This will bid up the price of other securities and lower the rate of interest. This would be the liquidity effect.

This is the effect which explains why academic economists, in general, will say offhand that an increase in the quantity of money will lower interest rates. In economic terminology, we would call this an effect through stocks. The financial economist or Federal Reserve economist will argue a little differently. He would expect an immediate effect through flows. He would say, "How is the rate of increase in the quantity of money stepped up?" He would say that in our kind of financial system ordinarily it will be stepped up by an increased rate of purchase of securities by the central banks, which in turn will add to the reserves of commercial banks which will expand by making additional loans. He would say that the very process of stepping up the quantity of money in our kind of financial system operates to raise the supply of loanable funds. That is entirely true of our kind of financial system.

It is interesting to note that discussions of the problem in earlier literature, for example, in John Stuart Mill's *Principles of Political Economy,* written over a century ago, very clearly stated that the first-round effect which was to be expected from a change in the quantity of money would be different as it occurred through the credit market or as it occurred through a change in gold production. It was argued that if it occurred through gold production, its first-order effect would be not on interest rates but on the wages of gold miners and the prices of commodities they bought and that it would spread from there. On the other hand, if the increase in the quantity of money occurred through the credit market, its first-round effect would be on interest rates.

These two factors—the effect on stocks and the effect through flows—would work in the same direction. However, the title "liquidity effect" under which I have included both is not an entirely descriptive term. Both factors tend to make for an initial decline in the rate of interest—the stock effect because of a movement along the liquidity curve and the flow effect because of a movement to the right in the supply of loanable funds. There is a difference. The flow effect would produce a decline in the interest rate which might be expected to happen immediately. As long as prices do not react, the effect through stocks will exert a continuing downward pressure on the interest rate. So it is not clear whether the liquidity effect would produce simply a sudden drop to a new level or a period during which interest rates fall, as I have shown it on Figure 2. That is the first effect—a liquidity effect.

Income-and-Price Level Effect

The next effect is the income-and-price level effect. As cash balances are built up, people's attempts to acquire other assets raise the prices of assets and drive down the interest rate. That will tend to produce an increase in spending. Along standard income and expenditure lines, it will tend to increase business investment. Alternatively, to look at it more broadly, the prices of sources of services will be raised relative to the prices of the service flows themselves. This leads to an increase in spending on the service flow and, therefore, to an increase in current income. In addition, it leads to an increase in spending on producing sources of services in response to the higher price which can now be obtained for them.

The existence and character of this effect does not depend on any doctrinal position about the way in which monetary forces affect the economy. Whether monetary forces are considered as affecting the economy through the interest rate and thence through investment spending or whether, as I believe, reported interest rates are only a few of a large set of rates of interest and the effect of monetary change is exerted much more broadly, in either case the effect of the more rapid rate of monetary growth will tend to be a rise in nominal income.

For the moment, let us hold prices constant and suppose that the rise in nominal income is entirely a result of rising output. What effect will that have? It will raise the demand curve for loanable funds. A business expansion is in process and the increasing level of income will raise the demand for loanable funds. This will exert a force tending to raise interest rates, or at least to counteract the downward pressure from the increasing stock of money. In addition, the rising incomes will tend to shift to the right the liquidity preference curve of Figure 1, since the higher the income, the larger the quantity of money demanded at each interest rate. (Strictly speaking, under our assumptions that the initial position was one of a 3 percent per year rate of growth in real income, the effect will be a still more rapid shift of the liquidity preference curve. Alternatively, we can interpret Figure 1 as representing a trend-corrected curve.)

Suppose the expansion in income takes the form in part of rising prices. This will not alter the tendency for the demand for loanable funds, expressed in nominal terms, to rise. But, if we measure the real quantity of money (M/P) on the horizontal axis of Figure 1, this tendency will affect that figure. Suppose prices go up as rapidly as the increased rate of monetary growth, in our assumed case, 2 percent. The real quantity of money will remain constant. If prices go up more rapidly than that, you will tend to move back along the curve. As income rises, whether or not prices rise, interest rates will turn around and go up, as a result of the rising demand for loanable funds, the shift of the liquidity preference curve, and the possible movement along it.

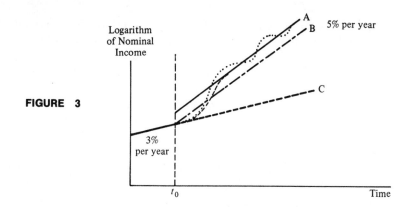

FIGURE 3

There are many reasons to believe that this rise in interest rates will go too far. It will overshoot. I cannot cover this point in full here, but let me suggest some reasons to expect even this short-run effect to overshoot.

In the first place, we started out by saying that prices will be slow to react and that the initial effect is the disturbance of portfolios. That means that there is some catching up to do. We can see what is involved most readily by looking at the ultimate long-run position.

If the rate of monetary growth stayed at 5 percent, the long-run equilibrium position would involve nominal income rising at 2 percent per year more than it did prior to the increase in the monetary growth rate. In Figure 3, Line C is a continuation of the orginal trend of rising income, let us say, at 3 percent a year. Line B shows a trend linked to the initial trend but with a rate of rise of 5 percent. If at first income proceeds along C but ultimately has to proceed along B, then for some period income will have risen more rapidly in order to catch up. That is one reason for a tendency to overshoot.

A second reason is a little more complicated. The true long-run equilibrium position of income will not be Line B but a higher line, say Line A. It will be a higher line because the amount of real balances that people want to hold will be smaller when prices are rising at 2 percent per year than when they are stable.

Price Anticipation Effect

This brings us to our third effect, the price anticipation effect. When prices are rising at 2 percent a year and people come to anticipate that they will continue to, this raises the cost of holding cash. Consequently, they will want to hold smaller balances relative to income. This is clearly the case and has been well-documented for hyper-inflation and substantial inflation. Phil Cagan's study on hyperinflation, which is by now a classic, documents very clearly that in such episodes, the higher the rate of change of prices, the higher is monetary velocity or the lower are real balances.

Studies for countries like Argentina and Brazil and Chile, countries that have had very substantial inflation, show the same phenomenon. For the United States, it has been much harder to pin down that phenomenon because our price movements have been mild.

In the study by Anna Schwartz and me, using averages for half-cycles, referred to earlier, we have been able for the first time to extract from the American data the same kind of response to the rate of change in prices as had been extracted for the more extreme inflationary episodes.

As a theoretical matter, the higher the rate of change of prices, the higher the velocity expected. This shows up as an empirical phenomenon. This is why the long period equilibrium will be a path like A in Figure 3 rather than like B. Therefore, even if there were no lag in the initial adjustment, at some time or other income or prices have to rise faster than the ultimate equilibrium rate of 2 percent per year in order to get up to this higher level. To digress for a moment, the phenomenon I have been describing is, in my opinion, the fundamental reason why a shift in the quantity of money tends to produce cyclical reaction patterns and not smooth movements. The dotted lines show two possible paths, one involving damped oscillations, the other a direct approach to equilibrium. But note that even the latter involves a cyclical reaction in the rate of change of income.

The price anticipation effect is the one that is most closely linked to Irving Fisher, that he investigated statistically, and that he introduced to explain the Gibson paradox.

If I may go back a moment, I am sliding over one point that I ought to make explicit. For simplicity, I have been talking as if the initial position we started from was one where there was reasonably full employment, so that while in the interim there can be a period with income increasing and prices stable, sooner or later the higher rate of rise in income will be translated into a higher rate of price increase. That really is not essential for my story at all.

It may be that part of the effect will be taken up in output rather than in prices. All that is essential is that there be some tendency for prices to rise somewhat more than they otherwise would, although I may say that, as an empirical matter, I would expect a shift from one fairly steady rate of monetary growth to another to be reflected fully, sooner or later, in prices.

Distinguish between Nominal, Real Rate of Interest

As long as there is some tendency for part of the increase in the rate of growth of the quantity of money to end up in a higher rate of price rise, sooner or later people will come to anticipate it. As people come to anticipate it, we introduce a distinction that I have so far kept out of the picture, namely, the distinction between the nominal rate of interest and the real rate of interest.

We are all very much aware of the distinction right now. It is also a distinction that goes back in our literature, at least to Irving Fisher who analyzed it most exhaustively. If the nominal interest rate is 4 percent per year and if prices over any period rise at the rate of 2 percent per year, then the realized real yield will be 2 percent, not 4 percent.

However, what matters for the market is not the *ex post* yield which is realized after the event but what people anticipate in advance. People today are buying bonds or other securities or making loans for the long-term future on the basis of what they anticipate will happen.

Let us designate the nominal interest rate by R_B (the B for bonds) and the real rate by R_E (E for equity). Now $1\ dP/P\ dt$ is the percentage rate at which prices are changing at time t. Let an asterisk attached to it stand for an anticipated rate, so $(1\ dP/P\ dt)^*$ is the anticipated rate of change in prices. Then, the relation Fisher developed is $R_B = R_E + (1\ dP/P\ dt)^*$. In other words, the nominal rate of interest on the market will be equal to the real rate of interest plus the anticipated rate of price change. Therefore, if R_E stays the same but the anticipated rate of price change goes up, the nominal interest rate will also go up. That is the third effect.

Returning to Figure 2, we see that if the whole of this 2 percent higher rate of monetary growth goes into prices, and if the initial equilibrium interest rate was 4 percent, then the new long-run equilibrium rate will be 6 percent. The interest rate pattern then will be something like that shown in Figure 2 and will ultimately get up to 6 percent.

What Theoretical Analysis Determines

That is the whole of the theoretical analysis that leads to tracing out a path of reaction in interest rates. I have exaggerated somewhat what can be traced out from the theoretical analysis alone since the fluctuations I have put in are not well determined. What is really determined by the theoretical analysis is an initial decline, a subsequent rise, and an ultimate attainment of a level about 2 percent higher than the initial one.

Let me give this theoretical analysis some empirical content. How long are these periods? What is their duration? Of the three studies that I have described, the one that Anna and I have done traces out the time pattern at the end, while Cagan's and Gibson's studies trace out the time pattern at the beginning. So far we have a missing link in between. The empirical work all three of us have done is entirely consistent with the pattern traced out in Figure 2. Empirically, there is a tendency for a rapid rate of monetary growth to be followed by a decline in interest rates and, after a lag, by a rise and then a final ultimate movement to a level higher than the starting point. The major patterns are recorded in the empirical evidence and do come out very clearly.

I have been talking about an increase in the rate of monetary expansion. Obviously, everything is reversed for a decrease, and our empirical studies, of course, cover both increases and decreases.

It turns out that the initial decline in interest rates after an acceleration of monetary growth lasts about six months. Clearly, there is variation but the average period is about six months. The time it takes to get back to the initial level is something like 18 months.

Long Period to Final Equilibrium Level

The period it takes to get to the final equilibrium level is very long. Fisher came out with a period of something like 20 years. He did a number of different studies which gave him estimates of 20 or 30 years. Our own estimates are about the same. They make a distinction which Fisher's did not. They suggest that the period is different for short rates than it is for long rates. Fisher did his studies for long rates and did not make that distinction.

As a purely theoretical matter, one would expect that it would take longer for long rates than for short rates. When you are buying a security with a short life, you are really interested in extrapolating price movements over a shorter future period of time than when you are buying a very long-term security. It seems not unreasonable that if you are extrapolating for a short period, you will look back for a shorter period than when you are extrapolating for a longer period.

I regard it as very strong empirical confirmation of this interpretation of the evidence that it does turn out that the period it takes to get full adjustment tends to be much longer for long rates than it does for short rates.

In Figure 2, the time it takes to get to the final equilibrium level depends on how long it takes for a change in the rate of monetary change to produce general anticipation of further price rises. That implicitly means that it depends on how far back people look in forming their anticipations. The mean period of price anticipation turns out to be something like 10 years for short rates and 20 years for long rates. Since these are the average periods, they imply that people take an even longer period of past history into account. These results are wholly consistent with Fisher's.

One more interesting point—and here I am much more tentative—such evidence as I have seen suggests what is to be expected, namely, that the period it takes is much longer in a country which has experienced mild price movements than in a country which has experienced rapid price movements. In one of the South American countries where prices have moved much more rapidly, the period it takes appears to be much shorter. That is what is to be expected in a more variable world where anticipations would be formed over a briefer period of time.

Relationship between Analysis and Gibson Paradox

Let me tie this in to the Gibson paradox and show how this analysis is related to that. The explanation that Fisher offered for the Gibson paradox was the same as what I

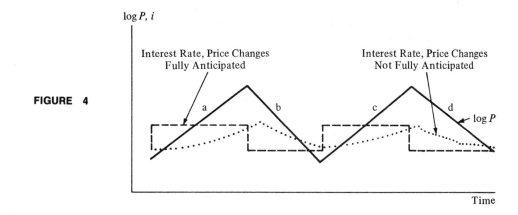

FIGURE 4

have called the third effect, but it hinges very much on how long it takes for people to form their anticipations. If price change were perfectly anticipated, if people instantaneously anticipated what was actually going to happen, high interest rates would be associated with rapid rates of price rise and low interest rates would be associated with low rates of price rise or with price declines, but there would be no reason to expect a connection between rising prices and rising interest rates.

Let me see if I can make this clear. Suppose that the historical record of prices was like that plotted in Figure 4, where the ordinate is the logarithm of the price, so that straight lines correspond to constant rates of price increase or decrease. If people fully anticipated this, the result would be that for periods a and c the interest rate would be high, for periods b and d the interest rate would be low—as shown by the dashed steps. There is no reason why rising prices should be associated with rising interest rates. Rising prices would be associated with high interest rates; falling prices with low interest rates. Yet the Gibson paradox is that rising prices are associated with rising interest rates and falling prices with falling interest rates.

In order to explain the Gibson paradox on this basis, Fisher says that if prices start to rise, people do not really believe it. It takes a long time before they accept the idea that prices are rising. Therefore, if we plot on Figure 4 not what the actual rate of change of prices is but what the anticipated rate of change of prices is, we find that it behaves like the wavy dotted line; the anticipated rate of change of prices starts being low, and only gradually rises, and keeps on rising for a time after actual prices start declining. Only after a lag will it start to decline, and then it will decline only gradually.

So, said Fisher, let prices start to rise when those prices have been stable. As prices rise, people gradually come to anticipate the rise. Only after prices have been rising for a long time will people take full account of the actual rate of rise.

Price Savings and Anticipation Time

In order for this delayed formation of anticipations to explain Gibson's paradox empirically, it is clear that there has to be a particular relation between the length of the period that it takes for people to form their anticipations and the actual long swings in prices. If people formed their anticipations very rapidly—much more rapidly than the length of a price rise or fall—then interest rates would rise for only a short period along with prices and soon would be high but constant. When prices started declining, interest rates would be low but constant. They would look more like the steps in Figure 4 than like the wavy dotted line. In order to have a close correlation between rising prices and rising interest rates, there must be a particular relation among the periods. It must be that the period of the long swings in prices is roughly comparable to the period of time which it takes for people to form anticipations.

That is what Fisher found. Indeed, that is the way in which he estimates the period it takes to form anticipation, and it is the way we have done it as well.

Fisher's conclusions as he presented them in the 1920s tended to be disregarded by almost all economists. Very few people paid any attention to him. The explanation is simple. People said, "That's silly theory, why should it take people 20 to 30 years to form anticipations about price changes? Surely, a theory which requires such a long period must be wrong."

What Anna Schwartz and I did was to recalculate the correlations for an additional 40 years or so beyond the period for which Fisher had data. The correlations are just as good for the additional 40 years as they were for the period before. This is a rare event in applied economics. All of us have had problems with spurious results. We try a dozen different correlations and finally get one that is satisfactory. How do we know it will hold for the future? It usually does not. But in this case, it so happens that Fisher studied this up through the '20s and we have about 40 more years of experience. Nobody since has paid any attention to this particular aspect of the data. Yet they show exactly the same thing for the period since then that they showed before, namely, a high correlation between the rate of change of prices and the rate of change of interest rates. The correlation is higher than the correlation between the level of interest rates and the rate of change of prices. That is to say, it is not the step relation in Figure 4 that dominates but the wavy one.

It is interesting to ask the question, "Why is it that it should take people so long to form anticipations?" I think another feature of the work that Anna and I did gives a very important clue to the answer and has importance beyond this particular problem. You will recall that I mentioned the repeated failure in former work to find a relationship between the rate of price change and velocity in the United States. In the study we made, we found it for the first time. The reason we did, I believe, is that we used as our unit of analysis the half-cycle. Ordinarily, in most such work when we introduce lags we tend to introduce constant chronological lags—one year, two years, three years.

When we started to work on this problem, we found ourselves introducing variable lags without intending to do so because if economic series are averaged over half-cycles, some half-cycles are short, some are long. Consequently, when we related velocity today to price change in a prior cycle phase, we implicitly had a lag that was long when the cycle phases were long and short when the cycle phases were short.

Distinction between Psychological, Chronological Time

What led me to continue along this line was the work that Maurice Allais described in his "A Restatement of the Quantity Theory of Money," recently published in the *American Economic Review* and in which he made a very basic and important distinction between psychological time and chronological time.

Let me translate this idea without going into Allais' particular way of putting it— though I believe his paper is one of the most important and original that has been written for a long time, not particularly because of its treatment of the demand for money but for its consideration of the problem of the formation of expectations.

People who are trying to form anticipations have some understanding of the nature of the society. They know that the economy goes in cycles and has its ups and downs. Suppose you are trying to form an anticipation about what is going to happen to prices. You will say, "I had better average out over these cycles. I had better look back to what was happening in a corresponding phase of the last cycle." If you are examining past history with the idea that there is some kind of cyclical pattern, it is perfectly reasonable for you to go back a roughly fixed number of cycles, not years.

That is exactly what our results suggested. Better results were obtained by taking as a unit of measurement the cycle and not the year. Let us apply this idea to the present problem. Let us say that you are going to buy a 40- or 50-year bond. You want to make a prediction for a long period on the basis of the past. It is reasonable for you to form your anticipation not on the basis of short-period data of the last few years but of a period that will encompass, as it were, full economic episodes.

Because of limitations of time, I am proceeding very dogmatically and sketchily, but this establishes a theoretical reason why it is not surprising to find that the period over which the anticipation is formed bears a relationship to the observed period of long swings in prices.

Correlation between Anticipation Period, Fluctuations

You might say that Fisher's result is a pure coincidence. His result depends on the periods of formation of anticipations being roughly as long as the periods of sustained price movements. Why should they be? If people are intelligently forming anticipations about the future on the basis of an analysis of the past, it is not a foolish thing for them to behave that way. That is why I believe that you will find that this period of anticipation is shorter in those countries which have sharper and more rapid fluctuations than in those which have slower and longer fluctuations.

I was very much struck with this point the other day when I was in New York acting as a representative of many of you at a College Retirement Equity Fund lunch. Some financial people started talking about the difference between the behavior of young people today and of their own behavior with respect to borrowing on credit. These people's behavior today was being very much influenced by what had happened in the 1930s. This was over a 30-year lag in their behavior.

Now of course the actual lag for the society is an average over all age classes and this is the longest lag, but once you start to look at it in that way, it does not seem to me too surprising that the lag should be so long.

Let me give you another empirical illustration. There is little doubt in my mind that the widespread expectation that prevailed in the United States after World War II that there would be a price fall involved using data going back roughly 150 years.

You ask yourself, "How shall I form an anticipation about what happens after a major war?" There is no use looking at what happened during peace time. It is better to look at what happened after earlier major wars. People who were forming these anticipations after World War II looked back at what happened after World War I, what happened after the Civil War, what happened after the War of 1812, and they found that in each of these cases, within about 10 or 15 years after the end of the war, prices were half what they had been at the end of the war. So it was not at all absurd for people to form their anticipations on the basis of a period stretching back over 100 years.

Recent Experience Illustrates Analysis

Let me conclude simply by applying this analysis to recent experience because it applies beautifully. When I say this analysis, I really am talking mostly about the short period analysis, not Fisher's long period analysis. Consider what happened in 1966 and 1967 because it was almost a perfect representation of the relationship I have shown in Figure 2.

There was a rapid rate of growth in money until April 1966. (The exact rate depends on whether you use a narrow or a broad definition of money but nothing I say will be affected by that because the patterns of behavior of the different rates are the same although the quantitative rates of change are different.) From April 1966 to about December 1966 there was a brief but sharp decline in the rate of monetary change.

From December 1966 or January 1967 through most of 1967, to something like October or November of 1967, there was an even more rapid rate of increase than before April 1966. Since about November 1967 there has been a tapering off in the rate of growth.

Delayed Impact of Earlier Monetary Growth

What happened to interest rates during that period? Prior to April 1966 interest rates were rising. Why were they rising? This was the delayed impact of the earlier high rate of monetary growth.

Suddenly there was a tightening of money—a sharp decrease in the rate of growth of the quantity of money. What does our theory say? Turn Figure 2 upside down. It says a rapid increase in interest rates would be expected because the delayed effect of earlier monetary ease is reinforced by the impact effect of monetary tightness. That, of course, is what happened. There was a very sharp rise in interest rates culminating in the so-called credit crunch.

The interesting thing is when did that culminate? In September or October 1966, several months before the reversal in monetary growth. That is exactly what our analysis would lead you to expect—a turnaround about six months after the shift in monetary growth.

At this point the tight money was having a depressing effect on interest rates. The liquidity effect had shot its bolt; the income effect was beginning to take over. That income effect resulted in a slowdown in the economy in the first half of 1967 which reduced the demand for loanable funds and so interest rates fell.

Then what happened? After monetary growth accelerated in January 1967, the short-term effects of easy money reinforced the delayed effect of the tighter money and so interest rates continued to fall. But this time the short-term effect was abnormally short—less than six months. Interest rates turned around some time in March or April that year and started to go up. These delayed effects of easy money were then reinforced in November 1967 by the tapering off of monetary growth.

Many Factors Affect Interest Rates

Obviously, I am not trying to say for a moment that monetary change is the only thing that affects interest rates. Do not misunderstand me. I am trying to isolate that part of the interest rate movement which is determined by monetary change. Many, many other things affect interest rates.

In particular, I have no reason to doubt that the sharp increase in the federal government's deficit, which meant an increase in the demand for borrowing by the federal government, was a factor which was raising interest rates through most of 1967. It may be that is why there was an abnormally short delay before the initial impact of easy money was reversed.

I should have made this qualification about other factors earlier. Our squared correlations are perhaps on the order of about 0.5 which means they account for half of the fluctuations in nominal interest rates. I do not for a moment want to suggest that if you understand the effect of monetary change on interest rates, you therefore have a theory of interest rates. In the first place, there are other forces which will change real interest rates. In the second place, there are undoubtedly other forces changing nominal interest rates, but it so happens that the major movements of nominal interest rates in 1966 and 1967 seem to have been dominated by the monetary effects so they serve to bring out very clearly the relations I have described.

One more word about the longer term relations. If this analysis is right, our present interest rates of 6 percent or 6.5 percent are still on the way up because they are still reflecting the building up of anticipations of price increases. Our present interest rates are extremely low—if you subtract the rate of price change, you have very low real interest rates. Therefore, if this analysis is right, the long-term trend of interest rates ought still to be up.

24

The Determination of Long-Term Interest Rates

Benjamin M. Friedman*

I. Introduction

The summer of 1974 brought record high yields on most long-term debt instruments publicly traded in the U.S. financial markets. As the accompanying Chart 1 shows, corporate bonds at 10.4 percent, U.S. Treasury bonds at 8.5 percent and Federal agency bonds at 9 percent all reached yield levels well in excess of their previous peaks achieved in the "squeeze" of 1969–1970, and municipal bonds at 6.9 percent came within 30 basis points of their 1970 peak. For the first time in U.S. history, high-grade corporate bonds, a primary source of investment capital supporting the core of American industry, came to market with double-digit coupons. All in all, 1974 proved to be an extraordinary episode for the bond market.

In light of the importance of long-term interest rates in determining the broader pattern of economic developments, the bond market's 1974 experience merits considerable attention in retrospect. What brought about these record high long-term yields?

Reprinted from Federal Reserve Bank of Boston, *New England Economic Review* (May-June, 1975), pp. 35-55, by permission of the publisher and the author. The footnotes and references were provided by the author for this volume.

*The author is currently engaged in research examining the determination of long-term interest rates and is grateful to the Federal Reserve Bank of Boston for its support of that research during the summer of 1974. The opinions expressed in this paper are the author's; they do not reflect the views, official or otherwise, of the Federal Reserve System or any of its officials.

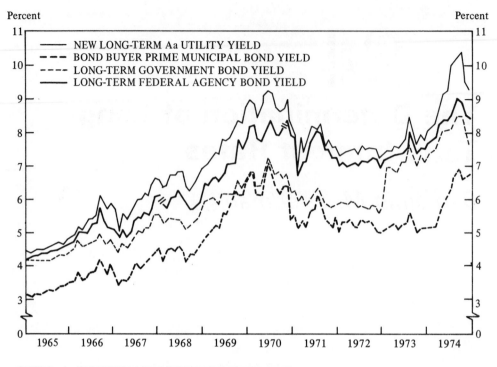

CHART 1 SELECTED LONG-TERM INTEREST RATES

Sources: Salomon Brothers, *An Analytical Record of Yields and Yield Spreads* and *Bond Market Roundup*.

Since the U.S. economy's financial markets and product and factor markets comprise an integrated overall system, one extraordinary economic circumstance is likely to occur in conjunction with others, and 1974 brought more unprecedented phenomena than simply the performance of the bond market. Other financial markets experienced their own forms of turbulence, as yields of money market instruments also reached record levels, while in the equity market the average price/earnings ratio for claims to American business fell to its lowest level since 1947. General price inflation also reached a double-digit pace for the first time in 1974, and particular raw material markets, such as those for agricultural products, experienced even more rapid inflation. The OPEC cartel unilaterally quadrupled the price of crude oil, and the higher oil price, together with the associated threat of quantity restrictions on U.S. access to imported oil, quickly became a dominating factor in many business and consumer contexts. In addition to the international political uncertainties which followed the action of the oil cartel, the denouement of the Watergate affair rendered 1974 a year also of unique strain for the domestic American political system itself.

How do all of these extraordinary features of 1974 contribute to explaining the emergence of record high long-term bond yields? What other factors were important? What, after all, are the interrelationships by which various key aspects of economic activity influence the bond market, and vice versa?

Economics has much to say about the determination of long-term interest rates. Indeed, economists have developed several different but not necessarily mutually exclusive explanations of this process, each emphasizing a distinct set of causal factors.

The object of this paper is to review the movement of long-term interest rates in 1974 through the eyes of each of these several plausible sets of explanations, reviewing in each case both the ideas involved and also the basic facts of the 1974 situation. Section II examines the choice, which is relevant both for investors and for seekers of funds, between bonds and alternative assets and liabilities. Section III focuses more directly on investors and analyzes the impact of risk and liquidity factors. Section IV turns to the borrower side of the market and considers the sources of the supply of securities. Sections V and VI, on price inflation and intermediation effects, respectively, review two more factors which are relevant both for investors and for seekers of funds. The paper's concluding section briefly draws together several of the major lessons of 1974 for the determination of long-term interest rates.

II. The Choice between Bonds and Other Assets and Liabilities[1]

Few investors place their entire portfolios in bonds. Most allocate their portfolios among some number of different assets, both financial and nonfinancial, investing only some fraction in bonds. While some investors perform this allocation according to an inflexible rule, such as placing a fixed dollar amount or a fixed proportion of their investible funds into bonds, most vary the allocation from time to time according to a host of considerations. At times these considerations may be quite complex.

Among those factors which influence investors' choices among various available assets, perhaps the most straightforward is the expected asset yield. For some choices, such as those between bonds and equities or between bonds and real estate, the direct comparison of expected yields may be only a minor element of the investor's decision, largely outweighed by other factors including some of those discussed in Sections III, V, and VI below. Choices between financial instruments and real assets, such as land or art objects, for example, may be extremely complicated, as may choices between equities and securities bearing nominal values and returns. The choice between bonds and shorter-term debt securities, however, typically depends heavily on yield considerations. Nevertheless, since instruments like certificates of deposit and open market paper mature relatively soon, while bonds mature only after quite a few years, the investment decision involved in choosing between bonds and

---

[1]For further reading on this subject, see, for example, Lutz [21]; Hicks [17], especially Chapter 11; Meiselman [23]; Wood [40]; Modigliani and Sutch [25]; Hamburger and Latta [16]; Sargent [31]; Modigliani and Shiller [24]; and Feldstein and Chamberlain [6]. (Here, as well as in footnotes 2–5, the numbers in square brackets refer to the references at the end of the paper.)

short-term instruments ought to depend upon a more sophisticated criterion than simply comparing the two alternative available yields-to-maturity.

Suppose, for example, that the investor actually anticipates keeping his funds invested for the long term. If he purchases a long-term bond, he knows relatively precisely what his investment will yield over this long period. By contrast, if he purchases a short-term security, he knows only what his investment will yield over the next few months; when this security matures, he must reinvest the proceeds at the then-prevailing market yield, which may well differ from the currently prevailing market yield. Judging the attractiveness of these two alternatives, therefore, involves making some guesses about the likely pattern of future yields. An investor who wants to place funds for a year, for example, does well to buy six-month paper yielding 8 percent per annum in preference to one-year paper yielding 9 percent per annum, if he is confident that he can reinvest in new six-month paper yielding substantially above 10 percent per annum when his first purchase of short-term paper matures.

Expectations of future yields are no less important if the investor anticipates keeping his funds invested only for the short term. In this case, if he purchases a short-term security with maturity equal to the length of time for which his funds are available, he knows exactly what his investment will yield over this period. His alternative is to purchase a longer-term bond and then sell it when he wants to withdraw the funds, in the interim collecting any associated coupon payments; the total net yield from this alternative plan clearly depends not only on the coupon and purchase price of the bond, both of which the investor knows at the outset, but also on the price to be realized from selling the bond. Given the inverse relationship between bond prices and bond yields, guesses about such future bond prices are, of course, equivalent to guesses about future yields. Once again, the investor's choice between debt securities of different maturity depends upon, among other considerations, expectations about some future yields.

The situation confronting a borrower, choosing between short- and long-term debt instruments as a vehicle for raising funds, is exactly analogous. No less than the investor deciding which security to purchase, the borrower deciding which security to issue must consider the same sorts of expectations about future interest rates.

Hence, the relevant yield criterion for choosing between bonds and short-term debt securities, either as assets or as liabilities, is not whether the two alternative *instruments* have equivalent yields but rather whether the two alternative *plans* have equivalent yields. Extending this logic of investor and borrower choice forward through the almost continuous spectrum of maturities which are available in the markets for publicly traded debt obligations in the United States implies that long-term interest rates to some extent reflect market expectations of the average future level of short-term interest rates. In particular, apart from the risk preference factors discussed below, the long-term interest rate is likely to be a geometric average of current and expected future short-term interest rates.

As a comparison of Charts 1 and 2 shows, long- and short-term interest rates have indeed tended to vary roughly together historically. If the market always expected the average future level of short-term yields to be identical to the currently prevailing

Percent

Percent

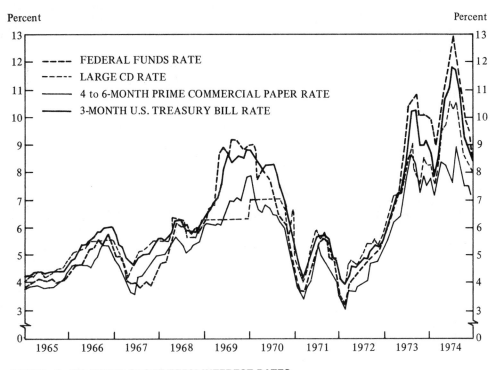

CHART 2 SELECTED SHORT-TERM INTEREST RATES

Note: The large CD rate is for 180–269 day negotiable CDs over $100,000 newly issued by New York City banks. This rate did not rise as much as other rates in 1969–70 because of Regulation Q ceilings.

Sources: Federal Reserve Bank of New York, unpublished data. Board of Governors of the Federal Reserve System, *Federal Reserve Bulletin.*

short-term yield, then the logic of alternative asset and liability choice implies that movements of the long-term yield would fully keep in step with movements of the short-term yield. In fact, closer inspection of Charts 1 and 2 reveals that long-term yields have typically fluctuated less widely than have short-term yields. Although it is impossible to observe directly the market's expectations, this evidence strongly suggests that the market does not fully adjust its expectations of the average future level of short-term interest rates whenever the currently prevailing short-term interest rate changes. Nevertheless, a change in the currently prevailing short-term yield, together with even a partial adjustment of expectations about future short-term yields, may significantly influence investors' and borrowers' choices between bonds and short-term securities.

Chart 2 shows that, in the summer of 1974, many U.S. money market instruments also reached record high yields. Prime commercial paper at 10.5 percent, bank certificates of deposit at 11.8 percent, and Treasury bills at 9 percent all represented not only inducements to investors to purchase money market instruments instead of bonds but also inducements to borrowers to turn to the bond market instead of the

Percent

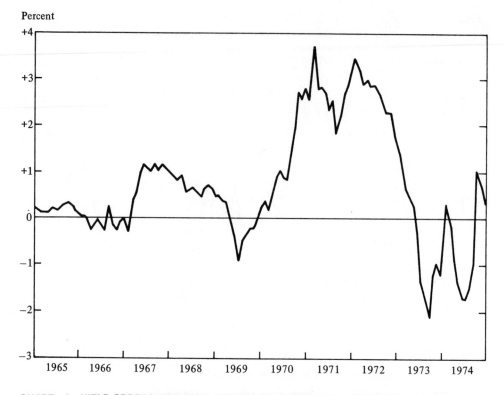

CHART 3   YIELD SPREAD BETWEEN CORPORATE BONDS AND COMMERCIAL PAPER

Sources: Salomon Brothers, *An Analytical Record of Yields and Yield Spreads* and *Bond Market Roundup.* Board of Governors of the Federal Reserve System, *Federal Reserve Bulletin.*

money market. Chart 3 shows that the yield spread between the six-month debt and the long-term debt of quality-credit U.S. corporations reached 170 basis points during the summer of 1974, a level exceeded only once during the past ten years—and then only for a single month (September 1973).

Two questions are immediately relevant to the emergence of this unprecedented situation in 1974. First, how did short-term yields become so high? Second, how did investors' and borrowers' choices between bonds and money market instruments respond to these high short-term yields?

As Chart 2 shows, short-term interest rates were actually falling at the beginning of 1974, as the economy moved into a period of decline at least partly due to the actual impact of and scare atmosphere associated with the OPEC oil embargo. By March, however, short-term interest rates had begun to rise again, and by mid spring their increase had achieved astounding speed. What happened? The basic explanation lies in some combination of demand and supply factors in the commercial bank loan market.

For some reason, still not very apparent, businesses' demand for bank loans began to increase dramatically at about this time. Observers have suggested a number of possible causes for the jump in loan demand—such as financing for rapidly inflating business inventories, commodity market speculative activity, lending to foreigners in the wake of the removal of the Federal Reserve's "voluntary" overseas credit restraint program, or additional lending to some companies which even then were having difficulties raising funds in the open credit markets—but no one has yet adequately explained the full extent of the increase which actually occurred. Commercial and industrial loans outstanding increased by a record $17.8 billion during the first six months of 1974, and other measures of commercial bank activity began to increase rapidly as well.

During the months of February through April 1974 the money stock increased at a rate of 8.7 percent per annum, somewhat above the Federal Reserve System's policy target. Misled—as at times in the past—by the inadequacies of its data reporting machinery for nonmember banks, however, as of the end of May 1974, the Federal Reserve mistakenly thought that the money stock had increased during those months at the more rapid rate of 11.2 percent per annum, well in excess of its policy target (see Table 1). This development was most unwelcome, given the emphasis which policy makers at that time placed on curbing price inflation. Highly sensitive to charges of mismanagement associated with erratic movements of the money stock during previous economic fluctuations, the Federal Reserve moved quickly to slow monetary growth. Since the willingness of businesses and households to hold cash balances depends on, among other factors, the level of short-term yields, the Federal Reserve conducted its open market operations in a way which rapidly escalated these yields to a level calculated so to discourage money demand as to bring monetary growth down to a more acceptable rate. The statistics available at the time indicated for some months—erroneously, in retrospect—that the excessive monetary growth was persisting, and so the Federal Reserve itself persisted until well through the summer in its policy of sharply restricting the supply of reserves to commercial banks. As a result of both demand and supply pressures which focused on the commercial banking system, therefore, short-term interest rates rose to the record levels shown in Chart 2.

Table 1. Money Stock Data Errors in Spring 1974

Months During 1974	M_1 Growth Rate Reported as of End of Last Month	M_1 Growth Rate Reported as of February 1975
February	14.2% per annum	10.2% per annum
March	11.1	9.6
February–March	12.4	9.9
April	8.1	6.3
February–April	11.0	8.7
May	5.3	4.4
February–May	9.7	7.6

Source: Federal Reserve *Bulletin.*

Investors responded to these high short-term yields, together with the probably higher expectations of future short-term yields, in the manner suggested by the asset-choice decision framework outlined above. Many pension funds and insurance companies, institutions which typically place about half of their investment funds into long-term bonds, became reluctant to commit funds to long-term securities at the prevailing yield levels and instead accumulated their cash flow in the form of open market paper, certificates of deposit, and other shorter-term instruments. Some of these institutions actually became net sellers of bonds into the secondary market. Similarly, borrowers responded by seeking funds in the long-term markets in a steady wave of bond issues on into the summer. Confronted by an excess of sellers (including both issuers of new bonds and some investment institutions) over buyers at current yield levels, investment bankers and bond dealers steadily lowered bid/ask quotations on the prices of outstanding bonds and raised offering yields on new bond issues. The result was the slow but steady emergence of the pattern of long-term interest rates shown in Chart 1.

III. Risk and Liquidity Factors[2]

Simple expected yield comparisons against alternative assets, such as those discussed in Section II, are typically not the only factors which influence investors' willingness to purchase bonds. If investors are sensitive also to the risk associated with holding capital assets, then they may actually choose low-yielding assets over higher-yielding ones, since indifference between two alternative assets implies equivalence of expected yields only on a risk-adjusted basis.

In theory either of two forms of risk may dominate investors' aggregate behavior toward debt securities. For investors who are certain that they can keep their funds committed for a long period of time, and whose investment goals focus primarily on the income stream generated by their assets, long-term debt securities often provide the surest returns; if these investors purchase short-term debt instruments such as commercial paper, they must face the uncertainty associated with continually having to roll over these instruments at unknown future yields. In contrast, investors who may want to sell their assets at some unknown time can typically reduce the uncertainty associated with the potential selling price of debt securities if the securities which they hold are short-term instruments. Although some groups of investors fall into one risk category and some into the other, in the aggregate investors seem to behave as if the capital uncertainty, associated with the variable price of long-term securities in the event of sale before maturity, predominates over the income uncertainty, associated with rolling over short-term securities at variable yields. Hence, investors typically require some form of yield premium, in excess of the expected average of future short-term yields, to attract them to long-term securities.

---

[2]For further reading on this subject see, for example, Keynes [19], especially Chapters 11-17; Hicks [17], especially Chapter 11; Tobin [35]; Fisher [9]; Sloane [34]; Kessel [18]; Arrow [1]; Leijonhufoud [20], especially Chapters 4 and 5; and Nelson [26].

The average upward slope of the yield curve over a long period of time may indicate a crude approximation to the average value of this liquidity premium associated with long-term securities, but there is no reason to assume that the premium itself is constant (either absolutely or as a fraction of total yield) over time. In particular, several factors which probably influence investors' views toward the increased riskiness of holding long-term bonds probably became even more pronounced than usual, in many investors' opinions, during 1974. To the extent that such risk and liquidity factors did become more important for investors' aggregate behavior in 1974, they contributed to the dramatic increase of bond yields shown in Chart 1. In order to analyze this aspect of the 1974 performance of the bond market, it is necessary to consider three separate dimensions of the riskiness of long-term bonds.

First, all debt securities which represent neither direct U.S. government obligations nor indirect U.S. government guarantees inherently bear some risk of default— i.e., of the obligor's failure to meet interest, sinking fund, and maturity payments according to schedule. Less creditworthy borrowers must typically pay higher interest rates to make their debt securities competitive with those of borrowers deemed to be of sounder credit quality. Furthermore, as Chart 4 shows, these yield differentials

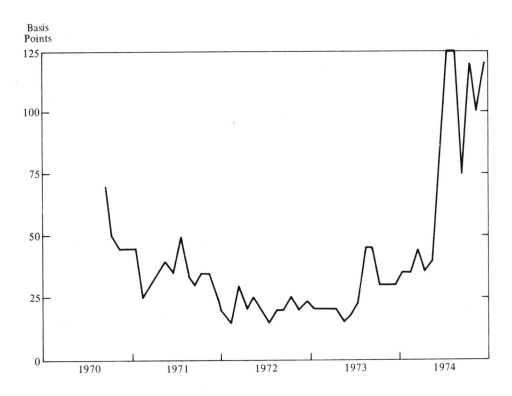

CHART 4 QUALITY YIELD SPREAD BETWEEN Aaa AND A CORPORATE BONDS

due to differences in creditworthiness are not constant but vary over time, at least in part as a result of changes in the public's attitude toward default risk. Periods of financial stringency, such as 1970 and 1974, inevitably lead to heightened concern over the ability of borrowers, especially the financially weaker ones, to meet their obligations. The increased apparent riskiness of many corporations' securities in 1974 reflected not only the publicity associated with a few major business failures, such as the Franklin National Bank, but also the tendency in recent years for corporations to allow their debt-equity ratios to rise and interest coverage to decline.

In addition to such broadly applicable fears of borrowers' defaults, the economic climate of the spring and summer of 1974 caused particular concern over the ability of many electric and gas public utility companies to remain solvent. Rapidly escalating fuel costs cut deeply into the earnings of many utilities, while some state regulatory agencies, partially in response to consumer pressure, granted rate increases only slowly. Consolidated Edison, for example, perhaps the single utility company most familiar to bond market investors, passed the spring dividend on its common stock amid a flurry of publicity. Consequently, during the summer of 1974, when market conditions were at their worst, even the most creditworthy utility companies experienced at least some difficulty in financing. In order to sell long-term debt securities, all but the few remaining triple-A rated utilities had to accept terms—such as shorter maturities, or ten years of call protection instead of the usual five—which represented concessions to the market. Several widely known and only moderately less creditworthy utility companies simply could not do their desired financing at any reasonable yield. In July Georgia Power, a familiar name in the bond market now rated A by both Moody's and Standard & Poor's, put up for competitive bid $130 million of 30-year bonds and 600,000 shares of preferred stock (par value $100); the company received no bids. Also in July Columbia Gas System, another familiar name now rated A by both Moody's and Standard & Poor's, put up for competitive bid 500,000 shares of preferred stock (par value $100); the company received a single bid, and that for only 200,000 shares. Wholly apart from the rationing phenomena indicated by these examples, it seems clear that investors' heightened fear of default increased the apparent riskiness of many bonds, thereby contributing to the rise in bond yields.

A second dimension of the liquidity of a security reflects not merely the security itself but also the institutional arrangements which exist for trading that security. Given the prevailing market institutions in the United States, some securities are more liquid in this sense than are others. The bid/ask spread associated with a multimillion dollar trade in Treasury bills, for example, is smaller than the bid/ask spread associated with a trade of comparable size in corporate bonds. In addition to this direct form of transactions cost, the ease of the transaction, in terms of rapid execution, varies considerably from one type of security to another. Like smallness of bid/ask spreads, the aspects of trading liquidity associated with ease of execution also typically favor bills over bonds and Treasury bonds over corporate bonds.

A problem currently attracting the attention of both the Securities and Exchange Commission and the U.S. Congress is the poor capitalization of the U.S. securities markets. Apart from those few securities firms which had the prescience or luck to offer their equity to the public in the better stock market climate of several years ago, most firms in these markets are privately held by relatively small numbers of individuals. As a result, these firms' ability and willingness to make markets—i.e., to take positions—in securities with volatile prices is limited. In 1974 many securities firms either ceased altogether or severely restricted their market-making activities in both bonds and equities. The result in the bond market was a slight widening of bid/ask spreads and a slight erosion of investors' overall ability to execute transactions. Although the actual decline in the liquidity of publicly traded bonds was small, these developments may have led many investors to fear that the U.S. bond market was beginning the course of trading erosion which has decimated European bond markets. To the extent that investors confronted such fears, they would have been less willing to purchase long-term bonds at any given yield.

The third—and probably most important—dimension of bonds' riskiness is the uncertainty with which investors hold the expectations of future yields discussed in Section II. Expectations of future bond yields are equivalent to expectations about future bond prices, and so uncertainty over future bond yields is analogously equivalent to uncertainty over future bond prices. For risk-averse investors who are sensitive to the possibility of having to sell long-term debt securities before maturity, uncertainty over the price to be realized from such a sale renders these securities less attractive at any given yield level.

Neither interest rate expectations nor the degree of uncertainty associated with those expectations is readily observable in the market. Nevertheless, several factors, including both economic and noneconomic developments, suggest that during 1974 market participants may have viewed future interest rates as being even more uncertain than usual. Price inflation was proceeding at a double-digit rate for the first time in U.S. peacetime experience; at the same time that the inflation itself was raising the level of uncertainty associated with risky assets, the steady weakening of the outlook for production and employment precluded confidence in the willingness of the political process to adopt and to maintain substantial restrictive measures in order to promote price stability. Furthermore, the recent sharp acceleration of price inflation had been at least partly related to movements of internationally traded raw commodity prices, poor harvests leading to high agricultural prices, and especially the OPEC countries' unilateral quadrupling of the price of oil; consequently, it was not clear how successful even a government single-mindedly devoted to price stability could be in promoting this goal. Both domestically, where a Constitutional crisis and change of Presidents dominated the news, and internationally, where continued tension in the Middle East kept open some question about future supplies of oil, political developments also added to the uncertainty. In the financial markets the record high interest rates themselves forced many institutions to chart new ground, as did the "petrodollar" flow problem discussed in Section VI below. For all of these reasons, investors may well have felt even less than usually able to form accurate expectations of future interest rates.

All three of these basic dimensions of the risk and liquidity associated with long-term debt instruments—default risk, tradability, and future price (yield) uncertainty—probably deteriorated during the course of 1974, with particular erosion during the period of severe market disarray which dominated the summer months. The reduced liquidity and increased riskiness of long-term bonds may well have led both individuals and institutional investors to avoid bond purchases and, in some cases, to sell their bond holdings, at the more moderate yields which prevailed at the beginning of the summer. In the absence of sufficient offsetting factors, the bond market moved rapidly to higher yield levels.

IV. The Supply of Securities to the Market[3]

Much of the discussion in Sections II and III focuses on investors' willingness to purchase and/or hold long-term bonds, given the availability of alternative financial and nonfinancial assets. The demand side of any market can, of course, be but half of the explanation of whatever market phenomena actually occur. If investors are willing to make only small net purchases of bonds at the prevailing market yield, the yield need not rise if bond issuers desire to sell only a small amount of net new offerings. Even if investors are unwilling, at the prevailing market yield, to hold the quantity of bonds already outstanding—i.e., if investors themselves become, in total, net sellers of bonds—it is at least conceivable that the market yield may not have to rise, if bond issuers retire more outstanding bonds than their gross offerings of new bonds.

In the United States four primary categories of long-term borrowing are predominant: Federal securities including obligations both of the Treasury and of the sponsored credit agencies (primarily the Federal Home Loan Bank Board and the Federal National Mortgage Association); state and local government obligations; corporate bonds; and mortgages, including those on both residential and commercial properties. Except for the Federal component, the supply of these securities is, to a greater or lesser extent in each particular case, sensitive to the yield which the borrower must pay. In 1974 the total net amount of new long-term securities supplied to the market was sufficiently large that yields had to rise to the levels shown in Chart 1 in order to induce investors to purchase the total supply. Furthermore, there is ground to suspect that, in some markets, credit rationing effects prevented yields from having to rise enough fully to equate supply and demand. It is a truism that, had the supply of long-term securities been either more sensitive to yield or simply smaller for any independent reason, long-term yields would have risen less. In seeking to understand why bond yields rose to their 1974 highs, therefore, it is useful to review in turn the 1974 experience of each of the four major categories of long-term borrowing. In so doing it is important to recall that, although the only quantities which can be observed are the actual amounts borrowed at the yields which finally

---

[3]For further reading on this subject see, for example, Wicksell [38]; Wicksell [39], especially Chapters 7 and 8; Cassell [4], especially Chapter 6; Robertson [29], especially Chapter 1; Tsiang [37]; Culbertson [5]; Malkiel [22], especially Chapters 6-8; Okun [27]; Bosworth [2]; Bosworth and Duesenberry [3]; and Friedman [10].

prevailed, a key factor determining these yields is the amount which market participants would have borrowed at any given yield other than the observed yield.

The U.S. government in 1974 moved toward a position of near balance of its budget for the first time in four years, as price inflation effects continued to increase Federal tax revenues rapidly while expenditures followed their somewhat more conservative recent course. As a result, overall net issues of Treasury securities, which had totaled over $23 billion in 1971, continued to decline until midyear 1974. In the first half of 1974 issues of long-term marketable Treasury securities totaled only $3 billion. Only after midyear did the Treasury significantly step up its issuance of long-term securities, and the nearly $9 billion issued in the second half of the year was still, on an annual rate basis, a smaller amount of long-term securities than the Treasury issued in 1971. Similarly, although the federally sponsored credit agencies borrowed at a record pace in the summer of 1974, most of their borrowing consisted of short-term instruments; the less than $6 billion of long-term securities issued by these agencies during 1974 was little more than the amounts issued in 1971 and 1973. As Chart 5 shows, therefore, the total net supply of long-term Federal securities seems to have become large only after midyear 1974. It is, of course, true that bond

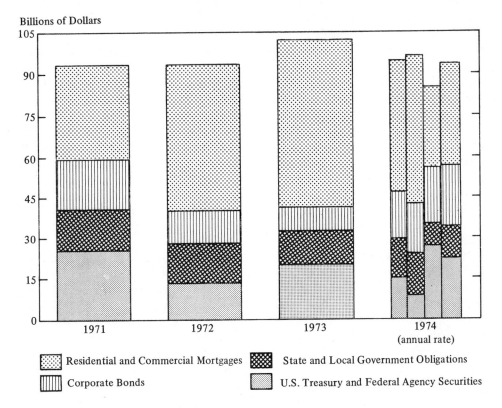

CHART 5 NET LONG-TERM BORROWING IN U.S. CREDIT MARKETS

yields in 1974 may have been lower had the Treasury and the sponsored agencies issued fewer long-term securities. Nevertheless, at least in comparison with historical standards, Federal long-term borrowings seem not to have been a major factor in causing the onset of high bond yields in 1974. At most they may have been a sustaining factor during the second half of the year.

State and local governmental units issued debt securities at a record pace in the spring of 1974, as the sum of their tax revenues, which largely rely on a rate structure significantly less progressive than that underlying the Federal personal income tax, plus Federal grants in aid failed to keep pace with inflating expenditures, and so budget surpluses shrank. The greater part of these securities issues were long-term obligations. Apart from budgetary considerations, it is worth noting that in many states and municipalities the interest ceiling laws, which effectively prohibited bond issues in the period of high interest rates in 1969 and 1970, were less a factor in 1974. Nevertheless, unlike the Federal government, which is almost totally insensitive to the yield which it must pay on its debt, voter referenda and other decision-making processes render at least some state and local governmental units reluctant to issue debt at very high interest costs. To some extent, therefore, the total net amount of state and local government bonds issued in 1974 would probably have been greater had interest rates been lower. In addition, the total net amount issued also reflected factors on the demand side of the bond market. In the first half of the year commercial banks were able to continue to add to their municipal bond portfolios, despite the tight money atmosphere, by raising funds in the certificate-of-deposit market at yields below the taxable-equivalent municipal yields. (This ability to expand bank credit rapidly against a slowly growing reserve base, largely by inducing depositors to shift from reserve-intensive demand deposits into certificates, was an element in the process by which restrictive monetary policy led to high short-term yields during this period, as described in Section II.) In the second half of the year, when short-term interest rates were higher and commercial banks became net sellers of state and local government bonds, net issues of these securities decreased sharply. Nevertheless, the mere willingness of state and local governments to issue almost $9 billion of long-term bonds during the second through fourth quarters of 1974, at the then-prevailing high interest rates, reflected at least some positive movement in their supply of securities to the market.

Net issues of long-term corporate bonds, which had proceeded at a rapid pace throughout the first half of 1974, decreased only slightly in the summer months. The source of this strong business supply of long-term debt securities is clear from an inspection of the aggregate U.S. corporate profit-and-expenditure account. Dominated primarily by physical investment in plant and equipment, corporate uses of funds have recently increased extremely rapidly. In contrast, corporations' internal generation of funds has increased more slowly, as the high reported profits have consisted to an ever greater extent (25 percent in 1974) of the price increase on finished inventories held and goods in process; since a business must continually replace inventories and working goods, these price gains do not represent any net gain of internal funds to be applied to other uses. Furthermore, to the extent that many corporations use first-in-first-out accounting methods for tax purposes, the taxability of such purely price components of corporate profits actually generates a net decrease in after-tax profits. Since several readily identifiable pressures—such as energy source problems, pollution control requirements, rising unit labor costs, and increasing foreign competition—have in many industries produced large incentives to undertake fixed investment, and since businesses typically prefer to finance fixed investment by long-term borrowing, the business sector's supply of securities to the market has increased. Wholly apart from credit rationing effects such as those discussed in Section III, the simple comparison of recent to historical net issue quantities, as in Chart 5, understates this supply increase, since the important factor is, once again, the willingness of business to issue long-term securities at any given market yield. Hence, the emergence in 1974 of a record volume of net new issues of long-term corporate bonds, despite the high level of corporate bond yields and despite any rationing which may have occurred, indicates a substantial positive shift of supply.

As Chart 5 shows, the net amount of mortgage borrowing by households and businesses in 1974 declined sharply from the 1973 level. In the case of the mortgage market, however, credit rationing effects, which were important but subsidiary qualifications in the discussions above of the bond issues of corporations and state and local governments, have been sufficiently widespread to preclude any such simple discussion of borrowers' willingness to seek mortgage credit. Since mortgage lending is today largely the province of specialized thrift institutions and since those thrift institutions encounter severe difficulty in attracting and retaining funds when readily available money market yields exceed by some margin the maximum yield which they can legally pay on deposit liabilities, the volume of funds available for mortgage lending typically contracts sharply at times of credit restraint such as 1974. For reasons largely related to tradition and to the current climate of financial overregulation, credit rationing and yield increases together determine the final outcome for the volume of mortgage credit in such periods. Primarily because of the decline in mortgage market borrowing, total net issues of long-term securities in 1974 were actually below prior years' totals. While it is, once again, difficult to infer ex ante borrowing intentions on the basis of ex post amounts borrowed, it is probably the case that the would-be supply of mortgages to the market also moved in 1974 so as to contribute to the rise in long-term interest rates.

As this brief review of the four major categories of long-term borrowing indicates, the total amount of long-term securities issued remained large in 1974 despite the record levels of long-term yields. Especially after allowing for credit rationing effects, it seems clear that, for a variety of reasons in specific sectors, the supply of long-term securities to the market—i.e., the amount of securities which borrowers would intend to supply at any given yield—rose substantially in 1974. Since supply must equal demand (apart from credit rationing), this positive supply movement was a key element in the summer's dramatic rise in long-term interest rates.

V. Expectations of Price Inflation[4]

Although some financial market participants may remember 1974 as the year of record high interest rates, for the public at large the most memorable feature of the U.S. economy's performance in 1974 will probably prove to have been the record pace of price inflation. It is hardly surprising that the emergence of the record high interest rates shown in Charts 1 and 2 coincided with a period in which, as Chart 6 suggests, virtually all measures of aggregate prices rose at rapid and accelerating speeds.

A relationship between price inflation and nominal yields is a commonplace assumption among financial market participants and observers, as well as economists, but at times the notion is too vague to provide any valuable insight. Indeed, the crux of the relationship is not current price inflation but expectations of future price inflation; current or recent price movements influence interest rates primarily by

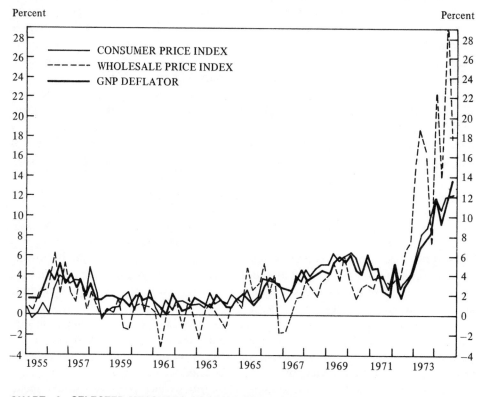

CHART 6   SELECTED MEASURES OF PRICE INFLATION
(Seasonally Adjusted Annual Rate)

[4]For further reading on this subject see, for example, Fisher [8], especially Chapters 2 and 19; Sargent [30, 32, 33]; Gibson [11, 12]; and Feldstein and Eckstein [7].

influencing market participants' expectations of future price movements. Even given the stipulation that it is expectations of future price inflation which matter, both market participants and others frequently simply accept the observed positive relationship without specifying the precise behavioral channels by which price expectations influence interest rates. It is clear that such an effect must depend upon these expectations' influencing the financial decisions made by at least some financial market participants; directly or indirectly, these decisions must then determine borrowers' willingness to issue bonds, or lenders' willingness to invest in bonds, or both.

Two such behavioral channels, by which expectations of future price inflation influence bond yields, merit particular attention. Each is symmetrical, in that it influences the behavior of borrowers and lenders in complementary ways.

First, expectations of future price movements may influence the demands for funds discussed in Section IV. Many business borrowers, for example, plan to use borrowed funds to purchase productive plant or equipment, and the use of these facilities will presumably generate output in the form of physical goods and services. If there is any nominal yield on borrowed funds, the purchase of plant or equipment is the more attractive the higher is the expected sale price of the output to be produced. If businesses come to expect an acceleration of general price inflation, therefore, then a larger amount of plant or equipment expenditures is likely to appear profitable at the given nominal yield, and so the demand for borrowings to finance such expenditures becomes greater. Similarly, if households expect the price of housing services to rise, they will be more willing to purchase houses at a given nominal yield on residential mortgages. In general, if borrowers anticipate more rapid price inflation, then the perceived real yield on borrowed funds declines unless the nominal yield rises in step with the increase in expected inflation. Unless some offsetting shift occurs in the supply of funds at the given nominal yield, demand for funds will exceed supply at that yield, and so some combination of nominal yield increase and credit rationing will be necessary to clear the market.

A slight variant of this effect of expected price inflation on borrowers' demand for funds occurs if the prices which businesses expect to rise are those of the production inputs themselves. In recent years, for example, construction costs have risen so rapidly that new installations have often doubled in cost within only a few years; businesses' and other borrowers' decisions to accelerate building programs as a cost-saving effort again lead to greater current demand for funds at given nominal yields. Households' decisions to accelerate purchases of homes have analogous effects. Similarly, the rapid rise of prices of some industrial goods and raw commodities in 1974 probably led businesses to accelerate purchases so as, in effect, to stockpile goods; this development may have been a major factor in the surge in bank loan demand discussed in Section II.

The same logic which leads borrowers to increase their demand for funds at a fixed nominal yield when they expect more rapid price inflation may symmetrically lead lenders to reduce their willingness to invest in fixed-yield debt instruments. It is important to emphasize that this effect on the lender side of the debt market can occur only to the extent either that investors have opportunities to invest in physical assets which they would expect to share in the general price rise or that the economy as a whole shifts its tastes from saving to consuming. An overall decline in the economy's thrift could probably occur only over a long period of time, even at the inflation rates which prevailed in 1974, and so the primary short-term effect of expected price inflation on the supply of funds must depend on investors' opportunities to shift from fixed-yield assets to physical goods or claims on physical goods. Nevertheless, since traffic in art objects and similar items is relatively small and since neither the equity market nor the real estate market appear to have faced a deluge of buyers in 1974, it is difficult to cite an investor shift toward physical assets as a major factor in the rise of interest rates during 1974.

Although in some situations the separate identity of borrowers and lenders is clear, in the more general context of this behavioral channel by which price expectations influence interest rates any sharp distinction between borrowers' behavior and lenders' behavior would be largely artificial. Many economic units are simultaneously borrowers and lenders. Furthermore, except for the case of pure financial intermediaries, the total amount of funds which economic units have available to invest in debt instruments or alternative assets typically depends on spending decisions comparable to those described above with reference to borrowers. Perhaps the simplest example of the blur between effects of price expectations on borrowers' behavior and analogous effects on lenders' behavior is the case of pure speculation—i.e., decisions by households or businesses to purchase physical goods which they never would have purchased at all in the absence of expectations of an accelerated rise in prices.

A second major behavioral channel by which price expectations influence interest rates also involves the decisions of borrowers and lenders in a symmetrical way. Section II explains in some detail how expectations of future interest rates affect both borrowers' and lenders' decisions in such a way as to produce a relationship between the currently prevailing long-term bond yield and a geometric average of expected future short-term yields. If market participants believe that price stability is a major objective of the central bank's monetary policy, then expectations of more rapid price inflation imply expectations of a tighter monetary policy. Regardless of whether the central bank formulates its policy operations in terms of interest rates or monetary and reserve aggregates, in any given situation a tighter monetary policy involves higher interest rates for at least some period of time. Expectations of greater future price inflation may, therefore, imply expectations of higher future interest rates; and, as Section II explains, expectations of higher future interest rates have a direct upward effect on current bond yields through the decisions of both borrowers and lenders.

Hence, the rapid price inflation which occurred in 1974 probably led to increased expectations of future price inflation, and these expectations, in turn, probably contributed to the rise of bond yields by two channels of influence on market participants' decisions. First, expectations of future price inflation were a key determinant underlying the demand for funds, or supply of securities to the market, described in Section IV. Second, in light of the central bank's concern with promoting price stability, which began to give way to an antirecessionary policy philosophy only late in the year, expectations of future prices contributed to the expectations of future interest rates described in Section II.

VI. Problems of Intermediation[5]

Although most of the discussion of Sections II-V analyzes the decisions of ultimate borrowers and ultimate lenders, only rarely do the two meet directly in highly developed financial markets such as those in the United States. Wholly apart from the services which specialists provide on an agency basis, most debt arrangements involve at least one intermediary acting as principal in the transaction. Typical examples of an intermediary acting as principal include a commercial bank which lends depositors' funds to businesses by extending commercial loans, a mutual savings bank which lends depositors' funds to households by extending mortgage loans, an insurance company which lends policy holders' funds to businesses by purchasing private placements of corporate debt, and a pension fund or mutual fund which lends shareholders' funds to businesses by purchasing publicly offered corporate bonds. Often the intermediation process is more complex, and an entire series of distinct intermediaries may participate in the process of transfering funds from an ultimate lender to an ultimate borrower.

In an economic sense, the essence of the intermediary's role is to take advantage of economies of scale so as to convert the liabilities issued by ultimate borrowers into its own liabilities in a form which will be more attractive to ultimate lenders. Sheer size permits most intermediaries to diversify their portfolios to an extent which would be impossible for all but a few ultimate lenders. In addition, the combination of size and some degree of credit market specialization permits intermediaries to take advantage of substantial economies of scale in the servicing of nonmarketable direct debt arrangements, such as commercial loans, mortgages, or corporate private placements. Economies of scale also render large intermediaries more able to stagger the maturity of debt instruments so as to provide a built-in assurance of continuous portfolio liquidity. Furthermore, in terms of the provision of liquidity, even those intermediaries whose liabilities are in liquid form may rely on the law of large numbers to render highly unlikely a simultaneous redemption of a great proportion of these liabilities; hence, the intermediary itself need not hold so liquid a portfolio as does each of the ultimate lenders from whom it draws its own funds.

The primary economic effect of financial intermediaries' conversion of direct liabilities into more attractive indirect liabilities is to reduce the yield which is necessary to make ultimate lenders willing to transfer their funds to ultimate borrowers. Consequently, any erosion of the ability of intermediary institutions to serve their customary function would imply some net increase in yields, in any given situation. Although changes in an economy's degree of financial intermediation—and, therefore,

---

[5]For further reading on this subject see, for example, Gurley and Shaw [13, 14, 15]; Tobin and Brainard [36]; and Patinkin [28].

in the associated yield reduction—usually occur only slowly over time, the developments of 1974 may well have led somewhat suddenly to anticipations of a weakened ability of the existing institutional structure to deal with increasing intermediation requirements. While the causal factors involved were still relatively small by the summer of 1974, many financial market participants may have feared that their increase over time would lead to a deterioration in the financial intermediation function, if not to some form of outright financial rupture.

Since demand for petroleum products is relatively insensitive to price, within a short time horizon, the increased price of crude oil in 1974 greatly increased the financial flows to oil exporting countries. Morgan Guaranty Trust Company has estimated total OPEC revenues from oil exports to have been $105 billion during 1974, with another $110 billion likely in 1975. After adding other sources of foreign exchange earnings such as investment income, and then subtracting imports, aid grants and other forms of foreign exchange disbursements, Morgan Guaranty has estimated the total OPEC current-account surplus to have been $65 billion in 1974 and has suggested another $60 billion surplus in 1975. In a longer time perspective, also, many knowledgeable sources expect these flows to continue to be very large. The Organization for Economic Cooperation and Development has projected that the OPEC accumulation of funds will total $300 billion by 1980, while the World Bank has estimated this total to be $650 billion; despite the extent of the disagreement, both institutions' estimates represent extraordinarily large flows by any historical standard.

If the OPEC countries were to invest their rapidly growing portfolios according to the behavior of an average investor in the countries from which their revenues came, then the resulting "petrodollar recycling" would have little structural impact on these countries' financial markets; various deposits and other claims would merely change ownership. Nevertheless, the major OPEC countries, including in particular the large Arab oil producers, have to date shown a marked preference for extremely liquid claims. Indeed, most of these countries' investments to date have taken the form of call money, government securities held under repurchase agreements, certificates of deposit of the few largest banks, and other extremely short-term assets bearing only minimum risk. Longer-term investment commitments of OPEC funds were beginning to become more prevalent by the end of 1974; [however] they still lagged far behind the total pace of accumulation of OPEC funds.

To the extent that OPEC countries, as investors, exhibit more risk aversion and preference for liquidity than does the typical investor in the U.S. financial markets, then the reinvested flow of oil payments, which transfers assets from other U.S. investors to the OPEC countries, has the effect of widening the gulf between the characteristics of the liabilities which ultimate borrowers issue and the characteristics of the assets which the representative ultimate lender is willing to hold. The adequacy of the existing intermediary institutions to bridge this widening gulf without unduly threatening their own solvency has increasingly come under question, both in general discussion and at meetings such as those of the International Monetary Fund and the OECD; and the United States and other governments, as well as a number of private groups, have suggested proposals for the development of further interme- diation facilities. In the absence of structural changes which increase the effectiveness of intermediation, however, the net effect of the shift toward greater liquidity prefer- ence among ultimate lenders will be some rise in yields.

It is unlikely that such direct effects of petrodollar recycling on financial interme- diation had yet reached large enough proportion to be a major factor generating the record high bond yields during the summer of 1974. Nevertheless, it is not unlikely that the prospect of the continuing rapid accumulation of funds among OPEC coun- tries influenced market participants' views of forthcoming developments. If market participants anticipated a continuation of these large-scale flows, without either a change in the portfolio preferences of the OPEC countries or offsetting institutional changes to assist the financial intermediation process, then their resulting expecta- tions of higher future interest rates would have contributed, as Section II indicates, to the rise in bond yields.

VII. Concluding Remarks

Sections II-VI present in some detail a group of interrelated economic factors, any one of which may have been the major cause of the record high bond yields which emerged in the summer of 1974. Expectations of higher short-term interest rates in the future, due to the recent rapid rise of money market yields, may have influenced both borrowers' and lenders' decisions in such a way as to raise bond yields. Devel- opments in the economy and in the pattern of corporate finance may have led lenders to regard certain borrowers' liabilities as more risky and, therefore, less attractive, at a given yield. Nonfinancial economic developments may have increased borrowers' supply of securities to the market, relative to lenders' overall ability or willingness to advance funds, at a given yield. By causing increased expectations of future price inflation, the rapid price inflation of 1974 may have either altered the supply of and demand for funds, so as to create upward pressures on nominal yields, or contributed to expectations of higher future yields due to anticipated policy responses. Similarly, the financial flows associated with the increased price of oil may also have contrib- uted to expectations of higher future yields, thereby exerting upward pressure on current bond yields.

Each of these explanations of the events of 1974 has some plausible appeal, and it would be difficult to choose among them. Nevertheless, as should by now be clear, these five explanations are by no means mutually exclusive. While some explanations were no doubt of greater significance than were others, there is no compelling reason for accepting some and rejecting others. As is typically the case in periods of high interest rates, during 1974 a number of potentially contributing factors occurred in conjunction.

The fact that most of these underlying developments tend over time to occur together is the chief reason why it is difficult, even using sophisticated statistical techniques, to determine which is of primary importance. Perhaps more to the point, however, the fact of joint occurrence of the likely underlying causes of high bond yields suggests that these causes themselves not only are not mutually exclusive but are not even mutually independent—that the causal factors described here are merely separate facets of an overall set of interrelated economic developments of which one sign is high and rising bond yields.

REFERENCES

1. ARROW, KENNETH J. *Aspects of the Theory of Risk Bearing.* Helsinki: Yrjo Jahnssonin Saatio, 1965.
2. BOSWORTH, BARRY. "Patterns of Corporate External Financing." *Brookings Papers on Economic Activity,* II (2, 1971), 253-279.
3. BOSWORTH, BARRY, and DUESENBERRY, JAMES S. "A Flow of Funds Model and Its Implications." Federal Reserve Bank of Boston, *Issues in Debt Management.* Boston: 1973.
4. CASSEL, GUSTAVE. *The Theory of Social Economy.* London: T. Fisher Unwin, 1923.
5. CULBERTSON, JOHN M. "The Term Structure of Interest Rates." *Quarterly Journal of Economics,* LXXI (November, 1971), 485-517.
6. FELDSTEIN, MARTIN S., and CHAMBERLAIN, GARY. "Multimarket Expectations and the Rate of Interest." *Journal of Money, Credit and Banking,* V (November, 1973), 873-902.
7. FELDSTEIN, MARTIN S., and ECKSTEIN, OTTO. "The Fundamental Determinants of the Interest Rate." *Review of Economics and Statistics,* LII (November, 1970), 363-375.
8. FISHER, IRVING. *The Theory of Interest.* New York: The Macmillan Company, 1930.
9. FISHER, LAWRENCE. "Determinants of Risk Premiums on Corporate Bonds." *Journal of Political Economy,* LXVII (June, 1959), 217-237.
10. FRIEDMAN, BENJAMIN M. "A Structural Model of the Long-Term Corporate Debt Market." Harvard Institute of Economic Research, Discussion Paper 348, 1974.
11. GIBSON, WILLIAM E. "Price-Expectations Effects on Interest Rates." *Journal of Finance,* XXV (March, 1970), 19-34.
12. GIBSON, WILLIAM E. "Interest Rates and Inflationary Expectations: New Evidence." *American Economic Review,* LXII (December, 1972), 854-865.
13. GURLEY, JOHN G., and SHAW, EDWARD S. "Financial Aspects of Economic Development." *American Economic Review,* LV (September, 1955), 515-538.
14. GURLEY, JOHN G., and SHAW, EDWARD S. "Financial Intermediaries and the Saving-Investment Process." *Journal of Finance,* XXV (March, 1956), 257-276.
15. GURLEY, JOHN G., and SHAW, EDWARD S. *Money in a Theory of Finance.* Washington: The Brookings Institution, 1960.
16. HAMBURGER, MICHAEL J., and LATTA, CYNTHIA M. "The Term Structure of Interest Rates." *Journal of Money, Credit and Banking,* I (February, 1969), 74-97.
17. HICKS, JOHN R. *Value and Capital.* London: Oxford University Press, 1939.
18. KESSEL, REUBEN A. *The Cyclical Behavior of Interest Rates.* New York: National Bureau of Economic Research, 1965.
19. KEYNES, JOHN MAYNARD. *The General Theory of Employment, Interest and Money.* New York: Harcourt Brace, and Company, 1936.
20. LEIJONHUFOUD, AXEL. *Keynesian Economics and the Economics of Keynes.* New York: Oxford University Press, 1968.

21. LUTZ, F. A. "The Structure of Interest Rates." *Quarterly Journal of Economics,* LIV (November, 1940), 36-63.

22. MALKIEL, BURTON GORDON. *The Term Structure of Interest Rates.* Princeton: Princeton University Press, 1966.

23. MEISELMAN, DAVID. *The Term Structure of Interest Rates.* Englewood Cliffs, N.J.: Prentice-Hall, 1962.

24. MODIGLIANI, FRANCO, and SHILLER, ROBERT J. "Inflation, Rational Expectations, and the Term Structure of Interest Rates." *Economica,* XL (February, 1973), 12-43.

25. MODIGLIANI, FRANCO, and SUTCH, RICHARD. "Innovations in Interest Rate Policy." *American Economic Review,* LVI (May, 1966), 178-197.

26. NELSON, CHARLES R. *The Term Structure of Interest Rates.* New York: Basic Books, 1972.

27. OKUN, ARTHUR M. "Monetary Policy, Debt Management, and Interest Rates: A Quantitative Analysis." Commission on Money and Credit, *Stabilization Policies.* Englewood Cliffs, Prentice-Hall, 1963.

28. PATINKIN, DON. "Financial Intermediaries and the Logical Structure of Monetary Theory." *American Economic Review,* LI (March, 1961), 95-116.

29. ROBERTSON, DENNIS H. *Essays in Monetary Theory.* London: Staples Press, 1946.

30. SARGENT, THOMAS J. "Commodity Price Expectations and the Interest Rate." *Quarterly Journal of Economics,* LXXXIII (February, 1969), 127-140.

31. SARGENT, THOMAS J. "Rational Expectations and the Term Structure of Interest Rates." *Journal of Money, Credit and Banking,* IV (February, 1972), 74-97.

32. SARGENT, THOMAS J. "Anticipated Inflation and Nominal Interest." *Quarterly Journal of Economics,* LXXXVI (May, 1972), 212-225.

33. SARGENT, THOMAS J. "Rational Expectations, the Rate of Interest, and the Natural Rate of Unemployment." *Brookings Papers on Economic Activity,* IV (2, 1973), 429-472.

34. SLOANE, PETER E. "Determinants of Bond Yield Differentials." *Yale Economic Essays,* III (Spring, 1963), 3-55.

35. TOBIN, JAMES. "Liquidity Preference as Behavior Toward Risk." *Review of Economic Studies,* XXV (February, 1958), 65-86.

36. TOBIN, JAMES, and BRAINARD, WILLIAM C. "Financial Intermediaries and the Effectiveness of Monetary Controls." *American Economic Review,* LIII (May, 1963), 383-400.

37. TSIANG, S. C. "Liquidity Preference and Loanable Funds Theories, Multiplier and Velocity Analyses: A Synthesis." *American Economic Review,* LVI (September, 1956), 539-564.

38. WICKSELL, KNUT. "The Influence of the Rate of Interest on Prices." *Economic Journal,* XVII (June, 1907), 213-219.

39. WICKSELL, KNUT. *Interest and Prices.* London: Macmillan, 1936.

40. WOOD, JOHN H. "The Expectations Hypothesis, the Yield Curve, and Monetary Policy." *Quarterly Journal of Economics,* LVIII (August, 1964), 457-470.

IV

MONETARY POLICY

A. The Implementation of Monetary Policy

The section begins with the official Federal Reserve version of how monetary policy is made. This selection not only describes the procedures by which policy decisions are made and carried out, but also discusses how the three major tools of monetary policy—open market operations, the discount rate, and reserve requirements—are currently manipulated. Of particular interest are recent revisions in regulations regarding member bank borrowing.

For over a decade many economists have argued that the official policy procedures described in the first reading in this section are not enough to insure economic stability. They have insisted that the Federal Reserve needs to specify a "strategy"—outlining its conception of the structure of the economy, its objectives for the performance of the economy, and the information constraints within which it must operate. The second article in this section by Raymond E. Lombra and Raymond G. Torto is an important step in this direction. Lombra and Torto provide an analytical view of Federal Reserve's "strategy." They show that an interest rate, the Federal funds rate, is still the (central) instrument of monetary policy in that strategy. They also show that despite the formal role of monetary aggregates as intermediate target-variables in that strategy, the Federal Reserve's concern over interest rate volatilily prohibits their use as such.

Richard G. Davis's survey article begins with an analysis of the merits of an interest rate versus a monetary aggregate instrument for monetary policy. Davis reviews some technical problems in choosing the best definition of the money supply. Then he goes on to examine the "costs of not controlling" money as well as an operational program for its control over various periods of time. In attempting to influence the money stock, as an intermediate target-variable, the policy maker can choose either an interest rate or a monetary aggregate as his policy instrument. Davis debates the problem of which instrument should be controlled and of which one should be allowed to fluctuate. A key to his considerations is an empirical test of how closely the money stock can be controlled using various instruments. He closes his survey with an examination of the optimum period of time over which to attempt to control the money supply, as an intermediate target-variable.

Many observers feel that the performance of the economy has been hampered by ineffective implementation of monetary policy. The fifth article in this section by Thomas H. Havrilesky, Robert H. Sapp, and Robert L. Schweitzer is a test of the response of the Federal Reserve to the state of the economy. The authors find that over the 1964–1974 period the Federal Reserve's reaction to the rate of inflation has waned considerably, but that its reaction to international economic conditions remained strong. Consistent with the assertions of the Lombra and Torto article earlier in this Section, they present evidence that the growth of monetary aggregates did not constrain short–run policy actions.

Tools of Monetary Policy

Board of Governors of the Federal Reserve System

Conduct of Open Market Operations*

The following exposition of the conduct of open market operations begins with a description of the organizational arrangements the System has developed for administering open market policy. After that there is a discussion of the process through which policy actions are decided, along with the types of information on which these actions are based. And finally there is a description of the operating techniques used by the Trading Desk for carrying out open market transactions.

Organizational Arrangements

By law, all open market operations of the Federal Reserve System must be directed and regulated by the System's Federal Open Market Committee, whose functions and composition were [already] noted.[1] The Committee meets approximately once a

Reprinted with deletions from the Board of Governors of the Federal Reserve System, *The Federal Reserve System: Purposes and Functions* (Washington, D.C.: Federal Reserve System, 1974), pp. 53-81, by permission of the publisher. Footnotes have been renumbered to follow the abridged text.

* The latter part of this article discusses the discount rate and legal reserve requirement tools of monetary policy.—Ed.

[1] The Committee's responsibility also encompasses operations in foreign currencies.

month to decide on its policy stance and objectives. It expresses these, for operating purposes, in the form of a directive issued to the Federal Reserve Bank of New York.

The Committee regularly designates the New York Bank to serve as its agent in executing whatever open market transactions the Committee authorizes. The Committee selects a Manager of the System Open Market Account, who is also a senior officer of that Bank and who has the immediate responsibility for carrying out open market operations. The System Account is participated in jointly by all 12 of the Federal Reserve Banks.

Coordination of the day-to-day operations with the directive is maintained by telephone through the medium of a daily conference call. Regular participants in this call are the System Account Management, senior staff at the Board of Governors, and a Reserve Bank president currently serving as a voting member of the Committee. Following this call, a memorandum is sent to all Committee members—by wire to all Reserve Bank presidents—informing them of action that the System Account Manager expects to take during the day in light of developing conditions and Committee objectives.

The staff at the Federal Reserve Bank of New York that assists the Account Manager in carrying out the FOMC's domestic policy directive operates through a "Trading Desk," which maintains direct telephone communication with about two dozen dealers located in New York City or outside. All of the Manager's puchase and sale orders for the Committee are executed through this Desk.

When the Account Manager seeks to execute an open market transaction, his staff contacts dealers in Treasury and Federal agency securities just as other investors do. In fulfilling their obligation to make regular markets, the dealers stand ready, when asked, to quote firm bids and offer prices on such securities and to do business at these prices on whichever side of the market the customer wishes. Since nearly two dozen dealers are now making markets in U.S. Government and Federal agency securities and are actively competing with one another for some share of the available business, the Trading Desk encounters no difficulty in completing its orders promptly. When its orders are large, as they usually are for the System's Account, the Trading Desk utilizes the auction method in distributing its orders among competing dealers.[2]

Policy Process

The process of formulating open market policy is a continuum that carries through successive meetings of the FOMC. It is a complex process because the quantity and

---

[2]Of those firms that were active as Government securities dealers in mid-1974, roughly half were special departments of major money market banks. Among the nonbank dealers, several were large, integrated brokerage houses that operate as investment bankers and traders in a number of different sectors of the securities markets—including equity as well as fixed-income securities. Other firms specialize mainly in the more active sectors of the Treasury and Federal agency markets. But most dealer houses participate in more than one market sector, and their close attention to changing yield relationships in the total structure of market rates helps to link developments in one sector to those in others.

the flow of money and credit not only affect all aspects of the economy's production and consumption activities but also are affected by them.

Discussion of policy at Committee meetings typically covers three general areas. First, there is a general expression of member judgments as to the state of the economy and the prospects for the future performance of such key economic variables as output, employment, prices, and the balance of payments in relation to desired goals. Second, there is a more explicit statement of member recommendations as to what the thrust of open market policy should be—both for the longer run and in the intermeeting period just ahead. Finally, the Committee engages in give-and-take discussion to synthesize its individual views into a consensus that can be expressed in sufficiently specific terms to provide meaningful guidance to the Manager in the conduct of day-to-day open market operations in the interim between Committee meetings.

Operating targets in recent years have included rates of growth in bank reserves and the monetary aggregates and associated ranges of tolerable changes in money market conditions. The key element in the latter is a permissible range of fluctuation in the Federal funds rate. This rate—essentially that at which banks are willing to lend or borrow immediately available reserves on an overnight basis—is a very sensitive indicator of tightness or of ease in bank reserves.

Individual members of the Committee may stress different operating targets as having key importance in the existing financial setting—depending in part on differences in their interpretation of recent and prospective developments and in part on their interpretation of the lessons of experience and economic theory. For this reason an extended discussion is sometimes needed to arrive at a consensus.

When a consensus has crystallized, the Committee formulates an instruction in the form of a domestic policy directive. The Committee also reaches an understanding with regard to the specific targets and ranges that will serve as guides to the Manager in implementing the directive.

By law, the Board of Governors is required to keep a record of the policy actions taken by the FOMC at each meeting and of the reasons underlying these actions, and to publish that record in its *Annual Report* to the Congress. In view of the strong emphasis that the Congress places on keeping the public informed about the activities of all Federal agencies and of the special interest that the financial community takes in the FOMC's policy process, the Board and the Committee regularly make the policy record for each meeting available to the public about 90 days after a meeting. The record summarizes the Committee's assessment of the country's economic and financial position at the time of the meeting as well as the Committee's views regarding the appropriate course for policy during the period ahead. Finally, it includes the policy directive adopted by the Committee at the meeting in question, together with a record of the votes; if there were any dissents, statements of the reasons for the dissents are also included.

Materials for Policy Making

In carrying out their decision-making responsibility, policy makers need a wide variety of background information. They must seek to make judgments as objectively as possible in the light of movements and interrelations in a wide array of statistical data that show how the economy is performing. Furthermore, they must assess such performance in relation to the national goals of sustained high employment, avoidance of marked inflationary or deflationary tendencies, and a balanced flow of U.S. payments with foreign countries. This need to consider current developments in relation to ultimate goals forces the Committee to look into the future with great care since actions to affect bank reserves today produce their ultimate impact on final spending, prices, and employment only after sizable time lags.

To meet the Committee's needs for an adequate factual foundation for diagnosing the recent performance of the economy and to provide an analytical framework for projecting how the economy is likely to perform in the future, a considerable amount of intensive and systematic staff preparation must precede each meeting of the FOMC. The results of this work are presented to Committee members in various forms, of which the following are most important:

1. Roughly three times a year, or more frequently if unusual developments require it, the staff provides the Committee with a full-scale projection of the domestic economic outlook. This presentation lays out expected levels and quarterly changes in all of the key sectors of the gross national product accounts—both in current and in constant dollars—for the next 12 to 18 months. It also provides projections of associated changes in key sectors of the Federal Reserve flow of funds accounts, plus a full review of expected developments in foreign trade and the balance of payments.

The projection is based on specific assumptions as to monetary, fiscal, and other Governmental policies. A monetary strategy is assumed that seems likely to come closest to achieving the Committee's policy goals during the period under consideration. To provide Committee members with a rough idea of trade-offs among policy goals that might result from alternative policy strategies, projections of key economic variables for alternative strategies are also provided. The particular estimates included in the projection are based on a blending of judgments reached by economic analysts experienced in making projections and of results from a large-scale econometric model of the U.S. economy.

2. Before each monthly meeting, Committee members receive a comprehensive staff document that reviews the facts and implications of recent domestic and foreign economic and financial developments, including the extent to which actual events seem to be confirming, or deviating from, the most recent economic projection. When significant deviations from the projection become evident, their implications for the longer run are evaluated and needed adjustments are made in the forecast.

3. To assist the Committee in formulating the short-run operating targets that lie behind its policy directive, the staff provides at each meeting a special document that serves as a basis for discussion of this subject. The document lays out several alternative sets of intermeeting operating targets. One set indicates what might be expected

or required for key financial variables if the prevailing longer-run policy strategy continues about unchanged; the others show what might develop if the policy strategy is revised. Each set of targets documents relationships among bank reserves, the monetary aggregates, and interest rates that would be expected to result from the particular strategy assumed.

4. The Account Manager provides detailed written reports, and also reports orally during the meeting, on his transactions since the Committee's last meeting; these reports include comments on any special problems that he has encountered in carrying out the Committee's instructions or in achieving the operational targets that the Committee specified for his guidance.[3]

5. Finally, Committee discussions at the monthly meetings are preceded by oral reports from the senior staff. These reports not only capsulize the highlights of the more comprehensive written materials the Committee has already received but also evaluate those aspects of the outlook, including the implications of alternative monetary policy strategies, that are believed to be of special significance to the Committee's current policy decision.

Manager's Operating Techniques

During the period between meetings, the System Account Manager is concerned with executing the Committee's latest domestic policy directive. His time horizon thus breaks down into the days and weeks in which he will be transacting operations, and he is constantly watching to see how the latest facts on bank reserves, the monetary aggregates, and interest rates seem to be relating to the Committee's operational targets.

The Federal Reserve engages in open market operations virtually every business day. The purpose of most of these operations, however, is to keep various technical (market) factors from introducing independent shifts in bank reserve positions that are inconsistent with the current aims of Federal Reserve policy or that may lead to larger and potentially destabilizing day-to-day fluctuations in money market conditions. Such technical market factors as changes in currency in public circulation, in Federal Reserve float, and in the Treasury's balance at the Federal Reserve can cause large day-to-day changes in bank reserve positions. Some of these changes are seasonal; others are unpredictable. The System's well-known practice of frequent open market transactions to offset the play of technical factors makes for a smoother day-to-day flow of money and credit to finance the nation's business.

The Manager receives information continuously during the day on conditions in both the money and securities markets. In addition he receives information daily— with a 1-day lag—on bank reserve positions, and his staff provides him with both daily projections for several weeks ahead of all of the technical factors expected to influence the supply of reserves and weekly projections of the money and credit aggregates. Data on the money stock and the bank credit proxy are made available

---

[3]The Special Manager for foreign currency operations provides similar reports on foreign exchange markets and on actions he has taken under the Committee's directive to him.

to the public weekly with a 1-week lag, although very rough preliminary data are available internally before that.

The Manager's operating techniques must be sufficiently adaptable for him to adjust to rapidy changing market forces and reverse the flow of reserves when the reserve effects of his transactions in preceding market days prove to have been too great or too little. Reflecting this need for adaptability, the Account Manager uses two general approaches to the execution of his operations. The approach that he selects depends on the expected duration of the particular reserve situation.

When projections of reserve factors indicate a net need to supply or to withdraw reserves for the banking system as a whole and this situation seems likely to persist for more than the current bank-statement-week, the Manager will generally buy or sell securities on an outright basis for prompt delivery. If the need is to withdraw reserves, he may also allow maturing securities to run off without replacement.

In situations where the need to provide (or withdraw) reserves seems only temporary—either because the projections suggest that reserves provided today will soon need to be withdrawn to offset expected seasonal movements in technical reserve factors, or because there is marked uncertainty about the near-term reserve outlook—the Manager will use special methods that have only a temporary effect on the aggregate supply of reserves. Thus, when the need is for temporary provision of reserves, he makes "repurchase agreements" with dealers; when it is for temporary withdrawal, he makes "matched sale-purchase transactions."

Outright Purchases and Sales

System transactions on an outright basis are typically made through an auction process in which all dealers are requested to submit bids or offers for securities of the type and maturity that the Manager has elected to sell or buy that day.[4] Once dealer tenders have been received, they are arrayed according to price. The Account Manager then accepts amounts bid or offered in sequence until his order is covered.

Not all "outright" transactions occur through the dealer market. If, on a day when the Manager sees a need to supply or absorb reserves, he has an order from a customer who uses the Federal Reserve as agent for transactions—say from a foreign account—that matches up with the System need, he may simply execute the order directly through the System Account. Since the staff of the Trading Desk keeps an hourly record of bid and offer prices being quoted by dealers for the full list of Treasury securities, foreign orders can be readily executed directly with the System's portfolio at the "best" market prices.

The great bulk of the System's outright transactions—whether in the dealer market or directly with official accounts—occur in Treasury bills since the Treasury bill sector is by far the most active part of the U.S. Government securities and Federal

---

[4]The System is prepared to do business with any dealer with adequate capital that demonstrates—through regular daily reports to the Federal Reserve Bank of New York on its positions and transactions—that it is regularly making markets in U.S. Government and Federal agency securities. Each dealer is also expected to submit at intervals financial statements certified by qualified public accounting firms.

agency markets. From time to time the System extends its purchases beyond the Treasury bill market to include intermediate- and long-term Government and agency issues. In recent years it has not had occasion to sell longer-term coupon issues, but it has sold short-term issues (those maturing in less than a year).

Buying of longer-term coupon issues is typically undertaken when the immediate market supply of Treasury bills is temporarily depleted and a supply of longer-term issues is available. Sometimes, the FOMC directs that longer maturities be purchased to help implement a particular interest rate strategy. But the impact of such transactions, in and of themselves, on yield spreads between short- and long-term issues tends to be quite marginal because the term structure of market yields is very strongly influenced by the consensus or interest rate expectations of market participants as a group. Nevertheless, at times when interest rates are already on the verge of a general decline—say, because of a threatened downturn in economic activity—System buying of longer-term maturities for the System account may influence the timing and sharpness of the decline in long-term rates.

Open Market Operations and Treasury Financings

Because the bulk of the System's open market operations are carried out in the market for U.S. Government securities, question is often raised as to how these operations relate to market borrowing by the Treasury. Treasury financings are of two types—(1) cash borrowings, which raise new money and expand the size of the outstanding public debt, and (2) refinancings, which roll over outstanding debt, as it matures, into new issues. The Treasury must undertake its financings in the open market. In the United States only a very limited amount of direct lending to the Treasury by the central bank is permitted since such direct lending would expand the supply of bank reserves and thus be potentially inflationary.[5] This insulates the Federal Reserve from any official pressure to assist in financing of Government deficits.

In Treasury refinancing operations, the Federal Reserve limits its participation to the amount needed to roll over System holdings of the maturing issue. If the System did not undertake to roll over such debt, its holdings of maturing debt would have to be redeemed, and this would cause a commensurate contraction in bank reserves. This could greatly complicate the Federal Reserve's task of managing bank reserves because of the very large size of System holdings of maturing Treasury debt; for example, holdings of maturing coupon issues at times may amount to as much as $6

---

[5]The law has usually permitted the Treasury to borrow up to $5 billion directly from the Federal Reserve. On the few occasions when such borrowing has occurred, it has taken the form of special Treasury certificates to be repaid within a few days. The purpose of such borrowing is to permit the Treasury to borrow for very short periods when its cash balance may be running low for technical reasons, such as at times just before large inflows of income tax receipts around quarterly tax-payment dates. The temporary borrowing privilege was suspended in the fall of 1973 and as of mid-1974 was awaiting congressional renewal.

billion. The sheer size makes simultaneous redemptions and concurrent market purchases to avoid unwanted reserve absorption impracticable.

The Account Manager may elect to redeem a small part of the System's holdings of a particular issue of maturing debt as a means of absorbing redundant reserves being otherwise generated at the time. These run-offs seldom exceed a few hundred million dollars, and they occur chiefly in connection with weekly Treasury bill auctions rather than in refinancings of Treasury coupon issues.

The net effect of these Federal Reserve practices is to require the Treasury to cover its financing needs in competition with other borrowers in the public securities market. To attract funds from the general public, the Treasury is obliged to pay the "going" rate of interest in the market.

The thrust of monetary policy is thus unaffected by Treasury financing operations. However, there are short periods from time to time when the Federal Reserve does take account of large-scale Treasury debt financing—particularly those involving issuance of intermediate- and longer-term debt—in the day-to-day conduct of policy. The term "even keel" is the shorthand expression that the market uses to describe such periods.[6]

The length of an even-keel period may vary from 1 to 3 weeks, depending on market conditions and attitudes at the time. Sometimes it may be only the very brief period between the announcement and the auction or subscription date. In others it may be the somewhat longer period until the date for payment. In a very few it may run somewhat beyond the payment date.

During an even-keel period, the Federal Reserve does not give up completely its freedom of maneuver in carrying out monetary policy. But it does not undertake any actions that, by themselves, would severely jolt market attitudes while a large U.S. Government financing is in process and thereby risk great unsettlement in securities markets generally. Nevertheless, swings in market rates of interest have sometimes been quite sizable during periods of even keel as well as outside of such periods. Thus, in no way does even keel provide a guarantee that the Federal Reserve will stabilize securities markets for Treasury financings at the expense of reserve objectives.

The Discount Rate and Reserve Requirements

Changes in the Federal Reserve discount rate and in member bank reserve requirements are the key instruments that the Federal Reserve uses along with open market operations to implement national monetary policy. All three affect the availability of bank reserves and money and the cost of credit generally.

In addition to these tools of general monetary policy, the Federal Reserve manages two other instruments, each of which has a more selective impact on deposits and credit flows. One is the setting of ceilings on the interest rates that member banks

---

[6]The concept of even keel does not apply to regular, repetitive auction financings such as those for weekly and monthly bills.

may pay to customers on their savings and time deposits; the other is the fixing of the initial margin requirement (down payment in cash or collateral) on credit-financed purchases of corporate stocks and convertible bonds. The interest rate ceilings limit the expansion of member bank savings and time deposits only when interest rates in the credit market are high relative to the ceilings. Margin requirements, in contrast, limit expansion of stock market credit at all times, although they are much more of a limitation the higher the required margin, which has been 50 percent or higher throughout the postwar period.

Operation of Reserve Bank Discount Window

The Federal Reserve lending mechanism, originally conceived as being the heart of the U.S. central banking operation, has long since been displaced in this role by open market operations. For some time it has served mainly as a complement to open market operations in the implementation of monetary policy.

The provision of Federal Reserve credit to member banks—at the initiative of the borrowing bank but subject to administrative constraints—serves essentially as (1) a source of temporary funds to help with large, unexpected deposit or portfolio adjustments that individual banks sometimes encounter and (2) a safety valve for member banks as a group during periods of monetary restraint. In addition, through lending operations the Federal Reserve provides somewhat longer-term credit to member banks that lack ready access to national money markets when these banks need help in covering recurring seasonal needs for funds. On rare occasions of emergency, when members confront urgent needs for liquefying their assets (such as needs arising from, say, unexpected developments in the local, regional, or national economy), they may obtain credit on a longer then temporary basis. Finally, nonmembers may borrow from the Federal Reserve under unusual and exigent circumstances in the financial markets, but at an interest rate that is above the discount rate available to member banks.

Mechanics of Borrowing

Technically, a member bank has two ways of borrowing funds from its Reserve Bank—by a discount or by an advance. Although the two methods are quite different, it has become customary to refer to both as "discounting."

A discount, in a technical sense, entails the sale of "eligible paper" to the Reserve Bank; all such paper carries the member bank's endorsement. An advance is a loan evidenced by a promissory note of the borrowing bank and secured by adequate collateral. At one time discounts were much the more important means of access to Federal Reserve credit, but today virtually all funds flow through the discount window by means of advances.

The law identifies three types of collateral for ordinary use in securing a member's borrowing—U.S. Government or Federal agency obligations (or other debt fully guaranteed by the U.S. Government or a federal agency); "eligible commercial, industrial, and agricultural paper"; and other security deemed satisfactory by the Reserve Bank. The major part of all borrowings are backed by U.S. Government obligations. Since many member banks leave their holdings of U.S. Government securities at Reserve Banks for safekeeping, it is a fairly simple matter to use such obligations as collateral.

Employing "eligible paper" is somewhat more complicated because such paper must be sent to the Federal Reserve Bank along with information that will permit the Reserve Bank to make a judgment concerning the eligibility and acceptability of the paper. Today, most private obligations held in bank portfolios are considered to be "eligible" for discount with a Reserve Bank if the remaining time to maturity is 90 days or less. Bankers acceptances and municipal warrants, however, may have a remaining maturity of up to 6 months, and agricultural loans may have as long as 9 months to maturity. Loans made for speculative purposes and bank finance bills (working capital acceptances) are not eligible.

Loans "secured to the satisfaction" of the Reserve Bank—that is, by other than U.S. Government or agency obligations or by eligible paper—are more common today than a decade or so ago. By law, the rate charged for such loans must be one-half of a percentage point higher than the rate on borrowing against collateral authorized by statute.

Adjustment Credit

Access to a Reserve Bank discount window is treated as a privilege of membership rather than as a right. An important reason for administrative restraint by the Federal Reserve on member bank borrowings is to maintain reasonable control over the volume of such borrowings and thus avoid excessive and unexpected fluctuations in the over-all volume of reserves being supplied by this means.

From the standpoint of an individual member bank, borrowing from the Federal Reserve can be an alternative to obtaining funds in the broad U.S. money market by borrowing overnight funds from other banks (so-called Federal funds), by selling securities from its asset portfolio, or (in the case of larger banks) by issuing large negotiable time CD's. For the banking system as a whole, however, there is an important difference between borrowing from the Federal Reserve and making adjustments through the market. Borrowing from the Federal Reserve increases the total reserves of banks and—if not offset by open market operations—provides the basis for an expansion of money and credit. Market adjustments, on the other hand, merely redistribute presently available reserve funds among banks.

Since membership in the Federal Reserve System in mid-1974 numbered about 5,800 banks with assets of more than $600 billion, it is apparent that the volume of borrowed reserves could vary widely if each member were free to tap its Federal

Reserve Bank discount window without restriction. A pattern of large and volatile borrowing by the member banks would run the risk of eroding the System's ability to control bank reserves and thereby to influence growth of money and credit in line with the nation's economic objectives. For these reasons administrative constraints on member bank borrowing have been developed.

As already indicated, most of the borrowing by member banks from the Reserve Banks is for quite short periods—usually no more than a few days—as banks seek funds to make temporary adjustments in their reserves. Such borrowing can be termed adjustment credit. Reasons for such borrowing that are considered appropriate generally include unexpected increases in loan demand, sudden deposit losses, or temporary and unexpected difficulties in obtaining funds through the facilities of the money market. Borrowing for the following purposes would be considered inappropriate: to finance speculative loans and investments, to substitute Federal Reserve credit for member bank capital, to finance lending in the Federal funds market, to acquire securities or other money market paper at a profit, or to refinance existing indebtedness to private lenders at the lower discount rate.

In judging whether a member bank is relying unduly on borrowing at the discount window, the Reserve Bank discount officer takes into account the amount of a member's indebtedness in relation to its required reserves, the frequency of the bank's borrowing, any need for funds that is attributable to computer breakdowns in transfers of funds, and any special circumstances affecting the current position of the bank.

As a general rule, larger member banks borrow to the next business day or for only a few days at a time since they manage their positions on a daily basis. Smaller banks usually borrow to the end of the reserve week, or for two reserve weeks. Even though requests for credit extensions are seldom denied, requests for renewals or too frequent requests for short-term discounting are closely scrutinized and under some circumstances are discouraged or even refused. If a particular member bank shows a pattern of borrowing that is characterized by frequent or continuing indebtedness over an extended period, the Reserve Bank lending officer will intervene and press the offending bank to repay its debt to the System, even though this may require the bank to reduce its assets and modify its loan and investment policies.

System guidelines for lending are interpreted by the Reserve Banks acting individually through their lending officers and credit committees. Policies with regard to such interpretations are coordinated by the System Conference of Lending Officers, which meets periodically and holds telephone conferences as needed. Through this type of coordination regional differences of interpretation are minimized. Since administration of the discount window is not normally intended to serve as an instrument of countercyclical monetary policy, lending guidelines are applied uniformly throughout the credit cycle—that is, during both periods of tight money and periods of easy money. However, since member bank borrowings are largest and most widespread during periods of credit restraint, more banks ordinarily become subject to administrative constraints at such times.

Seasonal Borrowing Privilege

In 1973 the Board of Governors, in consultation with the Reserve Banks, decided to formalize arrangements allowing for the extension of seasonal credit to member banks that lack effective access to national money markets. This decision was an outgrowth of the studies reappraising the discount mechanism undertaken by a special Federal Reserve committee in the late 1960's.

In its report this special committee noted that without an assured source of seasonal credit, smaller banks typically accumulated short-term securities as a pool of liquidity on which they could draw to meet peak seasonal needs for funds. To the extent that bank resources were tied up in this way during the off-peak season, there was a danger that some local credit needs for desirable projects would not be adequately accommodated. As a result of the 1973 changes in the regulation, which permit the Reserve Banks to supply credit to smaller banks to tide them over periods of peak seasonal need, banks are now able to use resources that they had previously placed in liquid assets to meet local needs.

To be eligible for the new seasonal borrowing privilege, a member bank must satisfy certain conditions:

1. Lack reasonably reliable access to national money markets;
2. Have a seasonal need that arises from a recurring pattern of movement in deposits and loans that persists for at least 8 weeks;
3. Meet from its own resources that part of the seasonal need equal to at least 5 percent of its average deposits over the preceding calendar year;
4. Arrange with its Reserve Bank for seasonal credit in advance of the actual need for funds.

Smaller banks that do a substantial volume of loan business in farm or resort areas are examples of institutions that may need to use the seasonal borrowing privilege, but they by no means exhaust the possibilities. For some banks, seasonal credits may remain outstanding for a number of months.

Emergency Credit

Emergency credit is made available to individual banks or groups of banks facing financial stringency caused by adverse local, regional, or national financial developments. In such operations the Federal Reserve serves its traditional role as the ultimate provider of liquidity—"lender of last resort"—to the economy.

A good example of this function is the action taken by the Federal Reserve in the summer of 1970 following insolvency proceedings by a major railroad corporation. When that corporation defaulted on its outstanding commercial paper, investors became generally concerned about the liquidity of a number of other large issuers of commercial paper, and as a result they cut back on their acquisitions of such paper. This forced issuers of maturing commercial paper to turn suddenly, and in volume, to their back-up credit lines at banks, thereby exerting a substantial squeeze on the resources and reserve positions of the banks involved. Since the problem was one of meeting a general demand for liquidity without adverse repercussions on business confidence and since the demands of the commercial paper issuers on banks did not represent a net expansion in the total demand for credit, the banks involved were allowed to cover some of their added needs for funds through special borrowings at Reserve Bank discount windows. Interest rate ceilings under Regulation Q on large CD's with relatively short maturities, which were below market rates of interest at the time, were also suspended, thus permitting banks to bid competitively for needed deposit funds in the market.

In its role as ultimate provider of liquidity the Federal Reserve also stands ready to provide credits to nonmember institutions under emergency conditions. Although no credits of the latter type have actually been provided in recent years, on several occasions—when it appeared that net deposit drains on nonmember banks, savings banks, or savings and loan associations might create general liquidity problems—the machinery for emergency lending was put in place on a contingency basis. Emergency lending to nonmember institutions is provided at a higher interest rate than to members and only after authorization by the Board of Governors.

Discount Rate

The cost of member bank borrowing is set by each Reserve Bank's discount rate—the rate of interest established by its board of directors, subject to review and determination by the Board of Governors. As envisioned in the original Federal Reserve Act, each Reserve Bank would set a discount rate in accord with its regional banking and credit conditions. In the early years of the System it was assumed that in its review process the Board would look particularly to regional banking conditions; but over the years, the progressive integration of regional credit markets into a fluid national market gradually produced a national perspective for discount rate determination. Establishment by Congress of national economic goals in the Employment Act of 1946 further enhanced the role of national considerations in proposals for changes in Reserve Bank rates and in the Board's determinations with respect to proposed changes.

Because the discount rate establishes the cost to members of reserves borrowed from Reserve Banks, it plays a significant role in the decisions that a bank makes about whether to borrow at the Federal Reserve discount window. Although bankers may be reluctant to borrow from the Federal Reserve and may do so only to cover temporary adjustment needs, a low discount rate in relation to other rates on money market claims makes it more likely that a bank will seek funds at the discount window instead of using alternative sources.

For example, if the rate on short-term Treasury bills is high in relation to the discount rate, a member bank may prefer to borrow from the Federal Reserve rather than sell Treasury bills from its portfolio. Similarly, if the rate charged for reserves obtained through the Federal funds market is high, a bank has an incentive to use the discount window. Or if rates are high on large time CD's, which may be sold in

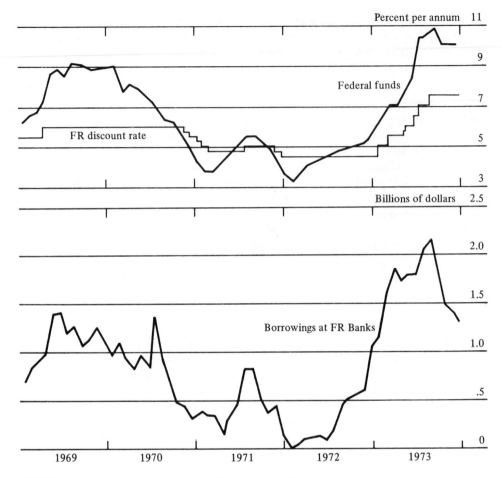

FIGURE A. Selected Interest Rates and Member Bank Borrowings

Monthly averages of daily figures.

some volume and relatively impersonally in the money market, the demand for borrowing from the Federal Reserve is stimulated. Consequently, when spreads in these various market rates over the discount rate make it profitable, and particularly if economic activity is buoyant and credit demands on banks are strong, member banks in need of funds tend to make increasing use of the discount window.

To help control the volume and profitability of borrowings at the discount window, the Federal Reserve adjusts the discount rate from time to time to relate it more closely to other money market rates. On occasion, however, changes in the discount rate may signal Federal Reserve concern over unfolding economic developments and a possible intent to alter current and future policy accordingly. Reactions of the financial community to such signals—"announcement effects"—may exert a significant impact on securities markets because market participants will tend to adjust their investment strategies in anticipation of coordinated System actions via other policy instruments. Changes in the discount rate, therefore, must be interpreted in terms of how they complement, or are likely to be complemented by, other policy actions.

Coordination of Discount and Open Market Operations

In gauging what volume of reserves to supply through open market operations to achieve monetary policy objectives, the FOMC must take account of the extent to which member banks may wish to borrow reserve funds from the Reserve Banks, or to repay outstanding borrowings. Member banks borrowings generally rise during periods of monetary stringency and fall during periods of monetary ease. These tendencies have to be taken into account in formulating open market strategy.

In periods of monetary restraint for example, if open market operations provide a smaller increase in nonborrowed reserves than the banks would like to have, given prevailing market conditions, the banks may offset this shortfall in desired reserves to a substantial extent, at least initially, by increasing their borrowing from the Reserve Banks. But because Federal Reserve credit is available only on a temporary basis, the upswing in such borrowing could moderate only temporarily the restraint being exerted on the availability of credit and money through open market operations. Rather, banks would soon need to obtain other funds to repay their debt to the System—by bidding more aggressively for funds in the money market, by liquidating assets such as Treasury bills, or by restricting the expansion of their loan portfolios. Efforts by banks to obtain funds through alternative money market transactions or by modifying loan policies would put upward pressure on short-term market rates, transmit reserve shortages to other banks, set in motion upward interest rate adjustments throughout credit markets, and lead in time to a slowing of expansion in the money stock.

Changes in Reserve Requirements

Legislation enacted in 1935, with subsequent amendments, gives the Board of Governors authority, within prescribed limits, to set minimum ratios for the reserves that member banks must hold against their demand and time deposits.[7] These limits range from 7 to 22 percent for demand deposits and from 3 to 10 percent for time deposits, depending on the size of the bank. Member bank reserves consist of cash held in member banks' vaults and of deposit balances held at Federal Reserve Banks.

---

[7]As banks have diversified their liabilities in recent years, the Federal Reserve has broadened the definition of deposits to cover such liabilities and bank-related claims as commercial paper issued by bank holding companies or nonbank subsidiaries to finance credit expansion by the affiliated bank or banks, liabilities of banks to their foreign branches (so-called Euro-dollar borrowings), and finance bills (working capital acceptances) issued by banks.

Actions by the Federal Reserve to change reserve requirements do not affect the total amount of reserve funds held by the member banks as a whole. Instead, they change the volume of deposits and the volume of loans and investments that member banks can support with the volume of reserves on hand. When required reserve ratios are raised, the amount of deposits a given supply of reserves can support is reduced. Correspondingly, when ratios are lowered, the volume of liabilities and credit the banking system can support on a given reserve supply is increased. Thus, an increase in reserve requirements is a restrictive action and a decrease an expansive action.

Use as a Policy Instrument

As an instrument of monetary management, adjustments in required reserve ratios are less flexible than open market operations or changes in the discount rate. There are two reasons for this. One is that changes in the ratio affect all member banks in a given class at once. The second is that for each member bank the required reserve ratio is the basis for current and forward decisions by the bank's management concerning the composition and maturity of liabilities and of loans and investments. Frequent changes in that ratio complicate in some degree the task of forward planning by the management.

Furthermore, even fairly small changes in reserve requirements, such as one-half of a percentage point, may result in relatively large changes in the margin between total reserves and required reserves. Thus, even a small change in the required reserve ratio may have a rather large potential impact on deposits and bank credit.

Changes in reserve requirements are normally undertaken as part of a monetary policy strategy that is designed to help moderate inflationary or recessive tendencies in the economy. Reserve requirement actions have an immediate impact on banking liquidity and on costs in all parts of the country. In contrast, if the same amount of reserve changes were effected through open market operations, there would be no announcement effect; instead, the impact would tend to be concentrated at first on banks at money market centers, filtering subsequently to smaller and more remotely located banks after some lag.

Some reserve requirement actions, however, are not designed to affect stabilization policy. For example, a cut in reserve requirements for member banks was implemented late in 1972 to realign reserve requirements among member banks on a more equitable basis and to compensate for a large, once-and-for-all reduction in bank reserve availability incident to a reform of the System's check-collection procedures. When changes in reserve requirements are made for purely structural reasons, the potential impact on credit market conditions and money growth can be offset by open market operations.

Regardless of the purpose of a particular change in reserve requirements—whether it be to support the thrust of monetary policy or to restructure requirements—it is always necessary to coordinate the reserve requirement changes closely with open market and discount operations. For instance, changes in reserve requirements may be timed to coincide with seasonal needs to supply or absorb reserves, thus replacing a certain amount of open market operations that otherwise would have been needed at the time. More generally though, the fact that the Federal Reserve can use offsetting open market actions and lending operations to adjust the net amount of reserves absorbed or provided by changes in reserve requirement ratios provides a cushioning mechanism that enables the banking system to make a smooth adjustment to a change in reserve requirements.

Additional flexibility may be provided by the reserve requirement instrument through selective changes in the structure of requirements. For example, in the new system of graduated requirements established in late 1972 for demand deposits, future changes may be limited to one or a few deposit-size categories or be made larger for some categories than for others. For other deposits, requirements have typically been different for savings and time accounts and have often been changed independently of one another. Similarly, for time deposits alone, requirements have been lower for small deposits, and additional size differentiations could, of course, be introduced.

Finally, the Federal Reserve established (effective in June 1973) a marginal reserve requirement on large time CD's of banks. This requirement applied to the marginal amount by which a bank's large CD's and related money-market-type liabilities issued to the public exceed the total that the bank had outstanding on a given base date. Earlier in 1973 major banks had been promoting large CD's aggressively as a source of funds to finance rapidly expanding loans to business. The marginal reserve requirement was introduced in an effort to dampen growth of business loans by raising the cost of CD funds being used to finance such loans.

The Strategy of Monetary Policy

Raymond E. Lombra and Raymond G. Torto*

I. Introduction

While much has been written over the years concerning monetary policy, there is apparently a discontinuity in the flow of information between policymakers, on the one hand, and academic researchers and participants in financial markets, on the other. Much of this lack of communication centers specifically on the formulation and implementation of monetary policy.** As a result, much of the research into the policy process is based on incorrect assumptions concerning how policy is managed. Sherman Maisel, a former member of the Federal Reserve Board of Governors, argues that the Fed itself is a source of this communications gap: "The Fed has always resisted being too specific about [its] methods and its goals, clothing its operations in a kind of mystique that left it more freedom to maneuver" [18, p. 26].

Reprinted from the Federal Reserve Bank of Richmond, *Monthly Review* (September/October, 1975), pp. 3–14, by permission of the publisher and the authors.

* The authors express gratitude to Charles Cathcart, Lauren Dillard, Cathy Gaffney, Gary Gillum, Herbert Kaufman, Donald Kohn, Thomas Mayer, John Pippenger, William Poole, Richard Puckett, Steven Roberts, and the staff of the Federal Reserve Bank of Richmond, particularly Alfred Broaddus and Joseph Crews, for very helpful comments that have materially improved the paper.

** In the next three articles different words are applied to the same concepts. "Operating targets" here is synonymous with "instruments" used elsewhere, e.g. article 28. "Intermediate target variables" used here is synonymous with "Objectives" used elsewhere (article 27). "Final target variables" used here is referred to as "goal variables" elsewhere (article 28).—Ed.

In the opinion of many policy observers, this communications failure has real costs, both in terms of public understanding and the effectiveness of policy. While the Fed is reluctant to specify its procedures too explicitly in order to protect its freedom of action, "its attempt to protect itself from both outside critics and internal disappointment . . . weakens its ability to improve its performance" [18, p. 311].

Recently a number of papers have been directed toward unraveling the mystique that surrounds monetary policy.[1] The purpose of this article is to synthesize and extend the recent literature on this subject and thereby provide an interpretation of the monetary policy process and a model of current open market strategy. Hopefully, this article will contribute to a better understanding of current policy procedures and will help to identify problem areas toward which further research should be directed.[2]

This article consists of seven sections. Section II presents the background to the current strategy. The following three sections describe long-run aspects of current policy formulation, the linkages between the long- and short-run policy process, and short-term open market strategy, respectively. An analysis of the effect of the constraint on interest rate volatility on short-run policy actions is presented in Section VI, followed by some final remarks in Section VII.

II. The Evolution of the Current Strategy

An important paper by Jack Guttentag, published in 1966, described the Federal Reserve's policy procedures of the 1950's and early 1960's as the money market strategy [10]. Under the money market strategy, the Federal Reserve's proximate focus was on the "condition of the money market"—generally understood to include the value of a constellation of interest rates, free reserves, and the inventory positions and financing costs of securities dealers. With such national economic goals as full employment and price stability remote in time and causal connection from conditions in the money market, the use of money market conditions as a proximate target tended to focus policy too narrowly. As a result, Guttentag argued:

> The main weakness of the [money market] strategy is its incompleteness, i.e., the fact that the Federal Open Market Committee (FOMC) does not set specific quantitative target values for which it would hold itself accountable for the money supply, long-term interest rates, or any other "strategic variable" that could serve as a connecting link between open market operations and system objectives; rather it tends to rationalize the behavior of these variables after the fact [10, p. 1].

---

[1]See, for example, the important articles by Axilrod and Beck [1], Brimmer [3], Kane [12], Maisel [17], Pierce [22, 23], Pierce and Thomson [25], Poole [26], and Tschinkel [29].

[2]This discussion is not meant to imply that all monetary research has been useless or that no one understands the essence of current policy procedures. With regard to the latter, it is clear that many financial market analysts have considerable expertise in assessing the implications of day-to-day Federal Reserve actions.

To correct the deficiencies in the money market strategy, Guttentag suggested that the Fed adopt a complete strategy—consisting of quantifiable targets specified over given control periods, with the sequence of targets linked empirically to the ultimate price and output goals of the economy. Targets are defined as strategic variables that policymakers can affect by manipulating policy instruments.[3] Included in the set of targets are both intermediate targets such as interest rates, bank reserves, and monetary aggregates, and longer-term final targets (or goal variables) such as output, employment, and prices. Instruments are the magnitudes under direct policy control and include open market operations, the discount rate, reserve requirements, and interest rate ceilings.

A control period is the time interval over which the attainment of targets is planned. A complete policy strategy involves a number of control periods, each giving primary emphasis to different target variables. For example, over a weekly control period, an operating target such as the Federal funds rate or nonborrowed reserves might receive emphasis; over a monthly or quarterly control period, an intermediate target such as the growth rate of M_1 might receive emphasis. In control periods as long as six months or a year, long-term target variables such as output and employment would be the major policy goals.

A strategy is complete if its intermediate target is a strategic variable, linked empirically to the economy's long-term output, price, and employment goals. This implies that the policymaker is cognizant of the linkages among the various elements of the strategy. In a more formal sense, a model of the monetary policy transmission mechanism such as: instrument→intermediate target→long-term target must be developed.[4]

Guttentag was careful to distinguish between policy strategy, which involves the selection of the target variables to be explicitly considered by policymakers, and policy formulation, which involves the setting of specific values, or *dial settings,* for the target variables. In selecting these values, the policymaker examines a set of policy determinants such as relevant financial and economic data and forecasts. Clearly the development of an overall policy strategy is logically prior to policy formulation, since the particular policy determinants that the policymaker considers are dependent upon the strategy being pursued and the transmission mechanism it embraces [7, pp. 6–11].

The thrust of the Guttentag critique was reinforced by a number of events that increased public awareness of monetary policy. In the late 1960's the economic stimulus provided by the Vietnam war and the delay of the 1968 tax surcharge and the intellectual stimulus of the monetarist counterrevolution served to focus increasing public attention on monetary policy. During the same period, the development of

---

[3]Discussions of monetary policy have long been plagued by semantic difficulties with such words as targets, indicators, guides, objectives, etc., with the same words having different meanings to different writers. Such problems have played a major role in several major controversies in monetary economics [20].

[4]The arrows indicate the direction of causation. See [7] for a clear discussion of the transmission mechanism in monetarist and nonmonetarist models. [See article 11 of this book.—Ed.]

large-scale econometric models reflected the substantial impact of monetary policy on economic activity and tended to emphasize quantification of policy targets. In view of these developments, it is perhaps not surprising that the Federal Reserve moved toward the development of a more complete strategy. In 1966 the FOMC added a "proviso clause" to its Directive, giving explicit weight to movements in bank credit in determining policy actions. In 1970 the FOMC first began to include explicit references to monetary aggregates in its instructions to the Trading Desk. An important step in this ongoing process was probably the appointment of Arthur Burns as Chairman of the Federal Reserve Board in early 1970. In this regard Maisel states: "From the first day in office [Burns] put the weight of his office behind greater quantification" [18, p. 70].

The result of this evolutionary process can be stated simply—monetary aggregates (e.g., M_1, M_2, M_3, and bank credit) now receive more weight in policy deliberations and actions. The Directive—the FOMC's instructions to the Manager of the Trading Desk—now includes *specific* values for various strategic target variables, such as the Federal funds rate, bank reserves, and the monetary aggregates.[5] It is useful for expository purposes to divide the discussion of current policy procedures and strategy into its long- and short-term aspects. A description of these components and their interrelationship begins in the next section.

III. A View of Long-Run Strategy

The policy process begins at the Federal Reserve Board with the development of staff forecasts for GNP, prices, unemployment, and other long-run targets four quarters into the future.[6] These basic forecasts are undertaken three or four times each year and are updated each month. The projections are referred to as consensus forecasts, since judgmental and econometric inputs are combined into a single forecast.

The econometric forecast is made using the Board's version of the SSRC–MIT–PENN (SMP) econometric model.[7] Initially, model simulations are conducted using expected values of exogenous variables not under Federal Reserve control, such as Federal Government outlays, and a trajectory for an intermediate target variable under potential Federal Reserve control, such as the growth rate of the money stock. The same money stock trajectory, for example a 5 percent annual

---

[5]The more specific the instructions contained in the Directive, the less discretion or latitude the Manager has in executing policy actions. One of Guttentag's criticisms of the Fed's operating procedures in the 1950's and 1960's was the ambiguity in the Directive. He stated: "It is natural and a type of poetic justice that the words used by the Committee in giving instructions to the Manager are thrown back to the Committee. If the Committee instructs him to follow an 'even keel tipped on the side of ease', for example, he can report back that he 'maintained an even keel . . .' and the Committee is not in a position to complain that it does not understand what these words mean" [10, p. 18].

[6]This discussion draws heavily from the work of former members of the Board staff: Pierce [23], Pierce and Thomson [25]; and the work of former Governors Brimmer [2, 3] and Maisel [17, 18].

[7]See [5], [7], and [9] for discussions of the policy transmission mechanism of the SMP model. *Editors' Note:* The latter two articles are reprinted in section II of this book.

growth rate, is also assumed by the judgmental forecasters. The judgmental forecast, prepared by staff economists in various sections of the Federal Reserve Board, is often more accurate in the near term than the model forecast [23, p. 12]. Differences in the econometric and judgmental forecasts are reconciled, and the consensus forecast is prepared.

One should not infer that the econometric projections are "pure" in the sense of a mechanical application of an existing model; as is true in most econometric work, a considerable degree of judgment is involved. This notion has been summarized by Hymans:

> No [model] operator—at least, one with much success as a forecaster—lets the computer center run his model. Rather, the operator considers the model to be nothing better than the best statement of the internal logic of the economy which he happens to have available. While he rarely tampers with the model's interactive logic, he recognizes that there are relevant factors which he thinks he knows, and which he is sure the model does not know, about current realities in the economy. In some way, he attempts to communicate this information to the model. . . . And what is most important, much of the relevant information which has to be communicated to the model is simply not contained in the values of the exogenous variables [11, p. 537].

For the sake of completeness, it should also be noted that the judgmental forecast is not independent of the econometric projections. The various forecasters interact continually and therefore a judgment about the path of economic activity (especially over a long time horizon) is no doubt influenced by the model simulations.

Following the development of the consensus forecast, the Board staff usually produces a number of alternative long-run scenarios of economic activity for evaluation by the FOMC. First, the consensus forecast is reproduced quarter-by-quarter, variable-by-variable with the econometric model by adjusting the constant terms in selected equations. Alternative trajectories of monetary growth are then fed into the model to produce a consistent set of monetary, GNP, price, and unemployment estimates.[8] The FOMC then evaluates these alternative scenarios and selects an explicit monetary growth path for the forthcoming six- or twelve-month period.

It is important to note that the implicit dial settings for the final targets embedded in the staff forecast may not, for a variety of reasons, be accepted by members of the FOMC. For instance, an individual member of the FOMC may not believe the staff forecast and may therefore foresee a different real sector outcome. Each Reserve Bank President has his own staff's view of the economic and financial outlook to consider, and it is possible that his staff has a forecast quite different from that of the

---

[8]As Pierce has discussed [23], a less extensive forecasting effort is made each month just prior to a FOMC meeting. This effort involves the updating of earlier forecasts through an extensive examination of incoming data and how they agree with, or have tended to modify, the projections presented in previous months. See also [2].

Board staff. More generally, there is no reason to assume that each member of the FOMC will embrace the estimates developed by the Board staff with regard to the impact of monetary policy on economic activity.[9]

Alternatively, an FOMC member may have a longer planning horizon for policy than the four- to six-quarter projection horizon and, therefore, might not believe that such a short-term projection should be a major determinant of current policy actions. In the current setting, for example, a policymaker may desire to drive unemployment down to 4 percent by mid-1976 but might feel that existing economic constraints, as well as structural relationships, make the risk of intensifying inflationary pressures under such a policy high. Hence, the return to full employment should be, in this member's view, more gradual and occur over a two- to three-year period.

Another possibility is that an FOMC member may have little faith in any of the assorted projections and instead may be strongly influenced by current economic and financial conditions. This view implies a shorter planning horizon than four to six quarters. Pierce has summarized some reasons why this last possibility may prevail from time to time:

> It is very difficult to convince a policymaker to move an instrument in what he views to be the wrong direction. That is to say, if income is expanding very rapidly and the models are predicting that it is going to fall in the future unless he eases up, it is very difficult to get him to ease up because that sort of policy recommendation is contrary to what is going on currently. I must say that until our models do a lot better, his wariness may be justified. Again, the problem is one of how to handle risk: what if the model were wrong? What if the economy were expanding very rapidly, the policymaker eases up, but economic expansion becomes more rapid? The cost of the error to the policymaker would be very large [23, p. 18].[10]

A Model of the Long-Run Strategy

The longer-term policy process described above conforms to a general class of constrained optimum problems. That is, policymakers may be viewed as maximizing a utility or preference function subject to the constraints imposed by the economic structure or by other considerations. Equation (1) states that the utility of the policymaker is a function of the deviation of the final targets from their desired levels, with

---

[9]In recent testimony by Chairman Burns before the Senate Banking Committee (July 24, 1975), members of the Senate Committee requested the release of the staff economic forecast conditional on a particular growth rate in the money stock. Chairman Burns did not appear to favor this suggestion, and his response emphasized some of the same points discussed in this and following paragraphs.

[10]The issue here is quite complex. The policymaker must act in the face of uncertainty over structural parameters and with the knowledge that there is a lag between actions and effects. In addition, there is the distinct possibility that incoming data may be revised substantially and thereby alter the appropriate policy response. Against this background, it is often difficult for policymakers to be convinced to move an instrument now to affect a final target one year in the future. Perhaps some of the recent applications of control theory to stabilization policy will prove helpful in educating both policy advisers and policymakers.

greater utility being associated with smaller deviations.[11] Let U represent the policy-maker's utility. Then:

$$\text{maximize} \qquad U = f_1 (Y^A - Y^*) \qquad (1)$$

$$\text{subject to} \qquad Y^A = f_2 (M_L, X_L) \qquad (2)$$

$$\text{and} \qquad \sigma_R^2 \leq \alpha \qquad (2a)$$

where Y is a vector of final target variables such as GNP and prices. The superscript A denotes the actual value of the variable, and the asterisk denotes a desired value. The symbol σ_R^2 represents the variance of some interest rate R, α is a constant, M is the money stock, X represents other determinants of the final targets, and the sub-script L is a distributed lag operator. The side constraints represented by equations (2) and (2a) reflect the limitations imposed on policymakers by the structure of the economy and by the volatility of interest rates.

The expected values of the final targets will generally depend upon the structure of the economy, the particular dial settings for the intermediate target variable selected by the central bank, dial settings for fiscal policy selected by Congress and the President, and the values of other determinants such as the level of consumer and business confidence, price expectations, the degree of capacity utilization, and inter-national developments. The forecast of final targets by the staff assumes specific dial settings for the intermediate target variables, e.g., the money stock, and also involves assumptions concerning all of the above determinants of economic activity not under the direct control of the Federal Reserve.[12] This process is summarized by equation (2), which condenses the SMP model and the consensus forecast for the final targets into a simple expression.[13] It is presumed that the policymaker believes that changes in the money stock lead in a systematic fashion, albeit with a lag, to changes in prices, output, and employment.[14]

Equation (2a) is included as a constraint to account for the Fed's ongoing desire to avoid disorderly conditions in financial markets that, in turn, might frustrate the

[11]To be more precise, (f_1) is an inverse function; that is, the policymaker is minimizing disutility (or "losses") by minimizing the deviations of the actual target values from desired levels.

[12]This being the case, the forecast may be wrong because the fiscal policy assumption is wrong, the Federal Reserve does not achieve the dial setting for the intermediate target, the structural parameters underlying the forecast are incorrect, or there is a stochastic shift in a behavioral relationship. One point relevant to this problem, which has received all too little attention in the literature, is the interdependence of stabilization policy actions. For example, if a restrictive monetary policy leads to a response by the Congress or the President to ease fiscal policy, the forecaster must anticipate this reaction.

[13]As noted above, each member of the FOMC might, in effect, have a different specification for equation (2) because of an alternative view of structural relationships. In this regard, equation (2), despite its simplicity, should not be mistaken for so-called reduced form models purporting to link the money stock or the monetary base to economic activity.

[14]Throughout this article error terms are generally ignored. Clearly, the staff should express the confidence intervals and standard errors around a particular forecast for the final targets.

achievement of the final targets. A discussion of the constraint on interest rate volatility is the subject of Section VI.

Before closing the discussion of the long-term strategy, it is important to emphasize that many members of the FOMC might object to the casual sequence that seems to underlie equation (2): open market operations→money stock→economic activity. More specifically, some might prefer:

$$Y^A = f_2(R_L, X_L)$$

where R is a short- or long-term interest rate, and the implied causal sequence is more like the transmission mechanism of the SMP model [7, pp. 7–9].

$$\begin{bmatrix} \text{Open} \\ \text{Market} \\ \text{Operations} \end{bmatrix} \rightarrow \begin{bmatrix} \text{Interest} \\ \text{Rates} \end{bmatrix} \rightarrow \begin{bmatrix} \text{Cost of Capital,} \\ \text{Household Net Worth,} \\ \text{Credit Availability} \end{bmatrix} \rightarrow \begin{bmatrix} \text{Economic} \\ \text{Activity} \end{bmatrix}$$

In part the issue involved here concerns the endogeneity or exogeneity of R and M and which variable ought to be the intermediate policy target [27]. For purposes of this article, this complex issue is sidestepped for two reasons. First, if one ignores the error term in the demand for money function, it may be solved in terms of the interest rate or the money stock, and either may be treated exogenously for forecasting purposes.[15] That is, a large macroeconometric model may contain a correctly estimated money demand function:

$$M = a_0 + a_1 y + a_2 R$$

where a_0, a_1, and a_2 are estimated parameters, M is money demand, y is nominal income, and R is the interest rate. The forecast for the final targets is independent of whether the money demand equation is solved for M or for R:

$$R = \frac{M - a_0 - a_1 y}{a_2}$$

Second, M is the assumed intermediate target variable in equation (2) because the FOMC has chosen to index its policy stance publicly in terms of M_1 and other monetary aggregates.[16] The use of the word "index" is meant to imply that even though members of the FOMC may have different views of the policy transmission mechanism in general, and the causal role of changes in the money stock in particular, the FOMC has been able to reach an agreement to express its policy in terms of growth rates in the monetary aggregates.

---

[15]Such a procedure would not be legitimate for estimation purposes because of the bias that would be introduced by treating a variable exogenously if in fact it were endogenous. See [16] for a discussion of this latter point and how it is related to models of money stock determination.

[16]See the "Record of Policy Actions" appearing each month in the *Federal Reserve Bulletin*.

IV. The Linkage between the Long- and Short-Run Strategy

Having selected a long-run dial setting for money stock growth, perhaps 5 percent over the next twelve months, the FOMC must now guide its open market operations monthly so as to achieve the desired long-run monetary growth path. It is important to recognize that there are an infinite number of monthly and quarterly patterns of monetary growth for the money stock that could turn out to *average* 5 percent over a full year. As will be shown, the monthly pattern desired by the FOMC will generally depend upon interest rate considerations and the current position of the money stock vis-à-vis the long-run target.

The relationship between the short- and long-run dial settings for M_1 is illustrated in Figure 1. It is assumed that a 5 percent long-run growth path for M_1 was adopted in December, and by the January FOMC meeting M_1 is well below its targeted long-run path. Under these circumstances the staff would normally prepare three (or more) alternative short-run money stock paths for FOMC consideration, each designed to return M_1 to the long-term path but each requiring successively longer adjustment periods.[17] With reference to Figure 1, a rapid return to the long-run path

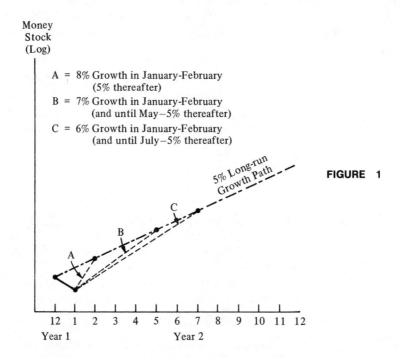

FIGURE 1

[17]Currently the control period for the FOMC's short-run strategy is two months—in December the control period is December-January, in January it is January-February, etc.

may require an 8 percent growth rate for M_1 in the January–February control period (A). Alternatively, slower growth rates of 7 and 6 percent in the January–February control period and in several successive periods would return M_1 to the long-run path in May (B) and July (C), respectively. The process underlying the selection of these alternative paths—i.e., the short-run formulation of policy and the actual short-run alternative selected by the FOMC—are discussed in the following sections.

V. A View of the Short-Run Strategy

The short-run strategy of the FOMC involves the selection of a short-run dial setting for the money stock and the development of an operating procedure for achieving the desired monetary growth path. The process begins with the staff presenting to the FOMC each month a set of alternative short-run (two-month) growth rates for the money stock. Associated with each alternative short-run path for the money stock will be a growth rate of bank reserves and a level of the Federal funds rate.

In formulating the short-run strategy, income movements are taken as given; that is, income for the coming two-month control period is interpolated from the quarterly projection of economic activity described earlier. The important assumptions underlying this procedure are that the quarterly projection and the monthly interpolation are correct and that there is no significant simultaneity problem over a one- or two-month period. To illustrate, again consider the example used in Figure 1. Assume that it is the end of January, that the consensus forecast specifies 5 percent monetary growth from December to July, and that the money stock actually declines in January. Normally, in the face of this one-month shortfall in the money stock, the staff would not revise its income projection for the coming months. This, in effect, assumes the policy lag is greater than one or two months and that subsequent policy actions will result in growth in the money stock that will overshoot the target by enough to offset the miss in the first month.

Given income and the current position of the money stock vis-à-vis the long-run target path as depicted in Figure 1, the staff might present at the January FOMC meeting a set of short-run alternatives, as in Table 1.[18]

The first row contains alternative short-run growth rates that will return the money stock to its long-run path. Alternative (A) and the staff discussion accompanying it would indicate that to achieve an 8 percent growth rate in M_1 and to return to the long-run path by February, the growth in reserves over the January–February period

[18]The alternatives, along with a discussion of the situation that might develop in financial markets under each option, appear in the "Bluebook," which is prepared monthly for the FOMC. See [2, p. 285]. The actual alternative selected by the FOMC is now published with a 45-day lag as part of the policy record. The alternatives contained in the Record of Policy Actions for the January 1974 FOMC meeting are the first available. In the discussion that follows we will, for simplicity, ignore M_2, even though it appears with M_1 under each alternative the FOMC considers.

Table 1. Alternative Short-Run Dial Settings
(Percent)

Target	Alternative		
	(A)	(B)	(C)
Money stock growth	8	7	6
Federal funds rate	6	7	8
Reserve growth	8	7	6

Note: The growth in reserves and the money stock are expressed at seasonally adjusted annual rates, while the funds rate is expressed as a level.

would have to be 8 percent and the level of the Federal funds rate required is 6 percent.[19]

The Federal funds rates, shown in row 2 of the table, are derived in two steps. First, assuming income given, a money demand function is solved for the short-term interest rate necessary to achieve the alternative short-run money path. The required Federal funds rate is then determined using a term structure equation relating it to the short-term interest rate. As was true in the forecast of economic activity, each alternative represents a staff consensus based on econometric models and judgmental considerations.[20]

The third row of the table could in theory be derived by solving a money supply function for the rate of growth in reserves necessary to achieve each money stock alternative. That is, if one viewed the money supply as the product of a reserve aggregate, such as reserves available to support private deposits RPD,[21] and a multiplier m, then the necessary growth in reserves could be obtained by estimating the multiplier, calculating the different February levels of the money supply M consistent with each money stock alternative, and dividing one by the other (RPD = M/m).[22]*

[19]It is worth noting that the FOMC has from time to time selected an alternative that has included, for example, the money stock under (A) and the funds rate under (B). In this case, the FOMC decided the staff had misspecified the relationship between the funds rate and monetary growth and has constructed a new alternative thought to be internally consistent. Thus, the FOMC is free to evaluate and to accept or reject the trade-offs among interest rates, reserves, and money stock growth implied by the staff estimates. See also n. 27.

[20]Monthly financial models developed at the Federal Reserve Board and the Federal Reserve Bank of New York are major inputs in this process. For a discussion of these models, see the papers by Pierce and Thomson [24, 25] and Davis and Shadrack [8].

[21]The reserve aggregate currently employed by the FOMC in its deliberations is called "reserves available to support private deposits" RPD. This magnitude is defined as total reserves minus required reserves against government and interbank deposits. It should be noted here that there is little objective evidence that RPD's have received much weight in the formulation or implementation of policy. Speaking of the 1973 period, Tschinkel said: "The Manager [reflecting the desires of the FOMC] found RPD of lesser importance in the determination of his response to the emerging patterns of monetary growth" [29, p. 10.]. See also the recent evaluation of Kane [12, pp. 841–43] and the discussion that follows.

[22]The particular reserve aggregate one chooses (e.g., total reserves, nonborrowed reserves, the monetary base, RPD, etc.) is not a critical issue here.

* Here the Federal funds rate and reserve aggregates play the role of what most literature refers to as "instruments" of monetary policy.—Ed.

In practice, as discussed by Axilrod and Beck [1], the approach is demand oriented. After projecting the interest rates consistent with the short-run money stock growth rate for each alternative, these rates are used to estimate bank demand for required and excess reserves [1, p. 89]. An important characteristic of this approach is that it results in the supply of reserves and money being perfectly elastic at the targeted level of the interest rate R and the volume of reserves and money, therefore, being demand determined. This is illustrated in Figure 2, where the demand for reserves is expressed as a function of the interest rate.[23] Assume the position and slope of the demand schedule for reserves TR_D have been estimated by the staff and that TR_1 is the level of total reserves in February that is derived from deposit demand consistent with a 6 percent growth rate in the money stock. Under the demand approach discussed above, the required interest rate is R_1, and the System will supply reserves elastically at that rate. Thus the supply function TR_S is horizontal. This means that stochastic shifts in the reserve demand (or money demand) function, an error in the income projection, or any other disturbance on the demand side will, in the first instance, alter the position of TR_D to TR'_D and lead to changes in the quantity of reserves to TR_2.[24]

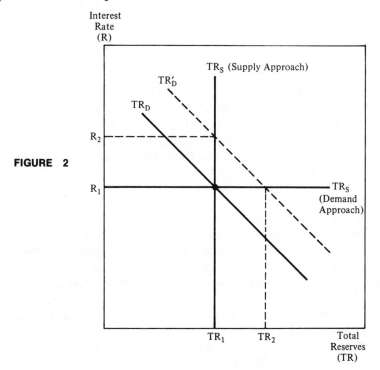

FIGURE 2

[23]While the following diagram relates the interest rate to reserves, one could just as easily substitute the money stock for reserves.

[24]While income is a shift parameter in this two-dimensional diagram, an increase in income would actually result in a movement along the demand function for demand deposits, time deposits, and reserves in three-dimensional space.

Table 2.   Short-Run Dial Settings for 1974*

Date of Meeting	2-Month Control Period	Money Stock Range (SAAR)	Actual Money Stock (SAAR)	RPD Range (SAAR)	Actual RPD (SAAR)	Federal Funds Rate Range (Percent)	Actual Federal Funds Rate (Percent)
Jan. 22, 1974	Jan.–Feb.	3.00 to 6.00	4.7	4.75 to 7.75	3.3	8.75 to 10.00	8.93 to 9.47
Feb. 20, 1974	Feb.–Mar.	6.50 to 9.50	11.8	3.50 to 6.50	5.8	8.25 to 9.50	8.81 to 9.33
Mar. 19, 1974	Mar.–Apr.	5.50 to 8.50	9.6	4.00 to 7.00	15.8	9.00 to 10.50	9.61 to 10.36
Apr. 16, 1974	Apr.–May	3.00 to 7.00	6.5	6.00 to 11.00	20.7	9.75 to 11.25[1]	10.78 to 11.46
May 21, 1974	May–Jun.	3.00 to 7.00	6.3	13.00 to 20.00	20.0	11.00 to 11.75[1]	11.45 to 11.85
Jun. 18, 1974	Jun.–Jul.	3.50 to 7.50	4.8	10.00 to 13.50	13.5	11.25 to 13.00[1]	11.97 to 13.55
Jul. 18, 1974	Jul.–Aug.	2.00 to 6.00	2.1	8.75 to 11.75	9.0	11.50 to 13.00	12.02 to 12.60
Aug. 20, 1974	Aug.–Sep.	4.75 to 6.75	1.5	7.75 to 9.75	7.7	11.50 to 12.50	11.48 to 11.84
Sep. 10, 1974	Sep.–Oct.	3.00 to 6.00	2.6	6.00 to 8.50	3.5	10.25 to 12.00[2]	10.11 to 11.41
Oct. 15, 1974	Oct.–Nov.	4.75 to 7.25	5.3	5.50 to 8.00	− 2.1	9.00 to 10.50	9.34 to 9.81
Nov. 19, 1974	Nov.–Dec.	6.50 to 9.50	4.5	2.50 to 5.50	3.2	8.50 to 10.00	8.72 to 9.46
Dec. 17, 1974	Dec.–Jan.	5.00 to 7.00	− 3.4	9.00 to 11.00	3.9	7.13 to 9.00[2]	7.17 to 8.45

*Short-run dial settings for the money stock and RPD are expressed as seasonally adjusted annual rates of growth (SAAR) averaged over two-month target period. The range for the Federal funds rate and the actual outcome apply to statement week averages during intermeeting period. Actuals for the money stock and RPD do not reflect benchmark revisions or revisions in the seasonal factors made following the period to which data relate.

[1] Upper limit of range raised between meetings to figure shown.

[2] Lower limit of range lowered between meetings to figure shown.

This can be contrasted with a supply approach to money stock control, which would lead to the interest rate being demand determined. Again with reference to Figure 2, the level of total reserves thought necessary to achieve the 6 percent growth in the money stock remains TR_1. Accordingly, the System would supply the volume of reserves represented by the vertical TR_S function. Any disturbance on the demand side will alter the interest rate to R_2 and leave the quantity of reserves (and money) unaffected. In the absence of any disturbance (i.e., in a deterministic system) both approaches yield the same result (R_1 and TR_1).

The point that must be emphasized is that one should not infer from the appearance of a reserve aggregate in Table 1 that the FOMC has adopted a supply approach to money stock control.[25] Evidence that the growth in reserves has had a low weight in the System's reaction function (i.e., in the formulation and implementation of policy) is easily obtained. Simply compare the specifications voted for reserves RPD, the money stock, and the funds rate in 1974 with the actual outcomes, shown in Table 2.[26] This exercise in revealed preference shows that the Federal Reserve rarely missed the funds rate range but allowed reserves and the money stock to move away from the specified range in about one-half of the two-month control periods. Assuming the initial specifications were internally consistent, the conclusion must be that in the short run disturbances were allowed to affect quantity and not price.

[25]Brunner and Meltzer, Friedman, and the St. Louis Federal Reserve Bank have long advocated such an approach.

[26]As detailed in Section VI, the short-run dial settings selected by the FOMC are actually expressed as ranges. The rationale for the ranges is explained in Section VI.

While this issue will be discussed in more detail in Section VI (of this article) the evidence in Table 2 suggests the System was not controlling reserves over the short run.[27]

A Model of the Short-Run Strategy

The following set of equations may be used to link the Federal funds rate to open market operations on the one hand and the money stock on the other:[28]

$$M_D = f_3 (y_L, R_L) \tag{3}$$

$$R = f_4 (RFF_L) \tag{4}$$

$$RFF = f_5 (TR_D, TR_S) \tag{5}$$

$$TR = NBR + MBB = ER + RR \tag{6a}$$

$$NBR = FR + RR \tag{6b}$$

where M_D is the demand for money, y is nominal income, R is a short-term interest rate such as the ninety-day commercial paper rate, RFF is the Federal funds rate, NBR is nonborrowed reserves, MBB is member bank borrowings, ER is excess reserves, FR is free reserves (ER − MBB), RR is required reserves, and TR_D is the demand for and TR_S the supply of total reserves. The first three relations are straightforward. Equation (3) is a standard money demand function; equation (4) is a term structure relation, where the short-term rate (e.g., the ninety-day commercial paper rate) is a function of a distributed lag on the funds rate (single-day maturity).[29] Equation (5) specifies the funds rate as a function of the demand for and supply of total reserves. In (6a) total reserves are divided into familiar components—required reserves and excess reserves—which, by definition, must equal reserves borrowed from the System and all other reserves (nonborrowed reserves). By rearranging terms, a convenient identity (6b) can be formed. This latter identity may be transformed into an equation with behavioral content by considering the right-hand side as reflecting the behavior of the public and the banks and the left-hand side as reflecting the behavior of the Fed. That is, the banks' demand for required reserves is derived from the public's demand for deposits. This, together with the banks' demand for free reserves, must equal the total of nonborrowed reserves supplied by the

[27]An interesting feature of this approach to policymaking is that a member of the FOMC might vote for alternative (A) in Table 1 even though he viewed monetary policy as operating primarily through interest rates and thus really preferred the interest rate under alternative (B). In other words, members of the FOMC may vote for individual elements in the table rather than columns. Support for this interpretation is provided by Maisel: "A possible side advantage of this strategy is that it can be followed even though it might be impossible to get agreement among the members of the FOMC either as to ultimate goals, or the form or level of an intermediate monetary variable, or as to how to define what strategy is being followed" [17, p. 154].

[28]For simplicity we will continue to ignore time deposits and therefore M_2.

[29]See [14] for evidence that a major portion of the variance in short-term rates can be explained by current and lagged movements in the Federal funds rate.

Federal Reserve open market operations.[30] Other factors, such as the gold stock, float, and Treasury deposits at the Federal Reserve, also affect the supply of nonborrowed reserves. However, holding these other factors constant or assuming that the System engages in so-called "defensive" open market operations to offset movements in these factors, NBR is controllable by policymakers. For present purposes, these other factors are held constant, and the change in nonborrowed reserves is assumed equal to the change in the System's holdings of securities. Therefore, the change in nonborrowed reserves directly reflects open market operations (i.e., ΔNBR = OMO). In summary, the funds rate is determined by the supply of nonborrowed reserves relative to the demand for required reserves and free reserves.[31]

To close the model, the System's short-run reaction function relating OMO to RFF must be specified. Ignoring for the moment the constraint on interest rate volatility, the desired level of the funds rate RFF* can be determined by solving equations (1) to (4) recursively for a relationship between long-run target values of the money stock and RFF:

$$RFF^* = f_6(M^*) \tag{7}$$

In practice it is the short-run target value for the money stock, rather than the long-run target value that would usually appear in equation (7). The reason, as discussed in Sections IV and VI, is that the change in the funds rate required to get the money stock back on the long-run path (assuming it is significantly off the path), is usually deemed too large and disruptive by the policymaker.

Once equations (1) to (4) have been solved for RFF*, equation (8) follows from equation (5) and the supporting identities:

$$\Delta NBR = OMO = f_7(RFF^* - RFF^A) \tag{8}$$

Simply put, the System will absorb (inject) reserves by selling (buying) securities when the funds rate is below (above) the desired level. This policy approach ensures that the supply of reserves is perfectly elastic at the desired funds rate and the quantity of reserves is demand determined. In the first instance, deviations in the demand for reserves from the FOMC specifications lead to an equivalent change in the stock of reserves but to no change in the funds rate.[32]

---

[30]See [5, Chapter 1] for a discussion of the key role of the free reserves equation in the financial sector of the SMP model.

[31]It should be emphasized that the set of equations presented is intended to be very general and should not be construed as a complete model of the financial sector and its interaction with Federal Reserve policy. This is a task beyond the scope of the present paper. As it stands the set of equations is underidentified, and no attempt is made to account for various aspects of simultaneity.

[32]A point worth mentioning in this context is that a change in reserve requirements has virtually no impact on reserves or the money stock unless accompanied by a change in the funds rate target. If, for example, the System lowers the reserve requirement on demand deposits, other things equal, this will push down the funds rate. However, as depicted in equation (8), this will result in the System selling securities and, therefore, absorbing the free reserves.

There is in theory a mechanism that limits the procyclical movement in reserves. The dynamics of the intermeeting phase of the short-run policy process are embedded in a feedback control loop that can be summarized by:

$$\Delta RFF^* = f_8(M^* - M^A) \qquad (9)$$

That is, movements in the funds rate depend upon deviations of the money stock from its desired value. To illustrate, assume incoming data on the money stock suggest that monetary growth over the short-run two-month target period will exceed the short-run dial setting selected at the last FOMC meeting. In response the Manager of the Trading Desk would be expected to increase the dial setting for the funds rate. In practice, however, the timing and magnitude of the Manager's initial response to apparent deviations of monetary growth from desired levels are often not so straightforward. If the tone of the securities markets is weak, for example, the FOMC might decide not to change the funds rate for the time being, even though the money stock is growing above the desired rate.[33]

A more difficult problem contributing to cautious adjustments of the funds rate is the uncertainty concerning the money stock forecasts. This uncertainty results from the fact that forecasts of the money stock over the short run (e.g., one to three months ahead) have not been very accurate [29]. This being the case, the FOMC often may delay its response to an apparent deviation of actual from desired monetary growth until more data are available to confirm the error. The rationale is that the policymaker prefers to avoid "whipsawing" the market—i.e., raising the Federal funds rate now if money growth appears to be exceeding desires and lowering it later if the money stock projections prove incorrect and actual money growth is found to be close to that desired. This, of course, is another facet of the System's desire to minimize short-run interest rate volatility and is discussed in the next section.

VI. The Constraint on Interest Rate Volatility and Its Interaction with Policy Targets

Within the FOMC's current strategy, the target values for the Federal funds rate, reserves, and the money stock are actually expressed as ranges. Referring back to Table 1, under alternative (A) for example, the entry for the money stock might be 7 to 9 percent and the entry for the Federal funds rate might be 5.5 to 6.5 percent. From the viewpoint of the staff, the ranges presented to the FOMC generally represent a standard error around a point estimate at the midpoint of the range. From the viewpoint of the FOMC, however, the ranges may have a somewhat different meaning. The range for the money stock is typically viewed as a range of tolerance. If the

---

[33]Thus, the Federal funds rate *is* the Federal Reserve's policy "instrument" and reacts to changes in the state of the economy reflected here in the "intermediate target variable" (M^*-M^A). Federal Reserve reactions are tested by Havrilesky et al. in article 28. Note that the Federal Reserve's structural hypothesis is ambiguous and thus prevents any suggestion that this (or any) instrument is an *optimal* one.—Ed.

money stock is expanding at a rate within its range, then the desired level of the Federal funds rate will probably not be altered to any significant degree.[34] Thus, in terms of equation (9), M^* is a range and ΔRFF^* equals zero unless M^A is outside the range.

The following quotations suggest there are at least two interpretations attached to the reasoning behind any given range for the money stock adopted by the FOMC: (1) "The inherent short-run volatility of the monetary aggregates is one reason why Committee expresses its short-run guides in terms of ranges of tolerance" [21, p. 334]. In this view the range implies a standard error around a point estimate. (2) "The Committee chose tolerance ranges for M_1 . . . that were at least as restrictive as the alternatives presented by the staff and reduced the lower ends of these ranges to indicate its willingness to accept substantially slower growth in the near term" [29, p. 108]. In this view the Committee skews its preferences, perhaps in response to previous deviations of actual from desired levels. Suppose the staff presents an alternative such as (C), which implies that an 8 percent Federal funds rate will translate into a 5-7 percent growth in the money stock, the point estimate being 6 percent growth. The FOMC, responding to past shortfalls in money stock growth, might then modify this alternative by changing the range to 5-8 percent, indicating its willingness to err on the side of more, rather than less, monetary growth relative to projected levels. Operationally, this means that if the money stock actually should grow at an 8 percent rate, this will not result in a raising of the desired Federal funds rate.

The significance of the Federal funds range is that it specifically limits the degree of response by the Manager to a deviation of monetary growth from the desired range. As shown in Table 2, this range in 1974 was typically 100-150 basis points. If the midpoint of the range selected is equal to the Federal funds rate prevailing just prior to the FOMC meeting, then the FOMC has typically been willing to tolerate a maximum change in the funds rate of 50-75 basis points in one direction over any given intermeeting period.[35] Against this background, it is interesting to note that the money demand functions that underlie the specifications presented to the FOMC exhibit very low interest elasticities [4; 8; 24; 25]. The monthly model discussed by Pierce and Thomson [25, p. 351], for example, indicates that, other things equal, a 100 basis point change in the Federal funds rate will lead to only about a 0.3 percentage point change in the annual growth rate of the money stock over a one-month period and only about a one percentage point change over a six-month period. Assuming the interest elasticities embedded in the monthly models are reasonably accurate, the constraint on the monthly movement in the Federal funds rate, as explicitly revealed by the range in the Policy Record for the funds rate, suggests that

---

[34]This discussion assumes that incoming data and forecasts of nonfinancial developments are consistent with the projections set out when the long-run trajectory for the money stock was first selected; as a result, the FOMC has not modified the long-run money stock target.

[35]From time to time the FOMC has been willing to change the upper or lower end of the range on the funds rate and thus permit a larger intermeeting movement in the funds rate. For a recent example, see the "Record of Policy Actions" of the FOMC in the *Federal Reserve Bulletin*, (February 1975), p. 88. In addition, if the funds rate prevailing at the time of the meeting is at the upper or lower end of the adopted range, it is possible that the full 100-150 basis point range could be used during the intermeeting period.

the FOMC is willing to tolerate relatively large short-run deviations of monetary growth from desired levels.[36]

Whether or not the constraint on month-to-month movements in interest rates has significant destabilizing effects on output and prices depends on the narrowness of the short-run constraint and whether or not it frustrates achievement of the long-run money stock target.[37]

With regard to the narrowness of interest rate tolerance bands, Pierce conducted some experiments with the SMP model and concluded: "The results indicate that the placement of sufficiently narrow bounds on the change in the bill rate can have a large impact on the simulated value of GNP" [22, p. 101]. It is worth emphasizing that *if the band on interest rate movements is fairly narrow and inflexible, it is reasonable to question whether or not the money stock is being "controlled" at all.**

In theory, at least, the current FOMC approach to the formulation of policy is designed to guard against short-run deviations of money stock growth affecting the achievement of the long-run money stock target. This is illustrated in Figure 3. Assume the FOMC selected a 4–6 percent long-run growth path for the money stock in month 1 of year 1, growth in the money stock in months 5 and 6 of year 1 has been 8 percent, and the FOMC is meeting at the beginning of month 7. Further, assume the prevailing Federal funds rate is 5 percent. As discussed in Section IV, the short-run alternatives for the money stock presented to the FOMC by the staff will typically be tied to a specific time path for returning the growth of the money stock to the desired range. For example, alternative (A) would envision only 2 percent growth in the money stock over the next two months and thus an early return to the range. This might require a sharp rise in the Federal funds rate to perhaps 7 percent. Alternative (B), however, would envision a slower return to the upper end of the desired range; the money stock might be expected to grow at a 5 percent rate for five months and return to the range by month 11. This alternative would require a smaller current rise in the Federal funds rate to perhaps 6 percent, possibly followed by further rises in subsequent months.[38] An examination of month-to-month movements in the funds rate and in monetary growth over the past several years suggests that the FOMC has in practice more often preferred to pursue an alternative such as (B).[39]

[36]In other words, short-run monetary control is considered too "costly" because of the volatility of interest rates that seems to be required. For a critical review of this issue see [15]. For some evidence that short-run deviations of monetary growth from the desired trajectory might not be "costly" in terms of missing price and output targets, see [6, p. 24].

[37]It also depends, of course, on the willingness of the FOMC to modify the constraint over time. In this regard, the FOMC has clearly been willing to tolerate larger swings in interest rates over the first half of the 1970's than it did over most of the 1960's.

* This raises questions as to whether money is actually serving as an intermediate target-variable despite lip-service given to its strategic role.—Ed.

[38]It should be noted that one alternative may envision an immediate return to the desired range without any significant change in the funds rate. The explanation accompanying such an alternative may be that the monthly pattern of income growth suggests smaller increases in coming months and thus less strength in money demand. Another possible explanation is that the current spurt in monetary growth is a random occurrence not likely to persist.

[39]The revealed tendency to view short-run deviations of monetary growth (and their mirror image, the short-run smoothing of interest rates) as costless is controversial. Within the Hicks-Hansen IS-LM framework, the presumption is that there are stochastic shifts in the LM curve that are larger than the random shifts of the IS curve. See Poole [27] and the pathbreaking report of Weintraub [30, especially pp. 63-66].

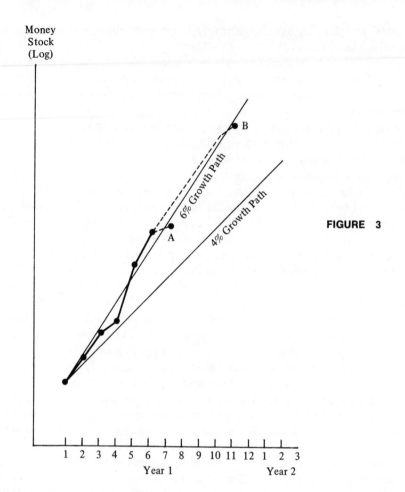

FIGURE 3

One significant area of concern with regard to this policy approach is the possible existence, from time to time, of a serially correlated error in the income projection. Suppose the staff is underestimating the strength in aggregate demand and the money stock is expanding more rapidly than desired. Since the growth of the money stock appears to be inconsistent with the income projection and the associated estimate of the demand for money, the initial tendency may be for the policymaker to discount the jump in monetary growth and wait for further data that would confirm greater strength in economic activity and money demand. The incorrect presumption is that the spurt in monetary growth is the result of a stochastic shift in money demand. The long-run implications of accommodating this growth are a more procyclical policy than desired and, given the lags in the effect of policy, the need later on for a very sharp tightening in policy to offset past excesses.

An important problem for monetary control that can result from a series of short-run deviations of monetary growth is that the FOMC might give up on the long-run

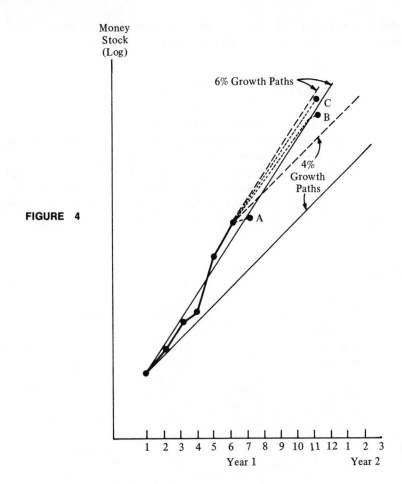

Money
Stock
(Log)

6% Growth Paths

C

B

4%
Growth
Paths

FIGURE 4

A

1 2 3 4 5 6 7 8 9 10 11 12 1 2 3
Year 1   Year 2

money stock target *de facto* by continually resetting the starting (or base) date of the control period over which the target value is to be attained. This might happen, for example, if the policymakers find it impossible to tolerate the large increases in interest rates necessary to offset past excesses in monetary growth. This is illustrated in Figure 4, which is similar to Figure 3 except that the FOMC is presumed to adopt alternative (C) at its meeting early in month 7. The long-run target remains 4-6 percent but is calculated from month 6 rather than from month 1.[40] Unfortunately,

[40]The FOMC recently made such a shift in the base of its current long-run money stock target. On May 1, 1975, Chairman Burns announced before the Senate Banking Committee that the FOMC planned money stock growth of 5 to 7.5 percent over the period March 1975-March 1976. On July 24, 1975, the Chairman announced before the House Banking Committee that the targeted growth rate was the same, but the period over which it was to be obtained was the second quarter of 1975 to the second quarter of 1976. Since the money stock grew at nearly a 9 percent rate in the second quarter of 1975, this change in the base, in effect, accepts much of the intervening monetary expansion.

this subtle ratcheting-up (or down) of the long-run monetary growth rate could exacerbate the cyclical swings in output and prices.[41]

VII. Some Final Remarks

This article has presented a view of the Federal Reserve's current approach to the formulation and implementation of monetary policy. It is hoped the general interpretation presented will be critically examined, the discussion of particular phases of the strategy carefully scrutinized, and the models that underlie the strategy empirically tested. This should result in a clearer understanding of current monetary policy procedures, more carefully developed advice for policymakers on how to improve their performance, and greater success in achieving the goals of monetary policy.

REFERENCES

1. AXILROD, STEPHEN and DARWIN BECK. "Role of Projections with Monetary Aggregates as Policy Targets," in *Controlling Monetary Aggregates II: The Implementation.* Federal Reserve Bank of Boston, 1973, pp. 81-102.
2. BRIMMER, ANDREW. "Tradition and Innovation in Monetary Management," in *Monetary Economics: Readings.* Ed. Alan Entine, Belmont, California: Wadsworth, 1968, pp. 273-89.
3. ———. "The Political Economy of Money: Evolution and Impact of Monetarism in the Federal Reserve System," *American Economic Review,* (May 1972), 344-52.
4. CICCOLO, JOHN H. "Is Short-Run Monetary Control Feasible?" in *Monetary Aggregates and Monetary Policy.* Federal Reserve Bank of New York, 1974, pp. 82-91.
5. COOPER, J. PHILLIP. *Development of the Monetary Sector, Prediction and Policy Analysis in the FRB-MIT-PENN Model.* Lexington: D. C. Heath, 1974.
6. CORRIGAN, E. GERALD. "Income Stabilization and Short-Run Variability in Money," in *Monetary Aggregates and Monetary Policy.* Federal Reserve Bank of New York, 1974, pp. 92-103.
7. CREWS, JOSEPH M. "Econometric Models: The Monetarist and Non-Monetarists Views Compared," *Monthly Review,* Federal Reserve Bank of Richmond, (February 1973), 3-12.
8. DAVIS, RICHARD and FREDERICK C. SCHADRACK. "Forecasting the Monetary Aggregates with Reduced-Form Equations," in *Monetary Aggregates and Monetary Policy.* Federal Reserve Bank of New York, 1974, pp. 60-71.
9. DE LEEUW, FRANK and EDWARD GRAMLICH. "The Federal Reserve-MIT Econometric Model," *Federal Reserve Bulletin,* (January 1968), 11-40.
10. GUTTENTAG, JACK. "The Strategy of Open Market Operations," *Quarterly Journal of Economics,* (February 1966), 1-30.
11. HYMANS, SAUL. "Comment" in *Econometric Models of Cyclical Behavior.* Ed. Bert Hickman, New York: National Bureau of Economic Research.

[41]See Poole's recent paper [26, pp. 25-30] for some further possible pitfalls within the current strategy.

12. KANE, EDWARD. "All for the Best: The Federal Reserve Board's 60th Annual Report," *American Economic Review,* (December 1974), 835-50.

13. ———. "The Re-Politicization of the Fed," *Journal of Financial and Quantitative Analysis,* (November 1974), 743-52.

14. LOMBRA, RAYMOND and LEIGH RIBBLE. "The Linkages Among Short-Term Interest Rates." Paper presented at the Eastern Economic Association Meetings. October 1974.

15. ——— and FREDERICK STRUBLE. "Monetary Aggregate Targets and the Volatility of Interest Rates." Unpublished manuscript, August 1975.

16. ——— and RAYMOND G. TORTO. "An Endogenous Central Bank and Its Implications for Supply and Demand Approaches to Money Stock Determination," *Quarterly Review of Economics & Business,* (Summer 1975), 71-79.

17. MAISEL, SHERMAN. "Controlling Monetary Aggregates," in *Controlling Monetary Aggregates.* Federal Reserve Bank of Boston, 1968, pp. 152-74.

18. ———. *Managing the Dollar.* New York: W. W. Norton, 1973.

19. ———. "The Economic and Finance Literature and Decision Making," *Journal of Finance,* (May 1974), 313-22.

20. MASON, WILL E. *Clarification of the Monetary Standard.* University Park: Penn State University Press, 1963.

21. "Numerical Specifications of Financial Variables and Their Role in Monetary Policy," *Federal Reserve Bulletin,* (May 1974), 333-37.

22. PIERCE, JAMES. "The Trade-off Between Short- and Long-term Policy Goals," in *Open Market Policies and Operating Procedures—Staff Studies.* Washington, D.C.: Board of Governors of the Federal Reserve System, 1971, pp. 97-105.

23. ———. "Quantitative Analysis for Decisions at the Federal Reserve," *Annuals of Economic and Social Measurement,* (March 1974), 11-19.

24. ——— and THOMAS THOMSON. "Some Issues in Controlling the Stock of Money," in *Controlling Monetary Aggregates II: The Implementation.* Federal Reserve Bank of Boston, 1973, pp. 115-36.

25. ——— and ———. "Short-Term Financial Models at the Federal Reserve Board," *Journal of Finance,* (May 1974), 349-57.

26. POOLE, WILLIAM. "The Making of Monetary Policy: Description and Analysis," *New England Economic Review,* Federal Reserve Bank of Boston, (March-April 1974), 21-30.

27. ———. "Optimal Choice of Monetary Policy Instruments in a Simple Stochastic Macro Model," *Quarterly Journal of Economics,* (May 1970), 197-216.

28. SIMS, CHRISTOPHER. "Optimal Stable Policies for Unstable Instruments," *Annuals of Economic and Social Measurement,* (January 1974), 257-65.

29. TSCHINKEL, SHEILA. "Open Market Operations in 1973," *Monthly Review,* Federal Reserve Bank of New York, (May 1974), 103-16.

30. WEINTRAUB, ROBERT. "Report on Federal Reserve Policy and Inflation and High Interest Rates," *Reserve Policy and Inflation and High Interest Rates.* U.S. Congress. House Committee on Banking and Currency, 93rd Congress (July-August 1974), pp. 31-76.

Implementing Open Market Policy with Monetary Aggregate Objectives

*Richard G. Davis**

The purpose of this paper is to survey recent research on some technical problems of implementing open market policy at a time when the proper intermediate policy objective is widely believed to be the behavior of the money supply and related monetary aggregates. The mere existence of a widely held preference for monetary aggregate targets in setting policy is a relatively recent development. Even five years ago, the notion that the money supply should be the primary target of monetary policy was a decidedly minority position. This was true not only of academic and business economists, but of policy makers and the interested general public as well. Ten to fifteen years ago, discussions of monetary policy were only rather rarely couched in terms of the money supply. Practical discussions of policy were framed mainly in terms of interest rates and credit market conditions.

Things are now quite different. If one asks the average bank or business economist what they think monetary policy should be over the coming months, most will eventually get around to saying that the money stock should grow at such and such a rate. The ensuing elaboration will often owe more to the familiar equation of exchange

Reprinted from the Federal Reserve Bank of New York, *Monetary Aggregates and Monetary Policy* (New York: The Bank, 1974), pp. 7-14, by permission of the publisher and the author.

*This paper was prepared for Second District economics professors attending a central banking seminar at this Bank on April 23, 1973. The views expressed are the responsibility of the author alone and do not necessarily reflect the views of the Bank or of the Federal Reserve System.

This article is reprinted, with minor revisions, from *Monthly Review* (Federal Reserve Bank of New York, July 1973), pages 170-82.

than to the Keynesian "IS-LM" analysis.[1] Similar comments could be made of discussions of monetary policy in the Congress and in the business press.

There is, to be sure, a danger of overdrawing this picture. Views on these matters are not and never have been uniform or monolithic. Yet, it is really striking the extent to which the monetarists have succeeded in shifting the focus of commonly received opinion on the role of money. One could, of course, ask whether this shift has been justified by an equally clear shift in the weight of the evidence. And one may entertain reservations on this score. However, the subject matter of the present paper is limited to the problems of implementing the monetarist program as regards using monetary policy to control the money supply and related monetary aggregates.

Money versus Interest Rates as Policy Targets: How Should the Choice Be Made?*

It is important to stress at the outset that the problem of choosing between the money supply (M), or some other related monetary aggregate as a policy target, on the one hand, and interest rates (r) and credit market conditions, on the other, is really quite distinct from any issue of "monetarism" versus "Keynesianism," "fiscalism," or what have you. One could perfectly well believe in the potency of fiscal policy and the importance of market interest rates, and, indeed, in the whole standard neo-Keynesian framework, and yet embrace the money stock rather than interest rates as the proper intermediate target for monetary policy. The question is, what is the most efficient target for policy makers to aim at in a world of uncertainties?

Recently, several papers have pointed out that even in the context of the standard neo-Keynesian IS-LM analysis, the choice between money stock targets and interest rate targets depends upon the relative importance of the various sources of instability in the economy.[2] Thus, for example, a money stock target may work quite badly in a

---

[1]In this algebraic summary of a simplified version of the Keynesian system, often used in the classroom, the so-called "LM" equation represents alternative combinations of GNP and the level of interest rates at which the supply and demand for money are equal. Similarly, the "IS" equation represents alternative combinations of GNP and interest rates at which the supply and demand for current output, including consumption goods, capital goods, and Government purchases, are equal. This solution of these two equations, the equilibrium value of the system as a whole, is that particular combination of income and interest rates for which *both* the supply and demand for money *and* the supply and demand for currently produced output are equal. Algebraically, the equilibrium values of GNP and interest rates are determined by the simultaneous solution of the two equations, LM and IS, each of which contains two unknowns, GNP and the level of interest rates (treated for simplicity as a single, "representative" interest rate). Graphically, the equilibrium values of the unknowns are shown by the intersection of the LM and IS lines (see Figure 1).

* In this article the author uses the label "operating targets" to refer to what the literature, cited in footnote 2 and the next reading, calls "instruments." The confusion arises because of the implicit definition of the policy control period. For very short periods many variables cannot be controlled and hence cannot qualify as "instruments." The label "objectives" used by Davis refers to what most of the literature calls "intermediate target variables." For further clarification, see the preceding reading, especially pages 423-425, and the following reading, especially pages 471-473.—Ed.

[2]See William Poole, "Optimal Choice of Monetary Policy Instruments in a Simple Stochastic Macro

world subject to large and unforeseen fluctuations in liquidity preference. If the money stock target is not adjusted for such shifts in the demand for money, the LM curve shifts (as in Figure 1-a) and the shifts in the demand for money are transmitted to interest rates and, ultimately, to aggregate demand. Conversely, if the major source of unforeseeable disturbances arises in the nonfinancial markets (i.e., from shifts in the IS curve), an interest rate target will work badly. Maintaining interest rates at a predetermined target (r* in Figure 1-b) in the face of such shifts in the IS curve will (as shown in Figure 1-b) allow these shifts to be transmitted fully into shifts in aggregate demand. A money stock target, in contrast, would limit the effects of shifts in the IS schedule on aggregate demand by allowing interest rates to rise or fall in an offsetting way.

In terms of this analysis, therefore, the choice of money versus interest rates depends upon the stochastic properties of the economy (that is, the sources and magnitudes of random disturbances) and not just upon its structural coefficients. Since Milton Friedman has identified belief in the stability of the demand for money as the

---

Model," *Quarterly Journal of Economics* (May 1970) and "Rules-of-Thumb for Guiding Monetary Policy" in *Open Market Policies and Operating Procedures* (Board of Governors of the Federal Reserve System, July 1971). See also John Kareken, "The Optimal Monetary Instrument Variable," *Journal of Money, Credit, and Banking* (August 1970). The argument made in these papers is as follows:

Let the demand for money function be

$$M = b_0 + b_1 Y + b_2 r + v$$

where Y and r are income and the interest rate and v is a random variable. With M given, the LM schedule becomes

$$Y = -\frac{b_0}{b_1} - \frac{b_2}{b_1} r + \frac{M}{b_1} - \frac{v}{b_1}.$$

Let the IS schedule be

$$Y = a_0 + a_1 r + u$$

where u is a random variable. The effect on income of using a money supply target (M*) is given by the reduced-form equation of the system,

$$Y = \frac{-a_1 b_0 + a_0 b_2}{a_1 b_1 + b_2} + \frac{a_1}{a_1 b_1 + b_2} M^* - \frac{a_1}{a_1 b_1 + b_2} v + \frac{b_2}{a_1 b_1 + b_2} u.$$

Now assume that the "loss" resulting from deviations of actual income from its target equals the square of these deviations. If M is used as the instrument, then the expected value of this loss is given by

$$\text{Var } Y_m = \frac{a_1^2}{(a_1 b_1 + b_2)^2} \sigma_u^2 + \frac{b_2^2}{(a_1 b_1 + b_2)^2} \sigma_u^2 - \frac{2a_1 b_2}{(a_1 b_1 + b_2)^2} \sigma_{uv}.$$

Inspection of the model makes it clear that the effect on income of an interest rate target (r*) is simply

$$Y = a_0 + a_1 r^* + u,$$

so that the variance of income is

$$\text{Var } Y_r = \sigma_u.$$

Comparison of the variances under M and r targets indicates that their relative size depends on the relative variances of the disturbance terms in IS and LM as well as on the values of the various structural parameters.

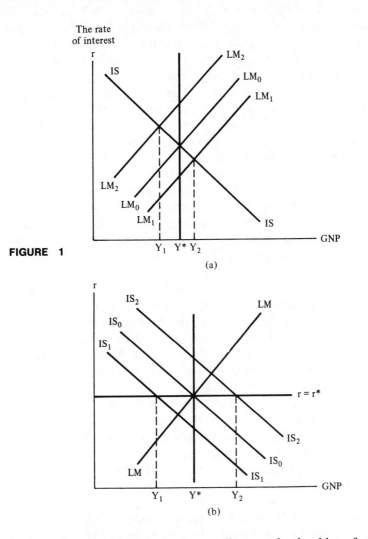

FIGURE 1

(a)

(b)

the hallmark of monetarism, monetarists, naturally enough, should prefer money. But, as noted earlier, Keynesians need not prefer interest rates. Indeed, given Keynes's emphasis on the volatile "animal spirits" of businessmen as a source of economic instability, it is by no means clear he would have thought IS more stable than LM and, therefore, r preferable to M as a policy target.

The Changing Role of Money Supply Targets in The United States

For better or worse, money supply targets have come to have a growing importance in policy making, as already indicated. Before turning to the technical problems raised by the attempt to implement such targets, however, it may be useful to sketch briefly how the role of money supply objectives in policy formulation has evolved in recent years. First, it should be noted that the very concept of a "money supply policy" is open to some ambiguities. The Federal Reserve, of course, does not control the money stock directly. The actual behavior of the money supply is the joint result of Federal Reserve actions with respect to its own instrument variables—its open market portfolio, discount rate, etc.—and the actions of the Treasury, of foreigners, of the banks, and of the nonbank public. Thus, both Federal Reserve and non-Reserve influences interact to make the money supply whatever it is at any given time. Under these circumstances, there can really only be a money supply "policy" if the Federal Reserve consciously seeks to achieve a certain path for money by using its instruments to offset the effects of actions taken by others

Prior to at least 1960, while there was much *"monetary policy,"* there can really not be said to have been much *"money supply policy."* The Federal Reserve, by and large, marched to a different drummer. The actual behavior of the money supply "fell out," for the most part an endogenous by-product of the System's actions with respect to whatever targets it *was* following and the actions of the public and the banks. To be sure, it can be argued—and has been by some—that whatever the System's *conscious* targets, the actual behavior of the money stock, or at least its broader and more significant movements, have been dominated all along by the behavior of the Federal Reserve's policy instruments rather than by the behavior of the public or the banks. But even if this were true, it would still imply only that the Federal Reserve *could* control the money stock if it chose to, not that it actually *did* so in any particular historical period.

As the 1960's wore on, the behavior of the money supply seemingly came to have increasing importance in the thinking of the policy makers, roughly paralleling developments in the economics profession and among the public generally. In the first instance, this meant that some individual members of the Federal Open Market Committee (FOMC) began to give more weight to money supply behavior in voting on specific policy alternatives. But despite this increased weight, it is probably fair to say that at no time in the 1960's did the recent and prospective behavior of the money stock become the dominant influence in the policy makers' thinking with regard to open market policy targets. Moreover, the FOMC continued to eschew any agreed-upon, formal money supply target. Actual policy alternatives continued to be stated in terms of money market conditions, as measured, for example, by free reserves and the levels of certain key money market interest rates.

Perhaps the earliest operational result, insofar as open market strategies were involved, of the increased concern over the behavior of the money supply and related monetary aggregates was the use by the FOMC, beginning in 1966, of the so-called "proviso clause." This was a clause included in the directive addressed by the FOMC at each of its monthly meetings to the Account Management at the Federal Reserve Bank of New York. It required the Account Management to shift money market targets from the levels initially directed by the Committee in an appropriately offsetting direction whenever growth in bank credit proved to be deviating significantly from the rates projected at the time of the previous meeting. The significance of this "proviso clause" as a step toward direct targeting of money supply and other aggregates was limited, however. First, it stopped short of committing the FOMC to an explicit target. Second, in practice it involved only quite gingerly and modest adjustments of "money market conditions" targets in response to unexpectedly rapid or slow growth in the bank credit proxy.

A more fundamental change took place in early 1970 when the Committee for the first time adopted explicit goals for the behavior of the narrow and broadly defined money supply (M_1 and M_2) and the bank credit proxy. At most of its meetings since early 1970 the Committee has continued to adopt explicit goals, covering varying time horizons, for the growth rates of one or more of these aggregates. At the same time, the Committee has experimented with various operational tactics to achieve these goals. However, this most emphatically does *not* mean that actual money supply behavior over the period since early 1970 can be interpreted as conforming to the FOMC's objectives in the short run. The bulk of the remainder of this paper is devoted to reasons why the money supply cannot, and perhaps even *should not,* be made to conform exactly to predetermined target values over short periods. Beyond this, however, goals for the growth rates of the monetary aggregates have seldom been the sole immediate objective of the FOMC even in the period since 1970. The Committee has generally retained concern for avoiding unstable conditions in the money markets and has also retained an interest in the behavior of short-term interest rates and money and capital market conditions generally.

The Choice of a Target among the Monetary Aggregates

Turning directly to some of the technical problems of implementing monetary policy where the intermediate objectives of policy are framed in terms of the monetary aggregates, several fairly basic questions come to mind immediately. The first might well be which monetary aggregate do you use: M_1, M_2, some measure of bank credit, total reserves, the monetary base (i.e., what is sometimes called "high-powered money," or total reserves plus currency in the hands of the nonbank public)? Without defending the point in detail, I would argue that, while measures of reserves and the monetary base may be useful in developing strategies to achieve goals for one of the other aggregates, these measures are not themselves the best choices for framing monetary policy goals. The basic point is that we are interested in influencing the economy at large, not the banking sector *per se.* Setting targets in terms of reserves would allow random developments within the banking sector—which might be summarized by movements in the reserve-deposit multiplier—to be transmitted to the overall economy, interfering with the achievement of the more basic goals for the gross national product (GNP) and similar variables.[3]

With regard to the remaining choices, between, say, M_1, M_2, and some measure of total bank credit, I would argue that this is essentially a second-order issue. It is, for example, very difficult to differentiate between these three aggregates in terms of the closeness of their relationship to GNP in the postwar period.[4] Real questions about which aggregate to use are, however, likely to develop during periods when Regulation Q ceilings are changed or when open market rates are rising above or falling below existing ceilings. Such "artificial" distortions in rate spreads induce marked decelerations or accelerations of time deposit growth and therefore distort the "normal" growth rate relationships among M_1, M_2, and bank credit.[5] For example, a rise in market rates above Regulation Q ceilings will cause the public to shift out of time deposits and into open market securities. The resulting slowdown in M_2 undoubtedly overstates the restrictiveness of monetary policy in such periods. The moral would seem to be that policy makers can, with reasonable safety, set goals either in terms of M_1, M_2, or bank credit during normal times (provided allowance is made for differences in trend growth rates), but careful interpretation of differential growth rates is imperative during periods when Regulation Q (or some other special disturbances that do arise from time to time) is a factor.[6]

---

[3]In "Improving Monetary Control" (*Brookings Papers on Economic Activity*, 2-1972), William Poole extends his analysis cited earlier to examine the situation where the central bank's options are not M and r, but the monetary base (B) and r. The additional variance introduced by the banking sector via the supply equation for money may make B targets inferior to r targets even where M targets would be superior to r targets. The argument against B targets is simply that the authorities ought to permit themselves maximum flexibility in adjusting as needed to variations in the relationship between B and M. As Poole points out, arguments for a steady rate of growth in M simply cannot be extended to a steady rate of growth in B.

[4]Michael Hamburger presents some results for changes in GNP regressed on current and lagged changes in various monetary aggregates in "Indicators of Monetary Policy: The Arguments and the Evidence," *American Economic Review* (May 1970). For the 1953-1968 period, the R^2's are 0.39 for M_1 and bank credit and 0.28 for M_2. However in the 1961-1968 subperiod, M_2 does much better than M_1 (0.43 versus 0.31) and only a little less well than bank credit (0.45). A paper by Frederick C. Schadrack, "An Empirical Approach to the Definition of Money" (June 1971), summarizes some previously published work of George Kaufman and Milton Friedman and Anna Schwartz and presents some new results using Almonized distributed lag techniques. For the period 1953-1968 there is very little to choose between M_1 and M_2, both including and excluding large CDs (all adjusted R^2's are around 0.55), though bank credit does a bit better at 0.61. Schadrack, however, expresses some preference for M_2 (excluding large CDs) on the grounds that its coefficients appear more stable over time.

[5]The view that Regulation Q provides the main reason for worrying about whether to use M_1 or M_2 was expressed as long ago as 1959 by Milton Friedman in *A Program for Monetary Stability*, page 91.

[6]Milton Friedman has recently expressed a preference for M_2 (excluding large CDs) over M_1 on the grounds that the income velocity of M_2 has shown essentially no trend since the early 1960's while the income velocity of M_1 has continued to show an uptrend of somewhat uncertain dimensions (see "How Much Monetary Growth" in the *Morgan Guaranty Survey*, February 1973). Friedman's argument is couched in terms of the substantially larger range of the *level* of the M_1 income velocity relative to the range of the *level* of the M_2 income velocity in the 1962-1972 period. The relevant issue, however, is the variance of the rates of growth of these two velocity measures—at least as far as setting intermediate-run or countercyclical monetary growth targets is concerned. To put it differently, what one cares about for these purposes is the closeness of fit of equations relating growth in nominal income to growth in money, not the size of the constant term in such equations.

How Large Are the Economic Costs of Failing to Hit Monetary Targets in the Short Run?

A second basic question with regard to implementing monetary aggregate targets for monetary policy is how long or short should the time horizon be for achieving these targets: i.e., should you try to set and meet targets for monetary growth over a month, a quarter, six months, a year? The answer to this question seems to depend essentially on two factors: (1) the decreasing feasibility of controlling the aggregates over successively shorter periods and (2) the increasing costs in terms of economic stability of failing to hit them over successively longer periods. This second aspect is examined first.

Just how much difference does it make to aggregate demand objectives if the M_1 target is missed by 2 percentage points over one month, over three months, etc.? The key to this question lies in the lag structure relating money growth to the behavior of the economy at large. If, for example, the influence of M on GNP were essentially instantaneous, deviations from monetary targets lasting even for very short periods could have a marked impact. On the other hand, if the influence of money operates with a long distributed lag, the impact of deviations from M_1 targets may be greatly attenuated. Suppose, for example, the Federal Reserve wants to hit a 6 percent money growth rate target. Suppose, instead, it actually hits 10 percent for two quarters in a row (as illustrated in Figure 2) and then drops down to 2 percent for the next two quarters. If the influence of money operates with a distributed lag—i.e., the effective impact of money at any point reflects a weighted average of past money supply growth rates—the overshoot effect of the two 10 percent quarters will never register its full impact on GNP. Long before this can happen, the *over*shoot effects will begin to be offset by the *under*shoot effects of the two 2 percent quarters. If lags are sufficiently long, the course of events in the economy may turn out to differ little from what would have happened had the 6 percent money target been successfully

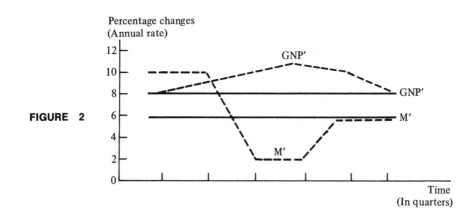

FIGURE 2

Percentage changes (Annual rate) — Time (In quarters) — GNP′ — GNP′ — M′ — M′

reached in each and every quarter instead of just on average over the whole four-quarter period.

One way to arrive at quantitative estimates of the costs of permitting M to deviate from target values over periods of varying lengths is to use econometric model simulations. Such simulations can be used to compare the results of steady monetary growth at an x percent rate with uneven monetary growth that averages out to the same rate over the longer run. One such simulation has been performed on a version of the well-known Federal Reserve Bank of St. Louis econometric equation.[7] In this equation, nominal GNP is determined mainly by the behavior of the money supply in the current and three prior quarters. The control simulation assumes a steady 6 percent rate of growth in M_1 in each quarter. Other simulations assume M_1 growth rates of 10 percent for one, two, and three quarters, respectively, followed by growth rates of 2 percent for an offsetting number of quarters, with M_1 returning to a 6 percent growth rate thereafter.

The results of these simulations (see Table 1) suggest that a one-quarter deviation of M_1 growth from target amounting to 4 percentage points or less would have essentially negligible effects on GNP. Deviations from target lasting for *two* quarters would have only moderate effects. In this case, the resulting deviations of GNP from the path implied by steady 6 percent M_1 growth path would reach a maximum of only about 1 percent of the level of GNP. Deviations of M_1 from its target growth rate amounting to 4 percentage points and lasting for as long as three quarters do have more serious effects, however.

Table 1.   Simulations of Gross National Product

Period	Control Simulation (Steady 6% M_1 Growth)		Simulation II		Simulation III		Simulation IV	
	%Δ M	Level of GNP (billions of dollars)	%Δ M	GNP Minus Control Simulation (billions of dollars)	%Δ M	GNP Minus Control Simulation (billions of dollars)	%Δ M	GNP Minus Control Simulation (billions of dollars)
1972: I	6	1,092.9	10	2.4	10	2.4	10	2.4
II	6	1,108.5	2	3.3	10	8.3	10	8.3
III	6	1,125.8	6	2.6	2	12.0	10	17.1
IV	6	1,145.6	6	1.1	2	10.3	2	22.6
1973: I	6	1,166.3	6	− 0.3	6	5.4	2	21.1
II	6	1,187.3	6	− 0.4	6	0.9	2	13.5
III	6	1,208.4	6	− 0.4	6	− 0.8	6	5.3
IV	6	1,229.7	6	− 0.4	6	− 0.8	6	0.5

Note: Simulations were performed with the equation described in "A Monetarist Model for Economic Stabilization" by L. Andersen and K. Carlson (Federal Reserve Bank of St. Louis *Review,* April 1970). The simulations are reported in James Pierce and Thomas Thomson, "Some Issues in Controlling the Stock of Money."

[7]See James Pierce and Thomas Thomson, "Some Issues in Controlling the Stock of Money," in *Controlling Monetary Aggregates II: The Implementation* (Federal Reserve Bank of Boston, 1972), pages 115–36.

Of course, these results are only as valid as the lag structures embodied in the underlying model. Probably most large-scale structural models incorporate somewhat longer lags in the money-GNP relationship than do St. Louis-type "reduced-form" equations. As a result, simulations with these models would no doubt suggest that deviations from target growth rates could occur over somewhat longer periods without serious consequences for aggregate demand objectives. For what they are worth, however, the available simulation results suggest that the FOMC need not be too concerned about even fairly sizable deviations from M_1 target growth rates lasting up to around six months—providing there is some subsequent undershooting. Putting it somewhat differently, the policy makers should perhaps not be too disturbed by sizable intrayearly fluctuations in M_1 growth, provided the average growth rate for the year as a whole comes out about on target.[8]

Achieving Monetary Objectives: The Need for Short-Run Operating Targets*

Having tried to establish some notion of the costs of failing to hit money supply targets over varying lengths of time, we address the next question, What operational procedures are available to achieve these M targets and how well can such procedures be expected to work? One begins from the obvious fact, noted earlier, that the Federal Reserve has direct control only over certain instrument variables, most notably the size of its open market portfolio of Government securities. To hit targets for any monetary variable—be it the money supply, the monetary base, or even member bank nonborrowed reserves—forecasts of noncontrolled factors influencing these variables must first be made. Next, the Federal Reserve's instrument variables must be adjusted in such a way as to take account of the movements of these noncontrolled factors. The harder the movements of these noncontrolled factors are to predict, or the more complex are their interaction with movements in the Federal Reserve's own instrument variables, the more difficult will it be to hit any given target.

---

[8]These conclusions are also supported by the results presented in "Income Stabilization and Short-run Variability in Money" by E. Gerald Corrigan, *Monthly Review* (Federal Reserve Bank of New York, April 1973), pages 87-98. In this paper, Corrigan first uses a "money-only" reduced-form equation to compare what GNP behavior would have been in 1970-1971 if M_1 had grown at a steady value equal to its average growth over the entire period relative to (a) the actual behavior of GNP over the period and (b) what the money-only equation would have projected for GNP given the actual behavior of M_1 over the period. Corrigan concludes that events would not have been very different with steady growth. In all but two quarters, GNP growth in the steady M_1 case would have differed by only 0.7 percent (annual rate) or less relative to the GNP growth indicated by the equation given the actual pattern of M_1 growth rates. The 1963-1965 period exhibits similar results. Simulations of the Board-MIT econometric model for 1970-1971 also indicate little difference between the results of smooth M_1 growth and the quite uneven quarterly pattern of M_1 growth rates that actually occurred—the largest difference for any quarter was a 0.6 percent annual rate of growth in GNP. Corrigan also runs simulations similar to the Pierce-Thomson simulations cited in Table 1 and the text, though using a money-only reduced-form equation. The results are essentially the same as the Pierce-Thomson results.

* See editors' note on page 445.

This is a complex matter, but the main points can be summarized as follows: to implement a money supply objective, defined, say, in terms of the desired M_1 growth rate over a month or period of months, an operationally meaningful strategy requires that week-to-week open market operations be laid out in terms of target values for other variables, variables easier to hit than the money supply itself. The targeted levels of these other variables must then be adjusted so that their achievement maximizes the likelihood of achieving the money supply target itself. In other words, one has to project, for example, the week-by-week levels of nonborrowed reserves that appear to be consistent with the desired money supply growth rate. Once this is done, the day-to-day decisions as to whether to buy or sell in the open market can be made in terms of the nonborrowed reserve objectives.[9]

As a practical matter, what variables are open to the Federal Reserve as feasible day-to-day and week-to-week operating targets? In practice, the number of available options is really rather small. First, one would have to rule out all total reserve and related measures, such as the total monetary base and the recently developed concept of RPD (total reserves behind private nonbank deposits). In practice, the Federal Reserve does not have the power to fix the levels of any of these measures within a given week. The problem is that changes in borrowings at the discount window, a magnitude over which the System exerts only the most general influence, will offset the effects on total reserves of System actions taken to change nonborrowed reserves.[10] However, by the same token, the various measures of nonborrowed reserves, including the nonborrowed monetary base and nonborrowed RPD, *are* feasible weekly operating targets. This is not to say the weekly targets for these nonborrowed reserve measures are easy to hit with accuracy. Quite the contrary. The non-Federal

---

[9]The problem of laying out short-term tactics for achieving the goals set in a money supply strategy is discussed in Richard G. Davis, "Short-Run Targets for Open Market Operations," in *Open Market Policies and Operating Procedures—Staff Studies* (Board of Governors of the Federal Reserve System, July 1971).

[10]This problem is examined in more detail in Davis (as cited above). If the Federal Reserve supplies nonborrowed reserves in excess of required reserves, which are fixed for a given reserve period under lagged reserve accounting, the result is likely to be mostly a paydown of outstanding borrowings and little if any buildup of excess reserves—at least up to the point where borrowings are reduced to frictional minima. On the other hand, reductions in the amount of nonborrowed reserves supplied are likely to lead to an offsetting increase in borrowings rather than a reduction in excess reserves. The point is simply that, in a period where excess reserves are very low and are probably very insensitive to money market rates in the short run, total reserves are fixed by required reserves (determined on the basis of deposit levels two weeks earlier) plus the frictional minimum level of excess reserves. (A regression of weekly levels of excess reserves on the weekly average Federal funds rate for 1970 and 1971 had a—nonsignificant—R^2 of only 0.005; the coefficient indicated that a full 1 percentage point increase in the Federal funds rate would reduce excess reserves by only $16 million.) Fluctuations in nonborrowed reserves lead to offsetting movements in the Federal funds rate and in borrowed reserves but not, to any significant extent, to fluctuations in total reserves. Precisely the same argument applies to the total reserve base and total RPD. Note that the situation under lagged reserve accounting, with the resulting fixity of required reserves in any given week, may not be much different from the situation where reserve requirements are determined by deposit levels in the same week if bank asset supplies are quite insensitive to money market interest rates over periods as short as one week.

Reserve-controlled factors affecting reserves, most notably float, are very difficult to predict accurately on a weekly basis.[11]

A different sort of weekly operational target that could be used to achieve the more basic money supply objectives is represented by money market interest rates, perhaps most notably the Federal funds rate (the rate on interbank overnight lending). On the one hand, this would be an operationally feasible target since the Trading Desk could feed funds into and out of the market as the actual market rate fell below or rose above the target rate. Thus, on a weekly average basis, say, it is possible to operate so that the average Federal funds rate will, most of the time, approximate a target rate. At the same time, the required weekly interest rate objective can be related to the more fundamental money supply target through forecasts of the demand for money at various interest rates. This problem is discussed further below.

In summary, to implement a money supply objective, the Federal Reserve must lay out a week-to-week program for operationally feasible short-run targets. It must set values for these targets that are projected to be consistent with the underlying money supply objective. If the projections prove wrong, the weekly target values will have to be adjusted. In practice, the Federal Reserve can use either a nonborrowed reserves measure or an interest rate measure, perhaps most especially the Federal funds rate, as its weekly operational target.

Relationship of Reserve and Interest Rate Operating Targets to Money Supply Objectives: A Simple Model of the Supply and Demand for Money*

Given the feasibility of either nonborrowed reserves or some measure of short-term interest rates as a week-to-week operating target, what is entailed in using these targets for achieving somewhat longer-run objectives for the money supply? To examine this, it is useful to set up an illustrative skeleton model of the supply and demand for money—or, to simplify matters somewhat, for deposits (D) alone. The demand equation for deposits in this model is the standard liquidity preference schedule. It includes a short-term interest rate (r) and some measure of transactions demand (Y). This latter variable can be treated as exogenous, given the short period purposes of the model. The supply of deposits is assumed to depend upon the level of nonborrowed reserves (Ru) and on the short-term interest rate (r). This latter dependency reflects the dependency of the banks' demand for borrowed reserves on short-term interest rates, the (smaller) dependency of their demand for excess reserves on

---

[11]In 1971, the average error in projecting market factors affecting nonborrowed reserves (float, currency in circulation, and the effects of Treasury and international transactions) as of the beginning of statement weeks was $275 million. See "Open Market Operations and the Monetary and Credit Aggregates—1971," *Monthly Review* (Federal Reserve Bank of New York, April 1972), pages 79-94.

* See editors' note on page 445.

rates, and the dependency on interest rates of the time-demand deposit mix. The latter of course has attendant effects on the banks' demand for reserves as a result of the difference in reserve requirement ratios for the two types of deposits. Thus, the model (in linear form) consists of

$$D = b_1 Y + b_2 r + u \qquad \text{(Demand)} \qquad (1)$$

$$D = c_1 Ru + c_2 r + e \qquad \text{(Supply)}, \qquad (2)$$

where u and e are random terms.

Now the choice of an interest rate operating target to achieve the broader money supply objectives is tantamount to treating the interest rate as an exogenous variable. In such a situation, nonborrowed reserves become *endogenous*, that is, such reserves are allowed to come out at whatever level proves necessary to achieve the interest rate target. The resulting reduced-form equation of the model is the same as the demand equation, i.e.,

$$D = b_1 Y + b_2 r^* + u, \qquad (3)$$

where r^* is the weekly interest rate target used by the Federal Reserve.

On the other hand, if the FOMC decides to work with a nonborrowed reserves operating target, the short-term interest rate becomes endogenous. The relevant reduced form for the reserve-target case is derived from the solution of the demand and supply equations as follows:

$$D = \frac{b_1 c_2}{c_2 - b_2} Y - \frac{b_2 c_1}{c_2 - b_2} R_u^* + \frac{c_2}{c_2 - b_2} u - \frac{b_2}{c_2 - b_2} e. \qquad (4)$$

A great deal of work has been done within the Federal Reserve System on estimating structural models of the type represented by equations (1) and (2)—though of course any realistic model requires far more than two structural equations—and reduced-form equations of the type represented by equations (3) and (4). While the estimation of these equations has raised the usual quota of econometric conundrums, some useful insights have been obtained from this work. Three areas in particular should be mentioned: (1) the different sorts of risk one is exposed to in using a nonborrowed reserves operating target as against an interest rate target, (2) the approximate limits of our ability to forecast and achieve money supply objectives with, respectively, these two types of operating targets, and (3) the existence of lags and their implication for policy making.

Sources of Error in Hitting Money Supply Objectives

As equation (3) indicates, the use of a short-term interest rate target entails making a short-term forecast of the demand for deposits. The interest rate target can then be set at the level that is expected to give the desired deposit behavior. (Of course, a formal econometric equation need not be used, but a judgmental forecast would require making much the same calculations implicitly.) There are two possible sources of error in picking the interest rate target needed to achieve the money supply goals: (1) random errors (or shifts in the demand equation) and (2) errors in forecasting Y—which is taken as exogenous for the short-term purposes at hand. Note that both types of error tend to be accommodated when using an interest rate target. That is, if the demand for money is greater than expected, for example, holding to the interest rate target (r* in Figure 3-a) will mean automatically supplying enough reserves to accommodate the demand.

This tendency for interest rate targets—and money market conditions targets generally—automatically to accommodate changes in the demand for money has been the chief complaint of monetarists about this type of target over the years. However, the complaint should not be leveled against interest rate operating targets *per se*. Rather, the complaint should have been, as applied to the procedures in use prior to 1970, (1) that the FOMC did not formulate explicit monetary growth rate objectives and (2) that it would not have been willing to move money market targets often enough, quickly enough, and decisively enough to achieve monetary growth objectives even if it had formulated them. Given the willingness to move interest rate targets as needed to achieve money supply objectives, such targets are a perfectly feasible way of operating open market policy to achieve money supply objectives.

As equation (4) indicates, the use of a nonborrowed reserves operating target can also be expected to lead to errors in controlling the money stock. The new element here is errors stemming from the supply side—errors which might be summarized in terms of unforeseen movements in the ratio of nonborrowed reserves to private deposits, i.e., unforeseen movements in the "deposit multiplier". Such movements can result, in turn, from unforeseen shifts in the banks' demand for excess and borrowed reserves and from unforeseen movements in the average required reserve ratio. This ratio is, of course, affected by shifts among the various categories of deposits and by movements of deposits between banks with different reserve requirement ratios. Another important potential source of error on the supply side can originate from unforeseen movements into and out of Treasury deposits at the commercial banks. These deposits absorb required reserves but are not themselves included in the money supply as usually calculated.

Relative to an interest rate target, nonborrowed reserves have some advantages and some disadvantages as an operating target for achieving money supply goals. Nonborrowed reserves are superior to interest rates in the face of a change in the demand for money. Such a change tends to get fully accommodated under an interest rate target, as already noted.[12] Under a nonborrowed reserves target, however, an increase in the demand for money will be accommodated only to the extent that the

---

[12]It should also be noted, however, that short-term, random, and reversible shifts in the demand for money *should* be accommodated since such accommodation prevents them from having any impact on real activity.

resulting upward pressure on money market rates engenders some elasticity of supply—to the extent, for example, that the banks themselves are induced by rising interest rates to accommodate the increase in demand by increasing borrowings from the Federal Reserve Banks or by drawing down excess reserves. Such offsets may not be too large, however, and will, in any case, not be complete. Thus, the money supply is likely to stay closer to target in the face of a demand shift if the Federal Reserve uses a nonborrowed reserves operating target than with an interest rate target.

On the other hand, a nonborrowed reserves target does not perform as well as an interest rate target in the face of an unforeseen shift in the average required reserve ratio—whatever its cause—or a shift in the banks' demand for excess and borrowed reserves. Such shifts will lead to a change in the actual money supply as long as the supply of nonborrowed reserves is held on target (see Figure 3-b). With an interest

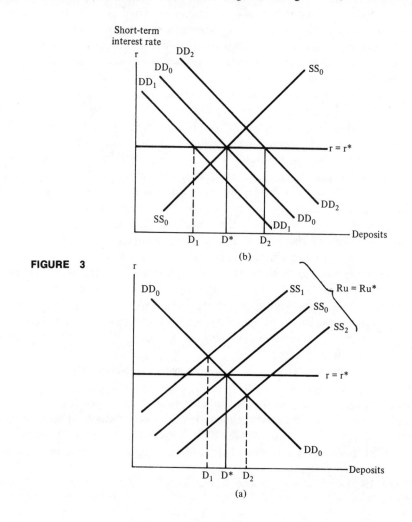

FIGURE 3

rate operating target, in contrast, the volume of nonborrowed reserves would automatically be adjusted to offset the impact on money of these changes in supply conditions. As a result, their distorting effects on the money supply would be neutralized.

Estimating Errors in Achieving Money Supply Objectives in the Short Run

In principle, then, either nonborrowed reserves or interest rates can be used as operating handles to achieve money supply goals; each has its own advantages and disadvantages.[13] Which can be expected to work better in practice, and how well each will work, are empirical questions. A fair amount of statistical work has been done in the Federal Reserve System on the probable size of errors in using these operating targets. Table 2 is fairly representative of the general thrust of the results—and it also gives some idea of the probable order of magnitude or errors in hitting money supply targets in the short run.

Three sets of forecasts are presented in Table 2.[14] The first two are based on reduced-form equations of the types suggested by equations (3) and (4) presented earlier. The first set uses changes in the Federal funds rate as the open market operating target: thus it is essentially a complex variant of equation (3) cited earlier.

[13]As a purely formal matter, the question of whether nonborrowed reserves or interest rates is the better instrument for controlling money can be treated with precisely the same analysis used by Poole to examine whether the money supply or the interest rate is the better handle to control GNP (see footnote 2). The question turns on the relative instability of demand (analogous to the IS curve in Poole's analysis) or supply (analogous to LM). The variance of deposits, using an interest rate target, depends on the variance in Y from forecast values and the variance of the error term u in equation (3) and on their covariances as well as on the income elasticity of demand. The variance of deposits, using a nonborrowed reserves target, depends on the variance of Y, the variances of the error terms in both supply and demand equations, their covariances, and the various income and interest rate elasticities in the supply and demand equations (see Pierce and Thomson, "Some Issues in Controlling the Money Stock"). Just as Poole's analysis has to be modified to allow for the possibility that M cannot be precisely controlled, however, the present analysis should really be modified for the possibility that nonborrowed reserves cannot be precisely controlled. In this case, nonborrowed reserves should be replaced in the supply equation with the sum of changes of Federal Reserve credit, the forecast value of operating factors affecting reserves, and a new random error term reflecting errors in forecasting operating factors. Some specialists object strongly to the proposition that nonborrowed reserves could be hit with any high degree of accuracy. They argue that under a pure nonborrowed reserves target, where the Federal funds rate could be expected to show much wider week-to-week movements than at present, the behavior of the Federal funds rate would no longer serve to assist the Open Market Account Management in warning when operating factors affecting reserves are going seriously off track. They argue that the margin of error in hitting the funds rate on average, week to week, would be much smaller. In that case, evidence purporting to compare nonborrowed reserves and the funds rate as competing targets for controlling money is seriously biased in assuming the two operating targets are themselves equally achievable

[14]These results represent an updating of material presented in a paper published in the November 1973 issue of the *Journal of Money, Credit, and Banking,* by Fred J. Levin, "Examination of the Money Stock Control Approach of Burger, Kalish, and Babb." See also A. E. Burger, L. Kalish III, and C. T. Babb, "Money Stock Control and Its Implications for Monetary Policy," *Review* (Federal Reserve Bank of St. Louis, October 1971).

Table 2. Errors in Forecasting M_1 Growth Rates, 1970–1972
(Seasonally adjusted annual rates; in percent)

Measure	Using Federal Funds Rate*	Using Nonborrowed Monetary Base†	FRB St. Louis Method‡
Mean absolute error of *ex post* monthly forecasts	2.91	3.47	6.33
Root mean square error of *ex post* monthly forecasts	3.60	4.22	8.61
Mean absolute error of *ex ante* monthly forecasts	3.36	3.61	§
Root mean square error of *ex ante* monthly forecasts	3.93	4.53	§
Mean absolute error of *ex ante* quarterly forecasts	2.10	2.13	§
Root mean square error of *ex ante* quarterly forecasts	2.34	3.08	§
Mean absolute error of *ex ante* six-month forecasts	1.19	2.10	§
Root mean square error of six-month *ex ante* forecasts	1.39	2.52	§

*Based on $\Delta M_1 = \sum_{i=0}^{7} b_i \Delta$ Federal funds rate $_{t-i} + \sum_{i=0}^{7} c_i \Delta$ business sales $_{t-i} + d \Delta$ Treasury deposits + constant. Estimated on 1965–69 data.

† Based on $\Delta M_i = \sum_{i=0}^{7} b_i \Delta$ nonborrowed monetary base $_{t-i} + \sum_{i=0}^{7} c_i \Delta$ business sales $_{t-i} + d \Delta$ Treasury deposits + constant. Estimated on 1965–69 data.

‡ See A. Burger, L. Kalish, and C. Babb, "Money Stock Control and Its Implications for Monetary Policy," *Review* (Federal Reserve Bank of St. Louis, October 1971).

§ Not available.

The second set of projections uses the nonborrowed monetary base as the operating target—i.e., it is a variant of equation (4). The third set is a method developed at the Federal Reserve Bank of St. Louis. It simply estimates the money-reserve base multiplier from a regression using a three-month moving average of past values of the multiplier, and adjustment for changes in legal reserve requirement ratios, seasonal dummies, and a measure of autocorrelation. The two reduced-form equations were estimated from 1965-1969 data, while the St. Louis method calls for updating the regression equation in each month. The forecasts were made for monthly changes in money supply (expressed as an annual rate of growth) over the 1970-1972 period. The forecasts labeled *ex ante* in the table are *ex ante* forecasts in the sense that all inputs were entered as of the estimates or projections that would have been available at the time.

Some interesting results emerge from Table 2. First, the forecasts using the nonborrowed monetary base and the Federal funds rate, respectively, do roughly equally well. Some other results (not presented in the table) which adjust nonborrowed reserves for required reserves against Treasury and interbank deposits (in other words, nonborrowed RPD) also seem to suggest a roughly comparable performance. This particular evidence, at least, does not provide a decisive case for or against any one of the potentially available operating targets.

A second point is that the two reduced-form equations forecast markedly better for this period than the St. Louis approach, which is essentially a purely autoregressive estimate of the money multiplier.

Finally, and most important, all three methods of projection do rather poorly in forecasting monetary growth rates for individual months. The same conclusion has to be drawn about attempts to forecast short-term growth rates judgmentally. Despite considerable investment of time and talent, all presently available techniques for making short-term projections of the monetary growth rate that would be associated with any particular setting of an operating target are subject to large errors on average and very large errors in many particular instances.

It is possible to be more optimistic when somewhat longer time horizons are considered, however. *Ex ante* forecasts for one quarter ahead have an average absolute error of 2.13 percent for the nonborrowed base equation and 2.10 percent for the Federal funds equation. Forecasts for six months ahead show corresponding average absolute errors of 2.10 percent and 1.19 percent, respectively. This means that for six-month periods, we seem to be able to get at least "ball park" estimates of the consequences for monetary growth rates of particular settings of open market operating targets. Even for these periods, however, the errors are clearly not negligible.

The Lags Between Federal Reserve Actions and Money Supply Response

Finally, with regard to the lags: All the econometric evidence available to us suggests that there is a lag between a change in operating targets and the full impact of that change on the money supply. Indeed both the Board staff's monthly money market model—a very complex version of structural equations (1) and (2)— and the reduced-form equations developed at this Bank—essentially complex versions of (3) and (4)—suggest that the effects may take on the order of six to eight months to work themselves out fully.[15] This means, for example, that a maintained step-up in the level of nonborrowed reserves will not have its full effect on the level of the money supply for several months. Similarly, a once-and-for-all increase in a Federal funds rate target will not have its full effect on the level of the money supply for several months.

Now it is of course true that the estimation of lag structures is a very uncertain business. The evidence that these lags are as long as six to eight months cannot be

[15]See "A Monthly Econometric Model of the Financial Sector" by Thomas Thomson and James Pierce, unpublished; and "Forecasting the Monetary Aggregates with Reduced-Form Equations" by Richard G. Davis and Frederick C. Schadrack.

considered at all firm. One possibility is that the use of monthly time units instead of shorter units may bias estimates of the lag upward; this sort of bias does seem to have turned up in some other areas of econometric work. However, the Board staff has also estimated a weekly model, and its lags, while not as long as those in the monthly model, are still substantial.[16] The point is that even if the true lags were, say, only one half the six- to eight-month range indicated by most of the econometric work, they would still have significant implications for policy.

The existence of these lags creates a potential control problem for the Federal Reserve in trying to hold monetary growth rates to any targeted rate. As indicated, these lags delay the ultimate impact on the money supply of a change in the operating target, be it nonborrowed reserves or short-term interest rates. By the same token, however, they also imply that an adjustment in the operating target large enough to produce a desired correction in the monetary growth rate *immediately* will ultimately overshoot this desired correction and will then have to be reversed (see Figure 4). For example, if M_1 is currently growing at 2 percent (January through March in Figure 4) and the Open Market Committee objective is 6 percent, the desired correction could be achieved by lowering a Federal funds rate target (labeled R_{ff} in the figure) or raising a nonborrowed reserves target (labeled Ru' in the figure). However, a reduction large enough to bring M_1 back to 6 percent within a month (April), would eventually (by June) push the monetary growth rate up to, say, 8 percent. At that point, a near-term correction back to 6 percent (in July) might require a drastic *increase* in the Federal funds rate target, one that might ultimately (in August and

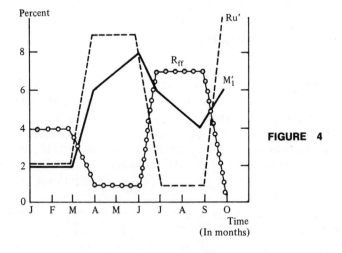

FIGURE 4

[16]Helen T. Farr, Steven M. Roberts, and Thomas D. Thomson, "A Weekly Money Market Model—A Progress Report" (June 1972, unpublished). The lags in the major structural equations of this model run from five to thirty-four weeks. Simulations performed by the authors indicate that an increase in nonborrowed reserves achieves its maximum effect on M_1 after about three months, while a decrease in the Federal funds rate produces its maximum impact after about six months.

September) push M_1 growth once more below the 6 percent target, and so on. Indeed, if the lag structure is sufficiently unfavorable, it would not be too difficult to imagine situations where explosive oscillations in the operational target would be required to hold the M_1 target, month by month, to a steady target growth rate.[17]

There appears to be a fairly clear moral to be derived from these implications of the existence of lags: policy makers should avoid taking too short a view in deciding where to set week-to-week operating targets. Even in a world where the money supply implications of a given target setting were known with certainty, operational targets should be set so as to achieve money supply goals *on average* over a period of time. Attempts to rejigger operating targets so as to hit the long-run money supply objectives in each and every month—assuming this to be possible at all—are likely to involve excessive volatility in the operating target. This volatility will mean excessive instability in money market rates. This will result directly, if the Federal funds rate is used as the operating target, and indirectly if some measure of nonborrowed reserves is used.

Similarly, when trying to speed up or slow down the monetary growth rate, the policy makers should keep in mind the fact that a movement in operating targets sharp enough to achieve this change rapidly will, because of lags, eventually overshoot. This overshooting will, in turn, require an eventual further adjustment of the instrumental target in the opposite direction. For this reason, it may well be desirable to take a somewhat gradualist approach to slowing down or speeding up monetary growth rates, aiming to accomplish the change over a period of months rather than immediately. Of course, in any particular situation, the right decision depends on for how long and by how much monetary growth has been deviating from what the

---

[17]In principle, at least, this proposition can be tested. First, reduced-form equations of the sort presented in Table 2, having been estimated statistically, can be solved for the current value of the instrument variable. Thus, for example, equation (1) in that table, where the Federal funds rate is the instrument variable, can be rewritten so that the current change in the Federal funds rate is the dependent variable and is a function of the current change in deposits, lagged changes in the Federal funds rate, and current and lagged changes in the exogenous variables. If we assume the current change in deposits equal to some given target value in each and every month, we then have a seventh-order difference equation in the Federal funds rate plus some exogenous variables. This equation tells us the change in the instrument variable—the Federal funds rate in this case—that will be required to hold M on target given the current values of the exogenous variables and the past history of these variables and the funds rate. Some preliminary analysis of this equation suggests that, under a fairly wide range of assumptions about the lag coefficients on the Federal funds rate in the original reduced-form equation, the time path of monthly changes in the funds rate needed to maintain changes in M at the targeted rate in each and every month would be oscillatory and explosive. Moreover, if one uses some plausible values for the behavior of the exogenous variables and initial conditions as of early 1972, simulations of the difference equation for constant monthly changes in the money supply did generate explosive oscillations in the Federal funds rate. Indeed, the simulation after just a few months involved a negative funds rate to hold changes in deposits on target, clearly an impossibility. While one would hardly want to jump to the conclusion that these simulations accurately reflect the way the world is actually constructed, their results are not really so implausible. There may be literally *no* way of getting M to grow by more than x percent next month. At some point, injections of nonborrowed reserves may drive the funds rate and borrowed reserves to zero, with further injections merely having the effect of piling up excess reserves. Of course, as these reserves begin to be utilized, with a distributed lag, money supply growth could subsequently become explosive, forcing the authorities to jump the funds rate up by amounts that would rock the structure of the money market—and so on.

policy makers consider desirable and how serious the economic consequences of these deviations seem likely to be if not corrected promptly.

In thinking about these matters, it quickly becomes apparent that the use of a money supply strategy for monetary policy confronts the policy makers with a very interesting and complex problem in control theory—one that is only just now beginning to be appreciated and explored. The policy maker is confronted with two sets of distributed lags. One set of lags, the one just discussed, relates operationally feasible open market target variables, such as nonborrowed reserves and the Federal funds rate, to the money supply. The other set, mentioned earlier, relates the money supply to the variables that ultimately matter. *Shortening* the attempted time horizon of monetary control increases the technical problems of monetary management and the likelihood of an unacceptable degree of money market instability. *Lengthening* the period of control increases the probable deviations of aggregate demand and related variables from desired behavior.

No doubt there is an optimum control period here somewhere. It was mentioned earlier that some calculations seem to suggest that, if monetary growth rate targets are hit on average over a year, deviations of GNP from the path it would follow with absolutely steady monetary growth might well remain within acceptable limits. However, if monetary growth rates have drifted off target over the first half of the year, for example, the authorities then have only six months in which to get the yearly average back on track. Thus it seems fairly clear that the authorities will have to be prepared to move their instrument variables with sufficient vigor to control average monetary growth rates over periods shorter than one year. Clearly, there are some messy problems here in this whole area. Quite possibly they have not yet even been clearly formulated—let alone solved.[18]

Conclusion

The main points made in this paper can be summarized as follows. The Federal Reserve has moved with the shift in the general climate of ideas over the past few years, putting increasing emphasis on the money supply and other monetary aggregates as intermediate objectives of monetary policy. The Federal Open Market Committee now sets explicit goals for the growth of the money supply and bank credit and issues operating instructions to the Account Management in New York that are drawn up largely with a view to achieving these objectives. The qualification

[18]It might be noted that these problems would not disappear though they might be simplified, if one were to adopt a steady growth of the money supply at some fixed rate à la Milton Friedman. In the first place, the economy would not "start out" on its long-run trend path with full employment and a history of steady monetary growth, sustainable real growth, and an "acceptable" rate of inflation. Consequently, one might want to approach the long-run monetary growth rate target only gradually. Secondly, all the technical problems of short-run control over the money supply would remain. Consequently, the actual growth rate could expect to go off track much as it does now. Therefore, the problems of an optimum control period, how to compensate for past errors, and how sharply to adjust operating targets to get back on track would still exist.

"largely" is necessary since the behavior of money and capital market conditions, and international financial developments, have also continued as a source of explicit concern to the Committee. At times, this concern has dictated operating decisions different from those that might have been made if hitting money supply objectives had been the sole aim. In trying to improve its ability to achieve money supply goals, the FOMC has experimented with alternative approaches to operating tactics. It has also made a substantial investment of research resources in the problems of monetary control.

The results to date suggest that attempts to forecast and control the money supply over short periods, whatever operating targets are used, will normally be subject to quite large errors. A rough judgment might be that reasonably close forecasts, and control, can be achieved over periods down to six months if the Committee is prepared to move its operating targets sufficiently vigorously to achieve the desired results.

Fortunately, the tentative evidence also suggests that very short-term control over the money supply is not necessary for satisfactory economic performance. Evidently, fairly large deviations from target may not do any significant harm, provided they do not last longer than a quarter or two and provided monetary growth rates average out about on target over longer periods of perhaps a year. None of these estimates can be regarded as firmly established, however.

In controlling money, shorter term operating targets that are more readily achievable than the monetary targets themselves are needed as a guide to day-by-day and week-by-week decisions. Various measures of nonborrowed reserves and short-term interest rates are available for this purpose. Each has advantages and disadvantages. The available evidence does not establish any clear overall superiority for any one of them.

Finally, it is clear that a great deal has been learned about the problems and possibilities of implementing money supply targets in the past few years. Virtually all of the research drawn upon in this survey is less than three or four years old. Many of the topics discussed would have seemed quite novel only a relatively short time ago. The progress in this area has been rapid. Indeed, one may wonder if diminishing returns may not already have begun to set in in some respects. Perhaps the direction in which research efforts will now move is to deal with the implications of the lags and uncertainties—in short the "control theory" issues mentioned earlier. What should be the time horizon for monetary control? How should targets be adjusted in response to the past "misses" that will inevitably arise? Work in this area will have to be sufficiently grounded in reliable evidence and sufficiently "robust" to be useful to properly skeptical policy makers. Nevertheless, we can be hopeful that further progress in this area will be forthcoming over the period ahead.

Tests of the Federal Reserve's Reaction to the State of the Economy: 1964–74

Thomas M. Havrilesky, Robert H. Sapp, and Robert L. Schweitzer[1]

This article reports estimates of the systematic reaction of the Federal Reserve System, as reflected in a variable that it purports to control (the Federal funds rate), to the state of the economy, as reflected by the price level, the level of unemployment, a measure of our country's international economic position, and the rates of growth of key monetary aggregates.

The "Laws of Economics"?

An entire generation of econometric models is premised on the assumption that either the money stock (more recently, the monetary base) or "the" interest rate is given by the monetary authority. Unfortunately, while certain monetary aggregates and/or interest rates may be controlled by the monetary authority, they are likely neither to remain fixed nor to be determined by processes that are random with respect to the other variables of the model, such as the price level and the level of unemployment. Thus, the assumption that a monetary control variable is "given"

Reprinted, with additions and deletions, from the *Social Science Quarterly*, 55, 4 (March, 1975), pp. 835–852, by permission of Southwest Social Science Association and the authors.

[1]The authors would like to thank James Dean, Neil de Marchi, Richard Froyen, Edward Kane, and Raymond Lombra for helpful comments.

can lead to serious bias in the estimation of macroeconomic models.[2] Reliable estimates of a systematic relationship between the state of the economy and the control variable(s) of monetary policy should, therefore, be of interest to individuals who depend on the predictions of these models.

Students of the Federal Reserve System have long noted the alacrity with which Federal Reserve officials allude, *ex post,* to a long list of variables in the macroeconomy to which they purport to attend. Yet, there is little evidence that these assurances are more than public relations pronouncements. In fact, for over a decade Fed watchers have been distressed by the reluctance of the monetary authority to commit itself explicity, *ex ante,* to specific macroeconomic goals and to a specific structural hypothesis in which these goals are contained.[3] This lack of open commitment has historically insulated the structural and policy-strategy conceptions of Federal Reserve officials from criticism and improvement (see footnote 6). In fact, this absence of openness enabled Federal Reserve officials to argue fallaciously that the unhappy condition of the economy in the early 1970's was explained, not by their dereliction or incompetence (which is consequently hard to uncover), but by the failure of "the laws of economics."[4]

In contrast, many critics have contended that the recent shortcomings of stabilization policy instead stem from the failure of the monetary authority to respond adequately to the state of the economy. They contend that if the Fed had truly been concerned about the rate of inflation, the money supply would have grown only moderately in the early 1970's. Instead, the annual rate of growth of the money supply jumped from 3.8 percent in the 1960's to approximately 7 percent in the 1970–1974 period.

Estimates of a systematic relationship between the state of the economy and the stance of monetary policy should shed additional light on this problem. For example, if tests indicate that the monetary authority's reaction to price inflation has deteriorated over the years, then in lieu of substantive evidence that the "laws of economics" have made it necessary to "live with" more inflation, inflationary distress would be attributable to the Federal Reserve's buckling under to pressure for rapid growth in the money supply. The impetus for "easy money" stems from the antipathy of certain vested interests and most political leaders to high and rising interest rates. In a nearly fully employed economy there will be continuing pressure on the Federal

[2]For example, consider the "reverse causation" problem discussed in Section II of this book. It can be seen that one cannot reasonably deal with "reverse causation" simply by assuming that the Federal Reserve completely offsets, through defensive operations, changes in the control-variable induced by changes in noncontrolled factors such as member bank borrowing. The true magnitude of these, probably incomplete, defensive reactions should be estimated. See Raymond E. Lombra, and Raymond G. Torto, "Federal Reserve 'Defensive' Behavior and the Reverse Causation Argument," *Staff Economic Study,* Board of Governors of the Federal Reserve System (Nov. 1972).

[3]Karl Brunner, "The Ambiguous Rationality of Monetary Policy," *Journal of Money, Credit and Banking,* 4 (Feb. 1972), pp. 3–12; Jack M. Guttentag, "The Strategy of Open Market Operations," *Quarterly Journal of Economics,* 75 (Feb. 1966), pp. 1–30; Thomas Havrilesky, "A New Program for More Monetary Stability," *Journal of Political Economy,* 80 (Jan.-Feb. 1972), pp. 171–175, and "A Skeptical View of the Brave New World of Monetary Policy Experiment," *Journal of Economic Issues,* 5 (Dec. 1971), pp. 109–113.

[4]Adam Smith, *Supermoney* (New York: Random House, 1972), p. 231.

Reserve to soften the short-run effect on interest rates of chronic government deficits. Increases in the growth rate of the money supply in the short run keep interest rates from rising far above the ceilings on rates that can legally be paid small savers thereby protecting savings and loan associations from competition and deposit outflows, bolster the housing market (which is largely financed by the savings and loan industry), and artificially stimulate the economy.

Unfortunately while "easy money" is often politically acceptable in the short run (e.g., during election years), in the long run it often has dire economic implications. In an overheated economy, the moderating effect of rapid money supply growth on interest rates tends to be only temporary. An increase in the growth rate of the money supply is quickly transmitted to a higher rate of price inflation and this, in turn, soon drives interest rates even higher. Periodic attempts to reduce inflation may result in recession.*

Therefore, econometricians and economists are not the only ones who have become concerned about the actual, *ex ante,* stabilization commitments of the monetary authority. There was increasing unease in the popular media with the theme, widely promoted in late 1973 by Arthur Burns, Chairman of the Federal Reserve System's Board of Governors, that the inflationary malaise was the by-product of hard luck and administrative ineptitude, as evidenced by currency devaluations, wheat deals, materials shortages, crop failures, and the machinations of supposedly sinister sultans of oil, energy oligops, and commodity speculators. As dissatisfaction with these *ad hoc* explanations of inflation continued to mount and as the public became aware that prices were accelerating long before the food and energy shortages, Congress and the electorate began to realize that a stricter control of money supply growth would help restrain the inflationary proclivities of government. In 1975 by Congressional Resolution the Federal Reserve was asked to choose and announce the specific money supply growth range that it would seek for as long as a year ahead.

Whether such announced growth ranges can be maintained under all economic conditions in face of the chronic "easy money" pressures discussed above is debatable.** If they cannot, a return to the unsatisfactory monetary policy reactions of the 1964–1974 period is rather likely. Therefore, it is instructive to estimate policy reactions of the monetary authority during the 1964–1974 decade when such monetary discipline was not maintained. Our procedure will allow us to test several hypotheses. For example, as suggested by an ex-Governor of the Federal Reserve System, we may be able to determine if, in the early 1970's, the monetary authority lost much of the anti-inflationary militance that it is purported to have had under William McChesney Martin in the 1960's. This, in turn, may clarify the allegations that the once hallowed role of the Federal Reserve as an independent monetary trustee has been lessened, perhaps by too close association of its Chairman and Governors with

---

*The uncertainties from resulting acceleration and deceleration of money supply growth, as discussed by Wood, Rasche and Humphrey in Section I and by Mayer, Kane and Friedman in Section IVC, may lead to an inefficient, recession-prone economy.—Ed.

**See the opinions of Paul Samuelson and Milton Friedman in Section IVC.—Ed.

the executive branch which traditionally is often wont to stimulate the economy and sustain low interest rates with inadequate regard for ultimate inflationary consequences.[5]

The Analytics of the Reaction Function

Our statistical work is not concerned with the potential strength of monetary policy to influence the macroeconomy; nor are we directly concerned with institutional constraints on that strength (such as too close ties to the executive branch) and the absence of strong incentives for Federal Reserve policymakers to improve their performance, for example by opening their views of the economic structure to critical inspection and debate. Both of these issues deserve critical inspection.[6]

Our purpose is to estimate the influence of the state of the economy on the policy actions of the Federal Reserve in times of announced "ease" and "tightness" under the regimes of two different chairmen and two different presidential administrations. We shall estimate, by ordinary least squares, the policy reactions of the monetary authority, as measured by a variable that is believed to have been closely, if not completely, controlled by the Fed, to the price level, the rate of unemployment, a measure of our country's international economic position, and the rates of growth of key monetary aggregates.

The *reaction function* of the monetary authority can be derived by maximizing its assumed utility function subject to its endowment of productive resources and a given hypothetical structure of the economy. This procedure is analogous to deriving a household's demand for a commodity by maximizing its utility function subject to its budget and a given hypothetical structure of the markets in which it buys and sells.

The coefficients of the reaction function do not directly reveal the weight that the Federal Reserve places on the explanatory variables; rather, they represent combinations of structural and utility parameters. Nevertheless, if we *assume* that the structure of the economy is unchanged between periods over the time span of our estimation, all changes in the coefficients of the reaction function, if statistically significant, will reflect changes in the monetary authority's preferences in terms of price inflation, unemployment, the international position of the dollar, and/or the growth rates of certain monetary aggregates. This is a rather strong assumption, and the reader

---

[5]For accounts of Martin's relative independence of and Burns' acquiescence to White House pressure for easy money, see Sherman J. Maisel, *Managing the Dollar* (New York: Norton, 1973), pp. 113-123; and Sanford Rose, "The Agony of the Federal Reserve," *Fortune* (July 1974), pp. 91-93, 180-190.

[6]As discussed above and pointed out in the Lombra and Torto reading earlier in this Section, the monetary policymaker has a decidedly eclectic attitude toward competing hypotheses about the structure of the economy. This lack of commitment makes it difficult for the Federal Reserve to choose between an interest rate and a monetary aggregate instrument. As a consequence considerable resources are allocated by the Federal Reserve to devise an optimal control (reaction) strategy for an essentially arbitrarily chosen, and hence probably suboptimal, control-variable (instrument). See, Thomas Havrilesky "The Optimal Reaction Function: Confluence of the Instrument Problem and the Target Problem" *Southern Economic Journal* (forthcoming).

should keep in mind that changes in structural parameters could also account for observed changes in the estimated reaction coefficients.

The Empirics of the Reaction Function

There have been several attempts to fit reaction functions to the data.[7] While it is not our purpose to review critically this literature, all articles of which we are aware suffer from one of two shortcomings. First, previous researchers have used, as dependent variables, measures, such as the monetary aggregates, that the Federal Reserve may not have attempted to control or may not have been able to control over reasonably short policy control periods.[*] Second, previous researchers have specified policy control periods that are quite long. This leads to a problem in ascribing one-way causality to the coefficients of the reaction function. For example, if the policy period were one quarter, it would be difficult to separate one flow of causation (from the state of the economy to the control-variable) from the other, reverse, flow of causation (from the control-variable to the state of the economy). In our research we assume a control or policy period of just one month and use monthly averages of the Federal funds rate as the policy control-variable or instrument.

As one of several money market variables (the Federal funds rate, borrowed reserves, free reserves, and the Treasury bill rate), the Federal funds rate is widely regarded as the single variable among all possible candidates that the Federal Reserve is most likely actually to have used as a control-variable. (We are not suggesting, however, that the Federal funds rate actually *is* an *optimal* control-variable for monthly policy control periods; to the contrary, cogent arguments can be made that a monetary aggregate is preferable in that it provides better information about what the effective stance of monetary policy really is. Moreover, in the long run an interest rate is not controllable as it is a market-determined, relative price.)[8] In addition, with practically every turning point in monetary policy (as determined from reading the minutes of the Federal Open Market Committee—FOMC—meetings in the 1960's) the Federal funds rate changed more pronouncedly in the expected direction in the weeks following the meeting than any other money market variable.[9] Moreover, it is

---

[7]For example, see James W. Christian, "A Further Analysis of the Objectives of American Monetary Policy," *Journal of Finance,* 23 (June 1968), pp. 465–477; Ann F. Friedlaender, "Macro Policy Goals and Revealed Preference," *Quarterly Journal of Economics,* 87 (Feb. 1973), pp. 24–43; Richard T. Froyen, "A Test of the Endogeneity of Monetary Policy," *Journal of Econometrics,* 2 (July 1974); Thomas Havrilesky, "A Test of Monetary Policy Action," *Journal of Political Economy,* 75 (June 1967), pp. 299–304; John A. Wood, "A Model of Federal Reserve Behavior," in George Horwich, ed., *Monetary Process and Policy: A Symposium* (Homewood, Ill.: R. D. Irwin, 1967), pp. 135–166.

[*]If the monetary instrument is not controlled but responds to the economy in an unconstrained fashion, we will have a "reverse causation" problem in econometric models that attempt to estimate the effect of that instrument on the economy. See footnote 2.—Ed.

[8]Much of the previous literature on the reaction function confuses the issue of what the *optimal* control variable would be for measuring the real thrust and appropriateness of monetary policy with the issue of estimating how the Federal Reserve *actually* reacted.

[9]The changes from ease to tightness or vice versa occurred in May 1960, June 1962, November 1966, December 1967, July 1968, December 1968, January 1970, August 1971, September 1972 and March 1974. Stephen H. Barnett, "The Monetary Indicators at Turning Points," *Financial Analysts Journal,* 26 (Sept.-Oct. 1970), pp. 29–32.

contended in numerous Federal Reserve publications that the monetary authority actually *does* try to effect close control over the Federal funds rate during relatively short policy control periods, such as a month or a week; therefore, even though the rate itself is influenced from the demand side, we assume that it is controlled by the monetary authority.*

What Are Monetary Targets, Instruments, and Indicators?

After the credit crunch of 1966, and especially after Arthur Burns became Chairman of the Board of Governors, attention in the financial press and in the writings of some Fed spokesmen seems to have focused on monetary aggregates (defined to include the bank credit proxy and various measures of reserves, the monetary base and the money stock). Labels such as guides, instruments, indicators, and targets have been attached to these monetary aggregates. For purposes of this paper and in most of the literature on the theory of monetary policy, the word "guide" is disregarded because it has little consistent, analytic meaning. The label "instrument" refers to a variable controlled by the policymaker over the policy control period and may be used interchangeably with the label, control-variable. Despite their theoretical superiority, for control periods such as a month or a quarter monetary aggregates do not seem actually to have been used as instruments by the Federal Reserve for the 1964–1974 period covered by this study. They are never referred to as strategic short-run instruments in Federal Reserve publications.**

Nor have the monetary aggregates, in our opinion, likely been used as true intermediate target-variables for shorter control periods such as a month or a quarter. Hypothetically, an optimal stabilization strategy under uncertainty would formulate the optimal reaction of monetary policy (the optimal instrument and optimal reaction of that instrument) to information about the state of the economy; in certain kinds of hypothetical structures information from one sector of the economy may be so superior to information from all other sectors that certain variables, endogenous to that sector, are controllable by monetary policy action. Under these circumstances, the optimal stabilization strategy may be to compensate for shocks to (to "track" on) these particular variables. In such cases, these variables are referred to in the theoretical literature as intermediate target-variables.[10]

---

* See the article by Lombra and Torto in this Section.—Ed.

**The Federal Reserve's failure to choose a monetary aggregate instrument in its short-strategy may stem from its lack of commitment to specific hypothesis about the structure of the economy. See footnote 6. Further discussion of the instrument and intermediate target problems and evidence of this lack of commitment is found in the articles by Davis and Lombra and Torto in this Section—Ed.

[10]The instrument problem is well understood. See John Kareken and Neil Wallace, "The Monetary Instrument Variable Choice: How Important?" *Journal of Money, Credit and Banking,* 4 (Aug. 1972), pp. 723–729. Also, William Poole, "Optimal Choice of Monetary Policy Instruments in a Simple Stochastic

Despite their semantic confusion, articles by Federal Reserve economists have placed the role of monetary aggregates in reasonable perspective; in several widely read articles it can be discovered that the monetary aggregates are used neither as instruments, as intermediate target-variables (in the rigorous sense described above), nor as indicators (in the sense made known by Brunner).[11]

Federal Reserve economists have very carefully explained that projected growth in certain monetary aggregates (such as Reserves to Support Private Deposits, RPD's) is based on quarterly projections of the growth of aggregate income generated by the FRB-MIT-Penn econometric model. The quarterly income projections are then placed on a monthly basis. Then, simulations of the growth rates of various monetary aggregates are made for alternative Federal funds rates. For a given Federal funds rate there will be a growth rate for each monetary aggregate.[12]

Thus, it is clear that in making the short-run projections the Federal Reserve assumes that the Federal funds rate will remain at a level predetermined by its stabilization policy decisions. Subsequent gaps between projected growth and actual growth of a monetary aggregate then simply tend to reflect how far the monetary authority's initial income projection is off. When the growth of a monetary aggregate is far out of line for several months, Federal Reserve economists sometimes indicate that corrective adjustments in the monetary policy instrument *may* be applied, that is, that the aggregates may be serving as intermediate target-variables in formal strategic models. However, in reality, wide swings in the growth rates of the monetary aggregates appear to be so tolerated that their role as intermediate target-variables must be doubted. Whether or not the growth of certain monetary aggregates historically constrained monetary policy actions over the 1964-1974 period is an emperical question. Nevertheless it should be clear that, despite recent improvement in policy strategy, monetary aggregates are not yet always perceived and used by the

---

Macro Model," *Quarterly Journal of Economics,* 84 (May 1970), pp. 197-216. The label "instrument" is sometimes confused with the label, "intermediate target", e.g., Harold Shapiro, and Robert Holbrook, "The Choice of Optimal Intermediate Targets," *American Economic Review,* 60 (Supplement, May 1970), pp. 40-46. For further clarification of the target problem, see Karl Brunner, *Targets and Indicators of Monetary Policy* (San Francisco: Chandler, 1969); Thomas Havrilesky, "Finding the Optimal Monetary Strategy with Information Constraints," *Journal of Finance,* 27 (Dec. 1972), pp. 1045-1056; and Thomas Havrilesky, "The Optimal Reaction Function; Confluence of the Instrument Problem and the Target Problem" *Southern Economic Journal* (forthcoming).

[11]A monetary indicator has a special theoretical meaning: when the structural hypothesis of the policy-maker is unspecified, an indicator may be used, nevertheless, to reflect the thrust of policy actions unambiguously and independently of the state of the economy. See Brunner, *Targets and Indicators.*

[12]Stephen H. Axilrod, "Monetary Aggregates and Money Market Conditions in Open Market Policy," and Richard G. Davis, "Short-Run Targets for Open Market Operations," *Open Market Policy and Operating Procedures*—Staff Studies, Board of Governors of the Federal Reserve System, 1971. Stephen H. Axilrod and Darwin L. Beck, "The Role of Projections and Data Evaluations with Monetary Aggregates as Policy Targets," and James L. Pierce and Thomas D. Thomson, "Some Issues in Controlling the Stock of Monetary Aggregates," *Controlling Monetary Aggregates II,* Federal Reserve Bank of Boston, 1972.

monetary authority as instruments, or intermediate targets in the proper short-run control-theoretic sense outlined above.*

Fitting the Reaction Function

As mentioned earlier, we assume that monthly data permit us to attribute unilateral causality to the reaction function (from the state of the economy to Federal Reserve action). The monthly specification also conforms to the monthly meetings of the FOMC. At these meetings data on the state of the economy, compiled since the last meeting, are discussed and policy decisions are rendered. Throughout the past decade forecasts of future economic activity are assumed not to have been systematically heeded by monetary policymakers. Policy actions for the four weeks following a meeting of the FOMC are carried out by its Account Manager. Thus, the average level of the Federal funds rate in any calendar month can be viewed as being dependent on the state of the economy, as viewed and interpreted by the policymakers, in the previous month. If the Chairman initiates or the Account Manager anticipates changes in policy before the actual meeting of the FOMC, the assumed one-month lag between a change in the state of the economy and policy action is still reasonable because of lags in reporting data. A final advantage of using monthly, rather than quarterly, data is that it allows researchers to pinpoint and estimate shifts from "tight" to "easy" policy and shifts associated with changes in the membership of the Board of Governors and in presidential administrations.

The explanatory variables in the reaction function (the state-of-the economy variables with which policymakers are assumed to have been concerned) are: the wholesale price index (P), the unemployment rate (U), an historically sensitive barometer of the international position of the dollar, the exchange rate of the Deutsche Mark (FX), and, for all periods after November 1966, the annualized rate of growth of one of three monetary aggregates: the adjusted bank credit proxy (BCP), the narrow money supply (M), and reserves available to support private deposits (RPD). All observations are monthly averages and enter the reaction function with a lag of one month.

Explanatory variables were not entered as differences between actual and desired (by the Fed) magnitudes because, in addition to its being unknown, subtracting a constant term from an observation vector which enters linearly, would add no variance and, therefore, would not affect the absolute magnitude of our estimates. In addition, the use of monthly data lagged only one period obviously means that our estimates do not reflect the *entire* (distributed lag) reaction of the Federal Reserve.

We do not introduce a measure of the need for "even-keeling" or other defensive operations by the monetary authority because even-keeling refers to adjustments in monetary aggregates such as reserves, the monetary base, Federal Reserve Credit, etc. (not to interest rate adjustments) by the central bank in the face of Treasury

---

*For fairly complete discussion of the monetary policymaker's strategy see the reading by Lombra and Torto earlier in this Section. There it is made clear that aggregates are not used as instruments and that the Federal Reserve is too concerned about interest rate volatility to use them as intermediate target-variables.—Ed.

funding and refunding. We assume that the Federal funds rate is controlled and, therefore, insulated from the influence of Treasury activities and other disturbances.

How the Federal Reserve Behaved

The Federal Reserve under Martin: Tightness before the Crunch, January 1964 to November 1966

Estimation begins with the first full calendar year of Lyndon B. Johnson's presidency. At this time William McChesney Martin was Chairman of the Board of Governors. In July 1962, according to the minutes of the FOMC, the Federal Reserve shifted from a policy of ease to a policy of tight money. Tight money policy seems to have persisted until shortly after the credit crunch of 1966.

In all equations that follow the figures in parenthesis are t-statistics, R^2 refers to the coefficeint of determination, F is the F-statistic, D-W is the Durbin-Watson test statistic, N is the number of observations, and the t subscript refers to the time period.

$$\text{Federal Funds} = -80.988 \quad -0.0365\ U_{t-1} + 0.5577\ P_{t-1} + 1.256\ FX_{t-1}$$
$$\text{Rate}_t \quad (-10.342)\ (-0.2603) \quad\quad (11.348) \quad\quad (3.593) \quad\quad (1)$$
$$R^2 = .98 \quad F^2 = 427.527 \quad D\text{-}W = 1.759 \quad N = 34$$

The results suggest that the Federal Reserve under Chairman Martin showed little concern for unemployment even though the unemployment rate did not fall below 4 percent until January 1966 and did not go below 3.7 percent until September 1966. The coefficient on the unemployment variable is statistically insignificant. The coefficient on the price level and exchange rate variables are both positive and significant at the .01 level. A one-point rise in the wholesale price index (P) appears to have induced a .56 percentage point rise in the Federal funds rate and a one-cent rise in the U.S. dollar price of the Deusche Mark seems to have induced a $1\frac{1}{4}$ percentage point rise in the Federal funds rate. The R^2 and F-statistics attribute high explanatory power to the equation and the D-W test statistic indicates an absence of autocorrelation in the residuals.

These results lend support to the widely held belief that the Federal Reserve under Martin was strongly anti-inflationary[13] and that the tight money period of the early 1960's was, in fact, partly brought on by the international weakness of the dollar.

The Martin Era: Ease after the Crunch, December 1966 to November 1967 and July 1968 to December 1968

The credit crunch of 1966 is alleged to have been instructive to monetary policymakers of the difficulties of singlehandedly attempting to cool the economy and

[13]Maisel, *Managing the Dollar*, pp. 60-69.

strengthen the dollar. Calls for fiscal restraint resounded about the nation and, spurred by the credit crunch and talk of a housing crisis brought about by interest rates that were "too high," the Federal Reserve was purported to have shifted to a policy of monetary ease in December 1966. (In addition, in June 1966 the bank credit proxy was first mentioned in the FOMC directive.)

By December 1967 it seemed apparent that fiscal restraint would not be forthcoming, that the Johnson Administration would not raise taxes to pay for resources diverted by the warfare-welfare state, and that the Vietnam War deficit would be quite sizable. The shift to tightness in December 1967 was short-lived because of the unexpected passage of the tax surcharge bill in mid-1968. The monetary authority shifted back to a policy of ease in June 1968. It turned out that the return to ease was a tactical mistake because the effect of the surchage was overestimated. With the arrival of the Nixon administration in January 1969 a policy of tightness was resumed.

Because the entire, post-crunch, Martin-Johnson period was one of ease, except for the December 1967 to June 1968 interlude, we consolidated the two subperiods of ease, December 1966 to November 1967 and July 1968 to December 1968.[14]

$$\text{Federal Funds Rate}_t = -20.247 - 1.714\ U_{t-1} + .3569\ P_{t-1} - .1765\ FX_{t-1} + .3968\ BCP_{t-1}$$
$$(-.884)\ (-2.185)\qquad (3.153)\qquad (-.2412)\qquad (.2009)$$

$$R^2 = .70 \quad F = 7.569 \quad D\text{-}W = .52 \quad N = 18 \tag{2}$$

The shift to ease is quite marked when compared to the pre-credit crunch results.[15] The coefficient on the rate of unemployment is now negative and statistically significant at the .01 level. The unemployment rate rose rather steadily from 3.5 percent in October 1966 to 4.3 percent in October 1967. For every one percent increase in the unemployment rate, the Federal funds rate would fall by approximately 1.71 percentage points. The shift to ease is further corroborated by the fact that the exchange rate coefficient is no longer statistically significant and that the coefficient on the price level variable, while still positive and significant, declines from .56 for the pre-crunch period to approximately .36; this indicates a .36 percentage point rise in the Federal funds rate for every one point increase in the wholesale price index. Establishing a pattern that was to be repeated during later periods of monetary tightness, a steady anti-inflationary monetary policy was apparently politically difficult to maintain in the face of rising unemployment and rising interest rates (even under William McChesney Martin). Despite the explicit mention given to the bank credit

[14]When the entire, post-crunch, pre-Nixon period, December 1966 to December 1968, is lumped together the result is similar to that reported here except that the coefficient on U_{t-1} is somewhat smaller.

[15]Because the R^2 and F-statistics are lower than the previous result, the explanatory power of the equations fall somewhat. The D-W statistic indicates autocorrelation in the residuals. When corrected by the Cochrane-Orcutt iterative technique, the signs and significance of the coefficients are unchanged and the R^2 rises to .97 with a D-W of 2.42.

To test our pooling procedure, we used Chow Tests. The results of the tests led us to reject at the .95 percent level the null hypothesis that the small subperiods obey the same relation over the whole sample period.

proxy in FOMC directives during this period,[16] the statistical results indicate that it did not elicit a systematic response from the monetary authority.

The Martin Era: Nixon's Game Plan I, January 1969 to January 1970 (and December 1967 to June 1968)

Richard Nixon was elected partly on the promise that he would cool an overheated economy. The Federal Reserve had begun the cooling process during the first half of 1968 only to move prematurely and mistakenly to a policy of ease because of the widespread overestimation of the depressive effect of the tax surcharge. Because this period of tightness in 1968 was so short (seven months), we consolidate it with the tight money period that began when Nixon assumed the presidency.[17]

$$\text{Federal Funds Rate}_t = -73.671 + .9767\ U_{t-1} + .8622\ P_{t-1} - 4.987\ FX_{t-1} + .7979\ BCP_{t-1}$$
$$(-10.570)\quad (1.524)\qquad (11.946)\qquad (-1.990)\qquad (.6500)$$

$$R^2 = .93 \quad F = 46.329 \quad \text{D-W} = .782 \quad N = 20 \tag{3}$$

That the period is one of tightness is suggested by the positive and significant (at the .99 level) sign on the coefficient of the price level variable. The coefficient indicates a .86 percentage point rise in the Federal funds rate for every single point rise in the wholesale price index; this is the largest value that we estimate for this coefficient in any subperiod of the entire 1964–1974 period.[18] In terms of the coefficient alone, one can infer that monetary policy was at its tightest during the first year of the Nixon administration.

The coefficients on the unemployment and exchange rate variables are both statistically significant at the .90 level, but possess the "wrong" signs. This suggests, somewhat anomalously, that a rise in the Federal funds rate was associated with a rise in unemployment and a decline in the Federal funds rate was associated with a rise in the price of foreign exchange during the year. Both the rate of unemployment and the exchange rate rose over the period (see note 23).

These phenomena can be explained by a steady rise in the *desired* level of unem-

---

[16]Maisel, *Managing the Dollar*, pp. 85, 230.

[17]When the January 1969 to January 1970 period is fit separately the results are:

$$FF_t = -111.067 + .3519\ U_{t-1} + 1.381\ P_{t-1} - 1.103\ FX_{t-1} + 1.6897\ BCP_{t-1}$$
$$(-4.930)\quad (.4041)\qquad (4.514)\qquad (-2.982)\qquad (1.1981)$$

$$R^2 = .85 \quad F = 11.175 \quad \text{D-W} = 1.4880 \quad N = 13.$$

Compared to the combined time periods, autocorrelation in the residuals does not appear to be a problem. Moreover, all signs are unchanged and only the coefficient of the unemployment variable loses significance.

[18]The fact that interest rates should rise with anticipated price inflation is of little concern here as the Federal funds rate is a control variable and thus is insulated from market forces.

ployment from, say 3.5 to 5 percent and a steady rise in the *desired* exchange rate against the Deutsche Mark during the period. In this way an unemployment rate that was below the desired rate would have caused the Federal funds rate to be raised since a higher Federal funds rate would take the economy closer to the Fed's assumed desired rate of unemployment. As the actual rate of unemployment rose, as it did over the period, the Federal funds rate would have been raised only if the desired rate of unemployment rose even faster. In this way, higher unemployment could have induced a higher Federal funds rate. Likewise, if the desired exchange rate was continuously raised, a rise in the actual price of foreign exchange, as long as it was below the desired rate, would have caused the Federal funds rate to have been lowered to take the monetary authority closer to its goal. As the actual exchange rate rose, the Federal funds rate would have been lowered only if the desired exchange rate rose even faster.

These interpretations are supported by widespread discussions, in the financial press during 1968 and especially 1969, of purposely imposing a cooling-off period on the economy and adopting a "more realistic" set of unemployment and exchange rate goals.

Finally, as in the previous results, the coefficient on the bank credit proxy was not statistically significant.[19]

The Federal Reserve under Burns: Nixon's Game Plan II, Pre-freeze Ease, February 1970 to July 1971

Once again, in 1970 the effect of monetary stringency on interest rates and unemployment became unpalatable to the administration. Even in 1969 formal and informal advisors were already suggesting that economic policy had shifted too far in the direction of tightness.[20] By 1970, while the rate of price inflation had slowed, the unemployment rate went rather steadily upward (rising from 4.2 percent in February 1970 to 5.6 percent in June 1971). "Gradualism" in the war against inflation would soon become the order of the day. As early as February 1970 it was favored by the Chairman of the Board of Governors, Arthur Burns. It was argued at the time that the wide gap between actual and potential output would *eventually* reduce the rate of inflation. Unfortunately, price and wage setters were learning that "gradualism" meant that the Nixon administration felt it could not allow the monetary authority to persist with a tight money policy long enough to dampen their inflationary practices. Consequently, "gradualism" was predicated on an invalid model of wage-price behavior.

True to form, early in 1971 President Nixon ordered increases in government spending to pump up the economy. Increases in government spending and borrowing would surely have meant higher interest rates unless the Federal Reserve complied with an easier monetary policy and comply it did. The old game plan was scuttled,

---

[19]This led us to introduce the growth of the narrowly defined money supply in place of the bank credit proxy. The results were quite similar to those reported above.
[20]Leonard Silk, *Nixonomics* (New York: Praeger, 1973), pp. 3-19.

and sentiment for anti-inflationary relentlessness in the conduct of monetary policy waned.[21]

Monetary ease was soon reflected in the growth rate of the money supply. During the 1960's money grew at the annual rate of 3.8 percent—in the 1970-1974 period it grew at a 7 percent rate. This quantum leap soon caused adherents to be attracted to the argument that the rate of growth of the money supply should be a constraint on monetary policy actions.

The results for the February 1970 to July 1971 period are:

Federal
Funds = 33.676   − 1.2596 U_{t-1} − .61965 P_{t-1} + 1.7359 FX_{t-1} + .17305 BCP_{t-1}
Rate$_t$ (2.0248) (− 2.5475)   (− 2.5585)   (2.5373)   (.14339)

$$R^2 = .93 \quad F = 41.424 \quad D\text{-}W = 1.266 \quad N = 18 \qquad (4)$$

Introducing a money supply constraint in place of the bank credit constraint yields:

Federal
Funds = 32.821   − 1.3635 U_{t-1} − .5806 P_{t-1} + 1.6289 FX_{t-1} + .79498 M_{t-1}
Rate$_t$ (2.2040) (− 3.2445)   (− 2.724)   (2.5773)   (1.3697)

$$R^2 = .94 \quad F = 47.791 \quad D\text{-}W = 1.352 \quad N = 18 \qquad (5)$$

The Federal funds rate fell steadily during this period. The shift to ease is marked notably by the negative and significant sign on the unemployment rate. The rate of unemployment rose from 4.2 percent in February 1970 to 5.6 percent in June 1971. The second equation indicates that a 1.36 percentage point decrease in the Federal funds rate occurred for each one percent rise in the unemployment rate.

The continual weakening position of the dollar abroad seems to have been of moment to the monetary authority. This entire period, especially the spring of 1971, featured growing pressure on the dollar and a rush of dollars into Deutsche Marks and other currencies (while government officials continued to insist on the strength of the dollar). The coefficient on the exchange rate variable is positive and statistically significant. In the second equation a one-cent rise in the price of the Deutsche Mark induced a 1.63 percentage point rise in the Federal funds rate.[22]

The bank credit proxy in the first equation is once again insignificant, but when the growth rate of the narrow money supply is introduced in its place in the second equation, the coefficient becomes statistically significant. A one percent increase in

[21]Maisel, *Managing the Dollar*, pp. 265-268. Silk claims the shift of Game Plan II occurred after the 1970 elections, in which the Republican party fared rather badly. Silk, *Nixonomics*, p. 68. It is often suggested that Richard Nixon was moved to stimulate the economy by memories of the 1959-1960 recession which thwarted his earlier bid for the presidency.

[22]The statistical result seems to contradict former Governor Maisel's contention that international considerations affected FOMC decisions only a few times during his tenure. Maisel, *Managing the Dollar*, p. 224.

the annual rate of growth of the narrow money supply induced the Fed to raise the Federal funds rate by .79 percentage points, presumably to keep the growth of the money supply within preconceived limits. This result obtains despite statements from Federal Reserve officials during the anxious months of the 1970 liquidity crisis disavowing a strict money supply constraint.[23]

Finally, once again we seem to have an anomalous result: the coefficient on the price level variable is negative and statistically significant. The wholesale price index was rising at an annual rate of about 4 percent during this period. This suggests that the Federal Reserve may have implicitly believed that a positive rate of price inflation was desirable in order to reduce unemployment and move leftward along a short-run Phillips curve by validating, rather than resisting, increases in the price level. Our conjecture is that there occurred over the period a gradual shift from zero desired inflation to a policy of encouraging an increase in the price level. Whether our conjecture is true or not,[24] the overall statistical results suggest a drastic change from the monetary policy of earlier periods. For example, when Martin was Chairman, while the shift to a policy of ease in 1967 and 1968 was marked by a reduction in the (reaction) coefficient of the price level variable, the coefficient was still positive and statistically significant.

Finally the R^2 and F-statistics indicate a reasonably good statistical fit and the D-W statistic falls in the inconclusive range.

The Burns Era: Nixon's New Economic Policy, August 1971 to September 1972.

By August 1971 government deficits and easy money had the domestic economy boiling again. The move to a policy of wage and price controls dramatically signaled a break with the previous policy of gradualism (Game Plan II). Estimates of the reaction function, using three different monetary aggregates as constraints are:

$$\begin{align} \text{Federal Funds Rate}_t = & -34.759 & -.0360\ U_{t-1} + & .6840\ P_{t-1} - 1.3053\ FX_{t-1} - .0277\ BCP_{t-1} \\ & (-1.5216)\ (-.0373) & (3.326) & (-5.5958) \qquad (-.0240) \end{align}$$

$$R^2 = .81 \quad F = 9.326 \quad \text{D-W} = 1.21 \quad N = 14 \tag{6}$$

$$\begin{align} \text{Federal Funds Rate}_t = & -37.459 & -.0410\ U_{t-1} + & .7053\ P_{t-1} - 1.3165\ FX_{t-1} - .3011\ M_{t-1} \\ & (-1.625)\ (-.0659) & (3.441) & (-5.764) \qquad (-.4978) \end{align} \tag{7}$$

$$R^2 = .81 \quad F = 9.689 \quad \text{D-W} = 1.21 \quad N = 14$$

[23]Silk, *Nixonomics*, p. 105.

[24]There are, of course, finite sample problems associated with all of our periods. In addition, some of the explanatory variables, for certain periods, are rather highly correlated. Therefore, under these conditions our results (especially the perverse signs we occasionally get) should be interpreted in a guarded fashion.

Federal
Funds $= -37.131 - .0417 \, U_{t-1} + .7049 \, P_{t-1} - 1.303 \, FX_{t-1} - 1.1661 \, RPD_{t-1}$
Rate$_t$ $\quad (-1.651) \, (-.0442) \quad (3.501) \quad (-5.785) \quad (-.6578) \qquad (8)$

$$R^2 = .82 \quad F = 9.939 \quad D\text{-}W = 1.30 \quad N = 14$$

Complete reliance on the freeze to hold prices down is not apparent because the coefficient on the price level variable is positive and significant, although not as great in magnitude as during the original Game Plan I period of 1969. As the price level rose, so too did the Federal funds rate. The results suggest that the monetary authority responded to the administration's signal and took firm action to restrict price inflation.

However, there seems to have been no concern for the prevailing level of unemployment in this period, the coefficient of the unemployment variable is statistically insignificant, suggesting that the Federal Reserve was willing to live with the 5.5 to 6 percent rate of unemployment that obtained. In fact, the unemployment rate stayed at the 5.8 to 6 percent level from August 1971 until June 1972.

Once again, the sign on the coefficient of the foreign exchange variable is significant but negative in sign. Again, this suggests that the central bank had gradually moved to even higher desired levels of exchange rates during this era. The result is consistent with the administration's policy of letting the dollar float during this period of actual and impending devaluations of the dollar and upward revaluation of several foreign currencies.

Finally, neither the rates of growth of bank credit, the money supply, nor reserves available to support private deposits (RPD's) prove to have been statistically significant constraints on monetary policy during the period, even though RPD's were announced to have become an "official" constraint on monetary policy in February 1972.

The Burns Era: Phase O(ut), a Return to the Old Game Plan? September 1972 to February 1974

The Federal funds rate lurched continually upward from September 1972 to September 1973 and leveled out late in 1973. Many interpreters would label this a sign of tightness. The abandonment of controls and this indication of tight money suggested to many observers a return to the old Game Plan I. Our results with respect to the coefficient of the price level variable would lead us to disagree.

Federal
Funds $= -6.3175 - 1.6929 \, U_{t-1} + .09838 \, P_{t-1} + .29339 \, FX_{t-1} - .75752 \, BCP_{t-1}$
Rate$_t$ $\quad (-1.1470) \, (-2.4571) \quad (4.5887) \quad (5.6079) \quad (-.63544)$

$$R^2 = .97 \quad F = 95.88 \quad D\text{-}W = 1.80 \quad N = 17 \qquad (9)$$

Federal
Funds = -6.2691 -1.7107 U_{t-1} + $.09584$ P_{t-1} + $.29508$ FX_{t-1} $-.12627$ M_{t-1}
Rate$_t$ (-1.0975) (-2.353) $\quad\quad\,$ (4.4398) $\quad\quad$ (5.3131) $\quad\quad$ $(-.18808)$

$$R^2 = .97 \quad F = 93.157 \quad D\text{-}W = 1.992 \quad N = 17 \tag{10}$$

Federal
Funds = -4.9535 -1.8633 U_{t-1} + $.10144$ P_{t-1} + $.26497$ FX_{t-1} + $.68347$ RPD_{t-1}
Rate$_t$ $(-.89241)$ (-2.6850) $\quad\quad$ (4.7861) $\quad\quad$ (4.4593) $\quad\quad$ (1.0631)

$$R^2 = .97 \quad F = 101.254 \quad D\text{-}W = 2.18 \quad N = 17 \tag{11}$$

As price controls were reduced (the shift to Phase III) in December 1972, the rate of price inflation accelerated. Even though the Federal funds rate rose steadily over the period, it did not respond as strongly to increases in the price level as in other periods. In the second and third equations a one-point rise in the wholesale price index generated, over the period, a mere .09 percentage point increase in the Federal funds rate—the lowest value of this coefficient for any period of our study, except for the pre-freeze expansionary period.

Once more, because of political antagonisms toward high and rising interest rates and the Fed's practice of smoothing changes in interest rates,[25] the Federal funds rate did not rise quickly enough as the demand for money increased. As a result of this weak reaction, there occurred in 1972 and 1973 a rapid acceleration of money supply growth. In an economy recovering from the doldrums of 1970 and early 1971, this virtually guaranteed enormous inflationary pressures in 1973 and 1974.

In contrast to the weak reaction to price inflation, there is a sizable negative and significant sign on the coefficient of the unemployment variable. In two of the three equations the coefficient has a greater absolute value than in any period of ease or tightness since 1964. Unemployment rates fell rather steadily from 5.6 percent in September of 1972 to 4.5 percent in October of 1973. The negative reaction of the Federal funds rate suggests, as with all results under the Nixon administration, a desired rate of unemployment in the areas of 5.5 percent, such that, when unemployment decreased, the Federal funds rate was raised.

Another element of tightness in the reaction function for this period is the positive and significant sign of the coefficient of the foreign exchange variable. Early in 1973 a wave of selling buffeted the U.S. dollar and the dollar was devalued. Nevertheless, in the period proceeding the devaluation and during the continued weakness of the summer of 1973, in accordance with the Smithsonian Agreement of 1971, our central bank took steps to bolster the exchange rate because it was believed that the dollar was temporarily undervalued. The statistical results indicate that these steps included letting interest rates rise to narrow the gap between foreign and domestic rates.

---

[25]Rose, "Agony of the Federal Reserve," argues that the Fed's propensity to stabilize upward interest rate movements (in order to protect the bond positions of the government securities dealers from capital losses) also helps account for the present inflation.

Finally, in all the equations the coefficient on the monetary aggregate was insignificant, suggesting that despite the upsurge of ballyhoo there was little systematic concern with the growth rate of monetary aggregates in this period (the only period in which the coefficient of one of these variables was significant and positive was the February 1970 to July 1971 interlude just after Arthur Burns became Chairman of the Board of Governors). On balance, the results for this subperiod suggest an apparent return to a posture of tight money mitigated by an extremely mild reaction to the enormous price inflation and rapid money supply growth that took place.

A Return to "The Old Time Religion": 1974–1975

In March 1974 the Federal funds rate moved very sharply upward but by early fall a small downward rebound occurred. This overall rise was widely interpreted as a spiritual reconciliation of the Nixon-(Ford)-Burns regime with the "old time religion" of a stable monetary policy. While the direction of the move in the Federal funds rate was surely appropriate, the magnitude and persistence of the increase in face of the recession that it caused was rather excessive, especially when contrasted to the preceeding years of excessive monetary ease.

Statistical estimation is not feasible because of the lack of sufficient data points. Nevertheless, since 1974 the Federal funds rate appears to have been reacting positively but a good deal more strongly to increases in the price level and negatively but considerably less strongly to the rising rate of unemployment than in any earlier period of monetary tightness under either Martin's or Burns' Chairmanship.

The adoption of a preannounced desired monetary growth range in 1975 was widely lauded. Nevertheless, there is skepticism regarding whether the Federal Reserve can sustain monetary restraint during periods of economic boom. If our impression from the preceding tests is correct, monetary stability in future periods will be, once again, challenged by pressures for a moderating influence on interest rates during periods of prosperity.

Summary of Statistical Results

The statistical findings for the 1964–1974 period indicate the Federal Reserve System under the chairmanship of William McChesney Martin reacted more strongly to price inflation than it did under the chairmanship of Arthur Burns in periods of tight money. A similar result holds for periods of easy monetary policy. This tends to corroborate the belief that the Federal Reserve lost much of its anti-inflationary militance when Burns was chairman.[26] Moreover, it is consistent with the near doubling of the rate of growth of the money supply that occurred under Burns by 1974.

[26]Two of the previous studies of the reaction function relate to the present research. When he uses the Treasury bill rate as the dependent variable, Christian's results attach reasonable signs to the explanatory variables, yet only the coefficient on the price level variable is significant for the 1952–1964 period. Unfortunately, Christian uses quarterly data.

Friedlaender's study employs simulation experiments to estimate impact multipliers. This allows her to

During the Johnson administration the statistical results suggest a desired unemployment rate in the area of 3.5 to 4 percent. Under the Nixon presidency results are consistent with the hypothesis that the desired rate of unemployment rose to approximately 5 percent during 1969, stayed at this level in 1970 and 1971, but was at the 5.5 to 6 percent level during the 1972–1974 period.

The international position of the dollar appears to have induced tightness by the Federal Reserve while Martin was chairman in the 1964–1966 period and while Burns was chairman during episodes of international pressure on the dollar when there was reluctance to let it float, as in early 1971 and early 1973. In all other periods the monetary authority either seemed to ignore the exchange rate or to encourage the value of the dollar to fall to more realistic levels, such as during late 1971 and early 1972.

Despite the tremendous eruption of Federal Reserve policy pronouncements concerning monetary aggregates, widespread arguments favoring their control seem to have systematically influenced monetary policy actions only during the first year and one half of the chairmanship of Arthur Burns; in all other periods statistically significant Federal Reserve reactions do not attach to the growth rate of the money supply, the bank credit proxy or reserves to support private deposits.

Overall, the results indicate that in the 1964–1974 decade the Federal Reserve responded to the state of the economy in a manner only very roughly consistent with its implicit mandate from Congress to stabilize the economy. Casual observation tells us that these responses have not resulted in an adequate performance of the economy in terms of price inflation. Our results suggest that the monetary authority in recent years has increasingly resigned itself, first, to "living with" higher inflation and, then, after short bouts of severe monetary stringency, to reacting less strongly to price inflation. Our conjecture is that such failure and fatalism are not the consequences of a much publicized breakdown of "the laws of economics," (except insofar as wage and price setters may have invalidated standard economic models by adapting their behavior to the Fed's failures). Nor are they consequences of special factors such as unavoidable materials shortages and crop failures. Rather, the poor performance simply reflects deterioration over the 1964–1974 period of the Federal Reserve's responsibility to sustain monetary stability.

---

separate estimated reduced form coefficients and utility weights in her regressions. Her results suggest that during the Kennedy-Johnson years price stability was more highly regarded by monetary and fiscal policymakers than unemployment, a result that is not inconsistent with ours.

B. Monetary Policy in an Open Economy

The final reading in the previous section by Havrilesky, Sapp, and Schweitzer indicated that the international position of the dollar had a significant statistical influence upon monetary policy during the 1964–1974 period. No longer can monetary economists regard lightly the effects of the growth of international economic interdependence on monetary policy. Together with the international oil crisis, recent changes in the exchange-rate system have greatly influenced the effectiveness of traditional monetary and fiscal policy.

The opening article in this section by Donald L. Kohn explores the implications of the growth of international interdependence, the move to flexible exchange rates, and the reduction in supply of a key commodity such as oil for monetary and fiscal policy in the countries initiating such actions and on other countries in the world. The second article by Donald S. Kemp presents the monetary theory of the balance of payments. This theory incorporates some of the fundamentals of money supply and money demand theory developed in Section III of this book. Comparison of the new monetary balance-of-payments theory with older theories is the theme of the third and final reading in this section by one of the originators of the monetary approach, Harry G. Johnson.

Interdependence, Exchange Rate Flexibility, and National Economies

Donald L. Kohn

Over the past 20 years, economic relations among countries have been marked by an increasing degree of interdependence. A rapid expansion has occurred in the quantity of goods and financial assets traded across international borders and these trade and capital flows have become quite sensitive to differences in price and interest rate levels. As a result of the growth of international transactions, countries have benefited greatly in the form of larger output through more efficient use of productive inputs.

The rise in interdependence, however, has made it increasingly difficult for a national economy to follow a path that is not consistent with worldwide economic conditions. That is, the costs of greater international trade and interdependence have been increased vulnerability to disturbances arising in other countries and a possible reduction of national autonomy in deciding on levels of domestic prices and economic activity. As a reaction, governments have increasingly accepted greater flexibility in their exchange rates in the hope that they might obtain better control of internal economic targets.

The growth of interdependence and exchange rate flexibility has important implications for the performance of a national economy. For one, the effectiveness of traditional monetary and fiscal tools in an open economy is greatly influenced by the

Reprinted from the Federal Reserve Bank of Kansas City, *Monthly Review* (April 1975), pp. 3-10, by permission of the publisher.

type of exchange rate system in operation. Even the channels through which these policies affect aggregate demand may be different when foreign trade and capital flows are important. Greater interdependence and exchange rate flexibility also affect how an economy will react to an economic event in another country.

This article explores some of the more important conceptual implications of the growth in interdependence and the move to flexible exchange rates. Monetary and fiscal policy actions are examined both for their effects in the country initiating such actions and for their impact on other countries of the world. Also examined is the impact that an abrupt shrinkage in the supply of an important commodity will have on countries importing that commodity. The consequences of these events will be compared under systems of fixed and flexible exchange rates. Throughout, it will be assumed that the markets for goods and services and credit are highly integrated. In such an environment, small deviations from the world levels of prices or interest rates will elicit very large flows of goods or capital moving from an area of low yield or price to one in which high yield or price prevails.[1]

Monetary Disturbance

Fixed Exchange Rates

When exchange rates are fixed, a monetary policy disturbance involving a change in the money stock at home or abroad tends to have little effect on income in its country of origin.[2] This is especially true of small countries with limited foreign exchange reserves. If the monetary authorities in such a country were to attempt to increase its money stock, they would first purchase securities so as to provide more bank reserves. The security purchase and money stock increase would put downward pressure on interest rates and cause capital to leave the country.[3] To prevent the exchange rate from falling below its fixed rate, the government of the expanding country must then meet the resulting new demand for foreign exchange with sales of

[1]This does not imply that price and interest rate levels cannot be changed by the actions of a large country which purchases a significant portion of world output, only that eventually the same prices or interest rates—at whatever level—will prevail throughout the world. No explicit distinction is made between stock and flow adjustments to price or yield changes. It is assumed that the stock adjustment is so large and persists for so long that in the intermediate term considered by this article it can be treated as a flow adjustment.

[2]The same type of analysis would hold for other monetary disturbances such as a change in people's desire to hold money.

Parts of this section follow the general outlines of the monetary theory of the balance of payments. See Harry G. Johnson, "The Monetary Approach to Balance of Payments Theory," *Journal of Financial and Quantitative Analysis,* March 1972, pp. 1555-72.

A summary of much of the research done on monetary and fiscal policy under fixed and flexible exchange rates can be found in Robert M. Stern, *The Balance of Payments* (Aldine, Chicago: 1973), especially Chapter 10.

[3]This ignores the possibility that the forward rate on the country's currency may adjust so as to allow it to maintain a different interest rate. The more exchange rates are really considered to be fixed and immutable, the more remote is this possibility.

its international reserves. This action, however, would reduce the reserves of the banking system and cause the money stock to contract. Hence, the initial increase in the money stock would tend to be offset by its susequent decline. The monetary authorities might try to maintain a higher money stock level by continuously injecting new reserves into the banking system. They would find, though, that their ability to sterilize the external deficit in this manner would be limited by their holdings of international reserves—for these reserves would continue to fall as long as the money stock and interest rates deviated from their initial levels.

If it took some time for capital flows to respond to lower interest rate levels, then the country might temporarily increase its demands for goods and services. In an open economy, at least part of that new demand would find an outlet in purchases from overseas. This would put additional downward pressure on the exchange rate, result in a further drop in international reserves, and speed the return of the money stock to its initial level. Monetary policy, therefore, changes the level of international reserves but has no more than a temporary impact on domestic money supply, prices, and incomes.[4]

If a large country increased its money supply, the results might be somewhat different. An increase in the money supply by a large country, i.e., one which purchases a significant amount of the world's output, would lead to an increase in demand for foreign goods and services and may raise the level of prices throughout the world. Similarly, an increase in that country's money stock would lower interest rates worldwide.[5] Consequently, the country would not be subject to the capital and product flows of the magnitude necessary to bring its income and interest rates back to their pre-expansion levels. Nonetheless, even a large country is likely to experience reserve outflows in response to a monetary expansion. The impact of the reserve outflow may be temporarily delayed if the country's foreign reserves are very large or if other countries hold the large country's currency as international reserves. In either event, the central bank could temporarily sterilize the reserve outflow and allow the money stock to remain higher for a considerable time period. In this interim period, the large country would then experience increased income and, if it is near full employment, increased prices. Eventually, the country would begin to run out of reserves and would be forced to reduce its money stock. But because of higher world prices and lower interest rates, reserve outflows would tend to cease when the money stock, income, and prices were above their previous levels. For the large reserve currency country, therefore, monetary policy can have a considerable shortrun impact on income and some smaller longrun effects, too.

When a large country acts to increase its money supply, smaller countries may be subject to some irresistible consequences of that action when exchange rates are fixed. The increase in demand by a large country would be felt by the rest of the

---

[4]For a country attempting to contract its money supply, the process would be a mirror image. A trade and capital account surplus would give rise to reserve inflows which would reexpand money. The central bank's ability to offset or sterilize this inflow would be limited by its holdings of domestic assets.

[5]If the money stock increase were continuous and inflationary, interest rates would eventually have to rise to incorporate revised inflationary expectations.

world as a rising demand for exports, which would cause rising pressures on prices and incomes worldwide. In addition, the reserve outflows of the large country would swell the reserves and money supplies in the rest of the world. Businesses and consumers would find that the initiating country's external deficits would provide them with the cash balances necessary to finance rising levels of expenditures. If a small country tries to resist these inflationary pressures by sterilizing the reserve inflows and keeping interest rates high, it would simply attract even more reserves. In brief, control over the money stock or inflation rate in the rest of the world could be greatly impaired. The inflation rate would be identical everywhere, tied to the monetary expansion of the large country.

These relationships were quite evident in the events of the mid-1960's through 1971. During that time, the United States was the dominant reserve currency country and, consequently, was in a position to incur large external deficits. In the late 1960's, many European countries complained that excessive monetary expansion and inflation in the United States were causing, through capital outflows and trade deficits, monetary expansion and demand pressures in the rest of the world. Foreign countries also found that their attempts to dampen internal demand to resist inflationary pressures only elicited larger reserve inflows. One response to this problem was the proliferation of controls on capital movements into European countries. These attempts to gain policy maneuverability by decreasing interdependence proved only temporarily successful, however, because the means of avoiding controls grew as quickly as the controls themselves.

The problem became more acute in 1970 and 1971 as the Europeans attempted to tighten their monetary policy while U.S. monetary policy was loosened in response to the U.S. recession. The Eurodollar market became a turntable on which dollar outflows from the United States were borrowed by European companies and converted into their own currencies for domestic use. Thus, integrated capital markets and fixed exchange rates meant that the European countries had largely lost control of internal monetary conditions and the ability to use monetary policy to achieve domestic income and inflation targets.

The United States, despite its large size and the special status of the dollar, found that it too was vulnerable to foreign capital flows that weakened monetary policy. In 1969, the Federal Reserve was trying to dampen inflation in the United States by reducing credit granted to American borrowers. The high interest rates and slow monetary growth in the United States, however, attracted capital from abroad, especially through the mechanism of U.S. bank borrowing in the Eurodollar market. For a time, therefore, U.S. banks were able to lessen the effects of the restrictive Federal Reserve policy by borrowing abroad and relending in the United States.

Flexible Rates

With flexible exchange rates, just as under fixed rates, a small country that increased its money stock would have a tendency toward lower interest rates and would incur capital outflows. Also, an increase in its money stock would cause its residents to demand more of all goods, including imports. Under fixed exchange rates, as described earlier, the deficit in trade and capital accounts would give rise to a reserve outflow that would tend to reverse the money supply increase. With flexible rates, however, the monetary authorities would not purchase or sell international reserves to keep the exchange rate within a prescribed fixed range. Consequently, the deficit would not lead to an offsetting reduction in bank reserves and the money stock. Rather, the country's increased demand for foreign currency would cause its own currency to depreciate, or decline, in price. As its currency depreciates, the country's exports become less expensive to foreigners, and imports cost its own residents more. As a result, both residents and foreigners demand more of the economy's output and nominal income rises. This is what the monetary authorities intended when they increased the money stock. Therefore, even though the traditional channels of monetary influence through interest rates would be eliminated by integrated capital markets, monetary policy can be quite effective by affecting import and export demand through changes in the exchange rate.

When exchange rates are flexible, monetary policy works in large countries in the same way it does in small countries. An increase in the money stock of the large country will result through trade and capital flows in the depreciation of its currency. This depreciation will stimulate production through its effects on internal demand. In the case of the large country, however, the capital outflow may be large enough to lower interest rates worldwide.

By allowing its exchange rate to fluctuate, a small country need not accept the effects of a monetary expansion transmitted from the larger country. The depreciation of the large country's currency and coincident appreciation of the small country's currency will prevent additional domestic demand in the large country from being translated into new demands for the small country's exports. Domestic producers in the large country will feel the entire impact of the monetary expansion. As a result, the large country may find that money stock increases produce greater inflation under flexible than fixed rates. For the small country, the exchange rate might appreciate so much that its income was reduced.[6] Under flexible exchange rates, however, the small country can increase its money stock to offset the effects of the excessive appreciation and retain control over its income level.

Expenditure Disturbance

Fixed Rates

An expenditure disturbance is a change in spending plans which is independent of a change in the money stock. One example of an expenditure disturbance would be a

---

[6]Appreciation beyond the level necessary to protect small country income from large country expansion may be made necessary by the new lower world interest rate which increases the demand for money at every income level. Sales of financial assets by small country residents to obtain higher money balances put upward pressure on interest rates which attracts capital and drives up the exchange rate thus reducing income.

change in fiscal policy—the taxing and spending decisions of government. Under fixed exchange rates, an increase in expenditures in a small country can be a very effective means of increasing income. As with an increase in the money supply, part of the increase in spending will be deflected to foreign commodities and result in higher imports. This will create a balance of payments deficit that will drain reserves, reduce the money stock, and counteract the expansive fiscal policy. But the increased spending will also put pressure on domestic credit markets and tend to raise interest rates above the worldwide level. This will promote an inward flow of foreign capital and a gain in international reserves. The latter reserve inflow will more than offset any tendency for reserves to decline due to the trade account deficit. That is because, if imports are a reasonably stable proportion of income, the trade deficit would be limited by the size of the rise in income. On the other hand, when capital markets are fully integrated, the tendency toward higher interest rates will call forth a flood of incoming capital. The net increase in international reserves—unless neutralized by the central bank through sales of domestic assets—will enable the money stock to increase, thereby validating and reinforcing the expansive thrust of fiscal policy. In brief, while monetary policy by itself is ineffective under fixed rates, an increase in the money stock which accompanies an expenditure shift can be quite powerful since it will not be subsequently offset by a reserve outflow.[7]

If a large country adopted an expansionary fiscal policy under fixed exchange rates, the same processes would work in the same directions as they do for a small country but the end result may differ. That is because the increased demand and subsequent net reserve inflow may have important effects on the rest of the world which, in turn, would feed back into the large country. As demand by large country residents for the products of other countries grows, total demand in other countries would also tend to expand. This would raise price and interest rate levels everywhere, but the impact would be greatest in the initiating country. Capital would flow into the large countries until its interest rates were reduced to the world level—now somewhat higher than they were initially. Because of the raised world interest rate level, the money stock and income increase in the large country would not be as great as it would have been had the country left the rest of the world unaffected.

The country facing an expenditure shift in a large country, especially an important trading partner, may experience important effects on its own economy. As pointed out earlier, interest rates in the smaller country would definitely be higher. Also, income in the smaller country would have two opposing forces working on it: the expansionary impact of demand from the country initiating the expenditure increase and the contractionary effects of a lower money supply due to a reserve outflow to

---

[7]This scenario and much of the ensuing discussion of expenditure disturbances assume that the government demands domestic, rather than foreign, output and that the existence of unemployed resources means that increases in domestic output can take place at a constant price level. See Robert Mundell, "Capital Mobility and Stabilization Policy under Fixed and Flexible Exchange Rates," reprinted as Chapter 18 of Robert Mundell, *International Economics* (New York: The Macmillan Company, 1968), p. 251. If there were any tendency for government purchases to raise prices, perhaps because the economy was near full employment, then imports would increase and the effect on income of the increase in government spending would be nullified by a larger trade deficit.

the larger country. Whether income in the smaller country will be higher or lower after the first expenditure change depends on the relative strength of these two forces.

Flexible Rates

Far different results would be obtained if a small country tried an expansionary fiscal policy under flexible exchange rates. The tendency toward balance of payments surplus under fixed rates would be translated into an appreciating exchange rate. This would dampen internal demand by reducing exports and increasing imports. Since no reserves can be gained or lost when governments do not intervene in the exchange market, the increased expenditures cannot be validated by increases in the money stock. The currency would continue to appreciate as long as expenditure demands were in excess of their old level. The process would stop when the currency appreciation had decreased demand by exactly the amount it had increased originally. When there are fluctuating exchange rates and integrated capital markets, fiscal policy tends to have no effect.

A large country would find its fiscal policy effectiveness reduced under flexible rates, but not eliminated. The initial increase in income in the large country increases demand in the rest of the world. Under flexible rates, however, the capital inflow would tend to appreciate the large country's currency. While the appreciation reduces demand on the large country's resources, it adds to the upward pressures on demand in the rest of the world by increasing their exports and decreasing their imports. Some of this foreign demand will return again to the large country as demand for its exports. If the countries are close to full employment, worldwide inflation will result. If unused capacity exists, real incomes will rise.

From the viewpoint of the small country facing a fiscal expansion in a large country, flexible rates would greatly increase its vulnerability to an unwanted rise in nominal income. Under fixed rates, the increase in demand in the small country was offset by a declining money supply. No such cushion exists with flexible rates. The large country's disturbance would have a considerable impact on the rest of the world.

This kind of business cycle transmission may have been operating at the end of 1974 and into 1975. The U.S. economy was declining more rapidly than that of most of the rest of the world. The decline was marked in part by slow monetary growth but even more importantly by downward expenditure adjustments in housing and durable goods purchases. The fall in demand resulted in lower interest rates and an outflow of capital from the United States. With exchange rates under a system of managed floating, the dollar began to depreciate against the currencies of most other industrialized countries. This development was beneficial to the United States as it tended to deflect foreign and domestic demand to U.S. products and so cushioned the fall in U.S. income. In other countries, the increased imports and decreased exports resulting from dollar depreciation tended to reduce income and output at a time when their economies were already weak. Consequently, they moved to support the dollar and control the appreciation of their own currencies.

Supply Disturbance

A supply disturbance is a sizable and unanticipated reduction in the supply, or an increase in the price, of an important international commodity. With the growth of interdependence, the potential for serious disturbances of this type has increased sharply. Important examples of supply disturbances have occurred recently in both food and petroleum products. Since food demand declines very little as its price rises, very large price increases were necessary to ration the shortfalls in supply. In the case of petroleum, the supply reductions occurred from a deliberate decision by many petroleum producing countries to band together to increase their profits. As with food, petroleum demand is not very responsive to price changes over the short run, so the producers found they could temporarily raise the price of oil substantially with only minor cutbacks in production.

From the viewpoint of the importing country, the effects of a supply disturbance in a commodity facing inelastic demands are many faceted and mostly bad. Given the short-run unresponsiveness of demand, the importing country will spend relatively more of its income on imports and domestic demand for internally produced goods will fall. As domestic demand falls, so will domestic incomes, unless the fall in demand is cushioned by the exporter spending its new export receipts in the importing country. This effect on income is analogous to a decline in planned expenditures or a tighter fiscal policy. There is also a monetary effect analogous to a reduction in the money supply. The monetary effect arises because the higher import prices cause an increase in the country's average price level.[8] At higher prices, there will be an increase in the demand for money balances to purchase the same level of real output. People desiring to increase their money balances will, in turn, tend to sell other financial assets and drive up interest rates. This increase in the demand for money caused by higher prices will have the same impact on the economy as a reduction in the supply of money.

For the importing countries, the supply disturbance can be viewed as a reduction in expenditure occurring simultaneously with a fall in the money stock. Under fixed rates, if the recessionary tendencies of the expenditure shift dominate—perhaps because the country spends a high proportion of its income on the particular product—the fall in domestic income will cause interest rates to fall, capital to flow out, and an ensuing decline in the money stock that will further reduce income. If the monetary effects dominate, lower domestic income will be accompanied by higher interest rates, capital inflows, and an expanding money stock. In this case, the capital inflows and expanding money stock with fixed rates will ameliorate the fall in internal demand.

When exchange rates are flexible, countries that would have been made worse off under fixed rates are helped by exchange rate movements. If the expenditure shift dominates, the fall in income will cause interest rates to fall, capital to flow out, and

---

[8]It is assumed that the fall in domestic demand is unlikely to cause much, if any, decline in domestic prices in the short run.

the exchange rate to decline. The ensuing increased demand for exports and import substitutes will then cushion the fall in internal demand. In this case, the country is better off under floating rates. When the monetary effect dominates, however, the fall in income will be accompanied by higher interest rates, capital inflows, and an appreciating exchange rate that will serve to further reduce income. In this case, the country is worse off under floating rates.

Whatever the exchange rate regime, a country facing a supply reduction is likely to experience a reduced level of real income and output for some time, especially when domestic prices and wages adjust slowly to changing demand conditions. To a lesser extent, it is also true over a longer term. Eventually, the pressure of falling domestic demand will tend to reduce domestic prices relative to import prices. Also, the investment of any capital inflows will reduce interest rates and stimulate interest sensitive spending. As a result, internal demand will rise. Even after full employment is attained, however, the importing country will be worse off than it was before foreign prices increased in that it would take a higher proportion of its production to purchase the same level of imports.

The behavior of income and trade balances in the wake of the petroleum price increases of 1973 and 1974 combine elements of adjustment under both fixed and flexible exchange rates. Petroleum producers accept payment in dollars, which are rarely converted into their own currencies. Consequently, the petroleum deficit cannot be offset by changing exchange rates. The petroleum exporters have little choice but to save much of their new income by investing their surpluses in the importing countries. The industrialized world as a whole has a petroleum deficit matched by a capital reflow of "petrodollars." This deficit is fixed in terms of dollars and is based on the price and quantity of oil purchased.

Exchange rates among oil-consuming nations do fluctuate and will rise or fall in part depending on a country's ability to attract capital to offset its trade account deficits. Countries with small capital inflows will find their currencies depreciating. Their oil imports will be offset by a rise in exports to other countries, and their short-run income adjustment may be relatively mild. Countries which attract a large inflow of petrodollars will have appreciating currencies. As a result, their trade deficits will tend to swell beyond that which can be attributed to oil imports. Floating rates in this hybrid system therefore serve to allocate the given petroleum deficit among consuming nations.

Conclusion

The integration of world markets for goods and credit has led to a heightened degree of economic interdependence among nations. Sensitive trade and capital flows govern the impact of economic events in their country of origin and facilitate their transmission to other countries of the world. The exact way in which countries interact in response to economic events depends, in part, on the exchange rate system under which they operate. A corollary notion is that countries might wish to choose their policy of exchange market intervention with an eye to the type of economic disturbances they expect to be most important at home and abroad.

If a country intended to rely on monetary policy to achieve its income, employment, and price targets, or felt it was subject to unwanted monetary influences from the actions of large and important trading partners, then it should choose to allow its exchange rate to fluctuate. Under flexible exchange rates, its own monetary policy gains effectiveness by inducing changes in exchange rates that push foreign and domestic demands on its resources in the desired direction. The country avoids importing monetary inflation or deflation by not letting its international reserves be changed and by allowing the exchange rate to neutralize potential changes in demand coming from abroad.

On the other hand, a country which felt it wanted to run an effective fiscal policy or felt most threatened by shifts in expenditure flows abroad might opt for a fixed exchange rate system. Fiscal policy in an integrated world is most effective under fixed rates because it will be accompanied by capital flows which validate and reinforce the initial fiscal policy impulse. When there are expenditure shifts in other countries, fixed rates will tend to minimize their effects at home because the capital and trade accounts will move in opposite directions.

No exchange rate system will protect a country against the effects of a sudden cutback in the supply of an important import. Countries that would tend to attract a lot of capital under these circumstances would find that fixed exchange rates will minimize the effect on income. Countries in which the trade deficit would dominate a capital inflow should choose fluctuating exchange rates.

In the 1970's there has been a pronounced movement toward increased flexibility in exchange rates. This is implicitly a concession that, at least over the long run, monetary disturbances and monetary policy dominate the determination of income. Within a shorter period, however, there may be some justification for exchange market intervention, if it is believed that expenditure shifts are pulling exchange rates away from levels consistent with long-run monetary equilibrium. Of course, no country can unilaterally decide its own exchange rate regime. The nature of the transactions in which one currency is traded for another requires at least implicit agreement by those on the other side of the trades. Countries must agree among themselves on the importance of various types of policies and disturbances and formulate an exchange rate system to maximize national decision-making-power, while retaining the fruits of an interdependent world economy.

30

A Monetary View of the Balance of Payments

Donald S. Kemp

In surveying the body of research dealing with the balance of payments, two major shortcomings are immediately apparent.[1] First, there are no widely accepted theories of the balance of payments which simultaneously incorporate both the current and capital account. The great majority of models used in payments theory consider either the capital account or the current account separately. Second, there have been very few attempts to include even the fundamentals of portfolio choice theory in balance-of-payments models. This is particularly surprising in view of the essentially monetary nature of payments theory.

This article presents an approach to payments theory which addresses both of these shortcomings. Since this essentially involves an extension of the rudiments of monetary theory to the area of the balance of payments, it is henceforth referred to as a monetary view of the balance of payments (MBOP).[2]

Reprinted from the Federal Reserve Bank of St. Louis, *Review* (April, 1975), pp. 14-22, by permission of the publisher and the author.

[1]For a lucid analysis of the current state of payments theory, see Anne O. Krueger, "Balance-of-Payments Theory," *The Journal of Economic Literature* (March 1969), pp. 1-26.

[2]The theoretical foundation of this approach to payments theory may be found in Robert A. Mundell, *Monetary Theory: Inflation, Interest, and Growth in the World Economy* (Pacific Palisades, California: Goodyear, 1971). The formal model, presented later in this article, draws extensively on work done at the University of Chicago Workshop in International Economics and the analysis presented in Harry G. Johnson, "The Monetary Approach to Balance-of-Payments Theory," *Further Essays in Monetary Economics* (Cambridge: Harvard University Press, 1973), pp. 229-49. This article is essentially a synthesis and extension of these previous works.

An Overview of the Theory

The MBOP may be summarized by the proposition that the transactions recorded in balance-of-payments (BOP) statistics reflect aggregate portfolio decisions by both foreign and domestic economic units. Under a system of fixed exchange rates, such as the gold standard or the type of arrangment set up in 1944 at Bretton Woods, overall net surpluses (deficits) in the trade and capital accounts are viewed as flows associated with either an excess demand for money on the part of domestic (foreign) economic units or an excess supply of money in foreign economies (the domestic economy). Consequently, in analyzing the rate of change of international reserves (the money account[3]) the monetary approach focuses on the determinants of the excess demand for or supply of money. According to this view, surpluses (deficits) in the money account measure the rate at which money balances are being accumulated (reduced) domestically. That is, a BOP flow is one of the mechanisms by which actual money balances are adjusted to their desired levels.

Suppose, for example, there is an autonomous increase in the money supply of country j, which leads to an increase in the demand for goods, services, and securities in that country. Under a system of fixed exchange rates, any such increase in domestic demand will result in a tendency for prices of domestic real and financial assets in country j to rise, in the short run, relative to those in foreign markets. Economic units in country j will react by decreasing their demands for domestic real and financial assets in favor of foreign assets while domestic suppliers of these assets will seek to sell more at home and less abroad. At the same time, foreign economic units will decrease their demands for the assets of country j, and foreign suppliers will attempt to sell more of their own assets in country j. All of these factors work in favor of an increase in imports and a decrease in exports in country j. The resultant deterioration of the BOP reflects the exchange of money balances for real and financial assets by economic units of country j. The foreign recipients of these money balances will convert them into their own currencies at their respective central banks. These foreign central banks will then present the balances to the central bank in country j in return for international reserves. Since international reserves are one of the components of a country's monetary base,[4] the effect of this transaction will be a decrease in the money supply of country j toward its level prior to the autonomous increase and an increase in the money supplies of its surplus trading partners.

Under a system of freely floating exchange rates, the required adjustment of mon-

---

[3]The overall net balance in the trade and capital accounts will henceforth be referred to as the money account. This reflects the fact that all transactions recorded below the line in this account have a direct impact on a nation's money supply. Under a pure gold standard, changes in official gold holdings are the only item below the line in this account. Under a Bretton Woods type system changes in official holdings of gold, SDRs, and foreign exchange and changes in the reserve position at the IMF are all included below the line in the money account.

[4]For a detailed discussion and analysis of the concept of the monetary base, see Leonall C. Andersen and Jerry L. Jordan, "The Monetary Base—Explanation and Analytical Use," this *Review* (August 1968), pp. 7-11.

ey balances is accomplished through movements in the exchange rate. Under such a system the BOP (on a money account basis) equals zero by definition, and there are no intercountry movements of international reserves. As such, required adjustments in money balances cannot be accommodated through balance-of-payments flows. In this case the adjustment of actual money balances to their desired levels is accomplished by changes in domestic prices and exchange rates (which change concomitantly with and accommodate the required movement in domestic price levels).

The above approach is in sharp contrast with what amounts to the current conventional wisdom of payments theory; namely, the elasticities and absorption approaches. Implicit in both of these approaches is the assumption that either there are no monetary consequences associated with the BOP or that, to the extent the potential for such consequences exists, they can be and are absorbed (sterilized) by domestic monetary authorities.[5]

The MBOP regards all BOP deficits and surpluses and movements in floating exchange rates as phases in a stock adjustment which are the result of a disparity between the demand for and supply of money. This approach asserts that, under a system of fixed exchange rates, there are inflows (outflows) of international reserves associated with BOP surpluses (deficits) and that these flows cannot be sterilized in the long run. Furthermore, because of the impact of these reserve flows on a country's monetary base, they will result in variations in the supply of money relative to the demand for it and thus have an equilibrating impact on the level of money balances and the BOP. According to this view, the only way to obtain persistent deficits or surpluses is to construct a model in which the need for stock adjustments is being continuously recreated.

The only solutions to these reserve flows are processes which facilitate the return of actual money balances to their desired levels. This adjustment can be accomplished either automatically, through inflows or outflows of international reserves, or through appropriate actions by the domestic monetary authorities which change some other component of the monetary base by the same amount. Under a system of freely floating exchange rates the adjustment is also accomplished either automatically by changes in domestic price levels and the concomitant changes in the exchange rate or again by the appropriate actions on the part of the monetary authorities. The only other potentially successful policy actions available are those which, in the end, have the same effect on money balances as those just mentioned.

---

[5]The elasticity and absorption approaches are theories of the trade account alone, and they neglect the issue of capital flows. For a discussion of the essentials of the elasticities approach, see Joan Robinson, "The Foreign Exchanges," *Readings in the Theory of International Trade,* Committee of the American Economic Association (Philadelphia: The Blakiston Company, 1949), pp. 83-103. For a discussion of the absorption approach, see Sidney S. Alexander, "Effects of a Devaluation on a Trade Balance," *Readings in International Economics,* Committee of the American Economic Association (Homewood, Illinois: Richard D. Irwin, Inc., 1968), pp. 359-73. For a discussion of the differences between the monetarists' approach and both the elasticities and absorption approaches to payments theory, see Johnson, "The Monetary Approach to Balance-of-Payments Theory," pp. 229-49.

Some Fundamental Propositions

In order to facilitate the development of a model later in this article, there are some fundamental propositions associated with the MBOP that should be discussed.

(1) The MBOP maintains that the transactions recorded in the balance of payments are essentially a reflection of monetary phenomena. As such, it places emphasis on the direct influence of an excess demand for or supply of money on the BOP.

Implicit in this approach is the assumption that the demand for and supply of money are stable functions of a limited number of variables. The MBOP does not imply that changes in the money supply are the only factors which affect the BOP. It, nevertheless, does say that the primary channel by which changes in any real variable affect the BOP is through their effects on the demand for or supply of money.[6] Thus, any analysis of the impact of a policy or other change must begin with an analysis of how this change generates a divergence between actual and desired money balances or affects such a divergence that already exists.

(2) In the analysis presented in this article, the crucial BOP concept is that which captures all transactions reflecting the adjustment of actual money balances to their desired levels. That is, the only transactions considered below the line are those which have an influence on domestic and foreign monetary bases and thus on domestic and foreign money supplies.[7]

The analysis presented here does not attempt to provide a theory of the individual subaccounts; it merely lumps the individual components (goods, services, transfers, short- and long-term capital) into a single category—"items above the line." This approach recognizes that an excess supply of or demand for money may be cleared through the markets for either goods, services, or securities.[8] Furthermore, if the BOP is viewed within this framework, the pitfalls of placing emphasis on any particular subaccount are obvious. For example, the effects on aggregate economic activity of a deficit in the merchandise trade account could be neutralized by a surplus in one of the capital accounts. In this case, any negative aggregate demand effects resulting from an increase in imports of goods would be offset by an inflow of capital and thus an increase in investment demand. The two effects would offset each other and aggregate money balances would be unchanged.

---

[6]For an analysis of the BOP effects of changes in a real variable (a change in tariff) within a monetarist's framework, see Michael Mussa, "A Monetary Approach to Balance-of-Payments Analysis," *Journal of Money, Credit and Banking* (August 1974), pp. 333-51.

[7]For a review of balance-of-payments concepts and their meaning, see John Pippenger, "Balance-of-Payments Deficits: Measurement and Interpretation," this *Review* (November 1973), pp. 6-14. For a discussion of which trasactions to include below the line, see footnote 3 of this article.

[8]This is not to say the MBOP framework would not be useful in analyzing individual subaccounts. However, such analysis would require a rigorous specification of the channels of monetary influence. For a survey and analysis of the literature pertaining to these channels, see Roger W. Spencer, "Channels of Monetary Influence: A Survey," this *Review* (November 1974), pp. 8-26. For an example of how this framework could be applied to the analysis of the capital account alone, see Pentti J. K. Kouri and Michael G. Porter. "International Capital Flows and Portfolio Equilibrium," *Journal of Political Economy* (May/June 1974), pp. 443-67.

(3) The MBOP relies on the assumption of an efficient world market for goods, services, and securities.[9] Under a system of fixed exchange rates, the price of any good or service in one country relative to its price in any other country can change only in the short run. Likewise, the rate of return on any asset can differ from the rate of return on assets of comparable risk and maturity in any other country only in the short run. It follows that in the long run price levels and interest rates in all countries must move rigidly in line with one another. In fact, in a fixed exchange rate regime it is the attempts to arbitrage intercountry price and interest rate differentials that are the driving force leading to the reduction or accumulation of money balances and a concomitant temporary BOP deficit or surplus.

Under a system of freely floating exchange rates, price levels may move at different rates between countries. However, the impact of these differential rates of change on individual relative prices between countries is offset by opposite movements in exchange rates. The same arbitrage opportunities that lead to reserve flows under fixed rates lead to exchange rate adjustments that exactly compensate for differential price level changes between countries.

(4) The MBOP is a theory of an automatic adjustment process. According to this theory, any BOP disequilibrium or exchange rate movement reflects a disparity between actual and desired money balances and will automatically correct itself. While the adjustment process is different under different exchange rate regimes, the implication is that the process is automatic and that its effects cannot be neutralized in the long run. Any BOP imbalance or exchange rate change is a phase in the automatic adjustment process and attempts to counter these processes merely increase the forces which give rise to the adjustment ultimately required for a return to equilibrium.

(5) The MBOP is concerned primarily with the long run. The approach recognizes that short run analysis is often complicated by the fact that the postulated adjustment behavior is incomplete in the short run. For example, the adjustment of actual money balances to their desired levels does not occur instantaneously, but rather requires the passage of time. As another example, it is possible that the monetary authorities may attempt to neutralize the impact of international reserve flows on their respective money supplies in the short run.[10] However, the MBOP asserts that governments cannot follow such policies in the long run. This seems reasonable because, in the long run, success in neutralizing the effects of international reserve flows implies that the governments of some (surplus) countries are willing to trade investment and consumption goods for foreign currency balances. The accumulation

---

[9]While it is acknowledged that there are some goods that are not traded internationally, there are limits to relative price changes between these nontraded goods and other (traded) goods. The higher the elasticities of substitution between these two classes of goods in both production and consumption, the smaller the scope for relative price changes and the more direct the international price interdependence.

[10]For an analysis of West German attempts to neutralize the effects of reserve flows, see Manfred Willms, "Controlling Money in an Open Economy: The German Case," this *Review* (April 1971), pp. 10-27.

of these balances by surplus country governments represents a nonmarket induced transfer of wealth away from domestic to foreign consumers. For whatever reason, it is unrealistic to suppose that a government would pursue such policies in the long run.

(6) An implication of this theory is that, under a system of fixed exchange rates, domestic monetary policy does not control a country's money supply. Excessive monetary expansion (contraction), via expansion (contraction) of some controllable component of the monetary base, will result in an outflow (inflow) of international reserves (an uncontrollable component of the monetary base) and a tendency for the money supply to return to its former level.[11] The resulting BOP deficit (surplus) is only a reflection of these uncontrollable international reserve outflows (inflows). Through this process, the inflationary or deflationary impact of domestic monetary policy is mitigated with respect to the domestic economy and is imposed on the rest of the world via intercountry flows of international reserves. At the same time, however, the domestic economy is subject to the influence of inflationary or deflationary monetary actions taken in other countries.

Under a system of freely floating exchange rates, the domestic monetary authorities retain dominant control over the money supply, while the interaction of domestic and foreign monetary policies determines the exchange rate rather than the BOP (which is now zero by definition). In this case, a country neither imports nor exports international reserves. As a result, the domestic economy is subjected to the full consequences of inflationary or deflationary domestic monetary policies and is insulated from the effects of monetary actions taken in other countries.

(7) Another feature of the MBOP is that it provides a framework within which one is able to assess the differential impact of monetary disturbances which occur in a world in which there is at least one reserve currency country (RCC) as opposed to those occurring in a world with no RCC's. An RCC is a country whose currency is held by others as a form of international reserves. It is this special status afforded to the currency of the RCC which leads to a slightly altered adjustment process for the world and the RCC itself.

The Special Case of a Reserve Currency Country

Because international reserves and reserve currencies exist only under a system of fixed exchange rates, the following analysis applies only to that case. For all non-RCCs, expansionary (contractionary) monetary policies are offset by a BOP deficit (surplus) and the resulting contraction (expansion) of the international reserve component of the monetary base. However, for an RCC this need not be the case. An expansionary (contractionary) monetary policy in the RCC may have no effect on its

[11]While this is true for most countries, it is not necessarily the case for a reserve currency country. The special case of a reserve currency country will be discussed in the next section.

BOP as defined in this article. However, the RCC's trading partners will always experience a BOP surplus (deficit) and an inflow (outflow) of international reserves as a result of such RCC policies.[12] The reason for this is that the RCC currency is held by foreign central banks as a form of international reserves. While non-RCC monetary authorities are not willing to accumulate large balances denominated in other non-RCC currencies, they are willing to accumulate large balances denominated in the RCC currency. Because these balances are themselves a type of international reserves, non-RCC monetary authorities may not be inclined to present them to the RCC authorities in exchange for other international reserves.

However, to the extent that the RCC loses no international reserves as a result of an increase in other components of its monetary base, it does experience an accumulation of liquid liabilities to foreign official holders.[13] As these liabilities of the RCC are regarded as assets by foreign official holders, their accumulation represents an inflow of international reserves and a BOP surplus for RCC trading partners.

The how and why of all of this can be brought out by reference to the balance sheets of the world's monetary authorities. While the following analysis applies to the case of expansionary monetary policy in the RCC, it is equally applicable to the analysis of contractionary monetary policy. In addition, in order to simplify the analysis, we will assume that foreign central banks invest *all* of their RCC currency holdings in government securities issued by the RCC. However, we fully recognize that this need not be the case. Non-RCC central banks can and frequently do invest their RCC currency holdings in other assets or simply allow them to accumulate as deposits at the RCC central bank. Whatever the non-RCC authorities decide to do, however, all that is crucial for our analysis to hold is that they do not accumulate deposits at the RCC central bank.

Illustration 1 indicates what happens to the monetary bases of all countries as a result of an attempt by the RCC monetary authorities to increase the domestic money supply in the face of a fixed demand for money. Tier (A) illustrates that the initial impact of such an undertaking is to increase the monetary base of the RCC only. Tier (B) illustrates what happens to the respective monetary bases as a result of the forthcoming intercountry reserve flows. Non-RCCs accumulate international reserves (R) in the form of deposits denominated in the RCC currency held at the RCC central bank. As long as these R are held in this form, the RCC monetary base decreases towards its initial level and the non-RCC monetary bases increase, just as in the case of a world in which there are no RCCs.

Since the non-RCCs view these reserve currency balances as R, they are willing to accumulate them in the same manner that they accumulate other R. However, these R differ from others in one significant aspect—namely, they can be invested in government securities issued by the RCC. When non-RCCs choose to do this, the effects

---

[12]Recall that the BOP concept used in this article is the balance in the money account. That is, the only items recorded below the line are those that affect the domestic money supply.

[13]While the accumulations or reductions of the holdings of liabilities do not affect the RCC balance of payments as defined in this article, they do affect some RCC balance-of-payments concepts. For example, such transactions would affect the Official Settlements Balance in the United States.

Illustration 1

Tier	RCC Monetary Authority's Balance Sheet		Collective Balance Sheet for All Non-RCC Monetary Authorities	
(A)	R(O) D(+) − OL(O)	DR(+) C(O)	R(O) D(O) − OL(O)	DR(O) C(O)
(B)	R(O) D(O) − OL(+)	DR(−) C(O)	R(+) D(O) − OL(O)	DR(+) C(O)
(C)	R(O) D(O) − OL(−)	DR(+) C(O)	R(O) D(O) − OL(O)	DR(O) C(O)
(NET)	R(O) D(+) − OL(O)	DR(+) C(O)	R(+) D(O) − OL(O)	DR(+) C(O)

where

R = official holdings of international reserves

D = domestic credit; this consists of central bank holdings of securities, discounts and advances, and float.

− OL = other liabilities of the monetary authorities (including foreign deposits at Federal Reserve Banks). These items conventionally appear on the source side of the base as a negative item. They are subtracted from other items in calculating the source base.[1]

C = currency held by the public

DR = reserves of the domestic banking community

[1] See Albert E. Burger, *The Money Supply Process* (Belmont, California: Wadsworth Publishing Company, 1971), p. 38.

are as illustrated in tier (C). When non-RCC monetary authorities purchase RCC government securities, the OL entry in the RCC balance sheet is drawn down. This has the effect of increasing the monetary base of the RCC without causing a decrease in the monetary bases of the non-RCCs. The net effect of all of this is that the monetary bases of all countries have increased (as shown in the NET tier).

In view of the above analysis, a world in which there exists at least one RCC differs significantly from a world in which there are no RCCs. In a world with RCCs, BOP deficits and surpluses may by themselves decrease and increase the level of R in the world and in individual countries. In a world with no RCCs, BOP deficits and surpluses result in a redistribution of an existing stock of R among countries, but produce no change in the overall level. As a result, in a world with RCCs, the world and each individual non-RCC will ordinarily experience much more difficulty in controlling its money supply. Thus, the existence of RCCs compounds the problems of money stock control which are already inherent in any system of fixed exchange rates.

In addition, this analysis implies that the inflationary or deflationary impact of RCC monetary policy is spread over the entire world. Unlike the case of a non-RCC, however, there may be no mitigation of the impact on the domestic economy since the RCC may neither gain nor lose reserves. As a result, prices in the RCC could change by the same amount as they would under a system of freely floating exchange rates. What's worse, however, is that the rest of the world will gain or lose international reserves and bear the same price level impact as the RCC. Thus, the potential for large BOP surpluses and deficits and for worldwide inflations and deflations are greater under a fixed exchange rate system with RCCs than under any other system considered in this article.

A Monetary Model of the Balance of Payments

Now that the essential features of the MBOP have been spelled out, let us turn to the derivation of a model in which these features are expressed by a set of equations.[14] First, the model is derived for a non-RCC under a system of fixed exchange rates. Second, the same model is applied to the case of an RCC under fixed exchange rates. Finally, the model is applied to the case of freely floating exchange rates.

The common elements in each of these models are stable money demand and money supply functions.[15] The money supply function for each country may be stated as

$$MS_j = a_j [R_j + D_j] \qquad (1)$$

where

MS_j = money supply in country j
a_j = money multiplier in country j
R_j = official holdings of international reserves in country j; hereafter referred to as the international component of the monetary base.
D_j = all other components of the monetary base in country j; hereafter referred to as the domestically controlled component of the monetary base.
$D_j + R_j = MB_j$ = monetary base in country j

[14]In order to simplify the presentation, many of the steps in the derivation of the model have been bypassed in the text. For the interested reader, a more thorough presentation of the model is provided in an appendix, which is available from this Bank upon request.

[15]For an analysis of the development of the money supply function employed in this article, see Jerry L. Jordan, "Elements of Money Stock Determination," this *Review* (October 1969), pp. 10-19.

The demand for money in each country is assumed to be a function of real income, the nominal rate of interest, and prices.

$$MD_j = f_j[y_j, r, P] \tag{2}$$

where

MD_j = demand for money in country j
P = price index in the world and thus in country j[16]
y_j = real income in country j
r = nominal rate of interest in the world and thus in country j.

In accordance with the general monetarist framework of the model, country j is in equilibrium if and only if the growth of the supply of money equals the growth of the demand for money. We are able to specify the conditions necessary for fulfilling this requirement by expressing equations (1) and (2) in terms of rates of change and then equating the resulting expressions. This procedure allows us to derive an expression for the rate of growth of international reserves in country j.[17]

$$\frac{R_j}{MB_j} g_{R_j} = g_p + \alpha_j g_{y_j} + \beta_j g_r - \frac{D_j}{MB_j} g_{D_j} \tag{3}$$

where

α_j = income elasticity of demand for money in country j
β_j = interest rate elasticity of demand for money in country j.

We are able to derive an expression for the growth rate of world prices $[g_p]$ by summing the expressions for the growth rates of the demand for and supply of money over all countries and equating the resultant expressions.

$$g_p = \sum_{i=1}^{N} w_i g_{MS_i} - \sum_{i=1}^{N} w_i [\alpha_i g_{y_i} + \beta_i g_r] \tag{4}$$

where

$w_i = \dfrac{MS_i}{\displaystyle\sum_{i=1}^{N} MS_i}$ = weights calculated on the basis of money supplies converted by exchange rates to equivalent units of currency j.

---

[16]This reflects the assumption that under a system of fixed exchange rates, a country's price level and interest rates move in line with the world price level and interest rates. However, in the case of freely floating exchange rates the assumption regarding the price level is no longer valid. As such, the money demand function must be specified somewhat differently in that case.

[17]Henceforth in this article $g_x = d\ln x/dt$. That is, g_x is the expression for the continuous rate of growth of variable x.

Fixed Exchange Rates in A World with No RCCs

Recall that by definition $g_{Rj} = (1/R_j)(dR_j/dt)$. Under a system of fixed exchange rates in a world in which there are no reserve currency countries, dR_j/dt is the expression for the balance of payments in the money account. It represents the rate at which country j is either gaining or losing international reserves during a given time period (t). With this in mind, and upon making some simplifying assumptions regarding the interest and income elasticities of demand for money, we are able to substitute expression (4) into expression (3) and get an expression for the balance of payments in country j.[18]

$$\frac{1}{MB_j} BOP_j = \left[\sum_{i=1}^{N} w_i g_{MS_i} - \frac{D_j}{MB_j} g_{D_j} \right] + \left[g_{yj} - \sum_{i=1}^{N} w_i g_{yi} \right] \tag{5}$$

Expression (5) is essentially an embodiment of the features of the price specie flow mechanism, which operates under a system of fixed exchange rates in a world in which there are no reserve currency countries.[19] That is, expression (5) states that the BOP is a function of:

1. the rate of growth of real income in country j relative to the average rate of growth of real income for all countries, and

2. the rate of growth of the domestically controlled component of the monetary base in country j relative to an average rate of money growth for the whole world.

Fixed Exchange Rates in a World with at Least One RCC

In a world in which there is at least one RCC, expression (5) is still an appropriate representation of the forces giving rise to BOP flows in non-RCCs. However, for an RCC there may be no international reserve flows associated with the BOP accounts; in which case $g_{Rj} = 0$. In the case of an RCC, excessive expansion (contraction) of

---

[18]We have assumed that $\alpha_i = 1$ for all i and that $(\beta_j = \sum_{i=1}^{N} w_i \beta_i)$.
Neither of these assumptions are crucial to the analysis at hand. They are invoked here mainly to simplify the presentation. The assumption that $\alpha_i = 1$ is interpreted as assuming that the income elasticity of demand for money is unity in all countries. Assuming that $(\sum_{i=1}^{N} w_i \beta_i = \beta_j)$ means that the interest elasticity of demand for money in country j is equal to a weighted average of the interest elasticities of demand for money in all countries. A more restrictive implication of this assumption would be that the interest elasticities are equal in all countries.

[19]The price specie flow mechanism is an attempt to explain international gold flows under the gold standard. It is associated primarily with the work of David Hume in the eighteenth century. However, in our case the BOP includes more than just gold flows. It includes flows of all international reserves—gold, SDRs, foreign exchange, and reserve positions at the IMF.

the domestically controlled component of the monetary base need not lead to an offsetting contraction (expansion) of the international reserve component. At the same time, however, excessive expansion (contraction) of the domestically controlled component of the monetary base in the RCC will lead to an accumulation (reduction) of international reserves in all other countries. As mentioned previously, we will assume that these international reserves will be held in the form of securities issued by the RCC government to non-RCC official holders. For the RCC, it is the net accumulation or reduction of such liabilities that is determined by monetary actions in our model. This process can be captured in our model by setting $g_{RRCC} = 0$ (where the RCC is the jth country) and replacing the term $\sum_{i=1}^{N} w_i g_{MSi}$ in expression (5) with a more detailed formulation of the factors contributing to the growth of the money supply in all countries.

$$\frac{1}{MB_w} BOL_{RCC} = \left[\sum_{i=1}^{N} w_i \frac{D_i}{MB_i} g_{Di} - \frac{D_{RCC}}{MB_{RCC}} g_{DRCC} \right] + \left[g_{yRCC} - \sum_{i=1}^{N} w_i g_{yi} \right] \quad (6)$$

where

MB_w = the sum of the monetary bases of all countries in the world.
BOL_{RCC} = the net accumulation of claims against the RCC by foreign official institutions during time period (t).[20]

This expression states that the change in the level of the liabilities of the RCC to foreign official holders that results from domestic monetary policy in the RCC is determined by the following:

1. the rate of growth of the domestically controlled component of the monetary base in the RCC relative to a weighted average of its rate of growth in all countries.
2. the rate of growth of real income in the RCC relative to a weighted average of the rates of growth of real income in all countries.

Freely Floating Exchange Rates

For the case of freely floating exchange rates, two modifications of the model are necessary. First, the model must be adapted to reflect the fact that there are no international reserve flows, so that the growth rate of a country's money supply is determined solely by domestic monetary policy [g_{Dj}]. Second, the money demand

[20]For the United States this BOP concept closely resembles the balance on liabilities to foreign official holders. However, this account is distinctly different from the BOP concept utilized in (5). Expression (5) explains the balance in the money account, whereas the BOP concept used in expression (6) has no relation to the money supply.

function must be modified to reflect the fact that the rate of price level change in one country may differ from the rate prevailing in the rest of the world.

Upon incorporating both of these modifications into the model, we are able to derive an expression for the determination of movements in the exchange rate.

$$g_{E_j} = [g_{MS_{ROW}} - g_{MS_j}] + [g_{y_j} - g_{y_{ROW}}] \tag{7}$$

where

$$E_j = \frac{P_{ROW}}{P_j} = \text{the price of currency } j \text{ in terms of foreign currencies}$$

$$P_{ROW} = \sum_{i=1}^{N-1} h_i P_i = \text{the price level in the rest of the world; that is, a weighted average of the price levels in all other countries.}$$

$$h_i = \frac{y_i}{\sum\limits_{i=1}^{N-1} y_i} = \text{weights calculated on the basis of real GNP}$$

$$P_j = \text{price level in country } j$$

This expression states that the exchange value of currency j in terms of foreign currencies is determined by the rate of growth of the money supply and real income in country j relative to the rate of growth of the money supply and real income, respectively, in the rest of the world. As such, it implies that currency depreciations are the result of excessive monetary growth. It, therefore, supports the proposition that inflation causes depreciation of the domestic currency rather than vice versa.

Summary and Conclusions

The MBOP may be summarized by the proposition that the transactions recorded in balance-of-payments statistics reflect aggregate portfolio decisions by both foreign and domestic economic units. The framework presented in this article suggests some important policy considerations that cannot be addressed within the framework which characterizes most of the currently accepted body of payments theory.

The analysis presented here casts the balance of payments in the role of an automatic adjustment mechanism. Balance-of-payments deficits and surpluses, or movements in freely floating exchange rates, are viewed as being simultaneously both the result of a divergence between actual and desired money balances and a mechanism by which such a divergence is corrected. As such, persistent balance-of-payments deficits (surpluses) or depreciation (appreciations) of the foreign exchange value of a currency reflect a continual re-creation of a situation in which excessive monetary expansion in the country in question is greater (less) than the worldwide average. Furthermore, the only solution to such international disturbances are policies which facilitate the equalization of actual and desired money balances.

The futility of tariff and nontariff barriers to trade which attempt to alter balance-of-payments flows or exchange rate movements becomes readily apparent when one views them within the framework presented above. Suppose, for example, that an import tariff is imposed with the aim of reducing a balance-of-payments deficit in the money account. According to the MBOP, international reserve flows will assure that the balance-of-payments deficit disappears in the long run whether the tariff is imposed or not. That is, even if the tariff were not imposed, the excess money balances, and therefore the deficit, would disappear as a result of the outflow of international reserves. However, if the tariff is imposed, relative prices will be artificially altered from the levels consistent with the most efficient allocation of resources and maximum gains from trade. Furthermore, the situation is no better if the tariff is imposed in retaliation against restrictive trade practices on the part of other nations. In this case, all that the tariff accomplishes is to further distort relative prices and further reduce the welfare of all nations.

Another advantage of the MBOP is that it enables one to evaluate clearly the relative desirability of different exchange rate regimes in terms of their promotion of autonomy of domestic monetary policy and domestic as well as worldwide price stability. Under a system of freely floating exchange rates, a country retains dominant control over its money growth, incurs the full consequences of its domestic monetary policy, and is not subject to the effects of inflationary or deflationary monetary policies undertaken in other countries. Under a system of fixed exchange rates in a world in which there are no reserve currency countries, a country loses control of its rate of money growth, has the domestic impact of its monetary policy mitigated, and is subject to the effects of monetary policies pursued by other countries. Under a system of fixed exchange rates in a world in which there is at least one reserve currency country, we have the potential for the worst of both of the above systems. While the impact of expansionary (contractionary) monetary policies in the reserve currency country is imposed on the rest of the world, there may be no mitigation of their domestic impact. As a result, the entire world is prone toward large changes in its money supply which are initiated by actions taken in the reserve currency country. This conclusion appears to be consistent with the inflationary experiences of the Western world which began in the late 1960s.

Finally, if the balance of payments is viewed within the MBOP framework, the pitfalls of placing emphasis on any particular BOP subaccount are obvious. A deficit (surplus) in any one account need not have any effect on domestic aggregate economic activity if its impact on money balances is offset by a surplus (deficit) in another account.

This point is especially significant in view of the large merchandise trade deficits that many oil-consuming countries have been experiencing. The analysis presented in this article indicates that the impact of these deficits on money balances, and therefore on aggregate economic activity in the deficit countries, will be substantially reduced as a result of large inflows of capital from OPEC members. Of course, this does not mean that oil-consuming countries are no worse off now than they were prior to the fourfold increase in oil prices. The MBOP merely states that the impact on GNP will be mitigated through subsequent inflows of capital. The distribution of a given GNP between the residents of oil-consuming and oil-producing countries, however, is altered in favor of the oil producers.

31

The Monetary Approach to Balance-of-Payments Theory

Harry G. Johnson

My purpose in this paper is to outline a new approach to the theory of the balance of payments and of balance-of-payments adjustment (including devaluation and revaluation) that has been emerging in recent years from several sources. Concretely, this new approach is found in the change in policy orientation adopted by the British government under pressure from the International Monetary Fund after the devaluation of 1967 failed to produce the expected improvement in the British balance of payments. The theoretical basis for the new orientation can be traced back to the work of the Dutch economist J. J. Koopmans. The new approach is also evident in the theoretical work of my colleagues at the University of Chicago and R. A. Mundell and his students, although it is only fair to note that economists elsewhere have been working along similar lines. The essence of this new approach is to put at the forefront of analysis the monetary rather than the relative price aspects of international adjustment.

To put the new approach in perspective, it is helpful to go back to the origins of balance-of-payments theory in the work of David Hume and specifically his contribution of the analysis of the price-specie-flow mechanism. Hume was concerned about refuting the concentration of the mercantilists on the objective of accumulating precious metals within the country and their consequent recommendation of

Reprinted from the *Journal of Financial and Quantitative Analysis*, 7, 2 (March, 1972), pp. 1555–1564, by permission of the publisher and the author.

policies designed to bring about a surplus on the balance of payments. His analysis, couched in terms relevent to the emerging new approach to balance-of-payments theory, showed that the amount of money in a country would be adjusted automatically to the demand for it (through surpluses or deficits in the balance of payments) induced by the effects on relative national money price levels of excess supplies of or excess demands for money. Hence, the mercantilist desire to accumulate "treasure" was in conflict with the basic mechanism of international monetary adjustment and could only be *ephemerally* successful.

Three points are worth noting about the price-specie-flow mechanism. First, in contemporary terminology, it assumes (in line with the stylized facts of that time) that all money is "outside" money (precious metals). That is, there is no commercial or central banking system capable of creating money not backed by international reserves with domestic money and international reserves being the same. Second, the mechanism of adjustment focuses on international transactions in goods, as distinguished from securities; this has remained dominant in balance-of-payments theory. Third, in the detailed analysis of the mechanism there is a rather awkward compromise between the assumption of a closed and an open economy in which it is assumed that domestic prices can vary from purchasing-power-parity under the influence of imbalances between money demand and money supply, but such variations give rise to changes in trade flows which alter the balance of payments and hence the domestic stock of money in the longer run. As we shall see, the new approach to balance-of-payments theory, while basically Humean in spirit, places the emphasis not on relative price changes but on the direct influence of excess demand for or supply of money on the balance between income and expenditure, or more generally between total acquisition and disposal of funds whether through production and consumption or through borrowing and lending, and therefore on the overall balance of payments.

Hume's analysis was in terms of an automatic mechanism of international adjustment motivated by money flows and consequential changes in national money price levels. The subsequent elaboration of the theory, up to and partly through the 1930s, retained the general notion of automaticity while adding in the complications required by the existence of credit money provided by commercial banks and the existence of central banking based on partial international reserve holdings, and the complications required by the possible attraction of international short-term capital movements through international interest-rate differentials. In addition, Cassel contributed the purchasing-power-parity theory of the equilibrium determination of the values of floating exchange rates.

In the 1930's, under the stimulus, on the one hand, of the collapse of the international regime of fixed exchange rates and the emergence of mass unemployment as a major economic problem and, on the other hand, of the Keynesian revolution—which altered the basic assumptions of theory from wage and price flexibility with full employment to wage rigidity with normal mass unemployment—a new approach to balance-of-payments theory emerged, one which viewed international adjustment not as an automatic process but as a policy problem for governments. The key problem examined in Joan Robinson's classic article on the foreign exchanges was the conditions under which a devaluation would improve a country's balance of payments. In Keynesian assumptions of wage rigidity, a devaluation would change the real prices of domestic goods relative to foreign goods in the foreign and domestic markets, thereby promoting substitutions in production and consumption. In Keynesian assumptions of mass unemployment, any repercussions of these substitutions on the demand for domestic output could be assumed to be met by variations in output and employment, and repercussions of such variations onto the balance of payments could be regarded as secondary. Finally, in the same assumption together with the general Keynesian denigration of the influence of money on the economy and concentration on the short run, the connections between the balance of payments and the money supply and between the money supply and aggregate demand could be disregarded. Attention was, therefore, concentrated on the "elasticity conditions" required for the impact effect of a devaluation—that is, of the associated change in relative real prices—to be an improvement in the balance of payments. These conditions were (1) for a simple model with perfectly elastic supplies and initially balanced trade, that the sum of the elasticities of home and foreign demand for imports should exceed unity (the so-called "Marshall-Lerner condition"), and (2) for more complex models assuming independent elasticities of demands for imports and supplies of exports, that a fearfully complex algebraic expression should be satisfied but challenging to derive and explore. (Much of the interest in this body of work was in the related questions of whether a devaluation that improved the balance of payments would necessarily turn a country's terms of trade against it and increase domestic employment.)

The so-called "elasticity approach" to devaluation proved demonstrably unsatisfactory in the immediate postwar period of full and over-full employment because of its implicit assumption of the existence of unemployed resources that could be mobilized to produce the additional exports and import substitutes required to satisfy a favorable impact effect. Recognition of this by the profession came in three versions. The first version involved carping at the irrelevance of "orthodox theory" (which the elasticity approach really was not) generally associated with the recommendation of exchange controls and quantitative import restrictions as an alternative to devaluation. The second was S. S. Alexander's "absorption approach," which argued essentially that a favorable effect from devaluation alone, in a fully employed economy, depends not on the elasticities but on the inflation resulting from the devaluation in these conditions, producing a reduction in aggregate absorption relative to aggregate productive capacity. Foreshadowing the new approach to be discussed below, part of the mechanism in Alexander's analysis that might bring this about is the "real balance effect" by which the rise in price consequent on the excess demand generated by devaluation deflates the real value of the domestic money supply and induces a reduction in spending out of income.

The presentation of the "absorption approach" as an alternative to the "elasticity approach" led to considerable controversy and extensive efforts to reconcile the two. However, the truth lies in recognition that a fully employed economy cannot use devaluation alone as a policy instrument for correcting a balance-of-payments deficit. It must use a combination of devaluation (to obtain an allocation of foreign and domestic demand among domestic and foreign output consistent with balance-of-payments equilibrium) and deflation (to match aggregate domestic demand with aggregate domestic supply). More generally, it must use a proper combination of what I have elsewhere called "expenditure-reducing" and "expenditure-switching" policies. This general principle is developed at length in James Meade's classic book, *The Theory of International Economic Policy: The Balance of Payments.* This principle constitutes the third, and most useful, version of recognition of the inadequacies of the "elasticity approach." In addition, it provides a synthesis, between that approach and the "absorption approach," that is logically satisfactory (though not economically satisfactory from the point of view of the new monetary approach). Unfortunately, Meade presented his analysis in terms of a short-run equilibrium analysis and based it on the assumption that the policy makers understood the theory as well as he did, thus making the book extremely inaccessible to policy makers. This may help to account for the bumbling of British demand-management policy after the devaluation of 1967. Also, following the tradition of British central banking and monetary theory, Meade identified monetary policy with fixing the level of interest rates, a procedure that automatically excludes consideration of the monetary consequences of devaluation by assuming them to be absorbed by the monetary authorities. (This is the reason for the economic objection to the Meade synthesis mentioned above.)

Subsequent to the work of Meade and others in the 1950's, the main development in conventional balance-of-payments theory has been the development of the theory of the fiscal-monetary policy mix, following the pioneering contributions of R. A. Mundell. In the general logic of the Meade system, a country has to have two policy instruments if it is to achieve simultaneously internal and external balance (full employment and balance-of-payments equilibrium). In Meade's system, the instruments are demand management by fiscal and/or monetary policy and the exchange rate (or controls or wage-price flexibility). What if wages are rigid, and controls and exchange rate changes are ruled out by national and international political considerations? A solution can still be found, at least in principle, if capital is internationally mobile in response to interest rate differentials. Fiscal expansion and monetary expansion then have the same effects on the current account, increasing imports and possibly decreasing exports, but opposite effects on the capital account. Fiscal expansion, increasing domestic interest rates and attracting a capital inflow, has the opposite effect on monetary expansion, which lowers interest rates and repels capital so that the two policies can be "mixed" in order to achieve a capital account surplus or deficit equal to the current account deficit or surplus at the level of full employment of the economy. This extension of the Meade approach has lent itself to almost infinite mathematical product differentiation, with little significant improvement in quality of economic product, and will not concern us further, except to remind us that theoretical investigation of the model has led naturally to the question of what would happen if capital were prefectly mobile and specifically to the implications of this assumption for the ability of the monetary authority to control the domestic money supply.

To recapitulate, the essential structure of what may be termed the standard model of balance-of-payments theory is a Keynesian model of income determination in which flows of consumption and investment expenditure are determined by aggregate income and demand-management policy variables (taxes and expenditures and interest rates) and in which the level of exports and the division of total expenditure between domestic and foreign goods (imports) are determined by the exchange rate which fixes the relative real prices of exports relative to foreign prices and of imports relative to domestic prices. By choosing a proper mix of demand-management policies and the exchange rate, the authorities can obtain full employment consistent with any current-account surplus or deficit. The net current-account surplus (or deficit) is equal to the excess (or deficiency) of the economy's flow of production over its flow of absorption, or to the excess (or deficiency) of its exports over its imports, or to its net excess (deficiency) of the flow of savings in relation to the flow of investment. By convention, but by no means necessarily, the current-account surplus or deficit is identified with the overall balance-of-payments position; it is easy enough to add in the determination of the balance-on-capital account by the differential between domestic and foreign interest rates, as is done in the theory of the fiscal-monetary policy mix.

The basic assumption, on which rests this system of balance-of-payments analysis and which forms the point of departure for the new "monetary" approach to balance-of-payments theory, is that the monetary consequences of balance-of-payments surpluses or deficits can be and are absorbed (sterilized) by the monetary authorities so that a surplus or deficit can be treated as a flow equilibrium. The new approach assumes—in some cases, asserts—that these monetary inflows or outflows associated with surpluses or deficits are not sterilized—or cannot be, within a period relevant to policy analysis—but instead influence the domestic money supply. And, since the demand for money is a demand for a stock and not a flow, variation of the supply of money relative to the demand for it associated with deficit or surplus must work toward an equilibrium between money demand and money supply with a corresponding equilibration of the balance of payments. Deficits and surpluses represent phases of stock adjustment in the money market and not equilibrium flows and should not be treated within an analytical framework that treats them as equilibrium phenomena.

It should be noted, however, that this criticism applies to the use of the standard model for the analysis and policy prescription of situations involving deficits or surpluses. The standard model, when used for the analysis of policies required to secure balance-of-payments equilibrium, is generally not subject to this criticism because by assumption the domestic money market will be in equilibrium. But even in this case, the fiscal-monetary mix version of it is open to criticism for confusing stock adjustment in the market for securities, in response to a change in interest-rate differentials between national capital markets, with a flow equilibrium.

In order to obtain flow-equilibrium deficits or surpluses on the basis of stock adjustments in the money market (and also possibly the securities market), it is necessary to construct a model in which the need for stock adjustments is being re-created continuously by economic change—in other words, it is necessary to analyze an economy, or an international economy, in which economic growth is in progress. This is one of the important technical differences between the new "monetary" models of the balance of payments and the standard Keynesian model—and a potential source of difficulty in comparing the results of the two types of analysis.

Another difference between the two types of models is that the "monetary" models almost invariably assume—in contrast to the emphasis of the standard model on the influence of relative prices of trade flows—that a country's price level is pegged to the world price level and must move rigidly in line with it. One justification for this assumption is that, at least among the advanced industrial countries, industrial competition is so pervasive that elasticities of substitution among the industrial products of the various countries approximate infinity more closely than the relatively low numbers implicit in the standard model. Another more sophisticated justification is derivable from the general framework of the monetarist approach, namely, that changes in relative national price levels can only be transitory concomitants of the process of stock adjustment to monetary disequilibrium and that in the longer-run analysis of balance-of-payments phenomena among growing economies attention should be focused on long-run equilibrium price relationships—which for simplicity can most easily be taken as constant.

This point has sometimes been put in terms of the positive charge that the standard model rests on "money illusion," in the sense that it assumes that workers will accept a reduction in their real standard of living brought about by a devaluation which they would not accept in the form of a forced reduction of domestic money wages. An alternative version of this charge is that the standard model assumes workers can be cheated out of their real marginal product by devaluation. However, the charge is incorrect. If rectification of a balance-of-payments deficit requires that the domestic marginal product of labor in terms of foreign goods falls, because the price of domestic goods relative to foreign goods must be reduced in the foreign and home markets to induce substitution between these goods favorable to the balance of payments, it requires no money illusion but only economic realism for the workers to accept this fact. Applications of the standard model to the case of devaluation, however, do require the assumption of money illusion if the elasticities of substitution between domestic and foreign goods are in fact high (approximately infinite) and it is, nevertheless, assumed that wages will remain unchanged in terms of domestic currency. In this case it is expected that workers will be content to accept wages below the international value of their marginal product and that employers will not be driven by competition for labor in the face of this disequilibrium to bid wages up to their marginal productivity levels. The issue, therefore, is not one of the standard model wrongly assuming the presence of money illusion on the part of the workers but of its possibly wrongly assuming low elasticities of substitution between domestic and foreign goods—which is an error in empirical assumptions rather than in model construction.

One further difference between the two types of model of balance-of-payments theory is worth noting. Whereas the Keynesian model assumes that employment and output are variable at (relatively) constant prices and wages, the monetary models assume that output and employment tend to full-employment levels, with reactions to changes taking the form of price and wage adjustments. This difference mirrors a broader difference between the Keynesian and quantity theory approaches to monetary theory for the closed economy. The assumption of full employment in the monetary balance-of-payments models can be defended on the grounds that these models are concerned with the longer run and that for this perspective the assumption of full employment is more appropriate than the assumption of general mass unemployment for the actual world economy since the end of the second World War.

I now turn from the discussion of theoretical issues in model construction to an exposition of some monetarist models of balance-of-payments behavior in a growing world economy. The models to be constructed are extremely simple, inasmuch as they concentrate on the overall balance of the balance of payments, i.e., on the trend of international reserve acquisition or loss, and ignore the composition of the balance of payments as between current account, capital account, and overall balance, as well as the question of changes in the structure of the balance-of-payments accounts that may occur as a country passes through various stages of economic growth. Nevertheless, they will, I hope, provide some interesting insights into balance-of-payments phenomena.

To begin with, it is useful to develop some general expressions relating the growth rates of economic aggregates to the growth rates of their components or of the independent variables to which they are functionally related. These can be established by elementary calculus and are merely stated here. In the formulas g is the growth rate per unit of time of a subscripted aggregate or variable; A and B are components of an aggregate; f(A,B) is a function of A and B and η denotes the elasticity of the aggregate defined by the function with respect to the subscripted variable. Then we have

$$g_{A+B} = \frac{A}{A+B} g_A + \frac{B}{A+B} g_B$$

$$g_{A-B} = \frac{A}{A-B} g_A - \frac{B}{A-B} g_B$$

$$g_{AB} = g_A + g_B$$

$$g_{A/B} = g_A - g_B$$

$$g_{f(A,B)} = \eta_A g_A + \eta_B g_B,$$

where η denotes an elasticity.

I begin with a discussion of monetary equilibrium in a single country maintaining a fixed exchange rate with the rest of the world, assumed to be growing over time, and small enough and diversified enough in relation to the world economy for its price level to be the world price level and its interest rate the world's interest rate. (Differentials between domestic and foreign price indices, or between domestic and foreign interest rates, could readily be allowed for, provided they are assumed fixed by economic conditions.) In addition, it is assumed that the supply of money is instantaneously adjusted to the demand for it because the residents of the country can get rid of or acquire money either through the international market for commodities or through the international securities market. Which mechanism of adjustment of money supply to money demand prevails will determine the way in which monetary policy affects the composition of the balance of payments, but that is a question not pursued in the present analysis.

The consequence of these assumptions is that domestic monetary policy does not determine the domestic money supply but instead determines only the division of the backing of the money supply the public demands, between international reserves and domestic credit. Monetary policy, in other words, controls the volume of domestic credit and not the money supply, and control over domestic credit controls the balance of payments and thus the behavior of the country's international reserves.

The demand for money may be simply specified as

$$M_d = p \cdot f(y \cdot i),$$

where M_d is the nominal quantity of domestic money demanded; y is real output; i is the interest rate or alternative opportunity cost of holding money; p is the foreign and therefore domestic price level; and multiplication of the demand for real balances $f(y,i)$ by p assumes the standard homogeneity postulate of monetary theory. The supply of money is

$$M_s = R + D,$$

where R is the international reserve and D the domestic credit or domestic assets backing of the money supply. Since by assumption M_s must be equal to M_d,

$$R = M_d - D$$

and

$$g_R = \frac{1}{R} B(t) = \frac{M_d}{R} g_{M_d} - \frac{D}{R} g_D,$$

where $B(t) = dR/dt$ is the current overall balance of payments. Letting $r = R/M_s$ R/M_d, the initial international reserve ratio, and substituting for g_{M_d},

$$g_R = \frac{1}{r} (g_p + \eta_y g_y + \eta_i g_i) - \frac{1 - r}{r} g_D.$$

Simplifying by assuming constant world prices and interest rates,

$$g_R = \frac{1}{R} \eta_y g_y - \frac{1-r}{r} g_D,$$

that is, reserve growth and the balance of payments are positively related to domestic economic growth and the income elasticity of demand for money and are negatively related to the rate of domestic credit expansion. Simplifying still further by assuming no domestic growth ($g_y = 0$),

$$g_R = \frac{-1-r}{r} g_D,$$

that is, reserve growth and the balance of payments are inversely related to the rate of domestic credit expansion.

These results are contrasted with various Keynesian theories about the relation between economic growth and the balance of payments. According to one theory derived from the multiplier analysis, economic growth must worsen the balance of payments through increasing imports relative to exports. This theory neglects the influence of demand for money on export supply and import demand and on the international flow of securities. According to another more sophisticated theory, domestic credit expansion will tend to improve the balance of payments by stimulating investment and productivity increase, thus lowering domestic prices in relation to foreign prices and improving the current account through the resulting substitutions of domestic for foreign goods in the foreign and domestic markets. This theory begs a number of questions even in naive Keynesian terms; in terms of the present approach it errs in attempting to deduce the consequences of domestic credit expansion from its presumed relative price effects without reference to the monetary aspect of balance-of-payments surpluses and deficits.

C. Monetary Policy in Public Debate

Recent years have been troublesome for Federal Reserve leadership. Scored by Monetarists and some Keynesians for losing control of the money stock and thereby causing excessive inflation *and* unemployment, and threatened by Congress with proposals for a stricter policing of their organization and activity, the leadership resolutely tries to defend its positions.

Federal Reserve Chairman Arthur Burn's letter to Senator Proxmire is such a defense. It is followed by a critique by Milton Friedman who refuses to allow Burns to exonerate the system for the severe inflation of the early 1970's and inability to control effectively the money stock.

Should the Federal Reserve attempt to control the money supply? Not too closely in the short run argues Alan R. Holmes. He contends that there are certain operational difficulties interfering with money supply control and that focusing upon the money supply would result in undesirable variations in market rates of interest.

In contrast, the next two articles, by Thomas Mayer and Milton Friedman respectively, argue that the operational difficulties discussed by Holmes can easily be overcome. Mayer contends that there are even greater operational difficulties involved in trying to control interest rates. Friedman points out that most of the inability to control money arises from the Federal Reserve's short-run strategy. In the next article, Paul Samuelson agrees that the Federal Reserve should pay more attention to the money supply but objects to a steady growth rule. (The Friedman and Samuelson pieces were presented as testimony on the 1975 Congressional Resolution that the Federal Reserve state publicly its plans for money growth for a year ahead.)

In the sixth article in this section Arthur Okun essentially sides with Holmes rather than Mayer and Friedman on the degree to which the money supply should be controlled. Okun also counsels moderation in the fiscal policy.

In the face of this tide of criticism how does the Federal Reserve System manage to operate? William P. Yohe's survey of studies of Federal Reserve behavior provides a great deal of insight into this question. Edward J. Kane follows with a hardhitting rundown of why current reforms for stricter control of the Federal Reserve by Congress are doomed to ineffectiveness—basically because it is in the interest of neither the Congress, the Presidency nor the monetary authority itself to restrict Federal Reserve independence. Kane is skeptical of the notion that the 1975 Congressional Resolution is an adequate means of insuring stability in money supply growth.

The issues debated here relate closely to earlier Sections: the relationships between money and interest rates, wealth and the level of economic activity were examined in Section I; estimates of the strength of these relationships over time was the subject of Section II; Section III considered the closeness and stability over time of the link between monetary policy and various measures of the money supply and interest rates; finally Sections IV A and IV B consider in detail some constraints on closer control of the money stock. Therefore the debate over monetary policy with which we conclude is really a prologue to the continuing efforts of the many economists represented throughout this book.

The Role of the Money Supply in the Conduct of Monetary Policy

Arthur Burns

The following letter, dated November 6, 1973, by Arthur F. Burns, Chairman of the Board of Governors of the Federal Reserve System, was written in response to inquiries by Senator Proxmire regarding criticisms of monetary policy during the past year.

The Honorable William Proxmire
United States Senate
Washington, D. C.

Dear Senator Proxmire:

I am writing in further response to your letter of September 17, 1973, which requested comments on certain criticisms of monetary policy over the past year.

As stated in your letter, the criticisms are: (1) "that there was too much variation from time to time in the rate of increase in the money supply, that monetary policy was too erratic, too much characterized by stops and starts"; and (2) "that the money

Reprinted from the Federal Reserve Bank of Richmond, *Monthly Review* (December, 1973), pp. 2-8, by permission of the publisher.

supply had increased much too much last year, in fact that the increase would have been too much even if we had been in the depths of a recession instead of enjoying a fairly vigorous economic expansion."

These criticisms involve basic issues with regard to the role of money in the economy and the role that the money supply should play in the formulation and execution of monetary policy. These issues, along with the specific points you raise, require careful examination.

Criticism of Our Public Policies

During the past two years, the American economy has experienced a substantial measure of prosperity. Real output has increased sharply, jobs have been created for millions of additional workers, and total personal income—both in dollars and in terms of real purchasing power—has risen to the highest levels ever reached.

Yet the prosperity has been a troubled one. Price increases have been large and widespread. For a time, the unemployment rate remained unduly high. Interest rates have risen sharply since the spring of 1972. Mortgage money has recently become difficult to obtain in many communities. And confidence in the dollar at home and abroad has at times wavered.

Many observers have blamed these difficulties on the management of public economic policies. Certainly, the Federal budget—despite vigorous efforts to hold expenditures down—continued in substantial deficit. There has also been an enormous growth in the activities of Federally sponsored agencies which, although technically outside the budget, must still be financed. The results of efforts to control wages and prices during the past year have been disappointing. Partial decontrol in early 1973 and the subsequent freeze failed to bring the results that were hoped for.

Monetary policy has been criticized on somewhat contradictory counts—for being inflationary, or for permitting too high a level of interest rates, or for failing to bring the economy back to full employment, or for permitting excessive short-term variations in the growth of the money supply, and so on.

One indication of dissatisfaction with our public policies was provided by a report, to which you refer in your letter, on a questionnaire survey conducted by the National Association of Business Economists. Of the respondents, 38 percent rated fiscal policy "over the past year" as "poor"; 41 percent rated monetary policy "over the past year" as "poor"; only 14 percent felt that the wage-price controls under Phase IV were "about right." If this sampling is at all indicative, the public policies on which we have relied are being widely questioned. Many members of the above group, in fact, went on record for a significant change in fiscal policy. In response to a question whether they favored a variable investment tax credit, 46.5 percent said "yes," 40 percent said "no," and 13.5 percent expressed "no opinion."

Let me turn now to the questions raised in your letter and in some other recent discussions about monetary policy. I shall discuss, in particular, the role of money supply in the conduct of monetary policy; the extent and significance of variability in the growth of the money supply; and the actual behavior of the money supply during 1972–1973.

Role of Money Supply

For many years economists have debated the role of the money supply in the performance of economic systems. One school of thought, often termed "monetarist," claims that changes in the money supply influence very importantly, perhaps even decisively, the pace of economic activity and the level of prices. Monetarists contend that the monetary authorities should pay principal attention to the money supply, rather than to other financial variables such as interest rates, in the conduct of monetary policy. They also contend that fiscal policy has only a small independent impact on the economy.

Another school of thought places less emphasis on the money supply and assigns more importance to the expenditure and tax policies of the Federal Government as factors influencing real economic activity and the level of prices. This school emphasizes the need for monetary policy to be concerned with interest rates and with conditions in the money and capital markets. Some economic activities, particularly residential building and State and local government construction, depend heavily on borrowed funds, and are therefore influenced greatly by changes in the cost and availability of credit. In other categories of spending—such as business investment in fixed capital and inventories, and consumer purchases of durable goods—credit conditions play a less decisive role, but they are nonetheless important.

Monetarists recognize that monetary policy affects private spending in part through its impact on interest rates and other credit terms. But they believe that primary attention to the growth of the money supply will result in a more appropriate monetary policy than would attention to conditions in the credit markets.

Needless to say, monetary policy is—and has long been—a controversial subject. Even the monetarists do not speak with one voice on monetary policy. Some influential monetarists believe that monetary policy should aim strictly at maintaining a constant rate of growth of the money supply. However, what that constant should be, or how broadly the money supply should be defined, are matters on which monetarists still differ. And there are also monetarists who would allow some—but infrequent—changes in the rate of growth of the money supply, in accordance with changing economic conditions.

It seems self-evident that adherence to a rigid growth rate rule, or even one that is changed infrequently, would practically prevent monetary policy from playing an active role in economic stabilization. Monetarists recognize this. They believe that most economic disturbances tend to be self-correcting, and they, therefore, argue that a constant or nearly constant rate of growth of the money supply would result in reasonably satisfactory economic performance.

But neither historical evidence nor the thrust of explorations in business-cycle theory over a long century give support to the notion that our economy is inherently stable. On the contrary, experience has demonstrated repeatedly that blind reliance on the self-correcting properties of our economic system can lead to serious trouble. Discretionary economic policy, while it has at times led to mistakes, has more often proved reasonably successful. The disappearance of business depressions, which in earlier times spelled mass unemployment for workers and mass bankruptcies for businessmen, is largely attributable to the stabilization policies of the last thirty years.

The fact is that the internal workings of a market economy tend of themselves to generate business fluctuations, and most modern economists recognize this. For example, improved prospects for profits often spur unsustainable bursts of investment spending. The flow of personal income in an age of affluence allows ample latitude for changes in discretionary expenditures and in savings rates. During a business-cycle expansion various imbalances tend to develop within the economy—between aggregate inventories and sales, or between aggregate business investment in fixed capital and consumer outlays, or between average unit costs of production and prices. Such imbalances give rise to cyclical movements in the economy. Flexible fiscal and monetary policies, therefore, are often needed to cope with undesirable economic developments, and this need is not diminished by the fact that our available tools of economic stabilization leave something to be desired.

There is general agreement among economists that, as a rule, the effects of stabilization policies occur gradually over time and that economic forecasts are an essential tool of policy making. However, no economist—or school of economics—has a monopoly on accurate forecasting. At times, forecasts based largely on the money supply have turned out to be satisfactory. At other times, such forecasts have been quite poor, mainly because of unanticipated changes in the intensity with which the existing money stock is used by business firms and consumers.

Changes in the rate of turnover of money have historically played a large role in economic fluctuations, and they continue to do so. For example, the narrowly defined money stock—that is, demand deposits plus currency in public circulation—grew by 5.7 percent between the fourth quarter of 1969 and the fourth quarter of 1970. But the turnover of money declined during that year, and the dollar value of GNP rose only 4.5 percent. In the following year, the growth rate of the money supply increased to 6.9 percent, but the turnover of money picked up briskly and the dollar value of GNP accelerated to 9.3 percent. The movement out of recession in 1970 into recovery in 1971 was thus closely related to the greater intensity in the use of money. Occurrences such as this are very common because the willingness to use the existing stock of money, expressed in its rate of turnover, is a highly dynamic force in economic life.

For this as well as other reasons, the Federal Reserve uses a blend of forecasting techniques. The behavior of the money supply and other financial variables is accorded careful attention. So also are the results of the most recent surveys on plant and equipment spending, consumer attitudes, and inventory plans. Recent trends in key producing and spending sectors are analyzed. The opinions of businessmen and outside economic analysts are canvassed, in part through the nationwide contacts of Federal Reserve Banks. And an assessment is made of the probable course of fiscal policy, also of labor-market and agricultural policies, and their effects on the economy.

Evidence from all these sources is weighed. Efforts are also made to assess economic developments through the use of large-scale econometric models. An eclectic approach is thus taken by the Federal Reserve, in recognition of the fact that the state of economic knowledge does not justify reliance on any single forecasting technique. As economic research has cumulated, it has become increasingly clear that money does indeed matter. But other financial variables also matter.

In recent years, the Federal Reserve has placed somewhat more emphasis on achieving desired growth rates of the monetary aggregates, including the narrowly defined money supply, in its conduct of monetary policy. But we have continued to give careful attention to other financial indicators, among them the level of interest rates on mortgages and other loans and the liquidity position of financial institutions and the general public. This is necessary because the economic implications of any given monetary growth rate depend on the state of liquidity, the attitudes of businessmen, investors, and consumers toward liquidity, the cost and availability of borrowed funds, and other factors. Also, as the nation's central bank, the Federal Reserve can never lose sight of its role as a lender of last resort, so that financial crises and panics will be averted.

I recognize that one advantage of maintaining a relatively stable growth rate of the money supply is that a partial offset is thereby provided to unexpected and undesired shifts in the aggregate demand for goods and services. There is always some uncertainty as to the emerging strength of aggregate demand. If money growth is maintained at a rather stable rate and aggregate demand turns out to be weaker than is consistent with the nation's economic objectives, interest rates will tend to decline and the easing of credit markets should help to moderate the undesired weakness in demand. Similarly, if the demand for goods and services threatens to outrun productive capacity, a rather stable rate of monetary growth will provide a restraining influence on the supply of credit and thus tend to restrain excessive spending.

However, it would be unwise for monetary policy to aim at all times at a constant or nearly constant rate of growth of money balances. The money growth rate that can contribute most to national objectives will vary with economic conditions. For example, if the aggregate demand for goods and services is unusually weak or if the demand for liquidity is unusually strong, a rate of increase in the money supply well above the desirable long-term trend may be needed for a time. Again, when the economy is experiencing severe cost-push inflation, a monetary growth rate that is relatively high by a historical yardstick may have to be tolerated for a time. If money growth were severely constrained in order to combat the element of inflation resulting from such a cause, it might well have seriously adverse effects on production and employment. In short, what growth rate of the money supply is appropriate at any given time cannot be determined simply by extrapolating past trends or by some preconceived arithmetical standard.

Moreover, for purposes of conducting monetary policy, it is never safe to rely on just one concept of money—even if that concept happens to be fashionable. A variety of plausible concepts merit careful attention because a number of financial assets serve as a convenient, safe, and liquid store of purchasing power.

The Federal Reserve publishes data corresponding to three definitions of money and takes all of them into account in determining policy. The three measures are (a) the narrowly-defined money stock (M_1), which encompasses currency and demand deposits held by the nonbank public; (b) a more broadly defined money stock (M_2), which also includes time and savings deposits at commercial banks (other than large negotiable time certificates of deposits); (c) a still broader definition (M_3), which includes savings deposits at mutual savings banks and savings and loan associations. A definition embracing other liquid assets could also be justified—for example, one that would include large-denomination negotiable time certificates of deposit, U.S. savings bonds and Treasury bills, commercial paper, and other short-term money market instruments.

There are many assets closely related to cash, and the public can switch readily among these assets. However money may be defined, the task of determining the amount of money needed to maintain high employment and reasonable stability of the general price level is complicated by shifting preferences of the public for cash and other financial assets.

Variability of Money Supply Growth

In the short run, the rate of change in the observed money supply is quite erratic, and cannot be trusted as an indicator of the course of monetary policy. This would be so even if there were no errors of measurement.

The record of hearings held by the Joint Economic Committee on June 27, 1973, includes a memorandum which I submitted on problems encountered in controlling the money supply. As indicated there, week-to-week, month-to-month, and even quarter-to-quarter fluctuations in the rate of change of money balances are frequently influenced by international flows of funds, changes in the level of U.S. Government deposits, and sudden changes in the public's attitude towards liquidity. Some of these variations appear to be essentially random—a product of the enormous ebb and flow of funds in our modern economy.

Because the demands of the public for money are subject to rather wide short-term variations, efforts by the Federal Reserve to maintain a constant growth rate of the money supply could lead to sharp short-run swings in interest rates and risk damage to financial markets and the economy. Uncertainties about financing costs could reduce the fluidity of markets and increase the costs of financing to borrowers. In addition, wide and erratic movements of interest rates and financial conditions could have undesirable effects on business and consumer spending. These adverse effects may not be of major dimensions, but it is better to avoid them.

In any event, for a variety of reasons explained in the memorandum for the Joint Economic Committee, to which I have previously referred, the Federal Reserve does not have precise control over the money supply. To give one example, a significant part of the money supply consists of deposits lodged in nonmember banks that are not subject to the reserve requirements set by the Federal Reserve. As a result there is some slippage in monetary control. Furthermore, since deposits at nonmember banks have been reported for only two to four days in a year, in contrast to daily statistics for member banks, the data on the money supply—which we regularly present on a weekly, monthly, and quarterly basis—are estimates rather than precise measurements. When the infrequent reports from nonmember banks become available, they often necessitate considerable revisions of the money supply figures. In the past two years, the revisions were upward, and this may happen again this year.

Some indication of the extent of short-term variations in the recorded money supply is provided below. Table 1 shows the average and maximum deviations (without regard to sign) of M_1 from its average annual growth rate over a three and a half year period. As would be expected, the degree of variation diminishes as the time unit lengthens; it is much larger for monthly than for quarterly data, and is also larger for quarterly than for semiannual data.

In our judgment, there need be little reason for concern about the short-run variations that occur in the rate of change in the money stock. Such variations have minimal effects on the real economy. For one thing, the outstanding supply of money is very large. It is also quite stable, even when the short-run rate of change is unstable. This October the average outstanding supply of M_1, seasonally adjusted, was about $264 billion. On this base, a monthly rise or fall in the money stock of even $2.5 billion would amount to only a 1 percent change. But when such a temporary change is expressed as an annual rate, as is now commonly done, it comes out as about 12 percent and attracts attention far beyond its real significance.

The Federal Reserve research staff has investigated carefully the economic implications of variability in M_1 growth. The experience of the past two decades suggests

Table 1. Deviations in M_1 from Its Average Rate of Growth, 1970 through Mid–1973

Form of Data	Annual Rates of Change in Percent	
	Average Deviation	Maximum Deviation
Monthly	3.8	8.8
Quarterly	2.4	5.5
Semiannual	1.8	4.1

that even an abnormally large or abnormally small rate of growth of the money stock over a period up to six months or so has a negligible influence on the course of the economy—provided it is subsequently offset. Such short-run variations in the rate of change in the money supply may not at all reflect Federal Reserve policy, and they do not justify the attention they often receive from financial analysts.

The thrust of monetary policy and its probable effects on economic activity can only be determined by observing the course of the money supply and of other monetary aggregates over periods lasting six months or so. Even then, care must be taken to measure the growth of money balances in ways that temper the influence of short-term variations. For example, the growth of money balances over a quarter can be measured from the amount outstanding in the last month of the preceding quarter to the last month of the current quarter or from the average amount outstanding during the preceding quarter to the average in the current quarter. The first measure captures the latest tendencies in the money supply, but may be distorted by random changes that have no lasting significance. The second measure tends to average out temporary fluctuations and is comparable to the data provided on a wide range of nonmonetary economic variables, such as the gross national product and related measures.

A comparison of these two ways of measuring the rate of growth in M_1 is shown in Table 2 for successive quarters in 1972 and 1973. The first column, labeled M, shows annual rates calculated from end-months of quarters; the second column, labeled Q, shows annual rates calculated from quarterly averages.

As may be seen, the quarterly averages disclose much more clearly the developing trend of monetary restraint—which, in fact, began in the second quarter of 1972. Also, the growth of M_1, which on a month-end basis appears very erratic in the first three quarters of 1973, is much more stable on a quarterly average basis. For example, while the level of M_1 did not expand significantly between June and September, the quarterly average figures indicate further sizable growth in the third quarter. For purposes of economic analysis, it is an advantage to recognize that the money available for use was appreciably larger in the third quarter than in the second quarter.

Table 2. Growth Rates of Money Supply to Two Bases

		Annual Rate of Change, in Percent	
		M	Q
1972	I	9.2	5.3
	II	6.1	8.4
	III	8.2	8.0
	IV	8.6	7.1
1973	I	1.7	4.7
	II	10.3	6.9
	III	0.3	5.1

Experience of 1972–1973

During 1972, it was the responsibility of the Federal Reserve to encourage a rate of economic expansion adequate to reduce unemployment to acceptable levels. At the same time, despite the dampening effects of the wage-price control program, inflationary pressures were gathering. Monetary policy, therefore, had to balance the twin objectives of containing inflationary pressures and encouraging economic growth. These objectives were to some extent conflicting, and monetary policy alone could not be expected to cope with both problems. Continuation of an effective wage-price program and a firmer policy of fiscal restraint were urgently needed.

The narrowly defined money stock increased 7.4 percent during 1972 (measured from the fourth quarter of 1971 to the fourth quarter of 1972). Between the third quarter of 1972 and the third quarter of 1973 the growth rate was 6.1 percent. By the first half of 1973 the annual growth rate had declined to 5.8 percent, and a further slowing occurred in the third quarter.

Evaluation of the appropriateness of these growth rates would require full analysis of the economic and financial objectives, conditions, and policies during the past two years, if not longer. Such an analysis cannot be undertaken here. Some perspective on monetary developments during 1972-1973 may be gained, however, from comparisons with the experience of other industrial countries, and by recalling briefly how domestic economic conditions evolved during this period.

Table 3 compares the growth of M_1 in the United States with that of other industrial countries in 1972 and the first half of 1973. The definitions of M_1 differ somewhat from country to country but are as nearly comparable as statistical sources permit. It goes without saying that each country faced its own set of economic conditions and problems. Yet it is useful to note that monetary growth in the United States was much lower than in other major industrial countries and that it also was steadier than in the other countries.

The next table [Table 4] shows, in summary fashion, the rates of change in the money supply of the United States, in its total production, and in the consumer price level during 1972 and 1973. The table is based on the latest data. It may be noted, in passing, that, according to data available as late as January 1973, the rate of growth of M_1 during 1972 was 7.2 percent, not 7.4 percent; and that the rate of increase in real GNP was 7.7 percent, not 7 percent. In other words, on the basis of the data

Table 3. Annual Percent Rates of Growth in Money Supply

	4th Quarter 1971 to 4th Quarter 1972	4th Quarter 1972 to 2nd Quarter 1973
United States	7.4	5.8
United Kingdom	14.1	10.0
Germany	14.3	4.2
France	15.4	8.7
Japan	23.1	28.2

Table 4. Money Supply, GNP, and Prices in the United States
(Percent change at annual rates)

	4th Quarter 1971 to 4th Quarter 1972	4th Quarter 1972 to	
		2nd Quarter of 1973	3rd Quarter of 1973
Money supply (M_1)	7.4	5.8	5.6
Gross National Product			
Current dollars	10.6	12.1	11.7
Constant dollars	7.0	5.4	4.8
Prices			
Consumer price index (CPI)	3.4	7.1	7.8
CPI excluding food	3.0	4.0	4.1

available during 1972, the rate of growth of M_1 was below the rate of growth of the physical volume of overall production.

The table indicates that growth in M_1 during 1972 and 1973 approximately matched the growth of real output, but was far below the expansion in the dollar value of the nation's output. Although monetary policy limited the availability of money relative to the growth of transactions demands, it still encouraged a substantial expansion in economic activity; real output rose by about 7 percent in 1972. Even so, unemployment remained unsatisfactorily high throughout the greater part of the year. It was not until November that the unemployment rate dropped below 5.5 percent. For the year as a whole, the unemployment rate averaged 5.6 percent. It may be of interest to recall that unemployment averaged 5.5 percent in 1954 and 1960, which are commonly regarded as recession years.

Since the expansion of M_1 in 1972 was low relative to the demands for money and credit, it was accompanied by rising short-term interest rates. Long-term interest rates showed little net change last year, as credit demands were satisfied mainly in the short-term markets.

In 1973, the growth of M_1 moderated while the transactions demands for cash and the turnover of money accelerated. GNP in current dollars rose at a 12 percent annual rate as prices rose more rapidly. In credit markets, short-term interest rates rose sharply further, while long-term interest rates also moved up, though by substantially less than short-term rates.

The extraordinary upsurge of the price level this year reflects a variety of special influences. First, there has been a worldwide economic boom superimposed on the boom in the United States. Second, we have encountered critical shortages of basic materials. The expansion in industrial capacity needed to produce these materials had not been put in place earlier because of the abnormally low level of profits between 1966 and 1971 and also because of numerous impediments to new investment on ecological grounds. Third, farm product prices escalated sharply as a result of crop failures in many countries last year. Fourth, fuel prices spurted upward, reflecting the developing shortages in the energy field. And fifth, the depreciation of the dollar in foreign exchange markets has served to boost prices of imported goods and to add to the demands pressing on our productive resources.

In view of these powerful special factors, and the cyclical expansion of our economy, a sharp advance in our price level would have been practically inevitable in 1973. The upsurge of the price level this year hardly represents either the basic trend of prices or the response of prices to previous monetary or fiscal policies—whatever their shortcomings may have been. In particular, as Table 4 shows, the explosion of food prices that occurred this year is in large part responsible for the accelerated rise in the overall consumer price level.

The severe rate of inflation that we have experienced in 1973 cannot responsibly be attributed to monetary management or to public policies more generally. In retrospect, it may well be that monetary policy should have been a little less expansive in 1972. But a markedly more restrictive policy would have led to a still sharper rise in interest rates and risked a premature ending of the business expansion, without limiting to any significant degree this year's upsurge of the price level.

Concluding Observations

The present inflation is the most serious economic problem facing our country, and it poses great difficulties for economic stabilization policies. We must recognize, I believe, that it will take some time for the forces of inflation, which now engulf our economy and others around the world, to burn themselves out. In today's environment, controls on wages and prices cannot be expected to yield the benefits they did in 1971 and 1972, when economic conditions were much different. Primary reliance in dealing with inflation—both in the near future and over the longer term—will have to be placed on fiscal and monetary policies.

The prospects for regaining price stability would be enhanced by improvements in our monetary and fiscal instruments. The conduct of monetary policy could be improved if steps were taken to increase the precision with which the money supply can be controlled by the Federal Reserve. Part of the present control problem stems from statistical inadequacies—chiefly the paucity of data on deposits at nonmember banks. Also, however, control over the money supply and other monetary aggregates is less precise than it can or should be because nonmember banks are not subject to the same reserve requirements as are Federal Reserve members.

I hope that the Congress will support efforts to rectify these deficiencies. For its part, the Federal Reserve Board is even now carrying on discussions with the Federal Deposit Insurance Corporation about the need for better statistics on the nation's money supply. The Board also expects shortly to recommend to the Congress legislation that will put demand deposits at commercial banks on a uniform basis from the standpoint of reserve requirements.

Improvements in our fiscal policies are also needed. It is important for the Congress to put an end to fragmented consideration of expenditures, to place a firm ceiling on total Federal expenditures, and to relate these expenditures to prospective revenues and the nation's economic needs. Fortunately, there is now widespread recognition by members of Congress of the need to reform budgetary procedures along these broad lines.

It also is high time for fiscal policy to become a more versatile tool of economic stabilization. Particularly appropriate would be fiscal instruments that could be adapted quickly, under special legislative rules, to changing economic conditions— such as a variable tax credit for business investment in fixed capital. Once again I would urge the Congress to give serious consideration to this urgently needed reform.

We must strive also for better understanding of the effects of economic stabilization policies on economic activity and prices. Our knowledge in this area is greater now than it was five or ten years ago, thanks to extensive research undertaken by economists in academic institutions, at the Federal Reserve, and elsewhere. The keen interest of the Joint Economic Committee in improving economic stabilization policies has, I believe, been an influence of great importance in stimulating this widespread research effort.

I look forward to continued cooperation with the Committee in an effort to achieve the kind of economic performance our citizens expect and deserve.

Letter on Monetary Policy

Milton Friedman

The following letter by Professor Milton Friedman, Department of Economics, University of Chicago, was written in response to a letter by Arthur F. Burns, Chairman of the Board of Governors of the Federal Reserve System.

The Honorable William Proxmire
Joint Economic Committee
United States Senate
Washington, D. C. 20510

Dear Senator Proxmire:

On September 17, 1973, you asked the Chairman of the Board of Governors of the Federal Reserve System to comment on certain published criticisms of monetary policy. On Nobember 6, 1973, the Chairman replied on behalf of the System. This Reply has been widely publicized by the Federal Reserve System. It was reprinted in the *Federal Reserve Bulletin* (November, 1973) and in at least five of the separate Federal Reserve Bank *Reviews.*

Reprinted from the Federal Reserve Bank of Richmond, *Monthly Review* (May–June, 1974), pp. 20–23, by permission of the publisher and the author.

The Reply makes many valid points. Yet, taken as a whole, it evades rather than answers the criticisms. It appears to exonerate the Federal Reserve System from any appreciable responsibility for the current inflation, yet a close reading reveals that it does not do so, and other evidence, to which the Reply does not refer, establishes a strong case that the Fed has contributed to inflation. The Reply appears to attribute admitted errors in monetary policy to forces outside the Fed, yet the difficulties in controlling and measuring the money supply are largely of the Fed's own making.

The essence of the System's answer to the criticisms is contained in three sentences, one dealing with the Fed's responsibility for the 1973 inflation; the other two, with the problem of controlling and measuring the money supply. I shall discuss each in turn.

Responsibility for Inflation

The severe rate of inflation that we have experienced in 1973 cannot responsibly be attributed to monetary management (italics added).

As written, this sentence is unexceptionable. Delete the word "severe," and the sentence is indefensible.

The Reply correctly cites a number of special factors that made the inflation in 1973 more severe than could have been expected from prior monetary growth alone—the worldwide economic boom, ecological impediments to investment, escalating farm prices, energy shortages. These factors may well explain why consumer prices rose by 8 percent in 1973 (fourth quarter 1972 to fourth quarter 1973) instead of, say, by 6 percent. But they do not explain why inflation in 1973 would have been as high as 6 percent in their absence. They do not explain why consumer prices rose more than 25 percent in the five years from 1968 to 1973.

The Reply recognizes that "the effects of stabilization policies occur gradually over time" and that "it is never safe to rely on just one concept of money." Yet, the Reply presents statistical data on the growth of money or income or prices for only 1972 and 1973, and for only one of the three monetary concepts it refers to, namely, M_1 (currency plus demand deposits), the one that had the lowest rate of growth. On the basis of the evidence in the Reply, there is no way to evaluate the longer-term policies of the Fed or to compare current monetary policy with earlier policy or one concept of money with another.

From calendar year 1970 to calendar year 1973, M_1 grew at the annual rate of 6.9 percent; in the preceding decade, from 1960 to 1970, at 4.2 percent. More striking yet, the rate of growth from 1970 to 1973 was higher than for any other three-year period since the end of World War II.

The other monetary concepts tell the same story. From 1970 to 1973, M_2 (M_1 plus commercial bank time deposits other than large C.D.'s) grew at the annual rate of 10.5 percent; from 1960 to 1970, at 6.7 percent. From 1970 to 1973, M_3 (M_2 plus

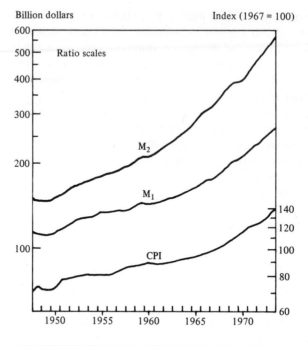

MOVEMENTS IN MONEY AND PRICES, 1948–1973

deposits at nonbank thrift institutions) grew at the annual rate of 12.0 percent; from 1960 to 1970, at 7.2 percent. For both M_2 and M_3, the rates of growth from 1970 to 1973 are higher than for any other three-year period since World War II.

As the accompanying chart demonstrates, prices show the same pattern as monetary growth except for the Korean War inflation. In the early 1960's consumer prices rose at a rate of 1 to 2 percent per year; from 1970 to 1973, at an average rate of 4.6 percent; currently, they are rising at a rate of not far from 10 percent. The accelerated rise in the quantity of money has clearly been reflected, after some delay, in a similar accelerated rise in prices.

However limited may be the Fed's ability to control monetary aggregates from quarter to quarter or even year to year, the monetary acceleration depicted in the chart, which extended over more than a decade, could not have occurred without the Fed's acquiescence—to put it mildly. And however loose may be the year-to-year relation between monetary growth and inflation, the acceleration in the rate of inflation over the past decade could not have occurred without the prior monetary acceleration.

Whatever, therefore, may be the verdict on the short-run relations to which the Reply restricts itself, the Fed's long-run policies have played a major role in producing our present inflation.

There is much evidence on the shorter-term as well as the longer-term relations. Studies for the United States and many other countries reveal highly consistent patterns. A substantial change in the rate of monetary growth which is sustained for more than a few months tends to be followed some six or nine months later by a change in the same direction in the rate of growth of total dollar spending. To begin with, most of the change in spending is reflected in output and employment. Typically, though not always, it takes another year to 18 months before the change in monetary growth is reflected in prices. On the average, therefore, it takes something like two years for a higher or lower rate of monetary growth to be reflected in a higher or lower rate of inflation.

Table 1 illustrates this relation between monetary growth and prices. It shows rates of change for three monetary aggregates and for consumer prices over two-year spans measured from the first quarter of the corresponding years. The average delay in the effect of monetary change on prices is allowed for by matching each biennium for prices with the prior biennium for money. Clearly, on the average, prices reflect the behavior of money two years earlier.

To avoid misunderstanding, let me stress that, as the table illustrates, this is an *average* relationship, not a precise relationship that can be expected to hold in exactly the same way in every month or year or even decade. As the Reply properly stresses, many factors affect the course of prices other than changes in the quantity of money. Over short periods, they may sometimes be more important. But the Federal Reserve and the Federal Reserve alone has the responsibility for the quantity of money; it does not have the responsibility, and certainly not sole responsibility, for the other factors that affect inflation. And the record is unmistakably clear that, over the past three years taken as a whole, the Federal Reserve System has exercised that responsibility in a way that has exacerbated inflation.

This conclusion holds not only for the three years as a whole but also for each year separately, as Table 2 shows. The one encouraging feature is the slightly lower rate of growth of M_2 and M_3 from 1972 to 1973 than in the earlier two years. But the

Table 1. Money and Prices

Dates for M_1, M_2, M_3	Annual Percent Rates of Growth from First Quarter to First Quarter of Indicated Years for				Dates for Consumer Prices
	M_1	M_2	M_3	Consumer Prices	
1959 to 1961	0.8	2.5	4.6	1.1	1961 to 1963
1961 to 1963	2.4	5.9	7.6	1.3	1963 to 1965
1963 to 1965	4.1	6.9	8.3	2.7	1965 to 1967
1965 to 1967	3.7	7.2	6.7	4.2	1967 to 1969
1967 to 1969	7.3	9.4	8.8	5.5	1969 to 1971
1969 to 1971	4.8	6.3	6.4	3.9	1971 to 1973
1971 to 1973	7.2	10.4	12.6	(9.1)*	1973 to

*First quarter 1973 to fourth quarter 1973.

Table 2. Recent Monetary Growth Rates

Calendar Year	Annual Percent Rate of Growth of		
	M_1	M_2	M_3
1970–1971	7.0	11.8	12.8
1971–1972	6.4	10.2	12.5
1972–1973	7.4	9.5	10.6

tapering off is mild, and it is not clear that it is continuing. More important, even these lower rates are far too high. Steady growth of M_2 at 9 and 10 percent would lead to an inflation of about 6 or 7 percent per year. To bring inflation down to 3 percent, let alone to zero, the rate of growth of M_2 must be reduced to something like 5 to 7 percent.

Controlling and Measuring the Money Supply

The conduct of monetary policy could be improved if steps were taken to increase the precision with which the money supply can be controlled by the Federal Reserve. Part of the present control problem stems from statistical inadequacies (italics added).

Again these sentences from the Reply are literally correct, but they give not the slightest indication that the difficulties of controlling and measuring the money supply are predominantly of the Fed's own making. The only specific problems that the Reply mentions are the "paucity of data on deposits at nonmember banks" and the fact that "nonmember banks are not subject to the same reserve requirements as are Federal Reserve Members."

Nonmember deposits do raise problems in measuring and controlling the money supply, but they are minor compared to other factors. The Reply's emphasis on them is understandable on other grounds. Almost since it was established in 1914, the Fed has been anxious to bring all commercial banks into the System and has been worried about the defection of banks from member to nonmember status. It has therefore seized every occasion, such as the Reply provides, to stress the desirability of requiring all banks to be members of the System or at least subject to the same reserve requirements as member banks.

Control

Nonmember banks raise a minor problem with respect to control. Their reserve ratios do differ from those of member banks. But nonmember banks hold only one-quarter of all deposits, this fraction tends to change rather predictably, and changes in it can be monitored and offset by open market operations.

A far more important problem with respect to control is the lagged reserve requirement that was introduced by the Fed in 1968. This change has not worked as it was expected to. Instead, by introducing additional delay between Federal Reserve open market operations and the money supply, it has appreciably reduced "the precision with which the money supply can be controlled by the Federal Reserve." Other measures taken by the Fed have had the same effect. In an article on this subject published recently, George Kaufman, long an economist with the Federal Reserve System, concluded, "by increasing the complexity of the money multiplier, proliferating rate ceilings on different types of deposits, and encouraging banks, albeit unintentionally, to search out nondeposit sources of funds, the Federal Reserve has increased its own difficulty in controlling the stock of money. . . . To the extent the increased difficulty supports the long voiced contention of some Federal Reserve officials that they are unable to control the stock of money even if they so wished, the actions truly represent a self-fulfilling prophecy."

Even more basic is the procedure used by the Open Market Desk of the New York Federal Reserve Bank in carrying out the directives of the Open Market Committee. These directives have increasingly been stated in terms of desired changes in monetary aggregates rather than in money-market conditions. However, the Desk has not adapted its procedure to the new objective. Instead, it tries to use money-market conditions (that is, interest rates) as an indirect device to control monetary aggregates. Many students of the subject believe that this technique is inefficient. Money-market conditions are affected by many forces other than the Fed's operations. As a result, the Desk cannot control money-market conditions very accurately and cannot predict accurately what changes in money-market conditions are required to produce the desired change in monetary aggregates.

An alternative procedure would be to operate directly on high-powered money, which the Fed can control to a high degree of precision. Many of us believe that the changes in high-powered money required to produce the desired change in monetary aggregates can be estimated tolerably closely even now. They could be estimated with still greater precision if the Fed were to rationalize the structure of reserve requirements.

Measurement

Repeatedly, in the past few years, the Fed's statisticians have retrospectively revised estimates of monetary aggregates, sometimes, as in December 1972, by very substantial amounts.

The one source of measurement error mentioned in the Reply is the unavailability of data on nonmember banks. This is a source of error because nonmember banks report deposit data on only two, or sometimes four, dates a year. The resulting error in estimates for intervening or subsequent dates has sometimes been sizable, but mostly it has accounted for a minor part of the statistical revisions. In any event, this source of error can be reduced drastically by sampling and other devices which the Fed could undertake on its own without additional legislation.

More important sources of error are seasonal adjustment procedures and the estimation and treatment of cash items, nondeposit liabilities, and foreign-held deposits.

It has long seemed to me little short of scandalous that the money supply figures should require such substantial and frequent revision. The Fed is itself the primary source of data required to measure the money supply; it can get additional data it may need; it has a large and highly qualified research staff. Yet for years it has failed to undertake the research effort necessary to correct known defects in its money supply series.*

Conclusion

For more than a decade monetary growth has been accelerating. It has been higher in the past three years than in any other three-year period since the end of World War II. Inflation has also accelerated over the past decade. It too has been higher in the past three years than in any other three-year period since 1947. Economic theory and empirical evidence combine to establish a strong presumption that the acceleration in monetary growth is largely responsible for the acceleration in inflation. Nothing in the Reply of the Chairman of the Federal Reserve System to your letter contradicts or even questions that conclusion. And nothing in that Reply denies that the Federal Reserve System had the power to prevent the sharp acceleration in monetary growth.

I recognize, of course, that there are now, and have been in the past, strong political pressures on the Fed to continue rapid monetary growth. Once inflation has proceeded as far as it already has, it will, as the Reply says, take some time to eliminate it. Moreover, there is literally no way to end inflation that will not involve a temporary, though perhaps fairly protracted, period of low economic growth and relatively high unemployment. Avoidance of the earlier excessive monetary growth would have had far less costly consequences for the community than cutting monetary growth down to an appropriate level will now have. But the damage has been done. The longer we wait, the harder it will be. And there is no other way to stop inflation.

The only justification for the Fed's vaunted independence is to enable it to take measures that are wise for the long run even if not popular in the short run. That is why it is so discouraging to have the Reply consist almost entirely of a denial of responsibility for inflation and an attempt to place the blame elsewhere.

If the Fed does not explain to the public the nature of our problem and the costs involved in ending inflation, if it does not take the lead in imposing the temporarily unpopular measures required, who will?

*On January 31, 1974, after this comment had been drafted, the Board of Governors of the Federal Reserve System announced "the formation of a special committee of prominent academic experts to review concepts, procedures and methodology involved in estimating the money supply and other monetary aggregates." I have agreed to serve as a member of this committee.

34

Operational Constraints on the Stabilization of Money Supply Growth

Alan R. Holmes

The Federal Reserve has frequently been accused of money market myopia. This is a false charge usually made by economists affected in some degree by a peculiar myopia of their own. The charge stems, or so it seems to me, in the first instance from a confusion between monetary policy decisions *per se* and the operational instructions given by the FOMC for the day-to-day conduct of open market operations.

The Federal Reserve has always maintained that money matters just as it believes that interest rates matter too, particularly given the institutional framework of our financial system. In reaching policy decisions, the Committee not only pays attention to the real economy—to current and prospective developments in employment, prices, GNP and the balance of payments—but it also considers a broad range of interest rates and monetary measures. Among the monetary measures, there are the various reserve measures—total reserves, nonborrowed reserves, excess reserves, and free or net borrowed reserves. Next are the measures of money ranging from M_1 on out. Finally, there are the credit measures, bank credit, the credit proxy—ranging on out to total credit in the economy and the flow of funds.

While I do not believe that research results to date justify adopting an operating policy designed solely to stabilize the monetary growth rate, I, nevertheless, believe that the research efforts stimulated by the monetary school have a real value. Out of

Reprinted with deletions from the Federal Reserve Bank of Boston, *Controlling Monetary Aggregates* (Boston: The Bank, 1969), pp. 65-78, by permission of the publisher and the author.

it all, there is bound to develop a better understanding of the relationships between monetary aggregates, interest rates, and the real economy. I suspect, however, that the underlying relationships are so complex that no simple formula can be found as an unerring guide to monetary policy. The psychology and expectations involved in private decision making are probably too complicated to compress into any such simple formula.

Thus, I think, the FOMC is right in paying attention to a broad range of reserve, money, and credit aggregates; in trying to understand why they are behaving as they are; and in assessing the implications of their past and prospective behavior for employment, prices, and GNP. Further, I think the Federal Reserve is right in not restricting itself to a single theory of money and in choosing the best from a number of theories.

In reaching a policy decision, the Committee pays close attention to a wide spectrum of interest rates, ranging from the Federal funds rate, through the short and intermediate term rates, out to rates in the long-term capital markets. One obvious problem with interest rates as either an indicator or target of monetary policy is that they may be measuring not only the available supply of money and credit but also the demand for money and credit. Obviously, a policy aimed at stabilizing interest rates in the face of rising demand will give rise to greater increases in the monetary aggregates than would be the case if demand were stable. Interest rates can also be misleading indicators of underlying conditions at times of special short-lived supply and demand relationships—of some fiscal policy development or of prospects for war or peace in Vietnam, to take some recent examples. But interest rates have the decided advantage of being instantaneously available, and they can often be excellent indicators that estimates of monetary aggregates, particularly reserve estimates, are wrong. The judicious use of interest rates as correctors of poor aggregative forecasting should not be underestimated.

Thus, when the FOMC reaches a policy decision, it is not thinking exclusively in terms of rates or of monetary aggregates, but of a combination of the two. A move toward a tighter policy would normally involve a decline in the rate of growth of the aggregates and an increase in rates. And a move toward an easier policy would normally involve an increase in aggregate growth rates and a decline in interest rates.

But, unfortunately, given the nature of our commercial banking system, money and credit flows cannot be turned off and on instantaneously. At any given point in time, banks have on their books a large volume of firm commitments to lend money. Also, potential borrowers may, if they surmise that the Federal Reserve is tightening policy, decide *en masse* to take down loans in anticipation of future needs. Hence, there may be, for a time, an undeterred growth in bank credit and the money supply. But this, in turn, should involve a more rapid and larger rise in interest rates than would otherwise have been the case. The point is that the Federal Reserve is always making a trade-off between aggregates and rates. It has, and takes, the opportunity at its FOMC meetings every three or four weeks to assess what has developed, what the impact has been on the real economy and on private expectations of the future, and to determine whether another turn of the screw—toward tightness or ease—is called for.

The moral of the story, if there is one, is that Federal Reserve policy should not be judged exclusively in terms of interest rates or in terms of monetary aggregates but by the combination of the two—and by the resultant impact of this combination on market psychology and expectations about the future and, ultimately, on the real economy. The weights placed on aggregates and rates, including those placed on individual components of either group, can and do vary from time to time. It is important to recognize that there is nothing in the present framework of Federal Reserve policymaking, or policy implementation, that would prevent placing still greater weight on aggregates if that should be considered desirable. I think it is obvious that aggregate measures of money and credit are getting their full share of attention at the present time.

Rates and aggregates, along with real economic developments and prospects, are the basic ingredients of any FOMC policy decision. They are also involved in the instructions that the FOMC gives to the Federal Reserve Bank of New York for the day-to-day conduct of operations in the interval between Committee meetings. Obviously, it would make little sense for the Committee to issue directives to the Desk in terms of the real economy with which it is basically concerned. Not only are open market operations in the very short run unlikely to have a major impact on the real economy, but adequate measures of economic change are unavailable in the short time span involved.

Thus, the Committee, in its instructions to the Manager, focuses on a set of money market conditions—a blend of interest rates and rates of growth of various reserve and credit measures—the Committee believes is compatible with its longer-run goals. At each FOMC meeting, the Committee has before it staff estimates of ranges for the Federal funds rate, the Treasury bill rate, bank borrowings from the Federal Reserve, and net borrowed reserves that the Staff believes compatible with an overall policy of no change or of greater tightness or ease, as the case may be. Additionally, the Staff prepares estimates of the money supply and the bank credit proxy that it believes likely to correspond to a given set of money market conditions. Needless to say, these forecasting techniques fall short of being an exact science, but their existence tends to focus attention on the vital interrelationships between interest rates and aggregates that will ensue from any policy decision.

As is well known, since the spring of 1966 the Open Market Committee has usually included in the directive a proviso clause with an explicit reference to one aggregate measure—the bank credit proxy—with specific instructions to modify open market operations if the proxy is tending to move outside a predicted or desired range. Thus the Committee expects to see money market conditions moving to the tighter end of the scale if the proxy is expanding too rapidly, or towards the easier end of the scale if the proxy is falling short.

How does this all work out in practice? First of all, the money and capital markets send out a constant stream of signals of interest rate developments that we can and do measure from day to day and hour to hour. If there are deviations from past patterns or levels (or from anticipated patterns or levels) of interest rates, we can usually find out a good deal about the source and meaning of the deviations.

Second, we have forecasts of the factors affecting bank reserves apart from open market operations—estimates of float, currency in circulation, gold and foreign exchange operations, and the level of Treasury balances at the Federal Reserve. These factors can and do supply or absorb hundreds of millions in bank reserves from day to day or week to week. The estimates are made at the Board and at the New York bank for the current statement week and for three weeks ahead, and they are revised daily on the basis of the inflow of reserve information available within the System each day.

Third, we have available an estimate once a week (on Friday) of the bank credit proxy and of the money supply for the current month; and, as we get toward the middle of the month, for the next month as well. And this estimate can be revised—at least informally—by the middle of a calendar week, after there has been time to analyze weekend deposit performance at Reserve City banks and a weekly sample of deposit data at country banks. We can then use these aggregate data—available less frequently and with a greater time lag than interest rate or reserve data—to modify subsequent open market operations with an impact on interest rates and the reserve supply.

In summary, there are four main points that I would like to draw from this abbreviated review of monetary policy formulation and implementation. First, monetary policymakers have always paid close attention to monetary aggregates—along with interest rates—in the formulation of policy decisions. It has been the interaction of the two on the real economy—on employment, prices, the GNP, and the balance of payments—that has been the focus of concern. Reluctance to adopt money supply as the sole guide to policy decisions has not stemmed from lack of concern about money but from the lack of evidence that the adoption of such a guide would give the desired results. Empirical research to date does not supply that evidence.

Second, it is incorrect to characterize monetary policy in terms of money supply alone. A rise in money supply—outside some specified range—does not necessarily mean easy money nor a decline of tight money. Policy has to be judged by a combined pattern of interest rates and monetary aggregates—and money supply is only one of those aggregates.

Third, since the spring of 1966 the FOMC has included an aggregate measure—the bank credit proxy—in its directive covering day-to-day open market operations. While use of the aggregates to shape interest rates and reserve measures has probably not been as aggressive as the monetarists would like to see (and, besides, it is the wrong aggregate according to some of them), it has been a useful adjunct to the directive.

Fourth, information on the performance of monetary aggregates . . . is available only with a time lag, and week-to-week forecasts of monthly data have tended to be erratic. This suggests that, in the short run, interest rate movements may provide a very useful indication of forecasting errors. It further suggests that aggregates can contribute more to the process of policy formulation—when there are opportunities to take a long-range view—than to the process of policy implementation as exemplified by the second paragraph of the directive. But current procedures for both policy formulation and policy implementation provide room for as much attention to monetary aggregates as may be required, and it is apparent that the aggregates are receiving a full measure of attention at the present time.

Operational Problems in Stabilizing Money Supply

In the absence of a concrete proposal, there are major difficulties in attempting to isolate the operational problems that would be involved in stabilizing the monetary growth rate to some targeted level. Much would depend on the definition of the money supply used, the time span over which the growth rate was to be stabilized, and whether the money supply was to be the sole indicator and/or target of monetary policy or mainly a primary indicator or target.

It obviously makes a great deal of difference whether the proposal is for a rigid monetary rule or whether there is room—and how much—for discretion. Some of the proposals for moving to the money supply as a target and indicator have been coupled with the complete abandonment of so-called "defensive" open market operations—a suggestion that raises a host of other problems that are not relevant to the main point at issue.

There is, of course, a strong temptation to pick and choose among the various suggestions and to erect a money supply target as a "straw man" that can be readily demolished. I shall try to resist that temptation and consider in more general terms the operational problems that would be involved if the FOMC were to move to money supply as the principal indicator of policy or target for open market operations.

But before setting straw men aside, it might be worthwhile to consider the proposition that open market operations should be limited to the injection of a fixed amount of reserves at regular intervals—say $20 million a week. So-called defensive operations—the offsetting of net reserve supply or absorption through movements in float, currency in circulation, gold or foreign exchange operations, etc.—would be abandoned, leaving the banking system to make its own adjustments to these outside movements. While such a system would certainly reduce the level of operations at the Trading Desk, it has never been quite clear how the banking system would make the adjustments to the huge ebb and flow of reserves stemming from movements in the so-called market factors. Either banks would have to operate with excess reserves amounting to many billion dollars at periods of maximum reserve supply by market factors or they would have to have practically unlimited access to the discount window. Neither possibility seems very desirable, if one is really interested in maintaining a steady growth rate in some monetary aggregate.

There is no reason to suppose that banks would, in fact, hold idle excess reserves in the amounts required. At times of reserve supply by market factors, attempts to dispose of excesses through the Federal funds market would drive the Federal funds rate down and generally lower dealer borrowing costs and the interest rate level. At other times, the reverse would happen. As a result, there would be either feast or famine in the money market, inducing changes in bank loan and investment behavior that would make it impossible to achieve the steady growth of financial aggregates that was presumably desired to begin with. The resultant uncertainty would undermine the ability of the money and capital markets to underwrite and to provide a means of cash and liquidity adjustment among individuals and firms.

The opening of the discount window, on the other hand, runs the risk that reserves acquired at the initiative of the commercial banks would be used to expand the total supply of money and credit and not solely to meet the ebb and flow of reserves through movement of market factors. As a result, the Federal Reserve would have to institute the same controls—in a decentralized fashion—at the various discount windows to limit the supply of reserves that are now provided in a more impersonal way through open market operations.

Consequently, it would appear wise to disassociate the debate over money supply from the problem of so-called defensive open market operations. There seems to be no reason why a seasonal movement of currency, a random movement of float, or a temporary bulge in Federal Reserve foreign currency holdings should automatically be allowed to affect the money market or bank reserve positions. There would seem to be no point in consciously reducing our efficient and integrated money and capital markets to the status of a primitive market where the central bank lacks the means and/or the ability to prevent sharp fluctuations in the availability of reserves—in the misguided attempt to hold "steady" the central bank's provision of reserves.

But the point remains that the ebb and flow of reserves through market factors is very large. While defensive operations are generally successful in smoothing out the impact of these movements on reserves, even a 3 percent margin of error in judging these movements would exceed a $20 million reserve injection in many weeks. Hence the small, regular injection of reserves, week by week, is not really a very practical approach.

The idea of a regular injection of reserves—in some approaches at least—also suffers from a naive assumption that the banking system only expands loans after the System (or market factors) have put reserves in the banking system. In the real world, banks extend credit, creating deposits in the process, and look for the reserves later. The question then becomes one of whether and how the Federal Reserve will accommodate the demand for reserves. In the very short run, the Federal Reserve has little or no choice about accommodating that demand; over time, its influence can obviously be felt.

In any given statement week, the reserves required to be maintained by the banking system are predetermined by the level of deposits existing two weeks earlier.

Since excess reserves in the banking system normally run at frictional levels—exceptions relate mainly to carryover excess or deficit positions reached in the previous week or errors by banks in managing their reserve positions—the level of total reserves in any given statement week is also pretty well determined in advance. Since banks have to meet their reserve requirements each week (after allowance for carryover privileges) and since they can do nothing within that week to affect required reserves, that total amount of reserves has to be available to the banking system.

The Federal Reserve does have discretion as to how the banks can acquire this predetermined level of needed reserves. The reserves can be supplied from the combination of open market operations and the movement of other reserve factors, or they can come from member bank borrowing at the discount window. In this context, it might be noted that the suggestion that open market operations should be used in the short run to prevent a rise in total reserves through member bank borrowing is completely illogical. Within a statement week, the reserves have to be there; and, in one way or another, the Federal Reserve will have to accommodate the need for them.

This does not mean that the way that reserves are supplied makes no difference nor that aggregate indicators cannot be used to influence the decision as to whether reserves will be supplied through open market operations or whether banks will be required to use the discount window. A decision to provide less reserves through open market operations in any given week, thereby forcing banks to borrow more at the window, could be triggered by a prior FOMC decision (based partly on a review of aggregate money and credit measures) to move to tighter money market conditions, or it might be occasioned by the implementation of the proviso clause if the bank credit proxy was exhibiting a tendency to expand more rapidly than the Committee deemed to be warranted.

No individual bank, of course, has unlimited access to the discount window. Borrowing from the Federal Reserve involves the use of adjustment credit that is limited in both amount and in frequency of use. Eventually, as the aggregate level of borrowing is built up, the discount officers' disciplinary counseling of individual banks that have made excessive use of the window will force the banks to make the necessary asset adjustments. Other banks, desirous of maintaining their access to the discount window intact for use in their own emergency situations, will try to avoid use of the window by bidding up for Federal funds or by making other adjustments in their reserve positions. In the process, interest rates, spreading out from the Federal funds rate, will have been on the rise. As pressure on the banks is maintained or intensified, the banking system as a whole is forced to adjust its lending and investment policies with corresponding effects on money and credit—and eventually on the real economy.

A switch to money supply as the target of monetary policy would, of course, make no difference in the process though which open market operations work on the banking system to affect monetary aggregates. But, depending on the time span over which it was desired to stabilize the rate of monetary growth and on whether money were to become the exclusive indicator and/or target, there would be a significant difference in the rate of interest rate variations. How great that variation might be would be a matter of concern for the Federal Reserve in the conduct of open market operations. I would like to return to that subject in just a few minutes.

First, however, it may be worthwhile to touch on the extensively debated subject whether the Federal Reserve, if it wanted to, could control the rate of money supply growth. In my view, this lies well within the power of the Federal Reserve to accomplish provided one does not require hair-splitting precision and is thinking in terms of a time span long enough to avoid the erratic, and largely meaningless, movements of money supply over short periods.

This does not mean that the money supply could be used efficiently as a target for day-to-day operations. Given the facts that adequate money supply data are not available without a time lag and that there may be more statistical noise in daily or weekly figures than evidence of trend, we would be forced to rely on our monthly estimates for guidance in conducting day-to-day operations. Projections of money supply—and other monetary aggregates—are, of course, an important ingredient of monetary policymaking. While I believe we have made considerable progress in perfecting techniques, forecasting is far from an exact science. Money supply forecasting is especially hazardous because of the noise in the daily data and because of the massive movements in and out of Treasury Tax and Loan accounts at commercial banks.

Let me illustrate the sort of problem that might be faced by citing some numbers representing successive weekly forecasts of annual rates of money supply growth for a recent month—admittedly not a good month for our projectors. The projections cited begin with the one made in the last week of the preceding month and end with the projection made in the last week of the then current month. The numbers are −0.5 percent, +4 percent, +9 percent, +14 percent, +7 percent and +4.5 percent. I might also note that, in the middle of that then-current month, the projections for the following month were for a 14 percent rate of growth. By the end of the month, the projection was −2.5 percent.

Assuming that the Desk had been assigned a target of a 5 percent growth rate for money supply, it seems quite obvious that, at mid-month, when the forecast was for a 14 percent growth rate for both the current and the following month, we would have been required to act vigorously to absorb reserves. Two weeks later, on the other hand, if the estimates had held up, we would have been required to reverse direction rather violently.

The foregoing should suggest that short-run measures of monetary growth do not provide a good target for the day-to-day conduct of open market operations. Use of such a target runs the serious risk that open market operations would be trying to offset random movements in money supply, faulty short-run seasonal adjustments, or errors of forecasting. In the process, offensive open market operations might have been increased substantially—and I have the uneasy feeling that financial markets might find such operations offensive in more than one sense.

While short-term measures of money supply growth appear to be too erratic to use as a primary target of open market operations, there are times when cumulative short-term evidence begins to build up—even between meetings of the FOMC—that strongly suggests that a deviation from past trends has gotten under way. Such evidence could of course be used, if interpreted cautiously, to modify operations in much the same way that the bank credit proxy is now used.

To return to the question of interest rate variation, there appears to be general agreement that variations would be greater with money supply as a guideline than they have been while the System was using multiple guidelines involving both monetary aggregates and interest rates. How great interest rate variations would be, would depend very much on how rigid the guideline was and how short the time horizon in which it was supposed to operate might be. The question of how great variations might be can probably never be resolved in the absence of any concrete experience.

Some exponents of the monetary school, however, seem to imply that interest rate variations make no difference at all—somehow the market is supposed to work everything out. It seems to me that there are serious risks in the assumption that the financial markets of the real world—in contrast to the markets of a theoretical model—can readily handle any range of interest rate variation. Pushing too hard on money supply control in the face of rapid interest rate adjustment could wind up by destroying the very financial mechanism which the monetary authority must use if it expects to have any impact on the real economy. Psychology and expectations play too great a role in the operations of these markets to permit the monetary authority to ignore the interpretations that the market may place on current central bank operations.

Thus, in the real world of day-to-day open market operations—theoretical considerations aside—the use of money supply as a target would appear to be too mechanistic and, in the short run, too erratic to be much use. The use of money market conditions—a blend of interest rates and reserve and credit measures—is a more realistic short-run guide, providing opportunities for trade-offs between interest rates and aggregates in the light of market psychology and expectations. Aggregate measures, including the money supply, are, of course, indispensable indicators for the monetary authorities as they reach policy decisions. But exclusive reliance on—or blind faith in—any single indicator does not appear justified by the current state of the arts.

As a description of Federal Reserve policy procedures this 1969 article is obviously dated (for a more up-to-date description the reader should examine the article by Lombra and Torto in Section IV A). Nevertheless, this article is an excellent representative of the body of opinion which objects to the "money supply only" school.—Ed.

35

A Money Stock Target

Thomas Mayer

Whether the Federal Reserve should aim at an interest rate target or a money stock target is one of the most important questions in macroeconomic policy. Unfortunately, the evidence is by no means all in yet. The choice between a money stock target and an interest rate target involves a number of separate issues. One of these is a measurement problem. Obviously, if one cannot adequately measure the interest rate—or the money stock—then this variable should not be used as the target of monetary policy. And there are serious problems in measuring both the money stock and the interest rate. As far as the money stock is concerned the measurement problem is mainly one of deciding whether to define money as M_1, M_2, or M_3. Since the growth rates of these magnitudes differ over time, a policy that may seem restrictive when money is defined as M_1 *might* seem loose when money is defined as M_2 or M_3. However, one should beware of exaggerating this problem. As Table 1 shows, although the growth rates of M_1, M_2, or M_3 did differ substantially during the last ten years, there was a high degree of correlation among the growth rates of all three measures. The years when M_1 grew unusually fast were, with a few exceptions, also years in which M_2 and M_3 grew unusually fast, and a similar thing applies to years of slow growth.

Reprinted, with deletions, from *Monetary Policy Oversight,* Hearings Before the Committee on Banking, Housing, and Urban Affairs, U.S. Senate, 94th Congress, First Session (1975), pp. 179-186, by permission of the author.
This reading is particularly closely related to the readings in Section IV A.—Ed.

Table 1. Growth Rates of M_1, M_2, and M_3, 1965–1974

	Growth Rate[1] (percent)			Rank of Growth Rate[2]		
	M_1	M_2	M_3	M_1	M_2	M_3
1965	4.6	8.7	8.5	7	6	5
1966	2.4	5.5	4.9	10	9	9
1967	6.6	10.0	9.8	3	3	3
1968	7.9	9.4	8.3	2	4	6½
1969	3.5	2.6	2.9	9	10	10
1970	6.1	8.4	8.3	5½	7	6½
1971	6.3	11.2	13.2	4	1	1
1972	8.7	11.1	13.1	1	2	2
1973	6.1	8.8	8.8	5½	5	4
1974 preliminary	4.5	7.3	6.7	8	8	8

Source: 1975 "Economic Report of the President," p. 310.
[1] December figure as percent increase over previous December.
[2] Starting with highest growth rate.

There is a substantial measurement problem for the interest rate too. The meaningful target is not the nominal rate of interest, but the expected *real* rate of interest; that is the stated interest rate minus the expected rate of change in prices. And while the actual change in prices can readily be measured, the *expected* rate of price change cannot. It is, therefore, tempting for the Federal Reserve, and others, to use the nominal rate instead. But this can be highly misleading. Suppose, for example, that the nominal rate of interest is 10 percent at a time when the public expects a 9 percent annual price increase over the life of the loan. Then, although the nominal rate of interest is high, the expected real rate is very low, being only one percent.

Second, while it is easy to talk about "*the* rate of interest" in the abstract, in reality there are many different rates of interest, and it is not clear how one should combine them into a single measure. For example, if the short-term rate and the intermediate-term rates are falling, while the long-term rate is rising, is "the rate of interest" rising or falling? Third, many interest rates are imputed rates which are not recorded in any market and therefore cannot be measured. Fourth, the rate of interest is but one dimension of the cost and difficulty of borrowing; the availability of funds is also important, and this is hard to quantify.

Another important aspect of the choice of the money growth rate or the interest rate as the monetary policy target involves a more abstract issue. Suppose that the Federal Reserve is trying to keep income constant, but that an increase in the profitability of new investment, or, for that matter, an increase in the government deficit, threatens to raise income. Such increases in expenditures raise the rate of interest. If the Federal Reserve follows an interest rate target, it responds to this by increasing the stock of money to keep the interest rate from rising. This means that the Federal Reserve is neutralizing an important automatic stabilizer, the rise in the interest rate, with its resulting tendency to reduce expenditures. It is, therefore, destabilizing the economy. On the other hand, if the Federal Reserve had followed a money stock target, it would have kept the money stock constant and allowed the interest rate to rise, which would have been stabilizing.

However, consider now a very different case where expenditure incentives are constant, but the amount of money the public wants to hold at the prevailing income level rises, perhaps because of greater uncertainty or perhaps because interest rates are falling. Such an increase in the demand for money lowers expenditures and hence income. In this case, if the Federal Reserve has a money stock target, it keeps the supply of money constant, and does not offset the greater demand for money. With the supply of money held constant, and the demand for money increasing, interest rates increase, and hence expenditures, and thus income, fall. On the other hand, if the Federal Reserve had followed an interest rate target, it would not have allowed the interest rate to rise but would have offset the rise in the demand for money by increasing supply. Thus, in this case, where the public's demand for money at each level of income increases, the Federal Reserve should follow an interest rate target, while in the previous case, where the demand for money increased because expenditure incentives and hence income rose, it should follow a money stock target.*

Unfortunately, the Federal Reserve does not have any reliable way of deciding which of these two cases it is facing at any particular time. It must follow either a money stock target and be wrong in some situations, or have an interest rate target and be wrong in some other situations. And, unfortunately, we do not have convincing evidence as to which of these two situations is the more common.

However, there is a third aspect to the choice between a money stock target and an interest rate target, and on this aspect the choice is clear; a money stock target is superior. This is the timing of policy. One very serious problem with the use of monetary policy as a stabilization device is that there are probably fairly long lags in its effectiveness. Hence, by the time a monetary policy becomes effective economic conditions may have changed enough for it to be destabilizing. And this is much more of a danger if the Federal Reserve uses an interest rate target than if it uses a money stock target. A money stock target speeds up the effectiveness of monetary policy. If the Federal Reserve increases the money stock, the fact that income does not respond right away means that the interest rate falls initially to a lower level than the level it will reach when income has fully responded. And this initial overshooting of the interest rate means that in the early stages of the monetary policy a greater stimulus to expenditures occurs, so that some of the impact of the policy is brought forward in time. On the other hand, if the Federal Reserve aims at a specific interest rate target, it brings the interest rate to that target right away and thus prevents the beneficial overshooting of the interest rate.[1]

On the other hand, it may seem that there are two advantages to following an interest rate target. One is the argument that the Federal Reserve can, in this way, reduce the high interest rates we have been experiencing. But this argument is open

---

*This problem is considered in detail in the first part of the Davis article in Section IV A.—Ed.
[1]Admittedly, the Federal Reserve could aim at an interest rate target which allows for an initial overshoot, but we cannot be sure that it will actually do so. And even if it does, it would not know how much of an overshoot to allow for.

to two fatal objections. One is that complaints about high interest rates ignore the distinction between real and nominal rates. The real rate of interest has not been high in recent years, it has been abnormally low. Thus, although the average *nominal* interest rate on short-term bank loans to business was 11.28 percent in 1974, the real rate (that is, the rate after subtracting the percentage increase in the private GNP deflator) was approximately zero. Despite the high nominal rate, 1974 was not a year in which lenders benefited at the cost of borrowers. The second argument against having the Federal Reserve follow the goal of keeping nominal interest rates low, is that such a policy would fail. The only way the Federal Reserve can, in the short run, keep the interest rate down is to have a very high growth rate of the money stock. But this would be highly inflationary, and inflation, in turn, raises the interest rate. Hence, a policy of keeping interest rates down could succeed only in the short run, and would do so only at the cost of greater and greater inflation.

So far, the discussion of the interest rate target has ignored a very important consideration. This is that using an interest rate target subjects the Federal Reserve to a temptation it seems to find hard to resist. This is to select as its interest rate target, not a rate which is appropriate to obtain the desired income level, but rather to choose an interest rate target which helps the Federal Reserve in certain primarily housekeeping tasks. And the interest rate target it thus selects is likely to be inappropriate from the point of view of income stabilization. Thus, the Federal Reserve is very concerned to prevent large fluctuations of the interest rate because it feels that major interest rate movements would hurt participants in the financial markets, such as government security dealers, and would thereby reduce the efficiency of the money market. Yet, if there is a large increase in, say, the incentives to invest, or in the deficit, a sharp rise in the interest rate may well be needed to stabilize income. The Federal Reserve as an agency in continual day-to-day contact with the money market places a much greater value on money market stability—relative to the stability of GNP—than seems warranted. It appears to suffer from that standard disease of bureaucracy, myopia.

Furthermore, the Federal Reserve has recently argued that it must avoid large declines in the interest rate to prevent a further fall in the dollar exchange rate. This appears to be one of the main reasons for the Federal Reserve's current highly restrictive policy. It furnishes a good example of the type of mischief an interest rate target is likely to cause. It is true that a decline in the dollar would have some disadvantages. It would antagonize foreign central banks, and also, by raising the cost of imports, it would raise the U.S. inflation rate. But, at the same time, a decline in the dollar would help the fight against the recession by stimulating exports and reducing imports, though admittedly with a lag. And beyond that, it requires a peculiar sense of priorities for the Federal Reserve to follow a highly contractive policy during the worst recession in the postwar period primarily in order to prevent a decline in the foreign exchange rate. It is this sort of thing which makes me believe that the Federal Reserve is abusing its independence. The adoption of flexible exchange rates should have freed the Federal Reserve from having to worry about international repercussions of monetary policy. And now we find the Federal Reserve sacrificing the domestic economy to foreign exchange considerations to a much greater extent than it has ever done before. It reminds one of the policy followed by the Bank of England in the 1920's, a policy which probably explains some of the difficulties the British economy faces even now.

For these reasons I believe that an interest rate target is inferior to a money stock target. Unfortunately, the Federal Reserve has a strongly ingrained tendency to use the interest rate as its target. Despite Federal Reserve statements that the money stock now receives more attention than it did in the past, when the chips are down, the Federal Reserve still appears to use an interest rate target. Hence, I believe that some mechanism such as the Concurrent Resolution is needed to stop the Federal Reserve's overemphasis on interest rates.

Can the Federal Reserve Control the Money Stock?

There is firm evidence that the Federal Reserve, if it *really* wants to, can control the money supply quite accurately over a period of, say, six months, and with moderate accuracy over a three-month period. Hence, I interpret the recent episode of money growth falling very substantially below the Federal Reserve's goal as reflecting the Federal Reserve's lack of sufficient determination. The Federal Reserve certainly would like the money stock to grow faster, but—and this is a big but—it also wants to avoid a large decline in interest rates. And, as I have pointed out above, one cannot attain both a money stock target and an interest rate target at the same time. By aiming at both, the Federal Reserve is compromising its money stock target. When the Federal Reserve says that it is trying to raise the money growth rate, this is certainly correct. But the answer is that, though it is "trying," it is not trying hard enough.

Both theoretical and empirical analyses tell us that the Federal Reserve could control the money stock if it were not distracted by its interest rate targets. To start with the theoretical analysis, the Federal Reserve can certainly control the stock of reserves. Now banks, as profit-maximizing institutions, have an incentive to use additional reserves they obtain to increase their loans and security holdings, since they earn nothing on excess reserves. To be sure, banks do want to hold a certain amount of excess reserves, but the Federal Reserve can provide them with more reserves than that, and once this is done banks have an incentive to use these additional reserves. At one time it was widely believed that during the 1930's banks had a completely insatiable demand for excess reserves, that however many reserves the Federal Reserve supplied to them, they would simply hold them as excess reserves. Monetary policy, it was said, was like pushing on a piece of string. But subsequent studies of excess reserve holdings in the 1930's have built a very persuasive case that this argument is invalid, that the demand for excess reserves was not insatiable, and that banks would have used additional reserves to expand the money supply.

Furthermore, the situation is now quite different than it was in the 1930's. Then, interest rates were so low that some people argued (mistakenly I believe) that it was not worth the trouble and costs for banks to buy securities. Interest rates are hardly that low now. Moreover, the argument in the 1930's was that although banks had the reserves to make more loans, the demand for loans was so small that banks could not find credit-worthy customers. Again, this is hardly the situation at present.

To be sure, we now hear again the argument that the amount of money in existence is determined, not by the potential supply, i.e., by the amount banks could create, but by the demand for money. But this argument is easily refuted by a diagram. Figure 1 shows the standard supply and demand curves for any good, including money. As this figure shows, a shift in the supply curve obviously results in an increase in the supply actually taken by the market, albeit at a lower price. To be sure, there is always a point of satiation when the public has all it wants. But this point is reached only when the price is zero. And this is hardly true of nominal interest rates at present.

Let us now turn to the empirical evidence on the postwar behavior of the money stock. There have been numerous empirical studies of the Federal Reserve's ability to control the money stock. And these studies, many of them done by the Federal Reserve's own staff, show that over a period of six months, or so, the Federal Reserve has quite good control over the money stock, and that it has fair control over a three month period.

To be sure, these studies relate to previous years, and one might argue—though this sort of argument is always suspect—that the present situation is different. But the evidence bearing directly on the current situation furnishes no support whatsoever to anyone who argues that the Federal Reserve cannot control the money supply. To this let us assume that the Federal Reserve, although it is really trying to control the money stock, is unable to do so, and [let us] see what the data would show if this were the case. We would then find that the Federal Reserve is providing banks with a large volume of reserves but that the banks are not making sufficient loans, or buying enough securities, to use up these reserves. Instead, they are holding a large

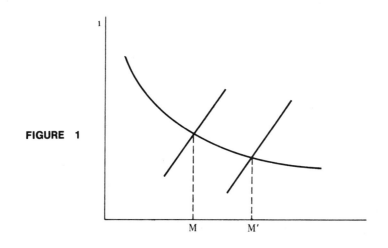

FIGURE 1

volume of excess reserves. Only in this case, where banks do not use the reserves supplied to them, could one argue that the Federal Reserve is impotent to expand the money supply since those reserves which *are* used (and are, therefore, not held as excess reserves) clearly result in an increase in the money stock.

Hence, we can see whether the Federal Reserve is, in fact, unable to raise the money growth rate by looking at what is happening to excess reserves. As Table 2 shows this is not the case. Excess reserves as a percent of required reserves were not large in 1974. In fact, they averaged somewhat less than they did for the last ten years. And, if one looks at the last quarter of 1974, a similar picture emerges; while excess reserves (as a percent of required reserves) in the last quarter of 1974 were somewhat higher than they were in the rest of the year, they were actually less than they were in the last quarters of 1972 and 1973. Yet, if the Federal Reserve were really trying to raise the money stock and was prevented from doing so by the reluctance of banks to expand their loans and security holdings, or by a reluctance of the public to hold additional deposits, then we would *have* to find that excess reserves were high and growing.

One might argue that the Federal Reserve is trying to present banks with more reserves but is unable to do so because the public is drawing currency out of banks at a rapid rate and also because banks are reducing their reserves by repaying borrowing. But this argument is completely invalid because the Federal Reserve can offset these two drains of reserves. Incidentally, as far as currency is concerned, the drain into circulation is not as horrendous as some stories seem to suggest. To be sure,

Table 2. Excess Reserves as Percent of Required Reserves

	Excess Reserves as Percent of Required Reserves
December:	
1965	2.03
1966	1.67
1967	1.38
1968	1.70
1969	.93
1970	.94
1971	.53
1972	.70
1973	.75
1974 preliminary	.93
Last quarter:	
1972	.81
1973	.64
1974 preliminary	.63

Source: 1975 "Economic Report of the President," p. 315. 1974 "Economic Report of the President," p. 315.

currency in circulation increased at a high rate (9.9 percent) in 1974, but this is not much greater than its rate of increase in 1973 and 1972 (8.3 percent and 8.2 percent, respectively). Similarly, while banks have substantially reduced their borrowing from the Federal Reserve, in December 1974 their outstanding borrowing (as a percent of required reserves) was not *very* much below its average for the Decembers of the last ten years (1.9 percent vs. 2.3 percent). In fact, in the last ten years there were three years when the figure was below what it was in 1974. Besides, the decline in bank borrowing from the Federal Reserve is not a factor completely exogenous to the Federal Reserve's policy, but is, at least to some extent, surely the result of the discount rate exceeding the Treasury bill rate by an unusually large margin so that banks have little incentive to borrow.

To be sure, there is some anecdotal "evidence" that banks are "awash with liquidity." But this is misleading. The bank credit market is not a perfect market with completely flexible prices. Hence, when the demand for loans falls, it first shows up by banks finding that they cannot make as many loans as they want to—at the prevailing interest rate—to customers who are as good and sound as their current customers. (This is similar to manufacturers who experience a recession first by their inventories increasing.) Hence, banks initially feel "awash with liquidity." But when they respond to changing credit market conditions by lowering their interest rates, and credit standards, their inventory of liquidity is no longer excessive. Hence, reports that, given prevailing interest rates and credit standards, banks are awash with liquidity do not tell us that bank reserves are ample but rather that the prevailing interest rates and credit standards are excessive.

Hence, I conclude that the evidence shows overwhelmingly that, *if* the Federal Reserve really wants to increase the money stock—and is willing to sacrifice its interest rate target—it can do so. And if the Federal Reserve tries to prevent interest rates from falling, then it should acknowledge that the decline in the money growth rate is a direct consequence of its policy, and not something beyond its control.

Statement on the Conduct of Monetary Policy

Milton Friedman

I am honored to testify before this committee on the conduct of monetary policy. In my opinion, House Concurrent Resolution 133 has produced the most important improvement in the institutional structure for the formation of monetary policy of the past four decades. Though the Federal Reserve System was established sixty-two years ago to provide long-term continuity in monetary policy, to the best of my knowledge, it has never before set itself quantitative objectives for as much as a year ahead. It never made its shorter-term objectives public in advance. On the contrary, it kept its policy directive secret as it still does for at least forty-five days. Finally, only in the past five years has it made the rate of growth in monetary aggregates an explicit target of policy.

The resolution changed matters in all these respects: it requires the Federal Reserve to state publicly its "objectives and plans" for growth in the monetary aggregates for a year ahead. This is salutary for the Federal Reserve itself. It should all along have been setting objectives for a considerable period in the future—far longer than twelve months. More important, for the first time it makes the Federal Reserve

Reprinted with deletions from *Second Meeting on the Conduct of Monetary Policy,* Hearings Before the Committee on Banking, Housing, and Urban Affairs, U.S. Senate, Ninety-Fourth Congress, First Session, November 4 and 6, 1975, pp. 42–48.

The next two readings are Senate testimony regarding the Congressional Resolution of 1975 that the Federal Reserve announced its desired money supply growth rates one year in advance. The background behind this Resolution is discussed by Edward J. Kane later in this Section.—Ed.

effectively accountable for its performance, which can be judged against quantitative objectives specified in advance.

The resolution is equally notable for its emphasis on the desirability that long-run monetary growth be commensurate with the economy's increase in productive potential—which implies steady growth, since the economy's productive capacity grows steadily.

1. The Background

The major defect in Federal Reserve performance over the whole of its history has been the erratic behavior of the monetary aggregates. Monetary growth has time and again moved from one extreme to the other: from unduly rapid growth to unduly slow growth. Periods of unduly rapid growth fueled the great inflations of World War I and World War II, and the more recent double-digit inflation of 1974. Periods of unduly slow growth or actual decline produced or deepened the sharp contractions of 1920-21, 1929-33, and 1937-38, as well as the milder recessions of the whole period.

This pattern of swinging from one extreme to the other has continued, as the accompanying table shows:

Table 1. Rates of Monetary Growth, 1970 to 1975

	Annual Rate of Growth of	
	M_1	M_2
June 1970 to June 1973	7.3	10.9
June 1973 to June 1974	5.6	8.7
June 1974 to Jan. 1975	0.9	5.1
Jan. 1975 to July 1975	8.6	12.0
July 1975 to 4 wks. ending Oct. 15	0.3	4.4

The rates of monetary growth over the three-year period from 1970 to 1973 were higher than for any other three-year period since the end of World War II. This rapid monetary growth undoubtedly helped produce the rapid inflation of 1973 and 1974, and even our current inflation. A change in monetary growth has a rapid effect on credit markets, but it generally takes some six or nine months before it affects total spending, and then the effect at first is mainly on physical output. In the U.S., it has generally taken some two years before a change in monetary growth has its main effect on prices.

The mild tapering off of monetary growth from 1973 to 1974 was long overdue and highly desirable. A reduction was essential to slow inflation. A gradual reduction was desirable to avoid a severe economic shock. This gradual reduction contributed to the mild recession that began in late 1973, but it also laid the basis for the tapering off of inflation we have been enjoying this year. Unfortunately, the Fed did not continue this gradual policy. In mid-1974, it enforced a sharp slowdown in monetary growth, which greatly deepened the recession beginning in late 1974. That deepening in the recession was the prelude to the concurrent resolution and no doubt did much to stimulate it.

Unfortunately, as the table shows, the concurrent resolution has not as yet ended the propensity for the Fed to swing widely from one extreme to the other. From January 1975 to July 1975, monetary growth jumped to an even higher rate than during the three years from June 1970 to June 1973. That monetary explosion helped end the recession and produce the vigorous recovery that has been in train since April or May, but it also threatened to produce a renewed acceleration of inflation. The slowdown in monetary growth beginning in July was therefore appropriate, but again it has been too abrupt and threatens to go too far. Were it to continue much longer, it would abort the current recovery and plunge us into renewed recession. I cannot believe that that will be permitted to happen. Indeed, I believe that the greater danger is another monetary explosion, another swing from one extreme to the other.*

The major current problem for monetary policy is to end these erratic swings from one extreme to the other, and to replace them by a steady rate of monetary growth that declines gradually over several years until it can be stabilized at a level consistent with no inflation.

The erratic swings in monetary policy have not reflected similar swings in the Fed's objectives, at least for the period for which the Fed has specified objectives in terms of monetary growth and for which we know what they were. The swings have rather reflected the failure of actual performance to conform to the stated objectives.

After a brief examination of the stated objectives of the Fed, I shall therefore devote most of my remarks to an examination of the reasons for the discrepancies between objectives and performance and for the changes in current procedure that are required in order to reduce those discrepancies. This seems to me the most urgent current problem in improving monetary policy so as to foster stable and non-inflationary economic growth.

2. The Stated Objectives

By requiring the Fed to specify objectives in terms of monetary growth for a considerable period ahead, and by linking the desirable rate of growth to the country's productive potential, the concurrent resolution has gone a long way to assure that the stated objectives will be reasonably well attuned to the economy's needs. That has certainly been the case on the two earlier occasions on which the Fed responded to the resolution. [This statement was prepared without access to the latest response.]

Personally, I have favored slightly lower rates of monetary growth than the 5 to 7-½ percent rate for M_1 and the 8-½ to 10-½ percent rate for M_2 specified by Chairman Burns on the first two occasions. However, my difference on this score is minor. Similarly, I fully endorse Chairman Burns's repeated emphasis that the maintenance

*In the period from July 1975 to January 1976 the M1 growth rate rose to 2.6 and the M2 growth rate rose to 7.1.—Ed.

for any long period of rates of monetary growth at these levels would mean an undesirably high rate of inflation, and hence that it is essential to move to sharply lower rates of monetary growth in order to establish the basis for steady non-inflationary economic growth.

The ultimate target should be a rate of growth in M_2 of roughly 3 to 5 percent a year. That would roughly match the rate of growth in our productive potential. Given the highly stable velocity of M_2 over more than a decade, it would be consistent with roughly stable prices.

Our present knowledge about the short-run effects of changes in the rate of monetary growth is too limited to yield any very precise estimate of how rapidly monetary growth should be reduced to the desired long-run rate. My own judgment is that a transition period of something like three to five years is a reasonable compromise between ending inflation rapidly and avoiding heavy transitional costs. This would require the stated rates of growth for M_2 to be reduced by one to two percentage points each year for the next three to five years.

This suggestion is not inconsistent with the verbal statements by Chairman Burns. An explicit numerical timetable along these lines would however be highly desirable. If the attainment of such a timetable can be made credible, it would provide a basis for private economic and financial planning. The salutary effect on inflationary anticipations would greatly ease the transition to a noninflationary environment.

My only other suggestion with respect to objectives is purely technical: the desirability of expressing them in terms not of rates of growth from a changing base, or not solely in those terms, but of a desired time path of each monetary aggregate plus and minus a percentage band. This suggestion is linked with the desirability of specifying a longer-range timetable. A range of monetary growth rates tied to an initial base produces numerical limits on the aggregate that widen indefinitely, the longer the time that elapses from the base.

3. Performance

When Chairman Burns testified before the House Banking Committee on July 24, 1975, both M_1 and M_2 were above both the original and revised upper limits of the Federal Reserve objectives. Just before his current testimony before this committee, the latest figures then available were below the lower limits, thanks to essentially zero growth from July to mid-October in M_1 and a 4 percent rate of growth in M_2.

As already noted, neither the initial overshooting nor the subsequent sharp retardation were intentional. Both reflected a failure of the Fed to achieve its stated objectives. These were only the latest of such failures.

Some observers have concluded from these failures that the Federal Reserve does not have the power to achieve its targets, that in this area it is a helpless giant. There is a sense in which that conclusion is correct, but a more fundamental sense in which it is wrong.

The conclusion is correct in the sense that the operating procedures now used by the Fed to implement its policy directives tend to produce major discrepancies between objectives and performance. So long as it continues to use those procedures, it will continue to fail to achieve its monetary growth objectives. But there are alternative operating procedures that have been extensively discussed and explored within and without the system and that are entirely feasible that would enable the Fed to reduce sharply the discrepancies between actual monetary growth and intended monetary growth.

These alternative procedures would of course not enable the Fed to hit its target on the nose day by day. There would still be sizable errors from week to week or month to month. But by comparison with present procedures, the errors would not be self-reinforcing. As a result the alternative procedures would enable the Fed to avoid the wide swings from one side to the other that have long characterized Fed performance.

The residual errors under the alternative procedure could be reduced still further by changes in Federal Reserve regulations, particularly with respect to required reserves, that are desirable on other grounds.

I shall elaborate these judgments by (a) explaining why present procedures are defective, (b) outlining the alternative procedures, and (c) suggesting the key changes in regulations that would be desirable to improve still further Federal Reserve control over monetary aggregates.

(a) Present Procedures*

Present procedures are an anachronistic survival of an earlier day. Their persistence is an extraordinary tribute to bureaucratic inertia. Before 1970, the Fed took as its prime objective "money market conditions," i.e., a collection of market interest rates. In 1970, it shifted to money aggregate targets. That was a major and salutary reform but it was stifled at its birth by the failure to adjust the operating procedures to the new target. Instead, the earlier procedures, designed to influence the "money market," were retained.

The way the Fed now operates is to convert its monetary growth objective into a Federal Funds rate which its staff estimates to be consistent with that rate of monetary growth. It then instructs the New York desk to keep the Federal Funds rate within a specified range. In this way, it tried to adapt the earlier procedure, which had been developed in order to influence money market conditions, to its new objective.

The rate of monetary growth is connected with the amount of reserves acquired by banks through a multiplier which determines the change in the quantity of money per dollar change in bank reserves. The amount of reserves banks wish to acquire at any time depends in turn on the relation between the rate of interest that they can earn on additional loans and the cost to them of acquiring funds. The Federal funds rate is one measure of this cost. In principle, therefore, there is a Federal funds rate at each point in time which, if attained, would lead banks to seek to acquire the amount of reserves that would produce any specified rate of monetary growth.

*For further detail on this subject see the Lombra and Torto article in Section IV A.—Ed.

Unfortunately, there are two large slips 'twixt that principle and Federal Reserve practice. The first slip is that the Fed cannot accurately predict the required Federal funds rate. In order to do so, it would have to predict the whole structure of rates of interest under alternative conditions. The Fed certainly can control the Federal funds rate if it wishes to. But it cannot control the many forces that impinge on the market for credit and that determine other interest rates, and it is the relation between these other interest rates and the Federal funds rate that is critical. Federal Reserve operations in the credit market are a minor element in the total credit market. That is why "money market conditions" have proved such a defective guide in the past. It is also why the Fed has such a poor record in estimating the Federal funds rate that will achieve a desired monetary growth rate.

In estimating the required Federal funds rate, the Fed uses a so-called "money market model" which, among other things, purports to predict the Treasury bill rate. Some years ago, I tested the model as it then was against the naive alternative model of assuming that next month's rate would be the same as this. The naive model gave more accurate predictions on the average than the Fed's sophisticated model. In short, its model had zero predictive power.

The second, and in some ways even more serious, slip is that if the Fed picks the wrong rate and sticks to it, the error cumulates and is self-reinforcing. Suppose, as occurred early this year, the Fed underestimates the required Federal funds rate, which is to say, that forces outside the control of the Fed, in this case the rebound from the severe recession, are tending to raise interest rates above the levels that the Fed's model predicts. At the pegged Federal funds rate, banks wish to add more to their reserves than is consistent with the desired rate of monetary growth. The Fed can peg the rate only by supplying those reserves. So long as it does so, the only sign that the rate is too low would be unduly rapid monetary growth. After an interval, the higher monetary growth will add further to the upward pressure on interest rates by stimulating spending and thereby raising the demand for loans. This interval used to be about six months. In recent years, however, the interval has shortened drastically as the market has come to understand the process. If the Fed continued to peg the rate, monetary growth would accelerate without limit. It was precisely this possibility that finally forced the termination of the World War II policy of pegging interest rates on government securities.

Of course the Fed will not continue down this road. Sooner or later, it will adjust its Federal funds target to try to get back to the desired monetary growth path. But the length of time required to detect that the Federal funds rate is set at the wrong level, the cumulative and self-reinforcing nature of the errors, and the Fed's commendable desire to change its Federal funds peg gradually combine to make this a difficult task, as experience has shown.

Consider just this past cyclical episode. In mid-1974, the Federal funds rate target was too high and produced a sharp decline in monetary growth. The Fed moved to reduce the Federal funds target. But the recession, and the intensification of the recession by the Fed's own mistake, kept driving market rates down. They kept falling from under the Fed's target as it were and the Fed kept trying to catch up. It did not do so until January 1975, but then it was not sure for a time that it had done so and kept reducing the Federal funds target until March, by which time it was too low. A monetary explosion ensued. However, having held the Federal funds rate too high for so long, the Fed was reluctant to change. Finally, it did so in June, and then, because of the delay, raised it by an unusually large amount. As a result, it overshot, which brought an abrupt monetary slowdown. In the past month or so, the New York City financial crisis has increased the demand for liquidity, by creating uncertainty, which has steepened the yield curve, and has shifted funds from municipals to other securities, which has driven rates on them down. These downward pressures on short-term market rates have reinforced the delayed effects of slow monetary growth, leaving the Federal funds target again too high. In order to peg it, the Fed has had to produce an absolute monetary contraction.

I believe, and hope, that this time the Fed will adjust its target Federal funds rate promptly.* But even if it does, we shall have had a wholly unnecessary and damaging swing from one extreme to the other. In principle, it is possible to balance an egg on its small end—but it takes extremely fine tuning to keep it balanced.

(b) Alternative Procedure

There is a far better procedure—comparable to letting the egg rest on its side. That procedure is to convert the desired monetary growth rate into the increase in the monetary base [roughly, currency plus deposits at Federal Reserve Banks] required to produce it; and instruct the New York desk to purchase or sell the amount of securities required to produce the requisite increase in the monetary base. In other words, eliminate entirely the extra step of what Federal funds rate is required to produce the necessary increase in reserves.

This procedure too is not perfect. The multiplier which connects the base to the money supply is not perfectly stable. It depends on the ratio of currency to deposits, the distribution of deposits between categories and banks subject to different reserve requirements, and the like. But the multiplier is fairly stable. Moreover, the ratios on which it depends tend to change slowly, so that changes in the multiplier can to some extent be predicted. Some twelve years ago, William Dewald demonstrated that simply assuming each ratio to be the same next month as this would produce adequately close control of the quantity of money. Since then, a number of careful empirical studies done within the Federal Reserve System have demonstrated that a more sophisticated version of this method of operation yields relatively small errors. Moreover, the residual errors could be reduced even further by some of the regulatory changes considered in the next sub-section.

Even if this procedure yielded as large an error for a brief period ahead as the present procedure, it would yet have one overwhelming advantage: the errors would not be cumulative and reinforcing; on the contrary, errors in successive weeks would be random and offsetting. An error in this procedure does not set in motion forces which lead to further and larger errors in the same direction. It is literally inconceiv-

*See footnote on page 558.—Ed.

able that if the Fed had followed this procedure during 1974 and 1975, it could have departed as far as it did from its own objectives.

The one serious objection to this procedure that I have seen is the contention that it would lead to more variability in interest rates over short periods than the present procedure. I have long believed that it would have precisely the opposite effect except possibly for very short periods, measured in a few days or perhaps several weeks. By delaying interest rate adjustments, the present procedure permits pressures to cumulate. I believe that it thereby produces more erratic and unstable interest rates than the alternative procedure. This judgment has recently been powerfully reinforced by an important paper by Professor William Poole, until recently a member of the research staff of the Board of Governors of the Federal Reserve, in which he reaches the same conclusion by a very different argument.

Under the alternative procedure, the Fed would have no need for any interest rate targets whatsoever. It could let the Federal funds rate, and other interest rates, be free market rates determined entirely by market forces. This would have the incidental great advantage that it would help to dissipate the mistaken belief that the Fed can or does control interest rates and the even more mischievous notion that "tight" money is to be identified with high interest rates rather than slow monetary growth and "easy" money, with low interest rates rather than rapid monetary growth.

I have long said that I will believe there has been a fundamental acceptance by the Fed of monetary growth as the appropriate target, rather than merely lip service, when I learn that on coming into his office in the morning, Alan Holmes's first action is something other than telephoning for interest rate quotes.*

One final comment on the techniques of control. Much work has been done inside and outside the System on a highly sophisticated level about the so-called problem of "optimal control." This work is important as well as intellectually fascinating but in my opinion is concerned with effects of a second order of magnitude. The urgent need is to introduce as rapidly as possible the alternative procedure to correct the first order defects of the present procedures. It will then be desirable and possible to proceed at more leisure to refine the procedures along the lines suggested by optimal control theory. We must not in this area as in others let the best be the enemy of the good.

(c) Desirable Changes in Regulations

Over the past decade, the Federal Reserve has introduced many changes in reserve requirements, in the classification of deposits subject to interest ceilings and the like, that have introduced additional variability into the multipliers connecting monetary aggregates with the monetary base. In an article on this subject published some years ago, George Kaufman, long an economist with the Federal Reserve System, concluded, "by increasing the complexity of the money multiplier, proliferating rate ceilings on different types of deposits, and encouraging banks, albeit unintentionally,

---

*Mr. Holmes, whose article appears earlier in this section, is Manager of the Federal Reserve System's Open Market Account.—Ed.

to search out non-deposit sources of funds, the Federal Reserve has increased its own difficulty in controlling the stock of money. . . . To the extent the increased difficulty supports the long voiced contention of some Federal Reserve officials that they are unable to control the stock of money even if they so wished, the actions truly represent a self-fulfilling prophecy."

The major change of this kind was the introduction of lagged reserve requirements in 1968. This change has not worked as it was expected to. Instead, it has introduced additional delay between Federal Reserve open market operations and their effect on the money supply, and has rendered such items as free reserves, excess reserves, member bank borrowing, and the like more variable. Perhaps the next most important change has been the proliferation of reserve categories.

It would be highly desirable for the Fed to reform basically the present system of reserve requirements. Three major changes are desirable: first, elimination of lagged reserve requirements; second, consolidation of reserve categories to move toward a single reserve requirement on all kinds of bank liabilities; third, introduction of staggered reserve adjustment periods, so that some banks end their reserve period on Monday, some on Tuesday, etc., instead of, as at present, all ending on Wednesday. Staggering reserve periods would eliminate a major part of the so-called "defensive" operations of the open market desk that arise from the intra-weekly cycle introduced as a result of all banks ending reserve periods on the same day. This proposal could be accompanied by a lengthening of the reserve period but need not be.

A more radical reform is to revise the reserve requirement lag by letting this week's required reserves be satisfied by last week's vault cash plus deposits at a Federal Reserve Bank. This ingenious proposal, suggested in an as yet unpublished paper by Robert Laurent of the Chicago Federal Reserve Bank, would greatly increase the precision with which the Fed could control the money supply. It deserves serious consideration.

I have not tried to be exhaustive but rather suggestive about the kinds of reforms needed. The issues involved are highly technical and detailed, but the general direction in which change is needed is not.

4. Conclusion

There is today a wide measure of agreement on the part of the Congress, the Federal Reserve System, and the financial and academic community, about the importance of monetary policy for economic stability, avoidance of inflation, and the fostering of healthy growth. There is still some disagreement about the specific policy that will best foster these objectives. However, I believe there has been growing support both for emphasis on monetary aggregates rather than interest rates as the major instrument of monetary policy and for a relatively steady and moderate rate of growth in monetary aggregates as the major objective. That is today the position of the Federal Reserve System itself as well as of many of the most severe critics of earlier Federal Reserve performance.

The major issue has shifted, I believe, from objectives to means. The present techniques of Federal Reserve operation are a survival of earlier practices and are not suited to present objectives. They have produced a dramatic discrepancy between the Federal Reserve's announced objectives and its actual performance. It is long past time that they were streamlined to accord with the change in objectives.

The Congress has played a major role in promoting a large measure of agreement on objectives. It could now play a major role by stimulating the Fed to adapt its procedures to its stated objectives.

Statement on the Conduct of Monetary Policy

Paul A. Samuelson

Let me conclude my prepared testimony with a few general philosophic remarks on monetary policy. I believe there is widespread agreement that money does matter much and I think there is widespread agreement among analysts that long continued rates of M growth, whether you use M-1 or M-2 or M-3 or some variant, which do greatly exceed the feasible real growth rates, that in the long run this will be associated with rising trends of prices. But I'm afraid that there the agreement ends.

I do not discern and I'm not now expressing my opinion about what I think ought to happen, but I'm simply trying to make a roundup of what I regard to be the trends of opinion. I do not see a converging pattern of agreement toward a money rule or tactic that calls for the same monetary aggregate target in season and out. I may say that I do not believe in such a target, but it is not that I believe that there should be an interest rate stabilization target. I think the monetarists' target would often be better than an interest rate target but still not as good as what I think is the feasible optimum. The optimum stabilizing target is essentially a leaning against the wind as best intelligence and analysis of the pattern of evidence based against past historical experience tells you that wind is going to be in the next six months and in the next nine months. I believe that the Federal Reserve would have a better record of performance if they adhered to such a general set of rules.

Reprinted with deletions from *Second Meeting on the Conduct of Monetary Policy,* Hearings Before the Committee on Banking, Housing, and Urban Affairs, U.S. Senate, Ninety-Fourth Congress, First Session, November 4 and 6, 1975, pp. 52-55.

Now addressing myself to the climate of opinion with respect to a monetary rule of constant growth applied to a money aggregate, it seems to me that the actual experiences of recent years have undercut rather than strengthened what I would regard as never a strong case for such a monetary rule.

Let me give some examples. Although I embrace the Clemenceau-like dictum that money is too important to leave to the monetarists, I never neglect help from any source. And so I monitor the money aggregates and I keep a trend rate of what's happening to the rate of growth of the money supply because I find that a much more useful thing to do than to keep my adrenalin running with what's happening to the rate of growth of a very choppy series in short periods. And my chart of that shows that as of mid-1974 the actual stock of money was hugging quite close, to my eye, to the trend. It's true that if I apply a ruler to the rate of growth it's choppy around the trend, but the Fed—perhaps because it's been given a proper fear of monetarists' criticism—tends, if it makes a tack in the wrong direction from the trend in one period, to make a tack in the next period in the opposite direction cancelling out extreme deviation.

I also have great confidence in free markets and I believe that free markets composed of intelligent people who have a lot of money riding on the outcome are perfectly capable of doing the smoothing and modulating if the Fed would continue to behave in such a fashion and not behave in the cum-cyclical way that it so often behaved between the wars, which was to create long undulations around no perceptible target.

So having these trend rates of growth, I apply various monetarists' equations to the mid-1974 data. Yet I have found no monetarists' equation with a good prediction performance over the extended past which came anywhere near to explaining the weakness in the economy that revealed itself shortly after the summer of 1974, from August on.

That shows to me that the economy in the recent period has had larger residuals of instability from non-monetary sources and that a money rule would have resulted, if followed, in larger than usual squared errors and a squared error of deviation in this case means things like human suffering and unemployment and untoward price behavior.

. . . If you look at the smoothed out changes in the money supply, look at annual data or use your own method of smoothing, if you consider the cost push and exogenous price elements that impinge upon the modern economy with stagflation and the other bad tradeoff patterns which we have experienced, then you must conclude that the major problem is not whether the Fed in one six month period is running ahead of some putative desirable long-run period and in some other period running behind. As a matter of fact, I think of those as largely self-cancelling errors, not doubled errors. I have confidence that the money market can adjust itself to that type of behavior.

What I object to and what I fear for the period ahead is cumcyclical reinforcement by the Federal Reserve. I would rather have neutral behavior than cumcyclical behavior. I think with an election year coming up there is plenty of evidence that governments can do things which can change the situation in six months, twelve months, eighteen months ahead, which have consequences for the period thereafter. So it seems to me that the proper behavior which I hope your committee and similar House committees will hold the Fed to, in season and out of season, is that they should not be deciding themselves what is the appropriate tradeoff between price inflation and unemployment; . . . I think that there is no fourth branch of government which is a central bank. I recognize the judiciary and the Congress and the Executive. I don't recognize the Federal Reserve as a fourth independent branch of government. I think that if the Fed is not going to be part of the Executive, it should be responsive to the Congress, not for its day to day scratching of its ears. It should be responsive to the Congress on monetary policy. And I think that its monetary policy should be a leaning against the winds as they can be expected by past evidence to prevail in the period ahead when the monetary actions of the Fed have their consequences.

So I want to go beyond the steady M-growth goal that's stated here by Professor Friedman to what seems to me to be an optimal goal. Now what I'm stating is not a fine-tuning goal. It's a mistake to try to fine-tune in an engineering situation where you have probability discrepancies, recorded over and over again in history, that you're not able to tell about at the beginning. What you do if you're an electrical engineering graduate student in optimal control, when you have a stochastic or change pattern, is to use your best judgment in identifying this mechanism and inferring what the past historical statistical patterns have been of the probabilistic influences. Then you devise a filter system which is not too fast and which is not too slow but one designed to give you the smallest squared error—which will still be a very large squared error of performance under many circumstances. I have tried again and again to find justifications for a stable rate of growth of the money supply under realistic circumstances. And I often find that a stable money supply is better than some very bad program. But it is not as good as what I think this Congress can expect from the Federal Reserve and which this Congress can in its testimony hold out as the proper strategies and tactics of Fed policy.

It is right for this kind of committee when the economy is in a recession, as we were last December, to be critical of the Federal Reserve. Just because it says it is lowering interest rates, that should not be good enough for you; when the Fed is unwilling to let interest rates go down faster, it is keeping the monetary aggregates growing so slowly. On such occasions the monetarists and people like myself come before this committee in agreement. If, however, in order to have what seems to me to be the feasible rate of real growth should require a rate of growth of the money supply in the best judgment based upon past patterns of experience of more than the 7½ percent upper limit, I think that it would be wrong to crucify mankind on a basis of a monetary rule. It's not the worst cross that the system might have to bear, but it's not a good way of running the system.

Rules and Roles for Fiscal and Monetary Policy

*Arthur M. Okun**

When economists write text books or teach introductory students or lecture to lay-men, they happily extol the virtues of two lovely handmaidens of aggregate economic stabilization—fiscal policy and monetary policy. But when they write for learned journals or assemble for professional meetings, they often insist on staging a beauty contest between the two. And each judge feels somehow obliged to decide that one of the two entries is just an ugly beast. My remarks tonight are in the spirit of bigamous devotion rather than invidious comparison. Fiscal policy and monetary policy are both beautiful; we need them both and we should treat them both lovingly.

The General Eclectic Case

In particular, both fiscal and monetary policy are capable of providing some extra push upward or downward on GNP. In fact, if aggregate stimulus or restraint were all that mattered, either one of the two tools could generally do the job, and the second—whichever one chose to be second—would be redundant. The basic general

Reprinted, with deletions, from James S. Diamond, ed., *Issues in Fiscal and Monetary Policy: The Eclectic Economist Views the Controversy* (Chicago: DePaul University, 1971), pp. 51-74, by permission of the publisher and author.
* The views expressed are my own and are not necessarily those of the officers, trustees, or other staff members of the Brookings Institution.

eclectic principle that ought to guide us, as a first approximation, is that either fiscal or monetary policy can administer a required sedative or stimulus to economic activity. As every introductory student knows, however, fiscal and monetary tools operate in very different ways. Monetary policy initially makes people more liquid without adding directly to their incomes or wealth; fiscal policy enhances their incomes and wealth without increasing their liquidity.

In a stimulative monetary action, the people who initially acquire money are not simply given the money; they must part with government securities to get it. But once their portfolios become more liquid, they presumably use the cash proceeds to acquire alternative earning assets, and in so doing they bid up the prices of those assets, or equivalently, reduce the yields. Thus, prospective borrowers find it easier and less expensive to issue securities and to get loans; and investors who would otherwise be acquiring securities may be induced instead to purchase real assets such as capital goods. Also, because market values of securities are raised, people become wealthier, if in an indirect way, and may hence increase their purchases of goods and services. Thus, many channels run from the easing of financial markets to the quickening of real economic activity.[1]

A stimulative fiscal action is appropriately undertaken when resources are unemployed; in that situation, an action such as expanded government purchases, whether for good things like hospitals or less good things like military weapons, puts resources to work and rewards them with income. The additional cash received by some people is matched by reduced cash holdings of those who bought government securities to finance the outlay. But the securities buyers have no income loss to make them tighten their belts; they voluntarily traded money for near money. In contrast, the income recipients become willing to spend more, and thus trigger a multiplier process on production and income. So, while fiscal and monetary routes differ, the ultimate destination—the effect on national product—is the same, in principle.

Indeed, the conditions under which either fiscal tools or monetary tools, taken separately, have zero effect on GNP are merely textbook curiosities rather than meaningful possibilities in the modern U.S. economic environment. For stimulative monetary policy to be nothing more than a push on a string, either interest rates would have to be just as low as they could possibly go, or investment and consumption would have to show zero response to any further reduction in interest rates. The former possibility is the famous Keynesian liquidity trap, which made lots of sense in describing 1936, but has no relevance to 1971. With prime corporations paying 8 percent on long-term bonds, interest rates are still higher than at any time in my lifetime prior to 1969.[2] There is plenty of room for them to decline, and, in turn, for states and localities, homebuyers and consumer installment credit users, as well as business investors, to be encouraged to spend more by lower costs of credit.

---

[1]There is general agreement between Keynesians and monetarists regarding the mechanism for transmitting monetary changes. See Milton Friedman and Anna J. Schwartz, "Money and Business Cycles," in Friedman, *The Optimum Quantity of Money and Other Essays* (Aldine, 1969), pp. 229-34. Reprinted from *Review of Economics and Statistics,* Vol. 45 supplement (February 1963), pp. 59-63.

[2]Even when any reasonable allowance is made for inflation, it is hard to view today's *real* rates as low by historical standards.

The opposite extreme, impotent fiscal policy, is equally remote. Fiscal policy must exert some stimulative effect on economic activity (even when the monetary policy makers do not accommodate the fiscal action at all) unless the velocity of money is completely inflexible so that no economizing on cash balances occurs. Though the money supply does not rise in a pure fiscal action, spending will tend to rise unless people are totally unable or unwilling to speed up the turnover of cash. And money holders do economize on cash to a varying degree—they do so seasonally and cyclically, and they do so dependably in response to changes in the opportunity cost of holding money. The holder of zero-yielding cash is sacrificing the opportunity to receive the going interest rates of earning assets. The higher interest rates are, the more he sacrifices; and hence, economic theory tells us, the more he will economize on his holdings of cash.

And the facts confirm the theory. The negative relationship between the demand for money and the rate of interest is one of the most firmly established empirical propositions in macroeconomics.[3] So a pure fiscal stimulus produces a speedup in the turnover of money and higher interest rates, and more GNP.

The fact that people do economize on cash balances in response to rises in interest rates demonstrates the efficacy of fiscal policy. Anybody who reports that he can't find a trace of fiscal impact in the aggregate data is unreasonably claiming an absolutely inflexible velocity of money—a vertical liquidity preference function[4]—or else he is revealing the limitations of his research techniques rather than those of fiscal policy.

A few other artful dodges, I submit, make even less sense. Try to defend fiscal impotence on grounds of a horizontal marginal efficiency schedule—that means investment is so sensitive to return that even the slightest interest variation will unleash unlimited changes in investment demand. Or make the case that people subjectively assume the public debt as personal debt and feel commensurately worse off whenever the budget is in deficit. Or contend that businessmen are so frightened by fiscal stimulation that their increased demand for cash and reduced investment spoils its influence.[5] Or use the argument that Say's law operates even when the unemployment rate is 6 percent.[6] It's a battle between ingenuity and credulity!

---

[3]See Okun, *The Political Economy of Prosperity* (Brookings Institution, 1970), p. 58, and the bibliography on pp. 146-47 for a list of articles reporting empirical results confirming this relationship. [See Section III B of this book for a survey of empirical results.—Ed.]

[4]For discussion of a model implying the existence of a vertical liquidity preference function, see Leonall C. Andersen and Jerry L. Jordan, "Monetary and Fiscal Actions: A Test of Their Relative Importance in Economic Stabilization," Federal Reserve Bank of St. Louis, *Monthly Review* (November 1968). [See Section II of this book for readings on the St. Louis model.—Ed.]

[5]See Roger W. Spencer and William P. Yohe, "The 'Crowding Out' of Private Expenditures by Fiscal Policy Actions," in Federal Reserve Bank of St. Louis, *Monthly Review*, Vol. 52, No. 10 (October 1970), pp. 17-24. [See Section I B of this book for articles on "crowding out."—Ed.]

[6]See "Interest Rates and the Demand for Money," Chapter 7 in Milton Friedman, *The Optimum Quantity of Money*. Reprinted from *The Journal of Law and Economics*, Vol. 9 (October 1966), pp. 71-85. So far as I can see, Friedman is invoking Say's Law. [See Section III C of this book for a closely related article by Milton Friedman.—Ed.]

The eclectic principle is terribly important, not because it answers any questions, but because it rules out nonsense questions and points to sensible ones. It warns us not to get bogged down in such metaphysical issues as whether it is really the Fed that creates inflation during wartime. Every wartime period has been marked by enormous fiscal stimulus, and yet that fiscal fuel-injection could have been neutralized by some huge amount of pressure on the monetary brakes. In that sense, the Fed could have been sufficiently restrictive to offset the stimulus of military expenditures. Anyone who chooses to blame the resulting inflation on not slamming on the monetary brakes, rather than on pumping the fiscal accelerator, can feel free to exercise that curious preference. Take another example: Did the expansion following the tax cut in 1964–65 result from monetary policy? Of course it did, the eclectic principle tells us. If the Fed had wished to nullify the expansionary influence of the tax cut, surely some monetary policy would have been sufficiently restrictive to do so. There is no unique way of allocating credit or blame in a world where both tools can do the stabilization job.

Side Effects as the Central Issue

So long as both tools are capable of speeding up or slowing down demand, the decisions on how to use them and how to combine them must be made on the basis of criteria other than their simple ability to stimulate or restrain. Nor do we typically get any help by considering *how much* work monetary or fiscal tools do, because usually the right answer is, "as much as needed," providing the shift in policy is large enough. In more formal terms, two instruments and one target produce an indeterminate system.

Of course, there are two basic targets of stabilization policy: price stability and maximum production. But the two tools will not serve to implement those two goals simultaneously. A pen and a pencil are one more tool than is needed to write a letter, but the second tool can't be used to mow the lawn. In the same way, fiscal and monetary policy can both push up aggregate demand or push down aggregate demand, but neither can solve the Phillips curve problem. Subject to minor qualifications,[7] the fiscal route to a given unemployment rate is neither less nor more inflationary than the monetary route to that same unemployment rate.

We can have the GNP path we want equally well with a tight fiscal policy and an easier monetary policy, or the reverse, within fairly broad limits. The real basis for choice lies in the many subsidiary economic targets, beside real GNP and inflation, that are differentially affected by fiscal and monetary policies. Sometimes these are labeled "side effects." I submit that they are the main issue in determining the fiscal-monetary mix, and they belong in the center ring.

[7]An unbalanced composition of demand among regions and industries means more inflationary pressure at a given overall utilization rate. Thus, particularly concentrated excess demands (e.g., for defense goods or for new homes) may harm the cause of price stability. But the degree of balance cannot be uniquely linked to fiscal-monetary choices.

Composition of Output

One of the subsidiary targets involves the composition of output among sectors. General monetary policy tools, as they are actually employed, bear down very unevenly on the various sectors of the economy. Home building and state and local capital projects are principal victims of monetary restraint. Although the evidence isn't entirely conclusive, it suggests that monetary restraint discriminates particularly against small business. In the field of taxation, we agonize about incidence and equity. The same intense concern is appropriate in the case of monetary restraint and, in fact, increasing concern is being registered in the political arena. In the 1969-70 period of tight money, many efforts (such as Home Loan Bank and Fannie Mae operations) were made to insulate housing from the brunt of the attack. But the impact on home building was still heavy. Moreover, there is considerable basis for suspicion that these actions defused—as well as diffused—the impact of monetary restraint. A more restrictive monetary policy, as measured in terms of either monetary aggregates or interest rates, is required to accomplish the same dampening effect on GNP if the sectors most vulnerable to credit restraint are shielded from its blows.

The concern about uneven impact may be accentuated because, in 1966 and again in 1969-70, monetary restraint hit sectors that rated particularly high social priorities. But that is not the whole story. Any unusual departure of monetary policy from a "middle-of-the-road" position may lead to allocations that do not accord with the nation's sense of equity and efficiency. For example, in the early sixties, it was feared that a very easy monetary policy might encourage speculative excesses in building because some financial institutions would be pressured to find mortgage loans in order to earn a return on their assets.

In the last few years, some economists—most notably, Franco Modigliani—have argued that monetary policy may have a significant impact on consumption through its influence on the market value of equity securities and bonds[8] in addition to its more direct impact through the cost and availability of installment credit. In my view, the jury is still out on this issue. On the one hand, it's easy to believe that a huge change, say, $100 billion, in the net worth of the American public, such as stock market fluctuations can generate, could alter consumer spending in relation to income by a significant amount like $3 billion, even though that change in wealth is concentrated in a small group at the very top of the income and wealth distribution.

[8]See Franco Modigliani, "Monetary Policy and Consumption—The Linkages Via Interest Rate and Wealth Effects in the Federal Reserve-MIT-Penn Model" (paper prepared for the Federal Reserve Bank of Boston Conference at Nantucket, Massachusetts, June 1971; offset), esp. part I.3. For earlier discussions of the effects of monetary policy as it operates in the Federal Reserve-MIT-Penn Model, see the following: Robert H. Rasche and Harold L. Shapiro, "The FRB-MIT Econometric Model: Its Special Features," in American Economic Association, *Papers and Proceedings of the Eightieth Annual Meeting, 1967* (*American Economic Review,* Vol. 58, May 1968), pp. 123-49; Albert Ando and Franco Modigliani, "Econometric Analysis of Stabilization Policies," in American Economic Association, *Papers and Proceedings of the Eighty-first Annual Meeting, 1968* (*American Economic Review,* Vol. 59, May 1969), pp. 296-314; Frank de Leeuw and Edward Gramlich, "The Federal Reserve-MIT Econometric Model," *Federal Reserve Bulletin,* Vol. 54 (January 1968), pp. 11-40; de Leeuw and Gramlich, "The Channels of Monetary Policy," *Federal Reserve Bulletin,* Vol. 55 (June 1969), pp. 472-91. [The article is reprinted in Section II of this book.—Ed.]

On the other hand, previous empirical work on this issue came up with a nearly unanimous negative verdict.[9] In 1966 and 1969, however, the timing of stock market declines and the sluggishness in consumer demand seemed to fit fairly well with the hypothesis. One would like to believe the wealth hypothesis because it would suggest that monetary policy has broad and sizable effects on consumption, especially on that of high-income consumers; monetary restraint would then be revealed as less uneven and less inequitable. But before embracing that judgment, one should wait for more decisive evidence.*

Interest Rates and Asset Values

Another major consideration in monetary policy is its effects on interest rates and balance sheets. Some economists may argue that the only function of interest rates is to clear the market and the only sense in which rates can be too high or too low is in failing to establish that equilibrium. Every Congressman knows better! Interest rates are a social target. That is the revealed preference of the American public, reflected in the letters it writes to Washington and the answers it gives to opinion polls. And this is no optical illusion on the part of the citizenry. They have the same good reasons to dislike rising interest rates that apply to rising prices—the haphazard, redistributive effects. And they are concerned about *nominal* interest rates just as they are concerned about prices. It is not clear that such major groups as businessmen or workers are particularly hurt or particularly helped by tight money (or by inflation), but the impacts are quite haphazard in both cases. The resulting lottery in real incomes strikes most Americans as unjust.

The largest redistributive effect of tight money, like that of inflation, falls on balance sheets rather than income statements. People care about their paper wealth and feel worse off when bond and equity prices nose dive. Even though society is not deprived of real resources when security prices drop, it is hard to find gainers to match the losers. Although Alvin Hansen stressed the social costs of distorted, fluctuating balance sheets in the 1950's,[10] this issue gets little attention from economists. But it never escapes the broader and keener vision of the American public.

Financial Dislocation

A restrictive monetary policy may also have important, dislocating effects on the financial system. The key function of a financial system is to offer people opportunities to invest without saving and to save without investing. If people want risky assets, they can acquire them beyond the extent of their net worth; if they wish to avoid risk, they can earn a moderate return and stay liquid. The trade of funds between lovers of liquidity and lovers of real assets produces gains to all. "Crunch"

---

[9]See John J. Arena, "The Wealth Effect and Consumption: A Statistical Inquiry," *Yale Economic Essays,* Vol. 3 (Fall 1963), esp. pp. 273-84, and "Postwar Stock Market Changes and Consumer Spending," *Review of Economics and Statistics,* Vol. 47 (November 1965), pp. 379-91; Saul H. Hymans, "Consumption: New Data and Old Puzzles," *Brookings Papers on Economic Activity* (1:1970), pp. 121-26.

* For further reading on the transmission of monetary policy, see Section I B of this book.—Ed.

[10]See, for example, *The American Economy* (McGraw-Hill, 1957), pp. 53-55.

and "liquidity crisis" are names for a breakdown in the functioning of the financial system. Such a breakdown deprives people of important options and may permanently impair their willingness to take risks and to hold certain types of assets. To the extent that very tight money curbs an inflationary boom by putting boulders in the financial stream, a considerable price is paid. And to the extent that extremely easy money stimulates a weak economy by opening the flood gates of speculation, that too may be costly.

Balance of Payments

The pursuit of a monetary policy focused single-mindedly on stabilization goals would have further "side effects" on the balance of payments, to the extent that it changes international interest rate differentials and hence influences capital flows. There are strong arguments for fundamental reforms of the international monetary system—especially more flexible exchange rates—that would greatly reduce this concern. But those reforms are not on the immediate horizon; nor is the United States prepared to be consistently passive about international payments.[11] Meanwhile, the external deficit casts a shadow that cannot be ignored in the formulation of fiscal-monetary policies.

Growth

A final consideration in the mix of stabilization tools is the long-run influence of monetary policy on the rate of growth of our supply capabilities. An average posture of relatively easy money (and low interest rates) combined with tight fiscal policy (designed especially to put a damper on private consumption) is most likely to produce high investment and rapid growth of potential. That becomes relevant in the short-run because the long-run posture of monetary policy is an average of its short-run swings. If, for example, the nation relies most heavily on monetary policy for restraint and on fiscal policy for stimulus, it will unintentionally slip to a lower growth path. The contribution of extra investment to growth and the value of the extra growth to a society that is already affluent in the aggregate are further vital issues. Recently, enthusiasm for growth-oriented policies has been dampened by the concern about the social fallout of rapid growth and by the shame of poverty, which calls for higher current consumption at the low end of the income scale. Nonetheless, the growth implications of decisions about the fiscal-monetary mix should be recognized.

In the light of these considerations, there are good reasons to avoid extreme tightness or extreme ease in monetary policy—even if it produces an ideal path of real output. Tight money can be bad medicine for a boom even if it cures the disease, just

---

[11]On the question of a passive stance, see Lawrence B. Krause, " A Passive Balance-of-Payments Strategy for the United States," *Brookings Papers on Economic Activity* (3:1970), pp. 339-60; and Gottfried Haberler and Thomas D. Willett, *A Strategy for U.S. Balance of Payments Policy* (American Enterprise Institute, February 1971).

as amputation of the hand is a bad remedy for eczema. The experience of 1966 provides an object lesson. Judged by its performance in getting GNP on track, the Federal Reserve in 1966 put on *the* virtuoso performance in the history of stabilization policy. It was the greatest tight-rope walking and balancing act ever performed by either fiscal or monetary policy. Single-handedly the Fed curbed a boom generated by a vastly stimulative fiscal policy that was paralyzed by politics and distorted by war. And, in stopping the boom, it avoided a recession. To be sure, real GNP dipped for a single quarter, but the unemployment rate did not rise significantly above 4 percent; the 1967 pause was as different from the five postwar recessions, including 1970, as a cold is different from pneumonia. Moreover, inflation slowed markedly in the closing months of 1966 and the first half of 1967. What more could anyone want? Yet, you won't find the 1966 Fed team in the hall of fame for stabilization policy. In the view of most Americans, the collapse of homebuilding, the disruption of financial markets, and the escalation of interest rates were evils that outweighed the benefits of the nonrecessionary halting of inflation. The Fed itself reacted by refusing to give an encore in 1967-68, accepting renewed inflation as a lesser evil than renewed tight money.

All of this leads up to my first rule for stabilization policy: *Keep monetary conditions close to the middle of the road.* Let me explain that, no matter how monetary policy affects GNP, the rule must be interpreted in terms of interest rates and credit conditions, and not in terms of monetary aggregates. Suppose, for a moment, that the monetary impact on GNP is so powerful and the growth rate of the money supply is so critical that a growth rate of money only a little bit below normal will offset the aggregate demand impact of a huge fiscal stimulus (just for example, a $25 billion Vietnam expenditure add-on). The results would still be very tight money in terms of credit conditions, interest rates, and the impact on the composition of output. The shift in financial conditions required to "crowd out" $25 billion of private expenditures can hardly be trivial—even if the needed shift in monetary growth were trivial.

The "middle of the road" is deliberately a vague concept, relying on the existence of some general long-run notion of appropriate and normal interest rates and liquidity ratios. To be sure, it is hard to tell when we are in the middle of the road, but it is easy to tell when we are far away from it.*

The Implications for Fiscal Policy

My second rule follows immediately from the first: *Operate fiscal policy to avoid forcing monetary policy off the middle of the road.* If fiscal policy is inappropriately stimulative or restrictive, a conscientious and (at least somewhat) independent monetary authority will be obliged to shoulder most of the burden for stabilizing the economy. In historical perspective, it is important to recognize that this sense of responsibility has not always prevailed. In World War II and again in the initial

---

* In Section IV A of this book several articles consider the effect of Federal Reserve concern over interest rate variations and other considerations, such as international economic concerns, in constraining monetary policy.—Ed.

stages of the Korean War, the Federal Reserve reacted to an inflationary fiscal policy simply by pegging interest rates and creating all the liquidity demanded in an inflationary boom. Through these actions, the Federal Reserve not only passed the buck right back to fiscal policy but became an active accomplice in the inflation, intensifying excess demand by holding nominal interest rates constant as prices accelerated. It was technically feasible for the Federal Reserve to behave similarly during the Vietnam war. The fact that it picked up the ball after the fiscal fumble of 1966 demonstrated a new and greater sense of responsibility by the central bank for overall stabilization. So long as both fiscal and monetary policy makers feel that responsibility, as they appropriately should, an inappropriate fiscal policy is bound to push monetary policy off the middle of the road. Obviously, fiscal buck passing can also occur in a situation when stimulus is in order. In 1971, a rather neutral fiscal program accompanied by ambitious targets for recovery threatens to overburden the Federal Reserve with the responsibility for stimulus.

Fiscal Tools and Composition

To avoid pushing monetary policy off the middle of the road, fiscal policy must itself depart from the middle of the road—turning markedly more stimulative or more restrictive than its normal long-run posture—when private demand is especially weak or especially strong. But such swings in fiscal policy must also be made in light of compositional constraints that apply to federal expenditures, and especially to federal purchases of goods and services. Our preferences about the composition of output imply some notion of appropriate levels of civilian public programs. No one would wish to double or halve the size of the Census Bureau or the Forest Service in order to accord with the cyclical position of the economy. Moreover, these limitations based on principle are reinforced by limitations of a practical character. First, federal civilian expenditures on goods and services involve a mere 2.5 percent of GNP and thus afford very little leverage for stabilization. Second, most federal programs involving purchases of goods and services have long start-up and shut-off periods that make it extremely difficult to vary timing greatly without impairing efficiency.

Popular discussions of fiscal stabilization tend to stress expenditure variation despite these clear constraints. Why are the lessons ignored? Could any informed person have seriously regarded a curb on civilian public programs during the Vietnam build-up period as a meaningful antidote to the stimulus of increasing military expenditures? Could anybody familiar with the history of the lags in public spending support a public works program as a way to create jobs and strengthen recovery in 1971 or 1972?[12] The evidence suggests that people with strong views on the desirable size of the public sector tend to invoke the cause of stabilization as a rationalization

[12]For a brief documentation of the disappointing results of the 1962 public works program, see Nancy H. Teeters, "The 1972 Budget: Where It Stands and Where It Might Go," *Brookings Papers on Economic Activity* (1:1971), pp. 232-33.

for the social preferences. To an advocate of additional government spending, a recession provides a useful additional talking point; to a crusader for cutbacks in government spending, excess demand inflation offers an excellent excuse.

Federal "transfer" programs, such as social security, unemployment compensation, and veterans' benefits, are not subject to serious implementation lags, but their room for maneuver is limited by the principle of intertemporal equity. The aged, the poor, or the unemployed cannot justifiably be treated better in a recession than in prosperity or in a boom. The unfortunate people who are jobless when the unemployment rate is low deserve no less generous benefits than those who are unemployed when the rate is high; indeed, if misery loves company, those unemployed in prosperity may suffer psychically because they have less of it.

Some significant elbow room, nevertheless, appears for varying such transfer programs. Society's agenda always contains some new initiative or additional step to strengthen transfer programs in a growing economy with growing overall income; and the next step can be timed to come a little sooner or a little later, depending on the economy's cyclical position. In the present context, the administration's family assistance program provides a good example. The proposed initial date for benefits is July 1, 1972, but the program could be made effective six months earlier. Similarly, there is some opportunity for varying the timing of benefit liberalization and of payroll tax increases with respect to the social security program. Congress displayed wisdom early in 1971 by deferring for a year the proposed increase in the maximum earnings base of the payroll tax.

While this pure timing flexibility is important, it may not provide enough leeway for a flexible fiscal policy to respond to the needs of a very slack or very taut economy. Beyond it, the most attractive fiscal tool is variation in personal income tax rates. In principle, significant and indeed frequent changes in these rates are acceptable. Because they affect the huge consumption sector most directly and because their impact is spread over Americans throughout the middle- and upper-income groups, personal taxes are an ideal instrument for flexibility. While the income tax is specifically aimed to redistribute income in a more egalitarian way, the basic function of taxation is simply to restrain demand, given the socially desired level of public expenditures. A prima facie case exists for suspending or repealing any tax (or tax rate) that is not essential for the purpose of restraining demand sufficiently to avoid both inflation and monetary restraint. Moreover, according to compelling historical evidence, changes in personal tax rates—upward or downward, permanent or temporary—have reasonably reliable effects on consumer spending and hence on GNP.[13]

Political implementation is the one troublesome problem with changes in personal tax rates. Obviously, unlike shifts in monetary policy, any change in tax rates requires legislative action. And the record of congressional response to presidential requests for such changes has left much to be desired. Many constructive proposals

[13]See my papers, "Measuring the Impact of the 1964 Tax Reduction," in Walter W. Heller (ed.), *Perspectives on Economic Growth* (Random House, 1968), and "The Personal Tax Surcharge and Consumer Demand, 1968-70," *Brookings Papers on Economic Activity* (1:1971), pp. 167-204.

have been made to improve that story. In 1961, the Commission on Money and Credit asked Congress to delegate authority for tax changes to the President subject to congressional veto; others have urged Congress to enact rules that would commit it to fast action—favorable or unfavorable—in response to a presidential request. Presidents Kennedy and Johnson made proposals for speeding the legislative process in their Economic Reports of 1962 and 1969, respectively. Herbert Stein presented a constructive proposal along similar lines in 1968. Even the Joint Economic Committee of the Congress expressed its concern in its 1966 report, "Tax Changes for Short-run Stabilization."[14] But the Congress has generally ignored these proposals, jealously guarding its prerogatives over taxation, and refusing to bind its own hands with respect to procedures.

Under the present rules of the game, the President must ask Congress to do what seems best for the country and must count on presenting the case persuasively. The discussion and debates of recent years have put Congress on its mettle to respond promptly and pragmatically to any presidential request for tax changes designed for short-run stabilization purposes. Moreover, the 1963 and 1967 stalemates reflected special factors that seem obsolete—budget orthodoxy in the earlier case and Vietnam strategy in the later one. Our traditional procedures deserve another try.

These thoughts on the uses of alternative fiscal tools can be summarized as my third rule: When additional fiscal stimulus or restraint is needed, opportunities for varying the timing of new initiatives in federal spending or tax programs should be the first line of attack: if these are inadequate to achieve the desired swing in fiscal policy, a change in personal tax rates should be sought. We must keep urging and prodding the Congress to respond more promptly when tax changes are proposed. And we must not give up, for it will heed this message eventually.

Full Employment Surplus

The problems of executive-legislative coordination apply to expenditures as well as taxes. The fractionated process by which appropriations are made on Capitol Hill leads to frightful difficulties in the overall control of federal spending. As I have suggested elsewhere, one path to improvement might involve the following procedures: The President would make explicit the fiscal decision underlying his budget; and the Congress would then focus on that decision, approving or modifying it; and it would then commit itself to undertake an iterative review of appropriations and

[14]Report of the Commission on Money and Credit, *Money and Credit—Their Influence on Jobs, Prices, and Growth* (Prentice-Hall, 1961), pp. 133-37; *Economic Report of the President together with the Annual Report of the Council of Economic Advisers, January 1962,* pp. 17-19, and *Economic Report,* January 1969, pp. 12-13; Herbert Stein, "Unemployment, Inflation, and Economic Stability," in Kermit Gordon (ed.), *Agenda for the Nation,* (Brookings Institution, 1968), pp. 292-93; *Tax Changes for Short-run Stabilization,* A Report of the Subcommittee on Fiscal Policy of the Joint Economic Committee, 89 Cong. 2 sess. (1966), p. 16.

tax legislation during the course of the year to assure that the budget stayed within the bounds.[15]

I believe that the concept of the full employment surplus can be extremely useful as the focus of the fiscal plan and review. It is a simple enough summary number of the budget's impact on the economy to be understood by the participants, and it is a good enough summary to serve the purpose. It permits the stimulus or restraint in the budget to be compared with that of the previous year and other relevant previous periods.[15a] While administration officials cannot hope to provide a scientific demonstration that the budget has the proper amount of stimulus or restraint, they can generate an informed discussion and enlightened decision process by explaining their forecast of the strength of private demand, the proper role for monetary policy, and the likely response of the economy to proposed fiscal changes.

The main function of the full employment surplus in policy discussion is to correct the misleading impression generated by the actual budget surplus or deficit when the economy is off course. In a weak economy, revenues automatically fall far below their full employment level and the budget is hence pushed into deficit. That automatic or passive deficit may be misread as evidence that the budget is strongly stimulating the economy and hence that further expansionary action is inappropriate. By the same token, a boom resulting from a surge in private demand or an easing of monetary policy would automatically swell federal revenues, thereby tending to produce a surplus in the budget. These automatic shifts in federal revenues are important and significant; such built-in stabilizers help to cushion cumulative declines and dampen cumulative upsurges, but they should be properly recognized as shock absorbers rather than either accelerators or brakes.

I believe the focus on the full employment budget by the administration this year has helped to raise the level of fiscal debate. It reveals that the big deficits of fiscal years 1971 and 1972 are symptoms of a weak economy rather than of a strong budget.

Guide vs. Rule

The full employment budget shows where the fiscal dials are set; but it cannot say where the dials *ought* to be set. It is an aid to safe driving much like a speedometer, but it cannot prescribe the optimum speed. That depends on road conditions. A maintained target for the full employment surplus represents a decision to drive by the dashboard and to stop watching the road. Road conditions do change significantly from time to time in our dynamic economy. The evidence of the postwar era suggests that zero is too low a full employment surplus for a period of prosperity and too high a full employment surplus for a period of slack and slump. From long-term saving-investment patterns, one might guess that a full employment surplus of one-half of one percent of GNP would be about right on the average to accompany a

[15]See Okun, *The Political Economy of Prosperity*, pp. 121-22.
[15a]Arthur M. Okun and Nancy H. Teeters, "The Full Employment Surplus Revisited," *Brookings Papers on Economic Activity* (1:1970), pp. 77-81.

middle-of-the-road monetary policy. But even that judgment would be highly speculative; and it would not tell us how to identify the rare case of an average year or how to quantify the departure of any particular year from the average. Economists have no right to be presumptuous about their ability to forecast in either the short run or the long run; and it is far more presumptuous to claim that the proper size of the full employment surplus can be determined for the long run than to believe that it can be nudged in the correct direction in any particular year on the basis of the evidence then at hand.

Adoption of a fixed full employment surplus implies a firm determination by fiscal policy makers to counteract any major surprises that arise *within* the federal budget. If Congress rejects the President's proposals for major expenditure programs such as revenue sharing or family assistance, the advocate of a fixed full employment surplus is committed to propose alternatives for those stimulative actions. Similarly, if uncontrollable expenditures spurt, some compensatory action is required to keep the overall full employment budget close to its original position.

At the same time, however, the advocate of the fixed full employment surplus is determined *not* to act in response to surprises in private demand or monetary policy, no matter how large or how definite these may be. The resulting decision rule is illogical and indefensible. Once it is recognized that some surprises within the federal budget are large enough to call for offsetting fiscal action, it must be conceded that some surprises in consumer spending, plant and equipment outlays, or Federal Reserve decisions might also point to shifts in the fiscal course.

In fact, the Nixon administration has not adopted a fixed full employment surplus but rather a rule that the full employment budget shall be *at least* in balance on the unified basis of budget accounting. The doctrine of balancing the full employment budget has obvious antecedents in the less sophisticated orthodoxy of balancing the actual budget. The new rule is far less harmful than its predecessor, but it is equally arbitrary. Its arbitrariness is perhaps illustrated by the fact that zero on the unified basis for the 1972 fiscal year turns out to be $7 billion on the national income accounts basis, which is the way Herbert Stein[16] first unveiled the concept and the way every economics student has learned full employment budgeting for a generation.

Statics vs. Dynamics

The rule really reflects the administration's concern about overdoing fiscal stimulus, and that concern has a valid basis. There is genuine danger that stimulative fiscal action appropriate to today's slack and sluggish economy could commit the nation to stimulative budgets in future years when they would be markedly inappropriate. We might then be obliged to offset that stimulus by relying on monetary restraint or by seeking tax increases or cutbacks in expenditure programs once the economy ap-

[16]Committee for Economic Development, *Taxes and the Budget: A Program for Prosperity in a Free Economy* (CED, November 1947), pp. 22–25; and Herbert Stein, *The Fiscal Revolution in America* (University of Chicago Press, 1969), esp. pp. 220–32.

proached full employment. Reliance on monetary restraint as an antidote to excessive budgetary stimulus violates rules one and two above. And to count on subsequent neutralizing measures of fiscal restraint is to ignore the serious doubts about the political feasibility of such legislative action. Congress is particularly unlikely to raise tax rates for the purpose of bailing out an overly enthusiastic antislump program that added mightily to federal spending. It would see such action as an open invitation to continued upward ratcheting of federal expenditures through time—with major expenditure initiatives in slumps and offsetting tax increases in booms. Whatever one's views on the appropriate size of the public sector, a cyclical ratchet is not a proper tool for decision making in the democratic process.

All of this argues for making stimulative fiscal policy with one eye on preserving our fiscal fitness for the next period of full employment. And that does require a rule, or at least some form of discipline that guards against excessive long-term commitments of revenue or expenditure. Hence, my fourth rule: *Stimulative fiscal programs should be temporary and self-terminating so that they don't jeopardize our future budgetary position.* The rule reminds us that the key issue is not whether full employment balance is maintained when the economy needs fiscal stimulus, but whether the budget remains in a flexible position from which it can be moved back readily into full employment surplus when restraint once again becomes appropriate.[16a] It cautions against permanent changes in the levels of taxation or expenditure programs for stabilization purposes; it puts a time dimension on the third rule, which identifies the types of fiscal variation consistent with compositional objectives. Both rules argue against public works as a tool for stabilization. They also cast doubt on the recent liberalization of depreciation allowances as a stabilization device; that measure sacrificed $4 billion of revenue annually on a permanent basis in order to get $2 billion into the economy in 1971.

The Dependence on Forecasting

The rule for relying on quick-starting and self-terminating fiscal measures is designed to ensure flexibility and thus to limit the time horizon over which the forecasting of aggregate demand is essential to policy decisions. But that time period remains substantial, and the success of policy remains dependent on the accuracy of economic forecasting. Tax cuts, for example, add cumulatively to aggregate demand for a considerable period after enactment. Thus, while they deliver some prompt stimulus to aggregate demand, they also involve a package of future add-ons to demand. The only way to lift the economy this quarter is through a tie-in sale that lifts the economy further for several subsequent quarters.

If any fiscal or monetary tool exerted its full impact instantaneously, stabilization policy making would be a different ball game. Indeed, this difference has been high-

[16a]See Frank Schiff's development of this point in "Control of Inflation and Recession" (speech delivered before the Seventy-fifth Annual Meeting of The American Academy of Political and Social Science, Philadelphia, April 1971; processed), pp. 12-16.

lighted by the Laffer model, which finds that the effects of a shift in the money supply on aggregate demand are concentrated in the very quarter of the policy action.[17] While GNP is determined by the money supply in the Laffer model, the implication for policy strategy is diametrically opposite to that of previous monetarist views. Because of its instantaneous total effects, the Laffer model issues an unequivocal mandate in favor of monetary fine tuning. Monetary policy makers are encouraged to take all the action appropriate to hit their economic targets today; and they should then wait for tomorrow and correct any errors by twisting the dials again. Unlike more traditional views about the timing impact of economic policies, the Laffer model finds no tie-in sale or longer-term commitment that would caution against large and abrupt changes in policy.

Because Keynesians and most monetarists agree that the time stream of economic impact following a policy action begins virtually at once but continues into the more distant future, they seat the forecaster at the right hand of the policy maker. When policy decisions necessarily affect the future, they must be made in light of uncertain forecasts of the future and not solely on the basis of the facts of the present. To act otherwise is to adopt implicitly the naive forecast that the future is going to be merely a continuation of the present. The historical record of economic forecasting in the past two decades demonstrates that professional forecasting, despite its limitations, is more accurate than such naive models.[18] Moreover, even the naive model that tomorrow will be like today is far more accurate than the supernaive or agnostic model that tomorrow's aggregate demand is just as likely to be below the social target as above it regardless of where today's aggregate demand stands. That agnostic model is the extreme point in the decision analysis set forth by Milton Friedman and William Brainard.[19] If forecasts could not beat the agnostic model, it would be important to do nothing. The stabilization policy maker should simply stay home, for action by him would be just as likely to push the economy in the wrong direction as in the right direction, and it could push the economy off the proper course when it would otherwise be there. ,

In fact, the professional forecaster can beat the agnostic model by a wide margin. I can think of only two years in the past twenty—1955 and 1965—when the January consensus prediction of economic forecasters would have led policy makers to ad-

[17]Arthur B. Laffer and R. David Ranson, "A Formal Model of the Economy" (paper prepared for the Office of Management and Budget, 1971; offset), pp. 25-27. [Michael Hamburger critiques the Laffer-Ranson model in Section II of this book.—Ed.]

[18]See Victor Zarnowitz, *An Appraisal of Short-term Economic Forecasts* (National Bureau of Economic Research, 1967), esp. pp. 6, 14-19, and 83-120; Geoffrey H. Moore, "Forecasting Short-Term Economic Change," *Journal of the American Statistical Association,* Vol. 64 (March 1969), esp. pp. 3-4 and 15; and Victor Zarnowitz, "Forecasting Economic Conditions: The Record and the Prospect" (paper prepared for the National Bureau of Economic Research's Colloquium on Business Cycles, September 24, 1970; offset).

[19]"The Effects of a Full-Employment Policy on Economic Stability: A Formal Analysis," in Milton Friedman, *Essays in Positive Economics* (University of Chicago Press, 1953), pp. 117-32; and William Brainard, "Uncertainty and the Effectiveness of Policy," in American Economic Association, *Papers and Proceedings of the Seventy-ninth Annual Meeting, 1966* (*American Economic Review,* Vol. 57, May 1967), pp. 411-25.

minister stimulants when they were inappropriate and no cases when the consensus forecast would have pointed toward sedatives when stimulants were really appropriate.

A Propensity to Overreact?

Nonetheless, the fact that forecasters can guide policy makers to the right choice as between sedatives and stimulants is not necessarily decisive. Even if some sedative medicine would help a patient, he may be better off with nothing than with a massive overdose of sedation. And it is sometimes claimed that policy makers tend to prescribe overdoses.[20] According to this claim, because their medicines operate only with a lag and because neither the time shape of that lag nor the total impact of the policy is readily determined in advance, the policy makers become impatient; hence, they continue to take more and more action until they have done too much of a good thing, which may be worse than nothing.

This intuitive argument has a certain appeal as a description of a human foible. We have probably all behaved in much this way in taking a shower. When the water is too cold, we turn up the hot faucet; and, if we are still cold ten seconds later, we may turn up the faucet some more, assuming that the first twist was inadequate. As a result of our first impatience, we may find ourselves scalded. And even after one or two experiences of this sort, we repeat that behavior and indeed find it difficult to discipline ourselves completely. If, indeed, fiscal-monetary policy makers have the same proclivities as the man in the shower, rules or discipline may help them to resist their impulses to overreact. But whether the Federal Reserve Open Market Committee or the Troika overtwist the faucets in their respective showers is an empirical issue, a proposition about their behavior that ought to be supportable or refutable by evidence. And I have yet to see evidence to support the proposition.

In the case of fiscal policy, I believe the record shows that policy makers generally have not behaved like the man in the shower. Below is a list of the major changes in fiscal policy during the past fifteen years, as defined by shifts in the full employment surplus,[21] and a capsule evaluation based on hindsight.

1. During 1958, the full employment surplus was reduced from more than 1 percent of GNP to near zero.

   Stimulative direction proper; inadequate size and timing delayed.

[20]See "The Role of Monetary Policy," Chapter 5 (esp. p. 109), in Friedman, *The Optimum Quantity of Money.* Reprinted from *American Economic Review,* Vol. 58 (March 1968), pp. 1-17.

[21]Okun and Teeters, "The Full-Employment Surplus Revisited," pp. 102-103; Teeters, "Budgetary Outlook at Mid-Year 1970,"*Brookings Papers on Economic Activity* (2:1970), p. 304; and Teeters, "The 1972 Budget: Where It Stands and Where It Might Go," p. 228.

2. In 1959-1960, fiscal policy was sharply reversed toward restraint with the full employment surplus reaching 2.5 percent of GNP in 1960.

   Inappropriate restraint.

3. During 1961-1962, that surplus was gradually trimmed.

   Stimulative direction proper; inadequate size and timing delayed.

4. After backsliding during 1963, fiscal policy became considerably more stimulative with the enactment of the tax cut at the beginning of 1964.

   Appropriate stimulus.

5. From the second half of 1965 to the end of 1968, the full employment budget was in deficit, reflecting the buildup of Vietnam expenditures.

   Inappropriate stimulus.

6. In 1969, as the result of the tax surcharge and expenditure cutbacks, a full employment surplus of 1 percent of GNP was restored.

   Appropriate restraint; much delayed timing.

7. In 1970 and the first half of 1971, fiscal policy was relaxed a bit with the full employment surplus roughly cut in half.

   Relaxation proper; inadequate size.

Items 1, 3, 6, and 7 all depart from the ideal in the direction of too little and too late rather than too much and too soon. In each of these cases moves that were larger or earlier or both would have produced better stabilization results. Item 5—the inappropriate fiscal stimulus of the Vietnam period—was not the overreaction of the man in the shower. The hot water was turned up, but not because anyone believed that the economy needed warming.

Item 2—the shift to restraint in 1959—can be viewed, in a sense, as a premature and excessive cooling of economic expansion. But that policy simply was not keyed to the general economic diagnosis or forecast, which saw the temperature as remaining extremely mild, but rather to a noneconomic budgetary orthodoxy. The full employment surplus was jacked up enough to balance the actual budget, as an end in itself rather than as a means to curb any present or prospective boom.

By any standard, the preponderant balance of mistakes in fiscal policy is revealed as errors of omission rather than commission—errors of doing too little too late, rather than too much too soon. Our fiscal man in the shower, in fact, tends to wait too long to ascertain that the water is really staying cold before he decides to turn it up. When he finally does turn the faucet, he acts timidly and hesitantly. When the water is hot, he also hesitates too long and moves indecisively. To shift metaphors, he is not trigger happy but, rather, slow on the draw. And so I come to my fifth rule: *Face the fact that policies must be made on the basis of a forecast, and don't be slow on the draw!*

My rules for fiscal discretionary judgment will work well only if stabilization policy is guided by the professional expertise of economists. Obviously, that has not always been the case; and when politics vetoed economics, serious fiscal destabilization resulted. Indeed, in the past generation, the economy has been more severely disrupted by government actions obviously inconsistent with the objective of economic stabilization than by autonomous shifts in private demand. The 1950–1951 Korean inflation, the 1953–1954 post-Korean recession, the 1960–1961 recession, and the Vietnam inflation were all government-induced fluctuations, in which the budget departed from any and all professional prescriptions for stabilization. In three of the four cases, swings in military expenditures created the problem; in the remaining case, it was caused by attachment to a taboo of budgetary balance. In light of these instances, one might well find that a fixed, moderate full employment surplus in peace and war, even years and odd years, would have yielded better overall results than those obtained from the actual fiscal process. But this is no argument for fixed parameters! The proposal to control political officials with a nondiscretionary rule reminds me of the suggestion to catch birds by pouring salt on their tails. Neither the political officials nor the birds will cooperate. If every economist in the nation had sworn (falsely) to Lyndon Johnson and Wilbur Mills that any deviation of the full employment surplus from 0.5 percent of GNP was a mortal sin, that wouldn't have changed fiscal policy in 1965–1968. Why not tell our statesmen the truth and try to convince them to heed professional advice on fiscal policy? As unpalatable as that message might be, it has more chance of convincing elected public officials than the rule of maintaining a fixed and rigid full employment surplus for all time. *And so I offer my sixth rule: Presidents should listen to the advice of their economists on fiscal policy and so should the Congress.*

Signals for the Monetary Authorities

Under the circumstances I envision, the tasks of the Federal Reserve would depend upon how well the fiscal rules operate. If the budget no longer generates disruptive shifts in aggregate demand and if it offsets, to some degree, any major autonomous shift in private demand, then the monetary policy makers may be able to hold money and credit conditions close to the middle of the road without much difficulty. Under those best of all possible circumstances, economists might begin to wonder what all the shouting was about in the debate on the relative importance of aggregate quantities and interest rates as guides to monetary policy. In 1962–1965, a monetary policy that was oriented toward interest rate targets did not produce large or abrupt shifts in the growth of the money stock, simply because the demand for money did not undergo enormous fluctuation. Presumably, if monetary policy had been pursued with respect to quantity rather than rate targets, those quantity guides would have left interest rates reasonably stable. If the demand for goods and the demand for money stay on course, then it makes little difference whether the directives to the trading desk are couched in terms of maintaining a given set of interest rates in the money markets or a given growth of the money supply.

It is not safe, however, to count on the world becoming that tranquil. Surprises will occur, and the policy makers will be forced to decide on the emphasis they wish to give to interest rates and aggregate quantities relative to one another. And it is a matter of degree—of relative emphasis. Anyone interested in diagnosing or influencing financial markets would obviously pay attention to both prices and quantities, just as he would in looking at any other market. Nobody has ever improved on Paul Samuelson's summary that Federal Reserve governors were given two eyes so that they could watch both yields and quantities.[22] In a more serious vein, James Duesenberry has recently sketched how the monetary authorities might appropriately be guided by both quantities and interest rates.[23] At a theoretical level, William Poole has shown the conditions for preferring rate-oriented, quantity-oriented, or mixed monetary strategies.[24]

Quite apart from the issue of appropriate guides, the chief problem facing the monetary authority is likely to be when and how much to depart from a "normal" or average posture in order to provide additional stimulus or restraint to economic activity. Monetary policy can and should find some elbow room without major deviations from the middle of the road. For one thing, monetary policy is light on its feet; the short implementation lag in Federal Reserve decisions provides an enviable contrast with the long lags in the legislative process for altering fiscal policy. In nudging economic activity to offset modest surprises, the speed of implementation makes monetary policy particularly useful.

Second, there is a case for a belt-and-suspenders strategy of making fiscal and monetary changes in the same direction when stimulus or restraint is desired. The quantitative effect of specific fiscal and monetary changes on GNP is uncertain. Errors in the estimates of these effects are likely to be negatively related or at worst unrelated—if the economy's response to monetary changes is larger than expected, the response to fiscal swings seems likely to be less than our estimates. How extensive the monetary swings should be and at what point the benefits in aggregate stabilization are outweighed by the costs of the side effects discussed above are issues that require careful judgment and the best use of discretion.

[22]"Money, Interest Rates and Economic Activity: Their Interrelationship in a Market Economy," in American Bankers Association, *Proceedings of a Symposium on Money, Interest Rates and Economic Activity* (ABA, 1967), p. 44. [Judging from his paper in this Section Samuelson's view seems to have changed somewhat since 1967.—Ed.]

[23]"Tactics and Targets of Monetary Policy," in Federal Reserve Bank of Boston, *Controlling Monetary Aggregates,* Proceedings of the Monetary Conference, Nantucket Island, June 8-10, 1969 (FRB of Boston, 1969).

[24]"Optimal Choice of Monetary Instruments in a Simple Stochastic Macro Model," *Quarterly Journal of Economics,* Vol. 84 (May 1970), pp. 197-216. [A sketch of Poole's analysis appears in the Davis article in Section IV A.—Ed.]

Any recommendation for discretionary monetary policy runs into the contention that the Federal Reserve also shares a propensity to overreact; I find it more difficult to interpret that contention than the one regarding fiscal policy; but, as I read the evidence, it is also untrue. Whether judged in terms of interest rates or of aggregate quantities, I cannot see that the Federal Reserve has behaved like the man in the shower. It was not overly expansionary during most recessions and early recoveries. If the monetary policies of 1957–1958, 1960–1962, or 1970 could be replayed with the aid of perfect hindsight, monetary policy would surely be more expansionary than it was in fact. The only example of such a period that might stand on the opposite side is late 1954, when in retrospect the Fed seems to have been excessively generous.

Nor in periods of strong economic advance has the Fed generally applied the brakes too strongly or too soon. It may have done so in the case of 1959, but it clearly stayed off the brakes too long in 1965 and probably in 1955. Most clearly, the Federal Reserve has revealed the propensity to underreact to economic chill in late expansions and early stages of recession: with perfect hindsight, it is clear restriction was maintained too long in 1953 and again in 1957. In my judgment, the error in the 1969 performance should also be interpreted as unduly prolonged restraint—staying on the brakes too long and too hard late in the year—although others might argue that the restraint was applied too vigorously early in the year. There have been other mistakes in monetary policy, like the misdiagnosis of 1968, but they have little to do with either overreaction or underreaction, so far as I can see. Nor does the basic decision of 1967, which gave side effects priority over aggregate stabilization targets, reveal a propensity to overreact.

Thus I come to my final rule: *The makers of monetary policy should be guided by both aggregate quantities and interest rates and by the present and prospective state of aggregate demand; they will serve the nation best by using fully their capability to make small and prompt adjustments in light of the best current evidence and analysis.*

Federal Reserve Behavior

William P. Yohe*

Introduction

The political economy of monetary policy decisions is the topic of this article. This was such a new interest in monetary economics in the 1960s that there was not a well-developed literature. What existed was an agglomeration drawn from history, political science, and economics. The modern computer did not make a noticeable impact on the literature of decision-making in the Federal Reserve System, except in a few instances. There was some impact on the broader literature dealing with the recognition and decision parts of the lags in monetary policy, and there was some impact on the models of decision-making, also as reviewed below. Further, there has probably been some impact on the desired qualifications of appointees to the Federal Reserve's decision-making bodies, as mentioned elsewhere [1, Sec. II].

An organization like the Federal Reserve System does not itself "behave," but rather the people who exercise power over decisions behave. The central policy-making body in the Federal Reserve is the Federal Open Market Committee

Reprinted from William J. Frazer, Jr., ed., *Crisis in Economic Theory* (Gainesville: University of Florida Press, 1974), pp. 189-200, by permission of the publisher, the editor and the author. The reference list has been extracted from the original, and reference numbers in text and footnotes have been adjusted accordingly.

*Most of this chapter was written while the author was serving as scholar in residence in the Research Department of the Federal Reserve Bank of St. Louis. He is especially indebted to Christopher Babb, Michael Keran, and Keith Carlson for helpful comments.

(FOMC), consisting of the seven members of the Board of Governors and the twelve Reserve Bank presidents. The committee is empowered by law to direct open market operations and has become by tradition a forum for the discussion of all aspects of system policy. Hence, most of the attention in studies of monetary policy-making has been concentrated on the FOMC. The basic raw materials for such studies are the personal papers of two former governors, the speeches and congressional testimony of FOMC principals, official Federal Reserve publications, the record of FOMC policy actions in the *Federal Reserve Bulletin* and *Annual Report,* and the FOMC minutes for 1936-1965, which have been released to the National Archives in stages since 1964.[1] The Federal Reserve publishes extensive financial and business statistics, many of which presumably influence policy deliberations. A number of studies have attempted to draw inferences about the timing of policy actions and the importance of various Federal Reserve goals from the statistical analysis of various time series.

In what follows, some of the historical and descriptive work on Federal Reserve organization and leadership is surveyed, empirical studies of FOMC behavior are reviewed, and more or less explicit models of FOMC decision-making are reviewed.

Federal Reserve Structure and Leadership

One of the most striking commentaries ever made on the critical role of a dominant leader in the conduct of Federal Reserve policy was reiterated by Friedman and Schwartz [2, p. 692]: "If Benjamin Strong [Governor of the Federal Reserve Bank of New York, who died in 1928] could 'have had twelve months more of vigorous health, we might have ended the depression in 1930, and with this the long drawn out world crisis that so profoundly affected the ensuing political developments.' "[2] Substantiating this assertion is a major theme of the Friedman and Schwartz account of the early years of the Great Depression.

Barger [3, Ch. 15] has written a brief account of the traditional conflict between the Federal Reserve Bank of New York and the Board in Washington and of the leadership exercised by Strong and his successor at the New York Bank, George L. Harrison, and by later Board Chairmen Marriner Eccles and William McC. Martin. The ability of Chairman Martin to accommodate both Republican and Democratic administrations is the subject of two articles [4, pp. 11-13; 5, pp. 11-14].

Political scientists have paid surprisingly little attention to Federal Reserve organization and functions. Their studies tend to be critical and to propose drastic reforms.

---

[1]There is a useful compendium of source materials by David P. Eastburn, *The Federal Reserve on Record* (Philadelphia: Federal Reserve Bank of Philadelphia, 1965). The 1936-1960 FOMC minutes were made available in 1964, the 1961 minutes in 1967, and the 1962-1965 minutes in 1970.

[2]Carl Snyder, in *Capitalism The Creator* (New York: Macmillan, 1940), made the original statement quoted by Friedman and Schwartz [No. 2]. See also Lester V. Chandler, *Benjamin Strong, Central Banker* (Washington D.C.: Brookings Institution, 1958).

Reagan investigated Federal Reserve structure for the Commission on Money and Credit nearly a decade ago and concluded [6, p. 75]:[3]

> Professionalization means orderly routines in procedure and hierarchy in organization, and an ethical code of commitments to professional standards and to organizational objectives—the characteristic virtues of bureaucracy. The Federal Reserve exhibits these virtues. But in the current context, professionalization also means institutional inbreeding, and, in turn, the growth of dogmas and a tendency to propagandize. The Federal Reserve exhibits these flaws. . . . In the wider political arena the System enjoys the general advantages that go with a reputation for expertise in an occult craft, so long as all goes well.*

Studies of Federal Reserve "politics" by economists are more numerous. In 1948, Bach wrote a report on the Board of Governors for the Hoover Commission, out of which evolved a book [7].[4] Many of the issues which Bach initially discussed, such as Federal Reserve "independence" and the lack of statutory objectives for monetary policy, were still current almost twenty years later! Whittlesey [8, pp. 33–34] has examined the effect of important changes in FOMC procedures in 1955 and after, and he concludes that the power of the chairman and the influence of economists has been enhanced. He has also studied [9, pp. 77–87] the origin and nature of Federal Reserve attempts to suppress any rapid and detailed disclosure of its policy actions. One of his principal conclusions [9, p. 87] is that the primary reason for central bank secrecy is "to avoid embarrassment later on in case it appears that a different course would have been wiser."

A few ex-Federal Reserve economists have written critical evaluations of monetary policy-making. The most scathing, perhaps, is "The Mysterious World of THE FED" by Hastings and Robertson [10, pp. 97–104].[5] The authors specify, in descending order, what they regard as the ten "nodes of power" within the Federal Reserve System, with the Chairman of the Board at the top, followed in order by the other governors, Board advisers, and the FOMC. Hastings and Robertson argue that the Chairman's influence is exercised primarily by his ability to determine FOMC decisions, regardless of the views of the majority of its members.

Dozens of Fed "insiders" and "outsiders" participated in the extensive 1964 congressional hearing [11]. A subsequent article [12, pp. 351–62] catalogs the rather diverse views expressed therein on various aspects of FOMC decision-making. A 1968 Joint Economic Committee report [13] revealed that the problems enumerated repeatedly in the 1964 hearings remained.

---

[3]Reagan's research paper for the Commission on Money and Credit has also been published: Michael D. Reagan "The Political Structure of the Federal Reserve System," *American Political Science Review*, 55:1 (March 1961), 361–402.

* For a recent study of the Federal Reserve's structure see Thomas Havrilesky, William Yohe and David Schirm "The Economic Affiliations of Directors of Reserve District Banks" *Social Science Quarterly* (December, 1973), pp. 608–622.—Ed.

[4]See also his later discussion [7, Ch. 7].

[5]The study was reprinted in the 1964 Patman *Hearings* [11, Vol. 2, pp. 1519–25].

Empirical Studies of FOMC Decisions

Quantitative work on FOMC deliberations and decisions may be conveniently grouped under three headings: (1) the measurement of decisions on the policy directive, (2) FOMC voting behavior, and (3) the length of the "inside lag" in monetary policy.

The principal "output" of FOMC deliberations is the economic policy directive to the manager of the Open Market Account at the Federal Reserve Bank of New York. For example, the directive[6] issued at the last meeting in 1970 [14, pp. 103-4] contained three parts: (1) a summary of recent changes in economic activity, prices, costs, interest rates, bank deposits, money supply, and bank credit; (2) the policy statement that the FOMC sought "to foster financial conditions conducive to orderly reduction in the rate of inflation, while encouraging the resumption of sustainable economic growth and the attainment of reasonable equilibrium in the country's balance of payments"; and (3) the charge that this policy should be implemented by "maintaining the recently attained money market conditions," with the proviso that operations could be modified if growth rates for money and bank credit were not at least as great as expected.

Note that there are numerous adjectives but no quantitative specifications of the desired changes in ultimate targets, financial conditions, or policy actions.* Two techniques have been used to try to measure the extent of a directive change. One is to use a quantitative proxy in the form of a readily available financial indicator that is quickly influenced by policy actions. Such a procedure is fraught with statistical problems. In addition, it is tangled up with the issue of what constitutes appropriate monetary policy indicators.

Another technique is to scale the directive itself to determine the magnitude of the intended policy change. An elaborate scheme for scaling directives was worked out by Deming [15], an economist who was president of the Federal Reserve Bank of Minneapolis, attended many FOMC meetings, and had access to all of the minutes. The state of monetary policy was scaled from $+3$ (greatest ease) to -3 (greatest) restraint), and substantive changes in a directive were considered as movements by one unit along the scale. In addition, he tried to account for "shades" in the directive—the addition of subsidiary instructions involving very slight policy changes without altering the substance of the directive. These were regarded as adding or subtracting a half point on the scale.[7] Unfortunately, Deming left the Federal Re-

---

[6]This directive touches upon two 1966 innovations: use of the "bank credit proxy" (member bank deposits) to estimate bank credit changes more quickly, and the "proviso clause" mentioned earlier. The directive also reflects an early 1970 innovation, the more direct statement of desires with respect to aggregates for bank credit and the money stock.

* In recent years Reserves to Support Private Deposits are mentioned and desired growth ranges for monetary aggregates are specified. See the Lombra and Torto article in Section IV A of this book for a detailed discussion.—Ed.

[7]For example, if past directives indicated a policy of moderate tightness (-2), then the injunction to maintain an "even keel" during an upcoming Treasury financing would temporarily move the scaling by a "shade" of $+\frac{1}{2}$.

serve before completing this work and never released his scaling of directives for the 1951–1962 period.

Brunner and Meltzer, in their 1964 work for the Patman Committee [16, 17, 18] devised a scale for measuring the extent of individual directive changes rather than the cumulative degree of tightness or ease [18, Appendix II].[8] Such changes were placed on a scale ranging from +1 (greatest change toward ease) to −1 (greatest change toward tightness). In the 1970 directive mentioned above, the change would be assigned the value 0. From about 1959 through the 1960s, changes in the directive were infrequent and mostly of an incremental nature, only ± ⅛ on the Brunner-Meltzer scale. Several studies by others have used this scale and will be mentioned later. Brunner and Meltzer have used their scalings primarily for work on "inside lags" and for demonstrating the close relationship between directive changes and changes in free reserves, as defined earlier.

Besides a summary of the discussion and the policy directive, the record of FOMC policy actions contains the voting outcome by the governors present and the Federal Reserve Bank presidents currently serving as voting members of the committee. While there is some question about the significance of the formal FOMC voting records [10, p. 101], such information represents the kind of data for which political scientists have developed various analytical techniques. Several of these techniques [19, pp. 396–405] were used to analyze the votes on the economic policy directive over the decade following the committee's reorganization in 1955. The most frequent outcome over this period was a unanimous decision not to change the previous directive. After 1959, policy changes were more incremental in nature, and dissent became more frequent as would be consistent with the rapid changes of the 1960s in the monetary area, although few Reserve Bank presidents seemed inclined to oppose Chairman Martin during his tenure.

A collection of hypotheses is presented in the previous study to account for the overwhelming occurrence of unanimous FOMC decisions. Canterbery [20, pp. 25–38][9] has attempted to elucidate the question of the Committee's nature. He specifically identified FOMC members by occupational background ("lawyer-bankers" and "economists"), specified corresponding a priori policy preferences under various economic conditions, and tested the predictions of his model against the actual voting record vis-à-vis contemporaneous economic conditions.

There have been several studies of the "inside lag" in monetary policy over the 1953–1960 period. The authors of the two earliest studies [21, pp. 62–97; 17, 37–47] did not have access to the FOMC Minutes; further (and related to this lack of access), they assumed the action lag to be zero, so that their estimates of the inside lag were synonymous with the recognition lag as defined earlier. Kareken and Solow [21] obtained the longest estimates of the lags (8.5 months, on the average, at business cycle peaks and 3 months at troughs); the excessive length of their lag measures

---

[8]For several later studies, Brunner and Meltzer have updated their scaling: Karl Brunner and Allan H. Meltzer, "The Appropriate Indicators of Monetary Policy," in *Savings and Residential Financing: 1969 Conference Proceedings* (Chicago: U.S. Savings and Loan League, 1969).

[9]See also E. Ray Canterbery, "Economics on a New Frontier," (Belmont, Calif.: Wadsworth, 1968), Ch. 12.

has been attributed to their choosing a monetary policy indicator (potential bank credit) that itself lags the taking of action [22, pp. 591-93].[10] Brunner and Meltzer [16, 17, 18], dating action by policy reversals in the Record of Policy Actions, found average lags of zero months at peaks and four months at troughs.

ler and Fand [23, pp. 21-35], using changes in the intended direction of the free reserves target to time the taking of action, have produced the shortest estimates of the inside lag (an average of two months at troughs and minus one month at peaks). Willes [22] has attempted to disaggregate the inside lags and separately estimate the recognition and action components. His results for the total inside lags are nearly the same as Brunner and Meltzer's [16, 17, 18], but he found two peaks for which the action lags were minus five or six months (action was taken considerably in advance of the upper turning points), which yielded slightly negative net lags when combined with positive recognition lags.

Hinshaw [24], on the other hand, sought to assess the forecasting ability of FOMC members vis-à-vis professional business cycle forecasters, by carefully studying the summaries of the remarks of each president and governor in the FOMC *Minutes*. He defined the recognition lag as the time elapsing between a turning point and the committee's assignment of 50 percent probability to the fact that a turning point had occurred. The "confirmation lag," however, is the time elapsing from a turning point until a 90 percent (nearly certain) probability is attached to the existence of a turning point. With a "certainty score" for every meeting, Hinshaw was able to relate the timing of policy reversals and major policy changes (using Brunner and Meltzer's scalings) to the committee's degree of certainty that a turning point had been reached. He concluded [24, pp. 120-21] that "the Committee changed policy at the peaks on less conclusive evidence than it required at troughs, and that its decision-making process in the vicinity of peaks proceeded by successive approximations."

Models of FOMC Decision-Making

The term "model" is used here in the general sense of a logically complete structure for explaining policy actions. The discussion will begin with more or less verbally specified models, proceed to the "reaction function" literature which attempts to infer the impact on policy actions of a variety of policy objectives, and conclude with more elaborate models for explaining Federal Reserve decision-making.

[10]All of the studies have used NBER turning points for dating peaks and troughs.

[11]A general discussion of the contents of the FOMC *Minutes* appears elsewhere (Opening the Books on Monetary Policy, Morgan Guaranty Survey, March 1965, pp. 3-15). A monetary historian, Elmus R. Wicker, was working on a detailed study of the *Minutes* in 1971. He presented a preliminary paper, "Reserve Supply Strategy, 1951-1957," at a seminar at the Federal Reserve Bank of Richmond, March 26, 1971.

Verbally Specified Models*

Replying to the frequent charges that the Federal Reserve has "money market myopia" and lacks any explicit analytical framework for making decisions, Koch [25, pp. 3-9, 12-15] of the research staff of the Board of Governors presented complicated flow charts to convey the Federal Reserve's conception of the policy transmission process and the sources of information (or indicators) to which it will respond. On the other hand, Guttentag [26, pp. 1-30], an economist formerly with the Federal Reserve Bank of New York, was a severe critic of the Federal Reserve's alleged preoccupation with a "money market strategy." He has attempted to conceptualize the policy-making process, distinguishing such components as policy determinants, policy formulation, operating targets, strategic (intermediate financial) targets, and a logically complete operating strategy. The "money market strategy" Guttentag asserted to be logically incomplete, since there is no particular conception of the linkages from money market conditions to ultimate targets.[12]

Drawing on his work on the inside lag, Mark Willes [27] has conceived the Federal Reserve as conducting monetary policy within what he called the "cyclical framework." As a consequence [27, p. 6], the Federal Reserve regards "cyclical peaks as signals for the need to begin an expansionary monetary policy and cyclical troughs as signals for the need to begin a restraining monetary policy." Willes proposed an alternative framework that sensitizes monetary policy actions directly to departures from unemployment, price-level, growth, and balance of payments objectives.

The "Reaction Function" Literature

The most extensive literature pertaining to Federal Reserve behavior concerns the estimation of a great variety of alternative "statistical reaction structures" and related "reaction functions." The U.S. studies stem from the original work done by Reuber for the Porter Commission in Canada [28, pp. 109-32]. A representative list of studies was cited earlier.

The simplest procedure is to select an intermediate financial target that the Federal Reserve presumably regards as critical in its operating strategy (money, bank credit, or some interest rate) and regress it on current values of various ultimate target variables and on the lagged intermediate target. The result is a geometrically decaying distributed lag structure [29, pp. 553-65], with the relative weight of independent variables in the past assumed to be reflected in the coefficient of the lagged dependent variable. The equation may be transformed into a reaction function by setting the lagged dependent variable equal to its current value (a presumed

---

* Within one year of the preparation of this article, several fairly explicit models of Federal Reserve behavior became available. For the most recent and by far the most complete example see the Lombra and Torto article reprinted in Section IV A of this book.—Ed.

[12]Sherman J. Maisel, "Controlling Monetary Aggregates" (Boston: Federal Reserve Bank of Boston, 1969) pp. 153-157, has drawn on a "personal construct" and Guttentag's framework to explain the FOMC's early 1969 variant of the "money market strategy"—the linkages from money market conditions (free and borrowed reserves and various short-term interest rates) to the "bank credit proxy" (member bank deposits).

condition for equilibrium) and solving for the intermediate target variable as a function solely of ultimate target variables. It is then possible to calculate implicit "trade-offs" among the ultimate targets—the rates at which changes in the ultimate targets could be exchanged without requiring any change in the intermediate target variable.

Dewald and Johnson [30] did such a study for the decade after the Treasury-Federal Reserve Accord of 1951. They experimented with a number of intermediate financial targets, ranging from free reserves to money and interest rate series, and they used as independent variables ("performance indicators") the real GNP, consumer price index, unemployment rate, and balance of payments deficit. The best statistical fit was obtained with the money supply (currency and demand deposits) as intermediate target. Substantial time lags for most of the responses in the intermediate targets were found in all of the regressions, and the balance of payments was not found to be significant in any of them. Several reaction functions were derived and the implicit trade-off rates among the ultimate objectives were calculated.

All of the subsequent studies involved attempts to overcome serious deficiencies in the Dewald-Johnson (DJ) work. These deficiencies and some of the proposed improvements may be summarized as follows:

1. Any one of the DJ equations may be regarded as a reduced-form equation for a (linear) structural model of the economy, combined with a preference function for the policy-maker. The coefficients of the ultimate target variables are thus a composite of the model's structure and the weights attached to each in the preference function.[13] The "trade-offs" calculated from the coefficients do not then reveal anything about the importance of particular objectives unless additional information is provided. Furthermore, it is doubtful that the "true" Federal Reserve preference function contains only current levels of ultimate targets and no deviations of a target's current level from some desired level.[14]

2. The selection of particular intermediate financial targets in the regressions raises the whole question of appropriate indicators for monetary policy. Other authors (Havrilesky [31], Buehler and Fand [23], and Keran and Babb [32] have preferred to use as a financial target a variable more proximate to policy actions than money or interest rates, that is, an "operating target" or instrument of monetary policy.

3. Not all movements in an intermediate financial target should be explicable on the basis of economic stabilization objectives. Open market operations, for example, are used for "defensive" purposes to offset seasonal and irregular shocks to the reserve base, to assist the Treasury in major refundings and cash borrowings, and to stabilize interest rates. Nonstabilization objectives ought to be more significant for a

[13]The first to raise this argument was John Wood [34], whose work will be discussed below.

[14]Havrilesky [31, p. 302], for example, includes the price level in his "policy action function" as the square of the difference between the actual index and a constant base period index. For an introduction to the theory of quantitative economic policy, see Bert G. Hickman, *Quantitative Planning of Economic Policy* (Washington D.C.: Brookings Institution, 1965), pp. 1-17.

study using monthly data than quarterly data, but significant effects have also been found in the latter [32, pp. 7–20].[15]

4. Single equations for the entire time period of study [33, p. 467] imply that the monetary authority has "a linear, temporally consistent set of decision rules and relative priorities for the achievement of different objectives."[16] Christian [33] has shown, however, that for subperiods of the DJ study, shifts in the importance of various objectives apparently did occur.

5. There is a presumption of strong multicollinearity among the independent variables in the regressions (movements in the price level, GNP, unemployment, and the balance of payments are not independent of each other). One solution would be to find a proxy variable to represent the state of all of the stabilization objectives. Thus, Keran and Babb [32, pp. 8–9] use free reserves as this proxy, citing the high correlation between changes in this series and changes in intended stabilization policy, as reflected in the FOMC directive. Even if distributed lags had been specified (which is not the case in Keran's and Babb's study), this procedure may obfuscate the use of the resulting reaction structures to provide information about the "inside lag."*

Some Elaborate Models

A somewhat more ambitious undertaking than estimating single equation statistical reaction structures is an attempt to infer the Federal Reserve's implicit decision rule (or reaction function) within a structural equations model which presumably reflects the policy-maker's conception of the linkages connecting policy actions and ultimate targets. Such projects have been completed by Wood [34] and Torto [35]. Wood [34, pp. 135–66] heroically assumes that the Federal Reserve seeks to optimize its policy actions subject to a quadratic preference function[17] containing the usual ultimate targets, short-term interest rates, and the Federal Reserve's government securities portfolio. Its conception of the "linear constraint" is represented by a crude model of the economy's structure in which current values of the target variables are deter-

---

[15]Wood's and Torto's works will be discussed below. Equations using monthly data information on the free reserve target from the FOMC *Minutes* have been estimated by John E. Buehler and David I. Fand "The FOMC Minutes and Monetary Policy," paper presented to the Southern Economic Association, November 17, 1967. There is also a question of whether the use of seasonally adjusted data eliminates most of the defensive operations (Wood [34] argues that it would, while Torto [35] demonstrates that it does not). For separate studies of defensive operations, see Leonall C. Andersen, "Seasonal Movements in Financial Variable—Impact of Federal Reserve and Treasury," *Business and Government Review,* University of Missouri (July-August, 1965), pp. 19–26; and see Charles Schotta and Vittorio Bonomo, "A Spectral Analysis of Post-Accord Federal Open Market Operations," *American Economic Review* (March, 1969).

[16]Besides an invariant policy-formulating framework, the lack of attention to the stability of regression coefficients in the DJ study carries implications about the linearity of the underlying model and the presumed reliability of the particular lag distributions estimated [33, pp. 465–67].

* A recent reaction function study of Federal Reserve behavior, reprinted in Section IV A of this book, satisfies all of these objections except the first and the last.—Ed.

[17]An introductory essay by Henri Theil, "Linear Decision Rules for Macrodynamic Policy Problems," in Bert G. Hickman, *Quantitative Planning of Economic Policy* (Washington D.C.: Brookings Institution, 1965) pp. 18–42, explains the approach used by Wood.

mined by extrapolations from the past values of the same variables, by current free reserves, and by current government budget and debt variables.

Torto [35] seeks to use a more refined model of the economy (an improved version of Goldfeld's model [36]) in which a behavioral equation for open market operations is specified and simultaneously estimated with the rest of the model, using two-stage least squares. Torto also attempted to distinguish "defensive" from "dynamic" open market operations (those directed toward stabilization). He runs a single equation estimate for open market operations, similar to the reaction structures discussed earlier, and compares the results with an equation simultaneously estimated with the complete model. Interestingly, the coefficients of the variables reflecting defensive operations are somewhat larger in the latter estimates. They are generally comparable to those obtained by Keran and Babb [32].[18]

Using computer techniques for analyzing and simulating sleep, another study views FOMC decisions as part of a stochastic (Markov) process [37].[19] Combined with changes in the domestic economy and balance of payments conditions, decisions on the policy directive comprise sequences of states, which may be tested for "memory" and used in various simulation experiments.

Work has been done on a different model for replicating FOMC decisions on the economic policy directive, based on inputs of a greater number of monthly data series [38, 39]. There the FOMC is conceived as a heuristic problem-solver which employs a network of simple rules of thumb to seek, process, and evaluate information about the state of its ultimate target variables and about the response of financial conditions to actions based on past decisions. An extension of the so-called "Carnegie Tech approach" to simulating decision-making by business firms [40], the model contains statements of FOMC objectives that are "satisficing"[20] rather than maximizing and contains procedures for limited search when conflicts arise between results and intentions and for the assessment of "slack" in the financial system.

Summary

The study of Federal Reserve behavior ranges from studies of the policy-making personnel and leaders, decision-making, bureaucratization, and Federal Reserve

---

[18]The equations in the two studies are specified somewhat differently, but the Federal Reserve is found to offset (with changes in government securities holdings), nearly dollar-for-dollar, shocks to bank reserve positions (variously specified).

The decision rule for open market operations derived by Torto also contains as independent variables the loan-to-deposit ratio of member banks and the changes in manufacturers' inventories, both of which are statistically significant. The former may be construed as a separate intermediate financial target, and the latter as a leading indicator of ultimate target variables. [A later version of this study is the basis of the Lombra and Torto article that appears in Section II of this book.—Ed.]

[19]A basic reference for this kind of approach is David Bartholomew, *Stochastic Models for Social Processes* (New York: John Wiley & Son, 1967).

[20]The term "satisficing" is used to indicate that behavior is directed not toward attaining an optimum, the path to which is unknowable, but toward the fulfillment of minimum standards (making ultimate target variables no worse or not so bad as before). For example, the unemployment target is attained so long as unemployment is not high and rising.

"politics," on one hand, to attempts to infer decision rules implicit in a structural equations model and to distinguish between "defensive" and "dynamic" open market operations, on the other.

There have also been studies of the minutes of the FOMC's meetings and the inside lag in monetary policy. In the first, there has been noticeable effort to measure the extent of the change in the FOMC's directive to the manager of the open market account. One procedure has been to use a proxy for the directive changes, but there are statistical problems and controversy over the selection of the appropriate indicator. Another procedure has centered about schemes for scaling and measuring directive changes. Brunner's and Meltzer's scheme has been widely cited. It is mentioned on other occasions.

Studies of the inside lag in monetary policy have been made with and without access to the FOMC's minutes, and some have attempted to construct models of FOMC decision-making. Apart from verbal models and the structural equations model mentioned above, attention has been drawn to "reaction functions" and their problems. These have failed to distinguish between "defensive" and "dynamic" objectives, and have presumed multicollinearity. Further study even attempts to extend a "Carnegie Tech approach" for simulating decision-making to FOMC decision-making in particular.

REFERENCES

1. FRAZER, WILLIAM J., JR., "Statement of William J. Frazer, Jr.," *Compendium on Monetary Policy Guidelines and Federal Reserve Structure,* Subcommittee on Domestic Finance of the Committee on Banking and Currency, House of Representatives (Washington, D.C.: U.S. Government Printing Office, December 1968).

2. FRIEDMAN, MILTON, and ANNA JACOBSON SCHWARTZ, *A Monetary History of the United States, 1867–1960* (Princeton, N.J.: Princeton University Press for the National Bureau of Economic Research, 1963).

3. BARGER, HAROLD, *The Management of Money: A Survey of American Experience* (Chicago: Rand McNally & Company, 1964).

4. ROSSANT, M. J., "Mr. Martin and the Winds of Change," *Challenge,* January 1964.

5. HARRIS, SEYMOUR E., "Monetary Policy Under Two Administrations," *Challenge,* February 1964.

6. REAGAN, MICHAEL D., "The Internal Structure of the Federal Reserve: A Political Analysis," *Monetary Management,* Frank M. Tamagna et al., eds. (Englewood Cliffs, N.J.: Prentice-Hall, Inc., 1963).

7. BACH, G. L., *Federal Reserve Policy-Making* (New York: Alfred A. Knopf, 1950).

8. WHITTLESEY, C. R., "Power and Influence in the Federal Reserve System," *Economica,* February 1963.

9. WHITTLESEY, C. R., "Federal Reserve Policy: Disclosure and Non-disclosure," *National Banking Review,* September 1963.

10. HASTINGS, DELBERT C., and ROSS M. ROBERTSON, "The Mysterious World of the Fed," *Business Horizons,* Spring 1962.

11. U.S. Congress, House, Subcommittee on Domestic Finance of the Committee on Banking and Currency, *Hearings, the Federal Reserve After Fifty Years* (Washington, D.C.: U.S. Government Printing Office, 1964).

12. YOHE, WILLIAM P., "The Open Market Committee Decision Process and the 1964 Patman Hearings," *National Banking Review,* March 1965.

13. U.S. Congress, Joint Economic Committee, *Report: Standards for Guiding Monetary Action* (Washington, D.C.: U.S. Government Printing Office, 1968).

14. Staff Editorial Committee, "Monetary Aggregates and Money Market Conditions in Open Market Policy," *Federal Reserve Bulletin,* February 1971.

15. DEMING, FREDERICK L., "Monetary Policy Objectives and Guides," paper given at the Commercial and Central Banking Seminar, University of North Carolina, August 28, 1963.

16. BRUNNER, KARL, and ALLAN H. MELTZER, *Some General Features of the Federal Reserve's Approach to Policy* (Washington, D.C.: U.S. Government Printing Office, 1964).

17. BRUNNER, KARL, and ALLAN H. MELTZER, *An Alternative Approach to Monetary Mechanism* (Washington, D.C.: U.S. Government Printing Office, 1964).

18. BRUNNER, KARL, and ALLAN H. MELTZER, *The Federal Reserve's Attachment to the Free Reserves Concept* (Washington, D.C.: U.S. Government Printing Office, 1964).

19. YOHE, WILLIAM P., "A Study of Federal Open Market Committee Voting, 1955-1964," *Southern Economic Journal,* April 1966.

20. CANTERBERY, E. RAY, "A New Look at Federal Open Market Voting," *Western Economic Journal,* December 1967.

21. KAREKEN, JOHN, and ROBERT M. SOLOW, "Lags in Monetary Policy," in Commission on Money and Credit, *Stabilization Policies* (Englewood Cliffs, N.J.: Prentice-Hall, Inc. 1963).

22. WILLES, MARK H., "The Inside Lags of Monetary Policy: 1952-1960," *Journal of Finance,* December 1967.

23. BUEHLER, JOHN E., and DAVID I. FAND, "The Federal Reserve and Monetary Policy," *Michigan Academician,* Spring 1969.

24. HINSHAW, C. ELTON, "The Recognition Pattern of the Federal Open Market Committee," in Rendigs Fels and C. Elton Hinshaw, *Forecasting and Recognizing Business Cycle Turning Points* (New York: National Bureau of Economic Research, 1968).

25. KOCH, ALBERT R., "An Approach to Monetary Policy Formulation," *Business Review,* Federal Reserve Bank of Philadelphia, February 1965.

26. GUTTENTAG, JACK M., "The Strategy of Open Market Operations," *Quarterly Journal of Economics,* February 1966.

27. WILLES, MARK H., *The Framework of Monetary Policy: A Staff Analysis of the Federal Open Market Committee in Its Conduct of Monetary Policy* (Washington, D.C.: U.S. Government Printing Office for the House Committee on Banking and Currency, 1967).

28. RUEBER, G. L., "The Objectives of Canadian Monetary Policy, 1949-1961: Empirical 'Trade-offs' and the Reaction Function of the Authorities," *Journal of Political Economy,* April 1964.

29. SIMS, CHRISTOPHER A., "Money, Income, and Causality," *American Economic Review,* September 1972.

30. DEWALD, WILLIAM G., and H. G. JOHNSON, "An Objective Analysis of the Objectives of American Monetary Policy, 1952-61," *Banking and Monetary Studies,* Dean Carson, ed. (Homewood, Ill.: Richard D. Irwin, 1963).

31. HAVRILESKY, THOMAS, "A Test of Monetary Action," *Journal of Political Economy,* June 1967.
32. KERAN, MICHAEL W., and CHRISTOPHER T. BABB, "An Explanation of Federal Reserve Actions, 1933-68," *Review,* Federal Reserve Bank of St. Louis, July 1969.
33. CHRISTIAN, JAMES W., "A Further Analysis of the Objectives of American Monetary Policy, 1952-61," *Journal of Finance,* June 1968.
34. WOOD, JOHN H., "A Model of Federal Reserve Behavior," *Monetary Process and Policy,* George Horwich, ed. (Homewood, Ill.: Richard D. Irwin, 1967).
35. TORTO, RAYMOND G., *An Endogenous Treatment of the Federal Reserve System in a Macro-Econometric Model* (unpublished dissertation, Boston College, 1969).
36. GOLDFELD, STEPHEN M., *Commercial Bank Behavior and Economic Activity: A Structural Study of Monetary Policy in the Postwar United States* (Amsterdam: North-Holland Publishing Company, 1966).
37. YOHE, WILLIAM P., "Federal Open Market Committee Decisions on a Markov Process," *Public Choice,* Fall 1971.
38. YOHE, WILLIAM P., "A Model of Federal Open Market Committee Decision Processes," a paper presented to the Panel on Nonmarket Decision-Making, Southern Economic Association, November 10, 1966.
39. YOHE, WILLIAM P., and LOUIS C. GASPER, "The 'Even Keel' Decisions of the Federal Open Market Committee," *Financial Analysts Journal,* November/December 1970.
40. CYERT, RICHARD, and JAMES G. MARCH, *A Behavioral Theory of the Firm* (Englewood Cliffs, N.J.: Prentice-Hall, Inc., 1963).

40

How Much Do New Congressional Restraints Lessen Federal Reserve Independence?

*Edward J. Kane**

Throughout his first 46 years in the U.S. Congress, Wright Patman waged a lonely crusade against the Federal Reserve's independent budgetary and decision-making status. Employing every rhetorical and investigative device he could muster, he sought unremittingly (though without much effect) to convince his fellow legislators to strip the Federal Reserve System of its unique bureaucratic privileges. Ironically, only in the current session of Congress after Patman himself was stripped of the powerful chairmanship of the House Banking, Currency, and Housing Committee did his campaign make noticeable legislative headway. In the early months of the 94th Congress, the same forces of congressional assertiveness that unseated Patman established for the first time a forward-looking channel for congressional surveillance of contemporaneous monetary-policy decisions.[1]

Reprinted from Challenge (Copyright © 1975 by International Arts and Sciences Press, Inc.), Vol. 18 No. 5 (November/December 1975), pp. 37–44, by permission of the International Arts and Sciences Press and the author.

*Everett D. Reese Professor of Banking and Monetary Economics, The Ohio State University. The author wishes to thank Kurt Dew, Thomas Havrilesky, Thomas Mayer, William Poole, and Robert Weintraub for their helpful comments on an earlier draft.

[1]At this writing, Congress is still considering a bill to require that the Fed submit its accounts to regular audit by the General Accounting Office and Senator Proxmire has announced his intention to introduce a bill to place an annual ceiling on Federal Reserve expenditures and to require Senate confirmation of the Board's Chairman and of all Bank Presidents.

It is easy to exaggerate the significance of this reputedly "historic" development. Contrasting the aims of the early drafts of the surveillance legislation with the resolution (House Concurrent Resolution 133) that finally passed the House and Senate in March 1975 underscores how little freedom of action—except in the realm of administrative privacy—the Fed finally had to surrender. In mandated quarterly hearings scheduled alternately before the House and Senate Banking Committees, the Fed must now document its policy goals and explain subsequent policy shortfalls more extensively than ever before. However, given the amplification of longstanding demands for more open government supplied by the Watergate scandal, maintaining administrative secrecy could easily have raised more public relations and legal problems for the Fed than it would have avoided.[2] Far more important are the areas of Fed autonomy that the legislation does not touch.

The Federal Reserve's Traditional Independence

To understand the changes the draft legislation went through, it is useful to establish some background. The Fed's position of bureaucratic privilege traces to the conscious efforts of the System's founders (greatly reinforced in the Banking Act of 1935) to insure that the U.S. central bank would be dominated neither by politicians single-mindedly seeking to win reelection through "popular but unsound" (i.e., *inflationary*) policies nor by private special interests (envisaged as a monstrous "money trust") seeking corruptly to use monetary controls to improve their competitive position. To insulate the U.S. central bank from partisan influences—both political *and* monied—Federal Reserve Governors are granted unparalleled autonomy in the form of long terms of appointment and an independent source of operating funds. The seven members of the Federal Reserve Board enjoy 14-year terms in office, staggered to prevent a President from being able (in his maximum eight years in office) to dominate the Board by threats of nonreappointment.[3] Perhaps most importantly, neither the President's Office of Management and Budget nor the Congress can influence Federal Reserve decisions through the conventional discipline of the budgetary process. The Federal Reserve is chartered as a quasi-private corporation in full control of the interest that accrues on its portfolio of over $85 billion in earning assets. Reversing the customary flow of government-agency funds, in recent years the Federal Reserve has turned over to the Treasury billions of dollars in earnings in excess of its self-determined operating expenses and net additions to capital accounts.[4]

[2]Consider, for example, the unfavorable publicity the System received during the Spring 1975 flap over Board statistician Carl Mintz' decision to leak survey information on bank loan rates to *Consumer Reports*.

[3]In practice, the frequency of early resignations has allowed two-term presidents to exercise considerable de facto influence through new appointments. The desire to screen new appointments to the Board has made most Board Chairmen a good deal more sensitive to Presidential wishes than they might have been otherwise.

[4]These payments have amounted to $39.9 billion since 1947, with almost $10 billion of this coming in the last two years.

Congressman Patman's Longstanding "Chess" Game

It is also useful to compare the mild changes in Fed autonomy wrought by the legislation of 1975 with the drastic changes sought by Wright Patman. Over the years, Congressman Patman pursued a strategy worthy of a chess grandmaster. He mounted a series of four interconnected legislative threats to the Federal Reserve's continued independence. Two of these threats were more obviously menacing than the other two, but each threat focused on a critical "square" in the Fed's checker-board charter of autonomy. Both sides suspected that the adoption of even the mildest of Patman's four reforms would make it harder in the future for Fed officials to defend their independence against an eventual Patman checkmate.

In order of increasing subtlety, Patman's catalogue of reforms called for (1) complete revocation of the Fed's charter as a quasi-private corporation; (2) cancellation of all U.S. government securities owned by the Fed, with a corresponding reduction in the national debt; (3) specification by Congress of precise year-to-year limits on interest rates and/or monetary expansion; and (4) periodic audits of the Fed's accounts by an independent government agency. The first reform would convert the Fed into a run-of-the-mill government agency, subject to the same budgetary discipline as any other. The second reform would leave the Fed formally independent but would deprive the Fed of sufficient earnings, thus forcing it into operating deficit. To finance these deficits, Fed officials would be forced to submit themselves to the congressional appropriations process. Ostensibly, the third and fourth reforms aim only at making Fed officials more directly "accountable" to the American people, but Patman wanted these small increases in accountability primarily as devices for generating embarrassing facts with which to harass Fed officials into a fatal public mistake.

The 1975 House and Senate Concurrent Monetary-Policy Resolutions

In contrast, the increase in accountability Congress imposed on the Fed in 1975 seems to have focused less on establishing a good framework for receiving information on future Fed operations than on increasing monetary growth in 1975 so as to increase the odds of incumbents' being reelected in 1976. Dissatisfied with current high and rising levels of unemployment, and to a lesser extent with the high level of interest rates and the defective pattern of procyclical variations in money-supply growth observed in recent years, new activist Chairmen of the three relevant oversight committees[5] sought to increase congressional influence on Fed policies but without forcing the System's budget to pass through the conventional appropriations

---

[5]Senator Hubert Humphrey, Joint Economic Committee; Senator William Proxmire, Senate Banking, Housing and Urban Affairs Committee; and Representative Henry Reuss, House Banking, Currency, and Housing Committee.

process. Uniting themselves with legislators from opposite ends of the ideological spectrum, they sponsored in each house concurrent resolutions designed to pressure the Fed into adopting an easier monetary policy in 1975.

These concurrent resolutions—expressing merely the "sense of Congress"—developed as a substitute for a Patman-type bill that would have set hard numerical limitations on the Fed's policy options and locked monetary policy into a narrow M_1 control framework. (M_1 is the sum of currency and checking accounts in the hands of the public.) Under a procedure proposed by Robert Weintraub (then a staff economist for the House Banking Committee and at this writing senior economist for the Senate Banking Committee), each year the Fed would have had to request permission from Congress to operate within specified upper and lower limits of money-supply growth. The thrust of the proposal was both to limit the Fed's freedom in periodic reports before Congress to explain away procyclical monetary growth after the fact and to make countercyclical monetary growth more likely by forcing the System Open Market Account to give up its apparent preoccupation with money-market interest rates.[6] The less ambitious bill (H.R. 212) introduced by Henry Reuss on January 14, 1975, "requested" Federal Reserve officials "to direct their efforts in the first half of 1975 toward maintaining an increase in the money supply (demand deposits and currency outside banks) of no less than 6 percentum at an annual rate, over each three-month period" and to report to the House Banking Committee whenever they failed to achieve the minimum target.

The concurrent resolution (H. Con. Res. 133) passed on March 4, 1975, by a vote of 367 to 55 proved much more permissive:

> Resolved that it is the sense of Congress that the Federal Reserve should conduct monetary policy in the first half of 1975 so as to lower long-term interest rates.[7]

It called further for the Federal Reserve to transmit quarterly reports "on its progress toward reaching this goal."

Similarly, a hard-line draft of the concurrent resolution originally written for the Senate by William Proxmire (S. Con. Res. 18, which portrayed the Fed as an "agent" to be brusquely ordered about) was softened in all important respects before being reported out by the Senate Banking Committee. Adopted by the Senate in an 86 to 0 vote, the language of this resolution was approved by the House in late March (1975). The resolution lays out a set of totally noncontroversial near-term and long-term guidelines to govern Fed policy decisions:

---

[6]This proposal would have updated and put teeth into a 1968 Joint Economic Committee "request" that the Fed "report promptly" to Congress whenever money growth fell outside a 2 to 6 percent range. (U.S. Congress, Joint Economic Committee, *Standards for Guiding Monetary Action, Report,* 90th Congress, Second Session, Washington: 1968, pp. 19–20.)

[7]In hearings before the Senate Banking Committee, Chairman Burns established the possible infeasibility of this particular target by pointing to the Fisher Effect. He stressed that the effects of monetary expansion on forecasts of future inflation could not be ignored. In certain circumstances, trying to drive down long-term nominal rates of interest by increasing the monetary growth rate could end up forcing these rates higher than they were in the first place.

1. Pursue policies in the first half of 1975 so as to encourage expansion in the monetary and credit aggregates appropriate to facilitating prompt economic recovery.

2. Maintain long-run growth of the monetary and credit aggregates commensurate with the economy's long-run potential to increase production. . . .

The last paragraph of the resolution maintains the call for quarterly oversight hearings (to be held alternately by the House and Senate Banking Committees) at which Fed officials will testify about their "objectives and plans with respect to ranges of growth or diminution of monetary and credit aggregates in the upcoming twelve months." However, the target ranges expressed would not be binding on Fed officials if they "determine that they cannot or should not be achieved because of changing conditions."

Why Didn't Congress Seek Tighter Oversight?

One has to ask why increased congressional oversight has been so long in coming and why in particular it came in 1975. One must also ask about the processes by which H. Con. Resolution 133 may be expected to influence future Fed decisions. The answer to the first question is that the case for having Congress make monetary policy is far from compelling. Merely increasing congressional scrutiny of Fed policy intentions (as voted in 1975) promises costs as well as benefits. The clearest benefit of increased oversight is informational. Forcing the Federal Reserve Chairman to appear each calendar quarter before a congressional committee to spell out the numerical range of growth rates in the monetary and credit aggregates planned for the next year will produce a better-informed citizenry. A clearer view of Fed reasoning and intentions will allow analysts to lay out more sharply the consequences of current Fed policies for public debate. This should hold down incidents of destabilizing interest-rate speculation by private investors (such as occurred in January 1974) based on false suppositions about the course of Fed policy over the immediate future. More important, public discussion of Fed plans should provide a reverse flow of information that would clarify the priorities of the public for Fed officials. Monetarist economists, especially, see a further benefit in the requirements both that the Fed plan a year ahead and especially that it focus upon its effects on monetary aggregates rather than upon its effects on interest rates (but they would have been more pleased if the term "credit aggregates" had not worked its way into the charge). Even nonmonetarist economists believe that the Fed's traditional concern with stabilizing day-to-day and week-to-week movements in money-market interest rates has prevented U.S. monetary policy from delivering its best countercyclical punch.

On the cost side, the issue turns on the degree of pressure and on the quality of economic statesmanship apt to be exercised by Congress, which depends, in turn, on the kinds of policies desired by the electorate. Everyone's worst fear is that perennial congressional preoccupation with winning reelection might further shrink and distort the Fed's policy horizon, accentuating what has come to be called "the political business cycle."[8] Pushing central-bank officials toward policies whose good effects promise to be felt before the ever approaching "next" election could result in huge overshoots in inflation or unemployment in the months immediately following election dates. Everyone is aware that substantially increasing the Fed's susceptibility to congressional direction could increase rather than lessen the amplitude of national economic fluctuations and impart to Fed decisions a secular bias in favor of inflation.* Whether or not politically motivated excesses might become endemic (assuming they are not already) would depend ultimately on the degree of economic sophistication attained by U.S. voters. Unless the electorate has the good sense to vote out congressmen who press poor policies on the Fed, Fed officials might be led to emphasize pleasing Congress in the short run over trying on their own to identify and to serve the public's long-term needs. Given U.S. citizens' low degree of macroeconomic literacy, only by paying great attention to the accurate economic education of laypersons could Fed officials hope to minimize these counterpressures. In view of the Fed's revealed preference for hiding its motives in clouds of smoke (consider, e.g., Fed discussions of discount-rate policy and its past success in confusing individual legislators without losing their support), one cannot expect it to excel quickly in this function.

However, in practice, the ponderous multilayered structure of congressional decision making and the economic naivete of the great preponderance of its members provide the most effective limitations on Congress' ability to dominate a reluctant Fed. Members whose ability to interpret current macroeconomic information is limited fear the possibility of a Fed counterattack that might label them as "inflationists," while the slowness and unwieldiness of the body virtually insure that its influence even on quarter-to-quarter decisions by the Fed will prove more apparent than real.

For all of these reasons, future Congresses may show much less taste for involving themselves in current monetary policy than this very special post-Watergate session has. Although the political benefit conferred on the Republican Party in 1972 by the Fed's excessive preelection expansion of the money stock has been very much on the minds of congressional Democrats, the current reforms are aimed not so much to punish the Fed specifically or to prevent it from repeating past mistakes as to increase incumbents' chances of reelection in 1976[9] and to symbolize the reduced policy autonomy of the Executive Branch generally. In trying to establish an activist

---

[8]See William D. Nordhaus, "The Political Business Cycle," *Review of Economic Studies,* 42 (April 1975), pp. 169-190, and Edward R. Tufte, "The Political Manipulation of the Economy—Influence of the Electoral Cycle on Macroeconomic Performance and Policy" (mimeographed, 1974).

*Evidence of this is reported in the reaction function study in Section IV A of this book.—Ed.

[9]During the February 19, 1975, hearings before the House Banking Committee, Democratic Congressman Henry Reuss addressed the following remarks to Chairman Burns: "I think a build up in the money supply during the Presidential election is a good thing. It would have helped in 1970, actually, but when you continued it into 1973 and made it worse, and continued in 1974, I and others did protest." (I am indebted to Kurt Dew for bringing this quote, which appears on p. 21 of the printed transcript, to my attention.)

image, the 94th Congress has systematically reasserted its authority over a number of areas that, as a practical matter, were formerly regarded to be under the dominion of the Executive Branch. In particular, oversight has been increased dramatically in the areas of foreign policy, the federal budget, and foreign and domestic intelligence activity.

Since participation in decision making leaves one less free after the fact to criticize mistakes, it is natural for incumbent congressmen to regard forging a formal association with current Fed decisions as a potential source of keen embarrassment. Whenever the unsatisfactory performance of the national economy has been a key election issue, incumbent congressmen have found it convenient to be able to blame everything on the "misguided" policies of an "independent" Federal Reserve System. The hypothesis that (aided by intensive Fed and commercial-bank lobbying) Congress increasingly recognized the value of having the Fed serve as a scapegoat explains the progressive blunting of the language of House and Senate draft legislation on monetary-policy guidelines as matters moved closer to a final vote.

In the end, Congress left the responsibility for monetary-policy *mistakes* where it has always been. The record of hearings generated by the surveillance legislation makes it clear that the 94th Congress explicitly backed off from enacting a symmetric "shared responsibility" for policy successes and failures.[10] Quarterly oversight hearings established under the concurrent resolution offer an opportunity for record building and public posturing that can allow clever congressmen and senators subsequently to credit policy successes to the influence of their wise advice on Fed thinking without sacrificing the Fed's traditional role as the scapegoat for policy failures. More than anything else, the continued survival of Fed independence is explained by the usefulness of having an allegedly nonpolitical entity on which incumbents of *both* parties can blame the aggregate economic ills of the country. If congressmen were ever to eliminate this useful independence, sooner or later they would want to reinvent it. Subtly or unsubtly, Federal Reserve lobbying pressure exploited precisely this point.

How The Fed Can Resist Close Oversight

Although the resolution adopted forces the Fed to reveal Federal Open Market Committee (FOMC) decisions that it would have preferred to keep secret, Congress' informational demands are neither onerous nor well defined. The Fed retains its traditional ability to confuse and confound outside observers with after-the-fact doubletalk.[11]

In Chairman Burns' first quarterly appearance under the resolution, on May 1,

---

[10]The hearings in question are those on H.R. 212 held between February 4 and 6, 1975, on H.R. 3160 held on February 19, 1975, and on S. Con. Res. 18 held on February 25 and 26, 1975.

[11]The bureaucratic usefulness of this power is stressed in J. F. Chant and K. Acheson, "Mythology and Central Banking," *Kyklos,* 26 (1973), pp. 362-379.

1975, he announced a 12-month target of 5 percent to 7.5 percent growth in M_1. He presented specific 12-month target ranges also for three other aggregates: M_2 (8.5 percent to 10.5 percent), M_3 (10 percent to 12 percent), and the bank credit proxy (6.5 percent to 9.5 percent).[12] Given the observed March 1975 level of each aggregate, this information is equivalent to having announced a March 1976 range of target levels for each aggregate. Table 1 translates the FOMC's growth-rate targets into this equivalent range of target levels.

As a device for establishing accountability, this reporting framework has three serious flaws. First, quarterly observations on 12-month targets provide no firm basis from which to assess whether any particular quarter's policy comes up on or off track. The FOMC will inevitably find itself in the position of having hit at least one of its announced targets and/or of having had plausible reasons for altering its plans in the direction of any observed miss. Before the banking committees can fulfill the oversight function the Concurrent Resolution appears to have delegated to them, the Fed must decompose its 12-month targets to display information on its interim intentions. Second, no indication is given as to whether or not the desired range is symmetric about the single most preferred growth rate. Near business-cycle turning points, especially, the FOMC may prefer values at one or the other end of the reported range. Third, the Fed is permitted at its own discretion to vary the composition of the set of monetary and credit aggregates about which it chooses to report. Target aggregates can be both as numerous and as diverse as the Fed finds convenient. This freedom to employ a wide range of instruments and indicators to interpret its policy intentions allows the Fed to describe its effects after the fact in a disingenuously favorable light.[13]

Bureaucratic organizations have a natural tendency to conceal both their mistakes and their priorities. The temptation to protect the System by exploiting these weaknesses in the reporting framework is likely to prove irresistible to Fed officials—all the more so since the Fed is almost certain to have embarrassing mistakes to conceal. Although the new reporting framework asks the Fed to focus on monetary and credit aggregates, it establishes no specific incentives or procedures to help the Fed to "kick" its longstanding addiction to interest-rate stabilization. Few facts of macroeconomic behavior are as well established as the Fed's procyclical weakness for smoothing the path of increases and decreases in money-market interest rates even at the expense of professed monetary-growth targets.[14]

[12]Partly in response to congressional complaints prior to this appearance, the FOMC also decided to cut the delay in releasing summaries of its meetings from 90 to 45 days.

[13]During the Senate Banking Committee's hearings on the Senate resolution, Allan Meltzer observed: "We have tried with different Federal Reserve chairmen to get a statement as to what it is that they are trying to do. Their statements are either vague or when they are descriptions of past policies, they use different measures. . . . There is at least one [measure] that always turns out to be an indication that what the Fed did was the appropriate thing to do. That was what they were trying to achieve. But it is a different indicator from one meeting to the next."

[14]In private correspondence, William Poole points out that the new congressional Budget Office's first report, *Inflation and Unemployment: A Report on the Economy* (June 30, 1975, pp. 64-65), draws the same inferences. After explicitly noting Burns' testimony on Fed plans, the staff projects 8.5 percent growth in M_1 as the likely FOMC response to developing interest-rate pressures.

Table 1. Range of FOMC March 1976 Target Levels Implicit in the May 1, 1975, Announced Targets for Growth Rates in Monetary and Credit Aggregates

(In billions)

Aggregate	Daily Average Value in March 1975*	Implicit Target Levels		
		Minimum	Midpoint	Maximum
M₁	286.1	300.4	304.0	307.6
M₂	626.4	679.6	685.9	692.2
M₃	1007.2	1107.9	1118.0	1128.1
Bank-Credit Proxy	498.1	530.5	537.9	545.4

*These are seasonally adjusted values taken from Federal Reserve Statistical Releases H.6 and H.3.

This behavior forms so repetitive and scriptlike a pattern that one must suppose that it develops as a systematic response to perceived incentives. The immediate screams of harried participants in the money markets (particularly of highly levered securities dealers) must weigh more heavily on the psyches of decision makers in the FOMC than the mere threat of subsequent barbs from congressmen and economists. To change so ingrained a response pattern, emphasis must be placed not on new reporting relationships with outsiders but on internal reforms designed to change incentives sufficiently that the FOMC and the Manager of the System Open Market Account in New York are driven to unlearn their old counterproductive habits. Even in the face of changes in FOMC decision making and execution processes that promised to work in this direction, a reasonable man might still doubt that monetary-growth rates would soon function as the dominant focus of U.S. monetary policy. But lacking such evidence, the possibility seems exceedingly remote.*

Did the FOMC Ease Policy between the First and Second Oversight Hearings?

Interpretive problems posed by this spring's sudden acceleration in monetary growth rates illustrate the ease with which the Fed can muddy the waters through which congressmen must peer. Figure 1 portrays three very different target paths for M₁, all of which are consistent with March-to-March growth of 6.25 percent in M₁. Without knowing which of the many possible interim "tracks" the FOMC desired, how are oversight committees to assess the roughly 11 percent per annum growth observed in M₁ during the March-to-June quarter of 1975? The $294.0 billion estimate for June, 1975 M₁ lies right on track B. To make up for past shortfalls, this track provides for a complete "front-end loading" of the planned monetary growth into the first half of the reporting period, with zero growth in M₁ over the last six months of the period.

* This opinion blends nicely with the thrust of the readings in Section IV A and earlier in this Section.—Ed.

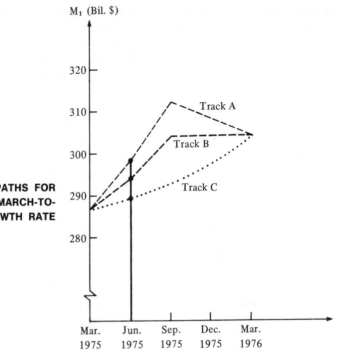

FIGURE 1 THREE INTERIM GROWTH PATHS FOR M₁ THAT ARE CONSISTENT WITH THE MARCH-TO-MARCH MIDRANGE FOMC TARGET GROWTH RATE ANNOUNCED ON MAY 1, 1975

However, the observed expansion would be excessive if the FOMC had wanted to follow the steady-growth track C and deficient if the desired path had been the deliberate-overshoot track A.

Since relevant control periods are much shorter than the period for reporting intentions to Congress, Banking Committee members were no better equipped in July 1975 to determine whether or not Fed policy intentions were realized during the March-to-June quarter than they had been in past periods. As before, legislators can be misled by a self-serving story so long as it is not downright implausible.

Fed spokesmen maintain that quarterly accelerations and decelerations in monetary growth represent short-run control errors that are best treated as water under the dam. This "forgiveness principle" lets the FOMC avoid the question of just what kinds of temporary disturbances should and should not be accommodated and leads to a continual displacement in the *base* to which FOMC growth-rate targets apply. If growth-rate targets are not themselves systematically adjusted in an opposite direction, forgiveness of errors amounts to shifting the intended future track for the various aggregates upward and downward with observed errors in control. For example, a vote to maintain, beginning from the June 1975 base, a 6.25 percent average expansion in M₁ between then and March 1976 would accept a March-to-March growth rate (7.9 percent) that lies outside the previously announced target range. To escape this implication, without changing the growth-rate targets Chairman Burns' July 24 testimony shifted the operative base from the average for March 1975 to the much lower average for the first quarter as a whole.

When control errors accumulate in a single direction for several months in a row (as is all too likely when FOMC policy pursues an interest-rate guide), the result can be a disastrously procyclical pattern of monetary fluctuations. For illustration, one has only to think of the downward deflection of the intended monetary track that occurred during the fall and early winter of 1974–1975. A growth-rate decision focus, combined with a liberal application of the forgiveness principle, tends to hide the quarter-to-quarter goals actually being pursued by the FOMC even from its own membership. Before congressional oversight of Fed intentions can have any substantial impact, the Banking Committees will have to push vigorously for an adequate framework for reporting Fed decisions.[15]

Summary

Compared to Patman's grand scheme or Weintraub's quest for a congressionally imposed money-supply rule, the increased congressional oversight adopted in 1975 constitutes a mild reform indeed. Its primary effect is to erect a framework for quarterly public hearings that allows concerned congressmen to monitor Fed policy decisions very loosely and to indicate their agreement or disagreement with the basic thrust of these decisions. Its secondary effects are to establish a weak discipline on the Fed to keep a closer eye on the movement of monetary and credit aggregates than it has in the past, to formulate its plans within the context of a one-year horizon, and to raise the possibility that the threat of congressional probing might be used to inhibit expressions of dissent within the FOMC.

Congress' short-run instructions (vague as they are) have already expired, leaving the hearings mechanism as the principal channel for transmitting future short-run congressional instructions. Far from establishing a shared responsibility, these hearings promise to provide little more than a convenient forum for legislative posturing. Fear of political abuse may lead Fed officials to adopt policies slightly more congenial to Banking Committee members than they might otherwise, but the major effect is simply to force the Fed to announce some loose numerical targets and, if it subsequently misses them badly, to discuss why. Although having to report this information dissipates the strict administrative secrecy that formerly surrounded Fed open-market decisions and leaves Fed officials more vulnerable to outside criticism, this event accords fully with preexisting trends toward greater disclosure enshrined in the Freedom of Information Act of 1966.

Especially in view of the framework established for reporting Fed intentions, the

---

[15]During the July 24 hearings, Congress focused instead on pressuring the Fed Chairman to supply projections of GNP, unemployment, and inflation implied by FOMC targets.

result is a significant change in Fed *procedures,* but by no means a structural change in the relation of the Fed to Congress. No firm contract has been struck as to how to measure future Federal Reserve policy performance. That such a contract, though sought explicitly, could not be won even from the unusually assertive 94th Congress suggests that the Fed's vaunted independence is a good deal less fragile than many of us have assumed.